BY
PANEL OF AUTHORS

DISCLAIMER

With the ambition of providing standard academic resources, we have exercised extreme care in publishing the content. In case of any discrepancies in the matter, we request readers to excuse the unintentional lapse and not hold us liable for the same. Suggestions are always welcome.

EDITION : 2021

ISBN : 978-93-91184-88-9

PRICE : ₹ 619.00

PRINTED AT : Upkar Printing Unit, Agra

PUBLISHED BY

OSWAL PUBLISHERS

Head Office: 1/12, Sahitya Kunj, M.G. Road, Agra - 282002

Phone : (0562) 2527771-4, +91 7534077222

E-mail : info@oswalpublishers.in

Website : www.oswalpublishers.com

The cover of this book has been designed using resources from Freepik.com

Preface

Based on the [CBSE/DIR (ACAD)/2021]
Circular No. Acad-75/2021, issued by the Board.

We at Oswal-Gurukul believe that preparation in the right direction is the key to avoid stress, and perform well in one's board exams. Therefore, in order to excel in exams we have compiled CBSE 36 Sample Question Papers for TERM I Examination of class XII. To provide best matter to students, subject-matter experts and the experienced teachers from across the country have collaborated to bring together this book.

This book comprises detailed solved Sample Question Paper by CBSE of each subject and sample papers of English Core, Physical Education, Accountancy, Business Studies and Economics according to the new SQP, explained in detail for better understanding of the concepts. We have made every attempt to cover as much ground as possible from the entire syllabus and to keep the language of the book lucid and crisp for easy grasping.

We sincerely hope that this book will prove to be a tool for effective time-management, as well as enable smart-study practices.

—The Publisher

SAMPLE QUESTION PAPERS MATHEMATICS ALSO AVAILABLE

oswal.io

create your own exam sample papers in 2 mins

Prepare a chapter, take practice test & get —— evaluated to perform better ——

Create unlimited tests based on the latest board paper pattern once you are done practicing the book questions

Scan the **QR code** and get instant access to **oswal.io** for **free**. Just register & get started!

A winning effort begins with daily practice of tests

Easy steps to follow :

Step 1 - In a few clicks, you can completely customize your test

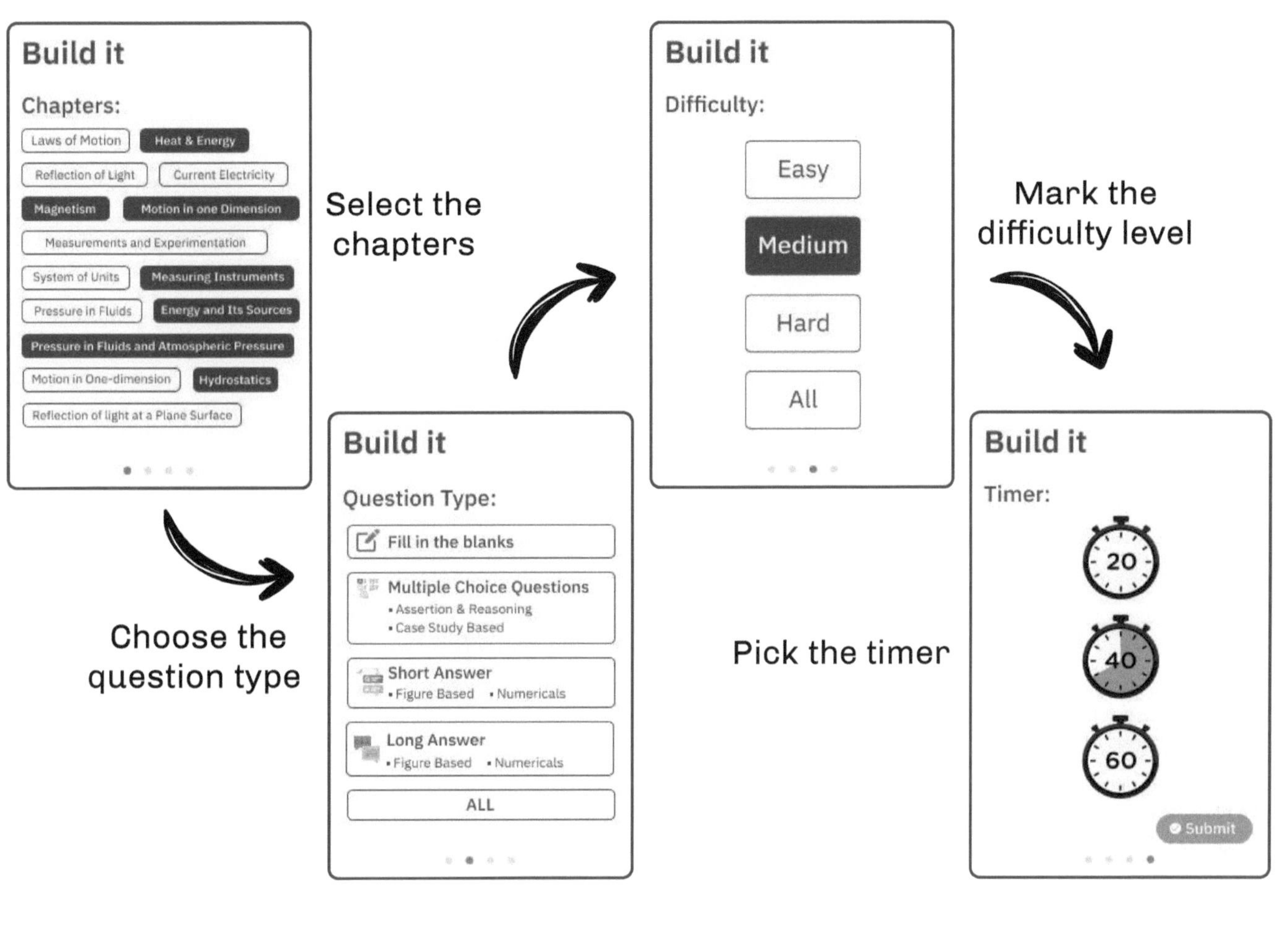

Step 2 - Test is based on the selected question type, chapters, difficulty, time

Step 3 - Click on start and type your answers in the given space

Step 4 - Use insert $\TeX$ equation editor to quickly & accurately insert the difficult math/physics/chem formulas

Step 5 - Skip any question if not sure, proceed to next & submit

Step 6 - You will get your result emailed right away

Contents

Economics 335–466

केन्द्रीय माध्यमिक शिक्षा बोर्ड
(शिक्षा मंत्रालय, भारत सरकार के अधीन एक स्वायत्त संगठन)
CENTRAL BOARD OF SECONDARY EDUCATION
(An Autonomous Organisation under the Ministry of Education, Govt. of India)

CBSE/DIR (ACAD)/2021

Date: 02-09-2021
Circular No. Acad-75/2021

All the Heads of Schools Affiliated to CBSE

**Subject: Sample Question Papers of Classes X and XII
for Term 1 Exams 2021-22**

Dear Principal,

The Sample Question Papers for classes X and XII Term 1 Exams 2021-22 are now available at CBSE website www.cbseacademic.nic.in at the link given below:

Sample Papers Class X:
http://cbseacademic.nic.in/SQP_CLASSX_2021-22.html

Sample Papers Class XII:
http://cbseacademic.nic.in/SQP_CLASSXII_2021-22.html

Dr. Joseph Emmanuel
Director (Academics)

'शिक्षा सदन' ,17 राऊज़ एवेन्यू ,इंस्टीट्शनल एरिया, नई दिल्ली–110002
'Shiksha Sadan', 17, Rouse Avenue, Institutional Area, New Delhi - 110002

फ़ोन/Telephone: 011-23212603,23233227 वेबसाइट/Website :http://www.cbseacademic.nic.in ई-मेल/e-mail: mailto:directoracad.cbse@nic.in.

NOTICE

Important Points for Sample Question Papers

The following points are to be noted while studying/referring to the Sample Papers for Classes X & XII Term 1 for the academic session 2021-22:

1. The Multiple Choice Questions given in the sample papers are not of one mark each for all papers.

2. In the SQPs of Mathematics and all languages except English, each question carries one mark.

3. For other subjects, each question carries equal marks viz.-a-viz. the total marks given i.e. 40 or 35 or 25 or 15 and the weight age of marks per question will be as follows:-

Max. Marks	No. of Questions to be attempted	Marks per Question
40	50	0.80
35	50	0.70
40	45	0.88
35	45	0.77
25	40	0.625
15	25	0.60

4. If total marks scored by a candidate is in fraction, then the same will be rounded off to the next higher numerical number, for example, if the child gets 16.1marks then the total marks will be rounded off to 17 and so on.

English Core

Sample Question Paper

English Core [Code (301)]

Term - I

Time : 90 Minutes **Max. Marks : 40**

General Instructions :

1. The Question Paper contains THREE sections.
2. Section A-READING has 18 questions. Attempt a total of 14 questions, as per specific instructions for each question.
3. Section B-WRITING SKILLS has 12 questions. Attempt a total of 10 questions, as per specific instructions for each question.
4. Section C-LITERATURE has 30 questions. Attempt 26 questions, as per specific instructions for each question.
5. All questions carry equal marks.
6. There is no negative marking.

READING

I. Read the passage given below.

I.   I got posted in Srinagar in the 1980s. Its rugged mountains, gushing rivers and vast meadows reminded me of the landscapes of my native place – the Jibhi Valley in Himachal Pradesh. Unlike Srinagar that saw numerous tourists, Jibhi Valley remained clouded in anonymity. That's when the seed of starting tourism in Jibhi was planted. I decided to leave my service in the Indian Army and follow the urge to return home.

II. We had two houses – a family house and a traditional house, which we often rented out. I pleaded with my father to ask the tenant to vacate the house so that I could convert it into a guesthouse. When my family finally relented, I renovated the house keeping its originality intact, just adding windows for sunlight.

III. I still remember the summer of 1992 when I put a signboard outside my first guesthouse in Jibhi Valley! The village residents, however, were sceptical about my success. My business kept growing but it took years for tourism to take off in Jibhi Valley. Things changed significantly after 2008 when the government launched a homestay scheme. People built homestays and with rapid tourism growth, the region changed rapidly. Villages turned into towns with many concrete buildings. Local businesses and tourists continued putting a burden on nature.

IV. Then, with the 2020-21 pandemic and lockdown, tourism came to a complete standstill in Jibhi Valley. Local people, who were employed at over a hundred homestays and guesthouses, returned to their villages. Some went back to farming; some took up pottery and some got involved in government work schemes. Now, all ardently hope that normalcy and tourism will return to the valley soon. In a way, the pandemic has given us an opportunity to introspect, go back to our roots and look for sustainable solutions.

V.   For me, tourism has been my greatest teacher. It brought people from many countries and all states of India to my guesthouse. It gave me exposure to different cultures and countless opportunities to learn new things. Most people who stayed at my guesthouse became my repeat clients and good friends. When I look back, I feel proud, yet humbled at the thought that I was not only able to fulfill my dream despite all the challenges, but also play a role in establishing tourism in the beautiful valley that I call home. (394 words)

Source: *https://www.outlookindia.com/outlooktraveller/explore/story/71458/how-one-mansconviction-put-jibhi-valley-on-the-world-tourism-map*

Based on your understanding of the passage, answer <u>any eight</u> out of the ten questions by choosing the correct option

Q.1. The scenic beauty of Srinagar makes the writer feel

    A.   awestruck   B. nostalgic   C. cheerful   D. confused

Ans. B. nostalgic

Q.2. A collocation is a group of words that often occur together.

The writer says that Jibhi valley remained <u>clouded in anonymity</u>.

Select the word from the options that correctly collocates with *clouded in.*

    A.   disgust   B. anger   C. doubt   D. terror

Ans. C. doubt

Q.3. Select the option that suitably completes the given dialogue as per the context in paragraph II.

Father: Are you sure that your plan would work?

Writer: I can't say (1) ....

Father: That's a lot of uncertainty, isn't it?

Writer: (2) .... , father. Please let's do this.

    A.   (1) that I would be able to deal with the funding (2) Well begun is half done

    B.   (1) anything along those lines, as the competition is tough (2) Think before you leap

    C.   (1) that, because it's a question of profit and loss (2) All's well that ends well

    D.   (1) I'm sure, but I can say that I believe in myself (2) Nothing venture nothing win

Ans. D. (1) I'm sure, but I can say that I believe in myself (2) Nothing venture nothing win

Q.4. Which signboard would the writer have chosen for his 1992 undertaking, in Jibhi Valley?

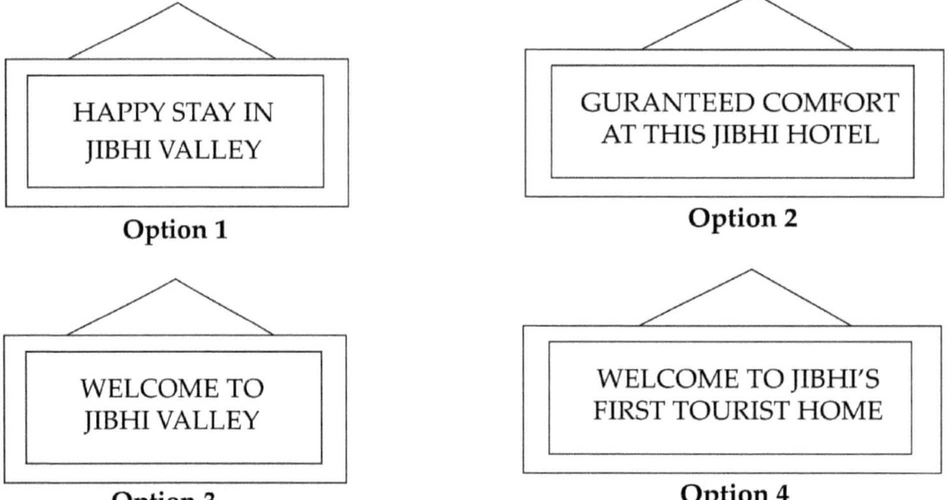

    A.   option 1   B. option 2

    C.   option 3   D. option 4

Ans. D. option 4

Q.5. Select the option that clearly indicates the situation before and after 2008, in Jibhi Valley.

A.

Before 2008	After 2008
picturesque landscapes	construction sites and commerce

B.

Before 2008	After 2008
zero tourism in the valley	sceptical villagers

C.

Before 2008	After 2008
buildings and hotels	profitable ventures

D.

Before 2008	After 2008
scenic surroundings	zero tourism in the valley

Ans. A.

Before 2008	After 2008
picturesque landscapes	construction sites and commerce

Q.6. What is the relationship between (1) and (2)?

    (1)   …tourism came to a complete standstill in Jibhi Valley.

    (2)   … tourism has been my greatest teacher.

    A.   (2) is the cause for (1).   B.   (1) repeats the situation described in (2).

    C.   (2) elaborates the problem described in (1).   D.   (1) sets the stage for (2).

Ans. D.   (1) sets the stage for (2).

Q.7. The writer mentions looking for sustainable solutions. He refers to the need for sustainable solutions because he realises that

    A.   even though all natural ecosystems are essential pillars of resilience, we need to focus on using their resources to address the economic needs of mankind, as a priority.

    B.   the exposures to pandemics are a reality and a big threat to the countries across the world.

    C.   for an economic recovery to be durable and resilient, a return to 'business as usual' and environmentally destructive investment patterns and activities must be avoided.

    D.   there is an increasing urgency in the climate movement and the need for collaborative action for the future.

Ans. C.   for an economic recovery to be durable and resilient, a return to 'business as usual' and environmentally destructive investment patterns and activities must be avoided.

Q.8. Select the option that lists the customer review for the writer's project.

    A.   Beautiful accommodation in the lap of nature. Luxurious cottage with indoor pool and garden.

    B.   Comfortable and peaceful. Neat room with ample sunlight. Pleasant and warm host.

    C.   Enjoyed the sprawling suite on the fifth floor. Great view. Professional service.

    D.   Remote locale, good food and clean room. Would have loved more natural light, though.

Ans. B.   Comfortable and peaceful. Neat room with ample sunlight. Pleasant and warm host.

Q.9. Which quote summarises the writer's feelings about the pace of growth of tourism in Jibhi Valley?

    A.   We kill all the caterpillars, then complain there are no butterflies.   *– John Marsden*

    B.   Nature will give you the best example of life lessons, just open your eyes and see.   *– Kate Smith*

    C.   We do not see nature with our eyes, but with our understanding and our hearts.   *– William Hazlett*

    D.   I'd rather be in the mountains thinking of God than in church thinking of the mountains.

                                                           – John Muir

Ans. A.   We kill all the caterpillars, then complain there are no butterflies.   *– John Marsden*

Q.10. Select the option that lists what we can conclude from the text.

    (1)   people of Jibhi Valley practiced sustainable tourism.

    (2)   the people of Jibhi Valley gradually embraced tourism.

    (3)   tourists never revisited Jibhi Valley.

    (4)   the writer was an enterprising person.

    A.   (1) and (2) are true.   B.   (2), (3) and (4) are true.

    C.   (2) and (4) are true.   D.   (1), (3) and (4) are true.

Ans. C.   (2) and (4) are true.

II. Read the passage given below.

    I.   Over the last five years, more companies have been actively looking for intern profiles, according to a 2018-19 survey by an online internship and training platform. This survey reveals that India had 80% more internship applications — with 2.2 million applications received in 2018 compared to 1.27 million in the year before. The trend was partly due to more industries looking to have fresh minds and ideas on existing projects for better productivity. What was originally seen as a western concept, getting an internship before plunging into the job market, is fast gaining momentum at Indian workplaces.

    II.   According to the survey data, India's National Capital Region has been the top provider of internships, with a total of 35% internship opportunities, followed by Mumbai and Bengaluru at 20% and 15%, respectively. This includes opportunities in startups, MNCs and even government entities. The survey also revealed popular fields to find internships in (Fig 1). There has been growing awareness among the students about the intern profiles sought by hiring companies that often look for people with real-time experience in management than B- school masters.

Internship Trends 2018
Popular fields to find internships in

Source: Internshala

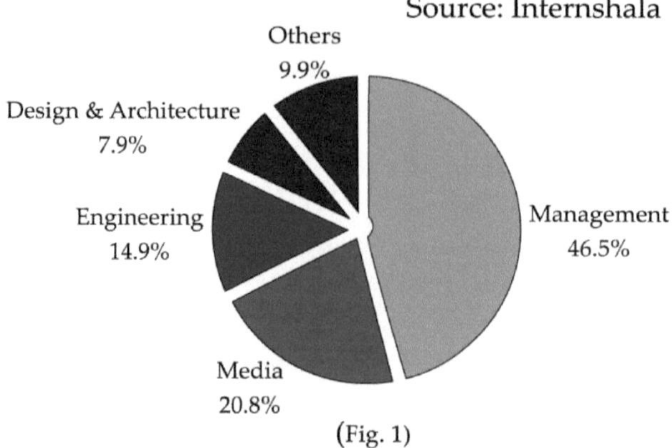

(Fig. 1)

III. The stipend has been an important factor influencing the choice of internships. The survey data reveals that the average stipend offered to interns was recorded as ₹7000 while the maximum stipend went up to ₹85,000. According to statistics, a greater number of people considered virtual internships than in-office internships. Virtual internships got three times more applications than in-office, since a large chunk of students were the ones already enrolled in various courses, or preferred working from home.

IV. Internship portals have sprung up in the last three to four years and many of them already report healthy traffic per month. Reports suggest that on an average, an internship portal company has around 200,000-plus students and some 8,000 companies registered on it. It gets around two lakh visits online every month. The Managing Director of a leading executive search firm says that though these web platforms are working as an effective bridge between the industry and students, most established companies are still reluctant to take too many interns on board for obvious reasons. (355 words)

Source:

(1) *https://www.businessinsider.in/internships-in-india-on-the-rise-with-startups-leading-theway/ articleshow/67655265.cms*

(2) *https://www.businesstoday.in/magazine/features/story/online-portals-helping-collegestudents-paid-internships-46215-2014-06-03*

Based on your understanding of the passage, answer <u>any six</u> out of the eight questions by choosing the correct option.

Q.11. Select the correct inference with reference to the following:

Over the last five years, more companies have been actively looking for intern profiles…

A. The past five years have seen active applications by interns to several companies.

B. The activity for intern profiling by the companies has reached a gradual downslide over the past five years.

C. There were lesser companies searching for intern profiles earlier, as compared to those in the recent five years.

D. Several companies have initiated intern profiling five times a year in the recent past.

Ans. C. There were lesser companies searching for intern profiles earlier, as compared to those in the recent five years.

Q.12. Select the central idea of the paragraph likely to precede paragraph I.

A. Process of registering for internships   B. Knowing more about internships

C. Dos and Don'ts for an internship interview   D. Startups and internships

Ans. B. Knowing more about internships

Q.13. Select the option that displays the true statement with reference to Fig 1.

A. Internships for Engineering and Management are the top two favourites.

B. Design & Architecture internships are significantly more popular than Others.

C. Internships for Media and Others have nearly equal popularity percentage.

    D.   Management internships' popularity is more than twice that for Media.

Ans. D.   Management internships' popularity is more than twice that for Media.

Q.14. Based on your reading of paragraphs II-III, select the appropriate counter- argument to the given argument.

    Argument: I don't think you'll be considered for an internship just because you've been the student editor and Head of Student Council.

    A.   I think I have a fair chance because I'm applying for a virtual position than an inoffice one.

    B.   I have real-time experience in managing a team and many companies consider it more meritorious than a degree in Management.

    C.   I know that my stipend might be on the lower side but I think that it's a good 'earn while you learn' opportunity.

    D.   Lot of metro-cities have a good percentage of positions open and I think I should definitely take a chance.

Ans. B.   I have real-time experience in managing a team and many companies consider it more meritorious than a degree in Management.

Q.15. Select the option that displays the correct cause-effect relationship.

A.

cause	effect
Several students had academic courses to complete	Students applied for online internship

B.

cause	effect
A large chunk of students preferred in-office internships	Applications were three times more than for virtual internships

C.

cause	effect
A greater number of students wanted to work from home	Several students had courses to complete

D.

cause	effect
Students applied for online internship	An equal number of students applied for work-from-home

Ans.

A.

cause	effect
Several students had academic courses to complete	Students applied for online internship

Q.16. The survey statistics mention the average stipend, indicating that

    A.   50% interns were offered ₹85,000.

    B.   ₹7,000 was the lowest and ₹85,000 was the highest.

    C.   most interns were offered around ₹7,000.

    D.   No intern was offered more than ₹7,000.

Ans. C.   most interns were offered around ₹7,000.

Q.17. The phrase 'healthy traffic' refers to the

    A.   updates from portals about health and road safety.

    B.   statistics about adherence to traffic rules by the portals.

    C.   sizeable number of visitors to the portal per month.

    D.   monthly data about the health of internship applicants.

Ans. C.   sizeable number of visitors to the portal per month.

Q.18. Read the two statements given below and select the option that suitably explains them.

    (1)   Established companies are reluctant to take too many interns on board.

    (2)   Probability of interns leaving the company for a variety of reasons, is high.

    A.   (1) is the problem and (2) is the solution for (1).

    B.   (1) is false but (2) correctly explains (1).

    C.   (1) summarises (2).

    D.   (1) is true and (2) is the reason for (1).

Ans. D.   (1) is true and (2) is the reason for (1).

WRITING

III. **Answer <u>any four</u> out of the five questions given, with reference to the context below.**

The President of R.W.A. Chelavoor Heights, Kozhikode, has to put up a notice to inform residents about a power-cut for their residential area.

Q.19. Select the appropriate title for the notice.

    A.   Choosing Own Power Cuts

    B.   Scheduled Power Cut

    C.   The Need to Save Power

    D.   Power and Resident Safety

Ans. B.   Scheduled Power Cut

Q.20. Select the option that lists the most accurate opening for this notice.

    A.   Greetings and attention please, to one and all in Chelavoor Heights.

    B.   This notice is written to share some news with you all about…

    C.   This is to inform all the residents of Chelavoor Heights about…

    D.   I wish to share with all officials of R.W.A. Chelavoor Heights that…

Ans. C.   This is to inform all the residents of Chelavoor Heights about…

Q.21. Select the option with the information points to be included in the body of the notice.

    (1)   Opinion about regular power cuts

    (2)   Resolution for power cuts

    (3)   Reason for the power cut

    (4)   Timings of the power cut

    (5)   Complaint against regular power cuts

    (6)   Date of the power cut

    A.   (1) and (4)   B. (2), (3) and (5)

    C.   (2) and (6)   D. (3), (4) and (6)

Ans. D.   (3), (4) and (6)

Q.22. Would this notice reflect the name of the R.W.A?

    A.   Yes, because it is the issuing body.

    B.   No, because it is understood through the signature.

    C.   Yes, because it makes it informal.

    D.   No, because the title makes it clear.

Ans. A.   Yes, because it is the issuing body.

Q.23. Select the appropriate conclusion for this notice.

    A.   Stay informed.   B. Collaboration solicited.

    C.   Stay prepared.   D. Inconvenience regretted.

Ans. D.   Inconvenience regretted.

IV. **Answer <u>any six</u> of the seven questions given, with reference to the context below.**

Venu is a member of Co-existence, a school club that actively promotes animal rights and care. He has to write an article emphasising the need for prevention of cruelty to animals and peaceful coexistence between animals and human beings.

Q.24. Select the option that lists an appropriate title for Venu's article.

    A.   Man and Animal-A Struggle to Co-exist

    B.   The Rehabilitation and Conservation of Species

    C.   Remodelling the Future by Peaceful Co-existence

    D.   Smart Moves- Survival of the Fittest

Ans. C.   Remodelling the Future by Peaceful Co-existence

Q.25. Which option (1-4), should Venu choose to elaborate on reasons for cruelty to animals?

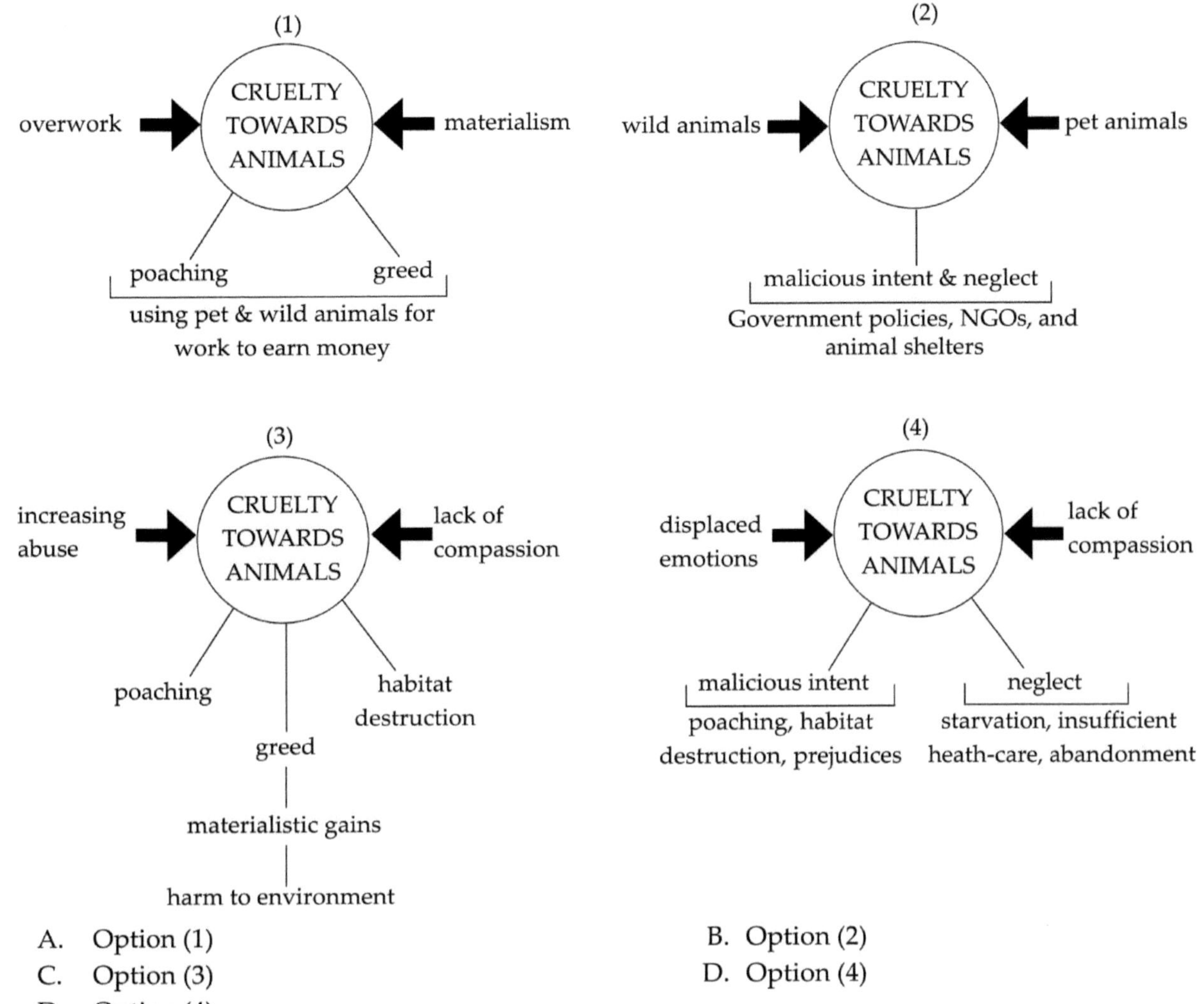

A. Option (1)	B. Option (2)
C. Option (3)	D. Option (4)

Ans. D. Option (4)

Q.26. Which option would help Venu with the appropriate organisation of relevant ideas for this article?

A. Expressing concern about several cases of cruelty to animals—Exploring the reasons—Stating the effects—Providing suggestions for peaceful co-existence— Presenting a conclusive outlook

B. Stating the effects of cruelty to animals— Presenting a concluding viewpoint—Providing suggestions for peaceful co-existence—Expressing concern for animal cruelty— Exploring the reasons for cruelty to animals

C. Introducing the purpose of the article—Information about policies and laws for animal protection—Exploring the reasons for the laws— Providing suggestions for peaceful co-existence —Presenting a pledge for awareness

D. Exploring the laws for animal protection—Questioning the efficacy of the laws—Providing suggestions for improvements in the behaviour towards animals— Introducing the purpose of the article—Appeal for joining Co-Existence

Ans. A. Expressing concern about several cases of cruelty to animals—Exploring the reasons—Stating the effects—Providing suggestions for peaceful co-existence— Presenting a conclusive outlook

Q.27. Which suggestions, from those given below, would be appropriate for Venu's article?

A. reducing human-wildlife conflict, banning habitat destruction, creating more wildlife sanctuaries

B. protecting the environment, penalising poachers

C. strengthening execution of animal rights' laws, increasing awareness, reducing human-wildlife conflict

D. creation of more wildlife sanctuaries and promotion of research on animals.

Ans. C. strengthening execution of animal rights' laws, increasing awareness, reducing human-wildlife conflict

Q.28. Read a sentence from Venu's article draft and help him complete it by selecting the most appropriate option.

As animals find their natural habitat shrinking daily, their interactions with humans keep rising, often to the (i)_________ of the humans and with (ii)_________ for the animals.

A.	(i) joy (ii) dangerous outcomes	B.	(i) thrill (ii) lethal consequences
C.	(i) irritation (ii) minimal effects	D.	(i) fear (ii) disastrous results

Ans. D. (i) fear (ii) disastrous results

Q.29. Which quote should Venu use to summarise the central idea of his article?

A. "Animals are such agreeable friends—they ask no questions; they pass no criticisms."

– George Eliot

B. "The greatness of a nation and its moral progress can be judged by the way its animals are treated."

– Mahatma Gandhi

C. A tiger may pray, "O Lord, how wicked are these men who do not come and place themselves before me to be eaten; they are breaking Your law." *– Swami Vivekananda*

D. "Clearly, animals know more than we think, and think a great deal more than we know."

– Irene M. Pepperberg

Ans. B. "The greatness of a nation and its moral progress can be judged by the way its animals are treated."

– Mahatma Gandhi

Q.30. Read the following options for the self-checklist for this article and select the option that includes the most appropriate self-checklist for this article.

(1)

MY ARTICLE CONTAINS	☑	☒
1. first person address to the audience as title		
2. content that lists the topical points		
3. opinions of stakeholders as by-line		
4. personal observations		
5. designation and date at the end		

(2)

MY ARTICLE CONTAINS	☑	☒
1. an eye-catching title that is thematically related		
2. content that offers a balanced view of the issue		
3. input for the cause-effect & suggestions		
4. a conclusion including personal observations		
5. a by-line		

(3)

MY ARTICLE CONTAINS	☑	☒
1. a thoughtful quote as title		
2. content that analyses pros and cons		
3. address of the writer		
4. a conclusion including published evidence		
5. expression of gratitude by-line		

(4)

MY ARTICLE CONTAINS	☑	☒
1. relevant data & by-line as title		
2. content that offers a balanced view of the issue		
3. name of the publishing body		
4. a conclusion including personal observations		
5. designation and date at the end		

A.	Option (1)	B.	Option (2)
C.	Option (3)	D.	Option (4)

Ans. B. Option (2)

LITERATURE

This section has sub-sections: V, VI, VII, VIII, IX. There are a total of 30 questions in the section. Attempt any 26 questions from the sub-sections V to IX.

V. **Read the given extract to attempt questions that follow:**

"I have nothing else to do," he mutters, looking away. "Go to school," I say glibly, realising immediately how hollow the advice must sound.

"There is no school in my neighbourhood. When they build one, I will go."

"If I start a school, will you come?" I ask, half-joking. "Yes," he says, smiling broadly.

A few days later I see him running up to me. "Is your school ready?"

"It takes longer to build a school," I say, embarrassed at having made a promise that was not meant. But promises like mine abound in every corner of his bleak world.

Q.31. Saheb's muttering and 'looking away' suggests his

    A. anger   B. shyness   C. embarrassment   D. anxiety

Ans. C. embarrassment

Q.32. Of the four meanings of 'glibly', select the option that matches in meaning with its usage in the extract.

    A. showing a degree of informality   B. lacking depth and substance

    C. being insincere and deceitful   D. speaking with fluency

Ans. B. lacking depth and substance

Q.33. Who do you think Saheb is referring to as 'they', in the given sentence?

"When they build one, I will go"

    A. The officials   B. The inhabitants

    C. The teachers   D. The journalists

Ans. A. The officials

Q.34. Select the option that lists the feelings and attitudes corresponding to the following:

    1. *I ask half-joking*

    2. *...he says, smiling broadly*

A.	(1) part arrogance, part seriousness		B.	(1) part amusement, part irritation
	(2) hesitation			(2) submissiveness

C.	(1) part concern, part hurt		D.	(1) part humour, part earnestness
	(2) pride			(2) self-belief

Ans.

D.	(1) part humour, part earnestness
	(2) self-belief

Q.35. Select the option that lists reasons why Saheb's world has been called 'bleak'.

    (1) The absence of parental presence   (2) The poor socio-economic conditions

    (3) His inability to address problems   (4) His lack of life-skills

    (5) The denied opportunities of schooling

    A. (1) and (4)   B. (2) and (5)

    C. (3) and (5)   D. (2) and (4)

Ans. B. (2) and (5)

VI. **Read the given extract to attempt questions that follow:**

Tiny vestiges of the old terror would return. But now I could frown and say to that terror, "Trying to scare me, eh? Well, here's to you! Look!" And off I'd go for another length of the pool. This went on until July. But I was still not satisfied. I was not sure that all the terror had left. So, I went to Lake Wentworth in New Hampshire, dived off a dock at Triggs Island, and swam two miles across the lake to Stamp Act Island. I swam the crawl, breast stroke, side stroke, and back stroke. Only once did the terror return. When I was in the middle of the lake, I put my face under and saw nothing but bottomless water. The old sensation returned in miniature.

Q.36. Why did Douglas go to swim at Lake Wentworth?

    A. To showcase his skills for all who had doubted him.

    B. To honour the efforts of his swimming instructor.

    C. To build on his ability of swimming in a natural water body.

    D. To know for sure that he had overcome his fear of drowning in water.

Ans. D. To know for sure that he had overcome his fear of drowning in water.

Q.37. Select the option that lists the correct inference based on the information in the extract.
    A. Triggs Island and Stamp Act Island are both located in Lake Wentworth.
    B. Lake Wentworth is a part of Triggs Island.
    C. Stamp Act Island is two miles away from New Hampshire.
    D. Lake Wentworth is connected via docks to New Hampshire.
Ans. A. Triggs Island and Stamp Act Island are both located in Lake Wentworth.
Q.38. What was the reason for the 'return' of terror?
    A. Superstitions about the dock at Triggs Islands   B. Recent reports about drowning incidents
    C. Prior drowning experiences   D. Warnings by experienced swimmers
Ans. C. Prior drowning experiences
Q.39. Douglas mentions that the *old sensation returned in miniature.*
    He means that he felt the familiar feeling of fear ………………
    A. at irregular intervals.   B. on a small scale.   C. repeatedly.   D. without notice.
Ans. B. on a small scale.
Q.40. How did Douglas handle the 'old sensation'?
    A. Addressed it.   B. Avoided it.
    C. Submitted to it.   D. Stayed indifferent to it.
Ans. A. Addressed it.
VII. **Read the given extract to attempt questions that follow:**
    The tall girl with her weighed-down head. The paperseeming
    boy, with rat's eyes. The stunted, unlucky heir
    Of twisted bones, reciting a father's gnarled disease,
    His lesson, from his desk. At back of the dim class
    One unnoted, sweet and young. His eyes live in a dream…
Q.41. The poet draws attention to the problem of __________ while describing the boy as *paper-seeming.*
    A. malnutrition   B. untidiness   C. isolation   D. abandonment
Ans. A. malnutrition
Q.42. Which option has the underlined phrase that applies the poetic device used for 'rat's eyes'?
    A. He shut up <u>like a clam</u> when interrogated.
    B. She runs <u>as swift as a gazelle</u>.
    C. He is considered the <u>black sheep</u> of the family.
    D. She ran away <u>chattering with fear</u>.
Ans. C. He is considered the <u>black sheep</u> of the family.
Q.43. Select the correct option to fill the blank.
    The tall girl's head is weighed down due to the__________ .
    A. effect of diseases   B. need for concentration
    C. desire to remain unnoticed   D. burdens of poverty
Ans. D. burdens of poverty
Q.44. The literal meaning of 'reciting' refers to delivering the lesson aloud. What does its figurative meaning refer to?
    A. Showing extra interest in the lesson.   B. Carrying his father's disease.
    C. Resigning to his disease and condition.   D. Voicing the poor conditions, he lives in.
Ans. B. Carrying his father's disease.
Q.45. How does the 'unnoted' pupil present a contrast to others?
    A. He appears to be in a world of dreams.   B. He struggles with the fulfilment of dreams.
    C. He seems taller than most.   D. He sits in the dimmest part of the classroom.
Ans. A. He appears to be in a world of dreams.
VII. **Read the given extract to attempt questions that follow:**
    He said I was unhappy. That made my wife kind of mad, but he explained that he meant the modern world is full
    of insecurity, fear, war, worry and all the rest of it, and that I just want to escape. Well, who doesn't? Everybody

I know wants to escape, but they don't wander down into any third level at Grand Central Station. But that's the reason, he said, and my friends all agreed. Everything points to it, they claimed.

My stamp collecting, for example; that's a 'temporary refuge from reality.' Well, maybe, but my grandfather didn't need any refuge from reality.

Q.46. Why did Sam's verdict make Charley's wife 'mad'?
- A.   It made it difficult for her to accept that Charley would consult a psychiatrist.
- B.   It seemed to suggest to her that she was the cause of Charley's unhappiness.
- C.   It made her aware of Charley's delicate state of mind.
- D.   It offended her that Charley and Sam collectively accused her.

Ans. B.   It seemed to suggest to her that she was the cause of Charley's unhappiness.

Q.47. Sam's explanation to the reaction of Charley's wife was ____________ in nat
- A.   critical   B.   aggressive   C.   clarifying   D.   accusatory

Ans. C.   clarifying

Q.48. Select the option that signifies the condition of people of the 'modern world' mentioned in the extract.
- (1)   unsure
- (2)   lazy
- (3)   offensive
- (4)   anxious
- (5)   afraid
- A.   (1) and (3)
- B.   (2) and (5)
- C.   (2), (3) and (4)
- D.   (1), (4) and (5)

Ans. D.   (1), (4) and (5)

Q.49. Select the option that displays a cause-effect set.

A.

Cause	Effect
Charley's stamp collecting	Wandering into the third level

B.

Cause	Effect
Everybody wants to escape	Modern world full of insecurity

C.

Cause	Effect
Charley's wandering into the third level	Charley's stamp collecting

D.

Cause	Effect
Modern world full of insecurity	Everybody wants to escape

Ans.

D.

Cause	Effect
Modern world full of insecurity	Everybody wants to escape

Q.50. Why didn't Charley's grandfather need refuge from reality?
- A.   He was too busy to bother.
- B.   He had chosen to deny his reality.
- C.   He lived in peaceful times.
- D.   He was a very secure person.

Ans. C.   He lived in peaceful times.

IX.   Attempt the following.

Q.51. In 'Keeping Quiet' the poet does not want the reader to confuse his advice for __________ with total inactivity.
- A.   experimentation
- B.   relaxation
- C.   isolation
- D.   introspection

Ans. D.   introspection

Q.52. On his way to school, Franz says that he had the *strength to resist* and chose to hurry off to school. The underlined phrase suggests that Franz was
- A.   hesitant.
- B.   threatened.
- C.   tempted.
- D.   repentant.

Ans. C.   tempted.

Q.53. Select the suitable option for the given statements, based on your reading of *Lost Spring*.
- (1)   The writer notices that Saheb has lost his carefree look.
- (2)   Saheb has had to surrender his freedom for ₹800 per month.

A. (1) is false but (2) is true. B. Both (1) and (2) are true.
C. (2) is a fact but unrelated to (1). D. (1) is the cause for (2).

Ans. B. Both (1) and (2) are true.

Q.54. Select the option that lists the qualities of Douglas' trainer.

(1) adventurous (2) generous
(3) patient (4) methodical
(5) encouraging (6) courageous

A. (1) and (6) B. (3), (4) and (5)
C. (2) and (5) D. (1), (4) and (6)

Ans. B. (3), (4) and (5)

Q.55. The metaphor 'lead sky', is used by Stephen Spender to bring out

A. the image of sky-high constructions in the slum.
B. a response to death and destruction.
C. the strong dreams and aspirations of the children.
D. a sense of hopelessness and despair.

Ans. D. a sense of hopelessness and despair.

Q.56. Sadao's servants leave his house, but none of them betrays the secret of the American P.O.W. Select the option that explains this.

A. The servants truly believed that they must not be a part of the household which sheltered a prisoner of war, but their love and loyalty to Sadao made them keep the secret safe.
B. The servants knew that any information about the P.O.W would result in punishment for them and their families which is why they revealed nothing.
C. The servants were superstitious and scared with a white man on the premises and consequently, chose to remove themselves and stay silent about the situation.
D. The servants did not want to incur the wrath of Dr. Sadao and lose their jobs, therefore they chose to exit instead, and return later.

Ans. A. The servants truly believed that they must not be a part of the household which sheltered a prisoner of war, but their love and loyalty to Sadao made them keep the secret safe.

Q.57. Classify (1) to (4) as fact (F) or opinion (O), based on your reading of *The Third Level*.

(1) First day covers are never opened. (2) Grand Central is growing like a tree.
(3) President Roosevelt collected stamps. (4) Sam was Charley's psychiatrist.

A. F-1,3,4; O-2 B. F-2, 3; O-1,4
C. F-2; O-1,3,4 D. F-3,4; O-1,2

Ans. A. F-1,3,4; O-2

Q.58. Identify the tone of Pablo Neruda in the following line:

Perhaps the Earth can teach us….

A. Confident and clear about the future events.
B. Dramatic about the prediction he made.
C. Convinced about the sequence of events to follow.
D. Uncertain, yet hopeful about the possibility.

Ans. D. Uncertain, yet hopeful about the possibility.

Q.59. Dr. Sadao mutters the word 'my friend' while treating the American P.O.W. in the light of the circumstances, we can say that this was

A. humourous. B. climactic. C. ironical. D. ominous.

Ans. C. ironical.

Q.60. The sight of young trees and merry children, on the way to Cochin, is ________ the poet's aging mother.

A. like a divine assurance for B. in sharp contrast to
C. a distraction from pain for D. the bridge between the poet and

Ans. B. in sharp contrast to

❑❑

Sample Paper 1

English Core

READING

I. Read the passage given below.

I. A bookshop is not something you find in every street or area these days. Books, which were once a permanent accompaniment for youngsters in their formative years, are fading out of their list of engagements.

II. Ask any youngster which is the latest book he has read and he will be baffled. Apart from a few consistent readers, others just befool themselves with a bookseller's name or lament the curriculum load for justifying themselves, like this seventeen-year-old school-goer who says, 'I just read my Physics book.'

III. Television has been blamed for this calamitous situation, which is producing square-faced people and a bookless society. Furthermore, today's children are under pressure to be smart and popular and to succeed on a social level. Parties, dancing and hanging out at different places begin early. Moreover, computers, video games, the Internet, swimming lessons, cricket and a youngster's passion for an hour-long tete-a-tete on the telephone with friends eat up all their leisure time.

IV. A child who is constantly under pressure to live up to his parents' expectations, which are at times unreasonable, does not like to throw himself into another set of books after the laborious school work, unless he comes from a family of readers where the engrossing work of Shakespeare and Dickens are just a matter of pulling them out from the shelves.

V. Many parents also believe that today's children have become more aware and demand logical reasoning for everything. They can no longer be fooled by fairy tales or animal stories, as they have not seen any fairies or animals except for those old and tired ones in the city zoo. This has made them more interested in movies or TV serials than a turtle talking to a rabbit or a frog changing into a prince.

VI. But a visit to the capital's leading bookstores presents a contrasting picture of youngsters' reading habits. These bookshops claim they are doing healthy business and have many regular buyers from this age group.

VII. Though the works of Shakespeare, Charles Dickens, Jane Austen and Mark Twain no longer interest teenagers, bestsellers from Daniel Steele, Sidney Sheldon and Jeffery Archer are on the list of all reading teens. Self-help books, such as those on personality development or relationship management, are also picked up by many of them.

VIII. Mystery books like Nancy Drew and Hardy Boys are popular with kids and Mills and Boons and other romance novels with their fairly predictable formula with teenage girls. For parents of children below ten, volumes of Panchatantra Stories, Amar Chitra Katha and other bedtime stories are worthy purchases as these teach the child what is wrong in their own special way. What seems to be the case is that parents have surrendered to others what was their most precious right—that of making their children what they should become. With the old techniques of child rearing losing ground, modern parents must consciously spend time with their children. Taste and enthusiasm for literature can be communicated artfully to children by reading bedtime stories to them, encouraging them to play historical characters and giving books as birthday gifts.

IX. The family reading which was once popular in the West could well be adopted here. Reading aloud the works of great men by parents to their children not only forms a warm bond between them but also attracts young minds to the world of books which gives them a chance to explore the sea of life.

Based on your understanding of the passage, answer <u>any eight</u> out of the ten questions by choosing the correct option.

Q.1. Choose the CORRECT option that takes away the teenagers from reading good books.

A.   Cinema   B.   Television

C.   Dance shows   D.   Music programs

Q.2. Select the option that would suitably complete the given dialogue between the parents and the child as per the context in paragraph 5.

Parents: Why don't read the books that we bought you? All you do is to look at the television the entire day!

Child: I don't (1) ....

Parents: And does the television provide you any logic to what you see?

Child: Yes! (2) .... I enjoy it.

A.   (1) want to read the books (2) they do.

B.   (1) understand the logics behind those fairy tales (2) the stories are realistic and well described through animations.

C.   (1) want to exhaust my mind thinking about the logic in them (2) totally.

D.   (1) like to read (2) it makes my imagination vivid.

Q.3. The passage uses a French word 'tete-a-tete'. This refers to:

A.   making group calls

B.   bad-mouthing people behind them

C.   having an argument

D.   having a private conversation between two people

Q.4. Select the CORRECT image of the activity that was once popular in the West.

A.   Option 1   B.   Option 2

C.   Option 3   D.   Option 4

Q.5. Select the correct hobby that youngsters use to posses before and the one they posses today.

Before	Today	Before	Today	Before	Today	Before	Today
Watching television	Reading books	Reading poetry	Reading novels	Reading books	Watching television	Watching movies on television	Watching movies online

           A.   B.   C.   D.

Q.6. What is the relationship between (1) and (2).

(1)   children have become more logic-demanding

(2)   children prefer watching television to reading fairy tales

A.   (1) is the cause of (2)   B.   (2) elaborates the affirmation of (1)

C.   (2) is the reason behind (1)   D.   (1) is the advice for (2)

Q.7. Based on information given in the passage, select the option that describes the cause of children ignoring books.

A.   They find them uninteresting   B.   They are more addicted to online entertainment

C.   They lament the curriculum load   D.   They don't have patience to read books

Q.8. Select the option that lists the importance of reading for writer.

A.   warms the bond between parents and children, attracts young minds to the world of books, a chance to explore the sea of life.

B.   bring harmony among people, create calm, keep people busy.

C.   makes people look trendy, learn something new, a chance to revive self.

D.   creates a huge burden on young minds, makes them anxious, an intense mind activity.

Q.9. Which quote summarizes the importance of the books as given in the last paragraph of the passage?

A.   *"You can swim all day in the Sea of Knowledge and still come out completely dry. Most people do."*

— Norton Juster

B.   *Sleep is good, he said, and books are better.*   *-George R.R. Martin*

C.   *If you don't like to read, you haven't found the right book.*   *-J.K. Rowling*

D.   *Books should go where they will be most appreciated, and not sit unread, gathering dust on a forgotten shelf, don't you agree?*   *-Christopher Paolini*

Q.10. Select the option that can be concluded from the text.

(1)   Youngsters are no longer interested in reading books

(2)   The number of Bookshops is increasing due to the increase in demand of the books

(3)   Shakespeare is the most beloved writer among the youngsters

(4)   Children desire logical content

A.   (1), (2) and (3) are true (4) is false   B.   (1) and (3) are true (2) and (4) are false

C.   (1) and (4) are true, (2) and (3) are false   D.   all are false

II. Read the passage given below.

I.   The passenger pigeon (Ectopistesmigratorius) was once found in huge numbers in North America. Records tell of passing flocks that darkened the skies for several days at a time. The species may have peaked at five billion individuals. A more conservative estimate is three billion.

II.   Within a short time, the species disappeared completely.

"Given the huge size of the population, it's simply amazing that the species disappeared so quickly," says Tom Gilbert. Gilbert is a professor at the University of Copenhagen's Centre for GeoGenetics, but he also has a part-time position as an adjunct professor at the Norwegian University of Science and Technology (NTNU).

III.   The history of the passenger pigeon is interesting, partly because it can tell us something about how and why species become extinct. Native Americans also relied on passenger pigeons for food. But at least in parts of the passenger pigeons' range, people had learned to harvest the species at a sustainable level that didn't threaten to eradicate it. It was common in some parts of North America to only eat young pigeons that were hunted at night, since this did not seem to scare away the adult birds or prevent them from re-nesting.

IV.   But starting around 1500, a more aggressive variant of humans came to the continent with the arrival of Europeans. The hunt for passenger pigeons grew and culminated in a massive hunt for the species throughout the 1800s, before the species finally collapsed and disappeared. In 2014, a study in published in the scientific journal PNAS strongly suggested that humans were simply the final straw in destroying a species that was already vulnerable and headed to oblivion.

The cladogram below follows the 2012 DNA study showing the position of the passenger pigeon among its closest relatives:

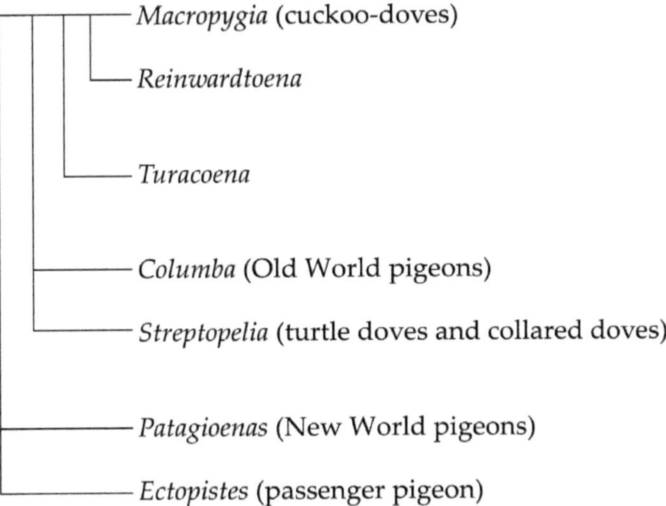

V.   The researchers asserted that despite their enormous numbers, the passenger pigeons were already in trouble. The population of the species varied greatly, similar to lemmings, but over a longer period of time. When the Europeans arrived, the species was already in a strong decline. The population was plummeting long before Europeans arrived, and perhaps Europeans even contributed to a short-term increase in numbers.

VI.   Studies of the genetic variation of the species using an investigative method called PSMC formed the background for these assertions. And now we have to concentrate a bit. The PSMC method can use the information in the genes of a single individual of a species to map the history of the species.

VII.   You should therefore be able to see how the species developed over many generations, and estimate how many individuals there were at any given time, all based on a single genome. Using this method, researchers found that the number of passenger pigeons was in free fall even before the arrival of the Europeans.

Although the species might not have become extinct, it would have shrunk significantly in any case, maybe to only a few hundred thousand individuals.

Based on your understanding of the passage, answer <u>any six</u> out of the eight questions by choosing the correct option.

Q.11. Select the correct inference with reference to the following.

"Records tell of passing flocks that darkened the skies for several days at a time."

A.   The innumerable individual passenger pigeons flocked the skies of North America.

B.   The black pigeons together turned the blue sky dark.

C.   When the pigeons passed through the skies of North America, the sky was covered with black clouds.

D.   The pigeons carried bad omens with them which were visible through the sky getting dark.

Q.12. According to cladogram 2012 DNA study in fig-1, the species that was famous among Old World pigeons were:

A.   Reinwardtoena   B.   Columba

C.   Patagioenas   D.   Turacoena

Q.13. Choose the correct cause and effect relationship from the given options.

Cause	Effect
The hunt for passenger pigeons grew and culminated in a massive hunt for the species throughout the 1800s.	The species finally collapsed and disappeared.

A.

Cause	Effect
The history of the passenger pigeon is interesting.	It can tell us something about how and why species become extinct

B.

Cause	Effect
The PSMC method can use the information in the genes of a single individual of a species.	Mapping the history of the species.

C.

Cause	Effect
Studies of the genetic variation of the species is using an investigative method called PSMC.	It formed the background for these assertions.

D.

Q.14. Select the central message in paragraph – II according to Tom Gilbert's study about Passenger pigeon.

It conclude that

A.   It's simply astonishing that the species found in large number, disappeared so quickly.

B.   It's pathetic that passenger pigeons were disliked by Europeans.

C.   It's incredible that the species flourished quickly.

D.   It's unbelievable that the species suddenly migrated.

Q.15. Based on your reading of paragraph III, select the appropriate counter- argument to the given argument.

Argument : The North Americans ate young pigeons that were hunted at night, since this did not seem to scare away the adult birds or prevent them from re-nesting.

A.   I think the North Americans could have eaten the birds at day too as it won't make any difference.

B.   I don't think that eating young birds at night wouldn't scare the adult birds. After all, they can sense fear and it is just an assumption of the North Americans.

C.   I feel that hunting adult birds could have been better because the young birds wouldn't have been able to judge the scene.

D.   I don't feel that what North Americans did was right.

Q.16. The phrase "The population was plummeting long before Europeans arrived" refers to:

A.   The number of migrating passenger pigeons was decreasing slowly.

B.   There was a rapid decrease in the population of passenger pigeons.

C.   The species of passenger pigeons were extinct.

D.   There was a rapid increase in the population of passenger pigeons.

Q.17. Based on the reading of the passage, choose the fact that the researchers find about the number of passenger pigeons.

A.   It's number started deteriorating with the arrival of Europeans.

B.   It was in free fall even before the arrival of the Europeans.

C.   It became extinct after the arrival of Europeans.

D.   It's species began to multiply with the arrival of Europeans.

Q.18. Read the two statements given below and select the option that explains them.

(1)   PSMC method uses the information in the genes of a single individual of a species.

(2)   It is important to map the history of the species to know more.

A.   (1) is the result of (2)   B.   (2) is the requirement for (1)

C.   (1) is true, (2) is false   D.   (2) is the research through (1)

WRITING

III.   Answer <u>any four</u> out of the five questions given, with reference to the context below.

Deepak Kumar, the Police Commissioner of Kanpur wants to write a notice advising the residents to drive carefully and use fog lights to prevent accidents

Q.19. Select the appropriate title for the notice.

A.   The Dense Fog   B.   Traffic Advisory

C.   Prevent accidents   D.   Be vigilant on roads

Q.20. Select the option that lists the most accurate opening for this notice.

A.   Greetings and attention please, to one and all….

B.   This notice is written to share some news with you all about…

C.   This is to notify that in view of …

D.   I wish to share this notice that ……

Q.21. Select the option with the information points to be included in the body of this notice.

(1)   Opinion about the weather

(2)   Resolution for accidents due to the fog

(3)   Reasons for the fog

(4)   Importance of fog lights for vehicles

(5)   Complaint against people without fog lights

A.   (2) and (4)   B.   (1), (3) and (5)

C.   (3) and (5)   D.   (2) and (3)

Q.22. What is the purpose of writing this notice?

A.   to threaten people   B.   to praise people

C.   to demean people   D.   to warn people

Q.23. Select the appropriate conclusion for this notice.

A.   Stay safe   B.   Don't panic

C.   Stay humble   D.   Inconvenience regretted

IV. **Answer <u>any six</u> of the seven questions given, with reference to the context below.**

You are Megha, a resident of Lodhi road, New Delhi. You have to write a letter to the editor bringing the issue of daylight robbery in your neighborhood into the view of concerned authorities.

Q.24. Choose the CORRECT start for the letter.

A. Please look at the daylight robbery in our area

B. Through the columns of your esteemed newspaper, I want to draw your kind attention towards the daylight robbery in our area

C. With your newspaper I want to open the eyes of the concerned authorities to the daylight robbery of the area

D. I want to complaint about the daylight robbery

Q.25. Pick the CORRECT tone in which this letter to the editor shall be ended.

"I hope that the concerned authorities may look into the matter at the earliest."

A. friendly and warm   B. cool and polite

C. polite and formal   D. rude and strict

Q.26. Choose the CORRECT option for the following.

"_______________: Need to take a strict action against the daylight robberies"

A. Subject   B. Topic

C. Salutation   D. Title

Q.27. Choose the option that shows what the letter to the editor would NOT do for Megha.

A. Bring changes in conditions

B. Take actions against the issue

C. Make her area safer to live

D. Getting a reward for her to bring it to the notice of concerned authorities

Q.28. Writing a letter to the editor will help Megha to _______________.

A.	B.	C.	D.
• vent out her frustration • Demean the police department	• look superior than other locals • Come out as a brave girl	• remove undeserving policeman from their job • Get hired instead	• Solve the robbery issues in the area by highlighting it in a newspaper • Make the area safe for people

Q.29. Megha shares some suggestions in her letter, to address the issue.

Select the option that helps her complete these suggestions, appropriately.

Much of this problem will be dealt if(i)_______________at the colony entrance. It will be so kind if the concerned authorities could provide at least two policemen to look around the area during the morning and the evening hours.

A. security guards are posted   B. arms are provided to the gatekeeper

C. restriction is made   D. there is a lock

Q.30. Which of the following approach is most appropriate for drafting a letter on the above subject?

A. Suggesting improvement methods—Introducing problem faced by the people—Conclusion.

B. Introducing problems faced by the people—Suggesting improvement methods—Conclusion.

C. Suggesting improvement methods—Conclusion—Introducing problems faced by the people.

D. Conclusion—Introducing problems faced by the people—Suggesting improvement methods

LITERATURE

This section has sub-sections: V, VI, VII, VIII, IX. There are a total of 30 questions in the section. Attempt any 26 questions from the sub-sections V to IX.

V. **Read the given extract to attempt questions that follow:**

Poor man! It was in honour of this last lesson that he had put on his fine Sunday clothes, and now I understood why the old men of the village were sitting there in the back of the room. It was because they were sorry, too, that

they had not gone to school more. It was their way of thanking our master for his forty years of faithful service and of showing their respect for the country that was theirs no more.

Q.31. The narrator referred to M. Hamel as 'Poor man!' because he:

A. empathised with M. Hamel as he had to leave the village.

B. believed that M. Hamel's "fine Sunday clothes" clearly reflected that he was not rich.

C. felt sorry for M. Hamel as it was his last French lesson.

D. thought that M. Hamel's patriotism and sense of duty resulted in his poverty.

Q.32. Choose the CORRECT idiom that describes the villagers' act of attending the last lesson most accurately.

A. 'Too good to miss'   B. 'Too little, too late'

C. 'Too many cooks spoil the broth'   D. 'Too cool for school'

Q.33. Choose the option that might raise a question about M. Hamel's "faithful service".

A. When Franz came late, M. Hamel told him that he was about to begin class without him.

B. Franz mentioned how cranky M. Hamel was and his "great ruler rapping on the table".

C. M. Hamel often sent students to water his flowers, and gave a holiday when he wanted to go fishing.

D. M. Hamel permitted villagers put their children "to work on a farm or at the mills" for some extra money.

Q.34. Select the option that most appropriately fills in the blanks, for the following description of the given extract.

The villagers and their children sat in class, forging with their old master a (i) ___ togetherness. In that moment, the class room stood (ii)___. It was France itself, and the last French lesson a desperate hope to (iii) ___to the remnants of what they had known and taken for granted. Their own (iv) ___.

A. (i) graceful; (ii) still; (iii) hang on; (iv) country

B. (i) bygone; (ii) up; (iii) keep on; (iv) education

C. (i) beautiful; (ii) mesmerised; (iii) carry on; (iv) unity

D. (i) forgotten; (ii) transformed; (iii) hold on; (iv) identity

Q.35. Identify the villagers' emotions from the extract.

A. happiness   B. desperation

C. depression   D. regret

VI. **Read the given extract to attempt questions that follow:**

"I will learn to drive a car," he answers, looking straight into my eyes. His dream looms like a mirage amidst the dust of streets that fill his town Firozabad, famous for its bangles. Every other family in Firozabad is engaged in making bangles. It is the centre of India's glass-blowing industry where families have spent generations working around furnaces, wielding glass, making bangles for all the women in the land it seems.

Mukesh's family is among them. None of them know that it is illegal for children like him to work in the glass furnaces with high temperatures, in dingy cells without air and light; that the law, if enforced, could get him and all those 20,000 children out of the hot furnaces where they slog their daylight hours, often losing the brightness of their eyes. Mukesh's eyes beam as he volunteers to take me home, which he proudly says is being rebuilt.

Q.36. The phrase 'Dream looms like a mirage amidst the dust of streets' signifies that

A. his dream was a reality, yet seemed distant.   B. his dream was lost in the sea of dust.

C. his dream was illusionary and indistinct.   D. his dream was hanging in the dusty air.

Q.37. Identify the emotions of Mukesh from the phrase: 'I will learn to drive a car'.

(1) arrogant   (2) hopeful

(3) sad   (4) ambitious

(5) sneaky

A. 1 and 5   B. 2 and 4

C. 2 and 5   D. 3 and 6

Q.38. Which of the following statements is NOT TRUE with reference to the extract?

A. Children work in badly lit and poorly ventilated furnaces.

B. The children are unaware that it is forbidden by law to work in the furnaces.

    C.   Children toil in the furnaces for hours which affect their eyesight.

    D.   Firozabad has emerged as a nascent producer of bangles in the country.

Q.39. *"Every other family in Firozabad is engaged in making bangles"*. What does this line highlight?

    A.   bangle making is the only industry that flourishes in Firozabad.

    B.   the entire population of Firozabad is involved in bangle making.

    C.   majority of the population in Firozabad is involved in bangle making.

    D.   bangle making is the most loved occupation in Firozabad.

Q.40. *"Mukesh's eyes beam as he volunteers to take me home."* This indicates that Mukesh was:

    A.   happy   B.   sad

    C.   gloomy   D.   dreamy

VII. **Read the given extract to attempt questions that follow:**

Driving from my parent's home to Cochin last Friday

morning, I saw my mother, beside me,

doze, open mouthed, her face ashen like that

of a corpse and realised with pain

that she was as old as she looked but soon

put that thought away,…

Q.41. Which of the following options best applies to the given extract?

    (1)   a conversation   (2)   an argument

    (3)   a piece of advice   (4)   a strategy

    (5)   a recollection   (6)   a suggestion

    A.   (1), (3) and (6)   B.   (2), (4) and (5)

    C.   Only (5)   D.   Only (1)

Q.42. Select the book title that perfectly describes the condition of the poet's mother.

Title 1	Title 2	Title 3	Title 4
You're Only Old Once! by *Dr. Seuss*	The Gift of Years by *Joan Chittister*	Somewhere Towards the End by *Diana Athill*	The Book You Wish Your Parents Had Read by *Philippa Perry*

    A.   Title 1   B.   Title 2

    C.   Title 3   D.   Title 4

Q.43. Choose the option that applies correctly to the two statements given below.

    Assertion: The poet wards off the thought of her mother getting old quickly.

    Reason: The poet didn't want to confront the inevitability of fate that was to dawn upon her mother.

    A.   Assertion can be inferred but the Reason cannot be inferred.

    B.   Assertion cannot be inferred but the Reason can be inferred.

    C.   Both Assertion and Reason can be inferred.

    D.   Both Assertion and Reason cannot be inferred.

Q.44. Choose the option that displays the same literary device as in the given lines of the extract.

her face

ashen like that

of a corpse…

    A.   Just as I had this thought, she appeared and…

    B.   My thoughts were as heavy as lead that evening when …

    C.   I think like everyone else who…

    D.   I like to think aloud when …

Q.45. Her face *'ashen like a corpse'*. The phrase here means:

    A.   there was ashes of smoke on her face

    B.   her face was full of dirt and dust

C.   her face was lifeless and dull like that of a dead person

D.   the wrinkles on her face made her looked ashen

VII.   Read the given extract to attempt questions that follow:

He was very light, like a fowl that had been half-starved for a long time until it is only feathers and skeleton. So, his arms hanging, they carried him up the steps and into the side door of the house. This door opened into a passage, and down the passage they carried the man towards an empty bedroom. It had been the bedroom of Sadao's father, and since his death it had not been used. They laid the man on the deeply matted floor. Everything here had been Japanese to please the old man, who would never in his own home sit on a chair or sleep in a foreign bed. Hana went to the wall cupboards and slid back a door and took out a soft quilt. She hesitated. The quilt was covered with flowered silk and the lining was pure white silk.

Q.46. The description of Sadao's father in the extract demonstrates that he was a ______________ person.

A.   witty

B.   modern

C.   traditional

D.   wacky

Q.47. 'She hesitated' means that Hana

A.   didn't want to carry the soldier as he had a limp in his leg

B.   didn't want to use her silk as he was their guest

C.   didn't want to use her white silk as the soldier was bleeding

D.   didn't like to share her stuff

Q.48. *"his arms hanging"* indicated the state of the soldier. Pick the option that correctly tells his state.

(1)   unconscious

(2)   weak

(3)   strong

(4)   rebellious

(5)   calm

(6)   conscious

A.   (1) and (2)

B.   (1) and (3)

C.   (5) and (6)

D.   (4) and (5)

Q.49. They avoided bringing the person home as he was

A.   foreigner, white, enemy

B.   enemy, soldier, Japanese

C.   Japanese, soldier, friend

D.   foreigner, friend, bleeding

Q.50. Select the option that displays a cause-effect set.

A.

Cause	Effect
Hana didn't want to use her beloved quilt for the American soldier.	She hesitated while taking it out.

B.

Cause	Effect
She hesitated while taking out quilt.	Hana didn't want to use her beloved quilt for an American soldier.

C.

Cause	Effect
Sadao's father was a traditional man.	He liked modern furniture in the house.

D.

Cause	Effect
He was not a true patriot.	Sadao was ready to treat the enemy.

IX.   Attempt the following.

Q.51. When M. Hamel addressed Franz saying, *"I've plenty of time, I'll learn"*, what does this imply?

A.   Self-realization

B.   Astonishment

C.   Lethargic responsibilities

D.   Evading responsibilities

Q.52. Which of the following profession is prevalent in Seemapuri?

A.   bangle making

B.   iron making

C.   rag picking

D.   pick pocketing

Q.53. *"Hi, Skinny! How'd you like to be ducked?"* This line shows that the speaker was a:

A.   trainer

B.   bully

C.   teacher

D.   swimmer

Q.54. The poetic device in the line *"wan, pale as a late winter's moon"* is:

    A. hyperbole   B. irony

    C. simile   D. metaphor

Q.55. The children's faces are compared to 'rootless weeds'. This means they are _______________.

    A. insecure   B. ill-fed

    C. wasters   D. dumb

Q.56. Select the suitable option for the given statements, based on your reading of *The Third Level*.

    (1) Charley's wife Louisa was always worried for her husband's distrainment.

    (2) Charley wanted to escape his depressing reality of life through the third level.

    A. (1) is false but (2) is true.   B. Both (1) and (2) are false.

    C. (2) is a fact but unrelated to (1)   D. (1) is the cause for (2).

Q.57. Dr. Sadao decided to help the man, irrespective of :

    A. not knowing the cure   B. being an American

    C. the fear of being caught   D. being a patriot

Q.58. Which of the following option does the poet NOT mean when he talks about 'keeping quiet'?

    A. total inactivity   B. contemplating

    C. self introspection   D. being calm

Q.59. Identify the tone of Kamala Das in the following line:

I saw my mother, beside me, doze, open mouthed….

    A. elated and excited   B. heartbroken and despaired

    C. scared and anxious   D. serene and satisfied

Q.60. Dr. Sadao didn't further his feelings for Hana before ensuring that she was a Japanese. This shows that Dr. Sadao was:

    A. fake   B. selfish

    C. confused   D. ethical

❑❑

Sample Paper 2

English Core

READING

I. Read the passage given below.

I. The Titanic, in its watery grave, is a great museum of human history and is at risk of being lost forever because of curious voyagers and treasure hunters, fears Bob Ballard, who first discovered the remains of the iconic ship in 1985. Famous for discovering the great ship, Ballard is a former US Navy Officer and a professor of oceanography.

II. "Titanic is a museum of human history without door and guard. I am deeply concerned about not only the Titanic but all the ancient history that is now at risk. If we cannot save this iconic ship, then there is a very little hope we can save ancient ships. The world should realize that you don't have to go down and take everything and you do not have to do a treasure hunt. This is a common heritage of all of us and if we really want to take steps to preserve human history in the ocean, we need to start with Titanic," Ballard said in a telephonic interview from London.

III. Ballard, as part of a tie-up, is presenting a documentary called "Save the Titanic" on the 100th anniversary of the sinking of the great ship – April 15, 1912. The ship and her fate continue to fascinate, largely because of the horror that took place that night, with 1,522 passengers and crew losing their lives.

IV. Ballard says that despite being on the ocean floor for 100 years, the ship is full of human footprints. "You will find pairs of shoes everywhere. The sea and the life below has claimed everything but they do not know what to do with shoes so you will find a pair of mother's shoes next to her little daughter and that's their grave-stone. At her wreckage, we almost felt that we were surrounded by the lifeboats of all the people that were in the water at that spot".

V. Ballard says that the fate of Titanic continues to fascinate so many years after it sank because it is "irony personified in history". "The story has all the ingredients to make it timelessly fascinating. You have this revolutionary ship that's unsinkable and carrying a cross-section of people in society. And then, it goes and hits an iceberg and sinks on its maiden journey. It's an irony personified in history".

VI. Talking about his discovery, which came after great research and 75 years later, Ballard, says it was a somber moment went they first spotted the boiler of the Titanic. "In the 90s, advanced technology gave us double diving capabilities in the Atlantic Ocean. I knew that the Titanic was sitting at almost 12,000 feet. What led me to her discovery was a simple technique that I followed. We decided to look for the debris trail instead of the ship".

VII. Ballard says the ship, if preserved well and not subjected to constant submarine journeys, will last for a long time on the Atlantic floor. "The deep sea, because of its darkness, its cold temperatures and its great pressure, creates a high state of preservation. With a little caution, we can protect the Titanic for future generations to visit."

VIII. Ballard has also connected to the people of Belfast, who refused to talk about the tragedy. "The ship's construction took place at Belfast. After the tragedy, families of the workers refused to talk about it because of the shame and sadness in the loss of life involved".

(**Source:** archive.indianexpress.com)

Based on your understanding of the passage, answer _any eight_ out of the ten questions by choosing the correct option.

Q.1. The vandalism on the remains of the Titanic ship by divers makes the writer feel:

A. shocked

B. concerned

C. awestruck

D. annoyed

Q.2. Euphemism is a word or phrase used to avoid saying an unpleasant or offensive word.

The writer says that the titanic is in its <u>watery grave</u>.

Select the word from the options that correctly translates to the euphemism presented here.

  A.　sunk   B.　saved

  C.　stopped   D.　sifted

Q.3. Select the option that suitably completes the given dialogue as per the context in paragraph VIII.

Writer: Are you related to the workers who made the Titanic?

Man from Belfast: Yes, but (1)..........................

Writer: I just wanted to know about the incident.

Man from Belfast: I am sorry but (2)..........................

  A.　(1) it wasn't me who made it (2) I am willing to tell you only if you pay me.

  B.　(1) I cannot recognize you (2) we don't disclose such confidential affairs.

  C.　(1) only distantly (2) you don't look like you care enough.

  D.　(1) why do you ask? (2) I would rather not talk about that unfortunate tragedy.

Q.4. What could've been the news headline when the writer first discovered the remains of the Titanic ship in 1985?

1. Titanic the unsinkable now in ruins.	2. Headed to the port, now in the ocean.	3. Titanic found preserved in its watery grave.	4. Positive news for voyagers, Titanic found.

  A.　option 1   B.　option 2

  C.　option 3   D.　option 4

Q.5. Select the option that clearly indicates the situation before and after Titanic was discovered in 1985.

	Before 1985	**After 1985**
A.	Ruins preserved in cold dark ocean.	Hunters and voyagers exploiting the ruins.
B.	Ruins sinking deeper into the ocean.	Hunters and voyagers bringing the entire ship out.
C.	Ruins remaining intact.	Ruins preserved untouched.
D.	Ship getting lost to sea creatures.	Conservationists saving the remains.

Q.6. What is the relationship between (1) and (2)?

(1) ....In the 90s, advanced technology gave us double diving capabilities in the Atlantic Ocean.

(2) ....We decided to look for the debris trail instead of the ship.

  A.　(2) is the cause of (1).   B.　(1) and (2) were independent of each other.

  C.　(2) did not cause (1).   D.　(1) is the cause of (2).

Q.7. The writer mentions the Titanic as a great museum of human history. He says so because he realises that:

  A.　No matter what may come, we should protect the Titanic as it is the only reminder of the greatest ship that sunk into the ocean.

  B.　Titanic contains hidden treasures from the century old rich passengers that boarded the ship.

  C.　The deep dark and cold conditions of the ocean has well preserved a century old specimen of human endeavour and failure which is an irony personified in history.

  D.　Titanic has been claimed by the sea life below so there's no point now in trying to salvage it from further disintegration.

Q.8. Select the option that lists the eulogy for the Titanic's passengers by the ship-makers from Belfast.

  A.　We are all grieving today for the greatest loss to mankind in recent history. We have failed all those on board by not building them a strong enough Titanic.

  B.　Loss to human life is the most miserable one can imagine, but remember it was the fury of nature that took it down, and nothing more.

    C.   Grieve we must yes! But life goes on for us unfortunates who are still alive and have to live with the horrors of this tragedy.

    D.   Titanic and its human companions are resting in the depths of the ocean. The tragedy has immortalized them all forever.

Q.9. Which quote summarises the writer's feelings about the conservation of Titanic as a cultural icon for human history?

    A.   The object of war is victory; that of victory is conquest; and that of conquest preservation.

—Montesquieu

    B.   The people without the knowledge of their past history, origin and culture is like a tree without roots.   *—Marcus Garvey*

    C.   Until the moment she actually sinks, the Titanic is unsinkable.   *—Julia Hughes*

    D.   Government has no other end, but the preservation of property.   *—John Locke*

Q.10. Select the option that lists what we can conclude from the text.

    (1) The writer has unrealistic expectations of protecting Titanic from degradation.

    (2) The writer is addressing all of us to be responsible in preserving our heritage.

    (3) The technologies haven't advanced much since the 90s to help save the ruins of the ship.

    (4) Before going for deep sea treasure hunting, one must understand the cultural impact of their actions.

    A.   (2) and (3) are true   B.   (2), (3) and (4) are true

    C.   (1) and (4) are true   D.   (2) and (4) are true

II. Read the passage given below.

    I.   NSYNC singer Lance Bass can't afford the $20 million price tag for a ride into space now, he should try again, in say, a decade. But within a decade or so, even some of Bass's fans could afford a quick and safe trip to the suborbital edge of space, roughly 50-60 miles above earth, says Frank Seitzen, President of the Space Transport Association.

    II.   "I think you're may be 10 or 12 years away from having companies that are reliable and that can go through that process for $5,000 or $10,000," Seitzen said. There's a hungry demand from would be space tourists and a $10 million prize is inspiring designers. The Prize, created in 1994 to spur the development of new space travel technologies, has attracted at least 21 space vehicle designs from people in five countries. The non-profit X Prize Foundation, founded by a group of donors inspired by the $25,000 Orteig Prize that Charles Lindbergh won in 1927, will give the prize.

    III.   Each design team is hoping to develop the first reusable rocket capable of blasting a pilot and two to five passengers to a height of 62 miles. NASA awards astronaut status for flights above 50 miles. Some design contestants boast that such trips will be available by 2005, although the first few travellers will face $100,000 bills until the market matures.

    IV.   Despite steep prices and lagging technology, Seitzen and others are convinced that a lucrative travel business awaits. Space Adventures, a travel agency that helped coordinate the first tourist trip to the International Space Station last year by US businessman Dennis Tito, claims it has collected $2 million in deposits from more than 120 would-be suborbital tourists. For client Wally Funk, who has paid her deposit, suborbital travel is a disappointing, yet feasible, alternative to decades of trying to reach space. Funk, a retired aviation safety investigator says, "I would do (a space station trip) in a heartbeat, but I can't because I'm not a millionaire."

    V.   Compared to Tito's groundbreaking effort last year, future suborbital flights look easy. Tito was subjected to rigid medical requirements and a gruelling six-month training course in Russia. But suborbital travellers will need only a few days of training and pending FAA approval, would have to pass a much lower bar for medical standards."We always say that if you can safely ride a roller coaster, then you are fit for a suborbital flight," says Space Adventures spokeswoman Tereza Predescu.

    VI.   Four commercial spaceports, which launch rockets into space like airports launch planes, are already licensed to operate by the FAA in Virginia, California, Alaska and Florida, and they are eager to welcome extra business from space tourists, negating the need to catch a ride to Russia. For those reasons, suborbital travel may represent a $1 billion in a year market, according to Space Adventures President and CEO Eric Anderson, that's 10,000 travellers paying $100,000 each during the first few years of adventure space travel.

(Source: auto.economictimes.indiatimes.com)

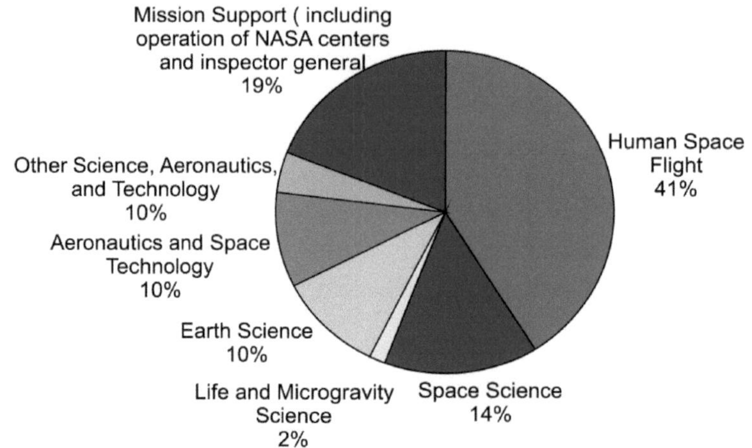

NASA budget for science-related programs and activities, FY 1997 (constant FY 1995 dollars)

Based on your understanding of the passage, answer <u>any six</u> out of the eight questions by choosing the correct option.

Q.11. Select the correct inference with reference to the following:

There's a hungry demand from would be space tourists and a $10 million prize is inspiring designers......

A. Space tourists have collectively bet a $10 million prize to anyone who can take them for a space trip.

B. Space tourists are demanding for restaurants in space to satiate a hungry stomach.

C. There's a potential for space tourism market but unfortunately no one is tapping into it.

D. Spacecraft designers are competing to bring the quickest and most affordable options for space tourism.

Q.12. Select the central idea of the paragraph I.

A. Space tourism may not be feasible as of now but next decade may prove more promising.

B. Space tourism is only for the super-rich, be it at present or in the next decade.

C. Space tourism is a wasteful venture of resources and fuels.

D. Space tourism is going to be accessible only through NASA.

Q.13. Select the option that displays the true statement with reference to the figure given.

A. NASA's budget lays more emphasis on the study of Life and Microgravity science.

B. NASA's budget for Human Space Flight and Mission Support are in the priority.

C. It is not possible to correctly tell NASA's preferences as everything is for science at the end.

D. Space Science and Earth Science are the highest funded NASA programs.

Q.14. Based on your reading of paragraphs IV-V, select the appropriate counter- argument to the given argument.

Argument: Space trips are an egotistical way to flaunt your wealth to the poor and middle class, because at the end of the day you're contributing nothing to science and advancement.

A. The wealthy have collected about $ 2 million for space travel, so they all are working together setting their egos aside.

B. It is not for us to judge what others are doing as long as they are aware of the carbon footprints they are going to leave behind.

C. History holds testimony that the rich has always had unrealistic tastes, earlier it was precious stones and ivory, now it is space travel.

D. The wealthiest are willing to fund for research and development in space science, so even if it is for their ego, it will still be a way for advancement in faster and cheaper technologies.

Q.15. Select the option that displays the correct cause-effect relationship.

	Cause	Effect
A.	$10 million prize for spacecraft designers.	Faster development of cost-effective space trips.
B.	Rising interest in space tourism.	Decrease in space science studies.
C.	Lower budget constraints for researchers.	Lesser productivity and slow advancements.
D.	Faster development of cost-effective space trips.	$10 million prize for spacecraft designers.

Q.16. The survey statistics mention the speculated average space flight budget, indicating that:

    A.   The ticket price can be either of $100,000 or $5,000.

    B.   The demand and development lack the potential to lower ticket price from $100,000 to $5,000.

    C.   The demand for a space flight is now saturating.

    D.   The demand and development have the potential to lower ticket price from $10,000 to $5,000.

Q.17. The phrase 'blasting a pilot' refers to the:

    A.   bombing the pilot into shreds.

    B.   launching a pilot into space.

    C.   shooting a pilot into space.

    D.   hurling a pilot into space.

Q.18. Read the two statements given below and select the option that suitably explains them.

(1) Each design team is hoping to develop the first reusable rocket.

(2) Suborbital travel may represent a $1 billion in a year market.

    A.   (2) is false but (1) is true.

    B.   (1) is true and (2) is the reason of (1).

    C.   (1) and (2) are false.

    D.   (2) and (1) are true but independent of each other.

WRITING

III.   Answer <u>any four</u> out of the five questions given, with reference to the context below.

General Manager of Digimart Infotech, New Delhi needs a marketing executive for the organisation.

Q.19. Which of the following title is suitable for this classified advertisement?

    A.   Bumper Vacancy

    B.   Want a job in a reputed Delhi based marketing company?

    C.   Position Vacant

    D.   Get your dream job.

Q.20. Which of the following details must be included in this advertisement?

    1.   Requirement

    2.   Eligibility

    3.   Daily roles and responsibilities.

    A.   1 only   B.   2 only

    C.   1 and 2 only   D.   2 and 3 only

Q.21. Which of the following is the most suitable starting line for this advertisement?

    A.   Wanted marketing executive for a reputed Delhi based organisation...

    B.   Want to become a part of a reputed Delhi based organisation?

    C.   Your dream job is calling you...

    D.   Make the most of this golden opportunity....

Q.22. Which of the following is not required in the above advertisement?

    A.   Address of the General Manager   B.   Eligibility criteria for applicants

    C.   Contact details   D.   Title of the advertisement

Q.23. Which of the following can't be skipped in the above advertisement?

    A.   UID details of the General Manager

    B.   Revenue earned by the company on yearly basis

    C.   Title of the advertisement

    D.   Address of the General Manager

IV.   Answer <u>any six</u> of the seven questions given, with reference to the context below.

Ravi is the member of Meghdhanush, a school club that actively promote mental health awareness. He has to write an article emphasizing need to consider mental health as essential part of our lives and stop stigmatizing the mental health patients.

Q.24. Select the most suitable title for the above article.

    A.   Subjective well-being   B.   Depression is lethal

    C.   Mental health – your greatest wealth   D.   Light at the end of the tunnel

Q.25. Which option (1-4), should Ravi choose to elaborate what mental health is?

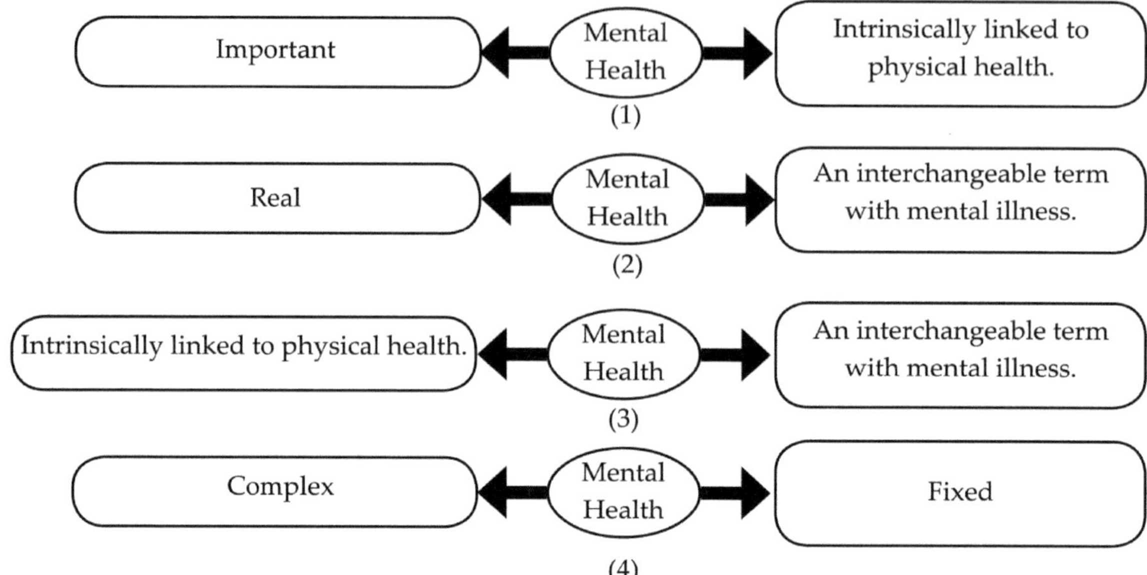

    A.   option 1   B.   option 2

    C.   option 3   D.   option 4

Q.26. Which option would help Ravi with appropriate organisation of relevant ideas for this article?

    A.   Expressing concern about several cases of suicide due to depression- exploring the reasons with factual support – stating the effects – providing the suggestion to create mental health awareness – presenting a conclusive outlook.

    B.   Exploring the reasons - Expressing concern about several cases of suicide due to depression - Providing the suggestion to create mental health awareness - Stating the effects - presenting a conclusive outlook.

    C.   Exploring the reasons - Stating the effects - Providing the suggestion to create mental health awareness - presenting a conclusive outlook.

    D.   Presenting a conclusive outlook - Stating the effects - Exploring the reasons - Providing the suggestion to create mental health awareness.

Q.27. Which of the following suggestion would be appropriate for Ravi's article?

    A.   Open more mental asylums.

    B.   Government should make budgetary allocations every year for dealing with mental health.

    C.   There should be compulsory mental health check up every year.

    D.   Individuals should understand the importance of mental health and society should be more sensitive towards such causes.

Q.28. Read the following sentence from Ravi's article draft and help him complete it by selecting the most appropriate term.

Reducing the _______ associated with mental health may enable more individuals to _______ from mental illness.

    A.   Medicines, infect   B.   Treatment, recover

    C.   Stigma, Recover   D.   Medicines, recover

Q.29. Which quote should be used to summarize the central idea of the article?

    A.   "It's okay to not to be okay"

    B.   "Mental health treatment is a science of uncertainty and art of possibility"

    C.   "There is no such problem like mental health; everything is simple made-up issue in mind."

    D.   "Unresolved issues lead to mental health"

Q.30. Select the most appropriate checklist for the above article.

A.   My article contains -

> 1. An eye-catching title
> 2. A by-line
> 3. Proper set of causes and effects for mental illness
> 4. Well deliberated suggestions
> 5. A quote to enhance the quality of the article
> 6. Factual information to support argument

B.   My article contains -

> 1. Quote as title
> 2. Opinion of experts
> 3. Aggressive arguments against those who stigmatize mental health.
> 4. Fact sheet to convince readers.
> 5. Free hand drawing at the end to make your article more eye catching
> 6. Date

C.   My article contains -

> 1. An eye-catching title
> 2. Opinion of doctors
> 3. Opinions of general public
> 4. Opinions of Mental health patients
> 5. Quote at the end
> 6. Date

D.   My article contains -

> 1. Causes for negligence of mental health
> 2. Suggestion to improve the condition
> 3. Three to four quotes.
> 4. By line
> 5. Date
> 6. Opinion of experts

LITERATURE

This section has sub-sections: V, VI, VII, VIII, IX. There are a total of 30 questions in the section. Attempt any 26 questions from the sub-sections V to IX.

V.   Read the given extract to attempt questions that follow:

Then all effort ceased. I relaxed. Even my legs felt limp; and a blackness swept over my brain. It wiped out fear; it wiped out terror. There was no more panic. It was quiet and peaceful. Nothing to be afraid of. This is nice... to be drowsy... to go to sleep... no need to jump... too tired to jump... it's nice to be carried gently... to float along in space... tender arms around me... tender arms like Mother's... now I must go to sleep... I crossed to oblivion, and the curtain of life fell.

Q.31. Choose the correct option with reference to the two statements given below.

Statement 1: The author tried his best to jump out of water.

Statement 2: After a while, the author was not anxious in water.

A.   If Statement 1 is the cause, Statement 2 is the effect.

B.   If Statement 1 is the effect, Statement 2 is the cause.

C.   Both the statements are the effects of a common cause.

D.   Both the statements are the effects of independent causes.

Q.32. The *'curtain (of life) fell'* corresponds to an aspect of:

A.   Geometry   B.   History

C.   Sports   D.   Drama

Q.33. The purpose of using "..." in the above passage is to:

A.   show omission   B.   indicate pauses

C.   shorten a dialogue   D.   replace an idea

Q.34. Which option indicates that the poet lost consciousness?

A.   *'It was quiet and peaceful.*   B.   *'I crossed to oblivion.'*

C.   *'Tender arms like Mother's.'*   D.   *'It wiped out fear.'*

Q.35. Why did a blackness swept over Douglas' brain?

1. He felt paralysed   2.   He felt drowsy

3. The water deep inside was black   4.   He began losing his memory

A. 1 and 3   B. 2 and 3
C. 3 and 4   D. 1 and 2

VI. Read the given extract to attempt questions that follow:

Thirty years later I visited his town and the temple, which was now drowned in an air of desolation. In the backyard, where lived the new priest, there were red and white plastic chairs. A young boy dressed in a grey uniform, wearing socks and shoes, arrived panting and threw his school bag on a folding bed. Looking at the boy, I remembered the prayer another boy had made to the goddess when he had finally got a pair of shoes, "Let me never lose them." The goddess had granted his prayer. Young boys like the son of the priest now wore shoes. But many others like the ragpickers in my neighbourhood remain shoeless.

Q.36. *"But many others like the ragpickers in my neighbourhood remain shoeless."* What does this line suggests about the author?

A. He is stating facts.

B. He is concerned about many others like the ragpickers.

C. He is indifferent towards it.

D. He is angry that the priest's son has got new shoes but ragpickers hadn't.

Q.37. Of the four meanings of 'desolation', select the option that matches in meaning with its usage in the extract.

A. encouragement   B. isolation
C. wilderness   D. joy

Q.38. Who do you think the author is referring to as 'his', in the given sentence?

"Thirty years later I visited his town and the temple"

A. Saheb   B. A man from Udipi
C. His friend   D. His Colleague

Q.39. Select the option that lists the feelings and attitudes corresponding to the following:

(1) *"Let me never lose them."*

(2) *"arrived panting and threw his school bag on a folding bed"*

A.	(1) self-belief	B.	(1) pride
	(2) arrogant and indifferent		(2) pride and arrogant
C.	(1) hope	D.	(1) seriousness
	(2) tired and oblivious		(2) tired and exhausted

Q.40. Select the option that lists reasons why the temple has been called *'drowned in an air of desolation'*.

1. Become old and dilapidated.

2. Has become more crowded.

3. People of all types visit there.

4. It has renovated a lot and attracts lot of tourists.

5. People no longer go to it.

A. 1 and 2   B. 1 and 5
C. 2 and 3   D. 1 and 4

VII. Read the given extract to attempt questions that follow:

And yet, for these

Children, these windows, not this map, their world,

Where all their future's painted with a fog,

A narrow street sealed in with a lead sky

Far far from rivers, capes and stars of words."

Q.41. Why are the windows of the classroom called the world of the children?

A. School going children have a bright future which can be seen through the windows

B. Their world is confined to the classroom windows full of poverty and diseases

C. These windows are full of hopes and aspirations for children

D. The world of the poor children living in slum is full of bounties

Q.42. How is the world of the slum children in contrast with the world of common people?
  A. With a bright prospect
  B. Dull and unpleasant
  C. Vibrant future
  D. Overall functioning

Q.43. Select the correct option to fill in the blank.
  A lead sky here suggests ____________.
  A. Dull and grey colour of the sky
  B. Sky which is loaded with clouds
  C. The dull life of the slum children
  D. Pollution in the sky

Q.44. Which option has the underlined phrase that applies the poetic device used for in *'Far far from rivers'*?
  A. She was <u>as red as a rose</u>
  B. He was <u>lion in the battle</u>
  C. The <u>Pied Piper of Hamelin</u>
  D. He was <u>swift like a Cheetah</u>

Q.45. The literal meaning of 'fog' refers to an atmospheric condition where visibility is reduced. What does its figurative meaning refer to?
  A. Future of the slum children is grey and not colourful
  B. Future of the slum children is unclear and uncertain
  C. Future of the slum children is blissful but cold
  D. Their future is clearly visible

VIII. Read the given extract to attempt questions that follow:

Have you ever been there? It's a wonderful town still, with big old frame houses, huge lawns, and tremendous trees whose branches meet overhead and roof the streets. And in 1894, summer evenings were twice as long, and people sat out on their lawns, the men smoking cigars and talking quietly, the women waving palm-leaf fans, with the fire-flies all around, in a peaceful world. To be back there with the First World War still twenty years off, and World War II over forty years in the future... I wanted two tickets for that.

Q.46. What do you think who is 'you' in the given sentence?
  'Have you ever been there?'
  A. Charley's psychiatrist, Sam Weiner
  B. Charley's wife, Louisa
  C. The reader
  D. Nobody in particular

Q.47. Choose the option that best describes the society represented in the above extract.
  A. content, peace-loving
  B. leisurely, sentimental
  C. orthodox, upper class
  D. comfortable, ancient

Q.48. Imagine that the city of Galesburg is hosting a series of conferences and workshops. In which of the following conferences or workshops are you least likely to find the description of Galesburg given in the above extract?
  A. Gorgeous Galesburg: Archiving a Tourist Paradise
  B. Welcome to the home you deserve: Galesburg Realtors
  C. Re-imagining a Warless Future: Technology for Peace
  D. The Woman Question: The world of women at home

Q.49. *"Tremendous trees whose branches meet overhead and roof the streets"* is NOT an example of:
  1. imagery
  2. metaphor
  3. alliteration
  4. anachronism
  A. option (1) and (2)
  B. option (1) and (3)
  C. option (2) and (3)
  D. option (2) and (4)

Q.50. Select the option that displays a cause-effect set.

	Cause	Effect
A.	The speaker wanted two tickets.	The World War was far off.
B.	The World War was far off.	The speaker wanted two tickets.
C.	The speaker wanted to be in a peaceful world.	He wanted two tickets to go there.
D.	He wanted two tickets to go there.	The speaker wanted to be in a peaceful world.

IX. **Attempt the following.**

Q.51. Repetition of the same word *'smile'* in the last line by Kamala Das implies that:

A. poetess was feeling happy
B. was hiding her feelings of fear
C. poetess was grinning from ear to ear
D. poetess was amused at what was happening

Q.52. *'They looked like little flags floating.'* What are referred to as flags by Alphonse?

A. copies of resignation letters
B. copies of written notes
C. notices on bulletin boards
D. flags of honour

Q.53. Which option has the underlined phrase that applies the poetic device that Stephen Spender used for *'stars of words'*?

A. He shut up like a clam when interrogated
B. She runs as swift as a gazelle.
C. He is considered the black sheep of the family.
D. She ran away chattering with fear.

Q.54. *"It's nice to be carried gently"*. What was carrying Douglas gently?

A. Water at Y.M.C.A swimming pool
B. Water at Lake Wentworth
C. Water at Tieton
D. Water at Maine lakes

Q.55. The poem *My Mother at Sixty-six* does not have full stop. What effect does this have?

A. a lucid flow of emotions
B. rhythmic flow
C. ambiguity of ideas
D. a sense of confusion

Q.56. Read the statements given below carefully. Choose the option that best describes these statements, with reference to the poem.

Statement-I: The poem *Keeping Quiet* calls for change as much in the individual as human society at large.

Statement-II: The poem *Keeping Quiet* implies that individual change will lead to bigger societal change.

Statement-III: Neruda believes that when people come together as a community, they will be able to bring a transformation in each person.

A. Statement I is True, Statement II is False, and Statement III cannot be inferred.
B. Statement I and II cannot be inferred, Statement III is True.
C. Statement I is True, Statements II and III cannot be inferred.
D. Statement I cannot be inferred, Statement II cannot be inferred, Statement III is False.

Q.57. Anees Jung says, *'But promises like mine abound in every corner of his bleak world'*. This suggests that:

A. there is no dearth of promises which remain unfulfilled.
B. there is a scarcity of people promising things for betterment.
C. people make a lot of promises which are often fulfilled.
D. promises made, live up to the expectations of people.

Q.58. *The Third Level* refers to the third level at the Grand Central Station. As a metaphor, which of the following would NOT be an appropriate explanation of the title?

A. The convergence of reality and fantasy.
B. The bridge between the past and the present.
C. The oppressive monotony of modern life.
D. The need for an alternate plane of understanding.

Q.59. How would you describe Charley's vision of his grandfather's life and times?

A. wistful escapism
B. idealized sentimentality
C. nostalgic simplicity
D. dreamy perfection

Q.60. *"Those scars,"* she murmured, lifting her eyes to Sadao.
The 'scars' DO NOT indicate:

A. torture perpetrated on prisoners of war.
B. superiority of Japan over America.
C. the quest for supremacy in war.
D. the rumours of torture often heard.

❑❑

Sample Paper 3

English Core

READING

I. Read the passage given below.

   I. No student of a foreign language needs to be told that grammar is complex. By changing word sequences and by adding a range of auxiliary verbs and suffixes, we are able to communicate tiny variations in meaning. We can turn a statement into a question, state whether an action has taken place or is soon to take place, and perform many other word tricks to convey subtle differences in meaning. Nor is this complexity inherent to the English language. All languages, even those of so-called 'primitive' tribes have clever grammatical components. The Cherokee pronoun system, for example, can distinguish between 'you and I', 'several other people and I' and 'you, another person and I'. In English, all these meanings are summed up in the one, crude pronoun 'We'. Grammar is universal and plays a part in every language, no matter how widespread it is. So, the question which has baffled many linguists is—who created grammar?

   II. At first, it would appear that this question is impossible to answer. To find out how grammar is created, someone needs to be present at the time of a language's creation, documenting its emergence. Many historical linguists are able to trace modern complex languages back to earlier languages, but in order to answer the question of how complex languages are actually formed, the researcher needs to observe how languages started from scratch. Amazingly, however, this is possible.

   III. Some of the most recent languages evolved due to the Atlantic slave trade. At that time, slaves from a number of different ethnicities were forced to work together under colonizer's rule. Since, they had no opportunity to learn each other's languages, they developed a make-shift language called a pidgin. Pidgins are strings of words copied from the language of the landowner. They have little in the way of grammar, and in many cases it is difficult for a listener to deduce when an event happened, and who did what to whom. Speakers need to use circumlocution in order to make their meaning understood. Interestingly, however, all it takes for a pidgin to become a complex language is for a group of children to be exposed to it at the time when they learn their mother tongue. Slave children did not simply copy the strings of words uttered by their elders, they adapted their words to create a new, expressive language. Complex grammar systems which emerge from pidgins are termed creoles and they are invented by children.

   IV. Further evidence of this can be seen in studying sign languages for the deaf. Sign languages are not simply a series of gestures; they utilise the same grammatical machinery that is found in spoken languages. Moreover, there are many different languages used worldwide. The creation of one such language was documented quite recently in Nicaragua. Previously, all deaf people were isolated from each other, but in 1979 a new government introduced schools for the deaf. Although children were taught speech and lip reading in the classroom, in the playgrounds they began to invent their own sign system, using the gestures that they used at home. It was basically a pidgin. Each child used the signs differently, and there was no consistent grammar. However, children who joined the school later, when this inventive sign system was already around, developed a quite different sign language. Although it was based on the signs of the older children, the younger children's language was more fluid and compact, and it utilised a large range of grammatical devices to clarify meaning. What is more, all the children used the signs in the same way? A new creole was born.

   V. Some linguists believe that many of the world's most established languages were creoles at first. The English past tense –ed ending may have evolved from the verb 'do'. 'It ended' may once have been 'It end-did'. Therefore, it would appear that even the most widespread languages were partly created by children. Children appear to have innate grammatical machinery in their brains, which springs to life when they are first trying to make sense of the world around them. Their minds can serve to create logical, complex structures, even when there is no grammar present for them to copy.

Based on your understanding of the passage, answer <u>any eight</u> out of the ten questions by choosing the correct option.

Q.1. The linguists are ……….. at the complexity of grammar.

    A.   annoyed   B.   bewildered

    C.   indifferent   D.   confident

Q.2. Circumlocution is the use of a large number of words to express an idea or thing.

The writer says that Sign languages are not simply a series of gestures.

Select from the options that is correctly circumlocutory for the word *gestures*.

    A.   systematic form of expressions by leg movements.

    B.   random actions performed to deliver messages.

    C.   expressing through different emojis.

    D.   systematic form of expressions by hand movements.

Q.3. Select the option that suitably completes the given dialogue as per the context in paragraph V.

Student: It is sometimes hardtop make sense how children can learn something as complex as grammar when even adults have a hard time getting it.

Professor: You mustn't underestimate a (1)……………………………

Student: How come a child sensibly understands grammar then?

Professor: (2)……………………………… in their brains!

    A.   (1) child's capability to learn new things (2) The whole magic lies

    B.   (1) human being like that even if it's a child (2) They have complex neurological connections

    C.   (1) child who wants to learn new things (2) They can have unlimited power

    D.   (1) child's ability to make sense of this world (2) They have an innate grammatical machinery

Q.4. Which signboard can be chosen for the government school for deaf in Nicaragua?

| 1. Government school for deaf, Nicaragua | 2. Public school for Nicaraguan studies. | 3. Government school for sign language, Nicaragua | 4. Sign language school for deaf and dumb, Nicaragua |

    A.   option 1   B.   option 2

    C.   option 3   D.   option 4

Q.5. Select the option that clearly indicates the situation before and after slave children were exposed to pidgin.

	Before exposure to pidgin	After exposure to pidgin
A.	Little complexity to the grammar.	Adapting new words to create a fresh expressive language.
B.	Grammar existent and full of big words.	Grammar became less expressive.
C.	Difficulty in understanding the language.	Language becomes more difficult and complex.
D.	Lack of words and inconvenience for landowners.	New words added for the sake of landowners.

Q.6. What is the relationship between (1) and (2)?

(1) …… the researcher needs to observe how languages started from scratch.

(2) ……. Complex grammar systems which emerge from pidgins are termed creoles.

    A.   (2) explains the question described in (1).   B.   (1) repeats the question in (2).

    C.   (1) is not the cause for (2).   D.   (1) and (2) are unrelated.

Q.7. The writer mentions looking at Atlantic slave trade for a better understanding of languages because he realises that:

A. Atlantic slave trade was filled with teachers who were well versed in linguistics.

B. It is the most effective way to check the linguistic development which requires no books.

C. It is the most recent and well documented form of linguistic study in how grammar is created.

D. Atlantic slave trade was a blotch in human history and should not be forgotten.

Q.8. Select the option that lists a linguist's review for the Nicaraguan sign language.

A. Children are not that silly when it comes to bringing up names or new words after all.

B. Interesting how something like the sign language made by children can be so inventive and fluid.

C. Needless to say that the children have done what their teachers couldn't have expected.

D. Each child was using the signs differently, and there was no consistent grammar.

Q.9. Which quote summarises the unmatched ingenuity of children?

A. "If a cluttered desk is a sign of a cluttered mind, of what, then, is an empty desk a sign?"

- Albert Einstein

B. "It is easier to build strong children than to repair broken adults."   *- F. Douglas*

C. "Children have real understanding only of that which they invent themselves."   *- Jean Piaget*

D. "By education I mean an all-round drawing out of the best in the child and man; body, mind and spirit."   *- Mahatma Gandhi*

Q.10. Select the option that lists what we can conclude from the text.

(1) Grammar develops over a generation gradually.

(2) Children are credited with new inventive forms of transforming languages.

(3) English grammar derives a lot from French and Germanic languages.

(4) Creole is a mix of different language forms.

A. (1), (2) and (3) are true.   B. (1), (2) and (4) are true.

C. (1) and (2) are true.   D. (3) and (4) are true.

II. Read the passage given below.

I. When plastic waste is burnt, a complex weave of toxic chemicals is released. Breaking down Poly Vinyl Chloride (PVC) used for packaging, toys and coating electrical wires. It produces dioxin, an organochlorine which belongs to the family of Persistent Organic Pollutants (POPs). A recent Dioxin Assessment Report brought out by the United States Environment Protection Agency (USEPA) says the risk of getting cancer from dioxin is ten times higher than reported by the agency in 1994.

II. Yet the Delhi government is giving the green signal to a gasification project which will convert garbage into energy without removing plastic waste. Former transport minister Rajendra Gupta, the promoter of this project, says this is not necessary.

He claims no air pollution will be caused and that the ash produced can be used as manure. An earlier waste-to-energy project set-up in Timarpur failed. The new one, built with Australian assistance, will cost ₹ 200 crore. It will generate 25 megawatts of power and gobble 1,000 tonnes of garbage everyday.

III. "Technologies like gasification are a form of incineration," says Madhumita Dutta, central coordinator with Toxics Link, New Delhi. Incineration merely transfers hazardous waste from a solid form to air, water and ash, she points out. Toxins produced during incineration include acidic gases, heavy metals as well as dioxins and furans. "The 'manure' will be hazardous and a problem to dispose," says Dutta.

IV. Municipal solid waste contains a mix of plastics. Breaking down this waste emits hydrochloric acid which attacks the respiratory system, skin and eyes, resulting in coughing, vomiting and nausea.

Polyethylene generates volatile compounds like formaldehyde and acetaldehyde, both suspected carcinogenic. Breathing styrene from polystyrene can cause leukaemia. Polyurethane is associated with asthma. Dioxin released by PVC is a powerful hormone disrupter and causes birth defects and reproductive problems. There is no threshold dose to prevent it and our bodies have no defence against it.

V. "Even the best run incinerators in the world have to deal with stringent norms, apart from contaminated filters and ash, making them hugely expensive to operate," says Dutta. In Germany, air pollution devices accounted for two-thirds the cost of incineration. Despite such efforts, the European Dioxin Inventory noted that the input of dioxin into the atmosphere was the highest from incineration.

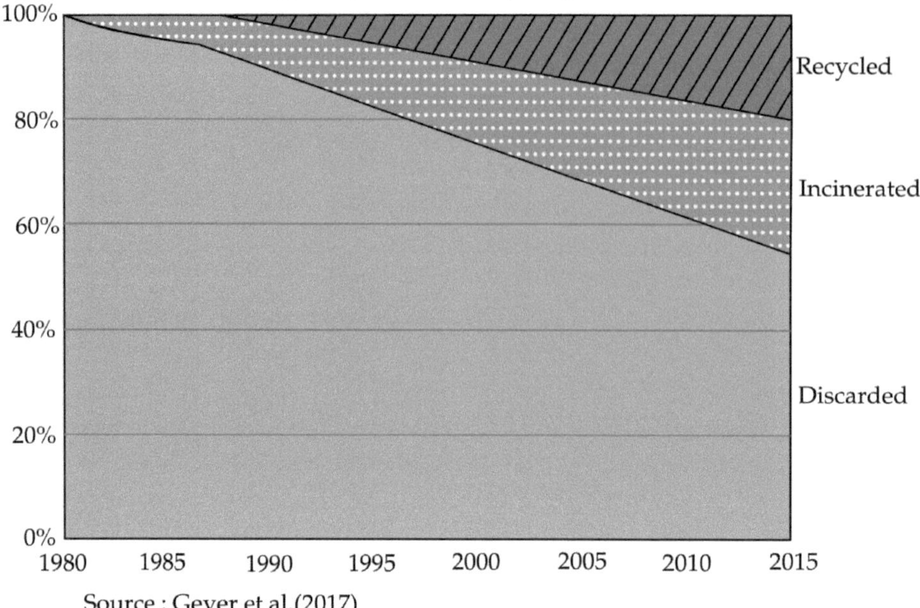

Source : Geyer et al.(2017)

VI. How has global plastic waste disposal method changed over time? In the chart, we see the share of global plastic waste that is discarded, recycled or incinerated from 1980 through to 2015. Prior to 1980, recycling and incineration of plastic was negligible; 100 percent was therefore discarded. From 1980 for incineration and 1990 for recycling, rates increased on average by about 0.7 percent per year. In 2015, an estimated 55 percent of global plastic waste was discarded, 25 percent was incinerated and 20 percent recycled.

VII. "India does not have the facility to test dioxin and the cost of setting one up is prohibitively expensive," says Dutta.Besides, Indian garbage has a low calorific content of about 800 cal/kg, since it has high moisture and requires additional fuel to burn. Toxics link calculates that the electricity generated from such technology will cost between ₹5-7 per unit, which is six times higher than conventional energy. India has chosen a dioxin preventive route and burning of chlorinated plastics is prohibited under Municipal Solid Waste and Biomedical Rules.

Nearly 80 percent of Indian garbage is recyclable or compostable. Resident associations, the informal sector and the municipal corporation can make Delhi's garbage disappear in a sustainable manner. "Instead, the government promotes end of pipeline solutions," says Dutta.

Based on your understanding of the passage, answer <u>any six</u> out of the eight questions by choosing the correct option.

Q.11. Select the correct inference with reference to the following:

Instead, the government promotes end of pipeline solutions.

    A.   Government is promoting solutions which can end the supply of garbage.

    B.   Government is planning to promote effective measures for waste disposal.

    C.   Government is planning to connect garbage disposal pipelines.

    D.   Government is promoting last stage actions instead of tackling the problem in initial steps.

Q.12. Select the central idea of the paragraph III.

    A.   Incineration is only going to bring more pollutants in the air.

    B.   Incineration will control the air quality index of Delhi.

    C.   Delhi air quality isn't improving anyway, so incineration will have little to no effect.

    D.   The benefits of incineration outweigh the risks in Delhi.

Q.13. Select the option that displays the true statement with reference to the given figure.

    A.   Incineration of plastic waste has stabilized since 1995.

    B.   Awareness towards recycling of plastic is reflected in recent years.

C.   The trend of discarding garbage hasn't changed much since 1980.

D.   Incineration of waste now is almost double that of discarded garbage.

Q.14. Based on your reading of paragraphs IV-V, select the appropriate counter- argument to the given argument.

Argument: Incineration is the quickest way of waste disposal, and even if it generates harmful toxins, proper measures can ensure that they don't escape in the environment.

A.   Recycling and reducing waste consumption are better options.

B.   Regulations are not enough to contain the toxic carcinogens it will generate along with a huge cost of operating it.

C.   Incinerators are a form of infrastructure development that is going to generate jobs.

D.   They are expensive to operate and do not generate enough electrical output.

Q.15. Select the option that displays the correct cause-effect relationship.

	Cause	Effect
A.	Burning of polyurethane.	Leukaemia.
B.	Emission of hydrochloric acid from wastes.	Birth defects and reproductive problems.
C.	Burning of polyethylene.	Release of formaldehyde and acetaldehyde.
D.	Wasteful consumption of products.	Dissatisfaction by the consumers.

Q.16. The survey statistics mention the global plastic waste disposal methods, indicating that:

A.   Prior to 1980, recycling and incineration of plastic was negligible.

B.   In 1990, recycling rates increased on average by about 7 per cent.

C.   In 2015, an estimated 55 percent of global plastic waste was recycled.

D.   100 per cent of garbage was incinerated in 1980.

Q.17. The phrase 'low calorific content' refers to the:

A.   lower calories for a healthy consumption   B.   lower content to remove all the moisture

C.   lower spectrum of behaving as toxin   D.   lower quality to burn as a fuel on its own

Q.18. Read the two statements given below and select the option that suitably explains them.

(1)   India has chosen a dioxin preventive route.

(2)   USEPA says the risk of getting cancer from dioxin is ten times higher than reported by the agency in 1994.

A.   (1) is the problem and (2) is the solution.   B.   (1) and (2) don't relate.

C.   (1) is true and (2) correctly explains it.   D.   (2) is false but (1) is true.

WRITING

III.   Answer <u>any four</u> out of the five questions given, with reference to the context below.

The Secretary of Panchsheel Apartments is supposed to publish a notice for the residents of society, about the electric power cut scheduled for tomorrow.

Q.19. Which of the following is the most suitable title for the notice?

A.   Summer, heat, and electric power cut

B.   This is the notice to inform about the scheduled power cut for maintenance

C.   Scheduled Power Cut

D.   The electricity will remain shut because of the maintenance related power cut

Q.20. Which of the following points must be necessarily included in this notice?

(1)   Time of power cut

(2)   Date of power cut

(3)   Reason for power cut

(4)   Technical details of maintenance work

A.   1 only   B.   1 and 2

C.   1,2 and 3   D.   1,2,3 and 4

Q.21. Which of the following is the most suitable opening line for this notice?

    A.   All society members are hereby informed about the scheduled power cut...

    B.   It is quite heart breaking to inform you all that ....

    C.   I, the secretary of Panchsheel society, feel privileged to inform....

    D.   Get ready to sweat dear society members as tomorrow there is a power cut...

Q.22. Should the notice contain the name of Panchsheel Apartments?

    A.   The notice must not have the name of publishing authority.

    B.   Can be published but not mandatory.

    C.   If Signature of publisher is given, then name of authority is not required.

    D.   Name of publishing authority must be given.

Q.23. Select the appropriate conclusion for this notice.

    A.   Pack your bags and plan a trip to some amusement spot nearby.

    B.   Residents are requested to be prepared for this problem.

    C.   Inconvenience regretted

    D.   Be informed

IV.   **Answer <u>any six</u> of the seven questions given, with reference to the context below.**

You are Aadarsh, Chairman of "Vidyamandir" an NGO that works for the upliftment of status of education in society. You are supposed to draft a letter to the editor of Navbharat Jansatta stating opinion on infrastructure requirements for learning and education in these changing COVID times.

Q.24. Which of the following can be the appropriate opening line for the above letter?

    A.   The world is changing so rapidly and the context that our schools confront is so dynamic that we, as educators....

    B.   As an editor of such a big media agency you should be aware that the teachers are distressed.

    C.   I hope you and other family members are doing fine.

    D.   I am extremely delightful to express my opinion on the matter...

Q.25. Which of the following is the most appropriate subject for the above letter?

    A.   Deterioration of the quality of education with COVID

    B.   How Corona ruined education and economy

    C.   Education infrastructure and its requirement in COVID era

    D.   Teachers are not to be taken for granted

Q.26. Which of the following approach is most appropriate for drafting a letter on the above subject?

    A.   Analysing change in education system—Suggesting Improvements in the system—Introducing problem faced by teachers—Conclusion

    B.   Introducing problems faced by teachers—Analysing change in education system—Suggesting improvements in the system—Conclusion

    C.   Analysing change in education system—Suggesting improvements in the system – Conclusion—Introducing problems faced by teachers

    D.   Conclusion—Introduction - Analysing change in education system—Suggesting improvements in the system.

Q.27. Complete the following phrase with the most appropriate terms.

Education system must ________ the change and ______ accordingly

    A.   Discard, be rigid   B.   Discard, Adjust

    C.   Accept, Adjust   D.   Accept, be rigid

Q.28. Which of the following is the most appropriate closing signature:

    A.   Your Loving subscriber   B.   Your Dearest Subscriber

        Aadarsh   Aadarsh

    C.   Yours Sincerely   D.   Forever Yours

        Aadarsh   Aadarsh

Q.29. Study the fragment of following draft and find out the error.

Teachers often feel they are not in power and yet in a position of great responsibility. The world is changing so rapidly and the context that our schools confront is so dynamic that we, as educators, must embrace change and make adjustments or potentially lose the franchise for preparing the next generation. Also, I strongly believe that Government should act proactively in this matter to facilitate teacher's fraternity.

Yours Sincerely

Aadarsh

A. Complementary closure is too formal

B. Closing signature must be on right

C. Closing signature is too formal

D. Language is too formal

Q.30. What is the type of the letter, which Aadarsh is about to draft?

A. Informal Letter

B. Technical Letter

C. Letter stating opinion on public interest

D. Letter of Resignations

LITERATURE

This section has sub-sections: V, VI, VII, VIII, IX. There are a total of 30 questions in the section. Attempt any 26 questions from the sub-sections V to IX.

V. **Read the given extract to attempt questions that follow:**

Then, as I hurried by as fast as I could go, the blacksmith, Wachter, who was there, with his apprentice, reading the bulletin, called after me, "Don't go so fast, bub; you'll get to your school in plenty of time!" I thought he was making fun of me and reached M. Hamel's little garden all out of breath. Usually, when school began, there was a great bustle, which could be heard out in the street, the opening and closing of desks, lessons repeated in unison, very loud, with our hands over our ears to understand better, and the teacher's great ruler rapping on the table.

Q.31. Franz's hurriedly walking towards the school suggests his ....

A. Fright

B. Diligence

C. Anxiety

D. Stress

Q.32. Which bulletin do you think blacksmith, Wachter had been reading?

A. School journal

B. Local news

C. Announcement from Berlin

D. Sports Day notice

Q.33. Select the option that lists the feelings and attitudes corresponding to the following:

(1) .... *Don't go so fast*

(2) .... *reached M. Hamel's little garden all out of breath.*

A.	(1) Sarcastic	B.	(1) Humorous
	(2) Carelessly		(2) Meticulous

C.	(1) Concern	D.	(1) Cheerful
	(2) Seriousness		(2) Miserable

Q.34. Select the option that tells the reason why Franz thought that the blacksmith was making fun of him?

(1) Franz's manner of running

(2) Blacksmith's practice of making fun of him

(3) Due to his frivolousness about studies

(4) Franz habit of being customarily late

A. 1 and 3

B. 2 and 3

C. 3 and 4

D. 1 and 4

Q.35. Of the four meanings of the phrase *'out of breath'*, select the option that matches in the meaning with its usage in the extract.

A. gasping for air

B. breathing fast with difficulty

C. without any breath

D. breathing effortlessly but awkwardly

VI. **Read the given extract to attempt questions that follow:**

My breath was gone. I was frightened. Father laughed, but there was terror in my heart at the overpowering force of the waves. My introduction to the Y.M.CA. swimming pool revived unpleasant memories and stirred childish fears. But in a little while I gathered confidence. I paddled with my new water wings, watching the other boys and trying to learn by aping them. I did this two or three times on different days and was just beginning to feel at ease in the water when the misadventure happened.

Q.36. Choose the correct option with reference to the two statements given below.

Statement 1: The author's father laughed to mock his son's inability to swim.

Statement 2: The author wanted to swim just to prove to his father that he can swim.

A.   Statement 1 is true but Statement 2 is false.

B.   Statement 1 is false but Statement 2 is true.

C.   Both Statement 1 and Statement 2 cannot be inferred.

D.   Both Statement 1 and Statement 2 can be inferred.

Q.37. *"My introduction to the Y.M.CA. swimming pool revived unpleasant memories and stirred childish fears."* It can be inferred that this was a clear case of ___________.

A.   suppression   B.   oppression

C.   depression   D.   repression

Q.38. The misadventure that took place right after the author felt comfortable was that:

A.   the author slipped and fell into the swimming pool.

B.   a bully tossed him into the pool for the sake of fun.

C.   his coach forgot to teach him how to handle deep water.

D.   his father couldn't help him from drowning into the water.

Q.39. Why is the fear "childish"?

A.   because it is from childhood   B.   because it was expected to go by now

C.   because it was not such a big fear   D.   because it was fear of a child

Q.40. What is the tone of the author?

A.   expository   B.   narrative

C.   ominous   D.   conservative

VII.   Read the given extract to attempt questions that follow:

"If we were not so single-minded

about keeping our lives moving,

and for once could do nothing,

perhaps a huge silence

might interrupt this sadness

of never understanding ourselves

and of threatening ourselves with death"

Q.41. The main focus of the poet is towards ___________.

A.   Peace, responsiveness, brotherhood   B.   Peace, humanity and brotherhood

C.   Brotherhood, desertion and fondness   D.   Humanity, isolation and brotherhood

Q.42. The literal meaning of '*do nothing*' refers to remain inactive. What does its figurative meaning refer to?

A.   Complete state of relaxation   B.   Experience the independence

C.   Enjoy the freedom   D.   Scrutinize our activities

Q.43. Which sadness is the poet referring to?

(1)   The sadness of remaining alone

(2)   The sadness that has made man self-absorbed

(3)   The sadness that has caused threat to man's own destruction

(4)   The sadness of not speaking to anyone

A.   1 and 3   B.   2 and 3

C.   3 and 4   D.   1 and 2

Q.44. Select the correct option to fill in the blank.

A huge silence can help in ___________.

A.   reconciliation   B.   reuniting with friends

C.   dealing with threats   D.   achieving goals of life

Q.45. What is the man *'single-minded'* about?
- A.   His own well-being and progress
- B.   Mindful of the destruction caused by human activities
- C.   Conscious about nature's advancement
- D.   Problems of the society and nation

VII.   Read the given extract to attempt questions that follow:

It was at this moment that both of them saw something black come out of the mists. It was a man. He was flung up out of the ocean .... flung, it seemed, to his feet by a breaker. He staggered a few steps, his body outlined against the mist, his arms above his head. Then the curled mists hid him again.

Q.46. Why did the figure of the man appear black?
- A.   Due to mist in the air
- B.   Because he was wounded
- C.   Because of the dark night
- D.   Because it was dark

Q.47. How would they have felt when they saw something black come out of the mists'?
- A.   terrified
- B.   shocked
- C.   happy
- D.   ignorant

Q.48. Select the option that signifies the walking style of the figure.
- A.   Elegant
- B.   Offensive
- C.   Stranded
- D.   Defensive

Q.49. Select the option that displays a cause-effect set.

A.

Cause	Effect
He was a prisoner.	Arms above head.

B.

Cause	Effect
Arms above head.	He was a prisoner.

C.

Cause	Effect
He flung out of the ocean.	He staggered.

D.

Cause	Effect
He staggered.	He flung out of the ocean.

Q.50. Pick the quote that best describes the theme of the story.
- A.   World belongs to humanity, not this leader, that leader or that king or prince or religious leader. World belongs to humanity.
- B.   You must not lose faith in humanity. Humanity is an ocean; if a few drops of the ocean are dirty, the ocean does not become dirt.
- C.   The purpose of human life is to serve, and to show compassion and the will to help others.
- D.   To deny people their human rights is to challenge their very humanity.

IX.   Attempt the following.

Q.51. *I looked again at her, wan, pale*

as a late winter's moon and felt that old

What is the literary device used in the lines?
- A.   metaphor
- B.   personification
- C.   anaphora
- D.   simile

Q.52. Why does Hamilton refer to prison in his speech?
- A.   to show knowing one's language is escape from exploitation
- B.   to argue in favour of liberal ways
- C.   to prove submission is the key to comfortable living
- D.   none of the above

Q.53. Identify the figure of speech used in the sentence *"Garbage to them is gold"*.
- A.   hyperbole
- B.   simile
- C.   synecdoche
- D.   personification

Q.54. *Keeping Quiet* uses fishermen to symbolize man's:
- A.   persistent pollution of the natural environment.
- B.   rapid degradation of human values.

C.   limitless exploitation of natural resources.

D.   constant participation in acts of terror.

Q.55. Spender's use of imagery in *"His eyes live in a dream, of squirrel game, in tree room, other than this"*, brings out:

A.   the similarity between the frail bodies of a squirrel and the children in the classroom.

B.   the contrast between studying in the dreary classroom and playing outside freely.

C.   the comparison of the dingy home of the squirrel and the dreary classroom.

D.   the difference between the games of the squirrel and those of the children.

Q.56. Choose the statement that is NOT TRUE with reference to Douglas.

A.   Douglas's fear kept him away from leisurely activities in water.

B.   The fall in the pool at YMCA taught Douglas a life lesson.

C.   The fear of drowning was the source of Douglas's anxiety and terror.

D.   Douglas decided to practice relentlessly to overcome his fear.

Q.57. The expression, *"Shakespeare's head"* in the poem *An Elementary School Classroom in a Slum* is an example of:

A.   pun.   B.   satire.

C.   parody.   D.   irony.

Q.58. *"He was very light, like a fowl that had been half-starved for a long time."* Which figure of speech is used by Buck in the given line?

A.   simile   B.   metaphor

C.   comparison   D.   paradox

Q.59. *He was taking out the packing now, and the blood began to flow more quickly.*

The underlined phrase suggests that the blood was:

A.   passive   B.   vigorous

C.   oozing   D.   dribbling

Q.60. Select the suitable option for the given statements, based on your reading of *The Third Level*.

(1)   Sam had a grain business.

(2)   Sam went back to his work to Galesburg, Illinois.

A.   1 is false but 2 is true.   B.   Both 1 and 2 are false.

C.   2 is a fact but unrelated to 1.   D.   1 is the cause for 2.

❑❑

Sample Paper 4

English Core

READING

I. Read the passage given below.

I. A bookshop is not something you find in every street or area these days. Books, which were once a permanent accompaniment for youngsters in their formative years, are fading out of their list of engagements.

II. Ask any youngster which is the latest book he has read and he will be baffled. Apart from a few consistent readers, others just befool themselves with a bookseller's name or lament the curriculum load for justifying themselves, like this seventeen-year-old school-goer who says, 'I just read my Physics book.'

III. Television has been blamed for this calamitous situation, which is producing square-faced people and a bookless society. Furthermore, today's children are under pressure to be smart and to succeed on a social level. Parties, dancing and hanging out at different places begin early. Moreover, computers, video games, the internet, swimming lessons, cricket and a youngster's passion for an hour-long tete-a-tete on the telephone with friends eat up all their leisure time.

IV. A child who is constantly under pressure to live up to his parents' expectations, which are at times unreasonable, does not like to throw himself into another set of books after the laborious school work, unless he comes from a family of readers where the engrossing work of Shakespeare and Dickens are just a matter of pulling them out from the shelves.

V. Many parents also believe that today's children have become more aware and demand logical reasoning for everything. They can no longer be fooled by fairy tales or animal stories, as they have not seen any fairies or animals except for those old and tired ones in the city zoo. This has made them more interested in movies or TV serials than a turtle talking to a rabbit or a frog changing into a prince.

VI. But a visit to the capital's leading bookstores presents a contrasting picture of youngsters' reading habits. These bookshops claim they are doing healthy business and have many regular buyers from this age group.

VII. Though the works of Shakespeare, Charles Dickens, Jane Austen and Mark Twain no longer interest teenagers, bestsellers from Daniel Steele, Sidney Sheldon and Jeffery Archer are on the list of all reading teens. Self-help books, such as those on personality development or relationship management, are also picked up by many of them.

VIII. Mystery books like Nancy Drew and Hardy Boys are popular with kids and Mills, Boons and other romance novels with their fairly predictable formula with teenage girls. For parents of children below ten, volumes of Panchatantra Stories, Amar Chitra Katha and other bedtime stories are worthy purchases as these teach the child what is wrong in their own special way. What seems to be the case is that parents have surrendered to others what was their most precious right, that of making their children what they should become. With the old techniques of child rearing losing ground, modern parents must consciously spend time with their children. Taste and enthusiasm for literature can be communicated artfully to children by reading bedtime stories to them, encouraging them to play historical characters and giving books as birthday gifts.

IX. The family reading which was once popular in the West could well be adopted here. Reading aloud the works of great men by parents to their children not only forms a warm bond between them but also attracts young minds to the world of books which gives them a chance to explore the sea of life.

Based on your understanding of the passage, answer <u>any eight</u> out of the ten questions by choosing the correct option.

Q.1. Society demands smart and successful people at present, which makes the children feel

   A.   relieved   B.   pressured

   C.   left out   D.   passionate

Q.2. Hyperbole is an exaggerated statement or emphasized claim, not meant to be taken literally.

The writer says that young people not reading books is a <u>calamitous situation</u>.

Select the word from the options that correctly replaces *calamitous situation*.

   A.   crisis   B.   misfortune

   C.   pandemic   D.   godsend

Q.3. Select the option that suitably completes the given dialogue as per the context in paragraph IV.

Parent: I've seen you spending your free time sleeping all the day. Why not do something productive?

Child: The school is laborious enough for me to (1)..............

Parent: That's not an excuse! How about reading some good novels to freshen up your mind?

Child: (2).................. I don't think I have the mental capacity to read more books.

   A.   (1) be active all the day (2) As if the school books weren't enough for me

   B.   (1) be a jack of all trades (2) You should understand that

   C.   (1) be a productive student (2) I am now a part of school's book club

   D.   (1) drain all my energy, I don't have time for additional activities. (2) I am already reading books in school

Q.4. Which signboard would the writer have chosen for his bookstore to attract young crowd?

1. Limited edition Jeffrey Archer, John Green and many more!	2. Shakespeare's classics now available!	3. Romantic novels from Jane Austin now in sale!	4. Best sellers from Charles Dickens for this season!

   A.   option 1   B.   option 2

   C.   option 3   D.   option 4

Q.5. Select the option that clearly indicates the situation before and after the introduction of television.

	Before television	After television
A.	Parents never felt the need to force kids to read books.	Parents are now pressuring kids to be smart and athletic.
B.	Family reading culture was popular in west.	Family reading culture is popular in east.
C.	Reading books was the usual hobby.	Reading books has become a rarity.
D.	Novels were not digitally printed.	Printing press is fully automated.

Q.6. What is the relationship between (1) and (2)?

(1)......... parents must consciously spend time with their children.

(2)......... children have become more aware and demand logical reasoning for everything.

   A.   (1) is the problem for (2).   B.   (2) sets the stage for (1).

   C.   (1) repeats what is said in (2).   D.   (1) and (2) are both independent.

Q.7. The writer mentions reading aloud the works of great authors by parents to their children, because he realises that

   A.   it not only forms a warm bond between them but also attracts young minds to the world of books which gives them a chance to explore the sea of life.

   B.   enthusiasm for literature can be communicated artfully to children by reading bedtime stories to them.

   C.   today's children are under pressure to be smart and to succeed on a social level.

   D.   it not only forms a warm bond between them but also attracts young minds to the world of possibilities which gives them a chance to excel in career.

Q.8. Select the option that lists the young reader's feedback for the writer's book awareness campaign.

    A.   I was surprisingly engrossed in the novel that I started to read, it isn't that boring or geeky as it sounds.

    B.   I just wanted to score some brownie points by being here, it reflects good on my CV.

    C.   I'm still indifferent to that fact that books can be interesting, I got bored after one page.

    D.   I don't get the need to read books when every information is at fingertips with internet.

Q.9. Which quote summarises the writer's feelings about the necessity of reading books?

    A.   "Fairy tales are more than true: not because they tell us that dragons exist, but because they tell us that dragons can be beaten."   *— Neil Gaiman*

    B.   "Outside of a dog, a book is man's best friend. Inside of a dog it's too dark to read."   *— Groucho Marx*

    C.   "I have always imagined that Paradise will be a kind of library."   *— Jorge Luis Borges*

    D.   "If you read a book, you will unlock unknown doors of your soul. And who knows; you can find a treasure inside…"   *— George Spyrou, Roxanne*

Q.10. Select the option that lists what we can conclude from the text.

    (1)   Children should not be swayed by any means if they are not into reading books.

    (2)   demand or classic authors is on an all-time high.

    (3)   contrary to popular belief, youngsters love reading.

    (4)   parents must add some efforts to raise a habit of reading in children.

    A.   (1), (2) and (3) are true.   B.   (3) and (4) are true.

    C.   (1) and (2) are true.   D.   (2), (3) and (4) are true.

II. Read the passage given below.

    I.   The passenger pigeon (*Ectopistes migratorius*) was once found in huge numbers in North America. Records tell of passing flocks that darkened the skies for several days at a time. The species may have peaked at five billion individuals. A more conservative estimate is three billion.

    II.   Within a short time, the species disappeared completely. "Given the huge size of the population, it's simply amazing that the species disappeared so quickly," says Tom Gilbert. Gilbert is a professor at the University of Copenhagen's Centre for GeoGenetics, but he also has a part-time position as an adjunct professor at the Norwegian University of Science and Technology (NTNU).

    III.   The history of the passenger pigeon is interesting, partly because it can tell us something about how and why species become extinct. Native Americans also relied on passenger pigeons for food. But at least in parts of the passenger pigeons' range, people had learned to harvest the species at a sustainable level that didn't threaten to eradicate it. It was common in some parts of North America to only eat young pigeons that were hunted at night, since this did not seem to scare away the adult birds or prevent them from re-nesting.

The cladogram below follows the 2012 DNA study showing the position of the passenger pigeon among its closest relatives:

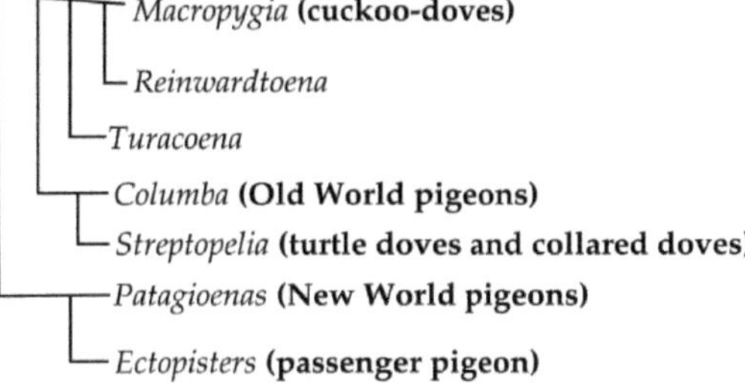

    IV.   But starting around 1500, a more aggressive variant of humans came to the continent with the arrival of Europeans. The hunt for passenger pigeons grew and culminated in a massive hunt for the species throughout the 1800s, before the species finally collapsed and disappeared. In 2014, a study published in the scientific journal PNAS strongly suggested that humans were simply the final straw in destroying a species that was already vulnerable and headed to oblivion.

The cladogram follows the 2012 DNA study showing the position of the passenger pigeon among its closest relatives:

    V.   The researchers asserted that despite their enormous numbers, the passenger pigeons were already in trouble. The population of the species varied greatly, similar to lemmings, but over a longer period of time. When the Europeans arrived, the species was already in a strong decline. The population was plummeting long before Europeans arrived, and perhaps Europeans even contributed to a short-term increase in numbers.

VI. Studies of the genetic variation of the species using an investigative method called PSMC formed the background for these assertions. And now we have to concentrate a bit. The PSMC method can use the information in the genes of a single individual of a species to map the history of the species.

VII. You should therefore be able to see how the species developed over many generations, and estimate how many individuals there were at any given time, all based on a single genome. Using this method, researchers found that the number of passenger pigeons was in free fall even before the arrival of the Europeans.

Although the species might not have become extinct, it would have shrunk significantly in any case, maybe to only a few hundred thousand individuals.

Based on your understanding of the passage, answer <u>any six</u> out of the eight questions by choosing the correct option.

Q.11. Select the correct inference with reference to the following:

The population was plummeting long before Europeans arrived.

A.   the population of passenger pigeons was at a rise way before Europeans arrived.

B.   passenger pigeons were thriving abundantly even before the arrival of the Europeans.

C.   the number of passenger pigeons was in free fall even before the arrival of the Europeans.

D.   Europeans killed the passenger pigeons and brought their population down.

Q.12. Select the central idea of the paragraph III.

A.   Native Americans practiced sustainable hunting, thus cannot be blamed for passenger pigeon extinction.

B.   Passenger pigeon extinction started during the times of Native American hunting.

C.   Passenger pigeons may have peaked at five billion individuals.

D.   Native Americans hunted passenger pigeons for their sport and thus, have a fair share of blame for their extinction.

Q.13. Select the option that displays the true statement with reference to the given figure.

A.   Turtle doves and Old world pigeons are from very different genetic branches.

B.   Cuckoo-doves and Old world pigeons are from similar branch.

C.   New world pigeons and Passenger pigeons had the closest DNA.

D.   Old world pigeons and New world pigeons share same DNA.

Q.14. Based on your reading of paragraphs VI-VII, select the appropriate counter- argument to the given argument.

Argument: The PSMC method proves the innocence of the Europeans that they had nothing to do with the decline in the population of passenger pigeons who were already doomed towards extinction.

A.   PSMC method does not tells the exact number of individuals left, it only gives an idea based on vague evidences, so it were actually the Europeans who drove them to extinction.

B.   It is not possible to see how the species developed over many generations, and estimate how many individuals there were at any given time.

C.   PSMC is a very recent technique that relies on assumption, so it is unfair to judge something that had already happened in the past based on it.

D.   There were still a few hundred thousand individuals left from the passenger pigeon population, which could've been easily saved by conservation programs, yet the Europeans hunted them all.

Q.15. Select the option that displays the correct cause-effect relationship.

	Cause	Effect
A.	PSMC method uses the genetic information of a single individual.	PSMC method can map the history of the species.
B.	Native Americans only hunted young pigeons.	Old pigeons died without raising any offspring.
C.	Passenger pigeons had an increase in number.	Passenger pigeons became extinct.
D.	Europeans relied on passenger pigeons for food.	There was a food shortage for Native Americans.

Q.16. The cladogram indicates that:
- A. new world pigeons is just another term for passenger pigeons.
- B. collared-doves are more closely related to old world pigeons, than they are to cuckoo-doves.
- C. passenger pigeons may have aroused independently from rest of the pigeons.
- D. turtle doves and collared-doves are totally different species.

Q.17. The phrase 'final straw' refers to the
- A. last of the event in the series of unfortunate trail of passenger pigeons.
- B. second last event before extinction of the passenger pigeons.
- C. final passenger pigeon that survived and kept the species alive.
- D. the last straw of food that the passenger pigeon ate before going extinct.

Q.18. Read the two statements given below and select the option that suitably explains them.
- (1) The hunt for passenger pigeons grew massively throughout the 1800s.
- (2) PSMC method formed the background for these assertions.
- A. (1) is false and (2) is the reason.
- B. (2) summarises (1).
- C. (1) is true and (2) explains it.
- D. (2) is false and (1) explains it.

WRITING

III. Answer <u>any four</u> out of the five questions given, with reference to the context below.

You are Ranjan/Ragini of Navi Mumbai. You wish to sell your ancestral property lying unattended in the locality nearby.

Q.19. Which of the following details must be included in this advertisement?
- I.   Location of Property
- II.   General layout/ rooms in house
- III. History of people lived in that house.
- A. I only
- B. II only
- C. I and II
- D. I, II and III

Q.20. Which of the following language is suitable for drafting the above advertisement?
- A. Sale, Sale, Sale, we present a golden opportunity to buy a house...
- B. Always dreamed of purchasing your own house? Your dream has come true...
- C. Available for sale a three room flat in ...
- D. Your sacred space is where you find yourself again and again. Make your sacred three-room space near Navi Mumbai.

Q.21. Which of the following is the most suitable title for this advertisement?
- A. Golden opportunity to buy a property
- B. Get your dream house
- C. Give your loved ones a gift for lifetime
- D. Sale and Purchase

Q.22. Which of the following is not required in the above advertisement?
- A. Address of Ranjan/Ragini
- B. Description of property
- C. Contact details
- D. Title of the advertisement

Q.23. Which of the following can't be skipped in the above advertisement?
- A. UID details of the Ranjan/Ragini
- B. Income earned by Ranjan/Ragini's family
- C. Title of the advertisement
- D. Address of the Ranjan/Ragini

IV. Answer <u>any six</u> of the seven questions given, with reference to the context below.

Sonam is a member of "Antheen" a college club that actively promote water conservation awareness. She has to write an article emphasizing the need to consider water conservation as essential part of our lives and promote domestic rainwater harvesting to increase ground water levels.

Q.24. Select the most suitable title for the above article.
- A. Water conservation
- B. Conserve water - No water no life
- C. Deserted Earth is not a good place to live
- D. Water helps human to survive

Q.25. Which option (1-4), should Sonam choose to elaborate on reasons for promoting domestic rainwater harvesting?

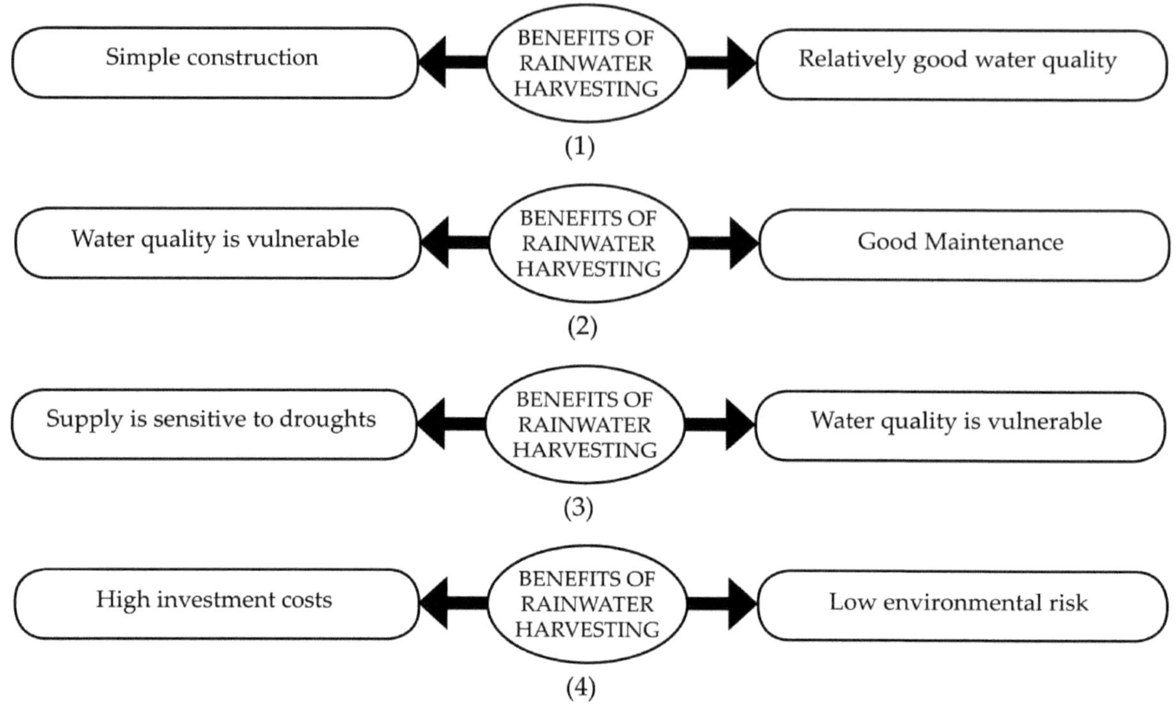

A. Option 1
B. Option 2
C. Option 3
D. Option 4

Q.26. Which option would help Sonam with appropriate organisation of relevant ideas for this article?

A. Expressing concern about several cases of land water depletion- exploring the reasons with factual support – stating the effects – providing the suggestion to create water conservation awareness– presenting a conclusive outlook.

B. Exploring the reasons - Expressing concern about several cases of land water depletion - providing the suggestion to create water conservation - Stating the effects - presenting a conclusive outlook.

C. Exploring the reasons - Stating the effects - providing the suggestion to create water conservation - presenting a conclusive outlook - Expressing concern about several cases of land water depletion.

D. Presenting a conclusive outlook - Stating the effects - Exploring the reasons - providing the suggestion to create water conservation.

Q.27. Which of the following suggestion would be appropriate for Sonam's article?

A. Everyone should have water wells in their houses
B. Submersible water pumps must be banned.
C. People wasting water should be sentenced to rigorous imprisonment.
D. Individuals should understand the importance of water conservation and do the needful.

Q.28. Read the following sentence from Sonam's article draft and help her complete it by selecting the most appropriate term.

There should be mass _______ about ways and means to __________ water.

A. Conscience, deplete
B. Conscience, Conserve
C. Awareness, deplete
D. Awareness, Conserve

Q.29. Which quote should be used to summarize the central idea of the article?

A. You never know the worth of water until the well runs dry.
B. I only feel angry when I see wastage of water
C. Time spent among tree is never a time wasted.
D. Environment is no one's property to destroy.

Q.30. Select the most appropriate checklist for the above article.

A.   My article contains -

1. An eye-catching title
2. A by-line
3. Proper set of causes and effects for water wastage
4. Well deliberated suggestions on water conservation
5. A quote to enhance the quality of the article
6. Factual information to support argument

B.   My article contains -

1. Quote as title
2. Opinion of experts
3. Aggressive arguments against those who waste water.
4. Fact sheet to convince readers.
5. Free hand drawing at the end to make your article more eye catching
6. Date

C.   My article contains -

1. An eye-catching title
2. Opinion of Geologists
3. Opinions of general public
4. Opinions of Government officials
5. Quote at the end
6. Date

D.   My article contains -

1. Causes for negligence of water wastage
2. Suggestion to improve the condition
3. Three to four quotes.
4. By line
5. Date
6. Opinion of experts

LITERATURE

This section has sub-sections: V, VI, VII, VIII, IX. There are a total of 30 questions in the section. Attempt any 26 questions from the sub-sections V to IX.

V.   Read the given extract to attempt questions that follow:

She still has bangles on her wrist, but no light in her eyes. "Ek waqt ser bhar khana bhi nahin khaya." she says, in a voice drained of joy. She has not enjoyed even one full meal in her entire lifetime-that's what she has reaped! Her husband, an old man with a flowing beard says, "I know nothing except bangles. All I have done is made a house for the family to live in." Hearing him one wonders if he has achieved what many have failed in their lifetime. He has a roof over his head! The cry of not having money to do anything except carry on the business of making bangles, not even enough to eat, rings in every home. The young men echo the lament of the elders. Little has moved with time, it seems in Firozabad, years of mind-numbing toil have killed all initiative and the ability to dream.

Q.31. *'She still has bangles on her wrist, but no light in her eyes.'* This implies that:

A.   she is married but has lost the charm in her eyes.

B.   she is a married woman who has lost her grace and beauty.

C.   though she is married, her eyes are devoid of happiness.

D.   she is a married woman who has lost her eyesight.

Q.32. *'He has a roof over his head!'* The tone of the author is:

A.   pessimistic

B.   empathetic

C.   sympathetic

D.   optimistic

Q.33. Choose the term which best matches the statement *'The young men echo the lament of their elders.'*

A.   acceptance

B.   reflection

C.   reiteration

D.   doubtfulness

Q.34. *'Years of mind-numbing toil have killed all initiative and the ability to dream'.* This shows that:

A.   the bangle makers are exhausted yet they are enterprising and have dreams.

B.   the drudgery of work has destroyed their willingness to improve their lot.

C.   the daily grind has stolen the dreams of the bangle makers and made them dull.

D.   the bangle makers have been working so hard that there's no time to dream.

Q.35. Select the option that lists the meaning of expression *'Little has moved with time'.*

A.   The speed of the bangle making has gradually zoomed up.

    B.   Nothing has changed at all.

    C.   There is a steady change in the condition of the bangle makers.

    D.   The state of bangle makers has changed completely.

VI.   **Read the given extract to attempt questions that follow:**

It was three months before the tension began to slack. Then he taught me to put my face under water and exhale, and to raise my nose and inhale. I repeated the exercise hundreds of times. Bit by bit I shed part of the panic that seized me when my head went under water.

Next he held me at the side of the pool and had me kick with my legs. For weeks I did just that. At first my legs refused to work. But they gradually relaxed; and finally I could command them.

Q.36. Of the four options given below, which one suits best to the explanation of *'I shed part of the panic'* in the extract?

    A.   The terror completely left   B.   Somewhat terror still left

    C.   Little fear was gone   D.   Major part of panic returned

Q.37. Select the option that lists the correct inference based on the information in the extract.

    A.   It took Douglas three months to get rid of his terror.

    B.   Three months ago, Douglas's tension began to reduce.

    C.   After three months of practice, Douglas got rid of his terror.

    D.   Within three months, Douglas was able to get over his fear.

Q.38. The qualities imbibed in the instructor helped Douglas turn into a good swimmer. What are these? Choose the correct options.

    I.   Practical   II.   Uncouth

    III.   Motivating   IV.   Punitive

    A.   I and II   B.   I and IV

    C.   II and III   D.   I and III

Q.39. Select the option that displays a cause-effect set.

A.

Cause	Effect
Douglas commanded over swimming skills.	The instructor taught Douglas.

B.

Cause	Effect
The instructor taught Douglas.	Douglas commanded over swimming skills.

C.

Cause	Effect
Douglas was completely dependent on instructor.	Douglas shed panic gradually.

D.

Cause	Effect
Douglas shed panic gradually.	Douglas was completely dependent on instructor.

Q.40. Choose the option which tells why Douglas had been under terror?

    A.   Once he was ducked by a big boy into deep water

    B.   His mother had terrorized him

    C.   No training by an instructor

    D.   Heard several drowning incidents

VII. **Read the given extract to attempt questions that follow:**

but after the airport's

security check, standing a few yards away, I looked again at her, wan, pale

as a late winter's moon and felt that old

familiar ache, my childhood's fear, but all I said was, see you soon,

Amma,

all I did was smile and smile and

smile.....

Q.41. *"all I did was smile and smile and smile"* -pick out from the following options the actual reason for the smile:

    A.   she was happy to board the plane   B.   hiding her fear from mother

    C.   was grinning with mirth   D.   was reassuring her mother

Q.42. The smile on the author's face at the end can be described as

    A.   all knowing

    B.   enigmatic

    C.   open and frank

    D.   untinged with sorrow

Q.43. How is the comparison of winter moon and face of mother appropriate here?

    A.   mother's face as round as moon's face

    B.   silvery hair matched with silver moon

    C.   lack of strength and colour

    D.   both are shining

Q.44. Kamala Das uses technique of the running over of a sentence from one poetic line to another- this is called ___________.

    A.   functional break

    B.   clear jump

    C.   enjambment

    D.   juxtaposition

Q.45. *"smile and smile and smile"* is a rhetoric device called:

    A.   onomatopoeia

    B.   alliteration

    C.   simile

    D.   repetition

VII. **Read the given extract to attempt questions that follow:**

The man moaned with pain in his stupor but he did not awaken. "The best thing that we could do would be to put him back in the sea," Sadao said, answering himself. Now that the bleeding was stopped for the moment he stood up and dusted the sand from his hands. "Yes, undoubtedly that would be best," Hana said steadily. But she continued to stare down at the motionless man. "If we sheltered a white man in our house we should be arrested and if we turned him over as a prisoner, he would certainly die," Sadao said. "The kindest thing would be to put him back into the sea," Hana said. But neither of them moved. They were staring with curious repulsion upon the inert figure.

Q.46. In which of the following options can the underlined words NOT be replaced with 'stupor'?

    A.   She hung up the phone feeling as though she had woken up from a <u>slumber</u>.

    B.   The manager complained about the employee's <u>sluggishness</u>.

    C.   He seemed to be in a <u>trance</u> when the doctor called upon him last week.

    D.   Seeing him in a <u>daze,</u> the lawyer decided not to place him in the witness box.

Q.47. Pick the option that best describes Sadao and Hana in the passage.

    A.   Sadao: scrupulous Hana: wary

    B.   Sadao: daring Hana: prudent

    C.   Sadao: prudent Hana: suspicious

    D.   Sadao: wary Hana: daring

Q.48. Pick the idiom that best describes the situation in which Sadao and Hana were in.

    A.   to be like a fish out of water

    B.   like water off a duck's back

    C.   to be dead in the water

    D.   to be in hot water

Q.49. Choose the correct option with reference to the two statements given below.

Statement 1: Sadao and Hana cared about the soldier but were worried about the consequences of being considerate.

Statement 2: Sadao and Hana wanted to shirk their responsibilities of looking after an injured soldier, who could be an American.

    A.   Statement 1 is true but Statement 2 is false.

    B.   Statement 1 is false but Statement 2 is true.

    C.   Both Statement 1 and Statement 2 are true.

    D.   Both Statement 1 and Statement 2 are false.

Q.50. Select the option that signifies the state of mind of Hana when she said *"If we sheltered a white man in our house we should be arrested…….."* in the extract.

    I.   anxious

    II.   compassionate

    III.   vigilant

    IV.   satisfied

    A.   I and III

    B.   II and IV

    C.   II and III

    D.   I and IV

IX. **Attempt the following.**

Q.51. Hamilton uses two words to define two beautiful linguistic characteristics of French . What are they?

    A.   Musical and rhythmic

    B.   Clear and logical

    C.   Lyrical and poetic

    D.   Prosaic and mundane

Q.52. The words *"sprinting and spilling"* are used to show:

A.   life and enthusiasm

B.   speed and tranquillity

C.   life and death

D.   surplus energy

Q.53. There is a difference in the fear of separation felt in the past and the present moment by Kamala Das. Which expressions bring out this in the best manner?

A.   Childish insecurity and knowledge born of maturity

B.   peevishness of a child left alone

C.   fear of getting neglected by her mother

D.   fear of temporary separation and permanent one.

Q.54. From the chapter *Lost Spring*, it is evident that the author has an attitude of:

A.   sympathy

B.   apathy

C.   empathy

D.   bewilderment

Q.55. Pick the quote that highlights the contrasting image portrayed in the poem *An Elementary School Classroom in a Slum*.

A.   'The worst form of inequality is to try and make unequal things equal.'

B.   'An imbalance between the rich and poor is the oldest and most fatal ailment of all republics.'

C.   'We must work together to ensure equitable distribution of wealth, opportunity and power in our society.'

D.   'No amount of artificial reinforcement can offset the natural inequalities of human individual.'

Q.56. Charley decided not to tell his psychiatrist friend about his idea. Choose the option that reflects the reaction Charley anticipated from his friend.

A.   "That's such a lovely comparison. Why don't you become a writer, Charley?"

B.   "Oh Charley. It is so sad to see your desperation to run away! So very sad."

C.   "Maybe that's how you entered the third level. Who would have thought?!"

D.   "You need help, my raving friend. You are way too invested in this crazy thought!"

Q.57. The chap that threw me in was saying, *"But I was only fooling."* Choose the option mentioning the personality traits of this 'chap'.

1.   persuasive

2.   irresponsible

3.   domineering

4.   manipulative

5.   callous

A.   1, 2, 4

B.   2, 4, 5

C.   2, 3, 5

D.   1, 3, 5

Q.58. *"Now I'll count up to twelve and you keep quiet and I will go."* Why does the poet wish to go at the end of the poem?

A.   The poet does not believe people will be quiet.

B.   The poet has already invested enough time.

C.   The poet will move on and seek to inspire others.

D.   The poet is marking the end of the poem by leaving.

Q.59. What does "blood" in the story *The Enemy* symbolise?

A.   racism

B.   prejudice

C.   unity

D.   nationalistic pride

Q.60. The fierce look of resistance upon Yumi's face was due to _________

A.   the thought of being declared as a traitor

B.   her willingness to turn over the prisoner to the officials

C.   the thought of her master's well being

D.   love and respect for her country

Sample Paper 5

English Core

READING

I. Read the passage given below.

I. The youth is a dynamo, an ocean, an inexhaustible reservoir of energy. But this energy cannot be kept caged in prison. Its basic nature is to flow, to express itself. The youth energy on the basis of the nature of its expression can be divided into four categories.

II. The vast majority of the youth today is with the establishment, whose formula of life is learn, earn, burn and enjoy. It means learn to operate the modern devices and employ them to earn the maximum amount of wealth to the point of burning the natural resources of the earth, as well as yourself out, and then enjoy your own funeral. This category of youth is intelligent, skillful and hardworking but it lacks insight and foresight. They are self-indulgent and any sense of moral code of conduct is alien to their nature. Neither are they able to see in depth, to find out whether there is a deeper meaning and purpose to their human life, nor have they the capacity to look beyond the tips of their nose to find out the consequences of their way and approach, where it is leading them to. They are the ends into themselves and enjoyment is the motto of their life.

III. The second category of youth in nature and approach is the same but as it is less privileged and less qualified and skilled; it has lesser opportunities for earning and enjoying. Such youth may be incited to be against the establishment. This opposition takes various forms. When it is well-organised and systemic it may take the form of political opposition and even go to the extent of expressing itself in unjust ways. When the opposition is not so intense and organised, it remains contended with giving verbal expression to its resentment periodically. The youth of the above two categories need to be shown the right path to positively channelise their energy.

IV. The third section of youth is a sober and thoughtful class of people, which objectively observes and studies the phenomenon of development of the world. These youth find that man in his insatiable thirst for consumption has become blind and lost the sense of distinction between milk and blood. Today man in his mad rush for exploitation is sucking the blood of Mother Earth; leading to their destruction and is thereby digging his own grave. This responsible category of young people is looking for an alternative mode of development based on co-operation between man and man. This development based on mutual love, friendship and harmony is not only sustainable but leading to endless prosperity mutually. To bring about his natural revolution from death-movement to life-movement is the aim of this group.

V. The fourth and most vital group of youth which is going to steer humanity into the third millennium and act as the pioneer for the future development of planetary life is engaged in evolving a new way of life and releasing a new principle of global consciousness through a fundamental research in the science of life. The science of life is a new branch of knowledge which takes the whole man into account without dividing him into subjective and objective halves of spirituality and physicality and does not treat him either as a refined (thinking) animal or an ethereal entity, having its base in some other non-physical world. It rather, recognises man as a basic unit of conscious life which has got immense, practically inexhaustible, possibilities and potentialities for evolution, development and growth.

As per the Vedic formula, man is the micro-cosmos and his fullest flowering and enfoldment lies in his identification with the cosmos.

Based on your understanding of the passage, answer <u>any eight</u> out of the ten questions by choosing the correct option.

Q.1. The writer feels that the youth's energy needs to be

   A. expressed   B. harnessed

   C. reserved   D. preserved

Q.2. Oxymoron is self-contradicting word or group of words.

The writer says that the vast majority of the youth today indulges to '_enjoy your own funeral_'.

Select from the options that correctly explains this oxymoron.

    A.   there is no deeper meaning and purpose to the human life.

    B.   formula of life is learn, earn, burn and enjoy.

    C.   self-indulgent people usually die alone and lonely.

    D.   The vast majority of the youth today lacks insight and foresight.

Q.3. Select the option that suitably completes the given dialogue as per the context in paragraph III.

Writer: So you're organizing a political rally today as I see. Any particular agenda that you're running for?

Youth leader: We are voicing our opinions (1)...............................

Writer: Well that sounds a bit extreme and unnecessary, don't you think?

Youth leader: (2)................................., we are doing what we feel is right.

    A.   (1) on the lack of proper garbage disposal bins in the city (2) Being conscious about climate change is good

    B.   (1) for building a new yoga center (2) a little bit of violence is ok if it is done for good

    C.   (1) against the promotion of only topper students (2) It is important that every child qualifies

    D.   (1) against unemployment, and we will barge into the DM office if need be (2) It is the only way the authorities will listen to us

Q.4. Which signboard would the writer have chosen for his description of the third section of youth?

1. Sober, sensitive and thoughtful youngsters.	2. Sober, selfish and thoughtful youngsters.	3. Drunk in power and self-indulgent youngsters.	4. Sensitive, grounded and delusional youngsters.

    A.   option 1   B.   option 2

    C.   option 3   D.   option 4

Q.5. Select the option that clearly indicates the comparison between first and fourth group of the youth.

	First group	Fourth group
A.	intelligent, skillful and insightful.	Mindful, intelligent and conscious.
B.	Sensitive, thoughtful and productive.	Immoral, unjust and self-indulgent.
C.	Self-absorbed, lacks insight and shallow.	Deep, insightful and thinking way ahead for the future.
D.	Rude, fast-paced and always in a hurry.	Pretentious, show-off and wannabe.

Q.6. What is the relationship between (1) and (2)?

(1)   .... but it lacks insight and foresight.

(2)   .... whose formula of life is learn, earn, burn and enjoy.

    A.   (2) is the cause for (1).   B.   (1) is the cause for (2).

    C.   (2) sets the stage for (1).   D.   (1) cannot describe (2).

Q.7. The writer mentions that man is the micro-cosmos and his fullest flowering and enfoldment lies in his identification with the cosmos, because he realises that:

    A.   Man is a basic unit of conscious life which has got immense potentialities for evolution, development and growth.

    B.   The youth needs to be shown the right path to positively channelise their energy.

    C.   The science of life is a new branch of knowledge which studies the development of planetary life.

    D.   Man should be divided into subjective and objective halves of spirituality and physicality.

Q.8. Select the option that lists the review for the writer's views on the second group of youth.

    A.   The writer clearly hates this group of youth the most as is clear with his choice of words for them.

    B.   The writer empathizes with this less privileged group and sees good potential in them if they are shown the right path.

C. The writer mocks them for being less qualified and skilled, and sees them as a potential threat to the society.

D. The writer is not much hopeful for this group of youth because they lack proper emotional intelligence.

Q.9. Which quote summarises the writer's feelings about the youth?

A. "Youth offers the promise of happiness, but life offers the realities of grief."   — *Nicholas Sparks*

B. "Older men declare war. But it is youth that must fight and die."   — *Herbert Hoover*

C. "What should young people do with their lives today? Many things, obviously. But the most daring thing is to create stable communities in which the terrible disease of loneliness can be cured."

     — *Kurt Vonnegut*

D. "Youth is wasted on the young."   — *George Bernard Shaw*

Q.10. Select the option that lists what we can conclude from the text.

(1) The youth is an inexhaustible reservoir of energy.

(2) The second category of youth is a sober and thoughtful class of people.

(3) The third section of youth may be incited to be against the establishment.

(4) The fourth group of youth is going to steer humanity into the third millennium.

A. (1) and (3) are true.   B. (2), (3) and (4) are true.

C. (1), (2) and (4) are true.   D. (1) and (4) are true.

II. Read the passage given below.

I. Over 100 persons have died in the floods in Assam so far while another 147 were killed in lightning strikes in Bihar last month. But with the monsoon season less than half way through, more loss of lives and property are expected if the trend in the past five years is anything to go by.

II. Take for instance human lives lost. In 2015, a little less than 1,000 persons died of flood and rain-related incidents, but in 2019, nearly 2,500 persons had lost their lives, according to government data. The loss of cattle also increased. While in 2015, less than 30,000 cattle died, in 2019, it was nearly 72,000.(See graphic 1)

III. To sum up the flood and its impact in the past five years, over 8,700 people were killed, over 2 lakh cattle died and more than 36 lakh houses were destroyed in floods. The cost of damage to property has also shot up in these five years. While in 2015, the damage suffered totalled ₹33,257 crore, in 2018, the last year for which data is available, it went up to ₹95,736 crore. The cost of damage is likely to be more in 2019 as over a dozen states, including Bihar, Assam, Himachal Pradesh, Kerala and Maharashtra, witnessed large-scale devastation.

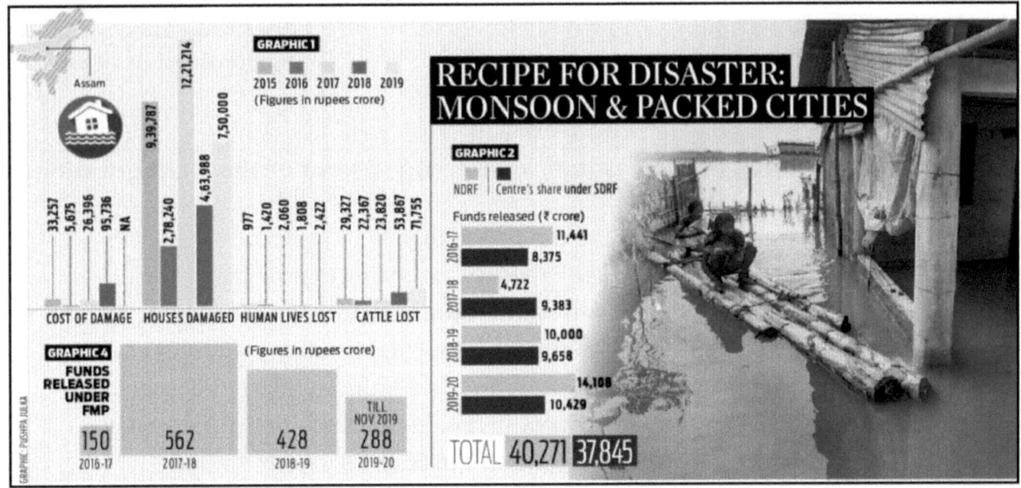

IV. Besides the rising damages, the cost to the exchequer towards relief work has also increased. In 2016-17, the Centre released ₹11,441 cr under the National Disaster Relief Fund while its share under the State Disaster Relief Fund was ₹8,375 crore. This increased to ₹14,108 cr and ₹10,429 cr respectively in 2019-20. (See graphic 2)

V. The flood's increasing loss of lives and property appears to make a mockery of all the expert committees, task forces and commissions the government has formed. In 1972, the Ganga Flood

Control Commission was set-up in Patna to address the flood problem and erosion in the Ganga basin states. In 1980, the Brahmaputra Board came into existence to address the flood erosion problem in the northeastern states and Sikkim. (See table)

VI. The government also launched a Flood Management Programme in the Eleventh Plan (2007-12) for providing financial assistance to state governments to undertake work related to river management, flood control, anti-erosion, drainage development, flood proofing, among others. The FMP was continued for three years under the Twelfth Plan from 2017-18 to 2019-20. It has subsequently been included as a component of the Flood Management and Border Areas Programme in the Ministry of Jal Shakti. But all these appear to have come to a naught as the government's approach is more reactive than proactive, according to experts. Instead of focusing on the real problem, it was only concerned about relief measures, they said.

VII. They pointed out that the area affected by floods has doubled since 1950. "The flood-affected area in 1950 was 25 million hectare, now it has doubled to nearly 50 million hectare. But, what is surprising is that nobody looks concerned about the real issues. Earlier, only villages used to be affected but now cities are also getting flooded. Chennai and Patna are just examples. I had written to the government in 2015, highlighting the poor drainage system in cities," said former IIT professor Dinesh Kumar Mishra.

Himanshu Thakkar, the coordinator of the South Asia Network of Dams, Rivers and People, said effective management of dams could bring down the damage caused by floods. "We have over 5,000 dams. Every dam can help moderate floods in the downstream area but only if it is operated properly," Thakkar said.

Committees & commissions	Aim	Work
Ganga Flood Control Commission	Flood, erosion in Ganga basin states.	Prepared 23 comprehensive master plans.
Rashtriya Barh Aayog	To evolve coordinated, integrated approach for flood control.	Submitted report in 1980 recommending measures Brahmaputra Board.
Brahmaputra Board	Flood, erosion problems in northeastern states.	Prepared 57 master plans for implementation.
Task Force-2004	Flood management and erosion control.	Submitted report in December 2004, recommending short, long-term measures.
Flood Management Programme	To provide financial assistance for river management, flood control, erosion.	Other than allocating financial aid, it is involved in flood forecasting.

Based on your understanding of the passage, answer <u>any six</u> out of the eight questions by choosing the correct option.

Q.11. Select the correct inference with reference to the following:

The government's approach is more reactive than proactive, according to experts.

A. Instead of focusing on the relief measures, the government is only concerned about real problem.

B. The government focuses more after damage rather than handling the root cause of the problem.

C. The government reacts in a proactive way which is commended by the experts.

D. The government focuses on the Ministry of Jal Shakti for such natural disasters.

Q.12. Select the central idea from the given table on the Committees & commissions.

A. These committees and commissions are only for North Indian rivers.

B. These committees and commissions are involved in flood forecasting.

C. These committees and commissions have a severe lack of infrastructure.

D. These committees are solely dedicated for flood and erosion relief with their financial aids.

Q.13. Select the option that displays the true statement with reference to figure given.

A. The cost of house damages was the highest in 2017.

B.   Cattle loss was highest in the flood of 2016.

C.   NDRF released the lowest funds for the year 2019-2020.

D.   Funds released under FMP were the highest for the year 2016-2017.

Q.14. Based on your reading of paragraphs III-IV, select the appropriate counter- argument to the given argument.

Argument: The damage relief fund costs are rising because of inflation. However, the overall loss of life and livestock is consistent.

A.   The rising costs are in no way related to inflation because Indian economy does not rely on global market for its currency value.

B.   Damage to property is greater as compared to loss of lives and livestock.

C.   Center isn't giving more relief funds for loss of life, so people have stopped reporting the dead.

D.   It is very clear that the rising damage costs are only because life and livestock damage have increased, because they are the indicator of fund prices.

Q.15. Select the option that displays the correct cause-effect relationship.

	Cause	Effect
A.	Cities are also getting flooded.	Poor drainage system in cities.
B.	Monsoon season caused flood in Brahmaputra valley.	Over 147 people die in Bihar last month.
C.	Flood and erosion in Ganga basin states.	Ganga Flood Control Commission prepared 23 comprehensive master plans.
D.	Government task forces are a mockery of all the expert committees.	More than 36 lakh houses were destroyed in floods.

Q.16. The survey statistics mention the funds released under NDRF, indicating that:

A.   The center's share under SDRF is always more than NDRF.

B.   The center's share under SDRF was more than NDRF in 2017-2018.

C.   The center's share under SDRF is almost similar to NDRF.

D.   The center's share under SDRF was more than NDRF in 2019-2020.

Q.17. The phrase 'exchequer' refers to the:

A.   former staff of bank who handles cheques.   B.   cheques that are given to victims.

C.   relief funds from NGOs.   D.   national government treasury.

Q.18. Read the two statements given below and select the option that suitably explains them.

(1)   Every dam can help moderate floods in the downstream area but only if it is operated properly.

(2)   Chennai and Patna have poor drainage systems.

A.   (2) is the problem and (1) is the solution for (2).

B.   (1) and (2) are both false.

C.   (1) is true but (2) is not the reason for (1).

D.   (2) is false and (1) explains it.

WRITING

III.   Answer <u>any four</u> out of the five questions given, with reference to the context below.

The Sports Secretary of St. George's School, Hyderabad, has to draft a notice for your school notice board informing the students about the sale of old sports goods of your school.

Q.19. Select the appropriate title for this notice.

A.   Sale of Old Sports Goods

B.   The Need to Sell Sports Goods

C.   Sports and More

D.   Good Quality Sports Goods at discounted price

Q.20. Select the option listing the most appropriate opening for this notice.

A.   Attention, students of all classes...

B.   We are writing this notice to inform you all that....

C. Students are hereby informed that...

D. I hereby wish to share with you all that...

Q.21. Select the option with the information points to be included in the body of this notice.

(1)	Information about the kind of goods	(2)	General opinion about old sports goods
(3)	Date of the sale	(4)	Reason for selling the old sports goods
(5)	Outcome of the sale	(6)	The place where the sale would be organised

A. 1 and 3   B. 1, 2 and 3

C. 5 and 6   D. 1, 3 and 6

Q.22. Should this notice include the name of the Sports Secretary?

A. Yes, because he is the one issuing the notice

B. No, because signature says it all

C. No, as the title itself is self-explanatory

D. Yes, because it makes it informal

Q.23. Select the appropriate conclusion for this notice.

A. All are welcome

B. Interested students are requested to visit during recess time

C. Collaboration solicited

D. Persuade your friends to attend to come forward

IV. **Answer <u>any six</u> of the seven questions given, with reference to the context below.**

While returning from school you happened to see plastic bottles being flung into the middle of the road from a speeding car. This made you think how people can be so devoid of civic sense. Write an article in 125-150 words on the lack of civic sense in our country and how civic sense can be inculcated in children at a very young age. You are Shiva/Shivani.

Q.24. Which suggestions would be appropriate for Shiva/Shivani's article?

A. We should inculcate civic sense right from childhood

B. Parents should ask children to take responsibility

C. Every demand of the child should not be met

D. Children should be encouraged to save money

Q.25. Select an appropriate title for this article.

A. Lack of Civic Sense   B. Save Environment

C. Ban Plastic   D. Let's Come Together

Q.26. Which option should the writer choose to elaborate on the reasons why use of plastic has risen?

1. 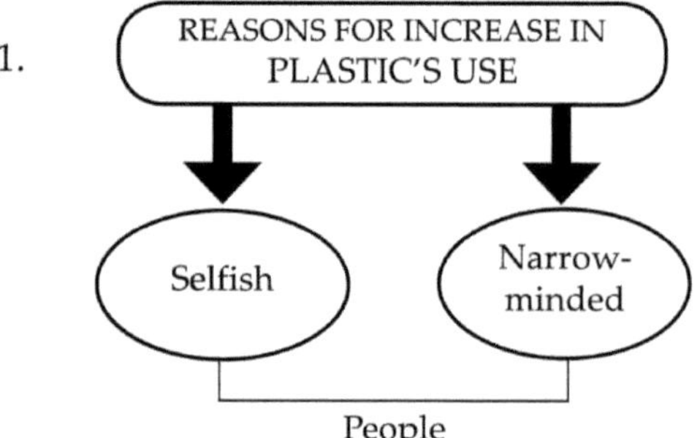

2. 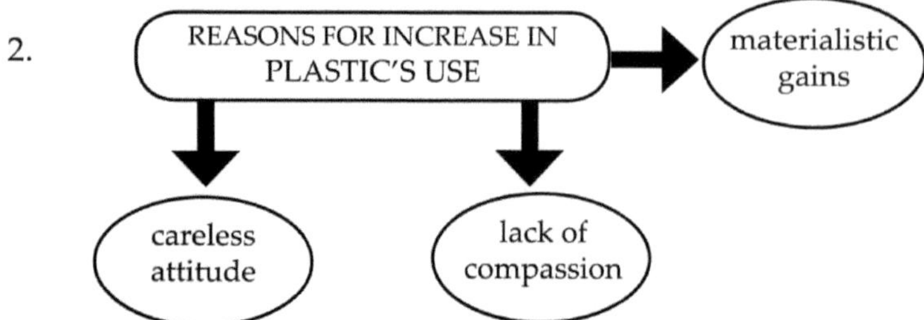

3. 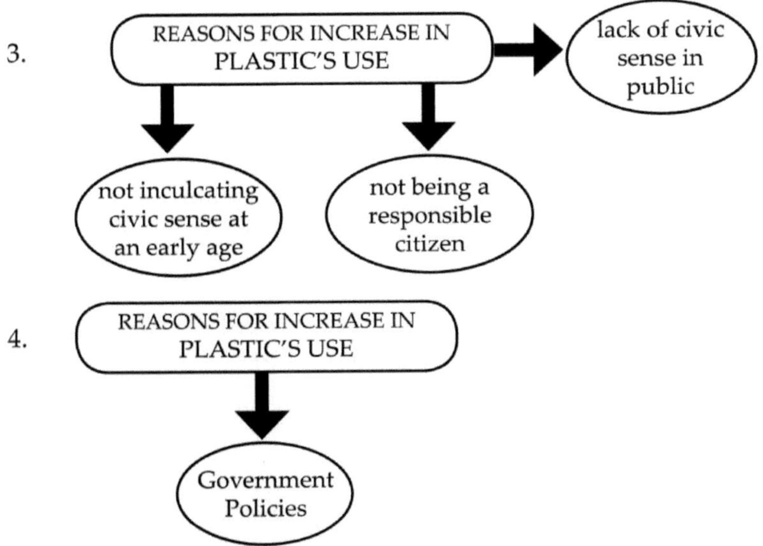

4.

A. Option 1	B. Option 2
C. Option 3	D. Option 4

Q.27. Which option would help Shiva/Shivani with the appropriate organisation of relevant ideas for this article?

A. Expressing concern about rise in use of plastic - looking at the reasons - presenting a concluding viewpoint - effects of the rise in use of plastic

B. Stating the effects of lack of civic sense - information about policies and laws - providing suggestions for saving the environment

C. Introducing the purpose of the article - presenting a pledge of saving environment - exploring the reasons for the laws - questioning the efficacy of laws

D. Showing the lack of civic sense in public - providing suggestions for improvements in the behaviour of people - talking about government policies - presenting a pledge for awareness

Q.28. Read a sentence from the article draft and complete it by selecting the most appropriate option.

Parents must (i) _____________ their children to keep their surroundings clean. All these things must be taught at (ii) _________.

A. (i) help (ii) school	B. (i) encourage (ii) at an early age
C. (i) ask (ii) childhood	D. (i) inculcate (ii) home

Q.29. Which quote summarises the central idea of the article?

A. Civic engagement is very important. We all live here together and we need to look out for one another. *—Elizabeth Goreham*

B. Civic education and civic responsibility should be taught in elementary school. *—Donna Brazile*

C. It seems to me that we are in danger of losing sight of certain basic civic values in society by allowing the growth of a whole generation of people who really have no sense of attachment to society. *—Alexander McCall Smith*

D. Without a sense of caring, there can be no sense of community. *—Anthony J D' Angelo*

Q.30. Read the options and select the option that includes the most appropriate self-checklist of the article.

A. My article contains -

1. First person address to the audience as title
2. Text that contains the topical points
3. Other people observation
4. Personal observations
5. Designation and date at the end

B. My article contains -

1. An eye-catching thematically related title
2. Content that offers a balanced view of the issue
3. Writer's opinion
4. Solution to the issue
5. A by-line

<table>
<tr><td>C. My article contains -</td><td>D. My article contains</td></tr>
<tr><td>

1. A quote as title
2. Date
3. A conclusion including published evidence
4. Expression of gratitude
5. A by-line

</td><td>

1. A content that analyses the pros and cons
2. Content that offers a balanced view
3. Input for the cause effect and suggestion
4. Name of the publishing body
5. Conclusion including personal observations

</td></tr>
</table>

LITERATURE

This section has sub-sections: V, VI, VII, VIII, IX. There are a total of 30 questions in the section. Attempt any 26 questions from the sub-sections V to IX.

V.   **Read the given extract to attempt questions that follow:**

"Will they make them sing in German, even the pigeons?" Whenever I looked up from my writing I saw M. Hamel sitting motionless in his chair and gazing first at one thing, then at another, as if he wanted to fix in his mind just how everything looked in that little school-room. Fancy! For forty years he had been there in the same place, with his garden outside the window and his class in front of him,.."

Q.31. What does the tone of Franz's question suggest?

    A.   sarcasm   B.   satire

    C.   cynicism   D.   caustic criticism

Q.32. Cooing is natural to pigeons. Similarly, what according to the context is as important to humans?

    A.   own language   B.   music

    C.   dreaming   D.   musing

Q.33. Mention the reason why Hamilton is sitting motionless in the chair.

    A.   He was memorising the lessons to be taught.

    B.   A recent development in his career came as a jolt from the blue.

    C.   He was trying to think what best lesson he should teach so that everyone remembers him.

    D.   He was worried about packing his things.

Q.34. Hamilton, in terms of his career, can be described as-

    A.   a novice   B.   a pioneer

    C.   a veteran   D.   a stickler

Q.35. Which of the following captions suits the theme of the story?

    A.   Mother tongue is to ordinary people what notes are to musicians

    B.   What is a Nation without mother tongue?

    C.   Rhythm is our universal mother tongue

    D.   Hearts can be ruled by imposing linguistic restrictions

VI.   **Read the given extract to attempt questions that follow:**

My acquaintance with the barefoot ragpickers leads me to Seemapuri, a place on periphery of Delhi yet miles away from it, metaphorically. Those who live here are squatters who came from Bangladesh back in 1971. Saheb's family is among them. Seemapuri was then a wilderness. It still is, but it is no longer empty. In structures of mud, with roofs of tin and tarpaulin, devoid of sewage, drainage or running water, live 10,000 ragpickers.

Q.36. The author used the word *'metaphorically'* for the location of Seemapuri. What does this suggest about the condition of the place?

    A.   Well located   B.   Lacking basic amenities

    C.   Advanced   D.   Retrograde

Q.37. Of the four meanings of 'wilderness', select the option that matches in meaning with its usage in the extract.

    A.   situated in woods   B.   located in a secluded area

    C.   full of wild animals   D.   occupied by tribal

Q.38. The author mentions that *'Those who live here are squatters who came from Bangladesh'.*

    She means that the people are __________ of Bangladesh.

A.	Ration card holders	B.	Trespassers
C.	Unlawful residents	D.	Native

Q.39. Select the option that lists the feelings and attitudes corresponding to the following:

(1) .... *barefoot rag pickers*

(2) .... *a place on periphery of Delhi yet miles away from it*

A.	(1) mocking		B.	(1) sympathetic	
	(2) figurative			(2) sarcastic	
C.	(1) remorseful		D.	(1) sympathetic	
	(2) sarcastic			(2) rhetorical	

Q.40. Select the option that lists reasons why rag pickers live in structures of mud, devoid of sewage, drainage or running water?

I.   no other option

II.   habitual of the atmosphere

III. like to live in such places as it would help in their livelihood

IV.   denied the opportunity to live in clean places

A.	I and III	B.	II and IV
C.	II and III	D.	I and IV

VII. **Read the given extract to attempt questions that follow:**

For once on the face of the Earth

let's not speak in any language,

let's stop for one second,

and not move our arms so much.

It would be an exotic moment

without rush, without engines,

we would all be together

in a sudden strangeness.

Q.41. The poet uses the word "let's" to ________.

    A.   initiate a conversation between the poet and the readers.

    B.   invite readers as part of the poem's larger call to humanity.

    C.   welcome readers into the world of the poem and its subject.

    D.   address readers as fellow members of the human race.

Q.42. Margaret Atwood said, *"Language divides us into fragments, I wanted to be whole."*

Choose the option that correctly comments on the relationship between Margaret Atwood's words and the line from the above extract – *"let's not speak in any language"*

    A.   Atwood endorses Neruda's call to not speak in any language.

    B.   Atwood justifies Neruda's request to not engage in any speaking.

    C.   Atwood undermines Neruda's intent to stop and not speak in any language.

    D.   Atwood surrenders to Neruda's desire for silence and not speak in any language.

Q.43. Why do you think the poet employs words like "exotic" and "strangeness"?

    A.   To highlight the importance of everyone being together suddenly for once.

    B.   To emphasize the frenetic activity and chaos that usually envelops human life.

    C.   To indicate the unfamiliarity of a sudden moment without rush or without engine.

    D.   To direct us towards keeping quiet and how we all would be together in that silence.

Q.44. Which option has the underlined phrase that applies the poetic device used for in 'sudden strangeness'?

A.	I had a <u>sleepless night</u>.	B.	The <u>trees whispered</u> their discontent.
C.	The <u>crazy lady was very lazy</u>.	D.	The <u>gentle giant jumped</u> with joy.

Q.45. The literal meaning of 'and not move our arms' refers to a condition when one sits without any movement of hands. What does its figurative meaning refer to?

A. exhibiting discipline

B. not use weapons to harm others

C. showing some kind of mourning

D. remain still in punishment

VII. Read the given extract to attempt questions that follow:

I turned into Grand Central from Vanderbilt Avenue, and went down the steps to the first level, where you take trains like the Twentieth Century. Then I walked down another flight to the second level, where the suburban trains leave from, ducked into an arched doorway heading for the subway and got lost! That's easy to do. I've been in and out of Grand Central hundreds of times, but I'm always bumping into new doorways and stairs and corridors. Once I got into a tunnel about a mile long and came out in the lobby of the Roosevelt Hotel. Another time I came up in an office building on Forty-sixth Street, three blocks away.

Q.46. The expression *'where you take trains like the Twentieth Century'* shows that the narrator....................

A. has confused state of mind

B. has habit of living in past

C. wants to deviate from the present situation

D. has been living in some unknown constant fear

Q.47. Select the option that lists the correct inference based on the information in the extract.

A. At the first level, suburban trains depart to subway.

B. First level and second level are connected by suburban trains.

C. Second level ends at subway.

D. For reaching second level, one must take a flight from first level.

Q.48. Select the correct option to fill in the blanks.

Charley's always bumping into new doorways and stairs and corridors suggest that _______.

A. it was the effect of his wife's behaviour towards him

B. he was becoming forgetful due to stress

C. Sam's behaviour had made him insane

D. he was under the impression that he had reached the third level

Q.49. Why did Charley come out in the lobby of a Hotel when he got into a mile long tunnel?

A. For a business meeting

B. He had lost his way

C. He was finding a refuge there

D. It was the only exit point where he could go

Q.50. Select the option that displays a cause-effect set.

A.

Cause	Effect
The narrator ducked into an arched doorway	He got lost

B.

Cause	Effect
The narrator got lost	He ducked into an arched doorway

C.

Cause	Effect
The narrator walked down another flight to the second level	The suburban trains leave from there

D.

Cause	Effect
The suburban trains leave from there	The narrator walked down another flight to the second level

IX. Attempt the following.

Q.51. The all- pervasive mood of the poem *My Mother at Sixty-six* can be best described as:

A. melancholic and cynical

B. nostalgic and enthusiastic

C. optimistic but tinged with fear

D. cynical and optimistic

Q.52. The style of *The Last Lesson* is

A. Descriptive

B. Narrative

C. Colloquial

D. Melodramatic

Q.53. Sadao was not able to kill the American prisoner or get him arrested. What could be the possible reason for this?

A. For the fear of getting arrested.

B. He recalled the courtesy of the American when he was in US.

C. It was against his profession.

D. The Americans might take revenge and declare war.

Q.54. Select the option that tells about the feelings which developed in Douglas' mind after being thrown away in the pool by a big boy?

    I.   Aversion from water

    II.   Liking for swimming

    III.   Lost confidence forever

    IV.   Terror seized him for a long time

    A.   I and II   B.   I and IV

    C.   II and III   D.   I and III

Q.55. *'Awarding the world its world'*, expression used by Stephen Spender illustrate that:

    A.   the world belongs to all equally

    B.   the world belongs to rich and influential

    C.   the world should be bestowed with bounties

    D.   the world should be reciprocated its resources

Q.56. Classify (1) to (4) as fact (F) or opinion (O), based on your reading of *The Third Level*.

    1.   Charley's three hundred dollars bought less than two hundred old style bills.

    2.   Charley was back on the second level.

    3.   I turned into Grand Central from Vanderbilt Avenue.

    4.   Charley never told his psychiatrist friend about his idea.

    A.   F-1, 3, 4; O-2   B.   F-1, 2, 3; O-4

    C.   F-3, 4; O-1, 2   D.   F-2; O-1, 3, 4

Q.57. Select the suitable option for the given statements, based on your reading of *Lost Spring*.

    1.   Many storms swept away Saheb's fields and homes.

    2.   Saheb didn't wear chappals.

    A.   (1) is false but (2) is true.   B.   Both (1) and (2) are false

    C.   (2) is a fact but unrelated to (1).   D.   (1) is the cause for (2).

Q.58. In 'Keeping Quiet' the poet induces a symbol in order to appeal that there can be life even without action. Which symbol is this?

    A.   water   B.   earth

    C.   air   D.   fire

Q.59. Inspite of complete defiance from the servants, Hana still helped Dr. Sadao in treating and serving POW. What does this reflect about her character?

    A.   Professionalism   B.   Humanitarianism

    C.   Selfishness   D.   Compulsion

Q.60. What could be the remedy of prevailing violence according to Pablo Neruda?

    A.   Refined and set language   B.   Speech therapy

    C.   Rehearsing silence   D.   Thorough wisdom

❑❑

Answers

Sample Paper 1

READING

Q.1. B. Television

Q.2. B. (1) understand the logics behind those fairy tales (2) the stories are realistic and well described through animations.

Q.3. D. having a private conversation between two people

Q.4. C. Option 3

Q.5.

	Before	Today
C.	Reading books	Watching television

Q.6. A. (1) is the cause of (2)

Q.7. A. They find them uninteresting

Q.8. A. warms the bond between parents and children, attracts young minds to the world of books, a chance to explore the sea of life.

Q.9. D. *Books should go where they will be most appreciated, and not sit unread, gathering dust on a forgotten shelf, don't you agree?*
-Christopher Paolini

Q.10. C. (1) and (4) are true, (2) and (3) are false

Q.11. A. The innumerable individual passenger pigeons flocked the skies of North America.

Q.12. B. Columba

Q.13.

	Cause	Effect
A.	The hunt for passenger pigeons grew and culminated in a massive hunt for the species throughout the 1800s.	The species finally collapsed and disappeared.

Q.14. A. It's simply astonishing that the species found in large number, disappeared so quickly.

Q.15. B. I don't think that eating young birds at night wouldn't scare the adult birds. After all, they can sense fear and it is just an assumption of the North Americans.

Q.16. B. There was a rapid decrease in the population of passenger pigeons.

Q.17. B. It was in free fall even before the arrival of the Europeans.

Q.18. D. (2) is the research through (1)

WRITING

Q.19. B. Traffic Advisory

Q.20. C. This is to notify that in view of …

Q.21. A. (2) and (4)

Q.22. D. to warn people

Q.23. A. Stay safe.

Q.24. B. Through the columns of your esteemed newspaper, I want to draw your kind attention towards the daylight robbery in our area

Q.25. C. polite and formal

Q.26. A. Subject

Q.27. D. Getting a reward for her to bring it to the notice of concerned authorities

Q.28. D.

> - Solve the robbery issues in the area by highlighting it in a newspaper
> - Make the area safe for people

Q.29. A.   security guards are posted

Q.30. B.   Introducing problems faced by the people—Suggesting improvement methods—Conclusion.

LITERATURE

Q.31. C.   felt sorry for M. Hamel as it was his last French lesson.

Q.32. B.   'Too little, too late'

Q.33. C.   M. Hamel often sent students to water his flowers, and gave a holiday when he wanted to go fishing.

Q.34. D.   (i) forgotten; (ii) transformed; (iii) hold on; (iv) identity

Q.35. D.   regret

Q.36. C.   his dream was illusionary and indistinct.

Q.37. B.   2 and 4

Q.38. D.   Firozabad has emerged as a nascent producer of bangles in the country.

Q.39. C.   majority of the population in Firozabad is involved in bangle-making.

Q.40. A.   happy

Q.41. C.   Only (5)

Q.42. B.   Title 2

Q.43. C.   Both Assertion and Reason can be inferred.

Q.44. B.   My thoughts were as heavy as lead that evening when …

Q.45. C.   her face was lifeless and dull like that of a dead person

Q.46. C.   traditional

Q.47. C.   didn't want to use her white silk as the soldier was bleeding

Q.48. C.   (a) 1 and 2

Q.49. A.   foreigner, white, enemy

Q.50.

	Cause	Effect
A.	Hana didn't want to use her beloved quilt for the American soldier.	She hesitated while taking it out.

Q.51. A.   Self-realization

Q.52. C.   rag picking

Q.53. B.   bully

Q.54. C.   simile

Q.55. B.   ill-fed

Q.56. A.   (1) is false but (2) is true.

Q.57. C.   the fear of being caught

Q.58. A.   total inactivity

Q.59. B.   heartbroken and despaired

Q.60. D.   ethical

Sample Paper 2

READING

Q.1. B.   concerned

Q.2. A.   sunk

Q.3. D.   (1) why do you ask? (2) I would rather not talk about that unfortunate tragedy.

Q.4. C.   option 3

Q.5.

	Before 1985	After 1985
A.	Ruins preserved in cold dark ocean.	Hunters and voyagers exploiting the ruins.

Q.6. D.   (1) is the cause of (2).

Q.7. C.   The deep dark and cold conditions of the ocean has well preserved a century old specimen of human endeavour and failure which is an irony personified in history.

Q.8. A.   We are all grieving today for the greatest loss to mankind in recent history. We have failed all those on board by not building them a strong enough Titanic.

Q.9. B.   The people without the knowledge of their past history, origin and culture is like a tree without roots.
—*Marcus Garvey*

Q.10. D.   (2) and (4) are true

Q.11. D.   Spacecraft designers are competing to bring the quickest and most affordable options for space tourism.

Q.12. A.   Space tourism may not be feasible as of now but next decade may prove more promising.

Q.13. B.   NASA's budget for Human Space Flight and Mission Support are in the priority.

Q.14. D.   The wealthiest are willing to fund for research and development in space science, so even if it is for their ego, it will still be a way for advancement in faster and cheaper technologies.

Q.15.

	Cause	Effect
A.	$10 million prize for spacecraft designers.	Faster development of cost-effective space trips.

Q.16. D.   The demand and development have the potential to lower ticket price from $10,000 to $5,000.

Q.17. B.   launching a pilot into space.

Q.18. B.   (1) is true and (2) is the reason of (1).

WRITING

Q.19. C.   Position Vacant

Q.20. C.   1 and 2 only

Q.21. A.   Wanted marketing executive for a reputed Delhi based organization...

Q.22. A.   Address of the General Manager

Q.23. C.   Title of the advertisement

Q.24. C.   Mental health – your greatest wealth

Q.25. A.   option 1

Q.26. A.   Expressing concern about several cases of suicide due to depression- exploring the reasons with factual support – stating the effects – providing the suggestion to create mental health awareness – presenting a conclusive outlook.

Q.27. D.   Individuals should understand the importance of mental health and society should be more sensitive towards such causes.

Q.28. C.   Stigma, Recover

Q.29. A.   "It's okay to not to be okay"

Q.30. A. My article contains -

> 1. An eye-catching title
> 2. A by-line
> 3. Proper set of causes and effects for mental illness
> 4. Well deliberated suggestions
> 5. A quote to enhance the quality of the article
> 6. Factual information to support argument

LITERATURE

Q.31. A. If Statement 1 is the cause, Statement 2 is the effect.
Q.32. D. Drama
Q.33. B. indicate pauses
Q.34. B. 'I crossed to oblivion.'
Q.35. D. 1 and 2
Q.36. B. He is concerned about many others like the ragpickers
Q.37. B. isolation
Q.38. B. A man from Udipi

Q.39. C.

> (1)   hope
> (2)   tired and oblivious

Q.40. B. 1 and 5
Q.41. B. Their world is confined to the classroom windows full of poverty and diseases
Q.42. B. Dull and unpleasant
Q.43. C. The dull life of the slum children
Q.44. C. The Pied Piper of Hamelin
Q.45. B. Future of the slum children is unclear and uncertain
Q.46. D. Nobody in particular
Q.47. C. orthodox and upper class.
Q.48. C. Re-imagining a Warless Future: Technology for Peace
Q.49. D. option (2) and (4)

Q.50.

	Cause	Effect
C.	The speaker wanted to be in a peaceful world.	He wanted two tickets to go there.

Q.51. B. was hiding her feelings of fear
Q.52. B. copies of written notes
Q.53. C. He is considered the black sheep of the family.
Q.54. A. Water at Y.M.C.A. swimming pool
Q.55. A. a lucid flow of emotions
Q.56. A. Statement I is True, Statement II is False, and Statement III cannot be inferred.
Q.57. A. there is no dearth of promises which remain unfulfilled.
Q.58. C. The oppressive monotony of modern life.
Q.59. B. idealized sentimentality
Q.60. B. superiority of Japan over America.

Sample Paper 3

READING

Q.1. B. bewildered

Q.2. D. systematic form of expressions by hand movements.

Q.3. D. (1) child's ability to make sense of this world (2) They have an innate grammatical machinery

Q.4. C. option 3

Q.5.

	Before exposure to pidgin	After exposure to pidgin
A.	Little complexity to the grammar.	Adapting new words to create a fresh expressive language.

Q.6. A. (2) explains the question described in (1).

Q.7. C. It is the most recent and well documented form of linguistic study in how grammar is created.

Q.8. B. Interesting how something like the sign language made by children can be so inventive and fluid.

Q.9. C. "Children have real understanding only of that which they invent themselves." *– Jean Piaget*

Q.10. B. (1), (2) and (4) are true.

Q.11. D. Government is promoting last stage actions instead of tackling the problem in initial steps.

Q.12. A. Incineration is only going to bring more pollutants in the air.

Q.13. B. Awareness towards recycling of plastic is reflected in recent years.

Q.14. B. Regulations are not enough to contain the toxic carcinogens it will generate along with a huge cost of operating it.

Q.15.

	Cause	Effect
C.	Burning of polyethylene.	Release of formaldehyde and acetaldehyde.

Q.16. A. Prior to 1980, recycling and incineration of plastic was negligible.

Q.17. D. lower quality to burn as a fuel on its own.

Q.18. C. (1) is true and (2) correctly explains it.

WRITING

Q.19. C. Scheduled Power Cut

Q.20. C. 1,2 and 3

Q.21. A. All society members are hereby informed about the scheduled power cut…

Q.22. D. Name of publishing authority must be given.

Q.23. C. Inconvenience regretted

Q.24. A. The world is changing so rapidly and the context that our schools confront is so dynamic that we, as educators....

Q.25. C. Education infrastructure and its requirement in COVID era

Q.26. B. Introducing problems faced by teachers – Analysing change in education system – Suggesting improvements in the system – Conclusion

Q.27. C. Accept, Adjust

Q.28. C. Yours Sincerely
Aadarsh

Q.29. B. Closing signature must be on right

Q.30. C. Letter stating opinion on public interest.

LITERATURE

Q.31. A. Fright

Q.32. C. Announcement from Berlin

Q.33. C.

(1)	Concern
(2)	Seriousness

Q.34. C.   3 and 4
Q.35. B.   breathing fast with difficulty
Q.36. C.   Both Statement 1 and Statement 2 cannot be inferred.
Q.37. D.   repression
Q.38. B.   a bully tossed him into the pool for the sake of fun.
Q.39. B.   because it was expected to go by now
Q.40. B.   narrative
Q.41. B.   Peace, humanity and brotherhood
Q.42. D.   Scrutinize our activities
Q.43. B.   2 and 3
Q.44. A.   reconciliation
Q.45. A.   His own well-being and progress
Q.46. A.   Due to mist in the air
Q.47. A.   terrified
Q.48. C.   Stranded

Q.49.

	Cause	Effect
A.	He was a prisoner	Arms above head

Q.50. C.   The purpose of human life is to serve, and to show compassion and the will to help others.
Q.51. D.   simile
Q.52. A.   to show knowing one's language is escape from exploitation
Q.53. A.   hyperbole
Q.54. C.   limitless exploitation of natural resources.
Q.55. B.   the contrast between studying in the dreary classroom and playing outside freely.
Q.56. D.   Douglas decided to practice relentlessly to overcome his fear.
Q.57. D.   irony.
Q.58. A.   simile
Q.59. B.   vigorous
Q.60. B.   Both 1 and 2 are false.

Sample Paper 4

READING

Q.1. B.   pressured
Q.2. A.   crisis
Q.3. D.   (1) drain all my energy, I don't have time for additional activities. (2) I am already reading books in school
Q.4. A.   option 1

Q.5.

	Before television	After television
C.	Reading books was the usual hobby.	Reading books has become a rarity.

Q.6. B.   (2) sets the stage for (1).
Q.7. A.   it not only forms a warm bond between them but also attracts young minds to the world of books which gives them a chance to explore the sea of life.
Q.8. A.   I was surprisingly engrossed in the novel that I started to read, it isn't that boring or geeky as it sounds.
Q.9. D.   "If you read a book, you will unlock unknown doors of your soul. And who knows; you can find a treasure inside…"
                                                        — *George Spyrou, Roxanne*
Q.10. B.   (3) and (4) are true.
Q.11. C.   the number of passenger pigeons was in free fall even before the arrival of the Europeans.
Q.12. A.   Native Americans practiced sustainable hunting, thus cannot be blamed for passenger pigeon extinction.

Q.13. C.   New world pigeons and Passenger pigeons had the closest DNA.

Q.14. D.   There were still a few hundred thousand individuals left from the passenger pigeon population, which could've been easily saved by conservation programs, yet the Europeans hunted them all.

Q.15.

	Cause	Effect
A.	PSMC method uses the genetic information of a single individual.	PSMC method can map the history of the species.

Q.16. B.   collared-doves are more closely related to old world pigeons, than they are to cuckoo-doves.

Q.17. A.   last of the event in the series of unfortunate trail of passenger pigeons.

Q.18. C.   (1) is true and (2) explains it.

WRITING

Q.19. C.   I and II only

Q.20. C.   Available for sale a three room flat in ...

Q.21. D.   Sale and Purchase

Q.22. A.   Address of Ranjan/Ragini

Q.23. C.   Title of the advertisement

Q.24. B.   Conserve water - No water no life

Q.25. A.   Option 1

Q.26. A.   Expressing concern about several cases of land water depletion- exploring the reasons with factual support – stating the effects – providing the suggestion to create water conservation awareness– presenting a conclusive outlook.

Q.27. D.   Individuals should understand the importance of water conservation and do the needful.

Q.28. D.   Awareness, Conserve

Q.29. A.   You never know the worth of water until the well runs dry.

Q.30. A.   My article contains -

> 1. An eye-catching title
> 2. A by-line
> 3. Proper set of causes and effects for water wastage
> 4. Well deliberated suggestions on water conservation
> 5. A quote to enhance the quality of the article
> 6. Factual information to support argument

LITERATURE

Q.31. C.   though she is married, her eyes are devoid of happiness.

Q.32. D.   optimistic

Q.33. C.   reiteration

Q.34. B.   the drudgery of work has destroyed their willingness to improve their lot.

Q.35. C.   There is a steady change in the condition of the bangle makers.

Q.36. C.   Little fear was gone

Q.37. C.   After three months of practice, Douglas got rid of his terror.

Q.38. D.   I and III

Q.39.

	Cause	Effect
B.	The instructor taught Douglas	Douglas commanded over swimming skills

Q.40. A.   Once he was ducked by a big boy into deep water

Q.41. B.   hiding her fear from mother

Q.42. B.   enigmatic

Q.43. C.   lack of strength and colour

Q.44. C. enjambment
Q.45. D. repetition
Q.46. B. The manager complained about the employee's <u>sluggishness</u>.
Q.47. C. Sadao: prudent Hana: suspicious
Q.48. D. to be in hot water
Q.49. A. Statement 1 is true but Statement 2 is false.
Q.50. A. I and III
Q.51. B. Clear and logical
Q.52. A. life and enthusiasm
Q.53. D. fear of temporary separation and permanent one.
Q.54. A. sympathy
Q.55. B. 'An imbalance between the rich and poor is the oldest and most fatal ailment of all republics.'
Q.56. D. "You need help, my raving friend. You are way too invested in this crazy thought!"
Q.57. C. 2, 3, 5
Q.58. C. The poet will move on and seek to inspire others.
Q.59. C. unity
Q.60. B. her willingness to turn over the prisoner to the officials

Sample Paper 5

READING

Q.1. A. expressed
Q.2. C. self-indulgent people usually die alone and lonely.
Q.3. D. (1) against unemployment, and we will barge into the DM office if need be (2) It is the only way the authorities will listen to us
Q.4. A. option 1

Q.5.

	First group	Fourth group
C.	Self-absorbed, lacks insight and shallow.	Deep, insightful and thinking way ahead for the future.

Q.6. B. (1) is the cause for (2).
Q.7. A. Man is a basic unit of conscious life which has got immense potentialities for evolution, development and growth.
Q.8. B. The writer empathizes with this less privileged group and sees good potential in them if they are shown the right path.
Q.9. C. "What should young people do with their lives today? Many things, obviously. But the most daring thing is to create stable communities in which the terrible disease of loneliness can be cured."
—*Kurt Vonnegut*

Q.10. D. (1) and (4) are true.
Q.11. B. The government focuses more after damage rather than handling the root cause of the problem.
Q.12. D. These committees are solely dedicated for flood and erosion relief with their financial aids.
Q.13. A. The cost of house damages was the highest in 2017.
Q.14. D. It is very clear that the rising damage costs are only because life and livestock damage have increased, because they are the indicator of fund prices.

Q.15.

	Cause	Effect
C.	Flood and erosion in Ganga basin states.	Ganga Flood Control Commission prepared 23 comprehensive master plans.

Q.16. B. The center's share under SDRF was more than NDRF in 2017-2018.
Q.17. D. national government treasury.
Q.18. C. (1) is true but (2) is not the reason for (1).

WRITING

Q.19. A.   Sale of Old Sports Goods

Q.20. C.   Students are hereby informed that...

Q.21. D.   1, 3 and 6

Q.22. A.   Yes, because he is the one issuing the notice

Q.23. B.   Interested students are requested to visit during recess time

Q.24. A.   We should inculcate civic sense right from childhood

Q.25. A.   Lack of Civic Sense

Q.26. C.   Option 3

Q.27. D.   Showing the lack of civic sense in public - providing suggestions for improvements in the behaviour of people - talking about government policies - presenting a pledge for awareness

Q.28. B.   (i) encourage (ii) at an early age

Q.29. B.   Civic education and civic responsibility should be taught in elementary school.   —*Donna Brazile*

Q.30. B.   My article contains -

1. An eye-catching thematically related title
2. Content that offers a balanced view of the issue
3. Writer's opinion
4. Solution to the issue
5. A by-line

LITERATURE

Q.31. A.   sarcasm

Q.32. A.   own language

Q.33. B.   A recent development in his career came as a jolt from the blue.

Q.34. C.   a veteran

Q.35. B.   What is a Nation without mother tongue?   **Q.36.** B.   Lacking basic amenities

Q.37. B.   located in a secluded area   **Q.38.** C.   Unlawful residents

Q.39. D.

(1)   sympathetic
(2)   rhetorical

Q.40. D.   I and IV

Q.41. B.   invite readers as part of the poem's larger call to humanity.

Q.42. A.   Atwood endorses Neruda's call to not speak in any language.

Q.43. B.   To emphasize the frenetic activity and chaos that usually envelops human life.

Q.44. D.   The <u>gentle giant jumped</u> with joy.

Q.45. B.   not use weapons to harm others

Q.46. C.   wants to deviate from the present situation

Q.47. D.   For reaching second level, one must take a flight from first level.

Q.48. D.   he was under the impression that he had reached the third level

Q.49. B.   He had lost his way

Q.50.

	Cause	Effect
D.	The suburban trains leave from there	The narrator walked down another flight to the second level

Q.51. C.   optimistic but tinged with fear   **Q.52.** B.   Narrative

Q.53. C.   It was against his profession.   **Q.54.** B.   I and IV

Q.55. B.   the world belongs to rich and influential   **Q.56.** A.   F-1, 3, 4 ; O-2

Q.57. C.   (2) is a fact but unrelated to (1)   **Q.58.** B.   earth

Q.59. B.   Humanitarianism   **Q.60.** C.   Rehearsing silence

❏❏

Physical Education

Sample Question Paper

Physical Education [Code (048)]

Term – I

Time : 1 hr 30 Minutes
Max. Marks : 35

General Instructions :
1. There are three sections in the questions paper namely Section A, Section B and Section C.
2. Section A consists 24 questions amongst which 20 questions have to be attempted.
3. Section B consists 24 questions amongst which 20 questions have to be attempted.
4. Section C consists 12 questions amongst which 10 questions have to be attempted.

Section – A

(KNOWLEDGE AND UNDERSTANDING)

1. What is the other name for Vitamin B_2?
   (a) Niacin   (b) Thiamin   (c) Folic Acid   (d) Riboflavin

Ans. (d) Riboflavin

2. What is the formula to divide an odd number of teams in the upper half for a knockout fixture?
   (a) N+1/2   (b) N–1/2   (c) N(N–1)/2   (d) N(N+1)/2

Ans. (a) N+1/2

3. Which test is developed to test fitness in senior citizens?
   (a) Harvard step   (b) Rikli and Jones   (c) AAHPER   (d) Rockport

Ans. (b) Rikli and Jones

4.

Which action is shown in the illustration?
   (a) Flexion   (b) Extension   (c) Adduction   (d) Abduction

Ans. (a) Flexion

5. Gliding movement occurs at which joint?
   (a) Knee   (b) Hip   (c) Wrist   (d) Elbow

Ans. (c) Wrist

6. Consolation tournaments are a part of which type of fixture?
   (a) Knockout   (b) league   (c) combination   (d) none of these

Ans. (a) Knockout

7. Which amongst these is not a macro mineral?
   (a) Calcium   (b) Potassium   (c) Phosphorus   (d) Iodine

Ans. (d) Iodine

8. Who discovered Vitamin A?
   (a) Dr. Mc Collum   (b) Dr. Coubertin   (c) Dr. J.B.Nash   (d) Dr. Harvard

Ans. (a) Dr. Mc Collum

9. Formula for determining the number of bye in the lower half of a knockout fixture when number of byes are odd?
   - (a) nb+1/2
   - (b) nb–1/2
   - (c) nb/2
   - (d) nb+1

Ans. (a) nb+1/2

10. What is the name of the postural deformity caused due to increase in the curve at the lumbar region?
    - (a) Knock knees
    - (b) Bow legs
    - (c) Kyphosis
    - (d) Lordosis

Ans. (d) Lordosis

11. Which test is used to test the functional ability amongst senior citizens?
    - (a) Rockport one mile test
    - (b) Harvard step test
    - (c) Rikli and Jones test
    - (d) Fitness Index score

Ans. (c) Rikli and Jones test

12. What is the test duration for the Arm curl test?
    - (a) 1min
    - (b) 2 min
    - (c) 30sec
    - (d) Number of repetitions

Ans. (c) 30sec

13. Which postural deformity has Convexities right or left?
    - (a) Flat foot
    - (b) Knock knees
    - (c) Kyphosis
    - (d) Scoliosis

Ans. (d) Scoliosis

14. Which motor skill is involved in Smashing volleyball?
    - (a) Gross motor skills
    - (b) Fine motor skills
    - (c) Cross motor skills
    - (d) Open skills

Ans. (b) Fine motor skills

15. Who gave Laws of motion?
    - (a) Galileo
    - (b) Pascal
    - (c) Newton
    - (d) Darwin

Ans. (c) Newton

16. Harvard step is performed to check which kind of fitness?
    - (a) Cardiovascular
    - (b) Explosive strength
    - (c) Muscular strength
    - (d) Reaction ability

Ans. (a) Cardiovascular

17. Which fixture is also known as 'Berger system '?
    - (a) Knockout fixture
    - (b) Round robin fixture
    - (c) Combination fixture
    - (d) Challenge tournament

Ans. (b) Round robin fixture

18. Which of the following is not a spinal curvature deformity?
    - (a) Kyphosis
    - (b) Scoliosis
    - (c) Lordosis
    - (d) Flatfoot

Ans. (d) Flatfoot

19. What according to you is the main cause for night blindness?
    - (a) Deficiency of Vit. E
    - (b) Deficiency of Vit. C
    - (c) Deficiency of Vit. A
    - (d) Deficiency of Vit. D

Ans. (c) Deficiency of Vit. A

20. Which law amongst the given ones is known as the First law of motion?
    - (a) Law of inertia
    - (b) Law of reaction
    - (c) Law of momentum
    - (d) Law of acceleration

Ans. (a) Law of inertia

21. What is the Ratio of carbon,hydrogen and oxygen in carbohydrates?
    - (a) $1:2:1$
    - (b) $2:2:1$
    - (c) $2:1:1$
    - (d) $1:2:2$

Ans. (a) $1:2:1$

22. The formula for determining the number of rounds in a single league fixture when the number of teams is even?
    - (a) N
    - (b) N–1/2
    - (c) N–1
    - (d) N(N–1)/2

Ans. (c) N–1

23. Which postural deformity is related to Posterior curve of the spine?

    (a) Scoliosis   (b) Kyphosis   (c) Lordosis   (d) Knock knees

Ans. (b) Kyphosis

24. Which movement is caused by Moving a body part away from the medial line of the body?

    (a) Flexion   (b) Extension   (c) Adduction   (d) Abduction

Ans. (d) Abduction

Section – B

(APPLICATION + HOTS)

25. Name the component which is measured by this test?

    (a) Endurance   (b) Speed

    (c) Flexibility   (d) coordinative ability

Ans. (c) Flexibility

26. Which exercise should be done to cure this deformity?

    (a) Skipping   (b) Walking on heels

    (c) Both (a) and (b)   (d) Hanging on horizontal bar

Ans. (c) Both (a) and (b)

27. Identify the component of fitness which is tested through this exercise

    (a) Maximum strength   (b) Explosive strength

    (c) Strength endurance   (d) Static strength

Ans. (b) Explosive strength

28. How many matches will be played if there are 22 teams for the knockout fixture?

    (a) 10   (b) 21   (c) 12   (d) 32

Ans. (b) 21

29. How many byes will be given if there are 8 teams in the league tournament?

    (a) 7   (b) 5   (c) 4   (d) 0

Ans. (d) 0

30. Halasana is used for curing which of the following deformities?

    (a) Kyphosis   (b) Scoliosis   (c) Lordosis   (d) Flatfoot

Ans. (c) Lordosis

31. Match the following:

1.	Vitamin B12	A. Thiamin
2.	Vitamin B3	B. Biotin
3.	Vitamin B7	C. Cobalamin
4.	Vitamin B1	D. Niacin

Choose the correct option from the following:

(a) 4 3 1 2

(b) 2 3 4 1

(c) 1 2 3 4

(d) 3 4 2 1

Ans. (a) 4 3 1 2

32. Match the following:

1.		A. lower body strength
2.		B. lower body flexibility
3.		C. upper body strength
4.		D. abdominal strength

(a) 3 1 4 2

(b) 4 1 3 2

(c) 3 2 4 1

(d) 4 2 3 1

Ans. (b) 4 1 3 2

33. Match the postural deformities with their remedial activity:

1.		A.
2.		B.

(a) 1 3 2 4
(b) 1 4 3 2
(c) 1 3 4 2
(d) 4 2 3 1

Ans. (c) 1 3 4 2

34. Match the following:

1.		A. Flexion
2.		B. Adduction
3.		C. Extension
4.		D. Abduction

(a) 3 2 1 4
(b) 2 3 1 4
(c) 4 2 3 1
(d) 4 1 3 2

Ans. (d) 4 1 3 2

35. Which statement is not true about protein?
(a) Protein forms new tissues
(b) Protein regulates the balance of water and acids
(c) Protein helps in production of hormones
(d) Protein makes antibodies.

Ans. (c) Protein helps in production of hormones.

36. How many rounds will be played if the number of teams are 29 in the knockout fixture?
(a) 5
(b) 6
(c) 7
(d) 3

Ans. (a) 5

37. Identify the odd one.

1.    2. 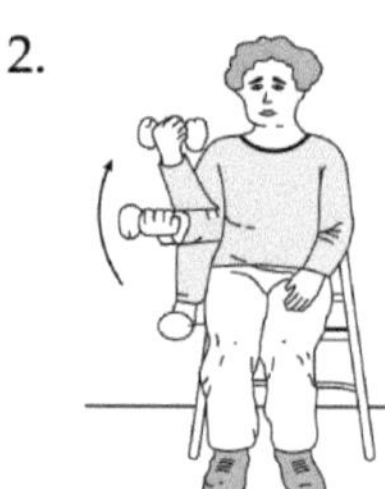   3.    4. 

(a) 4 (b) 3 (c) 2 (d) 1

Ans. (a) 4

38. Assertion (A): UNICEF says that water is not included in macro nutrients but USDA includes it as part of macronutrients.

Reason (R): Water must be taken in large quantities therefore it can be considered a macronutrient.

(a) Both (A) and (R) are true, but (R) is not the correct explanation of (A)

(b) (A) is true, but (R) is false

(c) Both (A) and (R) are true and (R) is the correct explanation of (A)

(d) (A) is false, but (R) is true

Ans. (c) Both (A) and (R) are true and (R) is the correct explanation of (A)

39. Assertion (A): Physical activities as corrective measure are very effective in functional deformity in comparison to structural deformity.

Reason (R): Muscles and ligaments are affected in functional deformity

(a) Both (A) and (R) are true, but (R) is not the correct explanation of (A)

(b) Both (A) and (R) are true and (R) is the correct explanation of (A)

(c) (A) is true, but (R) is false

(d) (A) is false, but (R) is true

Ans. (b) Both (A) and (R) are true and (R) is the correct explanation of (A)

40. Identify the movement

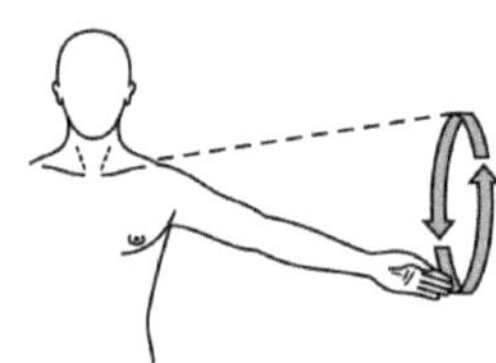

(a) Rotation (b) Circumduction (c) Flexion (d) Extension

Ans. (b) Circumduction

41. What will be the fitness index score of a girl if the test duration was 300sec and the pulse count(1min-1.5min) was 80.

(a) 73.2 (b) 62.8 (c) 68.1 (d) 85.3

Ans. (c) 68.1

42. Match the following

(a)	Technical committee	(i) To provide shifting facility
(b)	Finance committee	(ii) To resolve dispute
(c)	Transport committee	(iii) To deals with money and expenditure
(d)	First aid committee	(iv) To provide medical facilities.

(a) a–ii, b–iii, c–i, d–iv (b) a–iii, b–ii, c–i, d–iv

(c) a–ii, b–iii, c–iv, d–i (d) a–iv, b–iii, c–i, d–ii

Ans. (a) a–ii, b–iii, c–i, d–iv

43. Match the following vitamin with the disease caused due to their deficiency

1.	Vitamin A	A. Rickets
2.	Vitamin B	B. Night blindness
3.	Vitamin C	C. Beri beri
4.	Vitamin D	D. Scurvy

(a) 4 3 2 1
(b) 4 1 2 3
(c) 3 2 4 1
(d) 3 4 1 2

Ans. (b) 4 1 2 3

44. Starting a throwing event in athletics is an example of which law of motion.
(a) First law of motion
(b) Second law of motion
(c) Third law of motion
(d) First and third law of motion

Ans. (a) First law of motion

45. **Assertion (A):** "A change in the acceleration of an object is directly proportional to the force producing it and inversely proportional to its mass"
Reason (R): Lighter mass will travel at a faster speed
(a) Both (A) and (R) are true, but (R) is not the correct explanation of (A)
(b) Both (A) and (R) are true and (R) is the correct explanation of (A)
(c) (A) is true, but (R) is false
(d) (A) is false, but (R) is true

Ans. (b) Both (A) and (R) are true and (R) is the correct explanation of (A)

46. Identify which one of these is not the objective of Planning?
(a) Enhance creativity
(b) Increase efficiency
(c) Reduce chances of mistake
(d) Facilitates poor coordination

Ans. (d) Facilitates poor coordination

47.

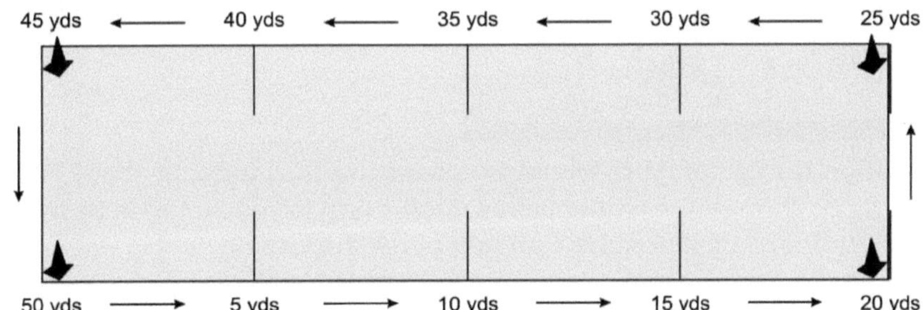

Identify the test for which this pattern is followed
(a) 600 mtr
(b) 50 yard dash
(c) 400 mtr
(d) 6 min walk

Ans. (d) 6min walk

48. Calculate the BMI of a girl and identify the category if her weight is 68 kg and height is 161 cm.
(a) Underweight
(b) Normal weight
(c) Overweight
(d) Obesity class I

Ans. (c) Overweight

Section - C

(CASE STUDIES)

49. Below given is the BMI data of a school's health check-up

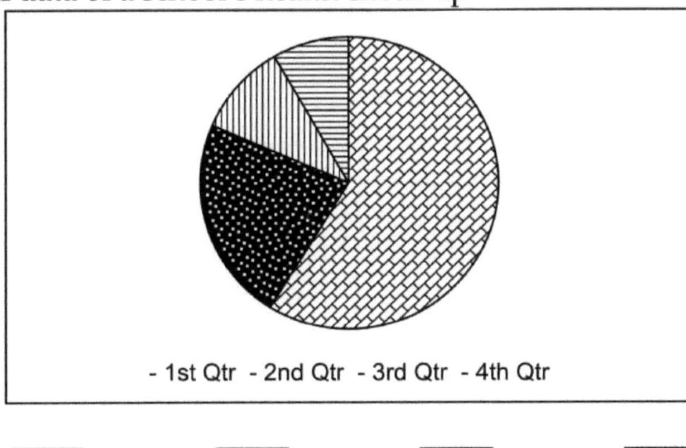

18.5-24.9   <18.5   25-29.9   30-34.9

In which category does the major student population fall into?

(a) Obese   (b) Normal weight
(c) Underweight   (d) Overweight

Ans. (b) Normal weight

50. Mr. Lakshman, aged 65 years worked as a civil engineer in a construction company .He had to walk and climb a lot as part of his job. After retirement, he settled with his son and spent time with his grandchildren. Nowadays he is experiencing difficulty in doing certain chores which involve physical movement.

The test shown in the picture is performed to assess which component?

(a) agility   (b) endurance   (c) speed   (d) strength

Ans. (a) agility

51. 

Physical education teacher of ABC school was teaching the students about Newton's Laws of Motion. While explaining he showed the students this picture and tried to explain how there is a difference in the speed of an object due to their weight. Can you name the Law?

(a) Newton's First Law of Motion   (b) Newton's Second Law of Motion
(c) Newton's Third Law of Motion   (d) Action Reaction

Ans. (b) Newton's Second Law of Motion

52. Jatin is a weightlifter in the 96 kg category. He has to participate in a weightlifting competition next week for which he is taking good care of his practice and diet. He has included all the essential nutrients in his diet. Based on this case, answer the following questions.

What do you think would be the most important component of Jatin's diet?

(a) Proteins   (b) Carbohydrates   (c) Vitamins   (d) Minerals

Ans. (a) Proteins

53. Rohan and Satish organized a Volleyball tournament on Knock out basis. They found that the spectators were losing interest in the tournament because two good teams were out of the tournament as they were defeated in the beginning.

Which provision could have avoided this kind of situation?

(a) Bye   (b) Seeding   (c) Pools   (d) Halves

Ans. (b) Seeding

54. Sandy is diagnosed with postural adaptation of the spine in lateral direction. The curve is identified as convexity right. It happened due to Sandy's underdeveloped legs and carrying heavy loads on one side only.

What kind of postural deformity doctors found in Sandy?

(a) Scoliosis   (b) Kyphosis   (c) Bow Legs   (d) Flatfoot

Ans. (a) Scoliosis

55. Motor develpoment only happens when the child is biologically and mentally ready for it. Motor development refers to the development of movement and various motor abilities from birth till death. It is the ability to move around and manipulate his/her environment. The first stage is marked by extremely rapid growth and development, as is the second stage. By the age of 2 years, this development has begun to level out somewhat. The final stage does not have any marked new development; rather it is characterized by the mastering and development of the skills achieved in the first two stages.

Which Factor affecting motor development
(a) Biological,environmental,nutrition,opportunity
(b) Obesity, postural deformities, physical activities
(c) Both (a) and (b)
(d) Technique, skill and style

Ans. (b) Both (a) and (b)

56. Harvard step test is also called the Aerobic Fitness Test. It was developed by Brouha and others in1943. It is used to measure aerobic fitness by checking the recovery rate.

Few students were asked to conduct Harvard step test for their classmates and they were asked to note down the complete details of their aerobic capacity. For conducting tests they required a bench separate for boys 20 inches and girls 16 inches with one stop watch to note down the timing and their recovery rate.

How many times is the reading taken for calculating a long term fitness index?

(a) 5   (b) 3   (c) 2   (d) 4

Ans. (b) 3

57. Rishi who was studying in class XII is a science stream student. During his Physical Education class, he got confused how Newton's laws of Motion are useful in sports and how they can be applied in sports. But his teacher explained these laws with help of examples from sports which proved to be very helpful for him

Swimming is the best example of which law of motion?

(a) Law of inertia   (b) Law of acceleration   (c) Law of reaction   (d) Both (a) and (c)

Ans. (d) Both (a) and (c)

58. Posture plays a very significant role in our daily activities. Correct posture means the balancing of the body in an accurate and proper manner. Various types of postural deformities can be identified in individuals.

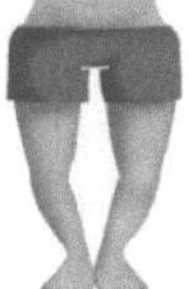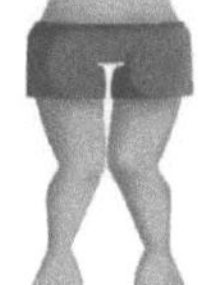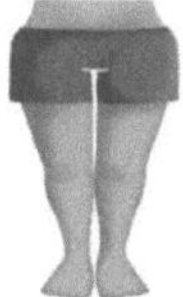

From the above given picture, the deformities seen on the left most is caused due to deficiency of which nutrient?

(a) Iron   (b) Calcium   (c) Vit D   (d) Both (b) and (c)

Ans. (d) Both (b) and (c)

59. Sohan, a new student in the school, was very much interested in sports and while learning various biomechanical aspects of the game including various movements he became curious to understand movements used in different games.

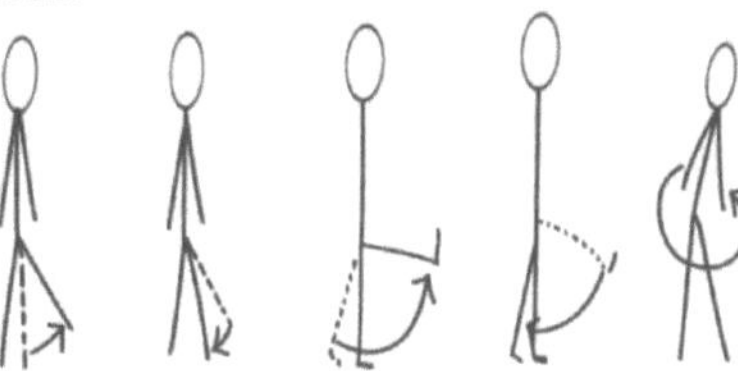

Flexion and extension comes under which movement.

(a) gliding   (b) angular   (c) rotation   (d) Circumduction

Ans. (b) angular

60. ABC School is one of the reputed schools in their location for the number of sports facilities it provides to its stake holders.Keeping that in consideration CBSE Sports cell has given them the responsibility of conducting CBSE Football cluster.35 teams have sent their entry for participation in the tournament.

A. Due to the large number of teams willing to participate the school should conduct the competition by which fixture?

(a) League   (b) Knock out   (c) Staircase   (d) Challenge

Ans. (b) Knock out

Sample Paper 1

Physical Education

Section – A

(KNOWLEDGE AND UNDERSTANDING)

1. What is Bye?
   (a) It's a method of drawing fixture.
   (b) Point system for team games.
   (c) Advantage given to a team to not play in initial round.
   (d) Placing of teams according to previous performance.

2. Which of the following food helps in sustaining prolonged routine of exercise?
   (a) Fats
   (b) Proteins
   (c) Vitamins
   (d) Carbohydrates

3. On average, how long does the statutory assessment process take?
   (a) Up to 26 weeks
   (b) Up to 12 weeks
   (c) Up to 8 weeks
   (d) Up to 52 weeks

4. Acceleration of an object will increase as the net force increases depending upon its:
   (a) Density
   (b) Mass
   (c) Shape
   (d) Volume

5. Which of the following treatments can be used to improve the processes underpinning motor skills?
   (a) Sensory integration therapy
   (b) Mathematic remediation programming
   (c) Exposure and operant conditioning
   (d) None of them

6. Vitamin E deficiency causes:
   (a) Anaemia
   (b) Weakness in heart and muscle
   (c) Both (a) and (b)
   (d) None of them

7. In normal walking at a person's preferred speed, the ratio of the durations of the stance and swing phases is roughly:
   (a) 1-1
   (b) 2-3
   (c) 2-1
   (d) 3-2

8. Partial curl up is to test.
   (a) agility and speed
   (b) leg strength and endurance
   (c) abdominal strength and endurance
   (d) upper body strength and endurance

9. Which of these are not gross motor skills?
   (a) Throwing a ball
   (b) Jumping
   (c) Balancing on one foot
   (d) Standing

10. A tournament where every team plays with every other team once and the number of matches is determined with the help of N(N-1) is called as:
    (a) Single league tournament
    (b) Double league tournament
    (c) Knock-out tournament
    (d) None of them

11. Vitamin E contributes to the production of __________, making our __________ system strong.
    (a) Strength, digestive
    (b) Antibodies, immunity
    (c) Both (a) and (b)
    (d) Hormones, muscular

12. Ramesh has to prepare formats of registration forms and batches for the participants. Which committee is Ramesh planning about?
    (a) Accommodation
    (b) Registration
    (c) Finance
    (d) Logistics

13. _________ Vitamin is a group of 8 water soluble vitamin which are important for cellular metabolism.
    (a) E   (b) B Complex   (c) C   (d) D

14. Which of the following players is associated with badminton?
    (a) Sania Mizra   (b) Saina Nehwal   (c) Karanam   (d) P.T.Usha

15. Which among the following is the next most important duty after planning
    (a) Feedback   (b) Organizing
    (c) Managing   (d) Planning

16. Rikli Jones test is conducted on:
    (a) Children   (b) Adults   (c) Adolescent   (d) Senior Citizens

17. Which method should he follow to improve the jump?
    (a) Flexibility   (b) Explosive power   (c) Push-ups   (d) Shuttle run

18. Which is the last function during an event organisation?
    (a) Organizing   (b) Planning   (c) Managing   (d) Feedback

19. Which of the following represents the smooth running of the event?
    (a) Managing   (b) Feedback   (c) Organizing   (d) Planning

20. Name the objective of planning shown in the figure given below:

    (a) Reduced mistakes   (b) Planning
    (c) Decision making   (d) None of them

21. Schedules fixed for the matches to be played their time, place, date and court, etc. known as:
    (a) bye   (b) fixture
    (c) advantage   (d) seeding

22. Allotment of bye is on basis of:
    (a) performance   (b) random draws
    (c) first come first serve   (d) pre-decided sequence

23. Select the correct development during infancy state.
    (a) Moral values   (b) Various senses
    (c) Fine motor skills   (d) Writing skills

24. The age of infancy is:
    (a) 0 to 1   (b) 0 to 2   (c) 0 to 3   (d) 0 to 4

Section – B

(APPLICATION + HOTS)

25. Which type of tournament is shown by the picture given?

    (a) League tournament   (b) Knock out tournament
    (c) Round robin tournament   (d) None of these

26. List the role of the following nutrients in the human body

    (a) Instant source of energy   (b) Muscle repair

    (c) Insulate the body   (d) None of them

27. Which of the following is an example of Lordosis?

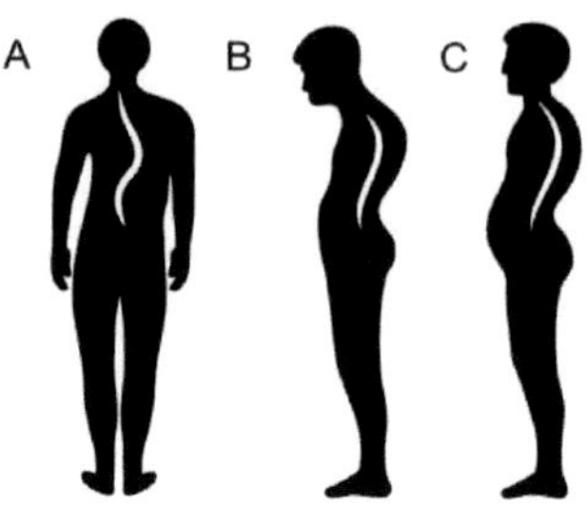

    (a) A   (b) B

    (c) C   (d) None of these

28. First step in sports management is :

    (a) planning   (b) organising

    (c) execution   (d) coordination

29. A _________ diet contains all the essential food constituents necessary for growth and maintenance of our body.

    (a) strict   (b) balanced

    (c) prescribed   (d) consistent

30. Fine motor development is involved in:

    (a) sitting   (b) walking

    (c) standing   (d) catching a ball

31. Match the following:

S. No.	LIST-I	LIST-II
1.	Abrasion	A. Joint Injuries
2.	Green stick fractures	B. Soft tissue injuries
3.	Shoulder Dislocation	C. Cause of sport injuries
4.	Lack of fitness	D. Bone injuries

Choose the correct option from the following:

    (a) 1–D, 2–A, 3–C, 4–B   (b) 1–B, 2–A, 3–C, 4–D

    (c) 1–B, 2–D, 3–A, 4–C   (d) 1–A, 2–D, 3–B, 4–C.

32. Match the following:

S. No.	LIST-I	LIST-II
1.	Technical committee	A. to provide shifting facility
2.	Finance committee	B. to resolve dispute
3.	Transport committee	C. to deals with money and expenditure
4.	First and committee	D. to provide medical facility

    (a) 1–B, 2–C, 3–A, 4–D   (b) 1–C, 2–B, 3–A, 4–D

    (c) 1–B, 2–C, 3–D, 4–A   (d) 1–D, 2–C, 3–A, 4–B.

33. Match the movements:

S. No.	LIST-I	LIST-II
1.	150° 180° 0°	A. Adduction
2.		B. Flexion
3.		C. Abduction

(a) 1–A, 2–B, 3–C
(b) 1–B, 2–C, 3–A
(c) 1–C, 2–A, 3–B
(d) 1–A, 2–C, 3–B

34. Match the movements:

S. No.	LIST-I	LIST-II
1.		A. Flexion
2.		B. Extension
3.		C. Abduction

(a) 1–A, 2–B, 3–C
(b) 1–C, 2–A, 3–B
(c) 1–B, 2–A, 3–C
(d) 1–A, 2–C, 3–B

35. Motor fitness test is a set of _________ tests.

(a) six (b) seven (c) eight (d) nine

36. The study of human body and various forces acting on it is:

(a) biology
(b) biomechanics
(c) physiology
(d) anatomy

37. Which of the following is not a cause of flat foot deformity?

(a) Body heaviness
(b) Standing for a long time
(c) Lack of vitamin D and calcium
(d) Faulty posture

38. **Assertion (A):** Physical Education is an elective discipline.

Reason (R): Physical Education borrows principles from other allied fields.

(a) Both (A) and (R) are true, but (R) is not the correct explanation of (A)
(b) (A) is true, but (R) is false
(c) Both (A) and (R) are true and (R) is the correct explanation of (A)
(d) (A) is false, but (R) is true

39. **Assertion (A):** The antibodies are created by the proteins in our body.

    Reason (R): Proteins are very important for the maintenance of our health.

    (a) Both (A) and (R) are true, but (R) is not the correct explanation of (A)

    (b) Both (A) and (R) are true and (R) is the correct explanation of (A)

    (c) (A) is true, but (R) is false

    (d) (A) is false, but (R) is true

40. Identify the following test:

    (a) Harvard step test

    (c) Partial curl up

    (b) Sit and reach

    (d) Chair stand test

41. Modified push ups are designed for:

    (a) volleyball player   (b) boys   (c) cricket player   (d) girls

42. Match the following:

S. No.	LIST-I	LIST-II
1.	600 m run/walk	A. Flexibility
2.	Sit and reach	B. Upper muscular strength
3.	Push ups (boys)	C. Agility
4.	4 × 10 m shuttle run	D. Aerobic capacity

    (a) 1–C, 2–B, 3–D, 4–A

    (c) 1–B, 2–C, 3–D, 4–A

    (b) 1–D, 2–A, 3–B, 4–C

    (d) 1–B, 2–A, 3–C, 4–D.

43. Match the movements and select the correct answer from the codes given below:

S. No.	LIST-I	LIST-II
1.	Extension	A. lifting the upper limb horizontally to form a right angle with the side of the body.
2.	Abduction	B. returning the upper limb from horizontal position to the side of the body.
3.	Adduction	C. bending the lower limb at the knee.
4.	Flexion	D. straightening the lower limb at knee.

    (a) 1–D, 2–C, 3–A, 4–B

    (c) 1–D, 2–A, 3–B, 4–C

    (b) 1–C, 2–B, 3–A, 4–D

    (d) 1–C, 2–A, 3–B, 4–D.

44. Which of the following methods helps best in maintaining a healthy body weight?

    (a) Leading an active lifestyle

    (c) Eating snacks frequently but no meals

    (b) Missing at least one meal every day

    (d) Reducing calories drastically in food eaten

45. **Assertion (A):** Test protocol is the correct procedure for carrying out a test.

    Reason (R): If a test is done incorrectly, it might affect the results.

    (a) Both (A) and (R) are true, but (R) is not the correct explanation of (A)

    (b) Both (A) and (R) are true and (R) is the correct explanation of (A)

    (c) (A) is true, but (R) is false

    (d) (A) is false, but (R) is true

46. The age group of middle childhood is ___________ .

    (a) 6-10 years

    (c) 7-12 years

    (b) 5-10 years

    (d) 9-13 years

47. What are the two types of motor development of muscles in the body?

    (a) Gross and fine   (b) Gross and net

    (c) Coarse and fine   (d) Gross and measured

48. Purpose of the test is measured through:

    (a) reliability   (b) validity

    (c) objectivity   (d) split half method

Section - C

(CASE STUDIES)

49. Given below is the graphical presentation of an event organization:

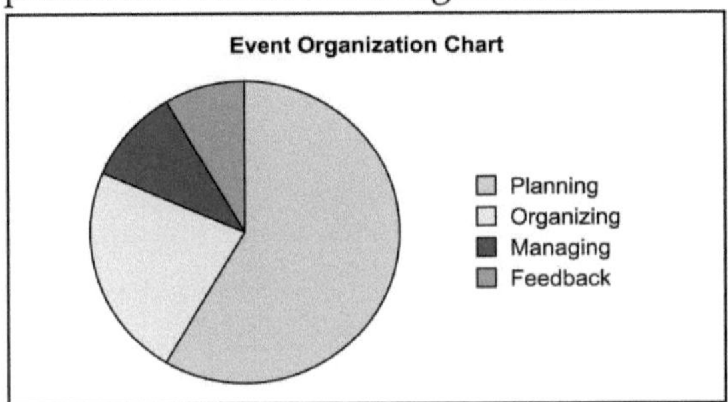

From the above diagram which of the following plays a major role in organizing an event?

    (a) Feedback   (b) Organizing   (c) Planning   (d) Managing

50. Ramesh is part of an event organizing team. He is appointed in the planning committee. Ramesh has to finalize a venue for the event. Which of the following points he must take into consideration?

    (a) Availability of the venue   (b) Capacity of the venue

    (c) Public access to the venue   (d) All of the above

51. XYZ event company's organizer Riya has to look after the finances of the event. Which of the following committee will she have to consult?

    (a) Finance and Budgeting   (b) Accommodation

    (c) Registration   (d) Transportation

52. Sports Minister, Mr. Kiren Rijuju has launched many sports schemes in India. Among these, one of the best schemes is Khelo India. Mr. Kannan, father of Kartik approached the PE teacher and enquired about the fitness levels of the students. PE teacher replied that Khelo India consisted of physical fitness tests for school children and they were analysing students' fitness through these tests.

To measure Lower body flexibility fitness, which one of the following is best?

    (a) Harvard Step test   (b) Sit and reach test

    (c) Barrow fitness test   (d) General fitness test

53. Below given is the Details of Different types of vitamins required for our body

The vitamins, minerals, and water collectively called as __________ food.

    (a) Body Building   (b) Defensive   (c) Energy Yielding   (d) Facilitating

54. Padma, a student of class XII, used to read books in the school library. One day she was studying the history of women participation in Indian Sports and felt that more girls and women must be encouraged to actively participate in sports. She believed that impossible things can be achieved through participating in sports. In which year did women first participated in Olympics?

    (a) 2000   (b) 1900   (c) 2012   (d) 1947

55. Rashmi is working on a project to collect data for assessing physical fitness amongst senior citizens at her residential complex. He plans to administer test for assessing upper body strength and upper body flexibility. Which of the following test should be conducted for assessing upper body flexibility?

    (a) Chair stand test
    (b) Arm curl test
    (c) Chair sit and reach test
    (d) Back scratch test

56. Mr. Sunder is a Physical Education teacher in a government school. Ramesh, a student is a long jumper but his landing is improper. So he could not win the event on sports day in the school. So Ramesh approached Mr. Sunder to seek his help to improve his performance. Mr. Sunder explained to Ramesh the proper technique to be followed so as to have the correct body posture while landing. Mr. Sunder also motivated Ramesh to constantly practise this technique to perfect it. After the one year of training, Ramesh won the gold medal in the Inter Zonal Athletic Meet. What was the problem faced by Ramesh?

    (a) Improper landing in long jump event
    (b) Not winning any medal
    (c) Improper performance
    (d) Incorrect body posture

57. Many children suffer from postural deformities. These can be corrected if recognised early and treated properly. Mahesh had a deformity in his spine which caused him to bend forward and his knees touched each other while he stood straight. What was the possible deformity Mahesh had?

    (a) Kyphosis
    (b) Scoliosis
    (c) Lordosis
    (d) Flat food

58. Sanaya got admission in Class XII in a reputed school. School is taking all the children on a picnic to Ramoji Film City. Sanaya suffered from a severe stomach ache on her journey. Immediately the class teacher consulted a Doctor who diagnosed the problem and told her that Sanaya had difficulty digesting a particular food. This can lead to symptoms such as intestinal gas, abdominal pain or diarrhoea. It is sometimes confused with or mislabelled as a food allergy. Food intolerance can cause:

    (a) Diarrhoea
    (b) Anaemia
    (c) Fatigue
    (d) Loss of Appetite

59. Kumar of XI-A is a great athlete. After the lockdown he went to see his Physical Education Teacher. Mr. Murugan, the PE teacher is shocked to see kumar, because Kumar has gained lot of weight. He also observed may other students have also gained weight. The PE teacher decided to conduct an 'Inter House Tournament' in the campus. Kumar requested PE teacher to conduct the tournament on league basis. Kumar feels that league method is best one for Inter house tournament. Why?

    (a) Less period required
    (b) Limited official
    (c) True winner
    (d) Players would be less tired

60. Below given is the tournament fixture procedure of a CBSE Volleyball National Competition.

```
1—2
1—3 2—3
1—4 2—4 3—4
1—5 2—5 3—5 4—5
1—6 2—6 3—6 4—6 5—6
```

    The formula for calculating number of matches in Round robin tournament are where 'N' is number of team is __________ .

    (a) N (N – 1)/2   (b) N   (c) (N – 1)   (d) (N + 1)

Sample Paper 2

Physical Education

Section – A

(KNOWLEDGE AND UNDERSTANDING)

1. In plantar flexion of the foot about the ankle joint:
   (a) The foot moves upwards towards the front of the calf
   (b) The foot moves upwards towards the rear of the calf
   (c) The foot moves sideways
   (d) None the above

2. The test duration for the Harvard fitness test is.
   (a) 3 minutes
   (b) 4 minutes
   (c) 5 minutes
   (d) 6 minutes

3. There are how many stages of motor development in children?
   (a) 3
   (b) 2
   (c) 4
   (d) 5

4. Which of the following is an example of food supplement?
   (a) Vitamins
   (b) Fatty acids
   (c) Both (a) and (b)
   (d) None of them.

5. A team which is defeated automatically gets eliminated from the tournament. It is known as:
   (a) League tournament
   (b) Knock-out tournament
   (c) Combination tournament
   (d) None of them

6. Before running a marathon, the trainer asked the athlete to monitor her vitamin and mineral levels to fight against free radicals which :
   (a) Damages cell
   (b) Limit conversion of proteins in ATP
   (c) Reduce effectiveness of electrolytes
   (d) Destroy stored glucose

7. Which is not an item of Barrow motor ability test?
   (a) Medicine Ball Put
   (b) Zig Zag Run
   (c) Standing Broad Jump
   (d) Push-ups

8. Development of a child's bone, muscles and ability to move around and manipulate their movement is referred to as:
   (a) Motor development
   (b) Physical activity
   (c) Both (a) and (b)
   (d) None of them

9. A league tournament is otherwise known as :
   (a) Round Robin tournament
   (b) Knock-out tournament
   (c) Combination tournament
   (d) None of them

10. Which of the following is a form of Fixtures?
    (a) Round Robin
    (b) League
    (c) Knock Out
    (d) All of the Above

11. Classes 8-12 should have exercises which help them in muscle training atleast:
    (a) 30 mins, twice a week
    (b) 60 mins, once a week
    (c) 60-120 mins, 3 days a week
    (d) 30 mins, 4 times a week

12. For Classes Nursery- Class 2, the PT period should have which of the following activities:
    (a) Endurance building, disciplined exercise
    (b) Running etc along with periodic completions
    (c) Movement based exercises coupled with recreative methods
    (d) None of these.
13. Ram is the seeded player, he played the next round and was eliminated. Which type of fixture were made for the tournament?
    (a) Knock Out   (b) League
    (c) Round Robin   (d) None of the above
14. Seema is a seeded player and she did not play the first round. Which of the following would be the reason?
    (a) She was not well   (b) She had a bye
    (c) She was a champion in the previous season   (d) She did not feel like playing
15. It is recommended to drink __________ of water daily.
    (a) 1-2 litres   (b) 2-3 litres
    (c) 1-1.5 litres   (d) 2-4 litres
16. Vitamins are called
    (a) Protective food   (b) Body Building food
    (c) Energy giving food   (d) Strong bones
17. In League tournaments the winner is decided by
    (a) British method   (b) American Method
    (c) No of Matches won   (d) Both (a) and (b)
18. Which of the following is Not a League Fixture Procedure?
    (a) Ladder method   (b) Stair method
    (c) Cyclic method   (d) Tabular method
19. What is the relationship between Mass and force?
    (a) Directly proportional   (b) No relationship
    (c) Inversely proportional   (d) Both (a) and (c)
20. Newton's second law is also known as
    (a) The law of reaction   (b) The law of inertia
    (c) The law of acceleration (d) None of these
21. Name the objective of planning shown in the figure given below:

    (a) Reduced mistakes   (b) Planning
    (c) Decision making   (d) None of these
22. Which committee selects various officials such as refress, judges, etc. in tournament?
    (a) Committee for publicity   (b) Reception committee
    (c) Committee for officials   (d) Transport committee
23. A balanced diet is complete, when it will be:
    (a) complex carbohydrates   (b) according to the needs of the person
    (c) animal fat rich   (d) 4 to 5 litter water
24. Out of them which is not the work of organising committee?
    (a) To draw fixture   (b) To decorate the tournament venue
    (c) To select referee panel for match   (d) To conduct the matches

Section – B

(APPLICATION + HOTS)

25. Which type of tournament is shown by the picture given?

(a) League tournament   (b) Knock out tournament

(c) Round robin tournament   (d) None of these

26. List the role of the following nutrients in the human body

(a) Intant source of energy   (b) Muscle repair

(c) Insulate the body   (d) None of them

27. Identify the following test:

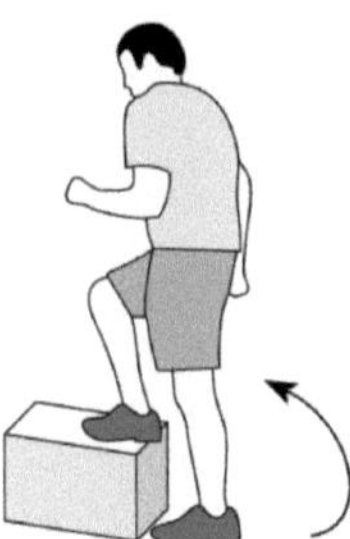

(a) Zig-zag run   (b) Harvard step test

(c) Standing broad jump   (d) None of these

28. Unit of energy that indicates the amount of energy contained in food.

(a) Label   (b) Food guide pyramid

(c) Calorie   (d) Basket

29. Which of the following is not a minerals?

(a) Fluorine   (b) Niacin   (c) Sodium   (d) Phosphorus

30. Obesity is a condition in which excess only body _________ has accumulated to the extent that it may have a negative effect on health.

(a) Carbohydrates   (b) Proteins   (c) Fats   (d) Minerals

31. Match the following:

S. No.	LIST-I	LIST-II
1.	Staffing	A. process of creating a comprehensive action
2.	Planning	B. all the processes that leaders create to monitor success
3.	Organizing	C. identifying key staff positions
4.	Controlling	D. distributing resources and organizing personnel

Choose the correct option from the following:

(a) 1–A, 2–B, 3–D, 4–C   (b) 1–C, 2–D, 3–A, 4–B

(c) 1–A, 2–D, 3–C, 4–B   (d) 1–D, 2–C, 3–B, 4–A

32. Match the following:

S. No.	LIST-I	LIST-II
1.	Arm curl test	A. Agility
2.	Eight foot up and go test	B. Upper body flexibility
3.	Chair Stand test	C. Upper body strength
4.	Back Scratch test	D. Lower body strength

(a) 1–C, 2–A, 3–B, 4–D   (b) 1–A, 2–B, 3–D, 4–C

(c) 1–B, 2–D, 3–A, 4–C   (d) 1–C, 2–A, 3–D, 4–B

33. Match the tests:

S. No.	LIST-I	LIST-II
1.	600 m run/walk	A. Cardiovascular fitness test
2.	Harvard step test	B. Rikli and Jones test
3.	Six minute walk test	C. Motor fitness test

(a) 1–C, 2–A, 3–B   (b) 1–A, 2–B, 3–C

(c) 1–C, 2–B, 3–A   (d) 1–B, 2–A, 3–C

34. Match the movements:

S. No.	LIST-I	LIST-II
1.	Abduction	A. Decreasing in Angle
2.	Newton's 2nd law	B. Frictional force
3.	Force that opposes	C. Away from midline movement
4.	Flexion	D. Law of Acceleration

(a) 1–C, 2–D, 3–B, 4–A   (b) 1–D, 2–C, 3–B, 4–A

(c) 1–D, 2–C, 3–A, 4–B   (d) 1–B, 2–D, 3–C, 4–A

35. What is Scoliosis?

(a) A heart disorder   (b) An ankle sprain

(c) Lateral curve in the spine   (d) Dislocated spine

36. __________ exercises are designed to correct the rotatory curvature of the spine.

(a) Kyphosis   (b) Scoliosis

(c) Lordosis   (d) Knock Knees

37. Which of the following is not a corrective measure for the postural deformity of knock knee?

(a) Keeping a pillow between the knees as much as possible

(b) Not standing for a long time

(c) Performing Padmasana and Gomukhasana

(d) Regular horse riding

38. **Assertion (A):** Testing motor fitness consists of measuring of all components of motor fitness.

Reason (R): Motor fitness test provides to the student a score regarding the level of fitness, effectiveness of any training programme.

(a) Both (A) and (R) are true, but (R) is not the correct explanation of (A)

(b) (A) is true, but (R) is false

(c) Both (A) and (R) are true and (R) is the correct explanation of (A)

(d) (A) is false, but (R) is true

39. **Assertion (A):** Sports biomechanics is a quantitative based study and analysis of professional athletes/ sports persons and sports activities in general.

Reason (R): In simple terms, it may be described as the physics of sports.

    (a) Both (A) and (R) are true, but (R) is not the correct explanation of (A)

    (b) Both (A) and (R) are true and (R) is the correct explanation of (A)

    (c) (A) is true, but (R) is false

    (d) (A) is false, but (R) is true

40. This is a side-to-side curvature of the spine.

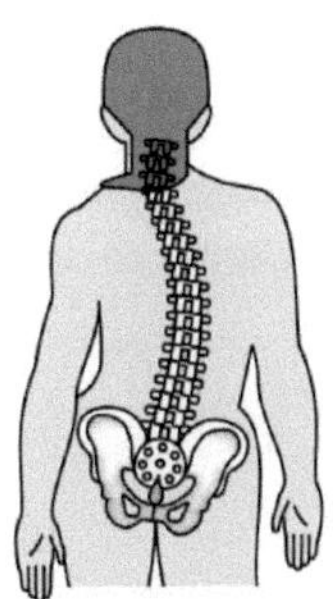

    (a) Lordosis   (b) Kyphosis   (c) Scoliosis   (d) Myosis

41. Modified push are designed for:

    (a) volleyball player   (b) boys   (c) cricket player   (d) girls

42. Match List-I with List-II:

S. No.	LIST-I	LIST-II
1.	Knock knees	A. Lack of exercise
2.	Lordosis	B. Lack of Vitamin D
3.	Flat foot	C. Heredity defects
4.	Scoliosis	D. Faulty posture

    (a) 1–B, 2–A, 3–C, 4–D   (b) 1–B, 2–A, 3–D, 4–C

    (c) 1–D, 2–C, 3–B, 4–A   (d) 1–D, 2–A, 3–C, 4–B

43. Match the following deformities with their respective symptoms:

S. No.	LIST-I	LIST-II
1.	Mechanical friction	A. Increased in angle
2.	Law of Inertia	B. Object are solid comes in contract
3.	Take off high jump	C. 3rd low of motion
4.	Extension	D. Things Remain in its position

    (a) 1–B, 2–D, 3–C, 4–B   (b) 1–D, 2–B, 3–C, 4–A

    (c) 1–D, 2–B, 3–A, 4–C   (d) 1–C, 2–B, 3–A, 4–D

44. Scoliosis deformity can be corrected by practicing.

    (a) Trikonasana and Ardh Chakrasana   (b) Halasana and paschimotanasana

    (c) Dhanurasana and Chakrasana   (d) Bhujangasana and Usthrasana

45. **Assertion (A):** Flat foot is a type of physical deformity.

    Reason (R): It occurs in athletes.

    (a) Both (A) and (R) are true, but (R) is not the correct explanation of (A)

    (b) Both (A) and (R) are true and (R) is the correct explanation of (A)

    (c) (A) is true, but (R) is false

    (d) (A) is false, but (R) is true

46. The vitamin necessary for coagulation of blood is:

    (a) Vitamin B   (b) Vitamin C

    (c) Vitamin K   (d) Vitamin E

47. Food passes through the stomach directly by:

    (a) the large intestine   (b) the small intestine

    (c) the heart   (d) the pancreas

48. Which food contains the most fat?

   (a) Graham crackers   (b) Brownies

   (c) Pudding   (d) Angle food cake

Section - C

(CASE STUDIES)

49. Data of number of students falling in different age groups was collected from ABC School in Agra. The PT teacher wants to design exercises for different age groups.

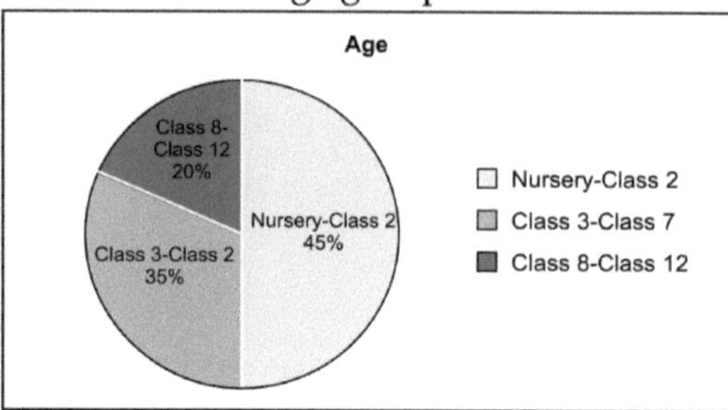

Nursery- Class 2 has children of the Age Group 3-7 years

Class 3-7 has children of age group 8-12 years

Class 8-12 has children of age group 13-18 years

Exercises like running, swimming, etc, which build agility, coordination and balance would be the most suitable for which age group?

   (a) Nursery- Class   (b) Class 3- Class 7

   (c) Class 8-Class 12   (d) Both (b) and (c)

50. Seema is a seeded player. But as per fixtures she did not play the first round while as she played the next round her opponent was eliminated. As she qualified to the 7th round she lost and she too was eliminated. The opponent was eliminated. What could be the reason?

   (a) Opponent Lost   (b) She did not want to play

   (c) Opponent was injured   (d) The referee gave a time out

51. The Ganga school teams have started the practice for Basketball Cluster Tournament. One day the school secretary visited the playground and watched the practice session. He felt that the players were weak. After discussion with the coach, he arranged a dietician to rectify the players' requirements. Which types of the nutrients are advisable for the player?

   (a) Proteins   (b) Minerals

   (c) Vitamins   (d) Carbohydrates

52. Below given is the Tournament fixture procedure of a CBSE Volley ball National competition

```
1—2
1—3  2—3
1—4  2—4  3—4
1—5  2—5  3—5  4—5
1—6  2—6  3—6  4—6  5—6
```

The formula for calculating number of matches in Round Robin tournament are where 'N' is number of teams is________

   (a) N(N – 1)/2   (b) N   (c) (N – 1)   (d) (N + 1)

53. During the physical education class Newton's Laws of motion were discussed and their practical application in sports events was explained to students. These laws are most relevant in sports as most of the actions in sports are related to these laws. Newton's First law of motion is also known as:

   (a) Law of inertia   (b) Law of Momentum

   (c) Law of reaction   (d) Law of acceleration

54. Gopichand, a student of class XII, has recently joined a gym near his house to get a toned and muscular body. He consults the gym trainer regarding his diet and is advised to increase the intake of protein in his diet. Proteins are also known as:
    (a) nitrogenous food
    (b) body building food
    (c) fatty food
    (d) both (a) and (b)

55. Sheethal spent her weekned checking the health status of all the security guards of her huge gates community as a part of project work assigned by PE teachers. She found out that more than half of them have shown a significant deformity in the upper part of their vertebral column. The term used to define this deformity is ____________ .
    (a) lordosis
    (b) scoliosis
    (c) kyphosis
    (d) both (a) and (b)

56. On the basis of given figures, answer the following questions:

    Both the test shown in the picture are conducted to check __________ fitness.
    (a) muscular
    (b) skeletal
    (c) cardiovascular
    (d) respiratory

57. Abhishek, the Class 12 monitor, was asked to speak on different types of movements possible in human body and their importance. He talked about four basic movements namely flexion, extension, abduction and adduction. Rest of the movements at different joints are combinations of these four basic movements. He also demonstrated about dorsiflexion and planter flexion movements. What movement that he demonstrated were possible at the shoulder joint?
    (a) Gliding
    (b) Angular
    (c) Circumduction
    (d) Rotation

58. ABC School is one of the reputed school in their location for the number of sports facilities it provides to its stakeholders. Keeping that in consideration CBSE Sports cell has given them the responsibility of conducting CBSE Football cluster. 35 teams have sent their entre for participation in the tournaments.
    Due to large number of terms willing to participate, the school is conducting the competition by ________ fixture.
    (a) league
    (b) knock-out
    (c) staircase
    (d) challenge

59. Your school has received an invitation for participation in a Badminton competition being organised by XYZ School. There is a entry fee for the competition due to which very few students have shown their willingness to participate. What is the disadvantage of using this particular fixture?
    (a) More time consuming
    (b) Less expenditure
    (c) More opportunities
    (d) Both (b) and (c)

60. Vikas, a state level wrestler has been advised by his coach to take adequate amounts of simple carbohydrates, vitamins, minerals and proteins in his diet along with the training schedule. He has also been advised to follow the diet plan and be aware of the drawbacks of unsupervised dieting. Glucose, Fructose, Lactose are __________ .
    (a) simple carbohydrates
    (b) complex carbohydrates
    (c) minerals
    (d) fats

Sample Paper 3

Physical Education

Section – A

(KNOWLEDGE AND UNDERSTANDING)

1. What is the primary nutrient that contributes to bone health ?
   (a) Iron
   (b) Potassium
   (c) Calcium
   (d) Phosphorus

2. Seeding method refers to :
   (a) Pairing of all weak teams together
   (b) Pairing of all strong teams together
   (c) Strong teams paired with weak or all strong teams grouped in upper half or lower half.
   (d) None of them

3. What is the weight of Medicine ball for boys in medicine ball put?
   (a) 1 kg
   (b) 2 kg
   (c) 3 kg
   (d) 4kg

4. Gross motor development skills, head control, and sitting are the exercise guidelines for children belonging to the age group of :
   (a) 1-2 years
   (b) 3-7 years
   (c) 8-12 years
   (d) None of them

5. Flexion and extension are:
   (a) Movements in the frontal plane about the sagittal axis
   (b) Movements in the sagittal plane about the frontal axis
   (c) Movements in the horizontal plane about the vertical axis
   (d) None of the above.

6. Writing, Holding, Catching, and Smashing are examples of:
   (a) Gross Motor Development
   (b) Fine Motor Development
   (c) Both (a) and (b)
   (d) None of them

7. The test duration for the Harvard fitness test is:
   (a) 3 minutes
   (b) 4 minutes
   (c) 5 minutes
   (d) 6 minutes

8. Internal and external rotation are movements in which anatomical plane ?
   (a) Sagittal
   (b) Frontal
   (c) Horizontal
   (d) None of these

9. A weight lifter should include ______________ in his/her diet.
   (a) Carbohydrate
   (b) Protein
   (c) Fat
   (d) Vitamins and minerals

10. In special seeding, the seeded players participate directly in the:
    (a) Finals
    (b) Semi-finals
    (c) Quarter-final or semi-final
    (d) None of them

11. Which of the following category of people are likely to live a healthy life style:
    (a) Under weight
    (b) Normal weight
    (c) Obese
    (d) Over Weight

12. Which category is related to underweight?
    (a) Obese
    (b) Over weight
    (c) Normal weight
    (d) Under weight

13. Which of the following is largely consumed but not neglected?
    (a) Minerals and Vitamins
    (b) Carbohydrates
    (c) Fats
    (d) Proteins

14. The acceleration of an object depends directly upon the net force acting upon the object and inversely upon the object's:
    (a) Weight   (b) Mass   (c) Height   (d) Density

15. The study of human body and various forces acting on it is:
    (a) Biology   (b) Biomechanics   (c) Physiology   (d) Anatomy

16. A high jumper can jump higher off a solid surface because it opposes his or her body with as much force as he or she is able to generate. This example refers to:
    (a) Law of conservation   (b) Law of inertia
    (c) Law of action and reaction   (d) Law of gravity

17. What could be the probable cause of this problem:
    (a) Weak muscles   (b) Sudden rise in body weight
    (c) Deficiency of Calcium, Vitamin D   (d) Only (a) and (b)

18. To rectify the problem of pain, which Yogasana would prove to be the most fruitful?
    (a) Gomukhasana   (b) Chakrasana
    (c) Halasana   (d) Vajrasana

19. Major portion of individuals diet constitute __________ nutrients
    (a) macro   (b) micro   (c) water   (d) roughage

20. Fat soluble vitamins are __________.
    (a) Vitamin A and D   (b) Vitamin A and K
    (c) Vitamin E and D   (d) Vitamin A, D, E and K

21. The body building nutrient is__________.
    (a) fat   (b) vitamin   (c) protein   (d) mineral

22. Ghee, Butter, Cheese and curds are rich sources of __________.
    (a) vitamins   (b) fats   (c) minerals   (d) proteins

23. Announcement of venue, date and events is done by ____________
    (a) Publicity committee   (b) Transportation committee
    (c) Ground committee   (d) Committee for officials

24. Name the objective of planning shown in the figure given below:

    (a) Reduced mistakes   (b) Planning
    (c) Decision making   (d) Goal oriented

Section – B

(APPLICATION + HOTS)

25. Which type of tournament is shown by the picture given?

(a) League tournament

(b) Knock out tournament

(c) Round robin tournament

(d) None of these

26. List the role of the following nutrients in the human body

(a) Instant source of energy

(b) Muscle repair

(c) Insulate the body

(d) None of them

27. This is humpback, abnormal outward curvature of thoracic spine.

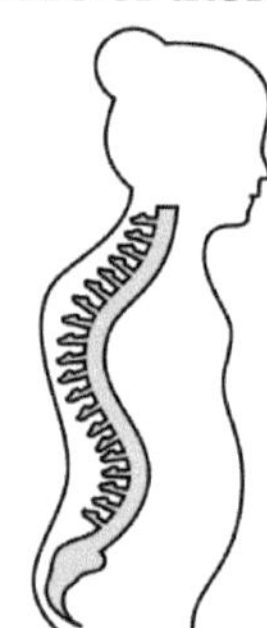

(a) Lordosis

(b) Kyphosis

(c) Scoliosis

(d) Myosis

28. Organising and conducting of sports events involve ___________.

(a) planning

(b) Forming committees

(c) both (a) and (b)

(d) only delegation

29. Complete responsibility for success of competition is taken by __________.

(a) Announcement committee

(b) Administrative director

(c) First aid committee

(d) Committee for officials

30. To prepare a proper score sheet for record is ________ responsibility.

(a) pre tournament

(b) during tournament

(c) Post tournament

(d) all of the above

31. Match the following:

S. No.	LIST-I	LIST-II
	Vitamin	Disease
1.	Vitamin A	A. Pyorrhea
2.	Vitamin B	B. Rickets
3.	Vitamin C	C. Beriberi
4.	Vitamin D	D. Night Blindness

(a) 1–D, 2–C, 3–A, 4–B

(b) 1–A, 2–B, 3–C, 4–D

(c) 1–C, 2–A, 3–B, 4–D

(d) 1–D, 2–A, 3–C, 4–B

32. Match the following:

S. No.	LIST-I	LIST-II
1.	Motor fitness test	A. Chair stand test
2.	Rikli and Jones test	B. 4 × 10 m shuttle run
3.	Cardiovascular fitness test	C. Rockport one mile test

(a) 1–A, 2–B, 3–C
(b) 1–C, 2–B, 3–A
(c) 1–B, 2–A, 3–C
(d) 1–B, 2–C, 3–A

33. Match the following;

S. No.	LIST-I	LIST-II
1.	Iron	A. Nervous system
2.	Sodium	B. Haemoglobin
3.	Fluorine	C. Strong bone
4.	Phosphorus	D. Enamel

(a) 1–C, 2–D, 3–B, 4–A
(b) 1–D, 2–A, 3–C, 4–B
(c) 1–A, 2–C, 3–B, 4–D
(d) 1–B, 2–A, 3–D, 4–C

34. Match the Diseases with their causes:

S. No.	LIST-I	LIST-II
1.	Dryness	A. Deficiency of calcium
2.	Anaemia	B. Deficiency vitamin A
3.	Decreased bone density	C. Lack of water during dieting
4.	Night blindness	D. Deficiency iron

(a) 1–D, 2–C, 3–A, 4–B
(b) 1–C, 2–D, 3–A, 4–B
(c) 1–A, 2–B, 3–C, 4–D
(d) 1–D, 2–C, 3–B, 4–A

35. Partial or complete absence of the enzymes accountable for breaking down or absorbing the food elements causes __________ .

(a) food intolerance
(b) bulimia
(c) ADHD
(d) dieting

36. In which category BMI comes in 30 BMI?

(a) Obesity II
(b) Over lead
(c) Obesity I
(d) Healthy weight

37. Karan wishes to serve his country by qualifying NDA, he clears all rounds but he is unable to qualify for the medical test. He was asked to run 100 metres and the examiner noticed he was unable to run properly and has knock knees. What precautions can be taken up at an early age to ensure that children do not develop this problem at a later stage in their lives:

(a) Balanced diet should be taken
(b) Babies and children shouldn't be forced to walk at an early age
(c) One should avoid sitting and walking in bent position
(d) Only (a) and (b)

38. **Assertion (A):** Sports biomechanics is limited to the study of those individuals who are involved in exercise or sports or any physical activity.

Reason (R): Performance enhancement is one of the area of the study in sports biomechanics.

(a) Both (A) and (R) are true, but (R) is not the correct explanation of (A)
(b) (A) is true, but (R) is false
(c) Both (A) and (R) are true and (R) is the correct explanation of (A)
(d) (A) is false, but (R) is true

39. **Assertion (A):** Knock Knee is the physical deformity.

Reason (R): Yogic exercise which help in treatment of knock knee are Padmasana (Lotus posture), Vatayanasan (Horse face posture), and Bhadrasana.

(a) Both (A) and (R) are true, but (R) is not the correct explanation of (A)
(b) Both (A) and (R) are true and (R) is the correct explanation of (A)
(c) (A) is true, but (R) is false
(d) (A) is false, but (R) is true

40. This is swayback, abnormal inward curvature of the lumbar spine.

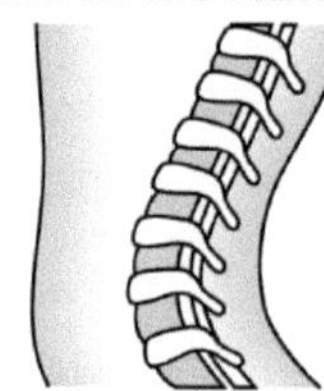

   (a) Lordosis   (b) Kyphosis

   (c) Scoliosis   (d) Myosis

41. Who is most likely to develop Scoliosis?
    (a) 30 year old woman
    (b) 9 year old boy
    (c) 12 year old girl
    (d) 20 year old man

42. Match the following:

S. No.	LIST-I	LIST-II
1.	Cyclic	A. Resolve dispute
2.	Technical committee	B. Arranging team
3.	Fixture	C. To avoid to meet in 1st round
4.	Seeding	D. League tournament

    (a) 1–C, 2–B, 3–A, 4–D
    (b) 1–B, 2–C, 3–A, 4–D
    (c) 1–D, 2–A, 3–B, 4–C
    (d) 1–D, 2–C, 3–B, 4–A

43. Match the following committee with their functions:

S. No.	LIST-I (Committee)	LIST-II (Function)
1.	Boarding and Lodging	A. Welcoming the chief guest
2.	Publicity	B. Making several announcements during the game
3.	Announcement	C. Providing accommodation and serving meals
4.	Reception	D. Announcement of date, venue to the public

    (a) 1–C, 2–A, 3–D, 4–B
    (b) 1–B, 2–D, 3–A, 4–C
    (c) 1–C, 2–D, 3–B, 4–A
    (d) 1–D, 2–A, 3–C, 4–B

44. How many byes will be given if 21 teams are participating in a knock-out tournament?
    (a) 11
    (b) 12
    (c) 10
    (d) 13

45. **Assertion (A):** To determine running speed and acceleration of a student.

    Reason (R): There will be distance of 50 meters between two straight lines.

    (a) Both (A) and (R) are true, but (R) is not the correct explanation of (A)
    (b) Both (A) and (R) are true and (R) is the correct explanation of (A)
    (c) (A) is true, but (R) is false
    (d) (A) is false, but (R) is true

46. If 8 teams are participating, the number of Knock-out matches will be:
    (a) 16
    (b) 8
    (c) 7
    (d) 9

47. In which tournament, strong teams may have the possibility to be eliminated in the preliminary round?
    (a) League tournament
    (b) Knock-out tournament
    (c) Challenge tournament
    (d) League cum league tournament

48. By which method the winner of a single league tournament is decided?
    (a) Percentage of matches won and drawn
    (b) Number of matches won
    (c) Percentage of matches won
    (d) All of these

Section – C

(CASE STUDIES)

49. Below given is the BMI data of general population's health check-up for the months of EBC (Economic Backward Class), Youth, Senior Citizens and Athletes:

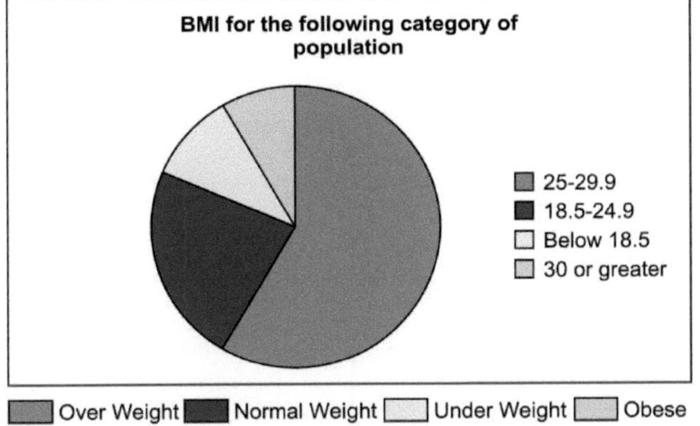

Which of the following category does most of the population fall into:

(a) Obese (b) Normal weight (c) Over weight (d) Under weight

50. The teachers as well as coaches always make their best efforts to improve the performance of their students in various competitive games and sports. They can help to improve the performance of students if they have adequate knowledge of biomechanics.

The more force one exerts on the downward bounce, the higher the ball bounces into the air. Which law is this statement being referred to?

(a) Newton's 1st law (b) Newton's 2nd law

(c) Newton's 3rd law (d) Law of gravitation

51. Suresh is extremely fond of Cricket as a sport, and wants to take it up as a profession. However, he always had pain whenever he would run and would sometimes also complain of pain after prolonged standing. Suresh dipped his feet in water and then walked on the floor, he did not obtain an arch, so he most likely has which one of the following problems

(a) Knock Knee (b) Scoliosis

(c) Flat foot (d) Bow Legs

52. Food is the basic requirement of every individual to fulfill the energy needs and to meet the development of the body. The nutritious diet directly affects the health of an individual. It contains various types of nutrients in it.

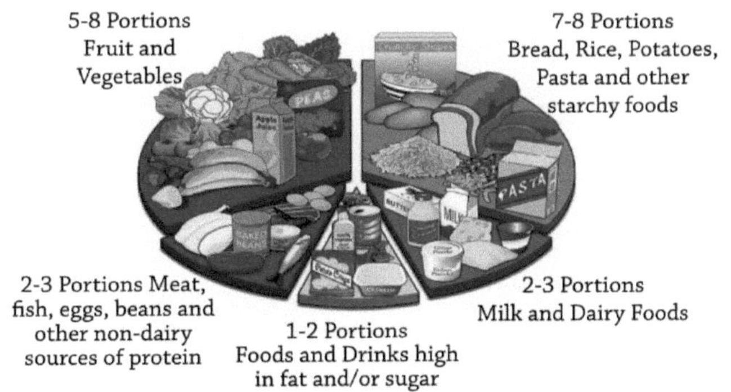

The bottom most part of the food pyramid is occupied by _________, indicating large quantities of intake.

(a) carbohydrates   (b) vitamins   (c) minerals   (d) fats

53. While organizing sports events for the Annual Sports Day, Arjun and Ravi being the captain and vice captain of sports, formed various committees as shown below.

The members of this committee are responsible for welcoming guests and spectators

(a) Decoration committee   (b) Reception committee

(c) Publicity committee   (d) Transportation committee

54. Your school has been given the responsibility to conduct Zonal basketball competition. As the Head boy/ Head girl of the student council you have been asked to make various teams of students to help teacher in changes for smooth conduct of the tournament. To help the terms to know about the food and stay arrangements a group of students will be assigned __________ committee.

(a) transport   (b) registration

(c) boarding and lodging   (d) decoration

55. Below given is the details of different types of vitamins required for our body:

The vitamins, minerals and water are collectively called as _________ food.

(a) body building   (b) defensive

(c) energy yielding   (d) facilitating

56. With the aim of promoting physical fitness and healthy lifestyle amongst students the Physical Education Teacher at XYZ School plans to organise intranural competitions at school. For conducting the event he has given this assignment to the students of class XII who have taken up Physical Education subject so that they can get first had experience of organising events.

    The work committees is divided into ____________ .

    (a) pre, during and post   (b) pre and post

    (c) pre and during   (d) during and post

57. A balanced diet refers to the intake of food constituting all the necessary nutrients. Ram shares his knowledge of 'food and nutrition' with neighbours while visiting his grandparents in a village. Ram notices that few people living in that village are suffering with goitre and severe anaemia. Minerals are placed under __________ nutrient category on the basis of required quantity.

    (a) micro   (b) macro

    (c) roughage   (d) non-nutritive

58. Mahesh, Physical Education teacher at XYZ School observed that Raju a student of class VI has outward curve of vertebral column at Thoracic region. He suggested some exercises to rectify this problem. What is this deformity know as?

    (a) Scoliosis   (b) Kyphosis

    (c) Lordosis   (d) Flat foot

59. During an athletic meet in stadium, eight women were on the starting line ready for the 100 metres race. With the sound of the pistal, all these woman started running.

    Hardly had they covered 15 metres, when accidently one woman slipped and fell, spraining her ankle, Due to pain the woman started crying. As soon as the other women heard her cry, all of them stopped running, stood for while, turned back, and ran towards her. They pacified her, joined their hands together, lifted her and walked together to reach the finishing line together. The officials were shocked to see such a demonstration of unity. Many eyes were filled with tears. What happened to one woman after she had covered a distance of 15 metres?

    (a) She started running

    (b) She started crying

    (c) She accidentally slipped and fell spraining her ankle

    (d) She fell down and broke her legs

60. Thomas went to and old age home on the occasion of his birthday. At that time all the inmates in the home were assembled in one place. When he enquired, they replied that they have as physical fitness test. Give any one standard physical fitness test for senior citizen.

    (a) Push ups   (b) Standing broad jump

    (c) Zig-zag run   (d) Chair sit and reach test

❑❑

Answers

Section - A

(KNOWLEDGE AND UNDERSTANDING)

1. (c) Advantage given to a team to not play in initial round.
2. (a) Fats
3. (a) Up to 26 weeks
4. (b) Mass
5. (a) Sensory integration therapy
6. (b) Weakness in heart and muscle
7. (d) 3-2
8. (c) Abdominal strength and endurance
9. (d) Standing
10. (a) Single league tournament
11. (b) Antibodies, immunity
12. (b) Registration
13. (b) B Complex
14. (b) Saina Nehwal
15. (b) Organizing
16. (d) Senior Citizens
17. (b) Explosive power
18. (d) Feedback
19. (a) Managing
20. (a) Reduced mistakes
21. (b) fixture
22. (b) random draws
23. (c) Fine motor skills
24. (b) 0 to 2

Section - B

(APPLICATION + HOTS)

25. (a) League tournament
26. (b) Muscle repair
27. (c) C
28. (a) planning
29. (b) balanced
30. (d) catching a ball
31. (c) 1–B, 2–D, 3–A, 4–C
32. (a) 1–B, 2–C, 3–A, 4–D
33. (b) 1–B, 2–C, 3–A

34. (c)   1–B, 2–A, 3–C
35. (c)   eight
36. (b)   biomechanics
37. (c)   Lack of vitamin D and calcium
38. (c)   Both (A) and (R) are true and (R) is the correct explanation of (A)
39. (a)   Both (A) and (R) are true, but (R) is not the correct explanation of (A)
40. (c)   Partial curl up
41. (d)   girls
42. (b)   1–D, 2–A, 3–B, 4–C
43. (c)   1–D, 2–A, 3–B, 4–C
44. (a)   Leading an active lifestyle
45. (a)   Both (A) and (R) are true, but (R) is not the correct explanation of (A)
46. (c)   7-12 years
47. (a)   Gross and fine
48. (b)   validity

Section - C

(CASE STUDIES)

49. (c)   Planning
50. (d)   All of the above
51. (a)   Finance and Budgeting
52. (b)   Sit and reach test
53. (b)   Defensive
54. (b)   1900
55. (d)   Back scratch test
56. (a)   Improper landing in long jump event
57. (a)   Kyphosis
58. (a)   Diarrhoea
59. (c)   True winner
60. (a)   N (N – 1)/2

Sample Paper 2

Section - A

(KNOWLEDGE AND UNDERSTANDING)

1. (b)   The foot moves upwards towards the rear of the calf
2. (b)   flexibility
3. (c)   4
4. (c)   Both (a) and (b)
5. (b)   Knock-out tournament
6. (a)   Damages cell
7. (b)   Zig Zag Run
8. (a)   Motor development
9. (a)   Round Robin tournament
10. (d)   All of the Above
11. (c)   60-120 mins, 3 days a week
12. (c)   Movement based exercises coupled with recreative methods
13. (a)   Knock out
14. (b)   She had a bye
15. (b)   2-3 litres

16. (a) Protective food
17. (a) British method
18. (a) Ladder method
19. (a) Directly proportional
20. (c) The law of acceleration
21. (c) Decision making
22. (c) Committee for officials
23. (b) according to the needs of the person
24. (b) To decorate the tournament venue

Section - B

(APPLICATION + HOTS)

25. (b) Knock out tournament
26. (a) Intant source of energy
27. (b) Harvard step test
28. (c) Calorie
29. (b) Niacin
30. (c) Fats
31. (c) 1–A, 2–D, 3–C, 4–B
32. (d) 1–C, 2–A, 3–D, 4–B.
33. (d) 1–B, 2–A, 3–C
34. (a) 1–C, 2–D, 3–B, 4–A
35. (c) Lateral curve in the spine
36. (b) Scoliosis
37. (b) Not standing for a long time
38. (a) Both (A) and (R) are true, but (R) is not the correct explanation of (A)
39. (b) Both (A) and (R) are true and (R) is the correct explanation of (A)
40. (c) Scoliosis
41. (d) girls
42. (b) 1–B, 2–A, 3–D, 4–C
43. (b) 1–D, 2–B, 3–C, 4–A
44. (a) Trikonasana and Ardh Chakrasana
45. (a) Both (A) and (R) are true, but (R) is not the correct explanation of (A)
46. (c) Vitamin K
47. (b) the small intestine
48. (b) Brownies

Section - C

(CASE STUDIES)

49. (d) Both (b) and (c)
50. (a) Opponent lost
51. (d) Carbohydrates
52. (a) N (N – 1)/2
53. (a) Law of inertia
54. (d) both (a) and (b)
55. (c) kyphosis
56. (c) cardiovascular
57. (c) Circumduction
58. (b) knock-out
59. (a) More time consuming
60. (a) simple carbohydrates

Sample Paper 3

Section – A

(KNOWLEDGE AND UNDERSTANDING)

1. (c) Calcium
2. (c) Strong teams paired with weak or all strong teams grouped in upper half or lower half.
3. (c) 3 kg
4. (a) 1-2 years
5. (b) Movements in the sagittal plane about the frontal axis
6. (b) Fine Motor Development
7. (c) 5 minutes
8. (c) Horizontal
9. (b) Protein
10. (c) Quarter-final or semi-final
11. (b) Normal weight
12. (a) Obese
13. (d) Proteins
14. (b) Mass
15. (b) Biomechanics
16. (c) Law of action and reaction
17. (d) Only (a) and (b)
18. (d) Vajrasana
19. (a) macro
20. (d) Vit A, D, E and K
21. (c) protein
22. (b) fats
23. (a) Publicity committee
24. (d) Goal oriented

Section – B

(APPLICATION + HOTS)

25. (a) League tournament
26. (c) Insulate the body
27. (b) Kyphosis
28. (c) both (a) and (b)
29. (b) Administrative director
30. (b) during tournament
31. (a) 1–D, 2–C, 3–A, 4–B
32. (d) 1–B, 2–C, 3–A
33. (d) 1–B, 2–A, 3–D, 4–C
34. (b) 1–C, 2–D, 3–A, 4–B
35. (a) food intolerance
36. (c) Obesity I

37. (d) Only (a) and (b
38. (a) Both (A) and (R) are true, but (R) is not the correct explanation of (A)
39. (b) Both (A) and (R) are true and (R) is the correct explanation of (A)
40. (a) Lordosis
41. (c) 12 year old girl
42. (a) 1–C, 2–B, 3–A, 4–D
43. (c) 1–C, 2–D, 3–B, 4–A
44. (a) 11
45. (a) Both (A) and (R) are true, but (R) is not the correct explanation of (A)
46. (c) 7
47. (b) Knock-out tournament
48. (d) All of the above

Section - C

(CASE STUDIES)

49. (c) Over weight
50. (c) Newton's 3rd law
51. (c) Flat foot
52. (a) carbohydrates
53. (b) Reception committee
54. (c) boarding and lodging
55. (b) defensive
56. (a) pre, during and post
57. (a) micro
58. (b) Kyphosis
59. (c) She accidentally slipped and fell spraining her ankle
60. (b) Chair sit and reach test

Accountancy

Sample Question Paper

Accountancy

Term - I

Time : 90 Minutes   Max. Marks : 40

General Instructions :

Read the following instructions very carefully and strictly follow them:

1. This question paper comprises three PARTS – I, II and III. There are 69 questions in the question paper.
2. Part – I is compulsory for all candidates.
3. Part – II Analysis of Financial Statement and Part – III Computerized Accounting. You have to attempt only one of the given OPTIONS.
4. There is an internal choice provided in each Sections.
   I.   Part-I, contains three Sections – A, B and C. Section A has questions from 1 to 18 and Section B has questions from 19 to 36, you have to attempt any 15 questions each in both the sections.
   II. Part I, Section C has questions from 37 to 41. You have to attempt any four questions.
   III. Part II, contains two Sections – A and B. Section A has questions from 42 to 48, you have to attempt any five questions and Section B has questions from 49 to 55, you have to attempt any six questions.
   IV. Part III, contains two Sections – A and B. Section A has questions from 49 to 62, you have to attempt any five questions and Section B has questions from 63 to 69, you have to attempt any six questions.
5. All questions carry equal marks. There is no negative marking.
6. Specific Instructions related to each Part and subdivisions (Section) is mentioned clearly before the questions. Candidates should read them thoroughly and attempt accordingly.

PART – I

Section – A

Instructions:

➤ *From question number 1 to 18, attempt any 15 questions.*

1. Gain / loss on revaluation at the time of change in profit sharing ratio of existing partners is shared by ___(i)______ whereas in case of admission of a partner it is shared by____(ii)_____.

   (A) (i) Remaining Partners, (ii) All partners.
   (B) (i) All Partners, (ii) Old partners.
   (C) (i) New Partner, (ii) All partner.
   (D) (i) Sacrificing Partner, (ii) Incoming partner.

Ans. (B) (i) All partners, (ii) Old partners.

2. Calculate the amount of second & final call when Abhijit Ltd., issues Equity shares of ₹ 10 each at a premium of 40% payable on Application ₹ 3, On Allotment ₹ 5, On First Call ₹ 2.

   (A) Second & final call ₹ 3.
   (B) Second & final call ₹ 4.
   (C) Second & final call ₹ 1.
   (D) Second & final call ₹ 14.

Ans. (B) Second & final call ₹ 4.

> **Explanation:**
> Issue price = ₹ 10
> Premium = 40% of ₹ 10 = ₹ 4
> Amount of Second & Final Call = ₹ 10 + ₹ 4 – ₹ 3 – ₹ 5 – ₹ 2 = ₹ 4

3. Anish Ltd., issued a prospectus inviting applications for 2,000 shares. Applications were received for 3,000 shares and pro-rata allotment was made to the applicants of 2,400 shares. If Dhruv has been allotted 40 shares, how many shares he must have applied for?

   (A) 40   (B) 44   (C) 48   (D) 52

Ans. (C) 48

> **Explanation:** Total shares applied = 3,000
>
> Shares on which Pro-rata allotment made = 2,400
>
> Total shares allotted = 2,000
>
> Shares allotted to Dhruv = 40
>
> Shares applied by Dhruv = $\dfrac{40}{2,000} \times 2,400 = 48$

4. Ambrish Ltd., offered 2,00,000 Equity Shares of ₹ 10 each, of these 1,98,000 shares were subscribed. The amount was payable as ₹ 3 on application, ₹ 4 an allotment and balance on first call. If a shareholder holding 3,000 shares has defaulted on first call, what is the amount of money received on first call?

   (A) ₹ 9,000   (B) ₹ 5,85,000   (C) ₹ 5,91,000   (D) ₹ 6,09,000.

Ans. (B) ₹ 5,85,000

> **Explanation:** Amount Payable per share on First Call
>
> $= ₹\, 10 - ₹\, 3 - ₹\, 4 = ₹\, 3$
>
> Amount Called on First Call = 1,98,000 × ₹ 3 = ₹ 5,94,000
>
> Amount Received on First Call = (1,98,000 − 3,000) × ₹ 3 = ₹ 5,85,000

5. What will be the correct sequence of events?

   (i) Forfeiture of shares   (ii) Default on Calls.

   (iii) Re-issue of shares   (iv) Amount transferred to capital reserve.

   Options:

   (A) (i), (iv), (ii), (iii)   (B) (ii), (iv), (i), (iii)

   (C) (ii), (i), (iii), (iv)   (D) (iii), (iv), (i) (ii)

Ans. (C) (ii), (i), (iii), (iv)

6. Arun and Vijay are partners in a firm sharing profits and losses in the ratio of 5:1.

Balance Sheet (Extract)

Liabilities	₹	Assets	₹
		Machinery	40,000

If the value of machinery reflected in the balance sheet is overvalued by $33\dfrac{1}{3}$ %, find out the value of Machinery to be shown in the new Balance Sheet:

   (A) ₹ 44,000   (B) ₹ 48,000   (C) ₹ 32,000   (D) ₹ 30,000

Ans. (D) ₹ 30,000

> **Explanation:** Value of Machinery in the Balance Sheet
>
> $= ₹\, 40,000$
>
> Value of Machinery in the Balance Sheet is overvalued by $33\dfrac{1}{3}\%$
>
> Value of Machinery to be shown in the New Balance Sheet
>
> $= \dfrac{40,000}{100 + \dfrac{100}{3}} \times 100$
>
> $= \dfrac{40,000}{400} \times 3 \times 100 = ₹\, 30,000$

7. Which of the following is true regarding Salary to a partner when the firm maintains fluctuating capital accounts?
   (A) Debit Partner's Loan A/c and Credit P & L Appropriation A/c
   (B) Debit P & L A/c and Credit Partner's Capital A/c
   (C) Debit P & L Appropriation A/c and Credit Partner's Current A/c
   (D) Debit P & L Appropriation A/c and Credit Partner's Capital A/c.

Ans. (D) Debit P & L Appropriation A/c and Credit Partner's Capital A/c.

8. At the time of reconstitution of a partnership firm, recording of an unrecorded liability will lead to:
   (A) Gain to the existing partners   (B) Loss to the existing partners
   (C) Neither gain nor loss to the existing partners   (D) None of the above

Ans. (B) Loss to the existing partners.

9. E, F and G are partners sharing profits in the ratio of 3:3:2. According to the partnership agreement, G is to get a minimum amount of ₹ 80,000 as his share of profits every year and any deficiency on this account is to be personally borne by E. The net profit for the year ended 31st March, 2021 amounted to ₹ 3,12 ,000. Calculate the amount of deficiency to be borne by E?
   (A) ₹ 1,000   (B) ₹ 4,000   (C) ₹ 8,000   (D) ₹ 2,000

Ans. (D) ₹ 2,000

> **Explanation:** Profit Sharing Ratio of E, F and G = 3 : 3 : 2
> Net Profit for the year ended 31st March, 2021
> $$= ₹ 3,12 ,000$$
> $$\text{G's share in profit} = ₹ 3,12,000 \times \frac{2}{8} = ₹ 78,000$$
> Profit guaranteed to G = ₹ 80,000
> Amount of Deficiency in G's profit share to be borne by E
> $$= ₹ 80,000 - ₹ 78,000 = ₹ 2,000$$

10. At the time of admission of a partner, what will be the effect of the following information? Balance in Workmen compensation reserve ₹ 40,000. Claim for workmen compensation ₹ 45,000.
    (A) ₹ 45,000 Debited to the Partner's capital Accounts
    (B) ₹ 40,000 Debited to Revaluation Account
    (C) ₹ 5,000 Debited to Revaluation Account
    (D) ₹ 5,000 Credited to Revaluation Account

Ans. (C) ₹ 5,000 Debited to Revaluation Account.

> **Explanation:** At the time of admission of a partner, excess of Workmen Compensation Reserve over Workmen Compensation Claim is debited to Revaluation Account.
> Balance in Workmen Compensation Reserve = ₹ 40,000
> Claim for Workmen Compensation = ₹ 45,000
> Excess of Workmen Compensation Reserve over Claim
> $$= ₹ 45,000 - ₹ 40,000 = ₹ 5,000$$

11. In the absence of partnership deed, a partner is entitled to an interest on the amount of additional capital advanced by him to the firm at a rate of:
    (A) entitled for 6% p.a. on their additional capital, only when there are profits.
    (B) entitled for 10% p.a. on their additional capital
    (C) entitled for 12% p.a. on their additional capital
    (D) not entitled for any interest on their additional capitals

Ans. (D) not entitled for any interest on their additional capitals.

12. Revaluation of assets at the time of reconstitution is necessary because their present value may be different from their:

   (A) Market Value   (B) Net Value   (C) Cost of Asset   (D) Book Value

Ans. (A) Market Value.

13. If average capital employed in a firm is ₹ 8,00,000, average of actual profits is ₹ 1,80,000 and normal rate of return is 10%, then value of goodwill as per capitalization of average profits is:

   (A) ₹ 10,00,000   (B) ₹ 18,00,000   (C) ₹ 80,00,000   (D) ₹ 78,20,000

Ans. (A) ₹ 10,00,000

> **Explanation:**
>
> $$\text{Average Capital Employed} = ₹\,8,00,000$$
> $$\text{Average of Actual Profits} = ₹\,1,80,000$$
> $$\text{Normal Rate of Return} = 10\%$$
>
> $$\text{Capitalized Average Profits} = \text{Average Profits} \times \frac{100}{\text{Normal Rate of Return}}$$
>
> $$= ₹\,1,80,000 \times \frac{100}{10}$$
>
> $$= ₹\,18,00,000$$
>
> $$\text{Value of Goodwill} = \text{Capitalized Average Profits} - \text{Average Capital Employed}$$
>
> $$= ₹\,18,00,000 - ₹\,8,00,000$$
>
> $$= ₹\,10,00,000$$

14. In which of the following situation Companies Act, 2013 allows for issue of shares at discount?

   (A) Issued to vendors   (B) Issued to public

   (C) Issued as sweat equity   (D) None of these

Ans. (C) Issued as sweat equity.

> **Explanation:** As per Companies Act, 2013, a company shall not issue shares at a discount except as provided in Section 54 for issue of sweat equity shares.

15. As per Section 52 of Companies Act, 2013, Securities Premium Reserve cannot be utilised for:

   (A) Writing off capital losses   (B) Issue of fully paid bonus shares

   (C) Writing off discount on issue of securities   (D) Writing off preliminary expenses

Ans. (A) Writing off capital losses.

16. Net Assets minus Capital Reserve is:

   (A) Purchase consideration   (B) Goodwill

   (C) Total assets   (D) Liquid assets

Ans. (A) Purchase consideration.

17. Kalki and Kumud were partners sharing profits and losses in the ratio of 5:3. On 1st April,2021 they admitted Kaushtubh as a new partner and new ratio was decided as 3:2:1. Goodwill of the firm was valued as ₹ 3,60,000. Kaushtubh couldn't bring any amount for goodwill. Amount of goodwill share to be credited to Kalki and Kumud Account's will be:

   (A) ₹ 37,500 and ₹ 22,500 respectively   (B) ₹ 30,000 and ₹ 30,000 respectively

   (C) ₹ 36,000 and ₹ 24,000 respectively   (D) ₹ 45,000 and ₹ 15,000 respectively

Ans. (D) ₹ 45,000 and ₹ 15,000 respectively.

Explanation: Old Profit Sharing Ratio of Kalki and Kumud $= 5 : 3$

New Profit Sharing Ratio of Kalki, Kumud and Kaushtubh $= 3 : 2 : 1$

$$\text{Kalki's Sacrifice or Gain} = \frac{5}{8} - \frac{3}{6} = \frac{15-12}{24} = \frac{3}{24} \text{ (Sacrifice)}$$

$$\text{Kumud's Sacrifice or Gain} = \frac{3}{8} - \frac{2}{6} = \frac{9-8}{24} = \frac{1}{24} \text{ (Sacrifice)}$$

$$\text{Sacrificing Ratio} = \frac{3}{24} : \frac{1}{24} = 3 : 1$$

Value of Goodwill of the Firm $= ₹\,3,60,000$

$$\text{Kaushtubh's share of Goodwill} = ₹\,3,60,000 \times \frac{1}{6} = ₹\,60,000$$

Goodwill to be Credited to Kalki's Account

$$= ₹\,60,000 \times \frac{3}{4} = ₹\,45,000$$

Goodwill to be Credited to Kumud's Account

$$= ₹\,60,000 \times \frac{1}{4} = ₹\,15,000$$

18. Sarvesh, Sriniketan and Srinivas are partners in the ratio of 5:3: 2. If Sriniketan's share of profit at the end of the year amounted to ₹ 1,50,000, what will be Sarvesh's share of profits?

(A) ₹ 5,00,000   (B) ₹ 1,50,000   (C) ₹ 3,00,000   (D) ₹ 2,50,000

Ans. (D) ₹ 2,50,000

Explanation: Profit Sharing Ratio of Sarvesh, Sriniketan and Srinivas $= 5 : 3 : 2$

$$\text{Sriniketan's Share of Profit for } \frac{3}{10} \text{th share}$$

$$= ₹\,1,50,000$$

$$\text{Firm's Total Profit} = ₹\,1,50,000 \times \frac{10}{3}$$

$$= ₹\,5,00,000$$

$$\text{Sarvesh's Share of Profit for } \frac{5}{10} \text{th share}$$

$$= ₹\,5,00,000 \times \frac{5}{10} = ₹\,2,50,000$$

Section – B

Instructions:

> *From question number 19 to 36, attempt any 15 questions:*

19. Angle and Circle ware partners in a firm. Their Balance Sheet showed Furniture at ₹ 2,00,000; Stock at ₹ 1,40,000; Debtors at ₹ 1,62,000 and Creditors at ₹ 60,000. Square was admitted and new profit-sharing ratio was agreed at 2:3:5. Stock was revalued at ₹ 1,00,000, Creditors of ₹ 15,000 are not likely to be claimed, Debtors for ₹ 2,000 have become irrecoverable and Provision for doubtful debts to be provided @ 10%.

Angle's share in loss on revaluation amounted to ₹ 30,000. Revalued value of Furniture will be:

(A) ₹ 2,17,000   (B) ₹ 1,03,000   (C) ₹ 3,03,000   (D) ₹ 1,83,000

Ans. (D) ₹ 1,83,000

Explanation:

Dr.			Revaluation Account		Cr.
Particulars	**Amount**		**Particulars**		**Amount**
	₹				₹
To Stock A/c	40,000		By Creditors A/c		15,000
To Debtors A/c	2,000		By Loss on Revaluation :		
To Provision for Bad Debts A/c	16,000		Angle's Capital A/c	30,000	
To Furniture A/c	17,000		Circle's Capital A/c	30,000	60,000
	75,000				**75,000**

Value of Furniture is reduced by ₹ 17,000.

$$\therefore \quad \text{Revalued value of Furniture} = ₹\, 2,00,000 - ₹\, 17,000$$
$$= ₹\, 1,83,000$$

Note : As profit sharing ratio of Angle and Circle is not provided in the question, so it is presumed they are sharing profits and losses equally.

20. Asha and Nisha are partner's sharing profits in the ratio of 2:1. Kashish was admitted for 1/4 share of which 1/8 was gifted by Asha. The remaining was contributed by Nisha. Goodwill of the firm is valued at ₹ 40,000. How much amount for goodwill will be credited to Nisha's Capital account?

(A) ₹ 2,500   (B) ₹ 5,000   (C) ₹ 20,000   (D) ₹ 40,000.

Ans. (B) ₹ 5,000

Explanation:

Old Profit Sharing Ratio of Asha and Nisha = 2 : 1

$$\text{Kashish's share} = \frac{1}{4}$$

$$\text{Kashish's share contributed by Asha} = \frac{1}{8}$$

$$\text{Kashish's share contributed by Nisha} = \frac{1}{4} - \frac{1}{8} = \frac{1}{8}$$

$$\text{Sacrificing Ratio} = \frac{1}{8} : \frac{1}{8} = 1 : 1$$

$$\text{Kashish's share of Goodwill} = ₹\, 40,000 \times \frac{1}{4}$$

$$= ₹\, 10,000$$

which will be contributed by Asha and Nisha equally,

i.e., $$₹\, 10,000 \times \frac{1}{2} = ₹\, 5,000$$

21. At the time of admission of new partner Vasu, Old partners Paresh and Prabhav had debtors of ₹ 6,20,000 and a provision for doubtful debts of ₹ 20,000 in their books. As per terms of admission, assets were revalued, and it was found that debtors worth ₹ 15,000 had turned bad and hence should be written off. Which journal entry reflects the correct accounting treatment of the above situation.

(A)	Bad Debts A/c	Dr.	15,000	
	To Sundry Debtors			15,000
	Provision for Doubtful Debts A/c	Dr.	15,000	
	To Bad Debts A/c			15,000
(B)	Bad Debt A/c	Dr.	15,000	
	To Sundry Debtors			15,000
	Revaluation A/c	Dr.	15,000	
	To Provision for Doubtful Debts A/c			15,000
(C)	Revaluation A/c	Dr.	15,000	
	To Sundry Debtors A/c			15,000
(D)	Bad Debt A/c	Dr.	15,000	
	To Revaluation A/c			15,000

Ans. (A)

		₹	₹
Bad Debts A/c	Dr.	15,000	
To Sundry Debtors			15,000
Provision for Doubtful Debts A/c	Dr.	15,000	
To Bad Debts A/c			15,000

22. Given below are two statements, one labelled as Assertion (A) and the other labelled as Reason (R).

Assertion (A): Transfer to reserves is shown in P & L Appropriation A/c.

Reason (R): Reserves are charge against the profits.

In the context of the above statements, which one of the following is correct?

Codes:

(A) (A) is correct, but (R) is wrong
(B) Both (A) and (R) are correct
(C) (A) is wrong, but (R) is correct
(D) Both (A) and (R) are wrong

Ans. (A) (A) is correct, but (R) is wrong.

Explanation: Any transfer to reserves is shown in Profit & Loss Appropriation Account. Reserve is not a charge against profit, as it is not meant to cover any known liability or expected loss in future, it is an appropriation of profit.

23. Anubhav, Shagun and Pulkit are partners in a firm sharing profits and losses in the ratio of 2:2:1. On 1st April 2021, they decided to change their profit-sharing ratio to 5:3:2. On that date, debit balance of Profit & Loss A/c ₹ 30,000 appeared in the balance sheet and partners decided to pass an adjusting entry for it. Which of the undermentioned options reflect correct treatment for the above treatment?

(A) Shagun's capital account will be debited by ₹ 3,000 and Anubhav's capital account credited by ₹ 3,000
(B) Pulkit's capital account will be credited by ₹ 3,000 and Shagun's capital account will be credited by ₹ 3,000
(C) Shagun's capital account will be debited by ₹ 30,000 and Anubhav's capital account credited by ₹ 30,000
(D) Shagun's capital account will be debited by ₹ 3,000 and Anubhav's and Pulkit's capital account credited by ₹ 2,000 and ₹ 1,000 respectively.

Ans. (A) Shagun's capital account will be debited by ₹ 3,000 and Anubhav's capital account credited by ₹ 3,000.

Explanation: Old Profit Sharing Ratio of Anubhav, Shagun and Pulkit = 2 : 2 : 1

New Profit Sharing Ratio of Anubhav,

Shagun and Pulkit = 5 : 3 : 2

Sacrificing Ratio = Old Ratio – New Ratio

$$\text{Anubhav's Sacrifice/Gain} = \frac{2}{5} - \frac{5}{10} = -\frac{1}{10} \text{ (Sacrifice)}$$

$$\text{Shagun's Sacrifice/Gain} = \frac{2}{5} - \frac{3}{10} = \frac{1}{10} \text{ (Gain)}$$

$$\text{Pulkit's Sacrifice/Gain} = \frac{1}{5} - \frac{2}{10} = \text{Nil}$$

Amount to be Compensated by Shagun to Anubhav

$$= ₹\,30,000 \times \frac{1}{10} = ₹\,3,000$$

24. A, B and C are partners, their partnership deed provides for interest on drawings at 8% per annum. B withdrew a fixed amount in the middle of every month and his interest on drawings amounted to ₹ 4,800 at the end of the year. What was the amount of his monthly drawings?

   (A) ₹ 10,000 (B) ₹ 5,000 (C) ₹ 1,20,000 (D) ₹ 48,000

Ans. (A) ₹ 10,000

Explanation: Rate of Interest on Drawings = 8% p.a.

B withdrew a fixed amount in the middle of every month, so interest will be calculated for an average period of 6 months.

$$\text{Interest on B's Drawings} = \frac{\text{B's Total Drawings} \times 8 \times 6}{100 \times 12}$$

$$₹\,4,800 = \frac{\text{B's Total Drawings} \times 8 \times 6}{100 \times 12}$$

$$\text{B's Total Drawings} = \frac{4,800 \times 100 \times 12}{8 \times 6} = ₹\,1,20,000$$

$$\therefore \quad \text{B's Monthly Drawing} = \frac{1,20,000}{12} = ₹\,10,000$$

25. Abhay and Baldwin are partners sharing profit in the ratio 3:1. On 31st March 2021, firm's net profit is ₹ 1,25,000. The partnership deed provided interest on capital to Abhay and Baldwin ₹ 15,000 & ₹ 10,000 respectively and Interest on drawings for the year amounted to ₹ 6,000 from Abhay and ₹ 4,000 from Baldwin. Abhay is also entitled to commission @10% on net divisible profits. Calculate profit to be transferred to Partners Capital A/c's.

   (A) ₹ 1,00,000 (B) ₹ 1,10,000 (C) ₹ 1,07,000 (D) ₹ 90,000

Ans. (A) ₹ 1,00,000

Explanation:

Net Profit	₹ 1,25,000
Less : Interest on Abhay's Capital	₹ 15,000
Interest on Baldwin's Capital	₹ 10,000
	₹ 1,00,000
Add : Interest on Abhay's Drawings	₹ 6,000
Interest on Baldwin's Drawings	₹ 4,000
	₹ 1,10,000
Less : Commission to Abhay	₹ 10,000
Net Divisible Profit	₹ 1,00,000

Commission to Abhay = 10% of Net Divisible Profit

$$= ₹\,1,10,000 \times \frac{10}{110} = ₹\,10,000$$

26. Given below are two statements, one labelled as Assertion (A) and the other labelled as Reason (R):

Assertion (A): Revaluation A/c is prepared at the time of Admission of a partner.

Reason (R): It is required to adjust the values of assets and liabilities at the time of admission of a partner, so that the true financial position of the firm is reflected.

In the context of the above two statements, which of the following is correct?

Codes:

(A) Both (A) and (R) are correct and (R) is the correct reason of (A)

(B) Both (A) and (R) are correct but (R) is not the correct reason of (A)

(C) Only (R) is correct

(D) Both (A) and (R) are wrong

Ans. (A) Both (A) and (R) are correct and (R) is the correct reason of (A).

> **Explanation:** At the time of admission of a new partner, the existing assets and liabilities are revalued and thus, revaluation account is prepared. By the time, the value of assets and liabilities may be altered from its book value, the value of some assets and liabilities increases while that of some decreases. Also, there must be some assets or liabilities that are not recorded in the books which need to be recorded.

27. Apaar Ltd. forfeited 4,000 shares of ₹ 20 each, fully called-up, on which only application money of ₹ 6 has been paid. Out of these 2,000 shares were re-issued and ₹ 8,000 has been transferred to capital reserve. Calculate the rate at which these shares were re-issued.

(A) ₹ 20 per share   (B) ₹ 18 per share   (C) ₹ 22 per share   (D) ₹ 8 per share

Ans. (B) ₹ 18 Per share

> **Explanation:**
>
> No. of Shares Forfeited = 4,000
>
> Issue and Called-up Amount per share = ₹ 20
>
> Paid-up Amount per share = ₹ 6
>
> Forfeited Amount on 4,000 shares = ₹ 6 × 4,000 = ₹ 24,000
>
> No. of Forfeited Shares Re-issued = 2,000
>
> Forfeited Amount on 2,000 shares = ₹ $24,000 \times \dfrac{2,000}{4,000}$ = ₹ 12,000
>
> Amount transferred to Capital Reserve = ₹ 8,000
>
> Loss on Re-issue of Shares = ₹ 12,000 – ₹ 8,000 = ₹ 4,000
>
> Price at which forfeited shares re-issued = ₹ $20 - \dfrac{₹\,4,000}{2,000}$ = ₹ 18

28. Which of the following statement is/are true?

(i) Authorized Capital < Issued Capital

(ii) Authorized Capital ≥ Issued Capital

(iii) Subscribed Capital ≤ Issued Capital

(iv) Subscribed Capital > Issued Capital

(A) (i) only   (B) (i) and (iv) Both   (C) (ii) and (iii) Both   (D) (ii) only

Ans. (C) (ii) and (iii) Both

29. Mickey, Tom and Jerry were partners in the ratio of 5:3:2. On 31st March 2021, their books reflected a net profit of ₹ 2,10,000. As per the terms of the partnership deed they were entitled for interest on capital which amounted to ₹ 80,000, ₹ 60,000 and ₹ 40,000 respectively. Besides this a salary of ₹ 60,000 each was payable to Mickey and Tom.

Calculate the ratio in which the profits would be appropriated.

(A) 1:1:1   (B) 5:3:2   (C) 7:6:2   (D) 4:3:2

Ans. (C) $7:6:2$

> **Explanation:** Ratio in which the Profits would be Appropriated
>
> $$= (80,000 + 60,000) : (60,000 + 60,000) : 40,000$$
> $$= 1,40,000 : 1,20,000 : 40,000$$
> $$= 7 : 6 : 2$$

30. Mohit had been allotted for 600 shares by a Govinda Ltd. on pro-rata basis which had issued two shares for every three applied. He had paid application money of ₹ 3 per share and could not pay allotment money of ₹ 5 per share. First and final call of ₹ 2 per share was not yet made by the company. His shares were forfeited. the following entry will be passed:

Equity Share Capital A/c	Dr. ₹ X	
To Share Forfeited A/c		₹ Y
To Equity Share Allotment A/c		₹ Z

Here X, Y and Z are:

(A) ₹ 6,000; ₹ 2,700; ₹ 3,000 respectively   (B) ₹ 9,000; ₹ 2,700; ₹ 4,500 respectively

(C) ₹ 4,800; ₹ 2,700; ₹ 2,100 respectively   (D) ₹ 7,200; ₹ 2,700; ₹ 4,500 respectively

Ans. (C) ₹ 4,800; ₹ 2,700; ₹ 2,100 respectively.

> **Explanation:**
>
> Shares Allotted to Mohit $= 600$
>
> Shares Applied by Mohit $= 600 \times \dfrac{3}{2} = 900$
>
> Amount paid by Mohit on Application $= 900 \times ₹\, 3 = ₹\, 2,700$
>
> Application Amount Due on Mohit's shares
> $$= 600 \times ₹\, 3 = ₹\, 1,800$$
>
> Excess money paid by Mohit on Application
> $$= ₹\, 2,700 - ₹\, 1,800 = ₹\, 900$$
>
> Allotment Amount Due on Mohit's shares
> $$= 600 \times ₹\, 5 = ₹\, 3,000$$
>
> Amount not paid by Mohit on Allotment $=$ Allotment Amount Due – Excess money paid on Application
> $$= ₹\, 3,000 - ₹\, 900 = ₹\, 2,100$$

31. Given below are two statements, one labelled as Assertion (A) and the other labelled as Reason (R):

    Assertion (A): In case of shares issued on Pro–rata basis, excess money received at the time of application can be utilised till allotment only.

    Reason (R): Company has to pay interest on calls in advance @ 12% p.a. for amount adjusted towards calls (if any).

    In the context of the above two statements, which of the following is correct?

    Codes:

    (A) Both (A) and (R) are true, but (R) is not the explanation of working capital management

    (B) Both(A) and (R) are true and (R) is a correct explanation of (A)

    (C) Both (A) and (R) are false

    (D) (A) is false, but (R) is true

Ans. (D) (A) is false, but (R) is true.

> **Explanation:** When the company issue shares on Pro-rata basis, excess money received at the time of application can be utilised on allotment and calls. And a company has to pay an interest @12% p.a. on calls in advance for amount adjusted towards calls (if any).

32. Ajay and Vinod are partners in the ratio of 3:2. Their fixed Capital were ₹ 3,00,000 and ₹ 4,00,000 respectively. After the close of accounts for the year it was observed that the Interest on Capital which was agreed to be provided at 5% p.a. was erroneously provided at 10%p.a. By what amount will Ajay's account be affected if partners decide to pass an adjustment entry for the same?

(A) Ajay's Current A/c will be Debited by ₹ 15,000

(B) Ajay's Current A/c will be Credited by ₹ 6,000

(C) Ajay's Current A/c will be Credited by ₹ 35,000

(D) Ajay's Current A/c will be Debited by ₹ 20,000

Ans. (B) Ajay's Current A/c will be Credited by ₹ 6,000.

Explanation:

Table showing Adjustment to be made

Particulars	Ajay's Current A/c		Vinod's Current A/c		Firm	
	Dr. (₹)	Cr. (₹)	Dr. (₹)	Cr. (₹)	Dr. (₹)	Cr. (₹)
Interest on Capital wrongly credited @ 10% p.a., now reversed	30,000		40,000			70,000
Interest on Capital credited @ 5% p.a.		15,000		20,000	35,000	
Profit credited to the partners in 3 : 2		21,000		14,000	35,000	
Total	30,000	36,000	40,000	34,000	70,000	70,000
Net Effect	Cr. 6,000		Dr. 6,000		–	

33. Vishnu Ltd. forfeited 20 shares of ₹ 10 each, ₹ 8 called-up, on which John had paid application and allotment money of ₹ 5 per share, of these, 15 shares were re-issued to Parker as fully paid up for ₹ 6 per share. What is the balance in the share Forfeiture Account after the relevant amount has been transferred to Capital Reserve Account?

(A) ₹ 0 (B) ₹ 5 (C) ₹ 25 (D) ₹ 100

Ans. (C) ₹ 25

Explanation:

No. of Shares Forfeited = 20

Called-up Amount per share = ₹ 8

Paid-up Amount per share = ₹ 5

Forfeited Amount on 4,000 shares = ₹ 5 × 20 = ₹ 100

No. of Forfeited Shares not Re-issued = 5

Balance in Share Forfeiture Account (on 5 shares)

$$= ₹ \, 100 \times \frac{5}{20} = ₹ \, 25$$

34. Newfound Ltd. took over business of Old land Ltd. and paid for it by issue of 30,000, Equity Shares of ₹ 100 each at a par along with 6% Preference Shares of ₹ 1,00,00,000 at a premium of 5% and a cheque of ₹ 8,00,000. What was the total agreed purchase consideration payable to Old Land Ltd.

(A) ₹ 1,05,00,000 (B) ₹ 1,43,00,000

(C) ₹ 1,40,00,000 (D) ₹ 1,35,00,000

Ans. (B) ₹ 1,43,00,000

Explanation:

Particulars	₹
Amount of Equity Shares issued = 30,000 × ₹ 100	30,00,000
Amount of 6% Preference Shares issued = ₹ 1,00,00,000 + 5% of ₹ 1,00,00,000	1,05,00,000
Amount of Cheque issued	8,00,000
Purchase Consideration	**1,43,00,000**

35. A and B are partners in the ratio of 3:2. C is admitted as a partner and he takes ¼th of his share from A. B gives 3/16 from his share to C. What is the share of C?

(A) 1/4

(B) 1/16

(C) 1/6

(D) 1/16

Ans. (A) $\dfrac{1}{4}$

Explanation: Since, C acquires 1/4th of his share from A, it means he acquires 3/4th (*i.e.*, 1 – 1/4th) of his share from B.

If $\dfrac{3}{4}$th share of C is 3/16 (Received from B)

$\therefore$
$$\text{C's share} = \frac{3}{16} \times \frac{4}{3} = \frac{1}{4}$$

36. Krishan Ltd. has Issued Capital of 20,00,000 Equity shares of ₹ 10 each. Till Date ₹ 8 per share have been called up and the entire amount received except calls of ₹ 4 per share on 800 shares and ₹ 3 per share from another holder who held 500 shares. What will be amount appearing as 'Subscribed but not fully paid capital' in the balance sheet of the company?

(A) ₹ 2,00,00,000

(B) ₹ 1,95,99,000

(C) ₹ 1,59,95,300

(D) ₹ 1,99,95,300

Ans. (C) ₹ 1,59,95,300

Explanation:

	₹	
Issued Capital :		
20,00,000 Equity shares of ₹ 10 each		2,00,00,000
Called-up Capital :		
20,00,000 Equity shares of ₹ 8 each		1,60,00,000
Subscribed but not Fully Paid Capital :		
19,98,700 Equity shares of ₹ 8 each	₹	1,59,89,600
1,300 Equity shares of ₹ 8 each	10,400	
Less : Calls-in-Arrears		
800 Equity shares of ₹ 4 each	3,200	
500 Equity shares of ₹ 3 each	1,500	5,700
		1,59,95,300

Section - C

Instructions:

> *From question number 37 to 41, attempt any 4 questions.*

Question no.'s 37 and 38 are based on the hypothetical situation given below.

Bright Star Limited is engaged in manufacture of high-end medical equipment. Considering the prospects of high growth in this segment the company has decided to expand and for this purpose additional investment of ₹ 50,00,00,000 is required. Directors have decided that 20% of this requirement would be financed by raising long term debts and balance by issue of Equity shares.

As per memorandum of association of the company the face value of Equity shares is ₹ 100 each. Also, considering the market standing of the company these shares would be issued at a premium of 25%. Directors decided to issue sufficient shares to collect the desired amount (including premium).

The prospectus was issued to public, and the issue was over subscribed by 2,00,000 shares which were issued letters of regret. Answer the below mentioned questions considering that the entire amount was payable on application.

37. What is the total amount collected on application?

   (A) ₹ 42,50,00,000   (B) ₹ 40,00,00,000

   (C) ₹ 32,00,00,000   (D) None of these

Ans. (A) ₹ 42,50,00,000

> **Explanation:** Additional Investment Required = ₹ 50,00,00,000
>
> 20% investment is financed by raising Long-term Debts and balance *i.e.,* 80% by issue of Equity shares.
>
> Amount of Equity Shares Issued = 80% of ₹ 50,00,00,000 = ₹ 40,00,00,000
>
> Equity Shares are issued at a premium of 25%
>
> $$\text{Number of Equity Shares Issued} = \frac{40,00,00,000}{100 + 25} = 32,00,000$$
>
> Number of Equity Shares Applied = 32,00,000 + 2,00,000 = 34,00,000
>
> Amount received on Application = 34,00,000 × ₹ (100 + 25) = ₹ 42,50,00,000

38. How many Equity shares were offered for issue by Bright Star Ltd.?

   (A) 40,00,000 shares   (B) 50,00,000 shares

   (C) 35,00,000 shares   (D) 32,00,000 shares

Ans. (D) 32,00,000 shares

> **Explanation:**
>
> Amount of Equity Shares Issued
>
> $$= 80\% \text{ of } ₹ 50,00,00,000 = ₹ 40,00,00,000$$
>
> Equity Shares are issued at a premium of 25%
>
> Number of Equity Shares Issued = 40,00,00,000/(100 + 25) = 32,00,000

Question no.'s 39, 40 and 41 are based on the hypothetical situation given below.

On 1st September 2020, twenty students of Modern College started their Partnership Firm in the name of "Be Safe" for selling sanitisers on digital mode. Since they were good friends of each other, they were not having any explicit agreement in place. All of them have agreed to invest ₹ 15,000/- each as capital. The books were closed on 31st March 2021, on which date the following information was provided by the firm:

PARTICULARS	AMOUNT (₹)
Sale of Sanitiser	1,20,000
Cost of goods Sold	50,000
Total Remuneration to Partners	2,000 per month

Rent to a Partner	1,000 per month
Manager's Commission	5,000
Closing Stock as on March 31,2021	9,000
6% Fixed Deposit (made on 31.3.2021)	20,000

39. Calculate the amount of profits to be transferred to Profit and Loss Appropriation Account.

(A) Profit ₹ 58,000

(B) Profit ₹ 44,000

(C) Profit ₹ 59,200

(D) Profit ₹ 58,700

Ans. (A) Profit ₹ 58,000

> **Explanation:** Profits to be transferred to Profit and Loss Appropriation Account = Sales – Cost of Goods Sold – Rent to a Partner – Manager's Commission
> $$= ₹\ 1,20,000 – ₹\ 50,000 – ₹\ (1,000 × 7) – ₹\ 5,000$$
> $$= ₹\ 58,000$$

40. On 31st March 2021, Remuneration to Partners will be provided to the partners of "Be Safe" but only out of:

(A) Profits for the accounting year

(B) Reserves

(C) Accumulated Profits

(D) Goodwill

Ans. (A) Profits for the accounting year.

41. On 01st December, 2020 one of the partners of the firm introduced additional capital of ₹ 30,000 and also advanced a loan of ₹ 40,000 to the firm. Calculate the amount of interest that Partner will receive for the current accounting period.

(A) ₹ 4,200

(B) ₹ 1,400

(C) ₹ 1,575

(D) ₹ 800

Ans. (D) ₹ 800

> **Explanation:** Additional Capital Introduced on 1st December, 2020
> $$= ₹\ 30,000$$
> Loan Advanced by Partner on 1st December, 2020
> $$= ₹\ 40,000$$
>
> As there is no information given in the question regarding the interest on capital, so no interest will be allowed on partners' capital and additional capital. Partner is only entitled to get interest on the loan advanced by him to the firm at the rate of 6% p.a. when the partnership deed is absent or in the absence of any information.
>
> $$\text{Interest on Loan Advanced by Partner} = ₹\ 40,000 × \frac{6}{100} × \frac{4}{12} = ₹\ 800$$

PART - II

Section - A

Instructions:

> *From question number 42 to 48, attempt any 5 questions.*

42. Given below are two statements, one labelled as Assertion (A) and the other labelled as Reason (R):

Assertion (A): The focus of calculation of working capital revolves around managing the operating cycle of the business.

Reason (R): It is because the concept of operating cycle is required to ascertain the liquidity of assets and urgency of payments to liabilities.

In the context of the above two statements, which of the following is correct?

Codes:

(A) Both (A) and (R) are true, but (R) is not the explanation of working capital management.

(B) Both(A) and (R) are true and (R) is a correct explanation of (A).

(C) Both (A) and (R) are false.

(D) (A) is false, but (R) is true.

Ans. (B) Both (A) and (R) are true and (R) is a correct explanation of (A).

> **Explanation:** Working capital indicates revolving a circular flow of cash starting with cash paid for purchase of material and ending with cash receipt after the sale of finished goods. And an operating cycle is the average amount of time it takes for the company's cash to be put into the business operations and then make its way back into the company's cash account.

43. Which of the following are included in traditional classification of ratios?

(i) Liquidity Ratios

(ii) Statement of Profit and loss Ratios

(iii) Balance Sheet Ratios

(iv) Profitability Ratios

(v) Composite Ratios

(vi) Solvency Ratios

(A) (ii), (iii) and (v)

(B) (i), (iv) and (vi)

(C) (i), (ii) and (vi)

(D) All (i), (ii), (iii), (iv), (v), (vi)

Ans. (A) (ii), (iii) and (v)

> **Explanation:** Traditional classification of ratios include : Statement of Profit and Loss Ratios, Balance Sheet Ratios and Composite Ratios. Functional or Modern classification of ratios include : Liquidity Ratios, Solvency Ratios, Activity Ratios and Profitability Ratios.

44. The following groups of ratios primarily measure risk:

(A) solvency, activity, and profitability

(B) liquidity, efficiency, and solvency

(C) liquidity, activity, and profitability

(D) liquidity, solvency, and profitability

Ans. (D) liquidity, solvency, and profitability.

45. Which one of the following is correct?

(i) A ratio is an arithmetical relationship of one number to another number.

(ii) Liquid ratio is also known as acid test ratio.

(iii) Ideally accepted current ratio is 1: 1.

(iv) Debt equity ratio is the relationship between outsider's funds and shareholders' funds.

In the context of the above two statements, which of the following options is correct?

(A) All (i), (ii), (iii) and (iv) are correct

(B) Only (i), (ii) and (iv) are correct.

(C) Only (ii), (iii) and (iv) are correct

(D) Only (ii) and (iv) are correct.

Ans. (B) Only (i), (ii) and (iv) are correct.

> **Explanation:** Liquid ratio is also known as acid test ratio or quick ratio,it measures the ability of a company to pay its short-term liabilities by having assets that are readily convertible into cash. Ideally accepted current ratio is 2 : 1. Debt-equity ratio indicates relative proportion of shareholders' equity and debt used to finance a company's assets.

46. Which of the following are the tools of Vertical Analysis?

(i) Ratio Analysis.

(ii) Comparative Statements.

(iii) Common Size Statements.

(A) Only (iii)   (B) Both (i) and (iii)   (C) Both (i) and (ii)   (D) Only (i)

Ans. (B) Both (i) and (iii)

> **Explanation:** Horizontal Analysis is undertaken to ascertain how the company performed over the years, for which comparative financial statements and trend analysis are used. Vertical analysis aims to ascertain the proportion of item, in relation to a common item in percentage terms, for which common-size financial statements and ratio analysis are used.

47. Match the items given in Column I with the headings/sub-headings (Balance sheet) as defined in Schedule III of Companies Act, 2013.

Column I	Column II
(I) Loose Tools	(a) Intangible fixed assets
(II) Patents	(b) Other current assets
(III) Prepaid insurance	(c) Long-term Borrowings
(IV) Debentures	(d) Inventories
(V) Machinery	(e) Tangible Fixed assets

Choose the correct option:

(A) (I)-(a), (II)-(b), (III)- (d), (IV)- (c), (V)-(e)

(B) (I)-(d), (II)- (a), (III)-(b), (IV)- (c), (V)-(e)

(C) (I)-(d), (II)- (a), (III)-(b), (IV)-(e), (V)-(c)

(D) (I)- (e), (II)- (d), (III)- (a), (IV)-(b), (V)-(b)

Ans. (B) (I)-(d), (II)- (a), (III)-(b), (IV)- (c), (V)-(e).

48. Which ratio indicates the proportion of assets financed out of shareholders' funds?

(A) Debt equity ratio

(B) Fixed assets turnover ratio

(C) Proprietary ratio

(D) Total assets to debt ratio

Ans. (C) Proprietary ratio.

Section – B

Instructions:

> *From question number 49 to 55, attempt any 6 questions.*

49. If Total sales is ₹ 2,50,000 and credit sales is 25% of Cash sales. The amount of credit sales is:

(A) ₹ 50,000   (B) ₹ 2,50,000   (C) ₹ 16,000   (D) ₹ 3,00,000

Ans. (A) ₹ 50,000

> **Explanation:**
>
> Total Sales = ₹ 2,50,000
>
> Credit Sales = 25% of Cash Sales
>
> Let Cash Sales be x
>
> Total Sales = Credit Sales + Cash Sales
>
> 2,50,000 = 25% of $x + x$
>
> 2,50,000 = 1.25 x
>
> $$x = \frac{2,50,000}{1.25} = 2,00,000$$
>
> Cash Sales = ₹ 2,00,000
>
> ∴   Credit Sales = 25% of ₹ 2,00,000 = ₹ 50,000

50. What will be the amount of gross profit of a firm if its average inventory is ₹ 80,000, Inventory turnover ratio is 6 times, and the Selling price is 25% above cost?

(A) ₹ 1,20,000   (B) ₹ 1,60,000   (C) ₹ 2,00,000   (D) None of these

Ans. (A) ₹ 1,20,000

Explanation:

$$\text{Inventory Turnover Ratio} = \frac{\text{Cost of Revenue from Operations}}{\text{Average Inventory}}$$

$$6 = \frac{\text{Cost of Revenue from Operations}}{80,000}$$

Cost of Revenue from Operations = 80,000 × 6 = ₹ 4,80,000

Selling price is 25% above cost, so gross profit percent is 25%.

$$\text{Gross Profit} = 4,80,000 \times \frac{25}{100} = ₹ 1,20,000$$

51. Which of the following statements are false?
    (a) When all the comparative figures in a balance sheet are stated as percentage of the total, it is termed as horizontal analysis.
    (b) When financial statements of several years are analysed, it is termed as vertical analysis.
    (c) Vertical Analysis is also termed as time series analysis.

    Choose from the following options:
    (A) Both (a) and (b)
    (B) Both (a) and (c)
    (C) Both (b) and (c)
    (D) All three (a), (b), (c)

Ans. (D) All three (a), (b), (c)

Explanation: In vertical analysis all the comparative figures in a balance sheet are stated as percentage of the total. In horizontal analysis financial statements of several years are analysed and it is also termed as time series analysis, as it ascertain the trend and changes in an item over time.

52. Given below are two statements, one labelled as Assertion (A) and the other labelled as Reason (R):

    Assertion (A): Increasing the value of closing inventory increases profit.

    Reason (R): Increasing the value of closing inventory reduces cost of goods sold.

    In the context of the above two statements, which of the following is correct?

    Codes:
    (A) Both (A) and (R) are correct and (R) is the correct reason of (A)
    (B) Both (A) and (R) are correct but (R) is not the correct reason of (A)
    (C) Only (R) is correct
    (D) Both (A) and (R) are wrong

Ans. (A) Both (A) and (R) are correct and (R) is the correct reason of (A).

Explanation: Increase in value of closing inventory increases the profit and at the same time decreases the cost of goods sold.

53. Given below are two statements, one labelled as Assertion (A) and the other labelled as Reason (R):

    Assertion (A): A high operating ratio indicates a favourable position.

    Reasoning (R): A high operating ratio leaves a high margin to meet non-operating expenses.

    In the context of the above two statements, which of the following is correct?

    Codes:
    (A) (A) and (R) both are correct and (R) correctly explains (A)
    (B) Both (A) and (R) are correct but (R) does not explain (A)
    (C) Both (A) and (R) are incorrect
    (D) (A) is correct but (R) is incorrect

Ans. (C) Both (A) and (R) are incorrect.

Explanation: A high operating ratio indicates that the expenses are more than the company's ability to generate sufficient revenue and it may be considered inefficient. And a high operating ratio leaves low margin to meet non-operating expenses.

54. Current ratio of Adaar Ltd. is 2.5:1. Accountant wants to maintain it at 2:1. Following options are available.
    (i)   He can repay Bills Payable
    (ii) He can purchase goods on credit
    (iii) He can take short-term loan
    Choose the correct option:
    (A) Only (i) is correct   (B) Only (ii) is correct
    (C) Only (i) and (iii) are correct   (D) Only (ii) and (iii) are correct

Ans. (D) Only (ii) and (iii) are correct

Explanation: Repay of Bills Payable will decrease the current assets and current liabilities with same amount, as a result current ratio will get improved. Purchase goods on credit will increase the current assets and current liabilities with the same amount, as a result current ratio will get reduced. Short-term loan taken will increase the current assets and current liabilities with the same amount, as a result current ratio will get reduced.

55. A company has an operating cycle of eight months. It has accounts receivables amounting to ₹ 1,00,000 out of which ₹ 60,000 have a maturity period of 11 months. How would this information be presented in the balance sheet?
    (A) ₹ 40,000 as current assets and ₹ 60,000 as non-current assets
    (B) ₹ 60,000 as current assets and ₹ 40,000 as non-current assets
    (C) ₹ 1,00,000 as non-current assets
    (D) ₹ 1,00,000 as Current assets

Ans. (D) ₹ 1,00,000 as Current assets.

Explanation: Expected receipt period of ₹ 60,000 is more than operating cycle but it is receivable within 12 months, so accounts receivables amounting to ₹ 1,00,000 will be presented in the Balance Sheet as Current Assets.

❑❑

Sample Paper 1

Accountancy

PART – I

Section – A

Instructions:

> *From question number 1 to 18, attempt any 15 questions.*

1. Which step is not involved in valuing the goodwill according to super profit method:
   - (a) Ascertain Average Profit
   - (b) Ascertain Super Profit
   - (c) Ascertain Normal Profit
   - (d) Multiply Super Profit with Number of years purchased

2. Maximum limit of premium on shares is :
   - (a) 32%
   - (b) 20%
   - (c) No limit
   - (d) 100%

3. Any change in the relationship of existing partners which results in an end of the existing agreement and enforces making of new agreement is called:
   - (a) Revaluation of partnership
   - (b) Reconstitution of partnership
   - (c) Realisation of partnership
   - (d) None of these

4. Balance Sheet prepared after new partnership agreement, assets and liabilities are recorded at:
   - (a) Revalued Figure
   - (b) Original value
   - (c) At realisable value
   - (d) None of these

5. The Need of revaluation of assets and liabilities on admission.
   - (a) Assets and Liabilities should appears at revised values
   - (b) Any profit and loss on account of change in values belong to old partners
   - (c) All unrecorded assets and liabilities get recorded
   - (d) None of the above

6. Actual number of shares offered to the public by the company for subscription is known as :
   - (a) Authorised Capital
   - (b) Subscribed Capital
   - (c) Issued Capital
   - (d) Paid-up Capital

7. A and B are partners in a firm sharing profits in 3 : 2 ratio . They admitted C as a new partner and the new profit sharing ratio will be 2 : 1 : 1 C brought in ₹ 40,000 as premium for goodwill for its share. What will be the journal entry for the premium of goodwill shared by old partners as per sacrificing ratio?

   (a)
	Dr.	40,000	
Premium for Goodwill A/c			
To A's Capital A/c			16,000
To B's Capital A/c			24,000

   (b)
A's Capital A/c	Dr.	16,000	
B's Capital A/c	Dr.	24,000	
To Premium for Goodwill A/c			40,000

   (c)
Premium for Goodwill A/c	Dr.	40,000	
To Bank A/c			40,000

   (d)
Bank A/c	Dr.	40,000	
To Premium for Goodwill A/c			40,000

8. Shares issued at more than face value:

   Following options are available:
   - (i) At discount
   - (ii) At premium
   - (iii) At par

Choose the correct option:

(a) Only (i) is correct

(b) Only (ii) is correct

(c) Only (i) and (ii) are correct

(d) Only (ii) and (iii) are correct

9. A, B and C share profits and losses in the ratio of 3 : 2 : 1. D is admitted with 1/6 share which he gets entirely from A. What will be the new ratio?

(a) 2 : 2 : 1 : 1   (b) 3 : 1 : 1 : 1   (c) 2 : 2 : 2 : 1   (d) None of these

10. In which of the following case, revaluation account is debited?

(a) When there is a increase in value of asset   (b) When there is a decrease in value of asset

(c) When there is a decrease in value of liability   (d) When there is a no change in value of assets

11. One of the partners (Mr. Dev) in a partnership firm has withdrawn ₹ 4,500 at the end of each quarter. Interest on his drawings is to be calculated at the rate of 6% per annum. Interest on his drawings will be________________.

(a) ₹ 810   (b) ₹ 400   (c) ₹ 405   (d) ₹ 304

12. Anthony Ltd. issued 40,000 equity shares of ₹ 20 each payable as ₹ 5 on application; ₹ 7 on allotment and ₹ 8 on final call. Company received the due amount but one shareholder holding 250 shares did not pay the allotment money and another shareholder holding 150 shares failed to pay the amount due on final call. Total amount of calls-in-arrears is:

(a) ₹ 1,750   (b) ₹ 3,200   (c) ₹ 6,000   (d) ₹ 4,950

13. If the new partner does not brings in his share of goodwill in cash so which account will be debited?

(a) Current A/c   (b) Capital A/c   (c) Revaluation A/c   (d) Balance Sheet

14. Partner's capital account are opened when their capital accounts are:

Following options are available:

(i) Fixed   (ii) Fluctuating

(iii) Both (i) and (ii)   (iv) None of these

Choose the correct option:

(a) Only (i) is correct   (b) Only (ii) is correct

(c) Only (iii) is correct   (d) Only (iv) is correct

15. What is Product Method?

Following options are available:

(i) Amount of drawing is uniform.

(ii) Amount of drawing is irregular.

(iii) Time intervals between the two drawings is also uniform.

Choose the correct option:

(a) Only (i) is correct   (b) Only (ii) is correct

(c) Only (i) and (ii) are correct   (d) Only (ii) and (iii) are correct

16. Green Ltd. had allotted 10,000 shares to the applicants of 14,000 shares on pro-rata basis. The amount payable on application is ₹ 2 per share. Mohan applied for 420 shares. The number of shares allotted to Mohan are:

(a) 60 shares   (b) 320 shares   (c) 340 shares   (d) 300 shares

17. Admission of a new partner:

Following options are available:

(i) With the consent of any existing partner

(ii) With the consent of all partners

(iii) With the consent of majority of existing partners

Choose the correct option:

(a) Only (i) is correct   (b) Only (ii) is correct

(c) Only (iii) is correct   (d) Only (i) and (ii) are correct

18. Which of the following statement is correct?

    (i) A company is legal entity quite distinct from its members.

    (ii) A company can buy its own share.

    (iii) A shareholder is the agent of the company.

    (iv) Same person can be agent and creditor of the company.

    (a) (i), (ii), (iii) are correct   (b) (iii), (iv), (i) are correct

    (c) (i), (ii), (iv) are correct   (d) All are correct

Section – B

Instructions:

> ➢ *From question number 19 to 36, attempt any 15 questions:*

19. On admission of a partner, which of the following items the Balance Sheet is transferred to the credit of Capital Accounts of old partners in the old Profit-sharing Ratio, if Capital Accounts are maintained following Fluctuating Capital Accounts Method.

    (a) Deferred Revenue Expenditure

    (b) Profit and Loss Account (Debit Balance)

    (c) Profit and Loss Account (Credit Balance)

    (d) Balance in Drawings Account of Partners

20. Current Accounts of the partners are opened:

    (a) When capital are fluctuating   (b) When capital are fixed

    (c) When fresh capital is introduced   (d) Whether capitals are fluctuating or fixed

21. Given below are two statements, one labelled as Assertion (A) and the other labelled as Reason (R).

    Assertion (A): Increase in value of assets is debited to revaluation account.

    Reason (R): Revaluation account is credited on increase in value of plant and machinery.

    Codes:

    (a) (A) is correct, but (R) is wrong   (b) Both (A) and (R) are correct

    (c) (A) is wrong, but (R) is correct   (d) Both (A) and (R) are wrong

22. At the time of reissue of all forfeited shares:

    (a) General reserve is debited with the credit balance left in the forfeited shares account

    (b) General reserve is credited with the credit balance left in the forfeited shares account

    (c) Capital reserve is debited with the credit balance left in the forfeited shares account

    (d) Capital reserve is credited with the credit balance left in the forfeited shares account

23. Virat and Anushka are partners in a firm sharing profit and losses in 2 : 1 ratio. Their capital balance were ₹ 10,00,000 and ₹ 8,00,000 respectively. The firm made profits during the year amounting to ₹ 3,45,000. Both partners are allowed salary of ₹ 2,500 per month. Interest on capital is allowed @ 5% on capital balance.

    Calculate Closing balance of capital for Virat and Anushka.

    (a) V = ₹ 12,10,000, A = ₹ 9,35,000   (b) V = ₹ 12,35,000, A = ₹ 9,10,000

    (c) V = 13,10,000, A = ₹ 9, 85,000   (d) None of these

24. X Ltd. forfeited 500 shares of ₹ 10 each, ₹ 7 called up, issued at a premium of ₹ 2 per share to be paid at the time of allotment for non-payment of first call of ₹ 2 per share. Entry on forfeiture will be:

			₹	₹
(a) Share Capital A/c	Dr.		3,500	
Securities Premium Reserve A/c	Dr.		1,000	
To Share First Call A/c				1,000
To Share Forfeiture A/c				3,500
(b) Share Capital A/c	Dr.		4,500	
Securities Premium Reserve A/c	Dr.		1,000	
To Share First Call A/c				1,000
To Share Forfeiture A/c				4,500

(c) Share Capital A/c	Dr.	4,500	
To Share First Call A/c			1,000
To Share Forfeiture A/c			3,500
(d) Share Capital A/c	Dr.	3,500	
To Share First Call A/c			1,000
To Share Forfeiture A/c			2,500

25. Given below are two statements, one labelled as Assertion (A) and the other labelled as Reason (R):

    Assertion (A): Operating ratio establishes the relationship between Operating profit and Revenue from operations.

    Reason (R): Operating ratio establishes the relationship between Operating Cost (Cost of revenue from operations + operating expenses) and Revenue from operations.

    Codes:

    (a) Both (A) and (R) are correct and (R) is the correct reason of (A)

    (b) Both (A) and (R) are correct but (R) is not the correct reason of (A)

    (c) Only (R) is correct

    (d) Both (A) and (R) are wrong

26. A company forfeited the following shares:

    200 shares of ₹ 10 each, called up ₹ 9 per share, paid up ₹ 7 per share. Journal entry for forfeiture will be:

    Share Capital A/c   Dr.   ₹ X

    To Share Forfeiture A/c   ₹ Y

    To Calls in Arrear A/c   ₹ Z

    Here X, Y and Z are:

    (a) ₹ 1600, ₹ 1,000, ₹ 600 respectively   (b) ₹ 2,000, ₹ 1,000, ₹ 1,000 respectively

    (c) ₹ 1800, ₹ 1,400, ₹ 400 respectively   (d) ₹ 1,800, ₹ 1,000, ₹ 800 respectively

27. **Sajal and Kajal are partners sharing profits and losses in the ratio of 2 : 1. On 1st April, 2018 their Capitals were: Sajal – ₹ 50,000 and Kajal – ₹ 40,000.**

    (i)   Interest on Capital is to be allowed @ 5% p.a.

    (ii) Interest on the loan advanced by Kajal for the whole year, the amount of loan being ₹ 30,000.

    (iii) Interest on partners' drawings @ 6% p.a. Drawings: Sajal ₹ 10,000 and Kajal ₹ 8,000.

    (iv) 10% of the divisible profit is to be transferred to Reserve.

    Net profit for the year ended 31st March, 2019 is ₹ 68,460. What amount of profit will be credited to Profit & Loss Appropriation A/c?

    (a) ₹ 68,460   (b) ₹ 66,660

    (c) ₹ 58,050   (d) ₹ 60,390

28. **Reya, Mona and Nisha shared profits in the ratio of 3 : 2 : 1. The profits for the last three year were ₹ 1,40,000; ₹ 84,000 and ₹ 1,06,000 respectively. These profits were by mistake shared equally to all, Journal entry for the same will be.**

(a)

Particulars		L/f	₹	₹
Nisha's Capital A/c	Dr.		55,000	
To Reya's Capital A/c				55,000
(Being adjustment entry passed)				

(b)

Particulars		L/f	₹	₹
Reya's Capital A/c	Dr.		55,000	
To Nisha's Capital A/c				55,000
(Being adjustment entry passed)				

(c)

Particulars		L/f	₹	₹
Mona's Capital A/c	Dr.		1,10,000	
Nisha's Capital A/c	Dr.		55,000	
To Reya's Capital A/c				1,65,000
(Being adjustment entry passed)				

(d)

Particulars		L/f	₹	₹
Nisha's Current A/c	Dr.		55,000	
To Reya's Current A/c				55,000
(Being adjustment entry passed)				

29. In case of change in profit sharing ratio, when revised values are not to be recorded in the books, then steps to be followed are:

(i)   Calculation of the net effect of revaluation.

(ii) To find share of sacrifice/(gain) by partners.

(iii) Calculation of proportional amount of net effect of revaluation.

(iv) Pass a single adjustment entry.

(a) (ii)-(iii)-(iv)-(i)   (b) (iii)-(ii)-(iv)-(i)   (c) (iv)-(iii)-(ii)-(i)   (d) None of these

30. The Earth Ltd. invited applications for 35,000 shares of ₹ 10 each and received applications for 40,000 shares along with the application money ₹ 4 per share.

Which of the following alternatives can be followed?

Following options are available:

(i)   Refund of excess application money and full allotment to the rest of the applicants.

(ii) Not to allot any share to some applicants, Full allotment to some applicants and pro-rata allotment to rest of the applicants.

(iii) Not to allot any shares to some applicants and pro-rata allotment to rest of the applicants.

(iv) Make pro-rata allotment to all the applicants and adjust the excess amount received towards call money.

Choose the correct option:

(a) Only (i)   (b) Both (i) and (iii)   (c) Only (ii)   (d) All of these

31. Given below are two statements, one labelled as Assertion (A) and the other labelled as Reason (R):

Assertion (A): Premium received on issue of shares, is credited to share premium account but not to Profit and Loss Account.

Reason (R): Since share premium is not a trading profit, it is not distributed to shareholders.

Codes:

(a) Both (A) and (R) are true, but (R) is not the explanation of (A)

(b) Both(A) and (R) are true and (R) is a correct explanation of (A)

(c) Both (A) and (R) are false

(d) (A) is false, but (R) is true

32. Ruchi, Pankaj & Tanmay are partners sharing profits and losses equally. Their Balance Sheet as at 31st March, 2021 stood as follows :

Liabilities		₹	Assets	₹
Sundry Creditors		140,000	Bank	75,000
Reserves & Surplus		60,000	Debtors	1,50,000
	₹		Copyrights	1,50,000
Capital	2,50,000		Stock	1,25,000
Ruchi	2,00,000		Land & Building	2,00,000
Pankaj	1,50,000	600,000	Machinery	1,00,000
Tanmay				
		8,00,000		8,00,000

From 1st April, 2021, the partners decide to share profits and losses in the Ratio of 3 : 2 : 1 and for that purpose the following revised value of assets were agreed upon:

(a) Land & Buildings ₹ 2,75,000/-,

(b) Machinery ₹ 90,000/-

(c) Copyrights ₹ 1,32,500/-,

(d) Stock ₹ 2,00,000/-,

(e) Prepaid Insurance ₹ 5,000/-, and

(f) Debtors ₹ 1,42,500/-

(g) Goodwill of the firm was valued at ₹ 60,000/-

Partners decided not to disturb the Reserves. What will be amount of Revaluation Profit or Gain.

(a) Loss on Revaluation ₹ 2,40,000

(b) Gain on Revaluation ₹ 1,20,000

(c) Gain on Revaluation ₹ 2,40,000

(d) Loss on Revaluation ₹ 1,20,000

33. S.K Ltd. invited application for 10,000 Equity Shares of ₹ 10 each. Applications were received for 15,000 shares and pro-rata allotment was made to all the applicants. If Mohan (one shareholder) was allotted 80 shares, find the shares applied by him.

(a) 80

(b) 100

(c) 150

(d) 120

34. A, B & C are partners sharing profit and losses in the ratio of 3 : 2 : 1. On 31st March they decided to share the profit and losses equally in future.

Balance Sheet			
Liabilities	₹	Assets	₹
Investment Fluctuation Reserve	12,000	Investments	1,00,000

Market value of Investment is ₹ 94,000/- what amount will be Credited/Debited to partner's Capital a/c?

(a) Investment Fluctuation Reserve Credited as ₹ 3,000 : ₹ 2,000 : ₹ 1,000

(b) Investment Fluctuation Reserve Debited as 3,000 : ₹ 2,000 : ₹ 1,000

(c) It will not be Debited to Capital A/c

(d) It will not be Credited to Capital A/c

35. A and B are partners sharing profits and losses in the ratio of 3 : 1. They admit C for 1/4th share in the future profits. The new profit sharing ratio will be :

(a) $A\frac{9}{16}, B\frac{3}{16}, C\frac{4}{16}$

(b) $A\frac{8}{16}, B\frac{4}{16}, C\frac{4}{16}$

(c) $A\frac{10}{16}, B\frac{2}{16}, C\frac{4}{16}$

(d) $A\frac{8}{16}, B\frac{9}{16}, C\frac{10}{16}$

36. A company issued 25,000 shares and received applications for 35,000 shares. Company wants to allot shares to everyone who has applied. What will be the ratio for allotment?

(a) 6 : 7

(b) 7 : 5

(c) 5 : 7

(d) 7 : 6

Section – C

Instructions:

➢ *From question number 37 to 41, attempt any 4 questions.*

Question no.'s 37 and 38 are based on the hypothetical situation given below.

Shivam, Paresh and Hariam are partners in a firm manufacturing furniture. They have been sharing profits and losses in the ratio of 5 : 3 : 2. From 1st April, 2018 they decided to share future profits and losses in the ratio of 2 : 5 : 3. Their balance sheet showed a debit balance of ₹ 12,000 in Workmen's Compensation Reserve. it was agreed that the goodwill of the firm be valued at ₹ 76,000. The stock (book balue of ₹ 40,000) was to depreciated by 8%. Creditors amounting to ₹ 900 were not likely to be claimed. Claim on Account of Workmen's Compensation amounted to ₹ 20,000. Investments (book value ₹ 38,000) were revalued at ₹ 40,000. Based on above information you are required to answer the following questions:

37. Loss on revaluation will be:

(a) ₹ 9,300

(b) ₹ 6,300

(c) ₹ 7,300

(d) ₹ 8,300

38. Shivam sacrificing ratio will be:

(a) 4/5

(b) 2/10

(c) 3/10

(d) 1/10

Question no.'s 39, 40 and 41 are based on the hypothetical situation given below.

X Ltd. is a reputed company invited application of 20,000 shares of ₹ 10 each payable as under ₹ 3 per share on Application; ₹ 3 per on Allotment; ₹ 2 per share on First Call; and balance on Final Call.

Prakriti an applicant of 100 shares failed to pay allotment money and first call money due from him. Rest of money is duely received.

39. What will be the amount received on share allotment?

   (a) ₹ 59,700   (b) ₹ 59,800   (c) ₹ 59,600   (d) ₹ 59,500

40. What will be the total amount (including allotment and first call) of calls in arrear?

   (a) ₹ 500   (b) ₹ 700   (c) ₹ 600   (d) ₹ 800

41. What will be the amount due on final call ?

   (a) ₹ 39,700   (b) ₹ 39,800   (c) ₹ 39,900   (d) ₹ 40,000

PART – II

Section – A

Instructions:

> *From question number 42 to 48, attempt any 5 questions.*

42. Given below are two statements, one labelled as Assertion (A) and the other labelled as Reason (R):

Assertion (A): Bills receivable is shown as trade receivable in the balance sheet.

Reason (R): Trade receivable include both debtors and bills receivable.

Codes:

(a) Both (A) and (R) are true, but (R) is not the explanation of (A).

(b) Both(A) and (R) are true and (R) is a correct explanation of (A).

(c) Both (A) and (R) are false.

(d) (A) is false, but (R) is true.

43. Which of the following capital is not shown in the company's Balance Sheet?

   (a) Authorised capital   (b) Issued & subscribed capital

   (c) Called-up & paid up-capital   (d) Reserve capital

44. Fixed assets of a company are increased from ₹ 3,00,000 to ₹ 4,00,000. What is the percentage change?

   (a) 25%   (b) 33.3%

   (c) 20%   (d) 40%

45. Higher the ratio, the more favourable it is, doesn't stands true for:

   (a) Operating ratio   (b) Liquidity ratio

   (c) Net profit ratio   (d) Stock turnover ratio

46. Which of the following analysis is considered as dynamic?

   (a) Horizontal   (b) Vertical

   (c) Internal   (d) External

47. Current Ratio of Vidur Pvt. Ltd. is 3 : 2. Accountant wants to maintain it at 2 : 1.

Following options are available:

(i) He can repay Bills Payable

(ii) He can purchase goods on credit

(iii) He can take short term loan

Choose the correct option:

   (a) Only (i) is correct   (b) Only (ii) is correct

   (c) Only (i) and (ii) are correct   (d) Only (ii) and (iii) are correct

48. Claim against the company not acknowledged as debts' is shown under:

   (a) Current Liabilities   (b) Contingent Liabilities

   (c) Non-current Liabilities   (d) Capital Commitments

Section - B

Instructions:
> ➤ *From question number 49 to 55, attempt any 6 questions.*

49. At the time of forfeiture of shares, share capital is debited with.

Following options are available:

(i) Amount received   (ii) Amount not received   (iii) Amount demanded

Choose the correct option:

(a) Only (i) is correct   (b) Only (ii) is correct   (c) Only (iii) is correct   (d) None of these

50. From the following information, you are required to compute profit after tax.

I.	Revenue from operation	= ₹ 80,00,000
II.	Cost of material consumed	= ₹ 10,00,000
III.	Purchase of stock-in-trade	= ₹ 30,00,000
IV.	Employees salary	= ₹ 4,00,000
V.	Tax rate	= 50%

(a) ₹ 20,00,000   (b) ₹ 24,00,000   (c) ₹ 15,00,000   (d) ₹ 18,00,000

51. Given below are two statements, one labelled as Assertion (A) and the other labelled as Reason (R):

Assertion (A): Reserve Capital is part of Share Capital that a company resolves not to call at any time it desires.

Reason (R): Reserve capital is a part of the Subscribed Capital that a company resolves, by a Special Resolution, not to call except in the event of Winding up of the Company.

Codes:

(a) Both (A) and (R) are correct and (R) is the correct reason of (A)

(b) Both (A) and (R) are correct but (R) is not the correct reason of (A)

(c) Only (R) is correct

(d) Both (A) and (R) are wrong

52. 500 shares on which final call not received.

Following options are available:

(i) Subscribed and fully paid   (ii) Subscribed but not fully paid

(iii) Uncalled capital

Choose the correct option:

(a) Only (i) is correct   (b) Only (ii) is correct

(c) Only (iii) is correct   (d) None of these

53. Given below are two statements, one labelled as Assertion (A) and the other labelled as Reason (R):

Assertion (A): Two persons can set up a business.

Reason (R): They also share the profits and losses equally.

Codes:

(a) (A) and (R) both are correct and (R) correctly explains (A).

(b) Both (A) and (R) are correct but (R) does not explain (A).

(c) Both (A) and (R) are incorrect.

(d) (A) is correct but (R) is incorrect.

54. If Current Ratio of a company is 3 : 2, identify which combination is correct.

(a) Current Assets ₹ 50,000 and Current Liabilities ₹ 50,000

(b) Current Assets ₹ 60,000 and Current Liabilities ₹ 50,000

(c) Current Assets ₹ 90,000 and Current Liabilities ₹ 70,000

(d) Current Assets ₹ 90,000 and Current Liabilities ₹ 60,000

55. Calculating Operating Ratio, if cost of revenue from operations ₹ 50,000, Revenue from operations ₹ 1,50,000 and Operating expenses ₹ 20,000.

(a) 45%   (b) 46.7%   (c) 48.1%   (d) 42.2%

❐❐

Sample Paper 2

Accountancy

PART – I

Section – A

Instructions:

> *From question number 1 to 18, attempt any 15 questions.*

1. Rajan Limited issued 50,000 shares at a price lower than the nominal value of the share. The shares issued are called:
   - (a) Sweat Equity Shares
   - (b) Redeemable Preference Shares
   - (c) Equity Shares
   - (d) Bonus Shares

2. In the event of change in profit sharing ratio, in which ratio the general reserve appearing in the balance sheet is transferred to the partners capital account?
   - (a) Sacrificing ratio
   - (b) Gaining ratio
   - (c) Old profit sharing ratio
   - (d) New profit sharing ratio

3. Interest on call in arrear:
   - (a) 5% per annum
   - (b) 6% per annum
   - (c) 9% per annum
   - (d) No interest

4. The Credit Balance of Profits and Loss appears in the books at the time of admission of partner will be transferred to :
   - (a) Profit and Loss Appropriation Account
   - (b) All Partner's capital Account
   - (c) Old Partner's capital Account
   - (d) Revaluation Account

5. Amount of money not received out of called up capital is :
   - (a) Added to share capital
   - (b) Subtracted from share capital
   - (c) Shown as current liabilities
   - (d) Shown as current asset

6. The ratio in which the continuing partners acquires the outgoing partners share is called:
   - (a) Gaining Ratio
   - (b) New Profit Sharing Ratio
   - (c) Old Profit Sharing Ratio
   - (d) None of these

7. A Company forfeited 4,000 shares of ₹10 each on which application money of ₹3 has been paid. Out of these 2,000 shares were reissued as fully paid up and ₹4,000 has been transferred to capital reserve.

   Calculate the rate at which these shares were reissued.
   - (a) ₹ 10 per share
   - (b) ₹ 9 per share
   - (c) ₹ 11 per share
   - (d) ₹ 8 per share

8. Current Accounts of the partners are opened:
   - (a) When capital are fluctuating
   - (b) When capital are fixed
   - (c) When fresh capital is introduced
   - (d) Whether capitals are fluctuating or fixed

9. A and B are partners sharing in the ratio 2 : 1. They decided to share in the ratio 3 : 2 in future. If the goodwill of the firm is valued at ₹60,000, how the adjustment in the profit will be affected?
   - (a) B pays A ₹4,000
   - (b) A pays B ₹4,000
   - (c) A pays B ₹6,000
   - (d) B pays A ₹6,000

10. Which of the following is not true with respect to Admission of a partner?
    - (a) A new partner can be admitted if it is agreed in the partnership deed.
    - (b) If all the partners agree, a new partner can be admitted.
    - (c) A new partner has to bring relatively higher capital as compared to the existing partners
    - (d) A new partner gets right in the assets of the firm

11. In which a company having at least 7 members?
Following options are available:
(i)   Private company
(ii) Public company
(iii) One person company
Choose the correct option:
(a) Only (i) is correct
(b) Only (ii) is correct
(c) Only (i) and (ii) are correct
(d) Only (ii) and (iii) are correct

12. In case of change in profit-sharing ratio, the accumulated profits are distributed to the partners in:
(a) New ratio
(b) Old ratio
(c) Sacrificing ratio
(d) Equal ratio

13. A Company invited applications for 1,00,000 shares and it received applications for 1,50,000 shares. Applications for 30,000 shares were rejected and the remaining shares were allotted on prorata basis. How many shares an applicant for 3,000 shares will be allotted?
(a) 2,500 Shares
(b) 3,600 Shares
(c) 4,500 Shares
(d) 2,000 Shares

14. If the partnership deed provides for payment of interest on capital of the partners, then interest can be paid only out of:
(a) Accumulated Profits
(b) Past Year's Profits
(c) Current Year's Profits
(d) General Reserve

15. A company issued 10,000 shares of ₹ 10 each. Amount is payable as ₹ 2 on Application, ₹ 5 on Allotment and ₹ 3 on first and final call. A shareholder who had 1,000 shares failed to pay allotment and first call amount on due date. After a month, he paid the due amount. What will be the amount received by company against issue of shares ?
(a) ₹ 92,000
(b) ₹ 90,000
(c) ₹ 1,00,000
(d) ₹ 80,000

16. If a fixed amount is withdrawn by a partner on the first day of every month for how many months interest on the total amount is charged?
(a) 6 months
(b) 6.5 months
(c) 4 months
(d) 12 months

17. Where the following will be shown ₹ 2,00,000 introduced by new partner?
Following options are available:
(i)   Partner's Capital Account
(ii) Balance Sheet
(iii) Profit & Loss Appropriation Account
(iv) Revaluation Account
Choose the correct option:
(a) Only (i) is correct
(b) Only (ii) is correct
(c) Only (i) and (ii) are correct
(d) Only (ii) and (iii) are correct

18. When the new partner brings additional cash other than his capital?
Following options are available:
(i)   Capital
(ii) Profit
(iii) Premium for goodwill
Choose the correct option:
(a) Only (i) is correct
(b) Only (ii) is correct
(c) Only (iii) is correct
(d) Only (i) and (ii) are correct

Section – B

Instructions:

> *From question number 19 to 36, attempt any 15 questions:*

19. Pragya Ltd. forfeited 8,000 equity shares of ₹ 100 each issued at a premium of 10% for non-payment of first and final call of ₹ 30 per share. The maximum amount of discount at which these shares can be reissued will be :
(a) ₹ 80,000
(b) ₹ 3,20,000
(c) ₹ 5,60,000
(d) ₹ 2,40,000

20. If at the time of admission if there is some unrecorded liability, it will be _________ to _________ Account.

    (a) Debited, Revaluation

    (b) Credited, Revaluation

    (c) Debited, Goodwill

    (d) Credited, Partners' Capital

21. When a company issue its share through IPO, it means shares are issued to:

    (a) Promoters

    (b) Creditors

    (c) Vendors

    (d) General Public

22. Given below are two statements, one labelled as Assertion (A) and the other labelled as Reason (R).

Assertion (A): The total capital of a company is divided to form the shares of that firm.

Reason (R): People contributing money via such shares are called shareholders.

Codes:

    (a) (A) is correct, but (R) is wrong

    (b) Both (A) and (R) are correct

    (c) (A) is wrong, but (R) is correct

    (d) Both (A) and (R) are wrong

23. Where are reserves and accumulated profits transferred to partners' capital accounts at the time of reconstitution?

    (a) Old Profit-Sharing Ratio

    (b) Sacrificing Ratio

    (c) Gaining Ratio

    (d) New Profit-Sharing Ratio

24. Pen and Pencil were two partners, they drew for their personal use ₹ 1,20,000 and ₹ 80,000. Interest is chargeable @ 6% p.a. on the drawings. What is the amount of interest chargeable from each partner?

    (a) ₹ 7,200 to Pen; ₹ 4,800 to Pencil.

    (b) ₹ 3,600 to Pen; ₹ 2,400 to Pencil.

    (c) ₹ 3,900 to Pen; ₹ 2,600 to Pencil.

    (d) ₹ 4,500 to Pen; ₹ 3,000 to Pencil.

25. Given below are two statements, one labelled as Assertion (A) and the other labelled as Reason (R):

Assertion (A): Partners create a firm.

Reason (R): These firms do not form any separate legal entities.

Codes:

    (a) Both (A) and (R) are correct and (R) is the correct reason of (A)

    (b) Both (A) and (R) are correct but (R) is not the correct reason of (A)

    (c) Only (R) is correct

    (d) Both (A) and (R) are wrong

26. When partnership deed does not provide interest on capital.

Following options are available:

    (i) Interest on capital is not allowed

    (ii) Interest on capital is allowed in all circumstances

    (iii) Interest on capital is allowed if only profit is their

Choose the correct option:

    (a) Only (i) is correct

    (b) Only (ii) is correct

    (c) Only (i) and (ii) are correct

    (d) Only (ii) and (iii) are correct

27. Issue of shares at discount is not allowed under which section of the Companies Act, 2013?

    (a) Section 52

    (b) Section 53

    (c) Section 54

    (d) Section 55

28. Lappy and Tappy are partners sharing Profit and Loss in the ratio 3 : 2 having Capital Account balances of ₹ 50,000 and ₹ 40,000 on 1st April, 2020. On 1st July, 2020, Lappy introduced ₹ 10,000 as his additional capital where-as Tappy introduced only ₹ 1,000. Interest on capital is allowed to partners @ 10% p.a. Interest on capital for the financial year ended 31st March, 2021 will be:

    (a) ₹ 5,750 for Lappy & ₹ 4,075 for Tappy

    (b) ₹ 5,000 for Lappy & ₹ 4,000 for Tappy.

    (c) ₹ 750 for Lappy & ₹ 75 for Tappy

    (d) None of these.

29. The profits for last 3 years were:

1st year = ₹ 6,000 (including abnormal gain ₹ 2,000)

2nd year = ₹ 4,000 (after charging abnormal loss ₹ 3,000)

3rd year = ₹ 2,500 (including abnormal income ₹ 1,500)

Calculate goodwill on the basis of 3 years' purchase of last 3 years profits and losses.

(a) ₹ 12,500   (b) ₹ 12,000   (c) ₹ 13,000   (d) ₹ 16,000

30. Which of the following are the characteristics of a company?

(i) Liability of the member is limited up to the face value of shares held by them.

(ii) A company is a separate body, can sue and be sued in its own name.

(iii) It is a voluntary association of persons.

(iv) Perpetual Sucession.

(a) (i), (ii), (iii)   (b) (i), (ii), (iv)   (c) (i), (iii), (iv)   (d) All of these

31. Given below are two statements, one labelled as Assertion (A) and the other labelled as Reason (R):

Assertion (A): Profit sharing ratio of all partners always remains constant.

Reason (R): Partners can enjoy this ratio either by contributing or not contributing in the firm's profit margin.

Codes:

(a) Both (A) and (R) are true, but (R) is not the explanation of (A).

(b) Both(A) and (R) are true and (R) is a correct explanation of (A)

(c) Both (A) and (R) are false

(d) (A) is false, but (R) is true

32. A, B & C were partners in the ratio of 3 : 2 : 1. As on 1st April they decided to alter their ratio. For this purpose A decided to give 1/4th share to B, and B decided to give 1/2 share to A & C equally. What will be the new ratio?

(a) 1 : 1 : 1   (b) 6 : 1 : 5   (c) 6 : 5 : 1   (d) 5 : 1 : 6

33. Neha, Nisha and Yamini are partners in a firm sharing profits and losses in the ratio of 5 : 3 : 2. They decided to share future profits and losses in the ratio of 3 : 2 : 1. Each partner's gain or sacrifice due to change in the ratio will be :

(a) Neha Sacrifice-1/30, Nisha Gain-1/30, Yamini-Nil

(b) Neha Gain-1/30, Nisha-Nil, Yamini Sacrifice-1/30

(c) Neha-Nil, Nisha Sacrifice-1/30, Yamini Gain-1/30

(d) Neha-Nil, Nisha Gain-1/30, Yamini Sacrifice-1/30

34. Which of the following is correct?

(i) Interest on calls in advance is 10% p.a.

(ii) Interest on calls in arrear is 12% p.a.

(a) Only I   (b) Only II   (c) Both are correct   (d) Both are incorrect

35. A and B are partners in a firm sharing profits in the ratio of 3 : 2. They admit C into partnership for 1/5th share. C brings ₹ 30,000 as capital and ₹ 10,000 as premium for goodwill. New profit sharing ratio will be 5 : 3 : 2. How much amount of premium is to debited/credited in B's Capital Account?

(a) Debit ₹ 3,000   (b) Credit ₹ 3,000   (c) Debit ₹ 5,000   (d) Credit ₹ 5,000

36. AK and BK are partners in a firm. They admit CK as a partner for 1/4th share in the profits of the firm. CK brings ₹ 2,00,000 as his share of capital. The value of total assets of the firm is ₹ 5,40,000 and outside liabilities are valued at ₹ 1,00,000 on that date. CK's premium share for goodwill:

(a) ₹ 30,000   (b) ₹ 90,000   (c) ₹ 50,000   (d) ₹ 60,000

Section - C

Instructions:

> *From question number 37 to 41, attempt any 4 questions.*

Question no.'s 37 and 38 are based on the hypothetical situation given below.

Pawan Ltd issued ₹10,00,000 new capital divided into ₹100 shares at a premium of ₹20 per share, payable as under:

On Application	₹10	
On Allotment	₹40	(including premium of ₹10 per share)
On First Call and Final	Balance	

Over – payments on application were to be applied towards sums due on allotment and first and final call. Where no allotment was made, money was to be refunded in full.

The issue was oversubscribed to the extent of 13000 shares. Applications for 12000 shares were allotted only 2000 shares and applications for 3000 were sent letters of regret and application money was returned to them.

All the money due was duly received.

37. What will the amount due on share capital?
    (a) ₹1,00,000 (b) ₹1,30,000 (c) ₹2,00,000 (d) ₹1,80,000

38. What amount of money will be credit to bank (returned)?
    (a) ₹30,000 (b) ₹50,000 (c) ₹1,00,000 (d) ₹1,10,000

Question no.'s 39, 40 and 41 are based on the hypothetical situation given below.

Opening Inventory	₹ 3,00,000
Closing Inventory	₹ 4,20,000
Purchases	₹ 14,00,000
Wages	₹ 3,70,000
Carriage Inwards	₹ 1,50,000
Administrative Expenses	₹ 84,000
Selling Expenses	₹ 36,000
Income Tax	₹ 1,00,000
Profit on sale of fixed assets	₹ 20,000
Revenue from operations (Sales)	₹ 2,40,000

Based on above information you are required to answer the following questions:

39. What will the amount received on share first and final call?
    (a) ₹6,20,000 (b) ₹6,80,000 (c) ₹6,60,000 (d) ₹6,40,000

40. Calculate Gross Profit Ratio.
    (a) 20% (b) 30% (c) 40% (d) 25%

41. Calculate Operating Ratio.
    (a) 30% (b) 25% (c) 80% (d) None of these

PART – II

Section – A

Instructions:

> ➢ *From question number 42 to 48, attempt any 5 questions.*

42. Two basic measures of liquidity are:
    (a) Inventory turnover and Current ratio
    (b) Current ratio and Quick ratio
    (c) Gross profit ratio and Operating ratio
    (d) Current ratio and Average Collection Period

43. Given below are two statements, one labelled as Assertion (A) and the other labelled as Reason (R):
    Assertion (A): Liquid ratio reveals strength of liquidity of a business unit.
    Reason (R): Liquid ratio analysis liquid assets and liquid liabilities of a business unit in order to assess the extent of liquidity.
    Codes:
    (a) Both (A) and (R) are true, but (R) is not the explanation of (A).
    (b) Both(A) and (R) are true and (R) is a correct explanation of (A).
    (c) Both (A) and (R) are false.
    (d) (A) is false, but (R) is true.

44. Main Objective of Analysis of Financial Statement is:
    (a) To know the financial strength
    (b) To make a comparative study with other firms
    (c) To know their efficiency of management
    (d) All of these

45. Which of the following is not a part of Finance Cost (in statement of profit and loss)?
    (a) Bank Charges
    (b) Interest paid on Debentures
    (c) Interest paid on Public Deposits
    (d) Loss on issue of Debentures

46. How many major head of the equity and liabilities side of a company's balance sheet are there ?
    (a) two   (b) six   (c) eight   (d) four

47. In which Sub-head "Interest on calls and advance" include?
Following options are available:
(i) Short-term provision
(ii) Other current liability
(iii) Long-term provision
Choose the correct option:
(a) Only (i) is correct   (b) Only (ii) is correct
(c) Only (i) and (ii) are correct   (d) Only (ii) and (iii) are correct

48. From following information, calculate other incomes.

Sales of product = ₹ 54,000
Sale of services = ₹ 60,000
Commission received = ₹ 1,20,000
Dividend from investment = ₹ 20,000

(a) ₹ 1,40,000   (b) ₹ 2,54,000   (c) ₹ (46,000) loss   (d) None of these

Section – B

Instructions:

> *From question number 49 to 55, attempt any 6 questions.*

49. Balance sheet of a company is required to be prepared in the format given in _________.
    (a) Schedule III Part II   (b) Schedule III Part I
    (c) Schedule III Part III   (d) Table A

50. Debt to Equity ratio =
Following options are available:
(i) Debt/Equity
(ii) Debt/Shareholders Fund
(iii) Total Assets/Debt
Choose the correct option:
(a) Only (i) is correct   (b) Only (iii)
(c) Both (i) and (ii) is correct   (d) None of these

51. The quick ratio of a company is 1.5 : 1. State with reason which of the following transactions would:
(i) increase the ratio (ii) decrease the ratio (iii) not change the ratio.
(A) Paid rent ₹ 3,000 in advance.
(B) Trade receivable included a debtor Shri Ashok who paid his entire amount due ₹ 9,700.
(a) (i) and (ii)   (b) (ii) and (iii)   (c) (i) and (iii)   (d) All of these

52. Assuming that the current ratio is 2 : 1 purchase of goods on credit would:
(a) Increase current ratio   (b) Decrease current ratio
(c) No effect on current ratio   (d) Decrease gross profit ratio

53. Given below are two statements, one labelled as Assertion (A) and the other labelled as Reason (R):
Assertion (A): The basic and formal annual reports are termed as financial statements.
Reason (R): It is used for the communication among the owners of the company and the external parties who invest in it.
Codes:
(a) Both (A) and (R) are correct and (R) is the correct reason of (A)
(b) Both (A) and (R) are correct but (R) is not the correct reason of (A)
(c) Only (R) is correct
(d) Both (A) and (R) are wrong

54. Activity Ratio also known as:
   (i)   Performance Ratio
   (ii) Turnover Ratio
   (iii) Operating Ratio
   Choose the correct option:
   (a) Only (i) is correct
   (b) Only (iii) is correct
   (c) Both (i) and (ii) is correct
   (d) None of these

55. Given below are two statements, one labelled as Assertion (A) and the other labelled as Reason (R):

Assertion: Tanmay Ltd. has a Proprietary Ratio of 25% to maintain this ratio at 30%, management may increase the current assets.

Reason: To increase the proprietary ratio the management may increase equity or reduce the debts increase of current asset will increase the ratio.

Code:
   (a) (A) and (R) both are correct and (R) correctly explains (A)
   (b) Both (A) and (R) are correct but (R) does not explain (A)
   (c) Both (A) and (R) are incorrect
   (d) (A) is correct but (R) is incorrect

□□

Sample Paper 3

Accountancy

PART – I

Section – A

Instructions:

> *From question number 1 to 18, attempt any 15 questions.*

1. Capital employed in a business is ₹2,00,000. Normal rate of return on capital employed is 15%. During the year, the firm earned a profit of ₹48,000. Calculate goodwill on the basis of 3 years purchase of super profit.
   - (a) ₹54,000
   - (b) ₹60,000
   - (c) ₹50,000
   - (d) None of these

2. Which of the following statement is false?
   - (a) A shareholder is the agent of the company.
   - (b) A company is a legal entity quite distinct from its members.
   - (c) A company can buy its own share.
   - (d) Same person can be agent and creditor of the company.

3. If the new partner brings any additional amount of cash other than his capital contribution then it is termed as :
   - (a) Capital
   - (b) Reserves
   - (c) Profits
   - (d) Premium for Goodwill

4. In case of change in profit-sharing ratio, the accumulated profits are distributed to the partners in:
   - (a) New Ratio
   - (b) Old Ratio
   - (c) Sacrificing Ratio
   - (d) Equal Ratio

5. Workmen Compensation Reserve stands at ₹72,000 at the time of admission of Z, and there is claim of ₹48,000 against it. The firm has two partners X and Y. Journal Entry will be :

		₹	₹
(a) Workmen Compensation Reserve A/c	Dr.	72,000	
To X's Capital A/c			36,000
To Y's Capital A/c			36,000
(b) Workmen Compensation Reserve A/c	Dr.	72,000	
To Workmen Compensation Claim A/c			48,000
To X's Capital A/c			12,000
To Y's Capital A/c			12,000
(c) X's Capital A/c	Dr.	36,000	
Y's Capital A/c	Dr.	36,000	
To Workmen Compensation Reserve A/c			72,000
(d) X's Capital A/c	Dr.	72,000	
To Y's Capital A/c			72,000

6. When nominal (face) value of a share is called up by the company, but as some shareholders did not pay the money, the shares are forfeited. The share capital is shown in the Balance Sheet (notes) of a company under the following heading:
   - (a) Subscribed and fully paid-up
   - (b) Subscribed but not fully paid-up
   - (c) Subscribed and called-up
   - (d) Subscribed but not called-up

7. A, B and C are partners sharing profits and losses in 5 : 4 : 1. On 1st April, 2020, they decided to share profits is 3 : 4 : 3. Which partner has sacrified his share?
   - (a) A sacrifice $\frac{1}{5}$
   - (b) B sacrifice $\frac{1}{5}$
   - (c) C sacrifice $\frac{1}{5}$
   - (d) None of these

8. A, B and C were partners in the ratio of 3 : 2 : 1. As on 1st April, they decided to share equally in future. What will be the Sacrificing or the Gaining Ratio?
   (a) Sacrifice A 1/6; B's Sacrifice Nil; C's Gain 1/6
   (b) Gain A 1/6; B's Sacrifice Nil; C's Sacrifice 1/6
   (c) Sacrifice A 1/3; B's Sacrifice 1/3; C's Gain 1/6
   (d) Sacrifice A 1/6; B's Sacrifice 1/3; C's Gain 1/3

9. P and Q are partners with a capital of ₹30,000 and ₹20,000 respectively. They are allowed interest @ 10% on the total capital. Interest allowed to P and Q will be:
   (a) ₹1,500, ₹1,000   (b) ₹3,000, ₹2,000   (c) ₹2,000, ₹3,000   (d) ₹1,000, ₹1,000

10. Interest on call in arrear:
    (a) 5% per annum   (b) 6% per annum   (c) 9% per annum   (d) No interest

11. In which ratio the general reserve existing in the Balance Sheet is transferred to capital accounts of partners in the event of change in profit sharing ratio?
    (a) Sacrificing ratio   (b) Gaining ratio
    (c) Old profit sharing ratio   (d) New profit sharing ratio

12. These shares which in addition to the fixed preference dividend, carry a right to participate in the surplus profits, if any, after dividend at a stipulated rate has been paid to the equity shareholders are called__________.
    (a) Participating preference shares   (b) Convertible preference shares
    (c) Redeemable preference shares   (d) Cumulative preference shares

13. Where will be the balance of Workmen Compensation Reserve transferred to at the time of admission of a new partner?
    (a) Old partners capital accounts in the old profit sharing ratio
    (b) Sacrificing partners capital accounts in the sacrificing ratio
    (c) Revaluation Account
    (d) All partners capital accounts in the new profit sharing ratio

14. What is Product Method?
    Following options are available:
    (i) Amount of drawing is uniform.
    (ii) Amount of drawing is irregular.
    (iii) Time intervals between the two drawings is also uniform.
    Choose the correct option:
    (a) Only (i) is correct   (b) Only (ii) is correct
    (c) Only (i) and (ii) are correct   (d) Only (ii) and (iii) are correct

15. If drawings of equal amount are made in the beginning of every month for 9 months ending 31st March, what will be the average period for which the interest on drawing will be calculated?
    (a) 5 months   (b) 6 months   (c) 4 months   (d) 12 months

16. When shares are forfeited which account is debited?
    Following options are available:
    (i) Share Capital A/c   (ii) Share Forfeiture A/c   (iii) Capital Reserve A/c
    Choose the correct option:
    (a) Only (i) is correct   (b) Only (ii) is correct
    (c) Only (iii) is correct   (d) Only (i) and (ii) are correct

17. What type of account is Revaluation Account?
    (a) Real   (b) Nominal   (c) Personal   (d) Liability

18. A company forfeited 4,000 shares of ₹ 10 each on which application money of ₹ 3 has been paid. Out of these 2,000 shares were re-issued as fully paid up and ₹ 4,000 has been transferred to capital reserve. Calculate the rate at which these shares were re-issued.
    (a) ₹ 10 per share   (b) ₹ 9 per share   (c) ₹ 11 per share   (d) ₹ 8 per share

Section - B

Instructions:

> *From question number 19 to 36, attempt any 15 questions:*

19. When the new partner brings additional cash other than his capital, it is:

    Following options are available:

    (i) Capital   (ii) Profit   (iii) Premium for goodwill

    Choose the correct option:

    (a) Only (i) is correct   (b) Only (ii) is correct

    (c) Only (iii) is correct   (d) Only (i) and (ii) are correct

20. When shares are forfeited, the Share Capital Account is debited with _______ and the Share Forfeiture Account is credited with _______.

    (a) Paid-up capital of shares forfeited; Called up capital of shares forfeited.

    (b) Called-up capital of shares forfeited; Calls-in-arrears of shares forfeited.

    (c) Called-up capital of shares forfeited; Amount received on shares forfeited.

    (d) Calls-in-arrears of shares forfeited; Amount received on shares forfeited.

21. When interest on drawing is charged by firm.

    Following options are available:

    (i) Credited to Partners' Capital A/c

    (ii) Debited to Partners' Capital A/c

    (iii) Debited to profit and Loss A/c

    Choose the correct option:

    (a) Only (i) is correct   (b) Only (ii) is correct

    (c) Only (iii) is correct   (d) None of these

22. Voluntary return of shares for cancellation by the shareholders is called:

    (a) Cancellation of shares   (b) Forfeiture of shares

    (c) Surrender of shares   (d) None of these

23. Given below are two statements, one labelled as Assertion (A) and the other labelled as Reason (R).

    Assertion (A): New partners compensate for the share of loss by the the old partners.

    Reason (R): It is the sacrifice done by the new partner as a result of which, it is denoted as sacrificing ratio.

    Codes:

    (a) (A) is correct, but (R) is wrong   (b) Both (A) and (R) are correct

    (c) (A) is wrong, but (R) is correct   (d) Both (A) and (R) are wrong

24. Which kind of Preference Share entitles its holders to receive arrear of dividends of previous years?

    (a) Cumulative Preference Share   (b) Non-Cumulative Preference Share

    (c) Convertible Preference Share   (d) Non-Convertible Preference Share

25. Kartik and Rana are partners sharing profits in the ratio of 4 : 1. Their capitals were ₹ 90,000 and ₹ 70,000 respectively. They admitted Kuldeep for 1/3rd share in the future profits. Kuldeep brought ₹ 1,00,000 as his capital. Firm's Goodwill is:

    (a) ₹ 40,000   (b) ₹ 1,40,000   (c) ₹ 3,00,000   (d) ₹ 2,60,000

26. Given below are two statements, one labelled as Assertion (A) and the other labelled as Reason (R):

    Assertion (A): Issued capital is that part of Authorised Share Capital which is issued for subscription whether subscribe or not.

    Reason (R): Issued capital is that part of Authorised Share Capital which is issued for subscription to the public which can be more than the subscription or equal to the subscription.

    Codes:

    (a) Both (A) and (R) are correct and (R) is the correct reason of (A)

    (b) Both (A) and (R) are correct but (R) is not the correct reason of (A)

    (c) Only (R) is correct

    (d) Both (A) and (R) are wrong

27. On Admission of a partner, building appreciated by ₹ 2,00,000 journal entry will be:

₹   ₹

   (a) Building A/c   Dr.   2,00,000
        To Old Partners' A/c   2,00,000

   (b) Revaluation A/c   Dr.   2,00,000
        To Building A/c   2,00,000

   (c) Building A/c   Dr.   2,00,000
        To Revaluation A/c   2,00,000

   (d) Old Partners' A/c   Dr.   2,00,000
        To Building A/c   2,00,000

28. 'A', 'B' and 'C' share profits and losses in the ratio of 3 : 2 : 1. 'D' is admitted with 1/6th share which he gets entirely from 'A'. New ratio will be:

   (a) 2 : 2 : 1 : 1   (b) 3 : 1 : 1 : 1   (c) 2 : 2 : 2 : 1   (d) None of these

29. A new company can issue shares:

Following options are available:

   (i) at par.

   (ii) at premium.

   (iii) at discount.

Choose the correct option:

   (a) Both (i) & (ii)   (b) Both (ii) & (iii)   (c) Only (i)   (d) All of these

30. 'A' and 'B' share profits in the ratio of 3 : 2. 'A's' capital is ₹ 40,000, 'B's' capital is ₹ 30,000. 'C' is admitted for 1/5th share in profits. What is the amount of capital which 'C' should bring?

   (a) ₹ 17,500   (b) ₹ 16,000

   (c) ₹ 1,00,000   (d) ₹ 64,000

31. A, B and C were partners sharing profit or loss in the ratio of 7 : 3 : 2. From Jan. 1, 2019 they decided to share profit or loss in the ratio of 8 : 4 : 3. Due to change in the profit sharing ratio, B's gain or sacrifice will be:

   (a) Gain 1/60   (b) Sacrifice 19/60

   (c) Gain 2/60   (d) Sacrifice 3/60

32. Given below are two statements, one labelled as Assertion (A) and the other labelled as Reason (R):

Assertion (A): Goodwill is easy to compute.

Reason (R): Only the old partners can perform this calculation.

Codes:

   (a) Both (A) and (R) are true, but (R) is not the explanation of (A).

   (b) Both(A) and (R) are true and (R) is a correct explanation of (A).

   (c) Both (A) and (R) are false.

   (d) (A) is false, but (R) is true.

33. Calculate net effect of revaluation when revised values are to be recorded in books.

   (i) Stock is to be valued at 10% less (Book value ₹ 3,00,000).

   (ii) Provision for bad debts is no more required, (Shown in Balance Sheet for ₹ 4,000).

   (iii) An outstanding salary which is unrecorded of ₹ 16,000.

   (a) ₹ 40,000 profit   (b) ₹ 42,000 profit   (c) ₹ 42,000 loss   (d) None of these

34. When a company issue shares at a premium, the amount of premium should be received by the company:

Following options are available:

   (i) Along with application money.

   (ii) Along with allotment money.

   (iii) Along with calls.

Choose the correct option:

(a) Only (i)   (b) Only (ii)   (c) Only (iii)   (d) All of these

35. The Net profits of Kala & Kand were ₹ 20,000. Gulaboo the manager was to be given the commission of ₹ 6,000; the distribution of profits will be done as:

(a) ₹ 10,000 to each   (b) ₹ 7,000 to each.   (c) ₹ 13,000 to each.   (d) None of these.

36. Shares can be forfeited:

(a) for non-payment of call money   (b) for failure to attend meetings

(c) for failure to repay the loan to the bank   (d) for which shares are pledged

Section – C

Instructions:

> *From question number 37 to 41, attempt any 4 questions.*

Question no.'s 37 and 38 are based on the hypothetical situation given below.

Nikhil and Pawan were partners in a firm sharing profit and loss in the ratio of 2 : 1 with capitals ₹60,000 and ₹50,000 respectively. Their Balance Sheet as on 31.03.2016 showed creditors ₹57,000; WCF ₹35,000 and General reserve ₹30,000. Their assets included banks ₹24,000; Profit and Loss (Dr.); Machinery ₹22,000; Investment ₹2,000. Debtors valued ₹44,000; Provision for Bad Debt ₹6,000; Building ₹1,35,000 and Stock ₹6,000.

Partners decide to admit 'Harshit' for 1/5 share future profit on the following terms:

Harshit acquire his share of profit from Nikhil.

Goodwill of the firm was valued at ₹60,000. Building to be over valued by ₹2,000. Provision on debtors should be maintained at 5%. Machinery to be reduced by 5%. Claim for WCF ₹17,000. Market value of investment ₹5,000 and taken by Nikhil at this value. Harshit bought ₹60,000, as a capital.

37. What will be new profit sharing ratio of Nikhil, Pawan and Harshit?

(a) 2 : 3 : 1   (b) 5 : 2 : 1   (c) 7 : 8 : 9   (d) None of these

38. After settlement of WCF claim how much remaining amount will be credited in Nikhil's And Pawan's Capital Account?

(a) Nikhil ₹17,000; Pawan ₹1,000   (b) Nikhil ₹10,000; Pawan ₹8,000

(c) Nikhil ₹12,000; Pawan ₹6,000   (d) None of these

Question no.'s 39, 40 and 41 are based on the hypothetical situation given below.

A Ltd. company was registered with an authorized capital of ₹2,00,000 of ₹10 per share, of these 6,000 shares were issued as fully paid to the vendors for the purchase of building. 8,000 shares were subscribed for by the public and during the first year ₹6 per share were called up, payable ₹3 on Application, ₹1 on Allotment, ₹1 on First Call, and ₹1 on Final Call. The amounts received in respect of these shares were as follows :

On 6,000 shares the full amount called.

On 1,200 shares ₹5 per share.

On 500 shares ₹4 per share.

On 300 shares ₹3 per share.

The directors forfeited 800 shares on which less than ₹5 per share had been paid.

39. What will be the amount due on share capital ?

(a) ₹48,000   (b) ₹25,000   (c) ₹80,000   (d) ₹84,000

40. What will be the total arrear amount (including First and Final Call)?

(a) ₹2,800   (b) ₹2,900   (c) ₹4,800   (d) ₹2,200

41. What will the amount of share forfeiture?

(a) ₹1,900   (b) ₹2,900   (c) ₹4,800   (d) ₹2,200

PART – II

Section – A

Instructions:

> *From question number 42 to 48, attempt any 5 questions.*

42. Which of the following is not a short-term borrowing?

(a) Deposits

(b) Loans repayable on demand

(c) Bank overdraft

(d) Trade receivables

43. Match the items given in column I with the headings/subheadings (Balance Sheet) as defined in schedule III of Companies Act 2013.

	Column - I		Column - II
I	Defirred Tax Liabilities	(a)	Long term borrowings
II	Bank overdraft	(b)	Intangible assets
III	Public deposits	(c)	Cash and cash Equivalent
IV	Trade marks	(d)	Long term provisions
V	Loose Tools	(e)	Non-Current liability

Choose the correct option:

(a) I-(e), II-(d), III-(a), IV-(d), V-(c)

(b) I-(a), II-(d), III-(b), IV-(e), V-(b)

(c) I-(b), II-(e), III-(a), IV-(c), V-(d)

(d) I-(c), II-(c), III-(d), IV-(a), V-(c)

44. Given below are two statements, one labelled as Assertion (A) and the other labelled as Reason (R):

Assertion (A): Proprietory ratio establishes relationship between proprietors fund and total assets.

Reason (R): The objective of calculating proprietory ratio is to measure proportion of fixed assets financed by shareholder's funds.

Codes:

(a) Both (A) and (R) are true, but (R) is not the explanation of (A).

(b) Both(A) and (R) are true and (R) is a correct explanation of (A).

(c) Both (A) and (R) are false.

(d) (A) is false, but (R) is true.

45. Two basic measures of liquidity are:

(a) Inventory turnover and Current ratio

(b) Current ratio and Quick ratio

(c) Gross profit ratio and Operating ratio

(d) Current ratio and Average Collection Period

46. What will be the area of interest for a creditor while analysing financial statements?

(a) Solvency (b) Liquidity (c) Profitability (d) Long-term solvency

47. Under which sub-head Provision for employees benefit to be settled within 12 months be shown.

Following options are available:

(i) Short-term Provisions

(ii) Short-term Borrowings

(iii) Other Current Liabilities

Choose the correct option:

(a) Only (i) is correct

(b) Only (ii) is correct

(c) Only (iii) is correct

(d) Only (i) and (ii) are correct

48. Under Financial Statement Analysis, this analysis is made to review and analyse the financial statements of one year only. Name of this analysis is:

(a) External Analysis (b) Internal Analysis (c) Horizontal Analysis (d) Vertical Analysis

Section – B

Instructions:

> *From question number 49 to 55, attempt any 6 questions.*

49. What is the analysis known as when financial statement for a single year is analysed?

    (a) Horizontal   (b) Internal   (c) Vertical   (d) External

50. When there is Profit on sale of investment it is included in:

    Following options are available:

    (i)   Other income

    (ii) Revence from operations

    (iii) Other expenses

    Choose the correct option:

    (a) Only (i) is correct   (b) Only (ii) is correct   (c) Only (iii) is correct   (d) None of these

51. Which of the following items is shown under the head 'Non-Current Assets' while preparing the Balance Sheet of a company?

    (a) Underwriting Commission   (b) Current Investment

    (c) Inventory   (d) Patents

52. Given below are two statements, one labelled as Assertion (A) and the other labelled as Reason (R):

    Assertion (A): Contingent liabilities are not shown in the Balance Sheet.

    Reason (R): Contingent liability is recorded in the Notes to Account.

    Codes:

    (a) (A) and (R) both are correct and (R) correctly explains (A)

    (b) Both (A) and (R) are correct but (R) does not explain (A)

    (c) Both (A) and (R) are incorrect

    (d) (A) is correct but (R) is incorrect

53. The two basic measures of operational efficiency of a company are:

    (a) Inventory Turnover Ratio and Working Capital Turnover Ratio

    (b) Liquid Ratio and Operating Ratio

    (c) Liquid Ratio and Current Ratio

    (d) Gross Profit Margin and Net Profit Margin

54. Trade Receivable includes:

    Following options are available:

    (i)   Debtors

    (ii) Bills Receivables

    (iii) Bills Payable

    Choose the correct option:

    (a) Only (i) are correct   (b) Only (iii) is correct

    (c) Both (i) and (ii) are correct   (d) None of these

55. Given below are two statements, one labelled as Assertion (A) and the other labelled as Reason (R):

    Assertion (A): Proposed dividend is a contingent liability.

    Reason (R): As per AS-4 Revised, Proposed dividend is shown as the contingent liability because it is subject to approval by the shareholders, who may reduce the amount of dividend to be paid.

    Codes:

    (a) Both (A) and (R) are correct and (R) is the correct reason of (A)

    (b) Both (A) and (R) are correct but (R) is not the correct reason of (A)

    (c) Only (R) is correct

    (d) Both (A) and (R) are wrong

Sample Paper 4

Accountancy

PART - I

Section - A

Instructions:

> *From question number 1 to 18, attempt any 15 questions.*

1. In a firm, 10% of net profit after deducting all adjustments, including reserve is transferred to general reserve. The net profit after all adjustments but before transfer to general reserves is ₹44,000. Calculate the amount which is to be transferred to reserve.
   (a) ₹2,500   (b) ₹4,000   (c) ₹4,400   (d) ₹2,200

2. A, B and D are partners in a firm sharing profits (losses) in the ratio of 3 : 2 : 1. They change their ratio into 2 : 1 : 2 for future profits. At that time their Balance Sheet shows the following balances.

   Investment Fluctuation Reserve = ₹6,000

   Investments = ₹25,000

   Now, the market value of investments is ₹22,000. Journal entry to distribute Investment Fluctuation Reserve among partners:

			₹	₹
(a)	Investment Fluctuation Reserve A/c	Dr.	6,000	
	To A's Capital A/c			3,000
	To B's Capital A/c			2,000
	To D's Capital A/c			1,000
(b)	Investment Fluctuation Reserve A/c	Dr.	6,000	
	To A's Capital A/c			6,000
(c)	A's Capital A/c	Dr.	6,000	
	To B's Capital A/c			3,000
	To D's Capital A/c			3,000
(d)	Investment Fluctuation Reserve A/c	Dr.	6,000	
	To Investments A/c			3,000
	To A's Capital A/c			1,500
	To B's Capital A/c			1,000
	To D's Capital A/c			500

3. A Company issued 10,000 shares of ₹10 each. Amount is payable as ₹2 on Application, ₹5 on Allotment and ₹3 on First and Final Call. A Shareholder who had 1,000 shares failed to pay allotment and first call amount on due date. After a month, he paid the due amount. What will be the amount received by company against issue of share?
   (a) ₹92,000   (b) ₹90,000   (c) ₹1,00,000   (d) ₹8,000

4. A and B carry on business and share profits and losses in the ratio of 3 : 2. Their respective capitals are ₹1,20,000 and ₹54,000. C is admitted for 1/5th share in profit and brings ₹1,20,000 as his share of capital. A and B decided to adjust their capitals is new profit sharing ratio. Calculate the amount required to be brought by A.
   (a) ₹30,000   (b) ₹1,68,000   (c) ₹60,000   (d) ₹28,000

5. A Company issued 25,000 shares and received applications for 35,000 shares. Company wants to allot shares to everyone who has applied. What will be the ratio for allotment ?
   (a) 6 : 7   (b) 7 : 5   (c) 5 : 7   (d) 7 : 6

6. Which of the following is not true with respect to Admission of a partner?
   (a) A new partner can be admitted if it is agreed in the partnership deed.
   (b) If all the partners agree, a new partner can be admitted.
   (c) A new partner has to bring relatively higher capital as compared to the existing partners.
   (d) A new partner gets right in the assets of the firm.

7. When the shares are issued at a price more than the face value, it is known as share issued at_________.
   (a) Premium   (b) Par   (c) Discount   (d) None of these

8. Which one of the following items is recorded in the Profit and Loss Appropriation Account?
   (a) Interest on loan   (b) Partner salary
   (c) Rent paid to partner   (d) Managers commission

9. When amount called but not paid by the shareholders:
   Following options are available :
   (i) Called-up Capital
   (ii) Calls-in-Arrears
   (iii) Calls-in-Advance
   Choose the correct option:
   (a) Only (i) is correct   (b) Only (ii) is correct
   (c) Only (iii) is correct   (d) Only (i) and (ii) are correct

10. A and B are partners in a firm sharing profits in 3 : 2 ratio . They admitted C as a new partner and the new profit sharing ratio will be 2 : 1 : 1. C brought in ₹40,000 as premium for goodwill for its share. What will be the journal entry for the premium of goodwill shared by old partners as per sacrificing ratio?

		₹	₹
(a) Premium for Goodwill A/c	Dr.	40,000	
To A's Capital A/c			16,000
To B's Capital A/c			24,000
(b) A's Capital A/c	Dr.	16,000	
B's Capital A/c	Dr.	24,000	
To Premium for Goodwill A/c			40,000
(c) Premium for Goodwill A/c	Dr.	40,000	
To Bank A/c			40,000
(d) Bank A/c	Dr.	40,000	
To Premium for Goodwill A/c			40,000

11. A and B are partners in a firm. They share their profits and losses in the ratio of 3 : 2. They have decided that their new profits (losses) sharing ratio will be 1 : 1. At that time their goodwill is valued at ₹30,000. Calculate amount of goodwill which will be given by B to A.
    (a) ₹2,500   (b) ₹2,400   (c) ₹2,800   (d) ₹3,000

12. In which ratio the reserves and accumulated profits are transferred to partners' capital accounts at the time of reconstitution?
    (a) Old Profit-Sharing Ratio   (b) Sacrificing Ratio
    (c) Gaining Ratio   (d) New Profit-Sharing Ratio

13. A Company invited applications for 1,00,000 shares and it received applications for 1,50,000 shares. Applications for 30,000 shares were rejected and the remaining shares were allotted on pro rata basis. How many shares an applicant for 3,000 shares will be allotted?
    (a) 2,500 Shares   (b) 3,600 Shares
    (c) 4,500 Shares   (d) 2,000 Shares

14. A and B are partners. A drew ₹32,000. If the rate of interest on drawings is 12% per annum, then what will be the amount of interest on drawings?
    (a) ₹1,920   (b) ₹19,200   (c) ₹1,820   (d) ₹16,200

15. In case of private placement of shares and company does not invite the general public for subscription of shares in that case, company instead of issuing prospectus:

   (a) prepares the statement in lieu of prospectus.

   (b) prepares the report

   (c) prepares the budget

   (d) prepares the asset side of balance sheet

16. If the new partner does not brings in his share of goodwill in cash, which account will be debited?

   (a) Current A/c   (b) Capital A/c   (c) Revaluation A/c   (d) Balance Sheet

17. Vinod Ltd. was formed with a Nominal Share Capital of ₹ 40,00,000 divided into 4,00,000 shares of ₹ 10 each. The Company offers 1,30,000 shares to the public payable ₹ 3 per share on Application, ₹ 3 per share on Allotment and the balance on First and Final Call. Applications were received for 1,20,000 shares. All money payable on Allotment was duly received, except on 2,000 shares held by Y. First and Final Call was not made by the Company. Call-in-arrears will be of:

   (a) ₹ 6,000   (b) ₹ 4,000

   (c) ₹ 5,000   (d) ₹ 7,000

18. When new partner is unable to bring his/her share goodwill in cash.

   Following options are available :

   (i)   New Partner's current A/c   Dr.
             To Sacrificing Partners Capital A/c

   (ii) Cash A/c   Dr.
             To Premium for Goodwill A/c

   (iii) No entry passed in the books of account.

   Choose the correct option:

   (a) Only (i) is correct   (b) Only (ii) is correct

   (c) Only (iii) is correct   (d) Only (i) and (ii) are correct

Section – B

Instructions:

   ➢ *From question number 19 to 36, attempt any 15 questions:*

19. Vinod Ltd. forfeited a share of ₹ 50 issued at a premium of 20% for non-payment of first call of ₹ 15 per share and final call of ₹ 5 per share. At what minimum price it can be re-issued?

   (a) ₹ 50   (b) ₹ 30   (c) ₹ 40   (d) ₹ 20

20. In case of change in profit sharing ratio, when revised values are not be recorded in the books, then steps to be followed are :

   Following options are available:

   (i)   Pass a single adjustment entry.

   (ii) To find share of sacrifice / (gain) by partners.

   (iii) Calculation of the net effect of revaluation.

   (iv) Calculation of proportional amount of net effect of revaluation.

   Choose the correct option:

   (a) (ii), (iii), (iv), (i)   (b) (iii), (ii), (iv), (i)   (c) (iv), (iii), (ii), (i)   (d) None of these

21. Goodwill appearing in the books (at the time of change in profit sharing ratio).

   Following options are available :

   (i)   Written off in new profit sharing ratio.

   (ii) Written off in old profit sharing ratio.

   (iii) Total Capital based on new partner share – Total of all partner's capital.

   (a) Only (i) is correct   (b) Only (ii) is correct

   (c) Only (iii) is correct   (d) Only (ii) and (iii) are correct

22. The shares on which there is no any pre-fixed rate of dividend is decided, but the rate of dividend is fluctuating every year according to the availability of profits, such share are called:

    (a) Equity Share
    (b) Non-cumulative Preference Share
    (c) Non-convertible Preference Share
    (d) Non-Guaranteed preference Share

23. Virat and Anushka are partners in a firm sharing profits and losses in 2 : 1 ratio. Their capital balance were ₹ 10,00,000 and ₹ 8,00,000 respectively. The firm made profits during the year amounting to ₹ 3,45,000. Both partners are allowed salary of ₹ 2,500 per month. Interest on capital is allowed @ 5% p.a. on capital balance.

    Calculate Closing balance of capital for Virat and Anushka.

    (a) Virat = ₹ 12,10,000, Anushka = ₹ 9,35,000

    (b) Virat = ₹ 12,35,000, Anushka = ₹ 9,10,000

    (c) Virat = 13,10,000, Anushka = ₹ 9, 85,000

    (d) None of these

24. Given below are two statements, one labelled as Assertion (A) and the other labelled as Reason (R).

    Assertion (A): A company cannot generate its own capital investment.

    Reason (R): The total collected investment is known as invested capital.

    Codes:

    (a) (A) is correct, but (R) is wrong
    (b) Both (A) and (R) are correct
    (c) (A) is wrong, but (R) is correct
    (d) Both (A) and (R) are wrong

25. A partner withdrew ₹ 4,000 per month from 1st July, 2016, in beginning of every month.

    Accounts are closed on 31st March, 2017.

    Calculate interest on drawings if the rate of interest is 10% per annum.

    (a) ₹ 1,600   (b) ₹ 1,800   (c) ₹ 1,500   (d) ₹ 2,200

26. According to Profit and Loss Account, the net profit for the year is ₹ 1,50,000. The total interest on partner's capital is ₹ 18,000 and interest on partner's drawings is ₹ 2,000. The Divisible profit as per Profit and Loss Appropriation Account will be:

    (a) ₹ 1,66,000   (b) ₹ 1,70,000   (c) ₹ 1,30,000   (d) ₹ 1,34,000

27. Given below are two statements, one labelled as Assertion (A) and the other labelled as Reason (R):

    Assertion (A): Partnership Act requires agreement which can be either written or oral.

    Reason (R): This is denoted as Partnership Deed.

    Codes:

    (a) Both (A) and (R) are correct and (R) is the correct reason of (A)

    (b) Both (A) and (R) are correct but (R) is not the correct reason of (A)

    (c) Only (R) is correct

    (d) Both (A) and (R) are wrong

28. For which purposes Securities Premium Reserve can be used:

    Following options are available:

    (i) For writing off the discount on debentures of the company.

    (ii) For writing off the preliminary expenses of the company.

    (iii) In providing for the premium payable on the redemption of preference shares.

    Choose the correct option:

    (a) Both (i) &(ii)
    (b) Both (i) & (iii)
    (c) Only (i)
    (d) All of these

29. 'B' and 'C' were partners sharing profits in the ratio of 3 : 2. They agreed to share their future profits in the ratio of 1 : 1. At that time their books showed the following balances:

Proit and Loss A/c (Cr.) = ₹ 60,000

General Reserve = ₹ 40,000

Pass necessary entry at the time of change in profit sharing ratio.

(a) C's Capital A/c   Dr. 10,000

      To B's Capital A/c   10,000

(b) General Reserve A/c Dr. 40,000

      To B's Capital A/c   20,000

      To C's Capital A/c   20,000

(c) Profit and Loss A/c   Dr. 60,000

    General Reserve A/c Dr. 40,000

      To B's Capital A/c   1,00,000

(d) Profit and Loss A/c   Dr. 60,000

    General Reserve A/c Dr. 40,000

      To B's Capital A/c   60,000

      To C's Capital A/c   40,000

30. The balance of Share Forfeiture Account can be used to:

(a) provide for discount given at the time of re-issue.

(b) write-off preliminary expenses.

(c) write-off bad debts.

(d) None of these

31. A and B are partners in a firm sharing profits in the ratio of 4 : 1. They decided to share future profits in the ratio of 3 : 2 w.e.f. 1st April, 2021. On that day, Profit and Loss Account showed a debit balance of ₹ 50,000. What will be the Sacrifice/Gain of B?

(a) Gain of 1/5   (b) Sacrifice of $\dfrac{3}{20}$ (c) Sacrifice of 1/5   (d) No sacrifice or gain

32. 'X' and 'Y' are partners sharing profits equally. 'Z' was admitted for 1/5 share. Calculate new profit sharing ratio.

(a) 2 : 3 : 1   (b) 3 : 3 : 1   (c) 6 : 5 : 2   (d) 2 : 2 : 1

33. Given below are two statements, one labelled as Assertion (A) and the other labelled as Reason (R):

Assertion (A): In case of change in profit sharing ratio, the old balances of reserves need not be transferred to partners' capital account in old profit sharing ratio.

Reason (R): If the partners decide not to distribute the reserves, the adjusting entry can be passed in sacrificing and gaining ratio to adjust the profit.

Codes:

(a) Both (A) and (R) are true, but (R) is not the explanation of (A)

(b) Both(A) and (R) are true and (R) is a correct explanation of (A)

(c) Both (A) and (R) are false

(d) (A) is false, but (R) is true

34. For which of the following situations, the old profit sharing ratio of partners is used at the time of admission of a new partner?

(a) When new partner brings only a part of his share of goodwill.

(b) When new partner is not able to bring his share of goodwill.

(c) When at the time of admission, goodwill already appears in the Balance Sheet.

(d) When new partner brings his share of goodwill in cash.

35. Which statements are correct?

    Following options are available:

    (i)   Payment of interest on call-in-advance is at the discretion of the company.

    (ii) A company can't raise funds beyond its authorized capital.

    (iii) Called up share capital is that part of subscribed capital that has been called up.

    Choose the correct option:

    (a) Both (i) & (ii)   (b) Both (i) & (iii)

    (c) Both (ii) & (iii)   (d) All of these

36. Asha and Nisha are partners sharing profit in the ratio of 2 : 1. Asha's son Ashish was admitted for 1/4 share of which 1/8 was gifted by Asha to her son. The remaining was contributed by Nisha. Goodwill of the firm is valued at ₹ 40,000. How much of the goodwill be credited to the old partners' capital account?

    (a) ₹ 2,500 each   (b) ₹ 5,000 each

    (c) ₹ 20,000 each   (d) None of these

Section – C

Instructions:

> *From question number 37 to 41, attempt any 4 questions.*

Question no.'s 37 and 38 are based on the hypothetical situation given below.

A and B are partners sharing the profits and losses in the ratio of 3 : 2 with the capitals of ₹2,00,000 and ₹1,00,000 respectively. Show the distribution of profits in each of the following alternative cases:

37. If the partnership deed is silent as to the interest on capital and the profits for the year are ₹50,000.

    (a) Profit transferred- ₹30,000, ₹20,000

    (b) Loss transferred- ₹30,000, ₹20,000

    (c) Interest on capital- ₹16,000, ₹8,000; Profit transferred- ₹15,600, ₹10,400

    (d) Interest on capital- ₹10,000, ₹5,000

38. If the partnership deed provides for interest on capital @ 8% p.a. and the losses for the year are ₹50,000.

    (a) Profit transferred- ₹30,000, ₹20,000

    (b) Loss transferred- ₹30,000, ₹20,000

    (c) Interest on capital- ₹16,000, ₹8,000; Loss transferred- ₹15,600, ₹10,400

    (d) Interest on capital- ₹10,000, ₹5,000

Question no.'s 39, 40 and 41 are based on the hypothetical situation given below.

Following are the information obtained from the books of Kamakshi Ltd.

	2016-17	2017-18
Inventory on 31st March	₹7,00,000	₹17,00,000
Revenue from Operations	₹50,00,000	₹75,00,000

(Gross profit is 25% on Cost of Revenue from Operations)

In the year 2016-17 inventory increased by ₹2,00,000.

39. What will be the Inventory Turnover Ratio for year 2017-18?

    (a) 4 times   (b) 2 times   (c) 3 times   (d) 5 times

40. What will be the Cost of Revenue from Operations for year 2016-17 ?

    (a) ₹10,00,000   (b) ₹40,00,000   (c) ₹20,00,000   (d) ₹30,00,000

41. What will be the Average Inventory for the year 2016-17?

    (a) ₹1,00,000   (b) ₹3,00,000   (c) ₹6,00,000   (d) ₹1,50,000

PART – II

Section – A

Instructions:

> *From question number 42 to 48, attempt any 5 questions.*

42. Given below are two statements, one labelled as Assertion (A) and the other labelled as Reason (R):

    Assertion (A): Financial statements include the monetary transactions performed during defined timeline.

    Reason (R): It is beneficial in ascertaining the financial situation of a company during that phase.

    Codes:

    (a) Both (A) and (R) are true, but (R) is not the explanation of (A).

    (b) Both(A) and (R) are true and (R) is a correct explanation of (A).

    (c) Both (A) and (R) are false.

    (d) (A) is false, but (R) is true.

43. Two basic measures of liquidity are:

    (a) Inventory Turnover and Current Ratio

    (b) Current Ratio and Quick Ratio

    (c) Gross Profit Ratio and Operating Ratio

    (d) Current Ratio and Average Collection Period

44. Bank Overdraft is shown in the Balance Sheet under the:

    (a) Short-term Borrowings

    (b) Non-Current Liabilities

    (c) Non-Current Assets

    (d) None of these

45. Higher the ratio, the more favourable it is, doesn't stands true for:

    (a) Operating ratio   (b) Liquidity ratio   (c) Net profit ratio   (d) Stock turnover ratio

46. What will happen to the accumulated profit or losses when the question is silent, and there is a change in profit sharing ratio?

    (a) Distributed   (b) Not distributed   (c) Adjusted   (d) None of these

47. Through which ratio earning capacity of a business is assessed through?

    (a) Profitability   (b) Solvency   (c) Current   (d) Debt

48. Working Capital Turnover Ratio is:

    Following options are available :

    (i) Current Assets / Current Liabilities

    (ii) Revenue from Operations / Working Capital

    (iii) Liquid Assets / Current Liabilities

    Choose the correct option:

    (a) Only (i) is correct

    (b) Only (ii) is correct

    (c) Only (i) and (ii) are correct

    (d) Only (ii) and (iii) are correct

Section – B

Instructions:

> *From question number 49 to 55, attempt any 6 questions.*

49. Current Ratio of Vidur Pvt. Ltd. is 3 : 2. Accountant wants to maintain it at 2 : 1.

    Following options are available:

    (i) He can repay Bills Payable.

    (ii) He can purchase goods on credit.

    (iii) He can take short-term-loan.

    Choose the correct option:

    (a) Only (i) is correct

    (b) Only (ii) is correct

    (c) Only (i) and (ii) are correct

    (d) Only (ii) and (iii) are correct

50. Consider the following information.

Long-term Borrowings	₹ 2,00,000
Long-term Provisions	₹ 1,00,000
Current Liabilities	₹ 50,000
Non-Current Assets	₹ 3,60,000
Current Assets	₹ 90,000

    Proprietary ratio will be:

    (a) 22.2%
    (b) 2.8%
    (c) 36%
    (d) None of these

51. Given below are two statements, one labelled as Assertion (A) and the other labelled as Reason (R):

    Assertion (A): A specified ratio is agreed in between the partners of the partnership firms.

    Reason (R): But, this ratio is not specified when a new member joins.

    Codes:

    (a) Both (A) and (R) are correct and (R) is the correct reason of (A).
    (b) Both (A) and (R) are correct but (R) is not the correct reason of (A).
    (c) Only (R) is correct.
    (d) Both (A) and (R) are wrong.

52. Preliminary expenses are those expenses which are paid before incorporation of a company. A company paid its preliminary expenses to its promoters. Accountant of company is in view that this is an expense, so it will be fully written-off in Statement of Profit and Loss. How this should have been shown?

    (a) Statement of profit and loss account by full amount
    (b) Current Asset
    (c) Deduct from Reserves and Surplus
    (d) None of the above

53. Given below are two statements, one labelled as Assertion (A) and the other labelled as Reason (R):

    Assertion (A): Security premium reserve is shown under the head share holders fund.

    Reason (R): Security premium reserve is that part of reserves hence it should be shown under the head reserves and surplus.

    Codes:

    (a) (A) and (R) both are correct and (R) correctly explains (A)
    (b) Both (A) and (R) are correct but (R) does not explain (A)
    (c) Both (A) and (R) are incorrect
    (d) (A) is correct but (R) is incorrect

54. The formula for calculating the Trade Receivables Turnover Ratio is:

    (a) $\dfrac{\text{Total Revenue from Operations}}{\text{Average Debtors}}$

    (b) $\dfrac{\text{Credit Revenue from Operations}}{\text{Average Debtors}}$

    (c) $\dfrac{\text{Net Credit Revenus from Operations}}{\text{Average Debtors} + \text{Average Bills Receivable}}$

    (d) None of these

55. Compute cost of material consumed from the following:

    Opening nuentory = ₹ 5,00,000

    Materials purchased = ₹ 40,00,000

    Closing Inventory = ₹ 6,00,000

    (a) ₹ 40,00,000
    (b) ₹ 39,00,000
    (c) ₹ 38,00,000
    (d) ₹ 41,00,000

Sample Paper 5

Accountancy

PART – I

Section – A

Instructions:

> *From question number 1 to 18, attempt any 15 questions.*

1. The valuation of goodwill is not necessary in sole trading:
   - (a) on closing the firm
   - (b) on making a firm
   - (c) on selling the firm
   - (d) None of these

2. Weighted Average Method of calculating goodwill is used when:
   - (a) Profit has decreasing trend
   - (b) Profit has increasing trend
   - (c) Both (a) and (b)
   - (d) None of these

3. A, B and C were partners in the ratio of 3 : 2 : 1. As on 1st April they decided to share equally in future. What will be the sacrificing or the gaining ratio?
   - (a) Sacrifice A 1/6; B's sacrifice Nil; C's Gain 1/6
   - (b) Gain A 1/6; B's sacrifice Nil; C's Sacrifice 1/6
   - (c) Sacrifice A 1/3; B's sacrifice 1/3; C's Gain 1/6
   - (d) Sacrifice A 1/6; B's sacrifice 1/3; C's Gain 1/3

4. Penalty for delay in refunding application money is charged:
   - (a) 6%
   - (b) 5%
   - (c) 15%
   - (d) 20%

5. The balance in the Investment Fluctuation Fund after meeting the fall in book value of investment, at the time of admission of partner will transferred to :
   - (a) Revaluation account
   - (b) Capital account of old partners
   - (c) General reserve
   - (d) Capital account of all partners

6. X and Y are partners sharing profits in the ratio of 3 : 1. They admit Z as a partner who pays ₹4,000 as Goodwill. New Profit-sharing Ratio being 2 : 1 : 1 among X, Y, Z. Goodwill will be credited to:
   - (a) X and Y as ₹3,000 and ₹1,000
   - (b) X only
   - (c) Y Only
   - (d) None of these

7. When nominal (face) value of a share is called-up by the company but as some shareholders did not pay the money, the shares are forfeited. The share capital is shown in the balance sheet (notes) of a company under the following heading:
   - (a) Subscribed and fully paid-up
   - (b) Subscribed but not fully paid-up
   - (c) Subscribed and called-up
   - (d) Subscribed but not called-up

8. A, B and C are equal partners, they wanted to change the profit sharing ratio to 4 : 3 : 2. They raised the goodwill to ₹90,000. The effected accounts will be:

		₹	₹
(a) C's Capital A/c	Dr.	10,000	
To A's Capital A/c			10,000
(b) B's Capital A/c	Dr.	10,000	
To A's Capital A/c			10,000
(c) C's Capital A/c	Dr.	10,000	
To B's Capital A/c			10,000
(d) A's Capital A/c	Dr.	10,000	
To C's Capital A/c			10,000

9. At the time of reconstitution of the firm in which ratio the reserves and accumulated profits are transferred to partners' capital accounts?
   - (a) Old Profit-Sharing Ratio
   - (b) Sacrificing Ratio
   - (c) Gaining Ratio
   - (d) New Profit-Sharing Ratio

10. Which of the following statements is/are correct?
    - (i) A company can issue redeemable equity shares.
    - (ii) A company can issue redeemable preference shares.
    - (iii) A company can issue redeemable debentures.
    - (a) Both (i) & (ii) are correct
    - (b) Both (ii) & (iii) are correct
    - (c) Both (i) & (iii) are correct
    - (d) All of these

11. What type of account is revaluation account?
    - (a) Real
    - (b) Nominal
    - (c) Personal
    - (d) Liability

12. A and B were partners in a firm. They share profits in 2 : 3 ratio. They close their accounts on 31st December every year. A withdraw a fixed sum of ₹2,000 at the beginning of every month starting from 1st July, 2017. You have to calculate interest on drawings while rate of interest is 12%. What is the interest of drawing?
    - (a) ₹420
    - (b) ₹720
    - (c) ₹440
    - (d) ₹580

13. Preference shareholders have:
    - (a) preferential right as to dividend only
    - (b) preferential right in the management
    - (c) preferential right as to repayment of capital at the time of liquidation of the company
    - (d) preferential right as to dividend and repayment of capital at the time of liquidation of the company

14. R and S are partners sharing profits equally. They admitted T for 1/3rd, share in the firm. What will be the new profit-sharing ratio?
    - (a) Equally
    - (b) Unequally
    - (c) 1 : 3
    - (d) 2 : 1

15. Unless otherwise stated, a preference share is always deemed to be:
    - (a) cumulative, participating and non-convertible
    - (b) non-cumulative, non-participating and non-convertible
    - (c) cumulative, non-participating and non-convertible
    - (d) non-cumulative, participating and non-convertible

16. What is the condition when closing stock are undervalued?
    Following options are available:
    - (i) Deducted to the current year and added to the previous year.
    - (ii) Added to the current year and deducted from previous year.
    - (iii) No effect.
    Choose the correct option:
    - (a) Only (i) is correct
    - (b) Only (ii) is correct
    - (c) Only (iii) is correct
    - (d) Only (iv) is correct

17. Goodwill appearing in the books (at the time of changes in PSR).
    Following options are available :
    - (i) Written off in new PSR.
    - (ii) Written off in old PSR.
    - (iii) Total Capital based on new partner share – total of all partner's capital.
    Choose the correct option:
    - (a) Only (i) is correct
    - (b) Only (ii) is correct
    - (c) Only (iii) is correct
    - (d) Only (ii) and (iii) is correct

18. A company purchased machinery for ₹ 6,00,000, out of which ₹ 1,00,000 was paid immediately and the balance amount was discharged by issue of equity shares of ` 10 each at 25% premium. How many shares will be issued by the company to the vendor?
    - (a) 50,000 shares
    - (b) 40,000 shares
    - (c) 60,000 shares
    - (d) 48,000 shares

Section - B

Instructions:

> *From question number 19 to 36, attempt any 15 questions.*

19. What are the treatment of general reserves on admission of a partner?

    Following options are available:

    (i)   No treatment required in partner's capital.

    (ii) Cr. in partner's capital account.

    (iii) Dr. in partner's capital account.

    Choose the correct option:

    (a) Only (i) is correct
    (b) Only (ii) is correct
    (c) Only (iii) is correct
    (d) None of these

20. Partner's capital account are opened when their capital accounts are:

    Following options are available:

    (i) Fixed
    (ii) Fluctuating
    (iii) Both (i) and (ii)
    (iv) None of these

    Choose the correct option:

    (a) Only (i) is correct
    (b) Only (ii) is correct
    (c) Only (iii) is correct
    (d) Only (iv) is correct

21. Which shareholders have a right to receive the arrears of dividend from future profits?

    (a) Redeemable Preference Shares
    (b) Participating Preference Shares
    (c) Cumulative Preference Shares
    (d) Non-cumulative Preference Shares

22. Given below are two statements, one labelled as Assertion (A) and the other labelled as Reason (R).

    Assertion (A): Partnership clauses can be changes with the consent of all partners.

    Reason (R): The documents are prepared as per the Stamp Act.

    Codes:

    (a) (A) is correct, but (R) is wrong
    (b) Both (A) and (R) are correct
    (c) (A) is wrong, but (R) is correct
    (d) Both (A) and (R) are wrong

23. A company purchased a building for ₹ 3,60,000 and issued as payment equity shares at 20% premium. Journal entry will be:

			₹	₹
(a)	Building A/c	Dr.	4,00,000	
	To Share Capital A/c			3,20,000
	To Securities Premium Reserve A/c			80,000
(b)	Share Capital A/c	Dr.	4,00,000	
	To Building A/c			3,60,000
	To Securities Premium Reserve A/c			40,000
(c)	Building A/c	Dr.	3,60,000	
	To Share Capital A/c			3,00,000
	To Securities Premium Reserve A/c			60,000
(d)	Building A/c	Dr.	3,60,000	
	To Share Capital A/c			60,000
	To Securities Premium Reserve A/c			3,00,000

24. 'A', 'B' and 'D' are partners in a firm sharing profits (losses) in the ratio of 3 : 2 : 1. They change their ratio into 2 : 1 : 2 for future profits. At that time their balance sheet shows the following balances.

    Investment Fluctuation Reserve = ₹ 6,000

    Investment = ₹ 25,000

    Now, the market value of investments is ₹ 22,000. Distribute Investment Fluctuation Reserve among partners.

			₹	₹
(a)	Investment Fluctuation Reserve A/c	Dr.	6,000	
	To A's Capital A/c			3,000
	To B's Capital A/c			2,000
	To D's Capital A/c			1,000
(b)	Investment Fluctuation Reserve A/c	Dr.	6,000	
	To A's Capital A/c			6,000
(c)	A's Capital A/c	Dr.	6,000	
	To B's Capital A/c			3,000
	To C's Capital A/c			3,000
(d)	Investment Fluctuation Reserve A/c	Dr.	6,000	
	To Investment A/c			3,000
	To A's Capital A/c			1,500
	To B's Capital A/c			1,000
	To D's Capital A/c			500

25. A company has issued 10,000 equity shares of ₹ 10 each and it has called the total nominal (face) value. It has received the total amount, except the final call of ₹ 3 on 500 equity shares. These 500 equity shares will be shown as:

(a) Subscribed and fully paid-up   (b) Subscribed but not fully paid-up

(c) Issued share capital   (d) None of these

26. Given below are two statements, one labelled as Assertion (A) and the other labelled as Reason (R):

Assertion (A): Partners always try to adjust the goodwill during the reconstitution.

Reason (R): Reconstitution is considered during the sale of the firm.

Codes:

(a) Both (A) and (R) are correct and (R) is the correct reason of (A).

(b) Both (A) and (R) are correct but (R) is not the correct reason of (A).

(c) Only (R) is correct.

(d) Both (A) and (R) are wrong.

27. Equity shares can be issued for the purpose of:

(i) Cash Receipt.

(ii) Purchase of Assets.

(iii) Redemption of debentures.

(iv) Distribution of Dividend.

(a) (i), (ii) & (iv)   (b) (ii), (iii) & (iv)

(c) (i), (ii) & (iii)   (d) All of these

28. The formula for calculating the sacrificing ratio is:

(a) New share – Old share   (b) Old share – New share

(c) Gaining Ratio – Old Ratio   (d) Old Ratio – Gaining Ratio

29. Arun and Vijay are partners in a firm sharing profits and losses in the ratio of 5 : 1.

Balance Sheet (Extract)

Liabilities	Amount (₹)	Assets	Amount (₹)
		Machinery	40,000

If value of machinery in the balance sheet is undervalued by 20%, then at what value will machinery be shown in new balance sheet:

(a) ₹ 44,000   (b) ₹ 48,000   (c) ₹ 32,000   (d) ₹ 50,000

30. A, B and C were Partners in a firm sharing profits in $3:2:1$ ratio. They admitted D for 10% profits. Calculate new Profit-Sharing Ratio.

(a) $15:9:8:7$ (b) $31:14:10:15$ (c) $9:6:3:2$ (d) $13:10:7:5$

31. Given below are two statements, one labelled as Assertion (A) and the other labelled as Reason (R):

Assertion (A): Capital that a company has not in the form of shares that have been completely paid for by shareholders.

Reason (R): It is not accessible by the partners.

Codes:

(a) Both (A) and (R) are true, but (R) is not the explanation of (A).

(b) Both(A) and (R) are true and (R) is a correct explanation of (A).

(c) Both (A) and (R) are false.

(d) (A) is false, but (R) is true.

32. Which of the following statements is/are correct?

Following options are available:

(i) A company is created by Companies Act.

(ii) The real owners of a Company are Board of Directors.

(iii) Company is a artifical person created by law.

(iv) The liability of a member in a company is unlimited.

Choose the correct option:

(a) (i), (ii), (iii) are correct   (b) (i), (ii), (iv) are correct

(c) (i), (iii), (iv) are correct   (d) All of these

33. A and B are partners sharing profits and losses as $2:1$. C is admitted and profit sharing ratio becomes $4:3:2$. Goodwill is valued at ₹ 94,500. C brings required goodwill in cash. Goodwill amount will be credited to:

(a) A ₹ 14,000 and B ₹ 7,000   (b) A ₹ 12,000 and B ₹ 9,000

(c) A ₹ 21,000   (d) A ₹ 94,500

34. A, B and C sharing profits in the ratio of $2:2:1$ have fixed capitals of ₹ 3,00,000, ₹ 2,00,000 and ₹ 1,00,000 respectively. After closing the accounts for the year ending 31st March 2019 it was discovered that interest on capitals was provided @ 12% instead of 10% p.a. the adjusting entry would be:

(a) Cr. A ₹ 1,200; Dr. B ₹ 800 and Dr. C ₹ 400   (b) Dr. A ₹ 1,200; Cr. B ₹ 800 and Cr. C ₹ 400

(c) Cr. A ₹ 800; Cr. B ₹ 400 and Dr. C ₹ 1,200   (d) Dr. A ₹ 800; Dr. B ₹ 400 and Cr. C ₹ 1,200

35. Star Ltd. issued 10,000 equity shares of ₹ 100 each at a premium of 20%. Mamta, who has been allotted 2,000 shares did not pay first and final call of ₹ 5 per share. On forfeiture of Mamta's shares, amount debited to securities premium reserve account will be:

(a) ₹ 5,000   (b) ₹ 10,000   (c) ₹ 15,000   (d) Nil

36. Answer and Question are partners from 1st April, 2020, without a Partnership Deed and they introduced capitals of ₹ 35,000 and ₹ 20,000 respectively. On 1st October, 2020, Answer advanced loan of ₹ 8,000 to the firm without any agreement as to interest. The Profit and Loss Account for the year ended 31st March, 2021 shows a profit of ₹ 15,000 but the partners cannot agree on payment of interest and on the basis of division of profits. What amount of profit will be distributed between them?

(a) ₹ 7,500 to each   (b) ₹ 7,380 to each   (c) ₹ 7,260 to each   (d) None of these

Section - C

Instructions:

> *From question number 37 to 41, attempt any 4 questions.*

Question no.'s 37 and 38 are based on the hypothetical situation given below.

A Ltd. makes an issue of 10,000 equity shares of ₹ 100 each, payable as follows:

On Application and Allotment	₹ 50
On First Call	₹ 25
On Final Call	₹ 25

Members holding 400 shares did not pay the second call and the shares are duly forfeited, 300 of which are re-issued as fully paid at ₹80 per share.

37. What will be the amount due on share application and allotment?

    (a) ₹ 5,00,000   (b) ₹ 2,50,000   (c) ₹ 7,50,000   (d) ₹ 4,50,000

38. What will the amount transferred to capital reserve?

    (a) ₹ 16,500   (b) ₹ 17,000   (c) ₹ 30,000   (d) ₹ 24,000

Question no.'s 39, 40 and 41 are based on the hypothetical situation given below.

Arun and Barun are partners in a firm sharing profits and losses. Their capitals on 1st April, 2015 were ₹ 4,80,000 and ₹ 5,40,000. On 1st October, 2015, they decided that the total capital of the firm should be ₹ 10,00,000 to be contributed equally by both of them. According to the partnerhip deed, interest on capital is allowed to the partners @ 6% p.a.

39. You are required to compute interest on capital for the year ending 31st March,2016.

    (a) ₹ 29,400; ₹ 31,200   (b) ₹ 14,400; ₹ 16,200   (c) ₹ 15,000; ₹ 15,000   (d) None of these

40. What would be the profit sharing ratio of Arun and Barun?

    (a) 1 : 1   (b) 2 : 3   (c) 3 : 2   (d) 3 : 4

41. What would be the interest on capital till 30th september, 2015?

    (a) ₹ 29,400; ₹ 31,200   (b) ₹ 14,400; ₹ 16,200   (c) ₹ 15,000; ₹ 15,000   (d) None of these

PART – II

Section – A

Instructions:

> *From question number 42 to 48, attempt any 5 questions.*

42. Given below are two statements, one labelled as Assertion (A) and the other labelled as Reason (R):

    Assertion (A): The process of evaluating business, projects, budgets and other finance related transactions to determine their performance and suitability is termed as horizontal analysis.

    Reason (R): It is performed by governmental institutions only.

    Codes:

    (a) Both (A) and (R) are true, but (R) is not the explanation of (A).

    (b) Both(A) and (R) are true and (R) is a correct explanation of (A).

    (c) Both (A) and (R) are false.

    (d) (A) is false, but (R) is true.

43. The ratio in which the continuing partners acquires the outgoing partners share is called:

    (a) Gaining Ratio   (b) New Profit Sharing Ratio

    (c) Old Profit Sharing Ratio   (d) None of these

44. Financial Analysis becomes useless because it:

    (a) Measures the profitability.   (b) Measures the solvency.

    (c) Lacks qualitative analysis.   (d) Makes a comparative study.

45. Bank Overdraft is shown in the Balance Sheet under the:

    (a) Short-term borrowings   (b) Non-current liabilities

    (c) Non-current assets   (d) None of these

46. Consider the following information:

Long-term borrowings	₹2,00,000
Long-term Provision	₹1,00,000
Current Liabilities	₹50,000
Non-current Assets	₹3,60,000
Current Assets	₹90,000

    Proprietary ratio will be:

    (a) 22.2%   (b) 21.8%   (c) 36%   (d) None of these

47. When financial statement for a single year is analysed, which analysis it is called?

    (a) Horizontal   (b) Internal

    (c) Vertical   (d) External

48. A company purchased a business of a firm. When accountant was tallying all assets and liabilities, he found that the company has paid more amount than the worth of it's assets. You are required to find what this difference be called and where it will be shown?

    (a) Capital Reserve, Reserve and Surplus

    (b) Goodwill, Intangible assets

    (c) Accountants totalling is wrong, assets and liabilities always tally without adjustment

    (d) None of the above

Section – B

Instructions:

    ➢ *From question number 49 to 55, attempt any 6 questions.*

49. If Debt equity ratio exceeds_____________, it indicates risky financial position.

    (a) 1 : 1   (b) 2 : 1   (c) 1 : 2   (d) 3 : 1

50. Under which sub-head Factory, Building under construction are include?

    Following options are available:

    (i) Fixed Assets –work in progress

    (ii) Other Non-current Assets

    (iii) Non-current Investment

    Choose the correct option:

    (a) Only (i) is correct   (b) Only (ii) is correct

    (c) Only (iii) is correct   (d) None of these

51. Under which sub-head Provision for employees benefit to be settled within 12 months.

    Following options are available:

    (i) Short-term provision

    (ii) Short-term borrowings

    (iii) Other current liabilities

    Choose the correct option:

    (a) Only (i) is correct   (b) Only (ii) is correct

    (c) Only (iii) is correct   (d) Only (i) and (ii) are correct

52. Given below are two statements, one labelled as Assertion (A) and the other labelled as Reason (R):

    Assertion (A): Gross Profit is the sum of revenue from operations and cost of revenue from operations.

    Reason (R): Gross profit helps in fixing selling prices and assessing efficiency of trading activities.

    Codes:

    (a) Both (A) and (R) are correct and (R) is the correct reason of (A)

    (b) Both (A) and (R) are correct but (R) is not the correct reason of (A)

    (c) Only (R) is correct

    (d) Both (A) and (R) are wrong

53. Operating ratio is:

    (a) Cost of revenue from operations + Selling expenses/Net revenue from operations

    (b) Cost of production + Operating expenses/Net revenue from operations

    (c) Cost of revenue from operations + Operating expenses/Net revenue from operations

    (d) Cost of production/Net revenue from operations

54. Given below are two statements, one labelled as Assertion (A) and the other labelled as Reason (R):

Assertion (A): The objective of computing operating ratio is to assess the operational efficiency of the business.

Reason (R): It shows the percentage of Revenue from operations that is absorbed by the cost of Revenue from operations and operating expenses.

Codes :

(a) (A) and (R) both are correct and (R) correctly explains (A).

(b) Both (A) and (R) are correct but (R) does not explain (A).

(c) Both (A) and (R) are incorrect.

(d) (A) is correct but (R) is incorrect.

55. Which of the following are limitations of ratio analysis?

Following options are available:

(i) Ratio Analysis is historical analysis.

(ii) Ratio analysis ignores qualitative factors.

(iii) Ratio Analysis ignores quantitative factors.

(iv) Ratio Analysis may result in false results if variations in price levels are not considered

Choose the correct option:

(a) A, C and D   (b) A, B and D

(c) A, B and C   (d) A, B, C, D

❑❑

Sample Paper  6

Accountancy

PART – I

Section – A

Instructions:

> *From question number 1 to 18, attempt any 15 questions.*

1. A partnership firm cannot have more than _____ partners and is prescribed in the ______.
   - (a) 50; Companies Act, 2013
   - (b) 30; Companies Act, 2013
   - (c) 40; Companies Act, 2013
   - (d) 20; Companies Act, 2013

2. Calculate the amount of second & final call when a company issue its shares @ ₹ 10 each at a premium of 30%. Payable on Application ₹ 4, On Allotment ₹ 4, On First call ₹ 2:
   - (a) Second and final call ₹ 3
   - (b) Second and final call ₹ 4
   - (c) Second and final call ₹ 1
   - (d) Second and final call ₹ 1

3. A Company invited applications for 1,00,000 shares and it received applications for 1,50,000 shares. Applications for 30,000 shares were rejected and the remaining shares were allotted on prorata basis. How many shares an applicant for 3,000 shares will be allotted :
   - (a) 2,500 shares
   - (b) 3,600 shares
   - (c) 4,500 shares
   - (d) 2,000 shares

4. A company issued 10,000 shares of ₹ 10 each. Amount is payable as ₹ 2 on Application, ₹ 5 on Allotment and ₹ 3 on First and Final call. A shareholder who had 1,000 shares failed to pay allotment and first call amount on due date. After a month, he paid the due amount. What will be the amount received by company against issue of shares?
   - (a) ₹ 92,000
   - (b) ₹ 90,000
   - (c) ₹ 1,00,000
   - (d) ₹ 8,000

5. What will be the correct sequence as types of "Share Capital"?
   - (i) Paid-up capital
   - (ii) Issued capital
   - (iii) Subscribed capital
   - (iv) Called-up capital

   Options:
   - (a) (ii), (iii), (iv), (i)
   - (b) (i), (iv), (ii), (iii)
   - (c) (ii), (i), (iii), (iv)
   - (d) (iii), (iv), (i), (ii)

6. Suraj, Mahesh and Tarun are partners sharing profits and losses in the ratio of 4:3:2. They decide to share future profits and losses in the ratio of 2:3:4 with effect from 1st April, 2018. An extract of their balance sheet as at 31st March, 2018 is as under:

Liabilities	Amount (₹)	Assets	Amount (₹)
Investment Fluctuation Reserve	36,000	Investment	4,00,000

   Market Value of Investment is ₹ 3,82,000. What amount will be Credited/Debited to Partner's Capital A/c?
   - (a) Investment Fluctuation Reserve Debited to ₹ 8,000, ₹ 6,000 ₹ 4,000
   - (b) Investment Fluctuation Reserve Credited to ₹ 8,000 ₹ 6,000 ₹ 4,000
   - (c) It will not be debited to capital A/c
   - (d) It will not be credited to capital A/c

7. Which of the following statement is true?
   (a) A minor cannot be admitted as a partner.
   (b) A minor can be admitted as a partner, only into the benefits of the partnership.
   (c) A minor can be admitted as a partner but his rights and liabilities are same of adult partner.
   (d) None of the above.

8. In case of Admission of a Partner, the entry for Unrecorded Investments is:
   (a) Debit Partners' Capital A/cs and Credit Investments A/c.
   (b) Debit Revaluation A/c and Credit Investments A/c.
   (c) Debit Investments A/c and Credit Revaluation A/c.
   (d) None of the above.

9. X, Y and Z are partners in a firm. At the time of division of profit for the year, there was dispute between the partners. Profit before interest on partner's capital was ₹ 6,000 and Y determined interest @ 24% p.a. on his loan of ₹ 80,000. There was no agreement on this point. Calculate the amount payable to X, Y and Z respectively.
   (a) ₹ 2,000 to each partner
   (b) Loss of ₹ 4,400 for X and Z; Y will take ₹ 14,800
   (c) ₹ 400 for X, ₹ 5,200 for Y and ₹ 400 for Z.
   (d) None of the above

10. X and Y are partners in the ratio of 3 : 2. Their fixed capitals are ₹ 2,00,000 and ₹ 1,00,000 respectively. After closing the accounts for the year ending 31st March 2019, it was discovered that interest on capital was allowed @ 12% instead of 10% per annum. By how much amount X will be debited/credited in the adjustment entry?
    (a) ₹ 600 (Debit)   (b) ₹ 400 (Credit)   (c) ₹ 400 (Debit)   (d) ₹ 600 (Credit)

11. The Partnership Agreement between Mahesh and Ramesh provides that:
    (i)   profits will be shared equally.
    (ii) Mahesh will be allowed a salary ₹ 400 per month.
    (iii) Ramesh is allowed a commission @ 10% on net profits before adjusting any remuneration.
    (iv) 10% per annum interest will be charged on drawings.
    (v)   their annual drawings were ₹ 16,000 and ₹ 14,000 respectively.
    (a) ₹ 34,200   (b) ₹ 32,700   (c) ₹ 47,300   (d) ₹ 29,700

12. On admission of a partner, which of the following items the Balance Sheet is transferred to the credit of Capital Accounts of old partners in the old profit sharing ratio, if Capital Accounts are maintained following Fluctuating Capital Accounts Method.
    (a) Deferred Revenue Expenditure   (b) Profit and Loss Account (Debit Balance)
    (c) Profit and Loss Account (Credit Balance)   (d) Balance in Drawings Account of Partners

13. 'A' and 'B' are partners in a firm. They share their profits and losses in the ratio of 3 : 2. They have decided that their new profits (losses) sharing ratio will be 1 : 1. At that time their goodwill is valued at ₹ 30,000. Calculate amount of goodwill which will be given by B to A.
    (a) ₹ 2,500   (b) ₹ 2,400   (c) ₹ 2,800   (d) ₹ 3,000

14. Which of the following capital is not shown in company's Balance Sheet?
    (a) Authorised capital   (b) Issued and subscribed capital
    (c) Called and paid-up capital   (d) Reserve Capital

15. Money received in advance from shareholders before it is actually called-up by the directors is:
    (a) debited to calls in advance account   (b) credited to calls in advance account
    (c) debited to calls account   (d) None of these

16. When the new partner brings cash for goodwill, the amount is credited to:
    (a) Realisation Account
    (b) Cash Account
    (c) Premium for Goodwill Account
    (d) Revaluation Account

17. 'A' and 'B' carry on business and share profits and losses in the ratio of 3 : 2. Their respective capitals are ₹ 1,20,000 and ₹ 4,000. 'C' is admitted for 1/5th share in profit and brings ₹ 1,20,000 as his share of capital. Capitals of 'A' and 'B' to be adjusted according to 'C's' share.

    Calculate the amount required to bring by 'A'.
    (a) ₹ 30,000   (b) ₹ 1,68,000   (c) ₹ 60,000   (d) ₹ 28,000

18. Average profit of firm is ₹ 3,00,000. Total tangible assets in the firm are ₹ 28,00,000 and outside liabilities are ₹ 8,00,000. In same type of business, normal rate of return is 10% of capital employed. Calculate goodwill by Capitalisation of Super Profit Method.
    (a) ₹ 14,00,000   (b) ₹ 16,00,000   (c) ₹ 18,00,000   (d) ₹ 10,00,000

Section – B

Instructions:

> *From question number 19 to 36, attempt any 15 questions.*

19. A, B, C, and D are partners in a firm sharing profits as 4 : 3 : 2 : 1 respectively. It earned a profit of ₹ 1,80,000 for the year ended 31st March, 2021. As per the Partnership Deed, they are to charge a commission @ 20% of the profit after charging such commission, which they will share as 2 : 3 : 2 : 3. What will be the amount of commission to be paid to the partners?
    (a) ₹ 7,500 each
    (b) ₹ 6,000; ₹ 9,000; ₹ 6,000; ₹ 9,000
    (c) ₹ 12,000; ₹ 9,000; ₹ 6,000; ₹ 3,000
    (d) None of these

20. Partners A, B and C share the profits of a business in the ratio of 3 : 2 : 1 respectively. They admit D who brings in ₹ 60,000 for his share of goodwill. A, B, C and D decide to share the profits respectively in the ratio of 5: 3 : 2 : 2. Credit will be given to:
    (a) A ₹ 6,000; B ₹ 6,000
    (b) A ₹ 30,000; B ₹ 18,000; C ₹ 12,000
    (c) A ₹ 30,000; B ₹ 20,000; C ₹ 10,000
    (d) A ₹ 30,000; B ₹ 30,000

21. 'A', 'B' and 'C' are partners sharing profits in the ratio of 2 : 2 : 1. At the time of Reconstitution of firm, they agreed to write off goodwill which is shown in balance sheet as an intangible asset amounting to ₹ 50,000. Journalise it.

(a) Goodwill A/c	Dr.	50,000	
To A's Capital A/c			20,000
To B's Capital A/c			20,000
To C's Capital A/c			10,000
(b) A's Capital A/c	Dr.	20,000	
B's Capital A/c	Dr.	20,000	
To Goodwill A/c			40,000
(c) A's Capital A/c	Dr.	20,000	
B's Capital A/c	Dr.	20,000	
C's Capital A/c	Dr.	10,000	
To Goodwill A/c			50,000
(d) A's Capital A/c	Dr.	10,000	
B's Capital A/c	Dr.	20,000	
To C's Capital A/c			30,000

22. Given below are two statements, one labelled as Assertion (A) and the other labelled as Reason (R).

    Assertion (A): X spends twice the time that Y devoted to business. X claims that he should get salary of ₹ 6,000 p.m. for extra time spent.

    Reason (R): As there is no partnership deed Partnership Act 1932 applies and as per the Act partners will not be allowed any salary of remuneration.

    Codes:

    (a) (A) is correct, but (R) is wrong

    (b) Both (A) and (R) are correct

    (c) (A) is wrong, but (R) is correct

    (d) Both (A) and (R) are wrong

23. Workmen Compensation Reserve (WCR) appears in the balance sheet of Rashmi and Suman, who share profits in the ratio of 2 : 3 at ₹ 80,000. Deepa is admitted and the new profit sharing ratio is 1 : 1 : 1. If the claim on account of WCR is estimated at ₹ 1,00,000, then.

    (a) The difference of ₹ 20,000 will be debited to revaluation account

    (b) The difference of ₹ 20,000 will be debited to Rashmi's capital account

    (c) The difference of ₹ 20,000 will be debited to Suman's capital account

    (d) None of the above

24. 'A' and 'B' were partners in a firm. They share profits in 2 : 3 ratio. They close their accounts on 31st Decermber every year. 'A' withdrew a fixed sum of ₹ 2,000 at the beginning of every month starting form 1st July, 2017. You have to calculate interest on drawings while rate of interst is 12% p.a.

    (a) ₹ 420   (b) ₹ 720   (c) ₹ 440   (d) ₹ 580

25. Seeta and Geeta are partners sharing profits and losses in the ratio 4 : 1. Meeta was manager who received the salary of ₹ 4,000 p.m. in addition to a commission of 5% on net profits after charging such commission of 5% on net profits after charging such commission. Profit for the year is ₹ 6,78,000 before charging salary. Find the total remuneration of Meeta.

    (a) ₹ 78,000   (b) ₹ 88,000   (c) ₹ 87,000   (d) ₹ 76,000

26. Given below are two statements, one labelled as Assertion (A) and the other labelled as Reason (R).

    Assertion (A): At the time of Admission of a partner, Accumulated profits and losses are transferred to Revaluation Account.

    Reason (R): At the time of Admission of a partner the Accumulated Profits & Losses are not transferred to Capital/Current account in old Profit Sharing Ratio.

    Codes:

    (a) Both (A) and (R) are correct and (R) is the correct reason of (A)

    (b) Both (A) and (R) are correct but (R) is not the correct reason of (A)

    (c) Only (R) is correct

    (d) Both (A) and (R) are wrong

27. S.K Ltd. invited application for 10,000 Equity Shares of ₹ 10 each. Applications were received for 15,000 shares and prorata allotment was made to all the applicants. If Mohan (one shareholder) was allotted 80 shares, find the shares applied by him.

    (a) 80   (b) 100   (c) 150   (d) 120

28. Which of the following is not a part of shareholder's fund?

    (i) Share capital

    (ii) Reserve and surplus

    (iii) Share application money pending allotment

    (iv) Money received against share warrants

    Choose the correct options:

    (a) Only (i)   (b) (i) and (iv) Both   (c) (ii) and (iii) Both   (d) (iii) Only

29. 'A' and 'B' are partners sharing profits and losses in the ratio of 5 : 3. On admission, 'C' brings ₹ 70,000 cash and ₹ 48,000 against goodwill. New profit sharing ratio between 'A', 'B' and 'C' is 7 : 5 : 4. The sacrificing ratio among 'A' and 'B' is:

    (a) 4 : 1   (b) 4 : 7   (c) 5 : 4   (d) 3 : 1

30. Singh who was allotted 200 equity shares of ₹ 20 each by a company, failed to pay ₹ 8 each on final call. Shares were re-issued to Kumar at ₹ 20 each. What will be the journal entry on re-issue?

Bank A/c	Dr.	₹	X
To Equity Share Capital A/c		₹	Y

Here X and Y are:

(a) ₹ 8,000, ₹ 8,000 respectively   (b) ₹ 4,000, ₹ 4,000 respectively

(c) ₹ 6,000, ₹ 6,000 respectively   (d) ₹ 5,000, ₹ 5,000 respectively

31. Given below are two statements, one labelled as Assertion (A) and the other labelled as Reason (R):

Assertion (A): Issued capital is that part of Authorised Share Capital which is issued for subscription whether subscribe or not.

Reason (R): Issued capital is that part of Authorised Share Capital which is issued for subscription to the public which can be more than the subscription or equal to the subscription.

Codes:

(a) Both (A) and (R) are true, but (R) is not the correct explanation of (A)

(b) Both(A) and (R) are true and (R) is a correct explanation of (A)

(c) Both (A) and (R) are false

(d) (A) is false, but (R) is true

32. There are two partners in a firm A and B. C is admitted into the firm for 1/3rd share of profit with the guaranteed profit of ₹ 1,800 p.a. The firm's total profit is ₹ 4,200. If A stood as guarantor of guaranteed profit to C, how much profit would be given to A?

(a) A's Capital A/c will be Debited by ₹ 2,000   (b) A's Capital A/c will be Debited by ₹ 1,500

(c) A's Capital A/c will be Debited by ₹ 1,000   (d) A's Capital A/c will be Debited by ₹ 1,800

33. A Ltd. forfeited 100 shares of ₹ 100 each issued at a premium of 50% to be paid at the time of allotment on which first call of ₹ 30 per equity share was not received, final call of ₹ 20 are yet to be made. These shares were reissued at ₹ 70 per share at ₹ 80 paid up. Calculate Gain on reissue.

(a) 1,000   (b) 3,000   (c) 4,000   (d) 2,000

34. ABC Ltd. purchased Furniture of ₹ 10,00,000 from KK Ltd. and paid 20% of the amount by accepting a bill of exchange in favour of KK Ltd. The remaining amount was paid by issuing Equity Shares of ₹ 100 each at a premium of 25% to KK Ltd. No. of Equity Shares to be issued?

(a) 6,000   (b) 6,400   (c) 10,000   (d) 7,000

35. A and B were partners in a firm sharing profits or losses in the ratio of 3 : 1. With effect from 1st January, 2021, they agreed to share profits in the ratio of 2 : 1. Due to change in profit sharing ratio, B's gain or sacrifice will be:

(a) Gain $\dfrac{1}{12}$ (b) Sacrifice $\dfrac{1}{12}$ (c) Gain $\dfrac{2}{60}$ (d) Sacrifice $\dfrac{2}{60}$

36. X Ltd. Forfeited 2,000 shares of ₹ 10 each (which were issued at par) held by Naresh for non-payment of allotment money of ₹ 4 per share. The called-up value per share was ₹ 9. On forfeiture, the amount debited to share capital account will be:

(a) ₹ 10,000   (b) ₹ 8,000   (c) ₹ 2,000   (d) ₹ 18,000

Section – C

Instructions:

> *From question number 37 to 41, attempt any 4 questions.*

Question no.'s 37 and 38 are based on the hypothetical situation given below.

Bindiya Limited was incorporated on 1st April 2019 with registered office in Mumbai. The capital clause of Memorandum of Association reflected a registered capital of 8,00,000 equity shares of ₹ 10 each and 1,00,000 preference shares of ₹ 50 each. Since some large investments were required for building and machinery the company in consultation with vendors, M/S. VPS Enterprises, issued 1,00,000 equity shares and 20,000 preference shares at par to them in full consideration of assets acquired.

Besides this the company issued 2,00,000 equity shares for cash at par payable as ₹ 3 on application, 2 on allotment, 3 on first call and 2 on second call.

Till date second call has not yet been made and all the shareholders have paid except Mr. Ajay who did not pay allotment and calls on his 300 shares and Mr. Vipul who did not pay first call on his 200 shares. Shares of Mr. Ajay were then forfeited and out of them 100 shares were reissued at ₹ 12 per share.

37. How many equity shares of the company have been subscribed?

    (a) ₹ 3,00,000   (b) ₹ 2,99,500

    (c) ₹ 2,99,800   (d) None of these

38. What amount of share forfeiture would be reflected in the balance sheet?

    (a) ₹ 600   (b) ₹ 900   (c) ₹ 200   (d) ₹ 300

Question no.'s 39, 40 and 41 are based on the hypothetical situation given below.

Feelgood enterprise is a partnership business with Gyan, Manya and Sania as partners engaged in trading business of Readymade Garments. They share profits and losses in the ratio of 3 : 2 : 1. Sania wants to change profit sharing ratio rest of the partners agreed upon and the new profit sharing ratio will be 1 : 1 : 1. For this purpose, goodwill is to be valued at two year's purchase of the average profit of last four years which were as follows:

Year ending on 31st March 2017 ₹ 1,00,000 (Profit)

Year ending on 31st March 2018 ₹ 2,40,000 (Profit)

Year ending on 31st March 2019 ₹ 3,60,000 (Profit)

Year ending on 31st March 2020 ₹ 1,60,000 (Loss)

On 1st October, 2018 a Motor bike costing ₹ 60,000 was purchased and debited to travelling expenses on which depreciation is to be charged @ 20% p.a. as per written down value method.

39. What will be the amount of Goodwill of firm?

    (a) ₹ 2,80,000   (b) ₹ 2,66,667

    (c) ₹ 2,70,000   (d) ₹ 3,25,000

40. Calculate the amount of motor car to be shown in Balance Sheet as on 31st March 2020?

    (a) ₹ 36,000   (b) ₹ 48,000   (c) ₹ 44,200   (d) ₹ 43,200

41. What will be the correct adjustment entry for Goodwill?

    (a) Sania's Capital A/c   Dr.   45,000

           To Gyan's Capital A/c   45,000

    (b) Manya's capital A/c   Dr.   60,000

           To Gyan's Capital A/c   45,000

           To Sania's Capital A/c   15,000

    (c) Manya's current A/c   Dr.   60,000

           To Gyan's Capital A/c   45,000

           To Sania's Capital A/c   15,000

    (d) Premium for Goodwill A/c   Dr.   60,000

           To Gyan's Capital A/c   45,000

           To Sania's Capital A/c   15,000

PART - II

Section - A

Instructions:

> *From question number 42 to 48, attempt any 5 questions.*

42. Given below are two statements, one labelled as Assertion (A) and the other labelled as Reason (R):

    Assertion (A): Horizontal analysis is also known as static analysis.

    Reason (R): Static analysis is made to review & analyse the financial statements of one year only.

    Codes:

    (a) Both (A) and (R) are true, but (R) is not the explanation of (A).

    (b) Both (A) and (R) are true and (R) is a correct explanation of (A).

    (c) Both (A) and (R) are false.

    (d) (A) is false, but (R) is true.

43 Which of the following are included in the Balance Sheet of a Company?

    Following options are available:

    (i) Long term Loan and Advances

    (ii) Revenue from operations

    (iii) Money Received against share warrant

    (iv) Current Assets

    (v) Other Income

    Choose the correct option:

    (a) (ii), (iii) and (v)   (b) (i), (iv) and (vi)

    (c) (i), (iii) and (iv)   (d) (iii), (i) and (v)

44. The following groups of ratios are primarily measure risk:

    (a) liquidity, activity and profitability   (b) liquidity, activity and inventory

    (c) liquidity, activity and debt   (d) liquidity, debt and profitability

45. Which of the following statements are true about ratio analysis?

    Following options are available:

    (i)   Ratio Analysis is useful in financial analysis.

    (ii) Ratio Analysis is helpful in communication and coordination.

    (iii) Ratio Analysis is not helpful in identifying weak spots of the business.

    (iv) Ratio Analysis is helpful in financial planning and forecasting.

    Choose the correct option:

    (a) (i), (ii) and (iv)   (b) (i), (iii) and (iv)

    (c) (i), (ii) and (iii)   (d) (i), (ii), (iii), (iv)

46. Which of the following transactions will improve the current ratio:

    Following options are available:

    (i)   Cash collected from trade receivables

    (ii) Purchase of goods for cash

    (iii) Payment to trade payables

    (iv) Credit purchase of goods

    Choose the correct option:

    (a) Only (iii)   (b) Both (i) and (iii)

    (c) Both (i) and (ii)   (d) Only (i)

47. Match the items given in the column I with the heading/subheadings (Balance sheet) as defined in schedule III of Companies Act 2013.

Column A	Column B
1. Public deposits	(i) Subscribed but not fully paid
2. Trade Mark	(ii) Ratio
3. 500 shares on which final call not received	(iii) Long term Borrowing
4. Financial Analysis	(iv) Intangible fixed assets

Choose the correct option:

(a) 1 – (iii), 2 – (iv), 3 – (i), 4 – (ii)   (b) 1 – (ii), 2 – (iii), 3 – (iv), 4 – (i)

(c) 1 – (iii), 2 – (i), 3 – (ii), 4 – (iv)   (d) 1 – (iv), 2 – (ii), 3 – (i), 4 – (iii)

48. In which of the following ratio ``Total Assets'' are used for calculation purpose:

(a) Proprietary Ratio   (b) Inventory Turnover Ratio

(c) Current Ratio   (d) Return on Investment

Section – B

Instructions:

> *From question number 49 to 55, attempt any 6 questions.*

49. Opening Inventory of a firm is ₹ 80,000. Cost of revenue from operations is ₹ 6,00,000. Inventory Turnover Ratio is 5 times. Its closing Inventory will be:

(a) ₹ 1,60,000   (b) ₹ 1,20,000   (c) ₹ 80,000   (d) ₹ 2,00,000

50. Total purchase ₹ 1,70,000, cash purchases ₹ 16,000, purchase return ₹ 8,000, creditors at the end of the year ₹ 32,000, creditors in the beginning ₹ 24,000. What will be the creditors turnover ratio?

(a) 5.12 times   (b) 5.16 times   (c) 5.21 times   (d) 5.25 times

51. Which of the following statement is not correct in case of Financial Statement Analysis?

Following options are available:

(i)   Horizontal Analysis is a part of comparison

(ii)   Vertical Analysis is a step towards comparison

(iii) Shareholders are the internal users

(iv) Ratio Analysis helps in understanding Cash inflows and Cash outflows

Choose the correct option:

(a) Both (i) and (ii)   (b) Both (i) and (iii)

(c) Both (ii) and (iii)   (d) (i), (ii), (iii) is correct and (iv) is incorrect

52. Given below are two statements, one labelled as Assertion (A) and the other labelled as Reason (R):

Assertion (A): Financial Statements are the end products of accounting process.

Reason (R): Financial Statements are the end products of accounting process. They provide information about the profitability and the financial position of a business.

Codes:

(a) Both (A) and (R) are correct and (R) is the correct reason of (A).

(b) Both (A) and (R) are correct but (R) is not the correct reason of (A).

(c) Only (R) is correct.

(d) Both (A) and (R) are wrong.

53. Given below are two statements, one labelled as Assertion (A) and the other labelled as Reason (R):

Assertion (A): Tanmay Ltd. has a Proprietary Ratio of 25% to maintain this ratio at 30%, management may decrease the current assets.

Reason (R): To increase the proprietary ratio the management may increase equity or reduce the debts increase of current asset will reduce the ratio.

Codes:

(a) (A) and (R) both are correct and (R) correctly explains (A)

(b) Both (A) and (R) are correct but (R) does not explain (A)

(c) Both (A) and (R) are incorrect

(d) (A) is correct but (R) is incorrect

54. Which of the following is not an indicator that a firm is overtrading?

(a) A sharp increase in sales

(b) Decreasing margins due to the use of discounts

(c) Increasing size of overdraft

(d) A decreasing debtor period

55. A company issued shares calling Application, Allotment and First and Final call. A holder of shares not paid allotments and first call. His shares are forfeited but not re-issued. As on balance sheet date, you are required to show these forfeited shares in the balance sheet of company under the head.

(a) Current Liablity

(b) Shareholders' Fund

(c) Current Assets

(d) None of these

56. Current ratio of Vidur Pvt. Ltd. is 3 : 2. Accountant wants to maintain it at 2 : 1.

Following options are available:

(i) He can repay Bills Payable

(ii) He can purchase goods on credit

(iii) He can take short term loan

Choose the correct option:

(a) Only (i) is correct

(b) Only (ii) is correct

(c) Only (i) and (iii) are correct

(d) Only (ii) and (iii) are correct

❑❑

Sample Paper 7

Accountancy

PART – I

Section – A

Instructions:

> *From question number 1 to 18, attempt any 15 questions.*

1. A company issued 50,000,12% preference shares of ₹ 100 each. Company received applications for 70,000 shares. This will be known as _________ of shares.

    (a) Over-subscription   (b) Under-subscription

    (c) Full subscription   (d) None of these

2. If a share of ₹ 10 issued at a premium of ₹ 2 on which the full amount has been called and ₹ 8 (including premium) paid is forfeited, the share capital account will be debited with:

    (a) ₹ 12   (b) ₹ 10   (c) ₹ 8   (d) ₹ 6

3. A company purchased machinery for ₹ 6,00,000, out of which ₹ 1,00,000 was paid immediately and the balance amount was discharged by issue of equity shares of ₹ 10 each at 25% premium. How many shares will be issued by the company to the vendor?

    (a) 50,000 shares   (b) 40,000 shares   (c) 60,000 shares   (d) 48,000 shares

4. The Directors of Axim Ltd. forfeited 20,000 equity shares of ₹ 10 each ,₹ 8 per share called-up for non-payment of ₹ 2 per share. Final call of ₹ 2 per share has not been yet called. Half of the forfeited shares were re-issued as fully paid-up for ₹ 15 per share. The amount transferred to capital reserve will be:

    (a) ₹ 2,00,000   (b) ₹ 60,000   (c) ₹ 1,20,000   (d) ₹ 40,000

5. What will be the correct sequence as types of 'Share Capital'?

    (i) Paid-up capital   (ii) Issued capital

    (iii) Subscribed capital   (iv) Called-up capital

    Choose the correct option:

    (a) (ii), (iii), (iv), (v)   (b) (i), (ii), (iii), (iv)   (c) (iii), (iv), (ii), (i)   (d) (iv), (iii), (ii), (i)

6. A, B & C are partners in the ratio of 3 : 2 : 1. On 31st March they decided to share equally in future.

Balance Sheet			
Liabilities	**Amount (₹)**	**Assets**	**Amount (₹)**
Workman Compensation Reserve	12,000		

Workman Compensation Claim was for ₹ 6,000/- what entry will be passed for the transfer of claim.

(a)   **Journal Entry**

Particulars		Amount (₹)	Amount (₹)
Workman Compensation Reserve A/c	Dr.	6,000	
To Provision for Works. Comp. Claim			6,000

(b)   **Journal Entry**

Particulars		Amount (₹)	Amount (₹)
Workman Compensation Reserve A/c	Dr.	6,000	
To A's Capital A/c			3,000
To B's Capital A/c			2,000
To C's Capital A/c			1,000

(c)

Journal Entry

Particulars		Amount (₹)	Amount (₹)
Workman Compensation Reserve A/c	Dr.	12,000	
To Provision for Works. Comp. Claim			12,000

(d)

Journal Entry

Particulars		Amount (₹)	Amount (₹)
Workman Compensation Reserve A/c	Dr.	12,000	
To A's Capital A/c			6,000
To B's Capital A/c			4,000
To C's Capital A/c			2,000

7. Which of the following statement is true regarding the Partner's Capital Accounts?

   (a) Fluctuating capital account can have a positive or a negative balance

   (b) Fixed capital account will always have a credit balance

   (c) Current account can have a positive or a negative balance

   (d) All of these

8. At the time of Admission of a Partner in which case sacrificing ratio is used to distribute?

   (a) Balance in profit and loss account   (b) Revaluation profit

   (c) Goodwill   (d) Reserves

9. A firm earns ₹ 1,20,000 as its annual profits. The normal rate of profit being 10%. Assets of firm are ₹ 14,40,000 and liabilities are ₹ 4,40,000. Find the value of goodwill by capitalisation method.

   (a) ₹ 4,00,000   (b) ₹ 2,80,000   (c) ₹ 2,00,000   (d) ₹ 3,60,000

10. Mona and Tina were partners in a firm sharing profits in the ratio of 3 : 2. Naina was admitted with 1/6th share in the profits of the firm. At the time of admission, Workmen's Compensation Reserve appeared in the Balance Sheet of the firm at ₹ 32,000. The claim on account of workmen's compensation was determined at ₹ 40,000. Excess of claim over the reserve will be:

    (a) Credited to revaluation account   (b) Debited to revaluation account

    (c) Credited to old partner's capital account (d) Debited to old partner's capital account

11. Calculate net effect of revaluation when revised values are to be recorded in books.

    Following options are available:

    (i) Stock is to be valued at 10% less (Book value ₹ 3,00,000).

    (ii) Provision for bad debts is no more required, (Shown in Balance Sheet for ₹ 4,000).

    (iii) An outstanding salary which is unrecorded of ₹ 16,000.

    Choose the correct option:

    (a) ₹ 40,000 profit   (b) ₹ 42,000 profit   (c) ₹ 42,000 loss   (d) None of these

12. If the purchase consideration is less than net worth then which account will be debited for the difference amount?

    (a) Vendor   (b) Goodwill   (c) Assets   (d) Capital Reserve

13. According to profit and loss account, the net profit for the year is ₹ 4,20,000. Salary of a partner is ₹ 5,000 per month and the commission of another partner is ₹ 10,000. The interest on drawings of partners is ₹ 4,000. The net profit as per profit and loss appropriation account will be:

    (a) ₹ 3,54,000   (b) ₹ 3,46,000   (c) ₹ 4,09,000   (d) ₹ 4,01,000

14. Which section of the partnership act defines partnership as the relation between person who have agreed to share the profit of the business carried on by all or any of them acting for all?

    (a) Section 61   (b) Section 130   (c) Section 4   (d) Section 48

15. When partner's capital accounts are fixed, which one of the following items will be written in the partner's capital account?

    (a) Partner's drawings.

    (b) Additional capital introduced by the partner in the firm.

    (c) Loan taken by partner from the firm.

    (d) Loan advanced by partner to the firm.

16. In case of fixed capitals, undistributed profits, general reserves, etc., are transferred to:

    (a) Partner's Capital Account

    (b) Partner's Current Account

    (c) Revaluation Account

    (d) Profit and Loss Adjustment Account

17. 'G' and 'B' are partners in a firm, 'G' withdraw ₹ 800 per month at the beginning of every month for 6 months ending on 31st December, 2017. 'B' withdraw ₹ 800 per month at the end of every month for 6 months ending on 31st December, 2017. Calculate interest on drawings @ 15% per annum on 31st December, 2017.

    (a) G = ₹ 320, B = ₹ 280

    (b) G = ₹ 180, B = ₹ 220

    (c) G = ₹ 720, B = ₹ 720

    (d) G = ₹ 210, B = ₹ 150

18. A and B contribute ₹ 1,00,000 and ₹ 60,000 respectively in a partnership firm by way of capital on which they agree to allow interest @ 8% p.a. Their profit or loss sharing ratio is 3 : 2. The profit at the end of the year was ₹ 2,800 before allowing interest on capital. If there is a clear agreement that interest on capital will be paid even in case of loss, then B's share will be;

    (a) Profit ₹ 6,000

    (b) Profit ₹ 4,000

    (c) Loss ₹ 6,000

    (d) Loss ₹ 4,000

Section – B

Instructions:

> *From question number 19 to 36, attempt any 15 questions.*

19. Milan, Khilan and Silam were partners sharing profits in the ratio of 2 : 2 : 1. They decided to share future profits in the ratio of 7 : 5 : 3 with effect from 1st April, 2019. After the revaluation of assets and re-assessment of liabilities, revaluation account showed a loss of ₹ 15,000. The amount to be debited in the capital account of Milan because of loss on revaluation will be:

    (a) ₹ 15,000

    (b) ₹ 6,000

    (c) ₹ 7,000

    (d) ₹ 5,000

20. Red, Blue and White were partners in a firm sharing profits in the ratio of 1 : 2 : 2. They decided to share future profits in the ratio of 7 : 5 : 3 with effect from 1st April, 2019. Their balance sheet as on that date showed a balance of ₹ 22,500 in deferred revenue expenditure account. The amount to be debited respectively to the capital accounts of Red, Blue and White for writing-off deferred revenue expenditure will be:

    (a) ₹ 7,500, ₹ 7,500 and ₹ 7,500

    (b) ₹ 4,500, ₹ 9,000 and ₹ 9,000

    (c) ₹ 10,500, ₹ 7,500 and ₹ 4,500

    (d) ₹ 11,250, Nil and ₹ 11,250

21. 700 shares of ₹10 each were issued as ₹ 9 paid-up for ₹ 7 per share. Entry for re-issue will be:

			₹	₹
(a)	Bank A/c	Dr.	4,900	
	Share Discount A/c	Dr.	1,400	
	To Share Capital A/c			6,300
(b)	Bank A/c	Dr.	4,900	
	Share Forfeiture A/c	Dr.	1,400	
	To Share Capital A/c			6,300
(c)	Bank A/c	Dr.	4,900	
	To Share Capital A/c			4,900
(d)	Bank A/c	Dr.	4,900	
	Share Forfeiture A/c	Dr.	2,100	
	To Share Capital A/c			7,000

22. Given below are two statements, one labelled as Assertion (A) and the other labelled as Reason (R).

Assertion (A): As a result in Change in Profit sharing ratio it results in Dissolution of the Partnership Firm.

Reason (R): As the old agreement comes to end as a result of any change in the partnership deed it ends up the old agreement and the new agreement is formed so it becomes the part of Reconstitution of the Partnership Firm ie Dissolution of the Partnership.

Codes:
(a) (A) is correct, but (R) is wrong
(b) Both (A) and (R) are correct
(c) (A) is wrong, but (R) is correct
(d) Both (A) and (R) are wrong

23. A, B and C are partners in a firm sharing profits and losses in 5:3:2 ratio. They decided to share future profits and losses in 3:2:1. Each partner's gain/sacrifice due to change in the ratio will be:
(a) A Gain-1/30, B-Nil, C Sacrifice-1/30
(b) A-Nil, B Sacrifice-1/30, C Gain-1/30
(c) A Sacrifice-1/30, B Gain-1/30, C-Nil
(d) A-Nil, B-Gain-1/30, C Sacrifice-1/30

24. A and B are partners in a firm having a capital of ₹ 54,000 and ₹ 36,000 respectively. They admitted C for $\frac{1}{3}$ rd share in the profit. C brought proportionate amount of capital. The capital brought in by C would be:
(a) ₹ 90,000
(b) ₹ 45,000
(c) ₹ 5,400
(d) ₹ 3,600

25. A and B are partners sharing profits in the ratio of 2 : 3. Their balance sheet shows machinery at ₹ 2,00,000; stock at ₹ 80,000 and debtors at ₹ 1,60,000. C is admitted and new profit sharing ratio is agreed at 6 : 9 : 5. Machinery is revalued at ₹ 1,40,000 and a provision is made for doubtful debts @ 5%. A's share in loss on revaluation amount to ₹ 20,000. Revalued value of stock will be:
(a) ₹ 62,000
(b) ₹ 1,00,000
(c) ₹ 60,000
(d) ₹ 98,000

26. Given below are two statements, one labelled as Assertion (A) and the other labelled as Reason (R):

Assertion (A): Issued capital can be more than the Authorised Capital.

Reason (R): Whenever the company wants it can issue shares to the public so it does not matter what the Authorised Capital is.

Codes:
(a) Both (A) and (R) are correct and (R) is the correct reason of (A)
(b) Both (A) and (R) are correct but (R) is not the correct reason of (A)
(c) Only (R) is correct
(d) Both (A) and (R) are wrong

27. Gopal Ltd. purchased machine of ₹ 1,15,000 from Indian Traders, payment of ₹ 10,000 was made by issuing cheque and the remaining amount by issue of equity shares of the face value of ₹ 10 each fully paid at an issue price of ₹ 10.50 each. Amount of securities premium will be:
(a) ₹ 6,000
(b) ₹ 7,000
(c) ₹ 5,000
(d) ₹ 4,000

28. Which of the following statement is true?
(a) Authorised capital > Issued capital
(b) Paid-up capital > Issued capital
(c) Authorised capital = Issued capital
(d) None of these

29. 'A', 'B' and 'C' share profits and losses in the ratio of 3 : 2 : 1. 'D' is admitted with 1/6th share which he gets entirely from 'A'. New ratio will be:
(a) 2 : 2 : 1 : 1
(b) 3 : 1 : 1 : 1
(c) 2 : 2 : 2 : 1
(d) None of these

30. A Company forfeited the following shares:

200 shares of ₹ 10 each; called-up ₹ 9 per share, paid-up ₹ 7 per share. Journal entry for forfeiture will be:

Share Capital A/c	Dr.	₹ X
To Share Forfeiture A/c		₹ Y
To Calls in Arrears A/c		₹ Z

Here X, Y and Z are:
(a) ₹ 2,000; ₹ 200; ₹ 1,800 respectively
(b) ₹ 2,000; ₹ 1,800; ₹ 200 respectively
(c) ₹ 1,800; ₹ 1,400; ₹ 400 respectively
(d) ₹ 1,800; ₹ 400; ₹ 1,400 respectively

31. Given below are two statements, one labelled as Assertion (A) and the other labelled as Reason (R):

    Assertion (A): Y wants that profits should be distributed in the ratio of capitals as he has invested more capital than X this dispute arises as the partnership deed was not there.

    Reason (R): As there is no partnership deed Indian Partnership Act, 1932 applies and as per the Act, Profits are to be distributed equally.

    Codes:

    (a) Both (A) and (R) are true, but (R) is not the explanation of (A).

    (b) Both(A) and (R) are true and (R) is a correct explanation of (A).

    (c) Both (A) and (R) are false.

    (d) (A) is false, but (R) is true.

32. A and B are partners sharing profits and losses in the ratio of 3 : 2. C is admitted into partnership for $\frac{1}{5}$th share in profit. He pays ₹ 1,00,000 as goodwill. The ratio of the partners A, B and C in the new firm would be 3 : 1 : 1. Goodwill will be credited to:

    (a) Only A ₹ 1,00,000

    (b) Only B ₹ 1,00,000

    (c) A ₹ 60,000; B ₹ 40,000

    (d) A ₹ 75,000; B ₹ 25,000

33. On an equity share of ₹ 20, the company called-up ₹ 16 but ₹ 14 has been received by the company, equity share capital account will be credited by:

    (a) ₹ 20   (b) ₹ 16   (c) ₹ 14   (d) ₹ 2

34. Vinod Ltd. is registered with 50,000 shares @ ₹ 10 each. It issued 40,000 shares to the public @ ₹ 10 each. Applications were received for 38,000 shares and allotment was made to all the applicants. The Authorised Capital of the company is:

    (a) ₹ 3,80,000

    (b) ₹ 4,00,000

    (c) ₹ 2,80,000

    (d) ₹ 5,00,000

35. A, B and C are partners sharing profits in ratio of 3 : 2 : 1. They agree to admit D into the firm. A, B and C agreed to give $\frac{1}{3}$rd, $\frac{1}{6}$th and $\frac{1}{9}$th share of their profit. The share of profit of D will be:

    (a) $\frac{1}{10}$ (b) $\frac{11}{54}$ (c) $\frac{12}{54}$ (d) $\frac{13}{54}$

36. The Directors of Vinod Ltd. forfeited 70,000 Equity Shares of ₹ 10 each, ₹ 10 called-up, for non-payment of final call of ₹ 1 per share. Half of the forfeited shares were reissued at ₹ 20 per share fully paid up. On reissue of forfeited shares, which of the following amount will be transferred to the Capital Reserve Account?

    (a) ₹ 70,000   (b) ₹ 1,40,000   (c) ₹ 4,20,000   (d) ₹ 3,15,000

Section - C

Instructions:

> *From question number 37 to 41, attempt any 4 questions.*

Question no.'s 37 and 38 are based on the hypothetical situation given below.

Himalaya Company Limited issued for public subscription of ₹ 1,20,000 equity shares of ₹ 10 each at a premium of ₹ 2 per share payable as under:

	(₹)
With Application	3 per share
On Allotment (including premium)	5 per share
On First Call	2 per share
On Second and Final Call	2 per share

Applications were received for ₹ 1,60,000 shares. Allotment was made on pro-rata basis. Excess money on application was adjusted against the amount due on allotment. Rohan to whom 4,800 shares were allotted, failed to pay for the two calls. These shares were subsequently forfeited after the second call was made. All the shares forfeited were reissued to Teena as fully paid at ₹ 7 per share.

37. What is the amount of discount on re-issue of shares?

    (a) ₹ 1,200   (b) ₹ 800   (c) ₹ 600   (d) ₹ 14,400

38. What is the amount to be left in Share forfeiture Account, which will be shown in the Balance Sheet?

    (a) ₹ 1,200   (b) ₹ 800   (c) ₹ 600   (d) NIL

Question no.'s 39, 40 and 41 are based on the hypothetical situation given below.

ERD Ltd. is a partnership business with Ram and Shyam as partners engaged in the production and sales of readymade garments.

Their initial capital contribution was ₹ 13,80,000 and ₹ 10,20,000 respectively with profit sharing ratio of 3 : 2. Firm's goodwill was valued at ₹ 10,00,000. Seeing the competition in the market they decided to expand their business. For this purpose, they Reeded machinery, more raw material etc. for which they needed more capital. Since they didn't have enough money and neither they wanted to take loan, they decided to admit Vijay as a partner who contributes ₹ 7,00,000 as capital and the required amount of goodwill for 1/5th share of profits to be acquired equally from Ram and Shyam.

The partners decided that capital accounts of old partners are to be adjusted on the basis of the proportion of Vijay's Capital to his share in the business.

Vijay accepted the offer. The terms of the offer were duly accepted and Vijay was admitted as a partner.

39. What will be the new profit sharing ratio of Ram, Shyam and Vijay?

    (a) 3 : 2 : 5   (b) 5 : 3 : 5   (c) 5 : 3 : 5   (d) 3 : 2 : 1

40. What is the amount of goodwill brought in by new partner?

    (a) ₹ 10,00,000   (b) ₹ 7,00,000   (c) ₹ 2,00,000   (d) ₹ 50,00,000

41. What is the value of total capital of the new firm?

    (a) ₹ 7,00,000   (b) ₹ 35,00,000   (c) ₹ 11,58,000   (d) ₹ 15,58,000

PART – II

Section – A

Instructions:

➢ *From question number 42 to 48, attempt any 5 questions.*

42. Given below are two statements, one labelled as Assertion (A) and the other labelled as Reason (R):

Assertion (A): Accounting ratio is a mathematical expression of relationship between one item of the group of item in the Financial Statement.

Reason (R): Accounting ratio is a mathematical expression of relationship between two items group of item in the Financial Statement.

Codes:

(a) Both (A) and (R) are true, but (R) is not the explanation of (A).

(b) Both (A) and (R) are true and (R) is a correct explanation of (A).

(c) Both (A) and (R) are false.

(d) (A) is false, but (R) is true.

43. Which of the following items is shown under the head Non-current Assets while preparing company's Balance Sheet as per Schedule III of Company Act, 2013?

Following options are available:

(i) Motor Vehicles   (ii) Stock in trade   (iii) Goodwill   (iv) Cash at bank

(v) Loose tools   (vi) Bills receivable

Choose the correct option:

(a) (i), (iii)   (b) (ii), (iv)   (c) (v), (vi)   (d) (i), (ii)

44. What is a measure of liquidity which excludes generally the least liquid assets?

   (a) current ratio, inventory   (b) liquid ratio, inventory

   (c) liquid ratio, accounts receivable   (d) current ratio, accounts receivables

45. Which of the following are limitations of ratio analysis?

   (i) Ratio analysis may result in false results if variations in price levels are not considered.

   (ii) Ratio analysis ignores qualitative factors.

   (iii) Ratio analysis ignores quantitative factors.

   (iv) Ratio analysis is historical analysis.

   In the context of the above four statements, which of the following options is correct?

   (a) (i), (ii) and (iv)   (b) (i), (iii) and (iv)   (c) (i), (ii) and (iii)   (d) (i), (ii), (iii), (iv)

46. In which of the following Liquid ratio is also known as:

   (a) Quick ratio   (b) Acid test ratio

   (c) Working capital ratio   (d) Stock turnover ratio

   Choose the correct option:

   (a) Only (i)   (b) Both (i) and (ii)   (c) Both (ii) and (iii)   (d) Only (iii)

47. Match the items given in Column A with the headings/sub-headings (Balance Sheet) As defined in Schedule III of Companies Act, 2013.

Column A	Column B
1. Share Capital	(i) Non-current Liabilities
2. Deferred Tax Liabilities	(ii) Current Liabilities
3. Short-term Provisions	(iii) Non-current Assets
4. Non-current Investments	(iv) Shareholder's Fund

Choose the correct option:

(a) 1-(i), 2-(iii), 3-(ii), 4-(iv)   (b) 1-(iv), 2-(i), 3-(ii), 4-(iii)

(c) 1-(iii), 2-(i), 3-(iv), 4-(ii)   (d) 1-(iv), 2-(iii), 3-(i), 4(ii)

48. A transaction involving decrease in current ratio and an increase in quick ratio:

   (a) purchase of stock-in-trade for cash   (b) sale of non-current assets for cash

   (c) sale of stock-in-trade at loss   (d) cash payment of non-current liability

Section – B

Instructions:

   ➤ *From question number 49 to 55, attempt any 6 questions.*

49. If Opening Inventory is ₹ 12,20,000, Cost of Revenue from Operations is ₹ 10,00,000 and Inventory Turnover Ratio is 5 times, then Closing Inventory will be:

   (a) ₹ 3,20,000   (b) ₹ 2,80,000   (c) ₹ 1,60,000   (d) ₹ 4,00,000

50. What will be the amount of Total current assets if a firm has current ratio of 4:1 and quick ratio of 2.5:1. Assuming inventories are ₹ 15,000?

   (a) ₹ 10,000   (b) ₹ 25,000   (c) ₹ 40,000   (d) ₹ 15,000

51. Which of the following is not included in short-term borrowings?

   Following options are available:

   (i) Loans repayable on demand.   (ii) Revenue from operations.

   (iii) Retirement benefits to employees.   (iv) Cash credit from bank.

   Choose the correct option:

   (a) Both (i) and (ii)   (b) Both (iii) and (iv)   (c) Both (ii) and (iii)   (d) Both (i) and (iv)

52. Given below are two statements, one labelled as Assertion (A) and the other labelled as Reason (R):

Assertion (A): Proposed dividend is a contingent liability.

Reason (R): As per AS-4 Revised, Proposed dividend is shown as the contingent liability because it is subject to approval by the shareholders, who may reduce the amount of dividend to be paid.

Codes:

(a) Both (A) and (R) are correct and (R) is the correct reason of (A)

(b) Both (A) and (R) are correct but (R) is not the correct reason of (A)

(c) Only (R) is correct

(d) Both (A) and (R) are wrong

53. Given below are two statements, one labelled as Assertion (A) and the other labelled as Reason (R):

Assertion (A): Proprietary ratio establishes relationship between proprietors fund and total assets.

Reason (R): The objective of calculating proprietary ratio is to measure proportion of fixed assets financed by shareholders funds.

Codes:

(a) (A) and (R) both are correct and (R) correctly explains (A).

(b) Both (A) and (R) are correct but (R) does not explain (A).

(c) Both (A) and (R) are incorrect.

(d) (A) is correct but (R) is incorrect.

54. Liquid ratio of 1.2:1, cash collected from debtors would:

Following options are available:

(i) Increase liquid ratio

(ii) Decrease liquid ratio

(iii) Have no effect on liquid ratio

(iv) Increase gross profit ratio

Choose the correct option:

(a) Only (i) is correct

(b) Only (iii) is correct

(c) Only (i) and (ii) are correct

(d) Only (iii) and (iv) are correct

55. A company has issued 2,00,000 equity shares of ₹ 10 each and it has called the entire nominal value of the share. It has received the entire amount except final call of ₹ 3 per share on 5,000 shares. Subscribed capital will be shown as follows:

	₹	₹
(a) Subscribed and fully paid		
2,00,000 Equity shares of ₹ 10 each	20,00,000	
Less: Calls-in-arrears	15,000	19,85,000
(b) Subscribed but not fully paid		
2,00,000 Equity shares of ₹ 10 each	20,00,000	
Less: Calls-in-arrears	15,000	19,85,000
(c) Subscribed and fully paid		
1,95,000 Equity shares of ₹ 10 each		19,50,000
Subscribed but not fully paid		
5,000 Equity shares of ₹ 10 each	50,000	
Less: Calls-in-arrears	15,000	35,000
		19,85,000

(d) None of the above

❑❑

Answers

Sample Paper 1

PART – I

Section – A

1. (a) Ascertain Average Profit

2. (c) No limit

3. (b) Reconstitution of partnership

4. (a) Revalued Figure

5. (b) Any profit and loss on account of change in values belong to old partners

6. (c) Issued Capital

7. (a)

Explanation:

Old ratio $= 3 : 2$

New ratio $= 2 : 1 : 1$

Sacrifice of A = Old share – New share

$$= \frac{3}{5} - \frac{2}{4} = \frac{2-10}{20} = \frac{2}{20}$$

$$\text{Sacrifice of B} = \frac{2}{5} - \frac{1}{4} = \frac{8-5}{20} = \frac{3}{20}$$

Hence, Sacrifice ratio $= 2 : 3$

And entry will be:

		₹	₹
Premium for Goodwill A/c	Dr.	40,000	
To A's Capital A/c			16,000
To B's Capital A/c			24,000

(Being premium for goodwill shared by old partners on the basis of sacrificing ratio *i.e.,* 2:3)

8. (b) Only (ii) is correct

9. (a) $2 : 2 : 1 : 1$

Explanation:

$$\text{A's share} = \frac{3}{6} - \frac{1}{6} = \frac{2}{6}$$

$$\text{B's share} = \frac{2}{6}$$

$$\text{C's share} = \frac{1}{6} \text{ and D's share} = \frac{1}{6}$$

New Profit Sharing Ratio $= 2 : 2 : 1 : 1$

10. (b) Decrease in value of asset

11. (c) ₹ 405

Explanation:

i.e., $$4,500 \times 4 = 18,000$$

Now $$= 18,000 \times \frac{6}{100} \times \frac{4.5}{12} = ₹\ 405$$

12. (d) ₹ 4,950

Explanation:

	(₹)
Calls-in-arrears:	
Allotment (250 × 7)	= 1,750
Final Call (250 × 8)	= 2,000
(150 × 8)	= 1,200
	= 4,950

13. (a) Current A/c

14. (c) Only (iii) is correct

15. (b) Only (ii) is correct

16. (d) 300 shares

Explanation: Calculation of shares alloted to Mohan:

$$= \frac{\text{Total number of shares alloted}}{\text{Total number of shares applied}} \times \text{shares applied by applicant}$$

$$= \frac{10,000}{14,000} \times 420$$

$$= 300$$

17. (b) Only (ii) is correct

18. (c) (i), (ii), (iv) are correct.

Section - B

19. (c) Profit and Loss Account (Credit Balance)

20. (b) When capital are fixed

21. (b) Both (A) and (R) are correct.

Explanation: When the value of assets increases it is debited to revaluation account. As plant and machinery is the assets, so when assets are increases, revaluation account is credited and assets are debited.

22. (d) capital reserve is credited with the credit balance left in the forfeited shares account.

23. (a) V = ₹ 12,10,000, A = ₹ 9,35,000

Explanation:

Particulars	Virat (₹)	Anushka (₹)
Opening Capital	10,00,000	8,00,000
(+) Salary to Partners	30,000	30,000
(+) Interest on Capital	50,000	40,000
(+) Divisible Profts (Total Profits– Salary – Interest on Capital) divided in 2 : 1 ratio [3,45,000 – 60,000 – 90,000] = 1,95,000 divided in the ratio of 2 : 1	1,30,000	65,000
Closing Capital	12,10,000	9,35,000

24.

		₹	₹
(d) Share Capital A/c	Dr.	3,500	
To Share First Call A/c			1,000
To Share Forfeiture A/c			2,500

25. (c) Only (R) is correct.

26. (c) ₹ 1,800, ₹ 1,400, ₹ 400 respectively

27. (c) 58,050

Interest on Loan advanced by Kajal is Charge against profit = ₹ 30,000 × $\dfrac{6}{100}$ = ₹ 1,800.

Profit to be Credited will be = ₹ 68,460 – ₹ 1,800 = ₹ 66,660

28. (a)

Particulars		L/f	₹	₹
Nisha's Capital A/c	Dr.		55,000	
To Reya's Capital A/c				55,000
(Being adjustment entry passed)				

Explanation:

Table Showing Adjustments					
Particulars		Reya	Mone	Nisha	Total
Distribution of Profits	Cr.	1,65,000	1,10,000	55,000	3,30,000
Reversal of Profits	Dr.	1,10,000	1,10,000	1,10,000	3,30,000
Difference		Cr. 55,000	–	Dr. 55,000	

29. (c) (iv)-(iii)-(ii)-(i)

Since revised values are not to be recorded in books, so profit or loss on revaluation is adjusted through capital accounts by passing a single adjustment entry.

30. (d) All of these

Explanation: Since all these options can be used by the company individually or in combination.

31. (a) Both (A) and (R) are true, but (R) is not the explanation of (A)

Explanation: A share premium account is recorded in the shareholders' equity portion of the balance sheet. The share premium account represents the difference between the par value of the shares issued and the subscription or issue price.

32. (b) Gain on Revaluation ₹ 1,20,000

Explanation:

Revaluation A/c				
Particulars	₹	Particulars	₹
---	---	---	---
To Machinery	10,000	By Land & Building	75,000
To Copyrights	17,500	By Stock	75,000
To Debtors	7,500	By Prepaid Insurance	5,000
To Gain Transferred to Capitals	1,20,000		
	1,55,000		**1,55,000**

33. (d) 120

Explanation: Calculation of shares applied by Mohan :

$$= \dfrac{\text{Total number of shares applied}}{\text{Total number of shares alloted}} \times \text{shares alloted to applicant}$$

$$= \dfrac{15,000}{10,000} \times 80$$

$$= 120$$

34. (a) Investment Fluctuation Reserve Credited as ₹ 3,000 : ₹ 2,000 : ₹ 1,000

Explanation:

Journal Entries

Particulars		₹	₹
Investment Fluctuation Reserve A/c	Dr.	6,000	
To Investments A/c			6,000
(Being the value of investment brought down to its market value)			
Investment Fluctuation Reserve A/c	Dr.	6,000	
To A's Capital A/c			3,000
To B's Capital A/c			2,000
To C's Capital A/c			1,000
(Being the surplus Investment Fluctuation Reserve transferred to partner's capital accounts)			

35. (a) $A\dfrac{9}{16}, B\dfrac{3}{16}, C\dfrac{4}{16}$

Explanation:

$$C's\ share = \frac{1}{4}$$

$$Total\ share = 1$$

$$Remaining\ share\ of\ A\ and\ B = 1 - \frac{1}{4} = \frac{3}{4}$$

$$A's\ new\ share = \frac{3}{4} \times \frac{3}{4} = \frac{9}{16}$$

$$B's\ new\ share = \frac{3}{4} \times \frac{1}{4} = \frac{3}{16}$$

$$C's\ new\ share = \frac{1}{4} \times \frac{4}{4} = \frac{4}{16}$$

$$\therefore \quad New\ profit\ sharing\ ratio = 9 : 3 : 4$$

36. (b) 7 : 5 (35,000 – 25,000) = 7 : 5

Explanation: The ratio is calculated as under:

$$Shares\ Applied : Shares\ Available$$
$$35,000 : 25,000$$
$$35 : 25$$
$$7 : 5$$

Hence, every person who applied for 7 shares will get 5 shares.

Section – C

37. (d) ₹ 8,300

38. (c) 3/10

39. (a) ₹ 59,700

40. (a) ₹ 500

41. (d) ₹ 40,000

PART - II

Section - A

42. (a) Both (A) and (R) are true, but (R) is not the explanation of (A)

43. (d) Reserve capital

44. (b) 33.3%

> **Explanation:** Percentage change $= \dfrac{\text{new value - old value}}{\text{old value}} \times 100$
>
> $= \dfrac{4,00,000 - 3,00,000}{3,00,000} \times 100$
>
> $= 33.33\%$

45. (a) Operating ratio

> **Explanation:** Operating ratio is a company's operating expenses as a percentage of revenue. Higher the operating ratio the less favourable it is because, it would leave a smaller margin to meet interest, dividend and other corporate needs.

46. (a) horizontal

47. (a) Only (i) is correct

48. (b) Contingent Liabilities

Section - B

49. (c) Only (iii) is correct.

50. (d) ₹ 18,00,000

> **Explanation:**
>
> **Statement of Profit and Loss**
>
> | Particulars | | Amount (₹) |
> |---|---|---|
> | Revenue from Operations | | 80,00,000 |
> | (–) Expenses | ₹ | |
> | Cost of Material Consumed | 10,00,000 | |
> | Purchase of Stock-in trade | 30,00,000 | |
> | Employees Benefit Expense | 4,00,000 | (44,00,000) |
> | Profit before Tax | | 36,00,000 |
> | (–) Tax @ 50% | | 18,00,000 |
> | Profit after Tax | | 18,00,000 |

51. (c) Only (R) is correct.

52. (b) Only (ii) is correct.

53. (d) Assertion is correct, but reason is incorrect.

> **Explanation:** when tow or more persons joins hands to set up a business and share its profit and losses, they are said to be in partnership. It is not mondatory for the partners to share profits and losses equally. The profit and losses will be shared equally only when they agree or when the partnership deed is silent in this respect.

54. (d) Current Assets ₹ 90,000 and Current Liabilities ₹ 60,000.

55. (b) 46.7%

Explanation:

$$\text{Operating Ratio} = \frac{\text{Cost of Revenue from Operations} + \text{Operating Expenses} \times 100}{\text{Revenue from Operations}}$$

$$= \frac{50,000 + 20,000}{1,50,000} \times 100 = 46.7\%$$

Sample Paper 2

PART – I

Section – A

1. (a) Sweat Equity Shares

2. (c) Old-profit sharing ratio

3. (a) 5% per annum

4. (c) Old partner's capital Account

5. (b) Subtracted from share capital

6. (a) Gaining Ratio

7. (b) ₹ 9 per share

Explanation:

Total forfeiture amount	= ₹ 6,000
(2,000 share @ ₹3 each)	
Less: Amount transfer to capital reserve	= (4,000)
Dicount allowed on re-issue of share	= 2,000

$$\text{Discount value of share} = 10 - \frac{2,000}{2,000} = 10 - 1 = ₹ 9 \text{ per share}$$

8. (b) When capital are fixed

9. (a) B pays A ₹ 4,000

Explanation:

Reason :	A	B
New Ratio	3/5	2/5
Old Ratio	2/3	1/3
Gaining/Sacrificing Ratio	(1/15)	1/15

i.e., B is the Gaining Partner while A is the Sacrificing Partner. Therefore, B will compensate A an amount equal to 1/15th of ₹ 60,000 *i.e.,* ₹ 4,000.

10. (c) A new partner has to bring relatively higher capital as compared to the existing partners

11. (b) Only (ii) is correct

12. (b) Old Ratio

13. (a) 2,500 shares

Explanation: Calculation of shares alloted :

$$= \frac{1,00,000}{1,20,000} \times 3000$$

$$= 2,500 \text{ shares}$$

14. (c) Current Year's Profits

15. (c) ₹ 1,00,000

Explanation: Amount due on total shares (10,000 × 10) ₹ 1,00,000 complete amount was received, one shareholder paid late, but at the end amount was received. Hence, complete amount received by the company will be ₹ 1,00,000.

16. (b) 6.5 months

17. (a) Only (i) is correct

18. (c) Only (iii) is correct

Section – B

19. (c) ₹ 5,60,000

Explanation: Maximum amount of discount at which these shares can be reissued are (8,000 × 70) = ₹ 5,60,000

20. (a) Debited, Revaluation

21. (d) General Public

22. (b) Both (A) and (R) are correct

Explanation: Shares, as applied to the capital of a company, refer to the units into which the total share capital of a company is divided. Thus, a share is a fractional part of the share capital and forms the basis of ownership interest in a company. The persons who contribute money through shares are called shareholders. Thus, both assertion and reason are correct and the reason is the correct explanation of the assertion.

23. (a) Old Profit-Sharing Ratio

24. (b) ₹ 3,600 to Pen; ₹ 2,400 to Pencil.

Explanation:

$$\text{Pen's Interest on Drawings} = ₹\,1,20,000 \times \frac{6}{100} \times \frac{6}{12} = ₹\,3,600$$

$$\text{Pencil's Interest on Drawings} = ₹\,80,000 \times \frac{6}{100} \times \frac{6}{12} = ₹\,2,400$$

25. (a) Both (A) and (R) are correct and (R) is the correct reason of (A).

Explanation: Persons who have entered into partnership with one another are individually called 'partners' and collectively called 'firm'. The name under which the business is carried is called the 'firm's name'. A partnership firm has no separate legal entity, apart from the partners constituting it. Thus, both assertion and the reason are correct and reason is the correct explanation of the assertion.

26. (a) Only (i) is correct

27. (b) Section 53

28. (a) ₹ 5,750 for Lappy & ₹ 4,075 for Tappy.

Explanation: Lappy's Interest on Capital = on ₹ 50,000 for 12 months = ₹ 50,000 × $\dfrac{10}{100}$ = ₹ 5,000

= on 10,000 for 9 months = ₹ 10,000 × $\dfrac{10}{100} \times \dfrac{9}{12}$ = ₹ 750

Total = ₹ 5,750

Tappy's Interest on Capital = On ₹ 40,000 for 12 months = ₹ 40,000 × $\dfrac{10}{100}$ = ₹ 4,000

= On 1,000 for 9 months = ₹ 1,000 × $\dfrac{10}{100} \times \dfrac{9}{12}$ = ₹ 75

Total = ₹ 4,075

29. (b) ₹ 12,000

Explanation:

$$\text{Average Profits} = \frac{\text{Total operating Profits}}{\text{Number of Years}}$$

$$\text{Average Profits} = \frac{(6,000-2,000)+(4,000+3,000)+(2,500-1,500)}{3} = ₹\,4,000$$

Goodwill = Average Profits × Number of Years' Purchase

Goodwill = 4,000 × 3 = ₹ 12,000

30. (d) All of these

31. (c) Both (A) and (R) are False

Explanation: The profit sharing ratio among the old partners will change keeping in view their respective contribution to the profit sharing ratio of the incoming partner. Hence, there is a need to ascertain the new profit sharing ratio among all the partners. Thus, assertion and reason are False.

32. (c) $6:5:1$

Explanation:

	A	:	B	:	C
Old Ratio	3	:	2	:	1
New Ratio	6	:	1	:	5

Sacrificing Ratio = Old Ratio – New Ratio.

Sacrifice of A = $\dfrac{1}{4}$ Gain of B = $\dfrac{1}{4}$

Sacrifice of B = $\dfrac{1}{2}$

Gain of A = $\dfrac{1}{2} \times \dfrac{1}{2} = \dfrac{1}{4}$

Gain of C = $\dfrac{1}{2} \times \dfrac{1}{2} = \dfrac{1}{4}$

New Ratio = Old Ratio – Sacrifice + Gain

$$A = \dfrac{3}{6} - \dfrac{1}{4} + \dfrac{1}{4} = \dfrac{6}{12}$$

$$B = \dfrac{2}{6} - \dfrac{1}{2} + \dfrac{1}{4} = \dfrac{1}{12}$$

$$C = \dfrac{1}{6} + \dfrac{1}{4} = \dfrac{5}{12}$$

33. (d) Neha-Nil, Nisha Gain-1/30, Yamini Sacrifice-1/30

Explanation: Sacrificing/(Gaining) Share = Old Share – New Share

$$\text{Neha} = \frac{5}{10} - \frac{3}{6} = \frac{15-15}{30} = \text{Nil}$$

$$\text{Nisha} = \frac{3}{10} - \frac{2}{6} = \frac{9-10}{30} = \left(\frac{1}{30}\right) \text{Gain}$$

$$\text{Yamini} = \frac{2}{10} - \frac{1}{6} = \frac{6-5}{30} = \frac{1}{30} \text{ Sacrifice}$$

34. (d) Both are incorrect.

35. (d) B's Capital Account is to be credited by ₹ 5,000.

Explanation: Calculation of scrificing ratio :

$$\text{A's acrifice} = \frac{3}{5} - \frac{5}{10} = \frac{1}{10}$$

$$\text{B's Sacrifice} = \frac{2}{5} - \frac{3}{10} = \frac{1}{10}$$

Sacrificing ratio = 1 : 1

Distribution of premium for goodwill :

$$\text{A's share} = 10,000 \times \frac{1}{2} = 5,000$$

$$\text{B's share} = 10,000 \times \frac{1}{2} = 5,000$$

36. (b) ₹ 90,000.

Section – C

37. (a) ₹1,00,000

38. (a) ₹30,000

39. (b) ₹6,80,000

40. (d) 25%

41. (c) 80%

PART – II

Section – A

42. (b) Current ratio and Quick ratio

43. (b) Both (A) and (R) are true and (R) is a correct explanation of (A).

Explanation: Liquidity measures a company's ability to utilize its resources available to meet its short term commitments. If a company cannot meet its short term commitments on time, it eventually becomes insolvent and may require reorganization or liquidation. Liquid assets are a measure of the near-term liquidity position of a firm. Liquid liabilities are debt obligations which a firm has to pay within a year. Thus, both assertion and reason are correct and reason is the correct explanation of the assertion.

44. (d) All of these

45. (a) Bank Charges

46. (d) four

47. (b) Only (ii) is correct

48. (a) ₹ 1,40,000

> **Explanation:** Other Incomes:
>
> (i)   Commission Received = 1,20,000
>
> (ii) Dividend from Investment Received =   20,000
>
> = 1,40,000
>
> Sale of products and services are revenue from operation and excise duty is revenue from operation in negative nature.

Section – B

49. (b) Schedule III Part I

50. (c) Both (i) and (ii) is correct

51. (b) (ii) and (iii)

> **Explanation:**
>
> (a) Decrease the ratio.
>
> **Reason:** Payment of advance rent of ₹ 3,000, will reduce the value of quick assets. Hence, the quick ratio is decreased.
>
> (b) Not change the ratio
>
> **Reason:** As there is a simultaneous increase and decrease in quick asset, i.e. cash and debtor, therefore, it will not affect the value of current asset.

52. (a) Increase current ratio

53. (a) Both (A) and (R) are correct and (R) is the correct reason of (A).

> **Explanation:** Financial statements are the basic and formal annual reports through which the corporate management communicates financial information to its owners and various other external parties which include: investors, tax authorities, government, employees, etc. Thus, both assertion and reason are correct and the reason is the correct explanation of the assertion.

54. (c) Both (i) and (ii) is correct

55. (c) Both (A) and (R) are incorrect

Sample Paper 3

PART – I

Section – A

1. (a) ₹54,000

> **Explanation:**
>
> Normal Profit = Capital Employed × Normal Rate of return
>
> $$= 2,00,000 \times \frac{15}{100} = ₹30,000$$
>
> Super Profit = Actual Average Profit – Normal Profit
>
> $$= 48,000 - 30,000 = ₹18,000$$
>
> Goodwill = Super Profit × Number of Year's Purchase
>
> $$= 18,000 \times 3 = ₹54,000$$

2. (a) A shareholder is the agent of the company.

3. (d) Premium for Goodwill

4. (b) Old Ratio

5.

		₹	₹
(b) Workmen Compensation Reserve A/c	Dr.	72,000	
To Workmen Compensation Claim A/c			48,000
To X's Capital A/c			12,000
To Y's Capital A/c			12,000

6. (a) Subscribed and fully paid-up

7. (a) A sacrifice $\dfrac{1}{5}$

> **Explanation:** Sacrificing Share = Old Share – New Share
>
> $$A = \frac{5}{10} - \frac{3}{10} = \frac{2}{10} = \frac{1}{5} \text{ Sacrifice}$$
>
> $$B = \frac{4}{10} - \frac{4}{10} = \text{Nil}$$
>
> $$C = \frac{1}{10} - \frac{3}{10} = \left(\frac{2}{10}\right) = \left(\frac{1}{5}\right) \text{ Gain}$$

8. (a) Sacrifice A 1/6; B's Sacrifice Nil; C's Gain 1/6

> **Explanation:**
>
> | | A | : | B | : | C |
> |---|---|---|---|---|---|
> | Old Ratio | 3 | : | 2 | : | 1 |
> | New Ratio | 1 | : | 1 | : | 1 |
>
> Sacrificing Ratio = Old Ratio – New Ratio
>
> $$\text{Sacrifice of A} = \frac{3}{6} - \frac{1}{3} = \frac{1}{6} \text{ Sacrifice}$$
>
> $$\text{Sacrifice of B} = \frac{2}{6} - \frac{1}{3} = 0$$
>
> $$\text{Sacrifice of C} = \frac{1}{6} - \frac{1}{3} = \left(\frac{1}{6}\right) \text{ Gain}$$

9. (b) ₹3,000, ₹2,000

10. (a) 5% per annum

11. (c) Old profit sharing ratio

12. (a) Participating preference shares

13. (a) Old partners capital accounts in the old profit sharing ratio

14. (b) Only (ii) is correct

15. (a) 5 months

16. (a) Only (i) is correct

17. (b) Nominal

18. (b) ₹ 9 per share

> **Explanation:**
>
> Total forfeiture amount (2,000 shares @ ₹ 3 each) = ₹ 6,000
>
> *Less:* Amount transferred to capital reserve = 4,000
>
> Discount Allowed on re-issue of share = 2,000
>
> $$\text{Re-issued value per share} = 10 - \frac{2,000}{2,000} = 10 - 1 = ₹\ 9 \text{ per share}$$

Section - B

19. (c) Only (iii) is correct

20. (c) Called-up capital of the shares forfeited; Amount received on shares forfeited.

21. (b) Only (ii) is correct

22. (c) Surrender of shares

23. (c) (A) is wrong but (R) is correct.

> **Explanation:** The new partner is required to compensate the old partners for their loss of share in the super profits of the firm for which he brings in an additional amount known as premium of goodwill. This amount is shared by the existing partners in the ratio in which they forego their shares in favour of the new partner which is called sacrificing ratio. Thus, assertion is wrong, but reason is correct.

24. (a) Cumulative Preference Share

25. (a) ₹ 40,000

26. (a) Both (A) and (R) true and (R) is the correct reason of (A).

> **Explanation:** Issued capital is a part of the Authorized capital, offered by the company for the subscription. This includes the allotment of shares. Generally a part of the authorised capital is issued to the public for subscription which is known as issued capital, *i.e.*, it is the nominal value of the shares which are offered to the public for subscription.

27.

	₹	₹
(c) Building A/c	Dr. 2,00,000	
To Revaluation A/c		2,00,000

28. (a) $2:2:1:1$

> **Explanation:**
>
> $$\text{'A' share} = \frac{3}{6} - \frac{1}{6} = \frac{2}{6}; \text{'B' share} = \frac{2}{6}; \text{'C' share} = \frac{1}{6} \text{ and 'D' share} = \frac{1}{6}$$
>
> $$\text{New Profit Sharing Ratio} = 2:2:1:1$$

29. (a) Both (i) & (ii).

30. (a) ₹ 17,500

> **Explanation:**
>
> | Particulars | Amount (₹) |
> |---|---|
> | 'A's' Capital | 40,000 |
> | 'B's' Capital | 30,000 |
> | Capital of 'A' and 'B' for $\frac{4}{5}$ share $\left(i.e., 1-\frac{1}{5}\right)$ | 70,000 |
> | Total Capital of firm $\left(70,000 \times \frac{5}{4}\right)$ | 87,500 |
> | 'C's' Share of Capital $\left(87,500 \times \frac{1}{5}\right)$ | 17,500 |

31. (a) Gain $\dfrac{1}{60}$

32. (c) Both (A) and (R) are false

Explanation: Since goodwill is an intangible asset it is very difficult to accurately calculate its value. Various methods have been advocated for the valuation of goodwill of a partnership firm. Goodwill calculated by one method may differ from the goodwill calculated by another method. Hence, the method by which goodwill is to be calculated may be specifically decided between the existing partners and the incoming partner.

33. (c) ₹ 42,000 loss

Explanation: To ascertain the effect of revaluation, revaluation account is to be prepared in the following manner.

Dr.   **Revaluation Account**   **Cr.**

Particulars	Amount (₹)	Particulars	Amount (₹)
To Stock A/c	30,000	By Provision for Bad Debts A/c	4,000
To Outstanding Salary A/c	16,000	By Loss on Revaluation to be transferred to Partners' Capital A/c	42,000
	46,000		**46,000**

34. (d) All of these

35. (b) ₹ 7,000 to each.

Explanation: Distributable Profit = 20,000 – 6,000 = ₹14,000
As the ratio is not given it will be distributed equally.

36. (a) for non-payment of call money

Section – C

37. (d) None of these

38. (c) Nikhil ₹12,000; Pawan ₹6,000

39. (a) ₹48,000

40. (a) ₹2,800

41. (b) ₹2,900

PART – II

Section – A

42. (d) Trade receivables

Explanation: Trade receivables are defined as the amount owned to a business by its customers following the sale of goods or services on credit. Also known as accounts receivables, trade receivables are classified as current assets on the balance sheet.

43. (a) I-(e), II-(d), III-(a), IV-(d), V-(c).

44. (a) Both (A) and (R) are true but (R) is not the explanation of (A).

Explanation: The proprietary ratio (also known as net worth ratio or equity ratio) is used to evaluate the soundness of the capital structure of a company. It is computed by dividing the stockholders' equity by total assets. Thus, both assertion and reason are correct statements, but reason is not the correct explanation of the assertion.

45. (b) Current ratio and Quick ratio

46. (a) Solvency

47. (a) Only (i) is correct

48. (d) Vertical Analysis

Section - B

49. (c) Vertical

50. (a) Only (i) is correct.

51. (d) Patents

52. (b) Both (A) and (R) are correct but (R) does not explain (A).

> **Explanation:** Contingent Liability is not recorded in the books of account but is disclosed in the Notes to Accounts for the information of the users.

53. (a) Inventory Turnover Ratio and Working Capital Turnover Ratio

54. (c) Both (i) and (ii) are correct

55. (a) Both (A) and (R) are correct and (R) is the correct reason of (A).

Sample Paper 4

PART - I

Section - A

1. (b) ₹4,000

> **Exaplanation:** 10% is to be transferred to general reserve after all adjustments (including such transfer). This can be ascertained using the following formula.
>
> $$\text{Transfer to General Reserve} = 44,000 \times \frac{10}{110} = ₹4,000$$

	₹	₹
2. (d) Investment Fluctuation Reserve A/c Dr.	6,000	
To Investments A/c		3,000
To A's Capital A/c		1,500
To B's Capital A/c		1,000
To D's Capital A/c		500

> **Explanation:** Investment Fluctuation Reserve is created as a safeguard against loss due to fluctuation in market price of investments. In the given example, ₹3,000 (₹25,000 – ₹22,000) will be used to cover loss due to fall in the price of investments and the balance ₹3,000 will be distributed among partners in their old ratio.

3. (c) ₹1,00,000

4. (b) ₹1,68,000

> **Explanation:** Old Ratio = 3 : 2, C's share = 1/5th, C's Capital = ₹1,20,000
>
> $$\text{Total Capital of firm based on C's share} = 1,20,000 \times \frac{5}{1} = ₹6,00,000$$
>
> $$\text{Remaining Share} = 1 - \frac{1}{5} = \frac{4}{5}$$
>
> $$\text{A's new share} = \frac{4}{5} \times \frac{3}{5} = \frac{12}{25}$$
>
> $$\text{B's new share} = \frac{4}{5} \times \frac{2}{5} = \frac{8}{25}$$

$$\text{C's new share} = \frac{1}{5} \times \frac{5}{5} = \frac{5}{25}$$

$$\text{New profit sharing ratio} = 12 : 8 : 5$$

$$\text{A's capital based on new share} = 6,00,000 \times \frac{12}{25} = ₹2,88,000$$

Hence, $\quad$ Capital to bring in by A $= 2,88,000 - 1,20,000 = ₹1,68,000$

5. (c) $5 : 7$

Explanation: The Ratio is calculated as under:

$$\text{Shares Available} : \text{Shares Applied}$$

$$25,000 : 35,000$$

$$5 : 7$$

Hence every person who applied for 7 shares will get 5 shares.

6. (c) A new partner has to bring relatively higher capital as compared to the existing partners.

7. (a) Premium

8. (b) Partner salary

9. (b) Only (ii) is correct

		₹	₹
10. (a) Premium for Goodwill A/c	Dr.	40,000	
To A's Capital A/c			16,000
To B's Capital A/c			24,000

Explanation:

$$\text{Old ratio} = 3 : 2$$

$$\text{New ratio} = 2 : 1 : 1$$

$$\text{Sacrifice of A} = \text{Old share} - \text{New share}$$

$$= \frac{3}{5} - \frac{2}{4} = \frac{12-10}{20} = \frac{2}{20}$$

$$\text{Sacrifice of B} = \frac{2}{5} - \frac{1}{4} = \frac{8-5}{20} = \frac{3}{20}$$

Hence, $\quad$ Sacrificing ratio $= 2 : 3$

And entry will be:

		₹	₹
Premium for Goodwill A/c	Dr.	40,000	
To A's Capital A/c			16,000
To B's Capital A/c			24,000

(Being premium for goodwill shared by old partners on the basis of sacrificing ratio *i.e.,* 2 : 3)

11. (d) ₹3,000

Explanation: $\quad$ Sacrifice Share = Old Ratio – New Ratio

$$\text{A's Sacrifice/Gain} = \frac{3}{5} - \frac{1}{2} = \frac{6-5}{10} = \frac{1}{10} \text{ (Sacrifice)}$$

$$\text{B's Sacrifice/Gain} = \frac{2}{5} - \frac{1}{2} = \frac{4-5}{10} = -\frac{1}{10} \text{ (Gain)}$$

So, B will give to A $= 30{,}000 \times \dfrac{1}{10} = ₹3{,}000$

12. (a) Old Profit-Sharing Ratio

13. (a) 2,500 Shares

14. (a) ₹1,920

15. (a) prepares the statement in lieu of prospectus.

Explanation: The statement in lieu of Prospectus is a document filed with the Registrar of the Companies (ROC) when the company has not issued prospectus to the public for inviting them to subscribe for shares. The Statement must contain the signature of all the directors or their agents authorized in writing.

16. (a) Current A/c

17. (a) ₹ 6,000

18. (a) Only (i) is correct

Section - B

19. (d) ₹ 20

Explanation: *i.e.,* 50 – 30 = ₹ 20

20. (b) (iii), (ii), (iv), (i)

21. (b) Only (ii) is correct

22. (a) Equity Share

Explanation: Equity shareholders are paid on the basis of earning of the company and do not get a fixed divided. They receive what is left after all other claims on the company's, income and assets have been settled. Through their right to vote, these shareholders have a right to participate in the management of the company.

23. (a) Virat = ₹ 12,10,000, Anushka = ₹ 9,35,000

Explanation:

Particulars	Virat (₹)	Anushka (₹)
Opening Capital	10,00,000	8,00,000
(+) Salary to Partners	30,000	30,000
(+) Interest on Capital	50,000	40,000
(+) Divisible Profits (Total Profits – Salary – Interest on Capital) divided in 2 : 1 [3,45,000 – 60,000 – 90,000] = 1,95,000 divided in 2 : 1	1,30,000	65,000
Closing Capital	**12,10,000**	**9,35,000**

24. (a) (A) is correct, but (R) is wrong.

Explanation: A company, being an artificial person, cannot generate its own capital which has necessarily to be collected from several persons. These persons are known as shareholders and the amount contributed by them is called share capital.

25. (c) ₹ 1,500

Explanation:

$$\text{Interest on Drawings} = \text{Amount} \times \text{Number of months of drawings} \times \text{Rate of Interest} \times \text{Average Period.}$$

Where

$$\therefore \quad \text{Interest on Drawings} = 4{,}000 \times 9 \times \frac{10}{100} \times \frac{5}{12} = ₹\ 1{,}500$$

$$\therefore \quad \text{Average Period} = \frac{\text{Time left after first drawings} + \text{Time left after last drawings}}{2}$$

$$= \frac{9+1}{2} = 5 \text{ months}$$

26. (d) ₹ 1,34,000

27. (a) Both (A) and (R) are correct and (R) is the correct reason of (A).

Explanation: Partnership comes into existence as a result of agreement among the partners. The agreement can be either oral or written. The Partnership Act does not require that the agreement must be in writing. But wherever it is in writing, the document, which contains terms of the agreement, is called 'Partnership Deed'.

28. (d) All of these

		₹	₹
29. (d) Profit and Loss A/c	Dr.	60,000	
General Reserve A/c	Dr.	40,000	
To B's Capital A/c			60,000
To C's Capital A/c			40,000

Explanation: Since, partners are changing their profit sharing ratio so, their all (accumulated) profits or losses will be distributed among them in their old ratio.

So, Total Accumulated Profit

$$\text{Profit and Loss A/c} = ₹\ 60{,}000$$
$$(+) \quad \text{General Reserve} = ₹\ 40{,}000$$
$$\overline{₹\ 1{,}00{,}000}$$

Distributed in 'B' and 'C' in old ratio

$$\text{'B'} = ₹\ 1{,}00{,}000 \times \frac{3}{5} = ₹\ 60{,}000$$

$$\text{'C'} = ₹\ 1{,}00{,}000 \times \frac{2}{5} = ₹\ 40{,}000$$

30. (a) provide for discount given at the time of re-issue.

Explanation: The balance of share forfeiture account can be only used to provide for discount given at the time of re-issue. The balance left after providing for discount is transferred to capital reserve account.

31. (a) Gain of 1/5

Explanation: B's Sacrifice/Gain = 1/5 – 2/5 = (1 – 2)/5 = 1/5 (Gain)

32. (d) $2 : 2 : 1$

Explanation:

$$\text{'Z's' share} = \frac{1}{5}$$

$$\text{Remaining share} = 1 - \frac{1}{5} = \frac{4}{5}$$

$$\text{'X's' and 'Y's' new share} = \frac{4}{5} \times \frac{1}{2} = \frac{4}{10} \text{ or } \frac{2}{5} \text{ each}$$

New profit sharing ratio of $X : Y : Z = 2 : 2 : 1$

33. (b) Both (A) and (R) are true and (R) is a correct explanation of (A)

34. (c) When at the time of admission, goodwill already appears in the Balance Sheet.

35. (c) Both (ii) & (iii).

36. (b) ₹ 5,000 each

Explanation:

$$\text{Asha's sacrifice} = \frac{1}{8}$$

$$\text{Nisha's sacrifice} = \frac{1}{4} - \frac{1}{8} = \frac{2-1}{8} = \frac{1}{8}$$

$$\text{Sacrificing ratio} = 1 : 1$$

$$\text{Ashish's share of Goodwill} = 40{,}000 \times \frac{1}{4} = ₹ 10{,}000$$

$$\therefore \text{Amount of goodwill credited to old partners' capital account} = 10{,}000 \times \frac{1}{2} = ₹ 5{,}000$$

Section - C

37. (a) Profit transferred – ₹30,000, ₹20,000

38. (c) Interest on capital- ₹16,000, ₹8,000; Loss transferred- ₹15,600, ₹10,400

39. (d) 5 times

40. (b) ₹40,00,000

41. (c) ₹6,00,000

PART – II

Section - A

42. (b) Both (A) and (R) are true and (R) is the correct explanation of (A).

Explanation: The chronologically recorded facts about events expressed in monetary terms for a defined period of time are the basis for the preparation of periodical financial statements which reveal the financial position as on a date and the financial results obtained during a period.

43. (b) Current ratio and Quick ratio

44. (a) Short-term Borrowings

45. (a) Operating ratio

46. (a) Distributed

47. (a) Profitability

48. (b) Only (ii) is correct

Section - B

49. (a) Only (i) is correct

50. (a) 22.2%

Explanation:

$$\text{Proprietary Ratio} = \frac{\text{Shareholders' Funds}}{\text{Total Assets}}$$

Shareholders' Funds = Total Assets* – Long-term Borrowings – Long-term Provisions – Current liabilities

$$= 4,50,000 - 2,00,000 - 1,00,000 - 50,000 = ₹\,1,00,000$$

Total Assets* = Non-Current Assets + Current Assets

$$= 3,60,000 + 90,000 = ₹\,4,50,000$$

$$\text{Proprietary Ratio} = \frac{1,00,000}{4,50,000} \times 100 = 22.2\%$$

51. (a) Both (A) and (R) are correct and (R) is the correct reason of (A).

Explanation: The ratio is normally clearly given as agreed among the partners which could be the old ratio, equal sacrifice, or a specified ratio. The difficulty arises where the ratio in which the new partner acquires his share from the old partners is not specified. Instead, the new profit sharing ratio is given.

52. (c) Deduct from Reserves and Surplus

53. (b) Both (A) and (R) are correct but (R) does not explain (A).

Explanation: As reserves and surplus is the sub head of shareholders fund so it has no difference if we use the main head shareholders fund or sub head Reserves and Surplus.

54. (c) $\dfrac{\text{Net Credit Revenue from Operations}}{\text{Average Debtors + Average Bills Receivables}}$

55. (b) ₹ 39,00,000

Explanation: Cost of material consumed :

Opening Inventory	=	5,00,000
+ Purchase	=	40,00,000
		45,00,000
(–) Closing Inventory	=	(6,00,000)
		₹ 39,00,000

Sample Paper 5

PART - I

Section - A

1. (b) On making a firm

2. (c) Both (a) and (b)

3. (a) Sacrifice A 1/6; B's sacrifice Nil; C's Gain 1/6

Explanation:

	A	:	B	:	C
Old Ratio	3	:	2	:	1
New Ratio	1	:	1	:	1
Sacrificing	$\dfrac{1}{6}$		$-\dfrac{1}{6}$		

$$\text{Sacrificing Ratio} = \text{Old Ratio} - \text{New Ratio}$$

$$\text{Sacrifice of A} = \frac{3}{6} - \frac{1}{3} = \frac{1}{6} \text{ Sacrifice}$$

$$\text{Sacrifice of B} = \frac{2}{6} - \frac{1}{3} = 0$$

$$\text{Sacrifice of C} = \frac{1}{6} - \frac{1}{3} = \frac{1}{6} \text{ Gain}$$

4. (c) 15%

5. (b) Capital account of old partners

6. (b) X only

7. (a) Subscribed and fully paid-up

8.

		₹	₹
(d) A's Capital A/c	Dr.	10,000	
To C's Capital A/c			10,000

9. (a) Old Profit-Sharing Ratio

10. (b) Both (ii) & (iii) are correct.

11. (b) Nominal

12. (a) ₹420

Explanation:

$$\text{Interest on Drawing} = 2{,}000 \times 6 \times \frac{12}{100} \times \frac{3.5}{12} = ₹420$$

$$\text{Average Time} = \frac{\text{Time left after First Drawing} + \text{Time left after Last Drawing}}{2}$$

$$= 6 + \frac{1}{2} = 3.5 \text{ months}$$

13. (d) preferential right as to dividend and repayment of capital at the time of liquidation of the company

14. (a) Equally

15. (c) cumulative, non-participating and non-convertible

16. (b) Only (ii) is correct

17. (b) Only (ii) is correct

18. (b) 40,000 shares.

Section – B

19. (b) Only (ii) is correct

20. (c) Only (iii) is correct

21. (c) Cumulative Preference Shares

22. (b) Both (A) and (R) are correct

Explanation: The clauses of partnership deed can be altered with the consent of all the partners. The deed should be properly drafted and prepared as per the provisions of the 'Stamp Act' and preferably registered with the Registrar of Firms.

23. (c)   Building A/c   Dr.   3,60,000

       To Share Capital A/c   3,00,000

       To Securities Premium Reserve A/c   60,000

24.   ₹   ₹

   (d) Investment Fluctuation Reserve A/c   Dr.   6,000

         To Investment A/c   3,000

         To A's Capital A/c   1,500

         To B's Capital A/c   1,000

         To D's Capital A/c   500

Explanation: Investment Fluctuation Reserve is created as a safeguard against loss due to fluctuation in market price of investments. In the give example. ₹ 3,000 (25,000- 22,000) will be used to cover loss due to fall in the price of investments and the balance ₹ 3,000 will be distributed among partners in their old ratio.

25. (b) Subscribed but not fully paid-up

26. (a) Both (A) and (R) are correct and (R) is the correct reason of (A).

Explanation: Goodwill is also one of the special aspects of partnership accounts which requires adjustment (also valuation if not specified) at the time of reconstitution of a firm.

27. (c) (i), (ii), & (iii) are correct

28. (b) Old share – New share

29. (d) 50,000

Explanation: Arun and Vijay $= 5 : 1$

$$\text{Machinery current value} = ₹\,40,000 + ₹\,40,000 \times \frac{20}{100-20}$$

$$= ₹\,40,000 + ₹\,40,000 \times \frac{20}{80}$$

$$= ₹\,40,000 + ₹\,10,000 = ₹\,50,000$$

30. (c) $9 : 6 : 3 : 2$

31. (c) Both (A) and (R) are false

Explanation: A company may reserve a portion of its uncalled capital to be called only in the event of winding up of the company. Such uncalled amount is called 'Reserve Capital' of the company. It is available only for the creditors on winding up of the company.

32. (c) (i), (iii), (iv) are correct.

33. (c) A ₹ 21,000

34. (b) Dr. A ₹ 1,200; Cr. B ₹ 800 and Cr. C ₹ 400

35. (d) Nil

36. (b) ₹ 7,380 to each.

$$\text{Interest on loan by Answer} = ₹\,8{,}000 \times \frac{6}{100} \times \frac{6}{12} = ₹\,240$$

$$\text{Net Profits} = ₹\,15{,}000 - 240 = ₹\,14{,}760$$

$$\text{This profit will be Distributed Equally} = \frac{14{,}760}{2} = ₹\,7{,}380 \text{ each}$$

Section - C

37. (a) ₹5,00,000
38. (a) ₹16,500
39. (a) ₹29,400, ₹31,200
40. (a) 1 : 1
41. (b) ₹14,400, ₹16,200

PART - II

Section - A

42. (c) Both (A) and (R) are false

Explanation: Financial analysis can be undertaken by management of the firm, or by parties outside the firm, *viz.*, owners, trade creditors, lenders, investors, labour unions, analysts and others.

43. (a) Gaining Ratio
44. (c) Lacks qualitative analysis
45. (a) Short-term Borrowings
46. (a) 22.2%

Explanation:

$$\text{Proprietary Ratio} = \frac{\text{Shareholders' Fund}}{\text{Total Assets}}$$

$$\text{Shareholders Fund} = \text{Total Assets} - \text{Long-term Borrowings} - \text{Long-term Provision} - \text{Current Liabilities}$$

$$= 4{,}50{,}000 - 50{,}000 - 1{,}00{,}000 - 2{,}00{,}000$$

$$= 1{,}00{,}000$$

$$\text{Total Assets} = \text{Non-current Assets} + \text{Current Assets}$$

$$= 3{,}60{,}000 + 90{,}000$$

$$= 4{,}50{,}000$$

$$\text{Proprietary Ratio} = \frac{1{,}00{,}000}{4{,}50{,}000} \times 100 = 22.2\%$$

47. (c) Vertical
48. (b) Goodwill, Intangible Assets

Explanation: When net assets are less and payment for business purchase is more, then it is called goodwill and it is shown under intangible assets.

Section - B

49. (b) 2 : 1
50. (a) Only (i) is correct
51. (a) Only (i) is correct

52. (c) Only (R) is correct
53. (c) Cost of revenue from operations + Operating expenses/Net revenue from operations
54. (a) (A) and (R) both are correct and (R) correctly explains (A).
55. (b) A, B and D

Sample Paper 6

PART - I

Section - A

1. (a) 50; Companies Act, 2013

2. (a) Second and final call ₹ 3

> **Explanation:** Total amount should be 10+30%
>
> *i.e.* $\qquad\qquad\qquad$ 10 + 3 = 13
>
> On Application ₹ 4
> On Allotment ₹ 4
> On First call ₹ 2
> Second and final call ₹ 3

3. (a) 2,500 shares

> **Explanation:** Applicants for 1,00,000 shares were alloted 1,50,000 shares
>
> 1 share must have been alloted $= \dfrac{1,50,000}{1,00,000}$ shares
>
> $\therefore$ 3000 shares must have been alloted $= \dfrac{1,50,000}{1,00,000} \times 3,000$ shares
>
> $= 2500$ shares

4. (c) ₹ 1,00,000

> **Explanation:** Amount due on total shares (10,000 × 10) is ₹ 1,00,000.
> Complete amount was received, one shareholder paid late, but at the end amount was received. Hence, complete amount received by the company will be ₹ 1,00,000.

5. (a) (ii), (iii), (iv), (i)

6. (b) Investment Fluctuation Reserve Credited to ₹ 8,000 ₹ 6,000 ₹ 4,000

Explanation:

Particulars	Amount (₹)	Amount (₹)
Investment Fluctuation Reserve A/c	36,000	
To Investments A/c (4,00,000 – 3,82,000)		18,000
To Suraj's Capital A/c		8,000
To Mahesh Capital A/c		6,000
To Tarun's Capital A/c		4,000
(Being the transfer of excess Investment Fluctuation Reserve to Partner's Capital Accounts in their old profit sharing ratio)		

7. (b) a minor can be admitted as a partner, only into the benefits of the partnership.

   Explanation: A minor partner shares only the profits of the firm and not the losses.

8. (c) Debit Investments A/c and Credit Revaluation A/c.

   Explanation: Unrecorded or Increase in Assets are debited in the Revaluation A/c.

9. (c) 400 for X, 5,200 for Y, 400 for Z

   Explanation: In the absence of partnership, deed profit and losses are shared equally. Interest on partner's loan is 6% p.a.
   Profit & Loss : [4,800 – 6,000] = 1,200 shared equally.
   4,800 to Y as interest on Loan.

10. (c) ₹ 400 (Debit)

Explanation: Table showing Adjustments

Particulars	X	Y	Total
Interest on Capital @ 12% p.a.	(24,000)	(12,000)	(36,000)
Interest on Capital @ 10% p.a.	20,000	10,000	30,000
	(4,000)	(2,000)	(6,000)
Profit to be distributed [3 : 2]	3,600	2,400	6,000
	(400) Dr.	400 Cr.	0

11. (b) ₹ 32,700

Explanation:

Particulars			Amount (₹)
Net Profits as per Profit and Loss Account			40,000
(+) Interest on Drawings:			
Ramesh	$\left(14,000 \times \dfrac{10}{100} \times \dfrac{6}{12}\right)$	700	
Mahesh	$\left(16,000 \times \dfrac{10}{100} \times \dfrac{6}{12}\right)$	800	1,500
(–) Salary to Mahesh (12 × 400)			(4,800)
(–) Commission to Ramesh $\left(40,000 \times \dfrac{10}{100}\right)$			(4,000)
Divisible Profits			32,700

12. (c) Profit and Loss Account (Credit Balance)

13. (d) ₹ 3,000

   Explanation: Sacrifice (Gain) Ratio = Old Ratio – New Ratio

   A's Sacrificing Ratio $= \dfrac{3}{5} - \dfrac{1}{2} = \dfrac{6-5}{10} = \dfrac{1}{10}$ Sacrifice

$$\text{B's Sacrificing Ratio} = \frac{2}{5} - \frac{1}{2} = \frac{4-5}{10} = \frac{1}{10} \text{ (Gain)}$$

So,
$$\text{'B' will give to 'A'} = ₹\,30,000 \times \frac{5}{1} = ₹\,3,000$$

14. (d) Reserve Capital

15. (b) credited to calls in advance account

16. (c) Premium for Goodwill Account.

17. (b) ₹ 1,68,000

Explanation:
$$\text{Old ratio} = 3 : 2; \text{ 'C's' Share} = \frac{1}{5}, \text{ Capital} = ₹\,1,20,000$$

$$\text{Total Capital of firm based on 'C's' share} = 1,20,000 \times \frac{5}{1} = ₹\,6,00,000$$

$$\text{Remaining share} = 1 - \frac{1}{5} = \frac{4}{5}$$

$$\text{New profit sharing ratio} = \text{'A's' new share} = \frac{4}{5} \times \frac{3}{5} = \frac{12}{25}; \text{ 'B's' new share} = \frac{4}{5} \times \frac{2}{5} = \frac{8}{25} \text{ and}$$

$$\text{C's' new share} = \frac{1}{5} \times \frac{5}{5} = \frac{5}{25}$$

$$\text{New profit sharing ratio} = 12 : 8 : 5$$

$$\text{'A's' Capital based on new share} = 6,00,000 \times \frac{12}{25} = ₹\,2,88,000$$

$$\therefore \quad \text{Capital to bring in by 'A'} = 2,88,000 - 1,20,000 = ₹\,1,68,000$$

18. (d) ₹ 10,00,000

Explanation:
$$\text{Capital Employed (Net Assets)} = \text{Total Assets} - \text{Total Liabilities}$$
$$= 28,00,000 - 8,00,000 = ₹\,20,00,000$$
$$\text{Normal Profit} = \text{Capital Employed} \times \text{Normal Rate of Return}$$
$$= 20,00,000 \times \frac{10}{100} = ₹\,2,00,000$$
$$\text{Super Profit} = \text{Actual Average Profit} - \text{Normal Profit}$$
$$= 3,00,000 - 2,00,000 = ₹\,1,00,000$$

So,
$$\text{Goodwill} = \frac{\text{Super Profit}}{\text{Normal Rate of Return}} \times 100$$
$$= \frac{1,00,000}{10} \times 100 = ₹\,10,00,000$$

Section – B

19. (b) ₹ 6,000; ₹ 9,000; ₹ 6,000; ₹ 9,000

Explanation:

$$\text{Commission} = ₹ 1,80,000 \times \frac{20}{120} = ₹ 30,000$$

$$\text{A's Commission} = ₹ 30,000 \times \frac{2}{10} = ₹ 6,000$$

$$\text{B's Commission} = ₹ 30,000 \times \frac{3}{10} = ₹ 9,000$$

$$\text{C's Commission} = ₹ 30,000 \times \frac{2}{10} = ₹ 6,000$$

$$\text{D's Commission} = ₹ 30,000 \times \frac{3}{10} = ₹ 9,000$$

20. (d) A ₹ 30,000; B ₹ 30,000

Explanation: Old Ratio (A : B : C) = 3 : 2 : 1
New Ratio (A : B : C : D) = 5 : 3 : 2 : 2
Sacrificing Ratio (O/R – N/R) = 1 : 1.
D's share of Goodwill = ₹ 60,000 in Sacrifing Ratio.

21. (c)

A's Capital A/c	Dr.	20,000	
B's Capital A/c	Dr.	20,000	
C's Capital A/c	Dr.	10,000	
To Goodwill A/c			50,000

Explanation: Old Partner's Capital A/c   Dr.
                To Goodwill A/c
            (Bing Goodwill writen off)

22. (c) (A) is wrong, but (R) is correct.

23. (a) The difference of ₹ 20,000 will be debited to revaluation account.

Explanation: If the claim is higher than the amount of Workman Compensation Reserve :
Workman Compensation Reserve A/c   Dr.
Revaluation A/c   Dr.
    To Provision for workmen Compensation Reserve A/c

24. (a) ₹ 420

Explanation:

$$\text{Interest on Drawings} = 2,000 \times 6 \times \frac{12}{100} \times \frac{3.5}{12} = ₹ 420$$

$$\text{Average Time} = \frac{\text{Time left after first drawing} + \text{Time left after last drawing}}{2}$$

$$= \frac{6+1}{2} = 3.5 \text{ months}$$

25. (a) ₹ 78,000

> **Explanation:**   (₹)
>
> Salary (4,000 × 12) = 48,000
>
> Commission $(6,78,000 - 48,000) \times \dfrac{5}{105}$ = 30,000
>
> Total Remuneration = 78,000

26. (d) Both (A) and (R) are wrong.

27. (d) 120 shares

> **Explanation:**
>
> | | Applied | Alloted |
> |---|---|---|
> | | 15,000 | 10,000 |
> | | x | 80 |
>
> On cross multiplying :
>
> $$15,000 \times 80 = 10,000 \times x$$
>
> $$\frac{15,000 \times 80}{10,000} = x$$
>
> $\therefore$ $x = 120$ shares.

28. (d) (iii) only

29. (d) 3 : 1

> **Explanation:**
>
> Sacrificing Ratio = Old Ratio − New Ratio
>
> 'A's Sacrifice $= \dfrac{5}{8} - \dfrac{7}{16} = \dfrac{10-7}{16} = \dfrac{3}{16}$ and
>
> 'B's Sacrifice $= \dfrac{3}{8} - \dfrac{5}{16} = \dfrac{6-5}{16} = \dfrac{1}{16}$
>
> Sacrificing Ratio = 3 : 1

30. (b) ₹ 4,000, ₹ 4,000 respectively

> **Explanation:** When shares are re-issued then money is received, so cash/bank will be debited as per accounting rule and equity share capital is increased, hence it will be credited.

31. (b) Both (A) and (R) are true and (R) is the correct explanation of (A).

32. (c) A's Capital A/c will be Debited by ₹ 1,000.

> **Explanation:** Total Profit of the firm = ₹ 4,200 (1 : 1 : 1)
>
> C was guaranteed = ₹ 1,800
>
> A, B & C's share of profits :
>
> A : (₹ 1,400 − 400) = ₹ 1,000
>
> B : ₹ 1,400
>
> C : ₹ (1,400 + 400) = ₹ 1,800

33. (c) ₹ 4,000

Explanation: Since premium has already been received, we will ignore it.

At the time of forfeiture :

₹ 100 is the nominal value of the share

₹ 20 has not yet been called for

₹ 80 remaining

Out of ₹ 80; ₹ 30 were not received.

∴ ₹ 50 was put in share forfeiture for each share.

At the time of re-issue :

₹ 70 received ₹ 10 discounted (share forfeiture)

∴ Profit on reissue = ₹ $(100 \times 50 - 100 \times 10)$

= ₹ (5,000 – 1,000)

= ₹ 4,000

34. (b) 6,400

Explanation: $10,00,000 - 20\%$ of $10,00,000 = ` 8,00,000$

No. of shares $\dfrac{8,00,000}{100 + 25} = \dfrac{8,00,000}{125}$

= 6,400 shares

35. (a) Gain $\dfrac{1}{12}$

$$\text{Sacrificing Ratio = Old Share – New Share}$$

$$A = \frac{3}{4} - \frac{2}{3} = \frac{9-8}{12} = \left(\frac{1}{12}\right) \text{ Sacrifice}$$

$$B = \frac{1}{4} - \frac{1}{3} = \frac{3-4}{12} = \left(\frac{1}{12}\right) \text{ Gain.}$$

36. (d) ₹ 18,000

Explanation: Share Capital A/c $(2,000 \times 9)$ Dr. 18,000

        To calls in Arrear A/c $(2,000 \times 4)$ 8,000

        To Share forfeiture A/c $(2,000 \times 5)$ 10,000

<h3 align="center">Section – C</h3>

37. (a) ₹ 3,00,000

Explanation:

     1,00,000 equity shares for consideration of assets

    + 2,00,000 equity shares directly

    ⎯⎯⎯⎯⎯⎯⎯

    3,00,000 equity shares

38. (d) ₹ 300

Explanation:

Share Capital A/c (300 × 8)	Dr.	2,400
To Calls in Arrear A/c (300 × 3)		900
To Share forfeiture A/c (300 × 5)		1,500

For 300 shares, forfeiture amounted to ₹ 900

For 1 share, forfeiture must amount to ₹ $\left(\dfrac{900}{300}\right)$

For 100 shares, forfeiture must amount to ₹ $\left(\dfrac{900}{300} \times 100\right)$

$$= ₹ 300$$

39. (c) ₹ 2,70,000

40. (d) ₹ 43,200

41. (a) (a) Sania's Capital A/c   Dr. 45,000

  To Gyan's Capital A/c   45,000

PART - II

Section - A

42. (d) (A) is false, but (R) is true.

Explanation: Horizontal analysis is known as dynamic analysis.

43. (c) (i), (iii) and (iv).

44. (d) liquidity, debt and profitability

45. (a) (i), (ii) and (iv)

46. (a) Only (iii)

47. (a) 1 – (iii), 2 – (iv), 3 – (i), 4 – (ii)

48. (a) Proprietary ratio

Section - B

49. (a) ₹ 1,60,000

50. (c) 5.21 times

Explanation:

$$\text{Net Credit Purchase} = \text{Total Purchase} - \text{Cash Purchase} - \text{Purchase Return}$$
$$= 1,70,000 - 16,000 - 8,000 = ₹ 1,46,000$$

$$\text{Average Trade Payable} = \frac{\text{Opening Trade Payable} + \text{Closing Trade Payable}}{2}$$
$$= \frac{24,000 + 32,000}{2} = 28,000$$

$$\text{Creditors Turnover Ratio} = \frac{\text{Net Credit Purchase}}{\text{Average Trade Payable}}$$
$$= \frac{1,46,000}{28,000} = 5.21 \text{ times}$$

51. (d) (i), (ii), (iii) is correct and (iv) is incorrect.

52. (a) Both (A) and (R) are correct and (R) is the correct reason of (A).

53. (c) Both (A) and (R) are incorrect.

54. (a) A decreasing debtor period.

55. (d) None of these

> **Explanation:** Share forfeiture is shown under the head "Share Capital".

56. (a) Only (i) is correct.

Sample Paper 7

PART – I

Section – A

1. (a) Over-subscription

2. (b) ₹ 10

3. (b) 40,000 shares

4. (b) ₹ 60,000

> **Explanation:**
>
> | | (₹) |
> |---|---|
> | Amount forfeited on 20,000 shares | |
> | (20,000 × 6) | = 1,20,000 |
> | (-) Amount forfeited on 10,000 shares | |
> | (1,20,000/20,000 × 10,000) | = (60,000) |
> | Capital Reserves | = ₹ 60,000 |

5. (a) (ii), (iii), (iv), (v)

6. (a)

Journal Entry

Particulars		Amount (₹)	Amount (₹)
Workman Compensation Reserve A/c	Dr	6,000	
To Provision for Works. Comp Claim			6,000

7. (d) All of these

8. (c) Goodwill

9. (c) ₹ 2,00,000

> **Explanation:**
>
> Capitalised Value of Firm = Actual profits / Normal Rate of Return
>
> = 1,20,000/10 x 100 = ₹ 12,00,000
>
> Net Assets of firm = Total Assets – Total Liabilities
>
> = 14,40,000 - 4,40,000 ₹ 10,00,000
>
> Goodwill = Capitalised Value of Firm – Net Assets of Firm,
>
> where
>
> Hence,   Goodwill = ₹ 12,00,000 – ₹ 10,00,000 = ₹ 2,00,000

10. (b) Debited to revaluation account

11. (c) ₹ 42,000 loss

Explanation: To ascertain the effect of revaluation, we will prepare revaluation account in the following manner.

Revaluation Account

Particulars	Amount (₹)	Particulars	Amount (₹)
To Stock	30,000	By Provision for Bad Debits	4,000
To Outstanding Salary	16,000	By Loss on Revaluation to be Partner's Capital A/c	42,000
	46,000		46,000

12. (d) Capital Reserve

13. (a) ₹ 3,54,000

Explanation:

$$\text{Net Profit} = [4,20,000 + 4,000 - (5,000 \times 12) - 10,000]$$
$$= ₹\ 3,54,000$$

14. (b) Section 130

15. (b) Additional capital introduced by the partner in the firm.

16. (b) Partner's Current Account

17. (d) G = ₹ 210, B = ₹ 150

Explanation: Interest on Drawings for G

$$= 800 \times 6 \times \frac{15}{100} \times \frac{3.5}{12} = ₹\ 210$$

Interest on Drawings for B

$$= 800 \times 6 \times \frac{15}{100} \times \frac{2.5}{12} = ₹\ 150.$$

18. (d) Loss ₹ 4,000

Explanation:

		(₹)
$A = 1,00,000 \times \dfrac{8}{100}$	=	8,000
$B = 60,000 \times \dfrac{8}{100}$	=	4,800
		12,800
(–) Profit		(2,800)
Loss		10,000

Share of Loss

		(₹)
$A = 10,000 \times \dfrac{3}{5}$	=	6,000
$B = 10,000 \times \dfrac{2}{5}$	=	4,000

Section – B

19. (b) ₹ 6,000

Explanation:

Particulars		L.F.	Amount (₹)	Amount (₹)
Milan's Capital A/c (15,000 × $\frac{2}{5}$)	Dr.		6,000	
Khilan's Capital A/c (15,000 × $\frac{2}{5}$)	Dr.		6,000	
Silam's Capital A/c (15,000 × $\frac{1}{5}$)	Dr.		3,000	
To Profit & Loss A/c				15,000

20. (b) ₹ 4,500, ₹ 9,000 and ₹ 9,000

Explanation:

Particulars		L.F.	Amount (₹)	Amount (₹)
Red's Capital A/c (22,500 × $\frac{1}{5}$)	Dr.		4,500	
Blue's Capital A/c (22,500 × $\frac{2}{5}$)	Dr.		9,000	
White's Capital A/c (22,500 × $\frac{2}{5}$)	Dr.		9,000	
To Deferred Revenue Expenditure A/c				22,500

21.

		₹	₹
(b) Bank A/c	Dr.	4,900	
Share Forfeiture A/c	Dr.	1,400	
To Share Capital A/c			6,300

22. (c) (A) is wrong, but (R) is correct.

23. (d) A-Nil, B-Gain-1/30, C Sacrifice-1/30

Explanation:

Sacrificing Ratio = Old Share – New Share
A = 5/10 – 3/6 = 15 – 15/30 = Nil
B = 3/10 – 2/6 = 9 – 10/30 = (1/30) Gain
C = 2/10 – 1/6 = 6 – 5/30 = 1/30 Sacrifice

24. (b) ₹ 45,000

Explanation:

$$(₹)$$
Capital of A = 54,000
B = 36,000
Total Capital = 90,000

Firm's share = $1-\dfrac{1}{3}=\dfrac{2}{3}$;

$$\text{Total Capital of Firm} = 90,000 \times \frac{3}{2} = ₹\,1,35,000$$

$$\text{C's Capital} = 1,35,000 \times \frac{1}{3} = ₹\,45,000$$

25. (d) ₹ 98,000

Explanation:

Dr.   **Revaluation Account**   Cr.

Particulars	Amount (₹)	Particulars	Amount (₹)
To Provision for Doubtful Debts (1,60,000 × 5%)	8,000	By Stock	18,000
To Machinery	60,000	By Loss on Revaluation:	
		A — 20,000	
		B — 30,000	50,000
	68,000		**68,000**

$$\text{B's share in loss} = 20,000 \times \frac{5}{2} \times \frac{3}{5} = ₹\,30,000$$

$$\text{Revaluation value of stock} = 80,000 + 18,000 = ₹\,98,000$$

26. (d) Both (A) and (R) are wrong.

27. (c) ₹ 5,000

Explanation: Securities Premium = 10,000 × 0.50 = ₹ 5,000

28. (a) Authorised capital > Issued capital

29. (a) 2 : 2 : 1 : 1

Explanation:

$$\text{'A' share} = \frac{3}{6} - \frac{1}{6} = \frac{2}{6};$$

$$\text{'B' share} = \frac{2}{6};$$

$$\text{'C' share} = \frac{1}{6}$$

and

$$\text{'D' share} = \frac{1}{6}$$

New Profit Sharing Ratio = 2 : 2 : 1 : 1

30. (c) ₹ 1,800; ₹ 1,400; ₹ 400 respectively

31. (d) (A) is false, but (R) is true.

32. (b) Only B ₹ 1,00,000

Explanation:

Sacrificing Share = Old Share – New Share

$$A = \frac{3}{5} - \frac{3}{4} = \frac{12-15}{20} = \left(\frac{3}{20}\right) \text{Gain}$$

$$B = \frac{2}{5} - \frac{1}{4} = \frac{8-5}{20} = \frac{3}{20}$$

C's share of goodwill *i.e.*, ₹ 1,00,000 will be credited to only B as he is the only sacrificing partner.

33. (b) ₹ 16

34. (d) ₹ 5,00,000

35. (d) $\dfrac{13}{54}$

Explanation:

$$\text{A sacrifice} = \frac{3}{6} \times \frac{1}{3} = \frac{1}{6}$$

$$\text{B sacrifice} = \frac{2}{6} \times \frac{1}{6} = \frac{1}{18}$$

$$\text{C sacrifice} = \frac{1}{6} \times \frac{1}{9} = \frac{1}{54}$$

$$\text{D's share} = \frac{1}{6} + \frac{1}{18} + \frac{1}{54}$$

$$= \frac{9+3+1}{54} = \frac{13}{54}$$

36. (d) ₹ 3,15,000

Section - B

37. (d) ₹ 14,400

38. (d) NIL

39. (b) 5 : 3 : 5

40. (c) ₹ 2,00,000

Explanation:

$$\text{Firm's Goodwill} = ₹\,10,00,000$$

$$\text{Vijay's Share in Goodwill} = 10,00,000 \times \frac{1}{5} = ₹\,2,00,000$$

41. (b) ₹ 35,00,000

Explanation:

$$\text{Vijay's Capital for } \frac{1}{5}\text{th share} = ₹\,7,00,000$$

$$\text{Total Capital of Firm} = 7,00,000 \times \frac{5}{1} = ₹\,35,00,000$$

PART - II

Section - A

42. (d) (A) is false, but (R) is true.

43. (a) (i), (iii)

44. (b) liquid ratio, inventory

45. (a) (i), (ii) and (iv)

46. (b) Both (i) and (ii)

47. (b) 1-(iv), 2-(i), 3-(ii), 4-(iii)

48. (c) sale of stock-in-trade at loss

Section – B

49. (b) ₹ 2,80,000

$$\text{Inventory Turnover Ratio} = \frac{\text{Cost of Revenue from Operations}}{\text{Average Inventory}}$$

$$5 = \frac{10,00,000}{\text{Average Inventory}}$$

$$\text{Average Inventory} = ₹\,2,00,000$$

$$\text{Average Inventory} = \frac{\text{Opening Inventory} + \text{Closing Inventory}}{2}$$

$$2,00,000 = \frac{1,20,000 + \text{Cl}}{2}$$

$$\text{Closing Inventory} = ₹\,2,80,000$$

Explanation:

50. (c) ₹ 40,000

Explanation:

$$\text{Current Ratio} = \frac{\text{Current Assets}}{\text{Current Liabilities}}$$

$$\Rightarrow \quad \frac{4}{1} = \frac{\text{CA}}{\text{CL}}$$

$$\therefore \quad \text{CA} = 4\text{CL} \qquad \text{...(i)}$$

$$\text{Quick Ratio} = \frac{\text{Quick Assets}}{\text{Current Liabilities}}$$

$$\Rightarrow \quad \frac{2.5}{1} = \frac{\text{QA}}{\text{CL}}$$

$$\text{QA} = 2.5\text{CL} \qquad \text{...(ii)}$$

$$\text{Inventories} = \text{CA} - \text{QA}$$

$$15,000 = 4\text{CL} - 2.5\text{CL}$$

$$15,000 = 1.5\text{CL}$$

$$\therefore \quad \text{CL} = \frac{15,000}{1.5} = ₹\,10,000$$

$$\text{CA} = 4\text{CL} = 4 \times 10,000 = ₹\,40,000$$

51. (c) Both (ii) and (iii)

52. (a) Both (A) and (R) are correct and (R) is the correct reason of (A).

53. (b) Both (A) and (R) are correct but (R) does not explain (A).

54. (b) (b) Only (iii) is correct

55. (c) Subscribed and fully paid

	₹	₹
1,95,000 Equity shares of ₹ 10 each		19,50,000
Subscribed but not fully paid		
5,000 Equity shares of ₹ 10 each	50,000	
Less: Calls-in-arrears	15,000	35,000
		19,85,000

Business Studies

Sample Question Paper

Business Studies

Term - I

Time : 90 Minutes   Max. Marks : 40

General Instructions :

1. The Question Paper contains 3 sections.
2. Section A has 24 questions. Attempt any 20 questions.
3. Section B has 24 questions. Attempt any 20 questions.
4. Section C has 12 questions. Attempt any 10 questions.
5. All questions carry equal marks.
6. There is no negative marking.

Section-A

1. "What distinguishes a successful manager from a less successful one is the ability to put the principles into practice." Which aspect of the nature of management is highlighted in the above statement?
   (a) Management as a science   (b) Management as an art
   (c) Management as a profession   (d) Management is an intangible force.

Ans. (b) Management as an art

   Explanation: Art implies application of knowledge & skill so that desired results are achieved. According to the feature of art **Practical Knowledge**, it is very important to know practical application of theoretical principles. A manager can never be successful just by obtaining degree or diploma in management; to be successful he must know how to apply various principles in real situations by functioning in capacity of manager.

2. ______________ provides a rational approach for setting objectives and developing appropriate courses of action for achieving predetermined objectives.
   (a) Directing   (b) Staffing   (c) Planning   (d) Controlling

Ans. (c) Planning

   Explanation: In planning process, firstly the objectives are set and premises are developed. Then, different ways of achieving the objectives are chosen and from them best alternative is chosen which is being implemented.

3. Marketing mix is the set of ______________ that the firm uses to pursue its marketing objectives in the target market.
   (a) Production tools   (b) Promotional tools
   (c) Marketing tools   (d) Selling tools

Ans. (c) Marketing tools

   Explanation: Marketing tools include product, price, place; and promotion.

4. Which level of management is responsible for the welfare and survival of the organisation?
   (a) Top Level of Management   (b) Middle Level of Management
   (c) Supervisory Level   (d) Both (b) and (c)

Ans. (a) Top Level of Management

   Explanation: As survival and growth is one of the function of Top level management with making policies and objectives, controlling activities of all departments.

5. Name the principle of management given by Fayol which when applied would mean that the workers and management both honour their commitments without any prejudice towards one another.
   - (a) Discipline
   - (b) Mental Revolution
   - (c) Remuneration of Employees
   - (d) Scalar Chain

Ans. (a) Discipline

   Explanation: Discipline requires good superiors at all levels, clear and fair agreement and judicious application of penalties. No discrimination while implementing penalties. Here 'discipline' means that workers and management both will honour their commitments.

6. A brand or part of the brand that is given legal protection is called ______________.
   - (a) Brand Mark
   - (b) Trademark
   - (c) Brand
   - (d) Brand name

Ans. (b) Trademark

   Explanation: A trademark is a recognised sign, symbol or expression which differentiates product or service from those of others. A trademark owner can be an individual, organisation or a legal entity.

7. Identify the dimension of the characteristic of management- "it is multidimensional", which specifies that the task of management is to make the strengths of human resources effective and their weaknesses irrelevant towards achieving the organisation's objectives.
   - (a) Management of work
   - (b) Management of people
   - (c) Management of operations
   - (d) Management of goals

Ans. (b) Management of people

   Explanation: Management as multidimensional includes Management of work, Management of people, and Management of operations.

   Management of people means dealing with employees as individuals and dealing with individuals as a group.

8. ______________ involves a variety of programmes designed to promote and protect a company's image and its individual products in the eyes of the public.
   - (a) Advertising
   - (b) Personal selling
   - (c) Publicity
   - (d) Public relations

Ans. (d) Public relations

   Explanation: Public relation is a strategic communication process that helps in building mutually beneficial relationships between organisations and their publics. That relation has an impact on the operations and plans of the organisation.

9. Which type of organisational structure will you suggest for a firm which has diversified activities and operations requiring a high degree of specialisation ?
   - (a) Centralised structure
   - (b) Decentralised structure
   - (c) Divisional structure
   - (d) Functional structure

Ans. (d) Functional structure

   Explanation: An organisation which uses functional structure is divided on the basis of functional areas, such as IT, finance, or marketing. This structure requires greater operational efficiency so they require specialised skilled persons.

10. "Changes or events cannot be eliminated but they can be anticipated and managerial responses to them can be developed." is suggested by the following importance of planning:
    - (a) Planning facilitates decision-making
    - (b) Planning promotes innovative ideas
    - (c) Planning provides direction
    - (d) Planning reduces the risks of uncertainty

Ans. (d) Planning reduces the risks of uncertainty

   Explanation: Planning is forward looking as it is done for future and future is uncertain. With the help of planning, future can be anticipated and planning can be done in that way. In this way, the risk of future uncertainties can be minimised.

11. "Grouping similar nature jobs into larger units called departments" is the step in the process of one of the functions of management. Identify the function of management.

    (a) Planning   (b) Organising   (c) Directing   (d) Staffing

Ans. (b) Organising

Explanation: "Grouping similar nature of jobs into larger units called departments", it is the second step in the process of organising after identification of work.

12. The Statement "Planning is a primary function", suggests that________

    (a) planning precedes other functions

    (b) planning requires logical and systematic thinking

    (c) plan is framed, it is implemented, and is followed by another plan, and so on

    (d) planning is required at all levels of management as well as in all departments of the organisation.

Ans. (a) planning precedes other functions

Explanation: Planning is considered as the primary function of management as it is the first function to be performed in any organisation and after that all other functions will follow.

13. A major decision area under one of the functions of marketing is the decision regarding marketing intermediaries to be used. Name the function.

    (a) Physical Distribution   (b) Gathering and Analysing market information

    (c) Promotion   (d) Transportation

Ans. (a) Physical Distribution

Explanation: Physical distribution is part of "distribution", which includes wholesale and retail marketing, as well the physical movement of products.

14. "The nature of the relationship of our country with foreign countries", is a major element of which of the following components of the Business Environment?

    (a) Social Environment   (b) Legal Environment

    (c) Political Environment   (d) Economic Environment

Ans. (c) Political Environment

Explanation: Political Environment includes the relation of one country with others.

15. Which of the following statements is incorrect?

    (a) Marketing is a social process.

    (b) Focus of the marketing activities is on customer needs.

    (c) Marketing is merely a post-production activity.

    (d) Marketing mix is a wider term than product mix.

Ans. (c) Marketing is merely a post production activity.

Explanation: No, market is not a post- production activity because there are multi-channels open to a marketer today. In today's era of earned and paid media, company can get engaged with the target audience in advance.

16. Planning is closely connected with ______________ and __________________.

    (a) Responsibility and accountability   (b) Delegation and decentralization

    (c) Stability and security   (d) Creativity and innovation

Ans. (d) Creativity and innovation

Explanation: Planning involves setting objectives and developing appropriate course of action to achieve the set objectives. Thus, to achieve the set objectives planning should be creative and innovative.

17. ______________ is an important function of marketing which is important not only for protection of the product but also serves as a promotional tool.

    (a) Grading   (b) Labeling   (c) Packaging   (d) Branding

Ans. (c) Packaging

Explanation: Packaging is important not only for protection of the products but also serves as a promotional tool. As, buyers assess the quality of the product is by the packaging of the product.

18. As part of regulations to be followed by advertisers, the advertisement for a new brand of baby food for infants provides important information for potential buyers that it is "Not recommended for infants under the age of four months". Which dimension of the business environment is highlighted in the above statement?

    (a) Social Environment
    (b) Legal Environment
    (c) Political Environment
    (d) Economic Environment

Ans. (b) Legal Environment

    Explanation: As, warning given on the pack is related to legal framework.

19. The principle of management given by Fayol which aims at preventing overlapping of activities is:

    (a) Division of Work
    (b) Unity of Command
    (c) Unity of Direction
    (d) Order

Ans. (c) Unity of Direction

    Explanation: According to this principle, each unit of the organisation should work towards a common objective and units having same goals should have a single head and plan which will help in eliminating overlapping of work.

20. ____________ensures that the subordinate performs tasks on behalf of the manager thereby reducing his workload and providing him with more time to concentrate on important matters.

    (a) Decentralization
    (b) Delegation of authority
    (c) Authority
    (d) Accountability

Ans. (b) Delegation of authority

    Explanation: Delegation of authority is the organisational process of a manager in which manager divides their own work among all their subordinates. On the other hand, decentralisation is systematic effort to delegate to the lowest level, all authority except which can be exercised at the central point.

21. ____________ is a process of classification of products into different groups on the basis of some important characteristics such as quality, size, etc.

    (a) Standardization
    (b) Grading
    (c) Product Development
    (d) Selling

Ans. (b) Grading

    Explanation: Grading is the procedure of categorisation of products into groups, on the basis of their significant characteristics such as quality, size etc.

22. The sum total of all individuals, institutions and other forces that are outside the control of a business enterprise but that may affect its performance is known as________________.

    (a) Business Environment
    (b) Social Environment
    (c) Political Environment
    (d) Economic Environment.

Ans. (a) Business environment

    Explanation: Business Environment is defined as the sum totals of all external factors (customers, competitors, suppliers, government, and the social, cultural, political, technological and legal conditions) to the business firm and that greatly influence their functioning.

23. Name the concept that refers to the number of subordinates that can be effectively managed by a superior and determines the number of levels of management in the organisation.

    (a) Organisation Structure
    (b) Span of Management
    (c) Hierarchy of Authority
    (d) Delegation of Authority

Ans. (b) Span of Management

    Explanation: Span of Management determines the level of interactions and responsibilities associated with employees and managers. The process is used to determine the management style and it also defines roles with the organisation.

24. Taylor believed that there was only one best method to maximise efficiency. This method can be developed through study and analysis. Identify the Principle of Scientific Management being discussed above:

    (a) Harmony not discord
    (b) Science not rule of thumb
    (c) Development of each and every person to his or her greatest efficiency and prosperity
    (d) Cooperation not individualism

Ans. (b) Science not rule of thumb

Explanation: In this principle, Taylor stressed on use and application of scientific methods and techniques in performing the activities and 'the dictatorship of the manager' which should be avoided. Mangers must be thinking before doing that is 'Trial and Error Method' or 'Hit and Miss Method' should be avoided, instead scientific and researched methods should be adopted for performing any activity.

Section-B

25. India has launched its most advanced Geo-imaging satellite which will allow better monitoring of the subcontinent, including its borders with neighbouring countries, by imaging the country 4-5 times a day. The satellite is capable of near real time monitoring of floods and cyclones. The factor constituting the Business Environment being discussed above is:

    (a) Social Environment
    (b) Economic Environment
    (c) Technological Environment
    (d) Political Environment

Ans. (c) Technological Environment

Explanation: Technological Environment refers to the changes in the output, production methods, use of equipment and quality of product. It includes forces related to scientific innovations and improvements in products as well as production technology. In this question, examiner has talked about "Geo Imaging satellite".

26. Which step in the process of planning will precede the step in which the manager is required to make certain assumptions about the future, which are the base material upon which the plans are drawn.

    (a) Implementing the plan
    (b) Identifying alternative courses of action
    (c) Setting objectives
    (d) Selecting an alternative.

Ans. (c) Setting objectives

Explanation: The step in which the manager is required to make certain assumptions about the future, which are the base material upon which the plans are drawn is Developing Premises (second step of Planning Process). The step before Developing Premises is setting objectives.

27. "Availability and affordability of the product were considered to be the key to the success of a firm." Identify the concept of marketing management highlighted by this statement.

    (a) Production concept
    (b) Product concept
    (c) Societal concept
    (d) Marketing concept

Ans. (a) Production concept

Explanation: According to Production Concept, customers will always buy those products which are available cheaper and more easily.

28. Aiming to revive Jammu and Kashmir's attraction as a top location for film shooting the J&K film policy, 2021 offers a host of incentives to the film makers, such as subsidies and low long-term interest rates, for films with patriotic and certain other themes shot in J&K, for giving work opportunities to local artistes, etc. This will have an impact on business enterprises in the state. Which component of business environment is highlighted above:

    (a) Specific and general forces
    (b) Technological environment
    (c) Economic environment
    (d) Totality of external forces

Ans. (c) Economic environment

Explanation: As the given question, talks about the subsidies and low long term interest rates which comes under economic environment.

29. The Topper group is looking to make a foray into manufacturing of semiconductors and it has set up a business to seize the business opportunity and add to its prospect in the long run. The company has already pivoted into a number of new projects like electronics, 5G network equipment, as well as semiconductors. Which economic objective of management does the business seek to fulfill?

    (a) Survival
    (b) Growth
    (c) Profit
    (d) Efficiency

Ans. (b) Growth

Explanation: As, Topper Group has already pivoted into a number of new projects like electronics, 5G network equipment, as well as semiconductors, this shows that company is growing.

30. Product cost sets the lower limits of the price, the utility provided by the product and the intensity of demand of the buyers sets the upper limit. So, in case of inelastic demand, total revenue .... when price increases:
    (a) Rises
    (b) Falls
    (c) Constant
    (d) Both (a) and (b)

Ans. (a) Rises

Explanation: The price of a product is affected by the elasticity of demand of the product. The demand is said to be elastic if a small change in price results in large change in the quantity demanded. Numerically, the price elasticity is greater than one. In case of inelastic demand, the total revenue increases when the price is increased and falls when the price is reduced. If the demand of the product is inelastic, the organisation can fix higher prices.

31. "A manager in a conscious manner has to ensure that even where members of a department willingly cooperate, coordination gives direction to the willing spirit." The characteristic of coordination being highlighted above is :
    (a) Coordination is the responsibility of all managers.
    (b) Coordination is a deliberate function.
    (c) Coordination integrates group efforts.
    (d) Coordination is a continuous process.

Ans. (b) Coordination is a deliberate function.

Explanation: In the given statement, manager has to make sure that each and every member of a department willingly cooperates.

32. For the following two statements choose the correct option:
    Statement I: Accountability can be delegated.
    Statement II: Responsibility can be delegated completely.
    Choose the correct option from the options given below:
    (a) Statement I is correct and II is wrong
    (b) Statement II is correct and I is wrong
    (c) Both the statements are correct
    (d) Both the statements are incorrect

Ans. (d) Both the statements are incorrect

Explanation: Accountability and Responsibility both cannot be delegated.

33. The CEO of Radhe Cycles Pvt Ltd. Mr. Kumar wants to get maximum output from the employees at a competitive cost. On the other hand Ramakaant, an employee of the company wants to get the maximum salary while working the least. The Principle of management given by Fayol being violated by Ramakaant is __________.
    (a) Remuneration
    (b) Equity
    (c) Discipline
    (d) Subordination of individual interest to general interest.

Ans. (d) Subordination of individual interest to general interest.

Explanation: Ramakaant wants to get the maximum salary while working the least. Doing so would not be in the general interest of the firm, as it would lose its competitiveness if it continues to pay too much to its employees. This means its violating the principle of Subordination of individual interest to general interest

34. Arrange the following steps in the process of organising in the correct sequence:
    (a) Assignment of duties
    (b) Departmentalisation
    (c) Identification and division of work
    (d) Establishing reporting relationship
    Choose the correct option:
    (a) (a) ; (b) ; (d); (c)
    (b) (c) ; (b) ; (a); (d)
    (c) (c) ; (b) ; (d); (a)
    (d) (b) ; (c) ; (a); (d)

Ans. (b) (c) ; (b) ; (a); (d)

Explanation: Process of organising
    (i) Identification and division of work.
    (ii) Departmentalisation.
    (iii) Assignment of duties.
    (iv) Establishing reporting relationship.

35. The production department at Karishmaa Ltd., a firm manufacturing readymade garments for men has an objective to increase production by 10% but the Sales department does not approve of the increase in production, till changes are brought about in the product to incorporate latest fashion. These kinds of

conflicts bring to light the following importance of the force that can help to accomplish the linking of activities of various departments:

(a) Growth in size   (b) Functional differentiation

(c) Specialization   (d) Efficiency

Ans. (b) Functional differentiation

Explanation: Functional differentiation ensure unity of action among interdependent departments like finance, production, marketing, etc.

36. Planning requires logical and systematic thinking rather than guess work. The feature of planning being referred to in the above statement is:

(a) Planning is a continuous process   (b) Planning is futuristic

(c) Planning is pervasive   (d) Planning is a mental exercise

Ans. (d) Planning is a mental exercise

Explanation: Logical and systematic thinking requires use of mind.

37. Silico Ltd. has appointed the former Consulting Executive of Shri Shakti Ltd. Rajan Bahl as its Vice President. What will be his basic task?

(a) To integrate diverse elements and coordinate activities of different departments.

(b) To carry out plans formulated by top managers.

(c) To oversee the efforts of the workforce.

(d) Help to maintain quality of output.

Ans. (a) To integrate diverse elements and coordinate activities of different departments.

Explanation: As Rajan Bahl has been appointed at Top Level Management

38. The marketing management philosophy which is based on the premise that any activity which satisfies human needs but does not pay attention to the ethical and ecological aspects of marketing cannot be justified is known as:

(a) Marketing concept   (b) Societal marketing concept

(c) Production concept   (d) Product concept

Ans. (b) Societal marketing concept

Explanation: According to this concept, human welfare should be given priority before profits and satisfying the wants.

39. Ravi joined a marketing firm as a Sales manager. On his first day in the company, during the orientation programme, the CEO of the company told Ravi that he will have to simultaneously perform the functions of management (planning, organising, staffing, directing, controlling) all the time. Which characteristic of management was the CEO referring to?

(a) Management is a continuous process   (b) Management is all pervasive

(c) Management is multidimensional   (d) Management is goal oriented

Ans. (a) Management is a continuous process

Explanation: Management is never ending process as it is concerned with continuous identification of the problem and solving them by taking adequate steps by performing all functions of management.

40. Unlike professions such as medicine or law which require a practicing doctor or lawyer to possess valid degrees, nowhere in the world is it mandatory for a manager to possess any such professional degree. Identify the characteristic of the profession being discussed above which is not being strictly met by management.

(a) Well defined body of knowledge   (b) Restricted Entry

(c) Professional Association   (d) Ethical Code of Conduct

Ans. (b) Restricted Entry

Explanation: To be manager, person or individual needs the managament degree. Most of the companies are trying to appoint a person as manager, who is having management degree.

41. "Following a pre-decided plan, when circumstances have changed, may not turn out to be in the organisation's interest." The limitation of planning being referred to in the above statement is_____________.

(a) Planning does not guarantee success

(b) Planning may not work in a dynamic environment

(c) Planning leads to rigidity

(d) Planning is a time consuming process.

Ans. (c) Planning leads to rigidity

Explanation: Once plans are made to decide the future course of action the manager may not be in a position to change them, as business environment is dynamic.

42. The technique of Scientific Management given by Taylor, which aims to establish interchangeability of manufactured parts and products is __________.

(a) Method Study

(b) Motion Study

(c) Standardization

(d) Differential piece wage system.

Ans. (c) Standardization

Explanation: Standardization of work is the technique of scientific management, which helps in establishing interchangeability of manufactured parts and products.

It is the process of setting standards for every business activity, process, raw materials, time, machinery and methods to achieve efficiency. Standardization of product implies that the size, design, quality, shape, etc. of the product should meet the requirements and tastes of consumers.

43. For the following two statements choose the correct option:

Statement I: Advertising is an impersonal form of communication.

Statement II: Advertising lacks direct feedback.

Choose the correct option from the options given below:

(a) Statement I is correct and II is wrong

(b) Statement II is correct and I is wrong

(c) Both the statements are correct

(d) Both the statements are incorrect

Ans. (c) Both the statements are correct

Explanation: As advertisement is impersonal form of communication so the feedback is also not being given directly.

44. KTX Group is rolling out an initiative to help create wealth for its employees through the implementation of Employee Stock Option. Through motivation and leadership the management will help individuals to develop team spirit, cooperation and commitment to the success of the group. The following importance of management is highlighted above:

(a) Management helps in achieving personal objectives

(b) Management helps in the development of society

(c) Management creates a dynamic organisation

(d) Management increases efficiency

Ans. (a) Management helps in achieving personal objectives

Explanation: KTX Group is rolling out an initiative to help create wealth for its employees through the implementation of Employee Stock option.

45. If there is a plan to increase production then more labour, more machinery will be required. This step in the process of planning will involve organising for labour and purchase of machinery. Identify the step in the planning process being discussed above:

(a) Identifying alternative courses of action

(b) Setting objectives

(c) Selecting an alternative

(d) Implementing the plan

Ans. (d) Implementing the plan

Explanation: If the organisation plan to increase production, on implementing this plan more labour, more machinery will be required.

46. Taylor proposed eight specialists from whom each worker will have to take orders from as part of the technique of Functional Foremanship specified by him. Those with technical, mastery, intelligence and grit may be given______work. Those with energy and good health may be assigned______work.

(a) Planning, Execution

(b) Execution, Planning

(c) Production, Planning

(d) Implementation, Production

Ans. (a) Planning, Execution

Explanation: As planning requires mastery and intelligence, energy is required for execution.

47. A person feeling hungry may get food by offering to give money or some other product or service in return to someone who is willing to accept the same for food. The important feature of marketing illustrated above is:

(a) Exchange mechanism
(b) Customer value
(c) Creating a market offering
(d) Needs and wants

Ans. (a) Exchange mechanism

Explanation: As the individual is getting one thing (Food) in exchange of another thing (Money/good)

48. **Assertion:** (A) Planning is futuristic.

Reason: (R) Planning is concerned with the future which is certain and does not require forecast.

(a) Both (A) and (R) are correct
(b) (A) is correct (R) is incorrect
(c) Both (A) and (R) are correct, and (R) is the correct explanation of (R)
(d) Both (A) and (R) are correct, and (R) is not the correct explanation of (R)

Ans. (b) (A) is correct (R) is incorrect

Explanation: Planning is futuristic means for future which is uncertain and require forecast.

Section-C

Read the following text and answer question number 49-54 on the basis of the same.

'Saarthi', the name has been associated with the manufacturing and sale of Fashion products since 1960, when Kapil Saarthi opened his first retail fashion clothing outlet in Ahmedabad. Sarthi Cosmetics was incorporated in India in 1940, and became a member of the S & M family of companies in 1959. Sarthi Perfumes began operations in Gujarat in an existing administrative S &M facility in 1985. An important difference between S &M and most other companies is that instead of operating as one large corporation it operates as 180 smaller companies each focused on a specific product and area, implying selective dispersal of authority, recognising the decision makers need four autonomy, as decision making authority is pushed down the chain of command. It enables the company to maintain short lines of communication with customers and employees, and accelerate the development of talent.

49. Identify the philosophy that is being followed by S&M through which it is dividing the decision making responsibilities among hierarchical levels.

(a) Delegation of Authority
(b) Decentralization of Authority
(c) Division of Work
(d) Span of Management.

Ans. (b) Decentralization of Authority

Explanation: Implying selective dispersal of authority, recognizing the decision makers need four autonomy, as decision making authority is pushed down the chain of command.

50. 'Why is there, need to apply the philosophy being followed by S&M, with caution?

(a) As it can cause a delay in communication
(b) As it can cause disintegration of the organisation
(c) As it can increase the workload of the top management
(d) As it can reduce the chances of growth of the firm

Ans. (b) As it can cause disintegration of the organisation

Explanation: S & M is a group of 180 companies if they operate together it become very difficult to maintain short times of communication with customers and employees. It becomes very difficult for the management to focus on each product line which may lead to disintegration of the organisation.

51. The application of the philosophy discussed above can foster a sense of competition amongst the departments, which in turn will help the firm in the following manner:

(a) Facilitates growth
(b) Better control
(c) Relief to top management
(d) Quick decision making.

Ans. (a) Facilitates growth

Explanation: If all the departments will work properly, there will be increase in production which will lead to profits, as a result growth of the organisation.

52. Quote the line from above which highlights the importance of the philosophy towards providing management education to employees.

(a) "Maintain short lines of communication"

    (b) 'Accelerate the development of talent'

    (c) 'Selective dispersal of authority'

    (d) 'Recognises decision makers need for autonomy'

Ans. (b) 'Accelerate the development of talent'

Explanation: Talent can be developed by providing more knowledge and skills.

53. As "The decision making authority is pushed down the chain of command" at S&M enterprises, it provides the benefit of quick decision making to the organisation because:

    (a) There is no requirement for approval from many levels

    (b) Organisation is able to generate more returns

    (c) There are innovative performance systems

    (d) It's a means of management education

Ans. (a) There is no requirement for approval from many levels

Explanation: In case of decentralisation, employees can take decisions themselves without taking appprovals from higher levels. The approval is required for big/important or strategic decisions.

54. The philosophy being followed by S & M is not followed by most other companies. This tells us that the philosophy is :

    (a) Optional

    (b) Compulsory

    (c) Limited to superior and his subordinate

    (d) Merely done to lessen the burden of the manager

Ans. (a) Optional

Explanation: The Philosophy being followed by S & M company is optional.

55. Mohammad Kanjiwal, a beekeeper since April 2021 is now part of the growing tribe of at least 50 urban dwellers across Maharashtra raising bees and harvesting honey in their balconies, rooftops and back gardens. As he had been focussed on eating right the thought of domesticating honey bees to promote healthy consumption habits and seeing honey being cultivated right before his eyes was mesmerising for him. Identify the factor constituting the general environment being discussed above.

    (a) Economic Environment   (b) Social Environment

    (c) Technological Environment   (d) Political Environment

Ans. (b) Social Environment

Explanation: "As he had been focused on eating right the thought of domesticating honey bees to promote healthy consumption habits".

56. Zolo, a marketer of cars having 40% of the current market share of the country aims at increasing the market share to 70% in next few years. For achieving this objective the manager of the company specified the action programme covering various aspects. Identify the function of marketing discussed above:

    (a) Customer support services   (b) Gathering and Analysing market information

    (c) Product designing and development   (d) Marketing Planning

Ans. (d) Marketing Planning

Explanation: Market planning is the process of organising and defining the marketing aims of a company and gathering strategies and tactics to achieve them. Zolo described his objective and action programme to achieve this objective

57. Style and Fit, a footwear manufacturing company has decided to offer 50% off on all its products due to the fall in demand of its products as more efficient substitutes have been introduced in the market. Identify the pricing objective included by the firm which has made the firm resort to discounting its product.

    (a) Obtaining market share leadership   (b) Surviving in the competitive market

    (c) Attaining product quality leadership   (d) Protect the interest of public

Ans. (b) Surviving in the competitive market

Explanation: As substitutes has been introduced and there is fall in demand. By reducing the price they might be able to attract customers.

58. A sanitizer manufacturing company wants to become a market leader. For this purpose the manager follows an activity with certain logical steps. The first step suggested by him is to increase profits by at least 30% in the next quarter. What will be the last step of the activity being followed by the manager.

(a) Follow-up action

(b) Identifying alternative course of action

(c) Setting objectives

(d) Evaluating alternative courses of action

Ans. (a) Follow-up action

Explanation: Process of Planning

(i) Setting objectives

(ii) Developing premises

(iii) Identifying alternative courses of action

(iv) Evaluating alternative courses of action

(v) Selecting one best alternative

(vi) Implementing the plan

(viii) Follow-up Action

59. In Shalleen Pvt. Ltd. there is one head Shalleen who has two lines of authority under her. One line consists of Sara-Rajat-Abhishek-Ismail-Chris. Another line of authority under Shalleen is Lata-Rupa-Geet-Hussain-Preeti. According to a Principle of Management given by Fayol, If Ismail has to communicate with Hussain who is at the same level of authority then illustrate the route he will have to traverse.

(a) Ismail-Abhishek-Rajat-Sara-Shalleen-Lata-Rupa-Geet-Hussain

(b) Hussain-Geet-Rupa-Lata-Shalleen-Sara-Rajat-Abhishek-Ismail

(c) Ismail-Chris-Shalleen-Preeti-Hussain

(d) Ismail-Abhishek-Rajat-Sara-Lata-Rupa-Geet-Hussain

Ans. (a) Ismail-Abhishek-Rajat-Sara-Shalleen-Lata-Rupa-Geet-Hussain

Explanation: In this question, they have talked about "Scalar Chain. According to this principle, the information should follow a pre-defined path so that any kind of ambiguity can be avoided. The information has to flow from supervisor to the one in lowest position.

60. According to the technique of Scientific Management "Differential Piece Wage system" How much more will a worker making 60 units earn as compared to a worker making 49 units? If the standard output per day is 50 units and those who make standard output or more than standard get ₹ 75 per unit and those below get ₹ 65 per unit.

(a) ₹ 4,500

(b) ₹ 3,185

(c) ₹ 1,315

(d) ₹ 3,250

Ans. (c) ₹ 1,315

Explanation: Calculations

$$\text{A worker making 60 units earn} = 60 \times 75 = ₹\ 4,500$$
$$\text{A worker making 49 units earn} = 49 \times 65 = ₹\ 3,185$$
$$\text{Difference between the two} = ₹\ 1,315$$

A worker making 60 units earn ₹ 1,315 more as compared to a worker making 49 units.

❑❑

Sample Paper 1

Business Studies

Section – A

1. "Diverse members of management work towards fulfilling the common organisational goals." Which point of features of management is discussed here ?
   - (a) Group activity
   - (b) Dynamic function
   - (c) Intangible force
   - (d) Continuous process

2. ____________ is an element of delegation.
   - (a) Accountability
   - (b) Formal organisation
   - (c) Functional structure
   - (d) Informal organisation

3. Advertising lacks____________.
   - (a) Reaching to a large number of people
   - (b) Covering market in short time
   - (c) Direct feedback
   - (d) Impersonal communication

4. Identify the level at which the directing function takes place in an organisation.
   - (a) Top level management
   - (b) Middle level management
   - (c) Lower level management
   - (d) All of these

5. Answerability of the subordinate about the final result of the assigned task. Identify the element of delegation.
   - (a) Authority
   - (b) Accountability
   - (c) Responsibility
   - (d) None of these

6. 'Doing the right task in management' means____________ .
   - (a) effectiveness
   - (b) efficiency
   - (c) both (a) and (b)
   - (d) none of these

7. "Personal selling creates effective demand which results in increase in income, with increase in income, there will be more products and services, which in turn brings economic growth". This statement signifies the importance of personal selling to:
   - (a) Businessman
   - (b) Customers
   - (c) Society
   - (d) None of these

8. ____________is a component of general forces of business environment?
   - (a) Employees
   - (b) Customers
   - (c) Technological conditions
   - (d) Investors

9. Management should find 'One best way' to perform a task. Which technique of Scientific Management is defined in this sentence?
   - (a) Time Study
   - (b) Motion Study
   - (c) Fatigue Study
   - (d) Method Study

10. "In order to be successful, an organisation must change its goals according to the needs of the environment." Which characteristic of management is highlighted in this statement?
    - (a) Dynamic function
    - (b) Group activity
    - (c) Continuous process
    - (d) Goal-oriented process

11. "All other managerial functions are performed within the framework of the plans drawn. Thus, it can be said that planning proceeds other functions." This statement describes which function of planning?
    - (a) Planning focuses on achieving objectives
    - (b) Planning is pervasive
    - (c) Primacy of planning
    - (d) Planning is futuristic

12. Planning is considered to be___________.
- (a) forward looking function
- (b) backward looking function
- (c) both (a) and (b)
- (d) none of these

13. According to which concept of marketing, availability and affordability of the product are considered to be the key to the success of the firm?
- (a) Production concept
- (b) Product concept
- (c) Sales concept
- (d) Marketing concept

14. 'Hora Ltd.' is growing. It has made new units. Each unit is self-contained and works as a profit centre. Which type of organisational structure is this ?
- (a) Decentralised organisation
- (b) Divisional organisation
- (c) Functional organisation
- (d) Centralised organisation

15. Which of the following does not characterise the business environment?
- (a) Employees
- (b) Uncertainty
- (c) Complexity
- (d) Relativity

16. ___________ is considered as father of Scientific Management?
- (a) Henry Fayol
- (b) Harold Koontz
- (c) F.W. Taylor
- (d) Gilbreth

17. ________is the process of planning, organising, directing and controlling the activities relating to exchange of goods and services.
- (a) Marketing management
- (b) Sales management
- (c) Personal management
- (d) Financial management

18. A company is manufacturing cosmetics, medicines, health products and skin care products. It has separate divisions headed by divisional heads. Each division consists of separate departments with respective departmental heads. Each department has different groups and units with their own goals and objectives. Which function of organisation structure is being highlighted in the above case:
- (a) Functional Structure
- (b) Divisional Structure
- (c) Decentralisation
- (d) None of these

19. Which of the following is not the component of specific forces of business environment?
- (a) Technology
- (b) Customers
- (c) Investors
- (d) Employees

20. To see whether plans are being implemented and activities are performed according to schedule is known as_________.
- (a) Objectives
- (b) Planning
- (c) Follow-up action
- (d) Premises

21. The term_____means the totality of all individuals, institutions and other forces that are outside a business.
- (a) internal environment
- (b) social environment
- (c) business environment
- (d) none of these

22. The business environment is_____in nature, so planning may not work in such in environment.
- (a) dynamic
- (b) creative
- (c) innovative
- (d) static

23. Name the technique of Scientific Management given by Taylor which helps to differentiate between the efficient and the inefficient workers.
- (a) Method study
- (b) Time study
- (c) Different piece wage system
- (d) Fatigue study

24. It helps the manager to extend his area of operations, as without it, his activities would be restricted to only what he himself can do. Identify the activity referred to in the above statement and state its elements.
- (a) Decentralisation
- (b) Delegation
- (c) Informal organisation
- (d) Divisional

Section - B

25. In a school, twelve students were given the work for the school library in the summer vacations. One afternoon they were told to unload the shipment of new releases, stock the book shelves and then dispose off all the waste. So instead of all students doing work in their own way they decided to make Vikas as their group leader to supervise the work by grouping students, dividing the work, assigning each group their quota and developing reporting relationship among them. Due to this, job was done in a faster manner. Identify the function of the management in this school.
    (a) Planning
    (b) Controlling
    (c) Organising
    (d) Staffing

26. Identify the correct sequence of steps involved in the planning process:
    (a) Evaluating alternative courses, Identifying alternative course of actions, Setting objectives, Developing premises
    (b) Setting objectives, Identifying alternative course of actions, Evaluating alternative courses, Developing premises
    (c) Setting objectives, Developing premises, Identifying alternative course of actions, Evaluating alternative courses
    (d) Setting objectives, Developing premises, Identifying alternative course of actions, Evaluating alternative courses

27. "The increase in the demand for many Ayurvedic medicines, health products and services in the past few months is related to the need for building immunity and an increased awareness for healthcare due to the spread of Corona Virus." Identify the feature of business environment being described above.
    (a) Specific and general forces
    (b) Interrelatedness
    (c) Relativity
    (d) None of these

28. Maestro Inc. is a multinational corporation that creates consumer electronics, personal computers, servers and computer software. The company also has a chain of retail stores known as Maestro Stores. Despite high competition, Maestro has succeeded in creating demand for its products, giving the company power over prices through product differentiation, innovative advertising and ensured brand loyalty. In the context of above case, name any one function of marketing that facilitates product differentiation.
    (a) Labelling
    (b) Branding
    (c) Product development
    (d) Customer support service

29. Tomato Ltd., a food delivery service application has recently faced criticism for the tampering of their product, by their boys. Tomato Ltd. has decided to put a hologram seal on the food packets in order to protect the contents from spoilage, leakage, pilferage, damage, along with a tag with a safety warning for the consumers to check the seal. Which concept of marketing discussed above is performing the important function of communicating with the potential buyer and promoting the sale?
    (a) Branding
    (b) Product designing and development
    (c) Labelling
    (d) Packaging

30. Manager is able to achieve the target production within the time, but after high wastage of resources. In this case, the manager is__________.
    (a) effective
    (b) efficient
    (c) both (a) and (b)
    (d) neither (a) nor (b)

31. "A popular brand of Hair Conditioners comes in different categories for different hair, say for normal hair and for other categories".
    Identify the function of labelling in the above example.
    (a) Providing information required by law
    (b) Describe the product and specify its contents
    (c) Grading of products
    (d) Promotion of products

32. For the following two statements choose the correct option:
    Statement I: The principles of management are in the continuous process of evolution.
    Statement II: The principles of pure science are considered to be rigid in nature.
    Choose the correct option from the options given below:
    (a) Statement I is correct and II is wrong
    (b) Statement II is correct and I is wrong
    (c) Both the statements are correct
    (d) Both the statements are incorrect

33. Atul was a pen manufacturer. He used to make ball point pens in a small factory in the basement of his house. Daily he would go to the market place and distribute pens to the retailers. Some of the pens were sold by him of his own by meeting persons on road. He had not kept any name for his pens. They were just blue, black and red pens. One of his friends suggested him to keep a good name of his pens. He kept his own name and started selling pens with the name of Atul Pens. Then there were three categories of pens – Atul red, Atul blue and Atul black. Gradually his business started to pick up even more and he made good revenue.

Which function of marketing is highlighted in the above case?

(a) Packaging
(b) Branding
(c) Labelling
(d) None of these

34. Arrange the following of Fayol's Principles of Management in the correct sequence:

(i) Division of work
(ii) Unity of direction
(iii) Unity of command
(iv) Stability of personnel

Choose the correct option:

(a) (i), (iii), (ii), (iv)
(b) (i), (ii), (iii), (iv)
(c) (ii), (iii), (i), (iv)
(d) (iv), (iii), (ii), (i)

35. After completing a course in travel and tourism, Amit started his own travel agency. For smooth functioning of his business, he decided to create fourteen job positions. Further, he divided them into four departments on the basis of functions namely, front office department including online queries, reservations, department for airways, railways and roadways, accommodation booking department and securing payments department. In order to avoid any interdepartmental conflicts, he decides to specify the lines of authority and areas of responsibility for each job position.

Identify the framework created by Amit within which all managerial and operating tasks are to be performed in his organisation.

(a) Organisational Structure
(b) Functional Structure
(c) Both (a) and (b)
(d) None of these

36. "Principles enable a better understanding of the relationship between human and material resources in accomplishing organisational purposes".

Which of the following characteristics of principles of management is reflected in the above statement ?

(a) Principles are flexible in nature
(b) Principles are contingent
(c) Principles are behaviourial
(d) General guidelines

37. Moon Private Ltd. decided to donate 2% of its sale to Sneha Foundation for improving the condition of children in India. This initiative by the company was appreciated by the public and their sales increased by 10%. Identify the objective of management depicted in the given case:

(a) Organisational objective
(b) Personal objective
(c) Social objective
(d) None of these

38. Some companies believe that it is easy to sell the products when products are inexpensive and are easily available. So the firms following production concept focus on lowering the cost of production by means of mass production and distribution but the drawback of this concept is that customers don't always buy products which are inexpensive and available. This concept is known as:

(a) Production Concept
(b) Product Concept
(c) Selling Concept
(d) Marketing Concept

39. Sunita took her niece, Aishwarya for shopping to 'Benetton' to buy her a dress on the occasion of her birthday. She was delighted when on payment for the dress she got a discount voucher to get 20% off for a meal of ₹ 500 or above at a famous eating joint. Identify the technique of sales promotion used by the company in the above situation.

(a) Rebate
(b) Discount
(c) Usable benefit
(d) Product combination

40. In order to make the 'Annual Day' of the school a successful event, the Headmistress of the school segregated all the activities into task groups each one dealing with a specific area. For instance, decorations, refreshments, backstage support, etc. Each group was put under the charge of one teacher. Identify the function of management performed by the Headmistress by dividing the activities and assigning the duties?

(a) Planning
(b) Organising
(c) Staffing
(d) Directing

41. "Most of the business firms are using social media sites (like Linked-in, Facebook, Twitter, Instagram. etc.) to promote their business". The dimension of business environment is __________.
    (a) economic environment
    (b) legal environment
    (c) technological environment
    (d) social environment

42. Mohan joined an organisation as a production manager. In order to ensure smooth flow of work, he decided to group similar activities into sections. The process carried out by him is known as________.
    (a) delegation
    (b) decentralisation
    (c) departmentalisation
    (d) formal organisation

43. For the following two statements choose the correct option:
    Statement I: Production concept is made to bring the cost of production to the minimum.
    Statement II: Selling concept states that customer satisfaction alone can ensure success.
    Choose the correct option from the options given below:
    (a) Statement I is correct and II is wrong
    (b) Statement II is correct and I is wrong
    (c) Both the statements are correct
    (d) Both the statements are incorrect

44. "Even a small production activity like loading pigs of iron into boxcars can be scientifically planned and managed. This can result in tremendous saving of human energy as well as wastage of time and materials." Which principle of scientific management is being highlighted in the given statement?
    (a) Harmony does not discord
    (b) Cooperation not individualism
    (c) Initiative
    (d) Science not rule of thumb

45. Sushmita is planning to start an online coaching centre. She wants to introduce innovative teaching techniques especially for slow learners. Therefore, she is constantly interacting with parents and encouraging them to share their ideas. This will make her aware of more alternatives. The step of planning being described in the given lines is______.
    (a) identifying alternative course of action
    (b) selecting the best course of action
    (c) evaluating the courses of action
    (d) follow up action

46. The target production of Surya Ltd. was 1,00,000 units in a year. Production Manager was able to cut down the cost but could not achieve the target. In this case, manager is________but not______.
    (a) efficient, effective
    (b) efficient, honest
    (c) effective, efficient
    (d) none of these

47. Priya purchased a bottle of tomato-sauce from the local grocery shop. The information provided on the bottle was not clear. She fell sick on consuming it. The function of management illustrated above is:
    (a) Labelling
    (b) Packaging
    (c) Branding
    (d) None of these

48. **Assertion:** Management as an art and science are not mutually exclusive, but complement each other.
    Reason: Managers work better if their practices are based on principles of management.
    (a) Both (A) and (R) are correct
    (b) (A) is correct (R) is incorrect
    (c) Both (A) and (R) are correct, and (R) is the correct explanation of (A)
    (d) Both (A) and (R) are correct, and (R) is not the correct explanation of (A)

Section – C

Read the following text and answer question no. 49-54 on the basis of the same:

After completing a diploma in interior decoration, Malini Birwal setup a small office at Chandigarh to render services. Being new in the field of entrepreneurship, she put in logical and systematic thinking involving foresight, intelligent imagination and sound judgement rather than guess work. She made certain assumptions as she knew that only accurate forecast will act as the base material upon which the plans are to be drawn. Her friend, Neeru Sharma, who has done MBA, advised her to do planning effectively as a good planning will help develop managerial response to deal with the changes and uncertain events. So, she acted in a conscious manner and made sub-plans for the juniors to follow.

49. Which feature of planning is highlighted in the above case study?
    (a) Planning is all pervasive
    (b) Planning is a mental exercise
    (c) Planning is a continuous process
    (d) Planning focuses on achieving objectives

50. Which importance of planning did Neeru hint at while guiding Malini?
    - (a) Planning facilities decision-making
    - (b) Planning promotes innovative ideas
    - (c) Planning reduces overlapping and wasteful activities
    - (d) Planning reduces the risks of uncertainty
51. Which steps of planning process was taken by Malini?
    - (a) Setting objectives
    - (b) Developing premises
    - (c) Selecting an alternative
    - (d) Follow up action
52. Which limitation of planning can you find in the above case study?
    - (a) Planning reduces creativity
    - (b) Planning involves huge costs
    - (c) Planning leads to rigidity
    - (d) Planning does not guarantee success
53. "Neeru Sharma, who has done MBA, advised her to do planning effectively as a good planning will help develop managerial response to deal with the changes and uncertain to deal with the changes and uncertain events". Which importance of planning is highlighted in the lines?
    - (a) It provides direction
    - (b) It reduces overlapping
    - (c) It reduces the risk of uncertaintly
    - (d) None of the above
54. Being new in the field of entrepreneurship, Malini put in logical and systematic thinking involving foresight, intelligent imagination and sound judgement rather than guess work. Which aspect of management is highlighted here:
    - (a) Planning
    - (b) Organising
    - (c) Staffing
    - (d) Directing
55. Saumya decided to start a business of selling dress material from her house. She did various online surveys to find out about the preferences of prospective customers. Based on this, she prepared a detailed analysis of the business. Then she made important decisions including deciding about the features, quality, packaging, labelling and branding of the dress material. Identify the element of marketing mix discussed in the given case.
    - (a) Promotion
    - (b) Market
    - (c) Product
    - (d) Place
56. A marketer of TV, having 10% of the current market share, aims to increase it to 20% in the next three years. For this, he needs to develop a complete marketing plan covering various important aspects and specify the action programmes to achieve these objectives. Which function of marketing is being discussed in the case?
    - (a) Standardisation and grading
    - (b) Gathering and analysing market information
    - (c) Product designing and development
    - (d) Marketing planning
57. 'Soft and Silk Crafts (India) Limited' has been manufacturing readymade textiles, maintains high reputation in the internatioal market and has been dumping its untreated poisonous chemicals and wastes in the river 'Yamuna' which has polluted the river and created many health problems for Delhiites. Identify the related environmental dimension.
    - (a) Political environment
    - (b) Social environment
    - (c) Legal environment
    - (d) Economic environment
58. To make the annual function of the school successful, the principal of the school divided all the activities into task groups each dealing with a specific area like rehearsals, decoration, state management, refreshments, etc. Each group was placed under the overall supervision of a senior teacher. Which step of organising is being discussed here?
    - (a) Division of work
    - (b) Departmentalisation
    - (c) Assignment of duties
    - (d) Reporting relationship
59. Swapnil Awasthi has recently joined Zincara Ltd, a company manufacturing washing machines. He found that his department was under-staffed and other departments were not cooperating with his department for smooth functioning of the organisation. Therefore, he ensured that his department has the required number of employees and its cooperation with other departments is improved. Identify, at which level Swapnil Awasthi was working in the organisation.
    - (a) Top level
    - (b) Middle level
    - (c) Lower level
    - (d) None of these
60. According to the technique of scientific management "Differential Piece Wage System" How much more will a worker making 60 units earn as compared to a worker making 39 units? If the standard output per day is 40 units and those who make standard output or more than standard get ₹75 per unit and those below get ₹ 65 per unit.
    - (a) ₹ 1575
    - (b) ₹ 1965
    - (c) ₹ 1365
    - (d) ₹ 1975

❑❑

Sample Paper 2

Business Studies

Section – A

1. "They don't sell what they can make, but they make what they can sell". Name the philosophy to which this statement is related.

   (a) Societal marketing concept
   (b) Marketing concept
   (c) Product concept
   (d) None of these

2. The process by which a manager synchronises the activities of different departments is known as ....

   (a) Coordination
   (b) Cooperation
   (c) Organising
   (d) Supervision

3. Planning function is performed by________

   (a) Top management
   (b) Middle management
   (c) Operative management
   (d) All of these

4. Priyansh works in cello limited. He is responsible for ensuring that his department has the necessary personnel. At what level of management Priyansh is working?

   (a) Top level
   (b) Middle level
   (c) Supervisory level
   (d) None of these

5. Telecall is a mobile company offers a discount of ₹1,000 to clear off excess inventory. Identify the method of sales promotion:

   (a) Discount
   (b) Rebate
   (c) Lucky draw
   (d) Usable benefit

6. Grouping of activities on the basis of product lines is a part of___________

   (a) Delegated organisation structure
   (b) Divisional organisation structure
   (c) Functional organisation structure
   (d) Autonomous organisation structure

7. "Once a plan is formed by the top management and is conveyed to the whole team, it is very difficult to alter it". Which limitation of planning is being indicated in the given statements?

   (a) Planning leads to rigidity
   (b) Planning is time-consuming
   (c) Planning reduces creativity
   (d) Planning does not guarantee success

8. While practicing principles of management______cannot be neglected as business have to fulfil social and ethical responsibility towards society.

   (a) techniques
   (b) programmes
   (c) actions
   (d) values

9. Customer feel more assured about quality and feel more comfortable if sponsors claim these benefits in advertising. Identify the features of advertising.

   (a) Enhancing customer satisfaction and confidence
   (b) Legitimacy
   (c) Expressiveness
   (d) Economy

10. "Firms believe that aggressive selling and promotional efforts will convince a customer to buy product". Which concept of marketing management is this?

    (a) Selling concept
    (b) Product concept
    (c) Production concept
    (d) Societal marketing concept

11. In urban areas, people are becoming diet conscious. They go to gym and avoid eating junk food due to which, there is less sale in fast food chain stores. Identify the dimension of business environment.
   (a) Political
   (b) Economic
   (c) Social
   (d) Technological

12. Planning helps in reducing the:
   (a) Direction for action
   (b) Decision-making
   (c) Memory
   (d) Risk of uncertainty

13. A man is running a fashion store. He sells variety of goods such as textiles, garments, cosmetics etc. He follows an organisation structure. Identify the organisational structure here.
   (a) Divisional structure
   (b) Functional structure
   (c) Both (a) and (b)
   (d) None of these above

14. Which of the following is not the function of packaging?
   (a) Product protection
   (b) Pricing objectives
   (c) Promotion
   (d) Product identification

15. Which of the following is not true regarding the objective of management?
   (a) Earning profits
   (b) Growth of an organisation
   (c) Providing employment
   (d) Policy-making

16. Foreman and Supervisors comprise____________
   (a) Top level management
   (b) Middle level management
   (c) Operational management
   (d) None of these

17. ________covers all the activities required to physically move the goods from manufacturers to customers.
   (a) Place mix
   (b) Price mix
   (c) Product mix
   (d) Promotion mix

18. Agro Limited has launched a new range of air conditioners in order to add value to the usability of the product. The new range of air conditioners has an inbuilt air purifier and is available in attractive colours. Identify the type of marketing philosophy being described in the above lines.
   (a) Product concept
   (b) Production concept
   (c) Marketing concept
   (d) Societal marketing concept

19. The process of classification of products into different groups on the basis of their important characteristics refers to which of the following marketing functions?
   (a) Grading
   (b) Standardisation
   (c) Product designing
   (d) Marketing planning

20. ________involves giving authority and responsibility to subordinates.
   (a) Division of work
   (b) Decentralisation
   (c) Delegation
   (d) Centralisation

21. Management is a ________function as it adapts itself according to the changing environment.
   (a) continuous
   (b) dynamic
   (c) pervasive
   (d) all of these

22. Which of the following is a feature of planning:-
   (a) Focuses on achieving goals
   (b) Pervasive
   (c) Mental exercise
   (d) All of the above

23. Name the technique of Taylor which is based on his scientific principles of management, 'science not rule of thumb'.
   (a) Standardisation and simplification
   (b) Functional foremanship
   (c) Method study
   (d) Time study

24. In order to get feedback about its recently launched immunity boosting Ayurvedic medicine, Atulya Limited conducted an online survery using a questionnaire, to gather customer reviews and opinions. Identify the marketing function being used by Atulya Limited.
   (a) Standardisation
   (b) Product designing
   (c) Customer support service
   (d) Gathering and analysing market information

Section - B

25. Ram, Shyam and Sunder are three brothers, who work in different MNCs as Managers. On dining table, every day they discuss about their day. One day they were having a conversation. Ram told that he face lot of problems in motivating people at shop floor. On the other hand, Shyam told that he face lots of problem in allocating the amount of finance required by each department. He has to tell different financial policies to the employees and have to coordinate with other departmental heads to know their financial requirements. Sunder told that he has to decide long term policies of the organisations and to scan the business environment. All these activities require lot of planning and logical thinking.

    If a person is maintaining the liaison with the outside world on the above case at which level he/she is working?

    (a) Top Level

    (b) Middle Level

    (c) Lower Level

    (d) None of these

26. To see whether plans are being implemented and activities are being performed according to schedule, is a step of planning process. Identify the step.

    (a) Choosing an alternative

    (b) Implement the plan

    (c) Identifying alternatives

    (d) Follow-up action

27. The government has directed all the leading companies to voluntarily participate in the Clean India Mission and asked them to make toilets in cities and villages. Identify the dimension of environment is affected due to such direction?

    (a) Technological environment

    (b) Social environment

    (c) Legal environment

    (d) Economic environment

28. In a popular advertisement on radio and television, Bollywood actress Vidya Balan talks about cleanliness and hygiene. The idea behind is to create awareness regarding having a toilet in each house instead of going out in the open. She included the advertisement with a punchline 'Jaha Soch Waha Shauchalay'. Identify what is being marketed by the famous actress in the above case.

    (a) Idea

    (b) Information

    (c) Experiences

    (d) Services

29. Any kind of external devices, like compact discs (CD's) for computer, have become obsolete. Google, with its Google Drive service, Apple with its Cloud offering, enables the users store documents, photos, music and movies on web-based servers. Identify the feature of business environment being described in the above lines.

    (a) Relativity

    (b) Dynamic nature

    (c) Uncertainty

    (d) Interrelatedness

30. "Even after opening up of the Indian Economy in 1991, foreign companies found it entremely difficult to cut through the bureaucratic red tape to get permits for doing business in India, which created a negative impact on business". Identify the dimension of the business environment which led to creation of the negative impact on business.

    (a) Social environment

    (b) Technological environment

    (c) Political environment

    (d) Legal environment

31. "Employee turnover should be minimised to maintain organisational efficiency." The principle of management is being highlighted above is:

    (a) Initiative

    (b) Stability of personnel

    (c) Order

    (d) Discipline

32. For the following two statements choose the correct option:

    Statement I : Organising involves identifying and dividing the work that has to be done in accordance with previously determined plans.

    Statement II : Identification and division of work is the first step in the process of organising.

    Choose the correct option from the options given below:

    (a) Statement I is correct and II is wrong

    (b) Statement II is correct and I is wrong

    (c) Both the statements are correct

    (d) Both the statements are incorrect

33. Joe Ltd. is a natural and ethical beauty brand famous for offering organic beauty products for men and women. The company uses plant based materials for its products and is the No. 1 beauty brand in the country. It not only satisfies its customers but also believes in the overall protection of the planet. Identify the marketing management philosophy being followed by 'Beauty Product Ltd'.

    (a) Production concept   (b) Product concept

    (c) Selling concept   (d) Societal marketing concept

34. Among the following elements of promotion in the correct sequence.

    (i) Public relations   (ii) Advertising

    (iii) Personal selling   (iv) Sales Promotion

    Choose the correct option:

    (a) (i), (ii), (iii),(iv)   (b) (ii), (iv), (i),(iii)

    (c) (ii), (iii), (iv),(i)   (d) (iv), (iii), (ii),(i)

35. Clean Sanity ware is a big company. Managing many employees at the same moment is a challenge which this company always faces. Since the company has many departments it is necessary for the company to ensure unity of action among various departments. The various departments are human resources, marketing, finance, operations and sales. The employees are always concerned about the company and are a useful resource to their organisation. Though they have diverse interests and have to perform different activities the management ensures that the efforts of the employees should be given a focus so as to achieve the organisation goals. The different departments have their own interests but due to proper coordination the conflicts of interest in the departments is minimized to a nil.

    Which characteristics of coordination have been highlighted in the above case?

    (a) Coordination ensures unity of action   (b) Development of personnel

    (c) Both of these   (d) None of these

36. While reading the label of a pack of aluminium foil, Rohan discovered that the product was manufactured at Hyderabad but was available for sale in many states across the country. Identify the function of marketing which has made this possible.

    (a) Grading   (b) Standardisation

    (c) Transportation   (d) Warehousing

37. Saleem keeps machines, materials, tools etc ready for operations by concerned workers. Whose work is described by this sentence under functional foremanship?

    (a) Repair boss   (b) Speed boss

    (c) Inspectors   (d) Gang boss

38. All organisations are set up to perform some task or goal. Management activities aim at achieving goals or tasks to be accomplished . The task or work depends upon the nature of business is known as

    (a) Management of work   (b) Management of operations

    (c) Management is pervasive   (d) Management is goal oriented process

39. Sona found a worm crawling out of a newly opened tetra pack of juice manufactured by a reputed company, Zest Ltd. She went back to the shopkeeper from whom the pack was purchased who directed her to call up the customer care centre. When all her efforts fell free, she went to a consumer activist group to seek their advice. The group decided to help Sona and take measures to impose restrictions on the sales of the firm's products of the particular batch and urge customers to refrain from buying the products of the company. Zest Ltd. Lost its image in the market. The CEO gave the responsibility of bringing back the lost image of the company to the manager. Identify the concept of marketing management which will help the manager to get the firm to get out of the crisis.

    (a) Public relations   (b) Sales promotion

    (c) Advertising   (d) None of these

40. Yash is a middle level manager. He keeps all his subordinates under a lot of discipline. His employees however complain of wastage of time and efforts as they feel that nothing is being assigned in a proper way and a proper place, also no proper schedule is made for working. Which principle of management is violated here?

    (a) Discipline   (b) Unity of command

    (c) Unity of direction   (d) Order

41. 'Mansi took her niece, Ridhima, for shopping to 'Mega Stores' to by her a bag for her birthday. She was delighted when on payment of the bag she got a pencil box along with the bag free of cost the technique of sales promotion used by the company in the above statement is__________.
    (a) Quality gift
    (b) Sampling
    (c) Product combinations
    (d) Usable benefits

42. Name the principle of management given by Fayol which when applied would mean that the workers and management both honour their commitments without any prejudice towards one another.
    (a) Discipline
    (b) Mental Revolution
    (c) Remuneration of employees
    (d) Scalar chain

43. For the following two statements choose the correct option:
    Statement I : Economic environment consist of economic policies and industrial policies.
    Statement II : Economic factors are a feature of the micro environment of an organisation.
    Choose the correct option from the options given below:
    (a) Statement I is correct and II is wrong
    (b) Statement II is correct and I is wrong
    (c) Both the statements are correct
    (d) Both the statements are incorrect

44. Himalaya Ltd. is engaged in manufacturing of washing machines. The target of the organisation is to manufacture 500 washing machines a day. There is an occupational specialisation in the organisation which promotes efficiency of employees. There is no duplication of efforts in such type of organisation structure. Identify the type of organisation structure described in this case.
    (a) Formal
    (b) Divisional
    (c) Functional
    (d) Informal

45. "An innovative course may be adopted by involving more people and sharing their ideas."
    Identify the step of planning function of management highlighted above.
    (a) Setting objectives
    (b) Developing premises
    (c) Identifying alternative courses of action
    (d) Selecting alternative courses

46. Derivation of principles of management may be said to be a matter of _____and its creative application may be regarded as an_______
    (a) Art, Science
    (b) Science, Art
    (c) Art, Profession
    (d) Profession, Science

47. The market is flooded with better quality toys of foreign origin. The result is fall in revenue of the indigenous or local companies as their products are much inferior and are also costlier in less demand in the market. Which dimension of business environment can be seen here affecting the local companies' revenue?
    (a) Social environment
    (b) Technological environment
    (c) Political environment
    (d) Legal environment

48. **Assertion:** Business environment is a relative concept
    Reason: It does not differ business in same country but differ from country to country.
    (a) Both (A) and (R) are correct
    (b) (A) is correct (R) is incorrect
    (c) Both (A) and (R) are correct, and (R) is the correct explanation of (R)
    (d) Both (A) and (R) are correct, and (R) is not the correct explanation of (R)

Section - C

Read the following text and answer the questions from 49-54 on the basis of the same:

'ABC' is a washing machine manufacturing company. The company decides to enter into music system manufacturing industry. The company has a committed top management. It knows that there are various challenges in the market where its decisions regarding the new industry might fail. Still the top management doesn't want to waste a lot of resources on its plans. It knows that sometimes plans take more time in making than getting implemented. However, the company wants to proceed with a positive approach. It has decided to study all the aspects of its competitors, to set all its objectives and to allocate the required resources. The company did well in its previous business. At that time they took planning very seriously as they knew everything the company had to do based on concrete plans. The company will start its operations from next month.

49. Which function of management has been discussed in the above case?
    (a) Planning
    (b) Organising
    (c) Directing
    (d) Controlling
50. Which limitation of planning has been highlighted in the above case?
    (a) Planning is a continuous process
    (b) Planning involves huge costs
    (c) Planning is a dynamic process
    (d) None of these
51. Which feature of planning is highlighted above?
    (a) Planning is a primary function of management
    (b) Planning does not guarantee success
    (c) Planning is a time consuming process
    (d) None of these
52. Importance of planning includes:
    (a) Planning is a primary function of management
    (b) Planning is a time consuming process
    (c) Planning provides direction
    (d) None of these
53. Planning is closely related with:
    (a) Creativity
    (b) Innovation
    (c) Both (a) and (b)
    (d) None of these
54. Planning has no meaning unless it contributes to the achievement of predetermined organisational goals. Identify the feature of planning from above statement:
    (a) Planning focuses on achieving objectives
    (b) Planning is futuristic
    (c) Planning is continuous
    (d) Planning is pervasive.
55. 'Yo Tummy' began its business by offering the classic combo of hamburgers and fries. But over time, their customers wanted healthier foods, so 'Yo Tummy' responded and began offering healthy alternatives such as salads, fruits, wraps and oat meal. If 'Yo Tummy' hadn't responded, they may have lost customers that wanted to eat healthier foods. The above case highlights one of the points related to the importance of business environment and its understanding by managers. Identify it.
    (a) It helps in coping with rapid changes
    (b) It helps in improving performance
    (c) It helps the firm to identify threats and early warning signals
    (d) It enables the firm to identify opportunities and getting the first mover advantage
56. Gagan Ltd. needed funds to fulfill a big order. The management of the company borrowed money from a financial institution @ 16% interest, while the prevailing rate of interest was 12%. As a result of the expensive funds, the company was able to achieve the target. According to you, management was:
    (a) effective
    (b) efficient
    (c) Inefficient
    (d) None of these
57. Super Fine Rice Ltd. has the largest share of 55% in the market. The company's policy is to sell only for cash. In 2020, for the first time company's number one position in the industry has been threatened because other companies started selling rice on credit also. But the managers of Super Fine Rice Ltd. continued to rely on its previously tried and tested successful plans which didn't work because the environment is not static. This led to decline in sales of Super Fine Rice Ltd. The above situation is indicating limitation of planning which led to decline in it sales, Identify it.
    (a) Planning leads to rigidity
    (b) Planning may not work in a dynamic environment
    (c) Planning is pervasive
    (d) Planning involves huge costs
58. Rahul decided to start a desert cooler manufacturing business. He sets the target of earning 20% profit on sales in the first year. He was very much concerned about the future prospects of the business, which were

uncertain. For this, he gathered information from the potential market and analysed that the demand for wall mounted coolers is increasing day by day. He used this information as the base for future planning. One the basis of the gathered information, he called a meeting in the following week to find new methods to achieve the objective.

Identify the function of management involved in the above case.

(a) Controlling

(b) Staffing

(c) Planning

(d) Organising

59. Mr. Amritansh Kapoor's father has a good business of iron and steel. He wants to go to the USA for his MBA but his father thinks that he should join the business. On the basis of emerging- trends, do you think that Mr. Kapoor should send his son to the USA?

(a) Yes because management is being recognised as a profession to a great extent

(b) No because management is an art rather than a profession

(c) Question is inappropriate

(d) None of these

60. "Seven Stars" is a well-known resort for organising parties, especially for children. However, in past 6 months its popularity has reduced considerably as a new resort with better ambience and facilities has opened within its vicinity. Name the related feature of business environment which has influenced the business of 'Seven Stars' adversely.

(a) Totality of external forces

(b) Dynamic nature

(c) Interrelatedness

(d) Uncertainty

□□

Sample Paper 3

Business Studies

Section – A

1. "Workers should be encouraged to develop and carry out their plans for development". Identify the principle of management formulated by Fayol.
   - (a) Espirit De Corps
   - (b) Initiative
   - (c) Stability of personnel
   - (d) Equity

2. The process of creating and producing package for a product is known as:
   - (a) Place or physical distribution
   - (b) Price
   - (c) Packaging
   - (d) Promotion

3. ___________management involves cost-benefit analysis and the relationship between inputs and outputs?
   - (a) Effectiveness
   - (b) Efficient
   - (c) Coordination
   - (d) Controlling

4. Which one of the following factors is not relevant to price fixation?
   - (a) Obtaining market leadership
   - (b) Age of an organisation
   - (c) Surviving in a competitive market
   - (d) Attaining product quality leadership

5. As a publisher, Mary has published a new book on marketing management. Identify which of the factors will she consider to determine the price of this book?
   - (a) Advertising
   - (b) Demand for the book
   - (c) Price of other competitive books
   - (d) Options (b) and (c)

6. _________is not a part of organising process?
   - (a) Assigning of duties
   - (b) Departmentalisation
   - (c) Decentralisation
   - (d) Establishing authority-responsibility relationship

7. "Planning involves foresightedness and imagination". Which feature of planning is highlighted here?
   - (a) Mental exercise
   - (b) Forward looking
   - (c) Decision-making
   - (d) None of these

8. "Planning requires lot of time and cost". This is one of the __________ of planning.
   - (a) advantages
   - (b) disadvantages
   - (c) both (a) and (b)
   - (d) none of these

9. A plan is framed; it is implemented and followed by another plan and so on. Which feature of planning is highlighted in the above sentence.
   - (a) Planning focuses on achieving objectives
   - (b) Planning is continuous
   - (c) Planning is the primary function of management
   - (d) Planning is pervasive

10. "It charges a comparatively higher price than its competitors." Which of the following component of marketing mix is shown in the above statement.
    - (a) Price
    - (b) Place
    - (c) Promotion
    - (d) Product

11. It has five of its own retail shops." Or "It also sells its products through various grocery shops." Identify the component of marketing mix highlighted the above statement.
    - (a) Price
    - (b) Place
    - (c) Promotion
    - (d) Product

12. Properly perform the assigned duty, is ____________
    - (a) accountability
    - (b) responsibilty
    - (c) authority
    - (d) none of these

13. A manager applies various theories of management in his/her unique personalised way. What aspect of nature of management does this statement indicate?
    - (a) Management as a Science
    - (b) Management as an Art
    - (c) Management of Amateurs
    - (d) Management as an Authority

14. It regularly uses different communication tools to increase its sales." Which of the following component of marketing mix highlighted in the above statement.
    - (a) Price
    - (b) Place
    - (c) Promotion
    - (d) Product

15. Which one of the following promotion tools has mass reach?
    - (a) Advertising
    - (b) Personal selling
    - (c) Sales promotion
    - (d) Public relations

16. Foreman and supervisors comprise________
    - (a) Top level of management
    - (b) Middle level of management
    - (c) Operational level of management
    - (d) None of these

17. ________is a process that initiates implementation of plans by clarifying jobs and working relationships and effectively deploying resources for attainment of identified and desired goals.
    - (a) Planning
    - (b) Organising
    - (c) Staffing
    - (d) Directing

18. Management principles increases managerial efficiency as the manager leaves routine meeting to his/her subordinates and deal with exceptional situations which require his/her expertise by following the principle of delegation. What does the above case signify about management?
    - (a) Meeting changing environment requirements
    - (b) Providing managers with useful insights into reality
    - (c) Fulfilling social responsibility
    - (d) Management training, education and research

19. Business environment includes which of the following forces?
    - (a) Socio-cultural
    - (b) Political
    - (c) Legal
    - (d) All of these

20. An organisational design that groups similar or related jobs together on the basis of function is known as__________
    - (a) Functional structure
    - (b) Divisional structure
    - (c) Organisation structure
    - (d) None of these

21. __________are related to delegation of authority.
    - (a) Authority and Responsibility
    - (b) Coordination
    - (c) Decentralisation
    - (d) None of these

22. ________is concerned with monitoring organisational performance towards the attainment of organisational goals.
    - (a) Organising
    - (b) Controlling
    - (c) Staffing
    - (d) Directing

23. The function of management which establishes relation between authority and responsibility is:
    - (a) Planning
    - (b) Organising
    - (c) Staffing
    - (d) Directing

24. Even a small production activity like loading pigs of iron into boxcars can be scientifically planned and managed. This can result in tremendous saving of human energy as well as wastage of time and materials. Which of the following Principle of management emphasize in above situation?
    - (a) Harmony, not discord
    - (b) Science not Rule of Thumb

(c) Initiative

(d) Development of each and every to her/his greatest efficiency and proficiency

Section - B

25. Tracy coolers are a very progressive company. The owners of the company feel that unless and until they contribute to the society it is worthless to exist. In a recent move by the government the organisation decided to help it. The company will be making five teams of hired environmentalists from foreign countries. This team will help the local people clean the portions of a polluted river in the country. The costs of this project will be borne by the company. Identify the marketing philosophy involved in the case above.

(a) Production concept

(b) Product concept

(c) Societal concept

(d) Marketing concept

26. To see whether plans are being implemented and activities are being performed according to schedule, is a step of planning process. Identify the step.

(a) Choosing an alternative

(b) Implement the plan

(c) Identifying alternatives

(d) Follow-up action

27. People think that it is the 'product' only that can be marketed. But something else can also be marketed *e.g.,* 'Visit Kerala for Health Tourism'. Identify what is being marketed here.

(a) Place

(b) Person

(c) Idea

(d) None of these

28. Ramesh is the owner of a printing press. The size of his organisation has increased during the recent past. There are many employees who work in his organisation. The organisation is considered good and has earned a lot of reputation in the market. However, when it comes to making key decisions in the organisation related to many things he never considers the opinions of his subordinates. Even though the size of organisation has increased yet he tries to take all key decisions on his own. Which principle of Fayol has been violated by Ramesh?

(a) Esprit de corps

(b) Equity

(c) Centralisation and Decentralisation

(d) Harmony Not discorded

29. Mother's Touch is a famous chain store selling a large variety of baby products in the Indian market. Their products include wipes, diapers, prams, stallers and toys. It charges a comparatively higher price than its competitors as it sells quality products. Besides, it offers regular discounts to its customers and easy credit terms to its retailers. It has five of its own retail shops. It also sells its products through various grocery stores so that the products are made available to customers at the right place, in the right quantity and at the right time. It regularly uses different communication tools to increase its sales.

Identify the variable highlighted in this line "Mother's Touch provide variety of products which include wipes, diapers, prams, stallers and toys".

(a) Price

(b) Promotion

(c) Place

(d) Product

30. Large scale production done to reduce the average cost of production is the essence of ________concept of marketing management.

(a) product

(b) selling

(c) production

(d) marketing

31. Thirthankar Pvt. Ltd. is a school bag manufacturing company. For the purpose of profit maximisation, Nisha added a laptop pocket to the existing bag design. Which marketing management philosophy is adopted by Nisha?

(a) Production concept

(b) Product concept

(c) Selling concept

(d) Marketing concept

32. For the following two statements choose the correct option:

Statement I : Marketing is the function of business concerned with fulfilling the needs and wants of the consumers.

Statement II : Marketing occupies an important position in the organisation.

Choose the correct option from the options given below:

(a) Statement I is correct and II is wrong

(b) Statement II is correct and I is wrong

(c) Both the statements are correct

(d) Both the statements are incorrect

33. After completing a course in travel and tourism, Amit started his own travel agency. For smooth functioning of his business, he decided to create fourteen job positions. Further, he divided them into four departments on the basis of functions namely, front office department including online queries, reservations, department for airways, railways and roadways, accommodation booking department, and securing payments department. In order to avoid any interdepartmental conflicts, he decides to specify clearly the lines of authority and areas of responsibility for each job position.

    Identify the framework created by Amit within which all managerial and operating tasks are to be performed in his organisation.

    (a) Organisational structure
    (b) Functional structure
    (c) Functional structure
    (d) None of these

34. Arrange the following principles of Fayol's principle of management.
    (i) Division of work
    (ii) Unity of direction
    (iii) Unity of command
    (iv) Scalar chain
    (a) (ii), (iv), (iii), (i)
    (b) (i), (iii), (ii), (iv)
    (c) (i), (iii), (iv), (ii)
    (d) (iv), (iii), (ii), (i)

35. With changes in the consumption habits of people, Neelesh, who was running a sweet shop, shifted to the chocolate business. On the eve of Diwali, he offered chocolates in attractive packages at reasonable prices. He anticipated huge demand and created a website chocolove.com for taking orders online. He got a lot of orders online and earned huge profits by selling the chocolate. Identify the two dimensions of business environment discussed in the above case.

    (a) Economic and Political Environment
    (b) Social and Political Environment
    (c) Social and Technological Environment
    (d) Legal and Political Environment

36. Planning is needed at all the levels of management. The feature of planning in being referred to in the above statement is:

    (a) Mental exercise
    (b) Continuous
    (c) Primary function
    (d) Pervasive

37. Due to proper organising and division of work, Lenux ltd goes for systematic arrangement of jobs among the employees, which importance of organising is highlighted here?

    (a) Benefits of specialisation
    (b) Clarity in working relationship
    (c) Adaptation of change
    (d) Effective administration

38. After production of goods the marketer needs to offer them to customers; for this he performs two basic functions. It includes all the activities which are undertaken to communicate with the customer and increase the sale is known as:

    (a) Pricing of products
    (b) Customer support services
    (c) Promotion and selling
    (d) Packaging and labelling

39. Ajeet is an energetic manager who makes plans and policies for his department. He tries to make best plans, for this he uses foresightedness and imagination. He has delivered many successful projects because of his good plans. He always makes alternative plans and selects the best out of them after evaluating their pros and cons. However, he knows all plans cannot be successful and requires a lot of time and energy. He also knows that the business environment is dynamic, it can change. One of his friend, suggested him to take suggestions from others when he makes his plans and also consider plans made by others.

    "He always makes alternative plans and selects the best out of them after evaluating their pros and cons." Which feature of planning is being highlighted here?

    (a) Forward Looking
    (b) Decision Making
    (c) Both (a) and (b)
    (d) None of these

40. In order to promote the habit of health and hygiene among weaker sections of the society. Abhyas Limited has launched low cost packs of hand wash. Identify the type of marketing philosophy being adopted by the company.

    (a) Product concept
    (b) Production concept
    (c) Marketing concept
    (d) Societal marketing concept

41. "A manager applies the acquired knowledge in a personalised and skillful manner in the light of the realities of a given in situation." The given statement indicates that management is:

    (a) a science
    (b) an art
    (c) a profession
    (d) none of these

42. "Manali, hill station in Himachal Pradesh, banned the sale of single use plastic items considering its negative impact on the environment". Which dimension of the business environment is discussed here.
   (a) Political
   (b) Legal
   (c) Technological
   (d) Social

43. For the following two statements choose the correct option:

   Statement I: Principles of management can be modified by the manager when the situation demands.

   Statement II: The principles of management enhance the understanding of relationship between human and material resources for the achievement of organisational goals.

   Choose the correct option from the options given below:
   (a) Statement I is correct and II is wrong
   (b) Statement II is correct and I is wrong
   (c) Both the statements are correct
   (d) Both the statements are incorrect

44. ABC group of companies decided to donate 3% of its sales to 'Child Rights an You (CRY)' for improving the condition of children in India. This initiative by the company was highly appreciated by the public and their sales increased by 10%. Identify the objective depicted in the given lines.
   (a) Social
   (b) Organisational
   (c) Personal
   (d) None of these

45. To see whether plans are being implemented and activities are being performed according to the schedule, is a step of planning process. Identify the step.
   (a) Selecting the best alternative
   (b) Implementing the plan
   (c) Follow up action
   (d) Evaluating alternative courses of action

46. ________is the right to give orders and obtain obedience, and ________is the corollary of authority.
   (a) Authority, responsibility
   (b) Responsibility, authority
   (c) Responsibility, accountability
   (d) None of these

47. With the introduction of mineral water bottle in India, Aqua was able to capture the big market share in India. Which importance of business environment is highlighted in the above case.
   (a) Helps in tapping resources
   (b) Help in policy-making
   (c) Improve performance
   (d) Help to identify opportunity and getting first mover advantage

48. **Assertion:** An establishment has a predefined set of fundamental goals which are the primary basis for its being.

   Reason: These must be easy and explicitly mentioned. Different establishments have different goals.
   (a) Both (A) and (R) are correct
   (b) (A) is correct (R) is incorrect
   (c) Both (A) and (R) are correct, and R is the correct explanation of R
   (d) Both (A) and (R) are correct, and R is not the correct explanation of R

Section – C

Read the following text and answer question no. 49-54 on the basis of the same:

Skin Care is a progressive company which has achieved new records in the field of cosmetics. Recently the company decided to hand over the decision making authority to the lower most level of employees. For this, the company went for a thorough planning. The positive results were noticed due to this change. The employees felt a lot of development in their skill and started taking first step to manage things on their own. Some major newspapers also covered this development. The production of the company increased. The company's top management could now focus on new areas of innovation as the employees turned more reliable. One day, it so happened that the company's manufacturing branch in North could not fulfill even half of its production target and the operations manager was held answerable for the assigned target. He was called in the office. When he was questioned, it was found that his right to command the workers was insufficient and it should have been more to create results. The management decided to listen to him and he was given more power. When he went to the shop floor he told the workers that the standard of behaviour of the workers should come from the official rules and procedures.

49. Identify the function of management performed by Skin Care:
    (a) Planning
    (b) Directing
    (c) Organising
    (d) All of these
50. Identify the concept of management used by Skin Care:
    (a) Coordination
    (b) Cooperation
    (c) Delegation of Authority
    (d) Decentralization
51. "The operations manager was held answerable for the assigned target". Which element of directing is being highlighted here?
    (a) Authority
    (b) Accountability
    (c) Responsibility
    (d) All of these
52. Planning precedes other functions as all the other managerial functions are performed within the framework of planning. Identify the feature of planning from above statement:
    (a) Planning is futuristic
    (b) Planning is continuous
    (c) Planning is primary function of management
    (d) Planning involves decision-making
53. Planning involves thorough examination and evaluation of each alternative and choosing the most appropriate one. Identify the feature from above statement:
    (a) Planning is pervasive
    (b) It is a mental exercise
    (c) It is continuous process
    (d) It involves decision-making
54. "When he was questioned it was found that his right to command the workers was insufficient". Which element of directing is being highlighted here?
    (a) Authority
    (b) Accountability
    (c) Responsibility
    (d) All of these
55. The Directors of 'Bhupendra Computers Limited', an organisation manufacturing computers, want to double the sales and have given this responsibility to their sales manager. The sales manager has no authority either to increase the sales expense or to appoint new salesman. Hence, he could not achieve his target. Identify the relevant principle associated in the above case.
    (a) Division of work
    (b) Authority and responsibility
    (c) Scalar chain
    (d) Remuneration
56. The marketing manager has allowed sales manager to give 8% discount, while finance department has ordered the sales manager not to offer more than 5% discount. Which principle of management is being violated?
    (a) Discipline
    (b) Authority and responsibility
    (c) Unity of direction
    (d) Unity of command
57. Suzen Ltd. wants to increase their market share by 5.4% in next two years. It spent a lot of money to hire specialised people for framing their plans, collecting important facts about environment who took lot of time to frame plans for the company. The competition has started increasing and it is not able to beat its competitors because it has already spent a huge amount. The plan failed and company suffered a huge loss. Identify the limitation of planning started in the given case.
    (a) Planning may not work in dynamic environment
    (b) Planning involves huge cost
    (c) Planning is a time-consuming process
    (d) All of these
58. A company wants to increase its market share from the present 10% to 25% to have a dominant position in the market by the end of the next financial years. Ms. Rajni, the Sales Manager had been asked to prepare a proposal that will outline the options available for achieving this objective. Her report included the following options. Entering new markets, expanding the product range offered to customers, using sales promotion teachings such as giving rebates, discounts or increasing the budget for advertising activities. Which step of the planning process has been performed by Ms. Rajni ?
    (a) Setting objectives
    (b) Development premises
    (c) Evaluating alternatives
    (d) Identifying alternatives
59. GMIR Internationals Ltd. is a well-known cement company in India. It is able to earn adequate revenues to cover costs. Its capital base, number of employees and production turnover has increased manifolds over the years. The rate of profitability of the business is also creditable. The employees of the company are happy and satisfied with their remuneration, working conditions, promotion policy etc. As a part of its

moral obligation, the company has taken many initiatives for providing employment to especially abled persons and promoting literacy in the villages adopted by it. Identify the objective being fulfilled by the GMIR Internationals Ltd.

(a) Personal objectives

(b) Organisational objectives

(c) Social objectives

(d) All of the above

60. Sawan Industries is a company dealing in office furniture. The company chose to diversify its operations to improve its growth potential and increase market share. As the project was important, many alternatives were generated for the purpose and were thoroughly discussed amongst the members of the organisation. After evaluating the various alternatives, Vishal, the Managing Director of the company, decided that they should add 'Home Interiors and Furnishings' as a new line of business activity.

Name the framework, which the diversified organisation should adopt, to enable it to cope with the emerging complexity?

(a) Functional structure

(b) Divisional structure

(c) Informal structure

(d) None of these

❑❑

Sample Paper

Business Studies

Section – A

1. "Managers in India do the same work as managers in USA or Japan or Germany." Which characteristic of management is highlighted in this statement?
   - (a) Management is a group activity
   - (b) Options (a) and (c)
   - (c) Management is all pervasive
   - (d) Management is effective

2. An art of completing the task on a right time or doing things right is known as__________
   - (a) coordination
   - (b) efficiency
   - (c) effectiveness
   - (d) none of these

3. _______refers to producing goods of predetermined specification, which helps in achieving uniformity and consisting in the output.
   - (a) Standardisation
   - (b) Grading
   - (c) Assorting
   - (d) Sorting

4. Which technique of Taylor separates Planning and Executive functions?
   - (a) Functional foremanship
   - (b) Fatigue work
   - (c) Standardisation
   - (d) Simplification

5. Name the type of organisational structure which makes training of employees easier, as the focus is only on a limited range of skills.
   - (a) Network structure
   - (b) Divisional structure
   - (c) Functional structure
   - (d) Matrix structure

6. _________refer that organising helps in optimum utlisation of resources. Which type of resources does it refer?
   - (a) Centralisation
   - (b) Delegation
   - (c) Development of personnel
   - (d) None of these

7. "Hence, she prepared an annual plan for production, sales and marketing through sales forecasting." Which feature of planning is depicted in the statement?
   - (a) Planning is continuous
   - (b) Planning is futuristic
   - (c) Planning involves decision-making
   - (d) Planning is a mental exercise

8. The main function of_______is to provide information required by law.
   - (a) labelling
   - (b) packaging
   - (c) branding
   - (d) both (a) and (b)

9. When the manager grants one month medical leave to a supervisor with pay and only one week medical leave to accountant. Which principle of management as given by Henri Fayol is being violated?
   - (a) Authority and Responsibility
   - (b) Equity
   - (c) Unity of command
   - (d) Scalar chain

10. "Tina observes at his office that there is a fixed place for everything and everyone". Identify the Principle of Management highlighted here.
    - (a) Equity
    - (b) Order
    - (c) Espirit de corps
    - (d) Unity of command

11. It is always noticed that efficient management motivates employees to adopt changes by convincing them. Which point of importance of management discussed here?
    - (a) Management helps in achieving personal objectives
    - (b) Management helps in the development of society
    - (c) Management helps in achieving group goals
    - (d) Management creates dynamic organisation

12. A brand or part of brand that is given legal protection is termed as__________.
   (a) brand name
   (b) brand mark
   (c) trademark
   (d) none of these

13. Sahil went to a mall to buy a TV. There he got to know an offer on TV which says worth ₹50,000 and get a holiday package worth ₹10,000 free. Identify the method of sales promotion.
   (a) Discount
   (b) Rebate
   (c) Product combination
   (d) Usable benefit

14. "Krishna shares with her that he always deals with lazy staff sternly to send the message that everyone is equal in his eyes". Identify the management principle.
   (a) Equity
   (b) Subordination of Individual interest to general interest
   (c) Scalar chain
   (d) None of the above

15. Which of the following is not a benefit of planning?
   (a) Planning reduces overlapping and wasteful activities
   (b) Planning is a mental exercise
   (c) Planning provides directions
   (d) Planning reduces the risks of uncertainty

16. A manager is required to make certain assumptions about the future which may be in the form of forecast. This step of planning is known as________.
   (a) Follow up
   (b) Developing premises
   (c) Evaluating alternative courses of action
   (d) Identifying alternative courses of action

17. ________is the process by which the manager brings order out of chaos, removes conflict among people over work or responsibility sharing and creates an environment suitable for teamwork.
   (a) Planning
   (b) Organising
   (c) Staffing
   (d) Controlling

18. Mansi took her niece Ridhima for shopping to 'Mega Stores' to buy her a bag for her birthday. She was delighted when on payment of the bag she got a pencil box along with the bag free of cost. Identify the technique of sales promotion used by the company.
   (a) Reducing sales price
   (b) Competitions or contests
   (c) Full finance
   (d) Product combination or free products

19. The Prime Minister has given a relief package of ₹10 crore. This is related to which dimension of business environment?
   (a) Political environment
   (b) Economic environment
   (c) Legal environment
   (d) None of these

20. ______refers to the important decisions related to the product such as quality, design, branding, product packaging, labelling, etc.
   (a) Marketing Mix
   (b) Product Mix
   (c) Promotion Mix
   (d) Marketing

21. ________management passes on the instructions of management to the workers.
   (a) Top
   (b) Middle
   (c) Supervisory
   (d) None of these

22. ________refers to the offer of sale in return of payment in easy installments without any interest charges thereon.
   (a) Full finance @ 0%
   (b) Sampling
   (c) Usable benefit
   (d) Quanity gift

23. "Thus, she identified and evaluated different alternatives through which the farms could be utilised throughout the year." Which feature of planning is depicted in the statement?
   (a) Planning is pervasive
   (b) Planning is continuous
   (c) Planning is futuristic
   (d) Planning involves decision-making

24. Since more number of people have become more beauty and health conscious, our economy has witnessed an unprecedented surge in the number of health and beauty spas and wellness clinics.

    Identify the feature of business environment being described in the above lines is.

    (a) Totality of external forces   (b) Dynamic nature

    (c) Inter-relatedness   (d) Relativity

Section – B

25. India's retail sector has been undergoing structural changes for the last two decades. On one hand, the 'mall culture' has gradually become a way of life, especially in the metros and mini-metros. On the other hand, there is accelerated growth in e-business as customers also prefer to buy products and services via the internet, telephone and television. However, operating in either of the segments is marked by the presence of strong competitors. Identify one component of specific force and one component of general force discussed in the case above.

    (a) Financiers and economic forces   (b) Customers and technological forces

    (c) Suppliers and political forces   (d) All of these

26. Which of the following steps of planning, will precedes the step of selecting an alternative?

    (a) Setting Objectives   (b) Developing Premises

    (c) Evaluating Alternative Courses   (d) Identifying Alternative Courses of Action

27. "For this purpose she set out specific goals, objectives and activities." Which features of planning is depicted in the statement?

    (a) Planning focuses on achieving objectives

    (b) Planning is a primary function of management

    (c) Planning is pervasive

    (d) Planning is continuous

28. Hero scooters are the leading manufacturers of scooters in the industry. They have the first mover advantage in the industry. When they started manufacturing scooters no other company was doing it. They manufacture scooters and the middle class purchases them in a high number. With each passing year the number of scooters sold is increasing. The company's main concern usually is to produce maximum number of scooters. Company's profit is governed by the maximum number of scooters they produce.

    (a) Production concept   (b) Product concept

    (c) Selling concept   (d) Societal marketing concept

29. Star Industries (India) Limited provides training based on one of the scientific principles of management to make the workers learn the best method of production which emphasises that each employee in the organisation should be scientifically selected and the work assigned to the employees should suit their physical, mental and intellectual capabilities.

    Which scientific principle of management is followed in the organisation?

    (a) Development of each and every person to his or her greatest efficiency and prosperity

    (b) Harmony, not discord

    (c) Science, not Rule of Thumb

    (d) Coorperation, not individualism

30. The government of India proposed to encourage e-transactions by encouraging the use of plastic money (through debit, credit and gift cards) or net banking by allowing deductions in usage charges, fees and income tax exemptions. The component of business environment is __________.

    (a) economic environment   (b) legal environment

    (c) political environment   (d) both (a) and (b)

31. "She used her foresight and logical and systematic thinking based on analysis of all facts and examined and evaluated all the alternatives." Which feature of planning is depicted in the statement?

    (a) Planning focuses on achieving objectives

    (b) Planning is a primary function of management

    (c) Planning involves decision-making

    (d) Planning is a mental exercise

32. For the following two statements choose the correct option:

Statement I : A product with a generic name can be advertised.

Statement II: Branding implies giving a unique name, sign, symbol or term for the identification of a product.

Choose the correct option from the options given below:

(a) Statement I is correct and II is wrong

(b) Statement II is correct and I is wrong

(c) Both the statements are correct

(d) Both the statements are incorrect

33. Ashutosh Goenka was working in 'Axe Ltd.', a company manufacturing air purifiers. He found that the profits have started declining from the last six months. Profit has an implication for the survival of the firm, so he analysed the business environment to find out the reasons for this decline. Identify the level of management at which Ashutosh Goenka was working.

(a) Top level

(b) Middle level

(c) Lower level

(d) All of these

34. Arrange the following steps of elements of Marketing Mix in the correct sequence:

(i) Promotion

(ii) Product

(iii) Place/Physical Distribution

(iv) Price

Choose the correct option:

(a) (ii) ; (iv) ; (iii) ; (i)

(b) (i) ; (ii) ; (iii) ; (iv)

(c) (iii) ; (ii) ; (iv) ; (i)

(d) (iv) ; (iii) ; (ii) ; (i)

35. Sanya bought multi-gym equipment from a renowned company. The company gave a warranty period of 1 year. Sanya used to work out on this equipment daily. Everything was going fine but one day some problem in the wire of the equipment occurred. Sanya called the company and told them that it is still in the warranty period. A service engineer from the company visited her home and fixed the problem. Sanya was further told that the maintenance service for 1 year is free of cost. Which element of marketing mix is maintained in the case above?

(a) Price

(b) Place

(c) Promotion

(d) Product

36. Planning cannot foresee everything, and thus, there may be obstacles to effective planning. Identify the related limitation of planning.

(a) Planning leads to rigidity

(b) Planning may not work in a dynamic environment

(c) Planning does not guarantee success

(d) Planning reduces creativity

37. Ramesh started a sarees showroom in Mumbai, India. He wants to sell sarees in France but he understands that conditions are different countries. Identify the feature of business environment highlighted here.

(a) Relativity

(b) Uncertainty

(c) Dynamic nature

(d) Complexity

38. Lower initial price to capture a large market. This forces the customers to buy the product and company can capture a very big share and leave very small share for competitors. This strategy is known as ____________.

(a) pricing strategies

(b) price skimming

(c) penetrating pricing

(d) none of these

39. Krishna and Saroj are both qualified CA and good friends. After obtaining a certificate of practice, they decide to pursue a career of their own choice. Krishna starts own practice in the city whereas Saroj joins a Government company. They meet after a long time in a party. Krishna invites Saroj to visit his office and she accepts his invitation. She observes at his office that there is a fixed place for everything and everyone and it is present there so that there is no hindrance in the activities of the office . Also, Krishna always tends to replace 'I' with 'We' in all his conversations with the staff members. Later on Krishna shares with her that he always deals with lazy staff sternly to send the message that everyone is equal in his eyes.

"Krishna always tends to replace 'I' with 'We' in all his conversations with the staff members". Which principle of management is being highlighted here?

(a) Stability of personnel

(b) Equity

(c) Espirit de corps

(d) None of these

40. In order to improve upon its competitive edge, Khushboo Limited has changed the packaging of its hair care products. They are now available in a consumer friendly design, which has a nozzle attached to the lid so that at the time of usage, the consumer doesn't need to open the cap of the bottle. Name the marketing function being explained in the given lines.
 (a) Product designing and development
 (b) Customer support services
 (c) Promotion
 (d) Physical distribution

41. Specialists tend to see different organisational processes and problem from their own point of view based on their fields of speciality. To achieve balance between these points of view, there arises a need for a concept known as__________.
 (a) coordination
 (b) efficiency
 (c) effectiveness
 (d) management by exception

42. Burger King, the fast food giant, made major changes in its menu to be able to survive in the Indian market. Which characteristic of management is highlighted?
 (a) Dynamic function
 (b) Practical knowledge
 (c) Group activity
 (d) Goal oriented

43. For the following two statements choose the correct option:
 Statement I : 'Rule of thumb' refers to use of personal judgement in handling management issues.
 Statement II : According to the principle of Co-operation, not individualism, scientific management has for its foundation the firm conviction that true interest of the management and workers are one and the same.
 Choose the correct option from the options given below:
 (a) Statement I is correct and II is wrong
 (b) Statement II is correct and I is wrong
 (c) Both the statements are correct
 (d) Both the statements are incorrect

44. Telecom sector was opened up to private sector as a reform under Economic Policy, 1991. Nokia became the first cellular company to operate in 1994 and dominated the market. Later, it lost its market share and was absorbed by Microsoft. The management of Microsoft examined the environment and made suitable change.
 Identify the point of importance of business environment with appropriate actions reflected in the above case.
 (a) It helps in identifying opportunities and getting first mover advantage
 (b) It helps in identifying threats and early warning signals
 (c) It helps in improving performance
 (d) It helps in tapping useful resources

45. A manager should have the right to punish a subordinate for willfully not obeying a legitimate order but only after sufficient opportunity has been given to a subordinate for presenting her/his case. Identify the step of principle of management highlighted above.
 (a) Authority and Responsibility
 (b) Discipline
 (c) Equity
 (d) Stability of Personnel

46. Quick foods Ltd. is a food delivery service app that has recently faced criticism for tampering of their products by their delivery boys. The company decided to put a hologram seal on the food packets in order to protect the contents from being tampered with along with a safety warning for the consumers to check the seal on delivery_____ concept of marketing has been discussed in this case which is not only performing an important function of communicating with the potential buyer but also promoting its sale.
 (a) Labelling
 (b) Product designing and development
 (c) Branding
 (d) Packaging

47. When Earita opened the door on hearing the doorbell, a person was standing who was selling Britannica is World 'encyclopedia'. Here Britanica is using which element of promotion mix?
 (a) Public relation
 (b) Sales promotion
 (c) Advertising
 (d) Personal selling

48. **Assertion:** The activities associated with managing a firm are familiar to all companies whether financial, cultural or civic.
 Reason: A petrol pump must be regulated as much as a school or a hospital. What managers do in India, Japan, Germany, or the USA is identical.

(a) Both (A) and (R) are correct

(b) (A) is correct (R) is incorrect

(c) Both (A) and (R) are correct, and (R) is the correct explanation of (R)

(d) Both (A) and (R) are correct, and (R) is not the correct explanation of (R)

Section - C

Read the following text and answer question no. 49-54 on the basis of the same:

Rayan decided to start a business of manufacturing toys. He identified the following main activities which he has to perform:(i) purchase of raw materials, (ii) purchase of machinery, (iii) production of toys: (iv) arrangement of finance; (v) sale of toys; (vi) identifying the areas where they can sell their toys; (vii) selection of employees. In order to facilitate the work he thought that four managers should be appointed to look after: (a) production (b) finance (c) marketing (d) personnel.

As planned, all this was executed and the business started doing well. But the manager of production department is overburdened with routine work and is unable to concentrate on core issues of the department. To overcome this problem, he entrusted some of his responsibility and authority to his immediate subordinate to share some of his routine work.

49. Identify the function of management involved in the above mentioned paragraph.

    (a) Planning   (b) Organising

    (c) Directing   (d) Controlling

50. Which concept/process is used by the production manager?

    (a) Decentralisation   (b) Delegation

    (c) Training   (d) Coordination

51. The concept identified in point (38), is an extension to one of the principles of management. Name that principle.

    (a) Authority and responsibility   (b) Division of work

    (c) Centralisation and decentralisation   (d) Unity of direction

52. Who will be accountable finally if the subordinate is unable to complete the task accordingly within time?

    (a) The manager   (b) The subordinate

    (c) Both (a) and (b)   (d) None of these

53. Organising is a process by which the manager:

    (a) establishes order out of chaos

    (b) removes conflict among people over work or responsibility sharing

    (c) creates an environment suitable for teamwork

    (d) all of the above

54. It is defined as the framework within which managerial and operating tasks are performed? Identity.

    (a) Span of management   (b) Organisational structure

    (c) Informal organisation   (d) None of these

55. The purchase, production and sales managers at Sharda Ltd., a firm manufacturing readymade garments are generally at a conflict, as they have their own objectives. Usually each thinks that only they are qualified to evaluate, judge and decide on any matter, according to their professional criteria. Name the concept, which will be required by the CEO Mr. Raman, to reconcile the differences in approach, interest or opinion in the organisation.

    (a) Coordination   (b) Cooperation

    (c) Planning   (d) Organising

56. It is heartening that the implementation of compliance requirements of the Companies Act, 2013 has progressed substantially with NIFTY 500 companies. Data shows a significant increase in women's participation in the top management of Indian Companies from 5% few years ago to 13% now. Even companies which are not in NIFTY 500 have undertaken drives to increase women's participation across different areas of work. The government had also announced that it would support such companies. Identify the dimension of business environment discussed above which brought about the change.

    (a) Technological environment   (b) Legal environment

    (c) Social environment   (d) Economic environment

57. It is interesting to known that the menu items of multinational food chains are customised to suit the general palates of the local people in the region. When McDonald's started its business in India in the year

1996, the company went through a complete localisation strategy. McDonald's changed its product menu to accommodate the vegetable burger given the large vegetarian population. It also altered its store design and even reduced the product price by close to 15% Also 'Mc Aloo Tikki Burger' is not available anywhere but in the Indian outlets of McDonalds.

Identify the relevant feature of business environment being discussed above.

(a) Inter-relatedness

(b) Complexity

(c) Relativity

(d) Uncertainty

58. Mahinder works in furniture manufacturing company. The company is now venturing into a new range of living room furniture. As the marketing manager of the company, he has been asked to devise a marketing plan for the proposed new range of furniture within a budget of ₹ 6 crores. Identity the step of planning function which is being discussed in the given lines.

(a) Setting objectives

(b) Developing premises

(c) Identifying alternative courses of action

(d) Follow up action

59. Sumit Rathore started a company 'Tesla Ltd' with ten employees to assemble economical computers for the Indian rural market. The company did very well in its initial years. As the product was good and marketed well, the demand went up. To increase production, the company decided to recruit additional employees Sumit Rathore, who was earlier taking all the decisions for the company, had to selectively disperse the authority. He believed that people are competent, capable and resourceful and can assume responsibility for the effective implementation of their decisions. This paid off and the company was not only able to increase its production but also expanded its product range with different features.

Identify the concept used by Sumit Rathore.

(a) Delegation

(b) Centralisation

(c) Decentralisation

(d) None of these

60. Rahul is working as a sales manager in a publishing house. In order to promote the new series of encyclopaedia, the company decides to undertake door to door selling in the city. As the sales manager, Rahul is given the target of selling 5000 units in one month. He appoints a team of five salesmen for the purpose. Each salesman is given the target of selling 1000 units. At the end of the month only 4800 units are sold as one of the salesman, Gaurav, fall ill during the last week and is able to sell only 800 units.

Identify, whether Rahul be still accountable for the performance of the assigned tasks to Gaurav.

(a) Yes

(b) No

(c) Question is insufficient

(d) None of these

❑❑

Sample Paper 5

Business Studies

Section – A

1. "The company has built India's largest e-waste recycling plant". Identify the dimension of business environment.
   - (a) Social environment
   - (b) Technological environment
   - (c) Legal environment
   - (d) None of these

2. Providing information to the customers about the product, its features, and quality etc are part of_________.
   - (a) Production
   - (b) Pricing
   - (c) Promotion
   - (d) None of these

3. Successful organisations do not achieve goals by chance but by following a deliberate process known as_________.
   - (a) Planning
   - (b) Co-ordination
   - (c) Controlling
   - (d) Management

4. Which limitation of planning suggests that the employees stop thinking and become the blind followers of the plan?
   - (a) Planning reduces creativity
   - (b) Planning does not work in dynamic nature
   - (c) Planning does not guarantee success
   - (d) Planning involves huge costs

5. Name the features of business environment being discussed in the given lines." The increase in the demand for many Ayurvedic medicines, health products and services in the past few months, is related to the need for building immunity and an increased awareness for healthcare due to the spread of Corona Virus".
   - (a) Specific and general forces
   - (b) Interrelatedness
   - (c) Relativity
   - (d) None of these

6. A paid form of non-personal communication undertaken by the marketers is known as _________.
   - (a) Advertising
   - (b) Sales promotion
   - (c) Personal selling
   - (d) None of these

7. 'Dreams can be turned into reality only when managers think in advance what to do and how to do it'. Identify the function of management indicated by the statement.
   - (a) Planning
   - (b) Organising
   - (c) Directing
   - (d) Controlling

8. "Equal pay to male and female workers for equal work" comes under________environment.
   - (a) political
   - (b) social
   - (c) technological
   - (d) economic

9. In an organisation Shyam and Ragini are working at the same posts but being a male employee Shyam has more rights than Ragini. State any one principle of management which is violated here?
   - (a) Principle of Equity
   - (b) Rule of Thumb
   - (c) Scalar Principle
   - (d) Unity of Command

10. "The company strives to be one of the leading players in this business which has huge potential not only in terms of generating huge revenues and profits but also wants to contribute to the environment issues that have become crucial worldwide". Which dimension of business environment is being referred here?
   - (a) Political environment
   - (b) Legal environment
   - (c) Social environment
   - (d) Economical environment

11. "To start the business, the company has obtained a licence from U. P. Pollution Control Board." Which dimension of business environment is being talked about?
   - (a) Economical environment
   - (b) Legal environment
   - (c) Both (a) and (b)
   - (d) Political environment

12. Coordination is not a separate function, but it is the ________ of management.
    (a) essence
    (b) step
    (c) process
    (d) both (a) and (c)
13. Identify the dimension of business environment, which focuses on laws and regulations on industrial development.
    (a) Economic environment
    (b) Legal environment
    (c) Political environment
    (d) All of these
14. "The company plans to make its millions by extracting metals such as gold and platinum from the e-waste piling up in the city." Which objective of business is being fulfilled?
    (a) Organisational objective
    (b) Social objective
    (c) Personal objective
    (d) All of these
15. Which of the following is not a principle of management given by Taylor?
    (a) Science, not rule of thumb
    (b) Functional Foremanship
    (c) Maximum, not restricted output
    (d) Harmony, not discord
16. Planning cannot foresee everything, and thus, there may be obstacles to effective planning. Identify the related limitation of planning.
    (a) Planning leads to rigidity.
    (b) Planning may not work in a dynamic environment.
    (c) Planning does not guarantee success.
    (d) Planning reduces creativity.
17. The basic role of firm under ________ concept is to identify a need and satisfy it better than competitors.
    (a) production
    (b) product
    (c) selling
    (d) marketing
18. Kingtech Ltd. is engaged in manufacturing televisions. The target of the organisation is to manufacture 500 TVs a day. There is an occupational specialisation in the organisation which promotes efficiency of employees. There is no duplication of efforts in such type of organisation structure. Identify the type of organisation structure described above.
    (a) Functional structure
    (b) Divisional structure
    (c) Decentralisation
    (d) Delegation
19. Mr. Kapil, an educationalist found that the teachers have to travel long to attend the workshops and they lose the opportunity to gain the knowledge on updates. He listed various alternatives and finally developed an app which could work on mobile and laptops to launch online sessions. Suggest which next step should he follow?
    (a) Developing premises
    (b) Identifying the alternative course of action
    (c) Implementation of plan
    (d) Follow up action
20. Which of the following is not a part of the business environment of business?
    (a) Customers
    (b) Suppliers
    (c) Competitors
    (d) All of the these
21. 'Determining in advance what is to be done and who is to be done it'. Highlights the ________ function of management.
    (a) directing
    (b) controlling
    (c) organising
    (d) planning
22. Identify the correct sequence of steps involved in the planning process.
    (a) Evaluating alternative courses, Identifying alternative course of actions, Setting objectives, Developing premises
    (b) Setting objectives, Identifying alternative course of actions, Evaluating alternative courses, Developing premises
    (c) Setting objectives, Developing premises, Identifying alternative course of actions, Evaluating alternative courses
    (d) Setting objectives, Developing premises, Identifying alternative course of actions, Evaluating alternative courses

23. Name the technique of scientific management which helps in establishing interchangeability of manufactured parts and products.
    (a) Standardisation
    (b) Functional Foremanship
    (c) Method study
    (d) Motion study
24. Ragini, the general manager of Fabmart, performs the managerial functions of planning, organising, staffing, directing, controlling as on ongoing process. Which management feature is highlighted here?
    (a) Management is multi-dimensional
    (b) Management is a dynamic function
    (c) Management is all pervasive
    (d) Management is a continuous process

Section – B

25. Delhi sports is a sports equipment company. It has different branches in different parts of the world. However the requirements of the sports equipment's are different in different branches. This is due to the change in cultures and lifestyles of people in the different countries. Company knows that the demand for these products is unpredictable as new designs keep on coming and the industry keeps on changing frequently. Identify the features of business environment highlighted here:
    (a) Relativity
    (b) Uncertainty
    (c) Dynamic nature
    (d) Complexity
26. What is the next step in the planning process after objectives are set and assumption are made?
    (a) Formulating derivative plans
    (b) Identify alternative courses of action
    (c) Developing planning premises
    (d) Evaluating the pros and cons
27. Pervasiveness of planning indicates that planning:
    (a) is a top management function.
    (b) extends throughout the organisation.
    (c) is a future-oriented activity.
    (d) is the first element of management process.
28. Find land Company is a reputed TV manufacturing firm. The owners of the company feel that unless and until they contribute to society it is worthless to exist as a company. In a recent move by the government the organisation has decided to help it. The organisation will be making five teams of hired environmentalists from foreign countries. This team will help the local people to clean the portions of a polluted river in the country. The costs of this project will be borne by the country. The costs of this project will be borne by the company. Identify the marketing concept.
    (a) Production concept
    (b) Product concept
    (c) Societal marketing concept
    (d) Marketing concept
29. 'Twinkle Stars' is a well-known resort for organising parties, especially for children. However, in past 6 months its popularity has reduced considerably as a new resort with better ambience and facilities has opened within its vicinity. Name the related feature of business environment which has influenced the business of 'Twinkle Stars' adversely.
    (a) Totality of external forces
    (b) Dynamic nature
    (c) Interrelatedness
    (d) Uncertainty
30. As the head of a financial consultancy firm, Mohit formulates the objectives for the whole year for the firm. The departmental managers on the other hand prepare the plans for their respective departments. The feature of planning being described in the given lines is________.
    (a) planning is futuristic
    (b) planning is pervasive
    (c) planning is goal-oriented
    (d) Both (a) and (b)
31. Managers in India do the same work as managers in USA or japan or Germany. Which characteristic of management is highlighted in this statement?
    (a) Management is a group activity
    (b) Both (a) and (c)
    (c) Management is all pervasive
    (d) Management is effective
32. For the following two statements choose the correct option:
    Statement I : Used and discarded packaging contributes significantly to the consumer protection problem.
    Statement II : Appropriate packaging contributes to the convenience in handling the product.
    Choose the correct option from the options given below:
    (a) Statement I is correct and II is wrong
    (b) Statement II is correct and I is wrong
    (c) Both the statements are correct
    (d) Both the statements are incorrect

33. "In today's time, Compact Disks (CD's) for computer, have become obsolete. Google with its Drive service, Apple with its icloud offering, enables the users to store documents, photos, music and movies on web based servers. This has adversely affected the producers of CD's. Identify the feature of business environment being described in the given lines.
    (a) Relativity
    (b) Dynamic nature
    (c) Uncertainty
    (d) Interrelatedness

34. Arrange the following of marketing management philosophies in the correct sequence:
    (A) Production concept
    (B) Product concept
    (C) Selling concept
    (D) Marketing concept
    (a) (i), (ii), (iii), (iv)
    (b) (ii), (iv), (i), (iii)
    (c) (i), (iii), (ii), (iv)
    (d) (iii), (iv), (ii), (i)

35. It requires application of mind involving foresight, intelligence, imagination and sound judgement. Which feature of planning is highlighted here:
    (a) Planning is pervasive
    (b) Planning is a mental exercise
    (c) Planning is futuristic
    (d) None of these

36. Customers will prefer creative and innovative products that are new or improved versions of existing products along with quality and performance. Which philosophy of management is this?
    (a) Product concept
    (b) Marketing concept
    (c) Societal concept
    (d) None of these

37. Mayra Ltd. is pursuing diversified activities which require a high degree of specialisation. Identity the type of structure that should be followed by Mayra Ltd.
    (a) Functional structure
    (b) Divisional structure
    (c) Both (a) and (b)
    (d) None of these

38. To became a Chartered Accountant in India, a candidate has to clear a specified examination conducted by the Institute of Chartered Accountants of India. Which features of profession is being revealed?
    (a) Ethical code of conduct
    (b) Restricted entry
    (c) Well-defined body of knowledge
    (d) Professional association

39. Shiba, a proofreader in ABC Publications, has been given a target of reading at least 30 pages per day. She has a habit of doing things differently. While doing her work, an idea struck her that a summary of a chapter in the form of a map where all the concepts related to that chapter would be interlinked, should be given in starting of each chapter. It will give students a list of chapter as well as provide a competitive edge over other publishers. But instead of appreciating her idea, her immediate boos scolded her and asked her to complete the work as per prescribed format. Out of the following, identify the limitation of planning stated in the given paragraph.
    (a) Planning reduces creativity
    (b) Planning involves huge cost
    (c) Planning is a time consuming
    (d) Planning does not work in dynamic environment

40. Indigo Limited has a staff of 300 people which is grouped into different departments. The organisational structure depicts that 100 people work in Production Department, 150 in Finance Department, 20 in Technology Department and 30 in Human Resource Department.
    Identify the type of organisational structure being followed by the company.
    (a) Functional structure
    (b) Divisional structure
    (c) Informal structure
    (d) None of the above

41. 'Bawa Cycles' was in the business of manufacturing racing cycles and had a monopoly in the market. The business was doing well and the company was consistently meeting its objective of 10% increase in sales every year. Encouraged by the good track record, the Managing Director of the company kept an ambitious target of 15% increase in sales for the next year. The same year, two competitors also entered the market and because of this the company was not able to meet target. Identify the limitation of one of the functions of management because of which the company was not able to achieve its target.
    (a) Planning may be rigid
    (b) Planning may not work in dynamic environment
    (c) Planning does not guarantee success
    (d) None of the above

42. XYZ Ltd. is manufacturing a new type of helicopter for elite people. The helicopters manufactured are patented products of the company. It is a unique product and no other company has made this type of helicopter yet. Thus, the company sells only on the basis of advance booking by the buyers. There has been excess demand since the company has launched the product. The company is in no need to market its product. It just has to see that it can make the helicopter available to people who can buy it.

_______marketing management philosophy is involved in the above case.

(a) Product
(b) Production
(c) Marketing
(d) Societal marketing

43. For the following two statements choose the correct option:

Statement I : Planning reduces overlapping & wasteful activities as it serves as the basis for coordinating the activities and efforts of different divisions and individuals.

Statement II : Planning is pervasive as it is required at all the levels of management but its scope may vary.

Choose the correct option from the options given below:

(a) Statement I is correct and II is wrong
(b) Statement II is correct and I is wrong
(c) Both the statements are correct
(d) Both the statements are incorrect

44. Uranus Limited is a company dealing in metal products. The work is mainly divided into functions including production, purchase, marketing, accounts and personnel. Identify the type of organisational structure followed by the organisation.

(a) Functional Structure
(b) Relational structure
(c) Divisional structure
(d) None of these

45. Renu went to purchase a car. There she got to know that due to Diwali the company is selling the car at a discount of ₹30,000 for a limited period. Identify the technique of sales promotion used by the company in the above situation.

(a) Rebate
(b) Discount
(c) Usable benefit
(d) Product combination

46. An IT company employing 4,000 people, plans to expand its business through diversification. It aims to become a global leader. To achieve this goal, It has started shifting to a ____________ management system from a centralised one. Thus, ____________function of management is being performed by the company to become a decentralised company.

(a) directing , centralised
(b) staffing , delegation
(c) organising , decentralised
(d) planning , decentralised

47. Priyanka, a manager, expects her subordinates to adapt to new environment and working conditions without giving them time to settle down. Which principle of management is being overlooked?

(a) Principle of decision-making
(b) Principle of not exact
(c) Principle of contingent
(d) None of these

48. **Assertion:** Thus Organising means establishing relationship between various factors of production and is concerned with establishing relationship amongst jobs, sections, departments and positions.

Reason: It involves identification and division of total work to be done into specific activities (called jobs) in accordance with previously determined plans.

(a) Both (A) and (R) are correct
(b) (A) is correct (R) is incorrect
(c) Both (A) and (R) are correct, and R is the correct explanation of (R)
(d) Both (A) and (R) are correct, and R is not the correct explanation of (R)

Section – C

Read the following text and answer question no. 49-54 on the basis of the same:

Yamuna Sharma, a small shopkeeper in Bikaner, Rajasthan used to sell the famous 'Bhujia-Sev'. It was a quick selling product for locals and foreign tourists. His second generation expanded the business and got 'Yamuna Ki Bhujia' registered with concerned authorities. Gradually, the brand offered a wide range of products to its customers like namkeen, sweets, bakery items, etc. However, 'Bhujia-Sev' remained the most popular products of the brand creating maximum revenue.

'Yamuna Ki Bhujia' offered its products at competitive prices even while offering customer services like gift packaging and free home delivery to become a household name. Now it has virtually become a synonym for 'Bhujia-Sev' in the market, so much so, that people ask for 'Yamuna Ki Bhujia' instead of 'Bhujia-Sev'. Yamuna Ki Bhujia' has developed a strong distribution network in India and abroad by setting up retail outlets and reaching out to the customer through internet selling.

Promotion of the brand had always been low profile, till the increase in competition pushed it to hire the services of a professional advertising agency, Vigyapan Pvt. Ltd. for promoting the product,. On the advice of Sewa Pvt. Ltd. 'Yamuna Ki Bhujia' has also worked upon managing public opinion by developing relations with the masses through sponsoring cultural and sporting events, maintenance of public parks, etc.

49. "His second generation expanded the business and got 'Yamuna Ki Bhujia' registered with concerned authorities.' With reference to the given text 'Yamuna Ki Bhujia' is a_______giving it a legal protection against its use by anyone else.
    (a) brand value
    (b) trademark
    (c) brand equity
    (d) brand mark

50. 'Yamuna Ki Bhujia' offered its products at competitive prices even while offering customer services like gift packaging and free home delivery to become a household name.
    Identify the factor affecting the element of marketing mix being discussed above.
    (a) Marketing methods used
    (b) Objectives
    (c) Extent of competition in the market
    (d) Product cost

51. 'Yamuna Ki Bhujia' has developed a strong distribution network in India and abroad by setting up retail outlets and reaching out to the customer through internet selling.
    Identify the decision related to the element of marketing mix being discussed above.
    (a) Storing and assorting products in order to create time utility
    (b) Regarding the channels or using intermediates
    (c) Both (a) and (b)
    (d) One regarding branding, packaging and labelling

52. On the advice of Sewa Pvt. Ltd. 'Yamuna Ki Bhujia' has also worked upon managing public opinion by developing relation with the masses through sponsoring cultural and sporting events, maintenance of public parks, etc. Name the department in the organisation which is generally responsible for performing the above important task of managing public opinion.
    (a) Marketing department
    (b) A separate department created in the firm for the purpose
    (c) An outside agency
    (d) Any of the above

53. Which one of the following is a marketing management philosophy?
    (a) Societal marketing concept
    (b) Distribution concept
    (c) Direct marketing concept
    (d) Channel concept

54. _______ ensures that products reach the ultimate customers from the manufacturers.
    (a) Selling
    (b) Marketing
    (c) Physical distribution
    (d) Sales promotion

55. The purchase, production and sales managers at Metcozy Ltd., a firm manufacturing readymade garments, are generally at a conflict, as they have their own objectives. Usually, each thinks that only they are qualified to evaluate, judge and decide on any matter, according to their professional criteria. Name the concept which will be required by the CEO, Mr. Mohan, to reconcile the differences in approach, interest or opinion in the organisation.
    (a) Coordination
    (b) Efficiency
    (c) Effectiveness
    (d) Planning

56. Karim decided to start a chocolates manufacturing business. He set the target of earning 10% profit on sales in the first year. As a good businessman, he was concerned about the future of the business, which was uncertain. He gathered the information that the demand for chocolates is increasing day-by-day. He

used this information as the base for future planning and shared it with his team. On the basis of the gathered information, he scheduled a meeting in the following week to find innovative ways to achieve the objectives. Write the first step, which has been followed by Karim that is related to the process of one of the functions of management.

(a) Setting objectives

(b) Development premises

(c) Evaluating alternatives

(d) Implementing the plan

57. Mohan decided to increase the production turnover of his business by 20% in the current year. Identify the step of planning being highlight in the above lines.

(a) Setting objectives

(b) Developing premises

(c) Identifying alternative course of action

(d) Follow up action

58. On the Introduction of GST act, experts in the field of business started analysing and forecasting its impact on various sectors and industries. Vivek, an established businessman attended a few seminar and conferences organised by such experts to familiarise himself with this information. He wanted to use these forecasts to reduce the uncertainty in making decisions for future in his business. Name the step of planning that will be followed after the step mentioned in the paragraph.

(a) Developing Premises

(b) Evaluating alternative courses of action

(c) Implementation of plan

(d) Identifying alternative course of action

59. According to the United Nations Environmental Agency, the world produces around 300 million tons of plastic each year, half of which constitutes single-use items. Ford is recycling over one billion plastic bottles every year to develop elements of the car's interior, reducing the amount of plastic ending up in a landfill. The American car maker has revealed that their Romanian-built Eco Sport SUVs' carpets are made using 470 recycled single-use plastic bottles. The process for making Ford Eco Sport carpets involves shredding bottles and their caps into tiny flakes and then heating them to 260° C.

Identify the related dimension of business environment.

(a) Economic dimension

(b) Social dimension

(c) Technological dimension

(d) Political dimension

60. Through this principle of management, Henri Fayol guides the managers to exhibit exemplary behaviour and advises that they should not fall into temptation of misusing their powers for personal benefit at the cost of general interest of the organisation.

Which principle of management is being described in the above statement?

(a) Remuneration of employees

(b) Centralisation and decentralisation

(c) Subordination of individual interest to general interest

(d) Equity

❏❏

Sample Paper **6**

Business Studies

Section – A

1. Under which function of management the best course of action is being chosen.
   - (a) Planning
   - (b) Controlling
   - (c) Organising
   - (d) None of the above

2. Organisational objective of management does not include_________.
   - (a) growth
   - (b) survival
   - (c) human betterment & social justice
   - (d) profit

3. According to _________ customer satisfaction alone can ensure market success.
   - (a) production concept
   - (b) societal marketing concept
   - (c) marketing concept
   - (d) product concept

4. Which aspect of management is concerned with the end result?
   - (a) Co-ordination
   - (b) Effectiveness
   - (c) Efficiency
   - (d) None of these

5. The Principle of Unity of Direction is concerned with:
   - (a) one head one plan
   - (b) one head different plans
   - (c) planning by employees
   - (d) one unit one plan

6. _________ ensures that the production reaches to the ultimate consumers from manufactures.
   - (a) Physical distribution
   - (b) Promotion
   - (c) Advertising
   - (d) Marketing

7. Management is equally important to run a political organisation or to run an economic organisation. Which feature of management is being reflected in the given statement?
   - (a) Management is goal oriented
   - (b) Management is group activity
   - (c) Management is pervasive
   - (d) Management is a continuous process

8. Organisation develops relationship between_________.
   - (a) People, work and resources
   - (b) Customer, supplier and resources
   - (c) Customer, people and work
   - (d) Work, people and supplier

9. Which of the following is a function of packaging?
   - (a) Product promotion
   - (b) Product identification
   - (c) Product protection
   - (d) All of the above

10. To meet the objectives of the firm, Ryan Ltd. offers employment to physically challenged persons. Identify the objective of management which is being highlighted here:
    - (a) Social objective
    - (b) Organisational objective
    - (c) Personal objective
    - (d) None of these

11. "The company has several departments: Production, Marketing, Finance and HR"? Which organisational structure is suitable for the company?
    - (a) Functional Structure
    - (b) Divisional Structure
    - (c) Both (a) and (b)
    - (d) None of these

12. Which of the following is not a benefit of planning?
    - (a) Reduces overlapping and wasteful activities
    - (b) Provides direction
    - (c) Reduces the risk of uncertainty
    - (d) Leads to rigidity

13. ABC Ltd. has decided to provide flat 10 % discount on all items. Identify the related function of marketing being highlighted here.
    (a) Packaging and labelling
    (b) Branding
    (c) Pricing
    (d) Promotion

14. "To increase the sales, the marketing manager, Mr. Gautam insists on offering 20% discount to customers". Which element of marketing mix is highlighted here?
    (a) Place
    (b) Promotion
    (c) Price
    (d) Product

15. Which of the following is not true with regard to concept of product?
    (a) It is a bundle of utility
    (b) Source of satisfaction
    (c) Confined to physical product
    (d) It includes both tangible and intangible attributes

16. "Planning provides the goals against which actual performance is measured". Identify the importance of planning highlighted in this point.
    (a) Planning helps in decision-making
    (b) Planning establishes standards for controlling
    (c) Planning provides direction
    (d) Planning promotes innovation

17. ___________ is the act of designing and producing wrapper of the product.
    (a) Labelling
    (b) Branding
    (c) Packaging
    (d) None of the above

18. The Prime Minister of India has announced an economic relief package of ₹ 50 crore. Identify the dimension of environment.
    (a) Political environment
    (b) Economic environment
    (c) Both (a) and (b)
    (d) None of the above

19. Principles of management are not:
    (a) applicable only in large firms
    (b) formed by practice and experience of managers
    (c) flexible
    (d) contingent

20. In the organisation, if there is increase in span of management, then the level of management will also________.
    (a) decrease
    (b) no effect
    (c) increase
    (d) either increase or decrease

21. ________ refers to the practice of managing the communication between public and organisation.
    (a) Public relation
    (b) Advertisement
    (c) Sales promotion
    (d) Branding

22. ________the separate divisions are created within the organisation for different product lines.
    (a) Divisional structure
    (b) Functional structure
    (c) Both (a) and (b)
    (d) None of these

23. If a statement is talking about the administrative orders and legislations, then it is indicating which dimension of business environment.
    (a) Political environment
    (b) Legal environment
    (c) Economical environment
    (d) Technological environment

24. Rama is working as a manager in Telco Ltd. In her team there are 15 members of different backgrounds and nationalities. While dealing with these 15 people she makes sure that she does not make any discrimination on the basis of caste, religion or gender etc. Which principle of Henry Fayol is being followed by Rama?
    (a) Discipline
    (b) Order
    (c) Espirit de Corps
    (d) Equity

Section – B

25. As consumers are becoming health conscious; this leads to change in taste and preferences, eating habits. The consumers are looking for more nutritious products. Now, the companies are trying to take leadership by providing better and nutritious products. Identify the related feature of business environment.

    (a) Interrelatedness
    (b) Relativity
    (c) Complexity
    (d) Dynamic

26. Identify the step in the process of planning which is considered as the "real point of decision making".

    (a) Developing premises
    (b) Evaluating alternatives
    (c) Follow-up action
    (d) Selection of best alternative

27. The part of a brand which can be spoken by the individual or targeted customer is:

    (a) Brand Name
    (b) Brand Mark
    (c) Trade Mark
    (d) Both (a) and (b)

28. Syska, a company manufacturing light bulbs incurred heavy expenditure on scientific Research and Development and discovered a technology that made it possible to produce an energy efficient light bulb that lasts at least ten times as long as a standard bulb. It resulted in growth and profitability of the company. Identify the dimension of business environment which has been referred in case of Syska.

    (a) Social environment
    (b) Legal environment
    (c) Political environment
    (d) Technological environment

29. A Company. is manufacturing garments. The manager wants to increase profits by purchasing new high speed machines or increasing the sale price or using waste materials in manufacturing stuffed toys. He decided that "using waste material" is the best solution for him. Identify the concept of management involved.

    (a) Effectiveness
    (b) Efficiency
    (c) Planning
    (d) All of these

30. Mansi, a shoe manufacturer for school students, decided to maximize her profit by producing and distributing at a large scale and thereby reducing the average cost of production. Mansi adopted ______ marketing management philosophy.

    (a) production
    (b) product
    (c) marketing
    (d) selling

31. The management of XYZ Ltd. strongly believes that the members of an organisation should work towards fulfilling the common organisational goals. This requires team work and integration of efforts of all individuals, departments and specialists. This is because all the individuals and departments depend on each other for information and resources to perform their respective activities. Managers need to reconcile differences in approach, timing, effort or interest. At the same time it should enable all its members to grow and develop. Thus, there is a need to harmonize individual goals and organisational goals.

    Identify the characteristic of management which is reflected by XYZ Ltd.

    (a) Management is continuous
    (b) Management is pervasive
    (c) Management is a group activity
    (d) Management increases the efficiency

32. For the following two statements choose the correct option:

    Statement I: Accountability cannot be delegated

    Statement II: Authority can be delegated

    Choose the correct option from the options given below:

    (a) Statement I is correct and II is wrong
    (b) Statement II is correct and I is wrong
    (c) Both the statements are correct
    (d) Both the statements are incorrect

33. Digital Ltd. has grown in size. Its market share starts declining with changes in business environment and with the entry of MNCs. To handle the situation CEO of Digital Ltd. starts delegating some of his authority to the General Manager, who also felt himself overburdened and with the approval of CEO disperses some of his authority to various levels throughout the organisation. Identify the concept of management discussed above.

    (a) Decentralisation
    (b) Delegation of authority

(c) Span of management   (d) None of these

34. Arrange the following in the process of Scientific Techniques in the correct sequence:
    (i)   Simplification of work   (ii) Functional foremanship
    (iii) Fatigue study   (iv) Standardisation
    Choose the correct option:
    (a) (i); (ii); (iii); (iv)   (b) (ii); (iv); (i); (iii)
    (c) (iv); (iii); (ii); (i)   (d) (ii); (iii); (i); (iv)

35. Radhika Ltd. has a plan of increasing profits by 10%. It has devoted a lot of time and money to this plan. But the competition increases and they were not able to change its plan to beat its competitors because huge amount of money had already been devoted to the pre-decided plan. Due to this company has to suffer losses. Which limitation of planning is being highlighted here?
    (a) Time consuming   (b) Involves huge cost
    (c) Rigidity   (d) Both (a) and (b)

36. Siddhartha is working in a MNC. One of his functions is to link between workers and middle level managers. At which level of management Siddhartha is working?
    (a) Lower level   (b) Middle level
    (c) Top level   (d) All of these

37. Amar Ltd. has appointed the former consulting executive of Shyam Ltd. Rajiv Bhatt as its Vice President. What will be his basic task?
    (a) To frame policies and plans
    (b) To see survival and growth of the company
    (c) Link between top level and lower level management
    (d) Both (a) and (b)

38. An automobile company has decided to launch electric charged vehicles. This will cost the company 200 crores annually. When the relationship manager of the company was asked about the reason of bearing so much extra cost he replied that the company considered environmental friendly techniques to reduce pollution. The company feels by bearing extra cost it is fulfilling its responsibility. Identify the market philosophy used by an automobile company.
    (a) Societal marketing concept   (b) Marketing concept
    (c) Selling concept   (d) Product concept

39. There is a famous manufacturing company where hundreds of workers are engaged in. All of them help each other which leads to a great environment in the company. However the company lacks professionalism. Most of the workers are school dropouts so they do not know how to synchronize the work. Failing of plans is common in this company.
    Identify the concept of management which is followed by the company.
    (a) Cooperation   (b) Coordination
    (c) Efficiency   (d) Effectiveness

40. Kalpana joins an IT firm as a System Analyst after completing his masters in Computer Science. She has to work in very close coordination with all the departmental heads. Very soon Kalpana realizes that each departmental head has its own individual style of working. They differ greatly in their day-to-day approach to complete the work. They tend to deal with a given situation, an issue or a problem through a combination of their own experience, creativity, imagination, initiative and innovation. In the context of the above case: Identify the nature of management highlighted in the above case.
    (a) Management as an art   (b) Management as a science
    (c) Management as profession   (d) All of the above

41. Vishal a worker, is given a target of assembling two computers per day. He got an idea which would not only reduce the assembling time of computers but would also reduce the cost of production of the computers. Vishal's supervisor instead of appreciating him, ordered him to complete the work as per the methods and techniques decided earlier as nothing could be changed at that stage. The limitation of planning being referred to in the above statement is that it_________.
    (a) rigidity   (b) time consuming

(c) may not work in dynamic environment   (d) reduces creativity

42. The principle given by Henry Fayol which aims employees should not be transferred frequently is _________.
   (a) equity
   (b) stability of personnel
   (c) order
   (d) subordination of organisational interest to general interest

43. For the following two statements choose the correct option:

   Statement I : Pricing is not a crucial decision regarding the product.

   Statement II : Pricing may influence the demand of the product.

   Choose the correct option from the options given below:
   (a) Statement I is correct and II is wrong   (b) Statement II is correct and I is wrong
   (c) Both the statements are correct   (d) Both the statements are incorrect

44. Namrata is the marketing manager of a company which sells laptops. She plans the target sale of 500 laptops per month. She allocates necessary resources to carry out the plan. She has six salesmen working under her. She works with them, guiding and motivating them to achieve the target sales. Identify the importance of management highlighted here.
   (a) Helps in achieving personal objectives   (b) Optimum utilisation of resources
   (c) Helps in achieving group goals   (d) Increases efficiency

45. If a company is evaluating the different options through which they can complete their target or achieve their objective. Then the next step to be followed by the company in planning will be:
   (a) follow-up   (b) implementation
   (c) developing premises   (d) setting objectives

46. Ratan works in a manufacturing company. His job is to keep machines, tools and materials ready. Identify the position held by Ratan according to functional foremanship described by F.W. Taylor.
   (a) Instruction card clerk   (b) Time and cost clerk
   (c) Speed boss   (d) Gang boss

47. Mahesh is planning to launch an online education portal. In order to understand the various needs of the students, she conducted an online survey. Based on the feedback of the survey, she had decided to offer educational packages to the prospective buyers. Identify the type of marketing concept been described in the given line.
   (a) Product concept   (b) Production concept
   (c) Marketing concept   (d) Societal marketing concept

48. **Assertion (A):** Planning is the foremost function in sports.
   Reason (R): Planning gives a view of future course of action.
   Pick the correct option:
   (a) Both (A) and (R) are correct
   (b) (A) is correct (R) is incorrect
   (c) Both (A) and (R) are correct, and R is the correct explanation of (A)
   (d) Both (A) and (R) are correct, and R is not the correct explanation of (A)

Section – C

Read the following text and answer question number 49-54 on the basis of the same.

After completing a course in travel and tourism, Mansi started her own travel agency name "Travel Organiser". She decided to create fourteen job positions divided into different departments on the basis of functions namely, front office department including online and offline queries, reservations department for airways, railways and roadways, accommodation booking department, and financial department for securing payments, operations department for smooth functioning of her business. She decides to specify clearly the lines of authority and areas of responsibility for each job position to avoid any interdepartmental conflicts. In the context of the above case:

49. Which function of management is being described in the above Paragraph?
    (a) Planning   (b) Organising
    (c) Directing   (d) Staffing

50. "She decided to create fourteen job positions divided into different departments" Which organisational structure is suitable for Shell Ltd?
    (a) Functional Structure   (b) Divisional Structure
    (c) Both (a) and (b)   (d) None of these

51. Identify the framework created by Mansi within which all managerial and operating tasks are to be performed in his organisation.
    (a) Organisational Structure   (b) Decentralised
    (c) Centralised   (d) None of these

52. Authority, Responsibility and Accountability are the three elements of:
    (a) Decentralisation   (b) Delegation
    (c) Hierarchy   (d) Span of Management

53. Which type of communication will take place between different departments in Travel Organiser
    (a) Formal Communication   (b) Informal Communication
    (c) Both (a) and (b)   (d) None of these

54. Responsibility is derived from:
    (a) Accountability   (b) Hierarchy
    (c) Authority   (d) None of these

55. In 1996, When McDonald's started its business in India the company went through a complete localisation strategy. McDonald's changed its product menu to accommodate the vegetable burger given to the large vegetarian population and even reduced the product price by close to fifteen per cent. "McAloo Tikki burger" is only available in the Indian outlets of McDonalds. Identify the relevant feature of business environment being discussed above.
    (a) Interrelatedness   (b) Complexity
    (c) Relativity   (d) Dynamic environment

56. Healthy Ltd., a sanitizer manufacturing company launched its products in time of Pandemic. To meet the increased demand, the company employed children from nearby villages. Although the product was in great demand, appropriate safety warning for use were not mentioned on the bottles that it should be used carefully.
    Identify the important product-related decision that was not taken into consideration by the company.
    (a) Packaging   (b) Branding
    (c) Labelling   (d) All of these

57. An ice-cream manufacturing company has found a new way to make ice creams by using an ingredient called 'ice structuring protein' which is widely found in nature especially, in fishes which allows them to survive in freezing arctic waters. Combining ISP with stabilizer technology allows to make ice creams that don't melt so easily thereby making it more convenient for small children and consumer in hot countries. In the context of above case:
    Identify the component of marketing mix being taken into consideration by the company.
    (a) Product   (b) Price
    (c) Promotion   (d) Place

58. XYZ company is manufacturing garments. The manager wants to increase profits by purchasing new high speed machines or increasing the sale price or using waste material in manufacturing stuffed toys.
    What will be the next step in process of planning?
    (a) Follow-up action   (b) Developing premises

  (c) Evaluating alternatives   (d) Implementing the plan

59. In MNC, there is one head Mr. Aman who has two lines of authority under him. One line consists of Atul-Saru-Anish- Iqbal-Chetan. Another line of authority has Lalit- Tanu- Vanshika-Nikita- Rajesh. According to a Principle of Management given by Fayol, If "Anish" has to communicate with "Vanshika" who is at the same level of authority then illustrate the route he will have to travlerse.

  (a) Anish-Iqbal-Chetan-Aman-Rajesh-Nikita-Vanshika

  (b) Anish-Iqbal-Chetan-Rajesh-Nikita-Vanshika

  (c) Anish–Saru-Atul-Aman- Lalit-Tanu-Vanshika

  (d) Anish-Aman- Vanshika

60. According to the technique of scientific management "Differential Piece Wage system" How much more will a worker making 50 units earn as compared to a worker making 39 units? If the standard output per day is 40 units and those who make standard output or more than standard get ₹55 per unit and those below get ₹ 45 per unit.

  (a) ₹2750   (b) ₹1800

  (c) ₹1755   (d) ₹995

❑❑

Sample Paper 7

Business Studies

Section – A

1. Successful management manifests itself in many positive ways like employees feel happy and satisfied. Identify the feature of management highlighted in this statement.
   - (a) Management is pervasive
   - (b) Management is dynamic
   - (c) Management is group activity
   - (d) Management is intangible

2. __________ is a systematic process of structuring, integrating, coordinating task, goals and activities to attain objectives.
   - (a) Planning
   - (b) Organising
   - (c) Coordination
   - (d) Management

3. It consists of all potential customers who have ability and willingness both to buy a product or service to satisfy their needs or wants. Identify the concept.
   - (a) Market
   - (b) Marketing
   - (c) Marketer
   - (d) Marketing management

4. Which level of management is responsible for providing good and healthy working conditions?
   - (a) Top level management
   - (b) Middle level management
   - (c) Lower level management
   - (d) All of the above

5. It is necessary that goods and services must available to the consumers at the right place, in the right quality and at right time. Name the concerned elements of marketing mix.
   - (a) Product mix
   - (b) Price mix
   - (c) Place mix
   - (d) Promotion mix

6. The basic purpose of ________ is to facilitate the decision making process for successful viability of goods and services of a business enterprise.
   - (a) market
   - (b) marketing planning
   - (c) both (a) and (b)
   - (d) market research

7. Identify the dimension of the characteristic of management- "it is multidimensional", Management translates the work to be done in terms of goals to be achieved and assigns the means to achieve it.
   - (a) Management of people
   - (b) Management of work
   - (c) Management of operations
   - (d) All of the above

8. ________ is paid form of non-personal communication to promote the sale of goods or services undertaken by an identified sponsor.
   - (a) Public relations
   - (b) Sales promotion
   - (c) Advertising
   - (d) Personal selling

9. Which of the following cases, would a continous study of business environment help in:
   - (a) raw material supplying company increases the price of raw material
   - (b) handset mobile phone manufacturer losing its market due to failure to introduce android mobile phones
   - (c) information that labour union is going on strike
   - (d) all of the above

10. Planning enables a manager to choose the best alternative which is best for the organisation growth and survival. Identify the feature of management highlighted in the given statement.
    - (a) Planning is pervasive
    - (b) Planning is primary function
    - (c) Planning is mental exercise
    - (d) Planning involves decision-making

11. Parul is working in JPL Ltd. and she has been assigned the task of arranging conference for 2 days for foreign delegates. She made two persons as coordinators to take care of activities related to refreshments and registration for smooth functioning of the event. Identify the function of management performed by Parul.
    (a) Planning
    (b) Organising
    (c) Directing
    (d) Staffing

12. __________ is deciding in advance what to do, when to do and how to do it.
    (a) Management
    (b) Planning
    (c) Organising
    (d) None of these

13. The term market may be understood in which of the following contexts?
    (a) Geographical area covered
    (b) Type of buyers
    (c) None of the above
    (d) Both (a) and (b)

14. The Economic survey, 2019 suggests that the psychological biases can be used in the realm of tax compliance. It is in favour of using religious norms such "dying in debt is a sin" to improve tax compliance. Identify the related dimensions of business environment.
    (a) Legal dimension and social dimension
    (b) Social dimension and economic dimension
    (c) Technological dimension and political dimension
    (d) Political dimension and economic dimension

15. Which of the following is not a component of specific forces of business environment.
    (a) Technological conditions
    (b) Customers
    (c) Employees
    (d) Investors

16. Planning is a __________ activity, as it contributes towards the realisation of predetermined goal.
    (a) purposeful
    (b) primary
    (c) predictable
    (d) perquisite

17. __________ refers to the set of activities performed by marketer to inform the targeted customers.
    (a) Promotion
    (b) Pricing
    (c) Marketing
    (d) Place

18. India's population is expected to grow under 0·5% during 2031-41 due to decline in fertility rate and increase in life expectancy. These changes in India's demography will also have implications such as the proportion of elementary school-going children will witness significant declines, lack of hospital beds and increase in retirement age. The related features of business environment being described in the above lines is:
    (a) Totality of external forces
    (b) Dynamic nature
    (c) Interrelatedness
    (d) Relativity

19. The Principle of Management is :
    (a) provide a solution
    (b) flexible
    (c) rigid
    (d) absolute

20. __________ gives shape to the organisational structure.
    (a) Organising
    (b) Hierarchy
    (c) Span of management
    (d) Number of employees

21. __________ refers to personal form of communication between seller and targeted customer.
    (a) Advertisement
    (b) Sales promotion
    (c) Public relations
    (d) Personal selling

22. The process of sharing some work and authority with subordinate is referred as__________.
    (a) Decentralisation
    (b) Delegation of authority
    (c) Span of management
    (d) Network structure

23. If a statement is talking about health attitudes, career attitudes and population shifts then the statement is indicating towards which dimension of business environment?
    (a) Economic environment
    (b) Social environment
    (c) Legal environment
    (d) None of these

24. "There should be feeling of mutual trust and belongingness among the employees of the organisation". Which principle is being highlighted here?
    (a) Equity
    (b) Subordination of individual interest to general interest
    (c) Espirit De Corps
    (d) Initiative

Section - B

25. As consumers are becoming health conscious; this leads to change in taste and preferences, eating habits. The consumers are looking for more nutritious products. Now, the companies are trying to take leadership by providing better and nutritious products. Identify the dimension of business environment.
    (a) Political environment
    (b) Technological environment
    (c) Economic environment
    (d) Social environment

26. Identify the correct sequence of steps involved in planning process:
    (a) Setting objectives, Developing Premises, Identifying alternative course of action, Evaluating alternative courses
    (b) Developing Premises, Setting Objectives, Identifying alternative course of action, Evaluating alternative courses
    (c) Identifying alternative course of action, Developing Premises, Setting Objectives, Evaluating alternative courses
    (d) Identifying alternative course of action, Evaluating alternative courses, Developing Premises, Setting Objectives

27. Folk Ltd. is a leather bags manufacturing company. The company is using prohibited animal skin to make leather bags, in order to satisfy some of its customers. Which marketing concept is being violated in the given case?
    (a) Product concept
    (b) Production concept
    (c) Societal marketing concept
    (d) Marketing concept

28. Two big banner movies were scheduled to be released on the same date. On the last moment release of one of the movies has to be postponed due to opposition of a group of people due to some unethical contents related to their religion was shown in that movie. The other movie released on time and made huge profit as there was no competition and movie which was postponed suffered loss. Identify the dimension of business environment, which delayed the release of movie.
    (a) Technological environment
    (b) Political environment
    (c) Economic environment
    (d) Social environment

29. Krishna is the manager of a MNC which manufacture clothes for kids. He plans to release his winter collection in the month of September itself. Then, he ensures that there is adequate workforce and production proceeds according to plans. He asks the marketing department to prepare their promotional and advertising campaigns also. Identify the concept of management explained in the above paragraph.
    (a) Planning
    (b) Organising
    (c) Coordination
    (d) Marketing

30. Nandini, a school bag manufacturer decided to improve the product for profit maximisation and thus added water bottle holder to the existing design. Nandini adopted _________ marketing management philosophy.
    (a) production
    (b) product
    (c) marketing
    (d) selling

31. Pankaj is a salesman in a company which deals in pet accessories and food. He has been given a target of selling 800 units of the food packets in a month by offering a maximum of 10% discount to his customers. In order to meet his monthly sales target, on the last two days of the months, he offers 15% discount to his customers. In which concept of management Pankaj lacks?
    (a) Effectiveness
    (b) Efficiency
    (c) Coordination
    (d) All of the above

32. For the following two statements choose the correct option:
    Statement 1: Responsibility flows, upwards from a subordinate to the superior.
    Statement 2: Accountability flows downwards from the superior to a subordinate.
    Choose the correct option from the options given below:
    (a) Statement I is correct and II is wrong
    (b) Statement II is correct and I is wrong
    (c) Both the statements are correct
    (d) Both the statements are incorrect

33. In Aakash Ltd., an employee has the objective of maximising his salary, whereas the objective of organisation is to maximise output at competitive cost. There was some dispute on this for a while. Eventually, the

organisation's interest was given priority over employee's interest. The principle related to this situation is__________.

(a) Remuneration

(b) Subordination of individual interest to general interest

(c) Equity

(d) Espirit de Corps

34. Arrange the following process of Top Level in the correct sequence:

(i) Framing plans and policies

(ii) Determining objectives

(iii) Assembling all the resources

(iv) Organising activities

Choose the correct options:

(a) (ii); (i); (iv); (iii)

(b) (i); (ii); (iiii); (iv)

(c) (i); (iii); (iv); (ii)

(d) (iv); (iii); (ii), (i)

35. The sales department accuses the production department for the poor sales due to late delivery of goods. The production department accuses the purchase department for not delivering the raw material in time and the purchase department accuses the finance department for not releasing funds on time. Which quality of management is missing in the above situation?

(a) Planning

(b) Management

(c) Coordination

(d) None of the above

36. Khush Ltd. set up the target of selling 500 units of fans per week and made all their plans to achieve this target. But due to change in technology adapted by competitors which leads to reduction in their (competitor) cost, the Khush Ltd. could not achieve their target. Identify the limitation of planning highlighted over here.

(a) Involves cost

(b) Time consuming

(c) Reduces creativity

(d) May not work in dynamic environment

37. Radhika is working as marketing manager of MNC in Delhi. What is the basic function of Radhika?

(a) To frame plans and policies

(b) Link between top and lower level management

(c) Link between workers and middle level management

(d) Responsible for survival and growth of company

38. A leather company is a very progressive company. The owners of the company feel that they should contribute to society otherwise it is worthless to exist as a company. The organisation will be making five teams of hired environmentalists from foreign countries. This team will help the local people in cleaning the polluted river in the country and the cost will be borne by the company. Identify the marketing management philosophy involved in the given case.

(a) Product concept

(b) Societal marketing concept

(c) Selling concept

(d) Marketing concept

39. There is a famous manufacturing company where hundreds of workers work. All of them help each other which lead to a great environment in the company. However the company lacks professionalism. Most of the workers are school dropouts so they do not know how to synchronize the work. Failing of plans is common in this company.

Identify the concept of management which is violated by the company.

(a) Cooperation

(b) Coordination

(c) Efficiency

(d) Effectiveness

40. Kapil is a well-known businessman in the field of Steel Industry. He owes the success of his business to his own education in business management and his team of certified management consultants. Therefore, he decides to send both his children Raghav and Ragini abroad to acquire a degree in business management in their individual area of expertise as there is restricted entry without the degree and one cannot become a manager. He feels that all over the world there is marked growth in management as a discipline.

Identify the nature of management being discussed here.

(a) Remanagement as an art

(b) Management as a science

(c) Management as profession

(d) All of the above

41. Mr. A is a very honest, sincere and hard-working manager. After implementation of his well chalked out plan he, from the start of July, decides to see in what ways and up to what accuracy has his plan been implemented.

    The step of the planning process will be involved by Mr. A from the starting of July is__________.

    (a) setting objectives   (b) developing premises

    (c) evaluating alternatives   (d) follow-up action

42. The scientific principle given by F.W.Taylor which says adopt a suggestion system or suggestions should be taken from employees is ___________.

    (a) harmony, not discord

    (b) cooperation, not individualism

    (c) science, not rule of thumb

    (d) development of workers to their greatest efficiency and prosperity

43. For the following two statements choose the correct option:

    Statement I : Packaging gives protection to the product.

    Statement II : Packaging does not help in promotion of product.

    Choose the correct option from the options given below:

    (a) Statement I is correct and II is wrong   (b) Statement II is correct and I is wrong

    (c) Both the statements are correct   (d) Both the statements are incorrect

44. Nishant is the marketing manager of a company which sells Air Conditioners. He plans the target sale of 2000 air conditioners per month. He has four salesmen working under him and he has allocated necessary resources to carry out the plan. At the end of the month, after comparison of actual sales with the target sales he found that actual sales exceeded the target sales. He rewarded the efficient employees to motivate them and others also. Identify the importance of management highlighted here.

    (a) Helps in achieving personal objectives   (b) Optimum utilisation of resources

    (c) Helps in achieving group goals   (d) Increases efficiency

45. The managers are required to make some assumptions regarding future, as future is uncertain. Identify the step in process of planning.

    (a) Setting objectives   (b) Developing premises

    (c) Evaluating alternatives   (d) Implementation of plan

46. According to Taylor, "even a small production activity like loading figures of iron into boxes can be scientifically planned and managed. This can result in tremendous savings of human energy as well as wastage of time and materials." Identify the related principle of scientific management.

    (a) Harmony, not discord

    (b) Science, not rule of thumb

    (c) Development of each and every person to get his/her greatest efficiency and prosperity

    (d) None of the above

47. In order to improve upon its competitive edge, Khushboo Ltd. has changed the packaging of its hair care products. They are now available in customer friendly design, which has a nozzle attach to the lid so that at the time of usage, the consumer doesn't need to open the cap of the bottle. Name the marketing function being explained in the given lines.

    (a) Product design and development   (b) Customer support services

    (c) Promotion   (d) Physical distribution

48. **Assertion (A):** Planning is time consuming.

    Reason (R): Planning requires lots of study, research and interpretation.

    (a) Both (A) and (R) are correct

    (b) (A) is correct (R) is incorrect

    (c) Both (A) and (R) are correct, and R is the correct explanation of (A)

    (d) Both (A) and (R) are correct, and R is not the correct explanation of (A)

Section - C

Read the following text and answer question number 49-54 on the basis of the same.

Naman works as a corporate event coordinator in an event management company. He has been made an overall official in-charge for organising a Press Conference for one of the clients of the company. For ensuring that the Press Conference takes place successfully, he identifies the various activities involved and divides the whole work into various task groups like seating arrangement committee, security committee and reception committee. In order to facilitate coordination within and among committees, he appoints a supervisor of each group. Each member in the group is asked to report to their respective supervisors and all the supervisors are expected to work as per Naman 's orders.

49. Which function of management is being performed by Naman?
    - (a) Planning
    - (b) Organising
    - (c) Directing
    - (d) Staffing

50. "He identifies the various activities involved and divides the whole work".
    Identify the step of process of organising highlighted:
    - (a) Division of work
    - (b) Establishing reporting relationships
    - (c) Assignment of duties
    - (d) None of these

51. "Divides the whole work into various task groups like seating arrangement committee, security committee and reception committee." Identify the step of process of organising highlighted:
    - (a) Division of work
    - (b) Establishing reporting relationships
    - (c) Assignment of duties
    - (d) Departmentalisation

52. "He appoints a supervisor of each group. Each member in the group is asked to report to their respective supervisors and all the supervisors are expected to work as per Naman's orders." Identify the step of process of organising highlighted:
    - (a) Establishing reporting relationships
    - (b) Assignment of duties
    - (c) Delegation
    - (d) None of these

53. __________ provides the framework which enables the enterprise to function as an integrated unit by regulating and coordinating the responsibilities of individuals and departments.
    - (a) Delegation of authority
    - (b) Organisational structure
    - (c) Span of management
    - (d) Decentralisation

54. Grouping of jobs of similar nature under functional is:
    - (a) Functional structure
    - (b) Divisional structure
    - (c) Hierarchy
    - (d) Both (a) and (b)

55. Even after opening up of Indian Economy, foreign companies found it extremely difficult to cut through the bureaucratic and red tapism in government offices. This discourages them from investing in India. Identify the dimension of environment highlighted here.
    - (a) Economic environment
    - (b) Technological environment
    - (c) Legal environment
    - (d) Political environment

56. Yummy Chocolates Ltd., a chocolate manufacturing company, launched some new products on the eve of Valentine in the market which attracted many buyers. To meet the increasing demand, the company employed people from nearby villages where there was a lot of unemployment. Because of the good behaviour of the management with the employees, more and more people wanted to join the company. As the products were in great demand in the market, a competitor imitated the products. The products of the competitor were not accepted by the consumers as it was a status symbol to buy the products of Yummy Chocolates Ltd. because of their standardised quality.

    Identify the product-related decision because of which consumers preferred the products of Yummy Chocolates Ltd.
    - (a) Branding
    - (b) Packaging
    - (c) Labelling
    - (d) All of these

57. CK Ltd. is a multinational corporation that creates consumer electronics, personal computers, servers and computer software. The company also has a chain of retail stores known as CK Stores. Despite high competition, CK has succeeded in creating demand for its products, giving the company power over prices through product differentiation, innovation advertising and ensured brand loyalty.

Identify the component of promotion mix being used by the company.

(a) Advertising

(b) Public relation

(c) Sales promotion

(d) None of these

58. Rahim wanted to start with a stationery business to reach the students of schools and colleges to provide stationery to them. He felt that students were not able to get the needed stationery easily and hence wanted to provide the stationery directly in the school. He listed out the various of setting up this business and finally selected the best way to set up this business by developing the app. Suggest what should be the next step to be followed by him:

(a) Identifying alternative courses of action

(b) Evaluating alternative courses of action

(c) Implementation of plan

(d) Follow up

59. In MNC, there is one head Mr. A who has two lines of authority under him. One line consists of P-Q-R-S-T Sara-Rajat-Abhishek-Ismail-Chris. Another line of authority has B-C-D-E-F Lata-Rupa-Geet-Hussain-Preeti. According to a Principle of Management given by Fayol, If "R" has to communicate with "D" who is at the same level of authority then illustrate the route he will have to traverse.

(a) R-S-T-F-E-D

(b) R-Q-P-A-B-C-D

(c) R-S-T-A-B-C-D

(d) R-Q-P-A-D

60. According to the technique of scientific management "Differential Piece Wage system" How much more will a worker making 45 units earn as compared to a worker making 35 units? If the standard output per day is 40 units and those who make standard output or more than standard get ₹ 50 per unit and those below get ₹ 40 per unit.

(a) ₹ 1600

(b) ₹ 2000

(c) ₹ 1800

(d) ₹ 450

❑❑

Answers

Section – A

1. (a) Group activity

> **Explanation:** Management always refers to a group of people involved in managerial activities. The management functions cannot be performed in isolation. Each individual performs his/her role at his/her status and department, and then only management function can be executed. Even the result of management affects every individual and every department of the organisation so it always refers to a group effort and not the individual effort of one person.

2. (a) Accountability

> **Explanation:** Accountability refers obligations to carry out assigned task.

3. (c) Direct feedback

> **Explanation:** It is very difficult to judge the effectiveness of an advertising message as there is no accurate feedback regarding its impact.

4. (d) All of these

> **Explanation:** Directing take place at the top, middle and bottom level of management .Directing takes place at all levels of management.

5. (b) Accountability

> **Explanation:** Accountability implies being answerable for the final outcome. Once authority has been delegated and responsibility accepted, one cannot deny accountability.

6. (a) effectiveness

> **Explanation:** According to the Modern concept of management says that employees must be effective as well as efficient. Effectiveness refers to completion of work or achievement of target on time.

7. (c) society

> **Explanation:** It serves society by converting latest demand into effective demand.

8. (c) Technological conditions

> **Explanation:** Technological conditions is a component of general forces that affect the business environment of an enterprises.

9. (d) Method Study

> **Explanation:** Management should find the best method to perform a particular task.

10. (a) Dynamic function

> **Explanation:** In this statement, characteristic of dynamic functioning of management is highlighted. The management is supposed to take decisions based on the changing business environment in order to survive.

11. (c)   Primacy of planning

> **Explanation:** Planning lays down the base for all other functions of management. All the other managerial functions are performed within the framework of the plans drawn. Since, planning precedes all the other function, it is called the primary function of management or primacy of planning.

12. (a)   forward looking function

> **Explanation:** Planning is considered to be forward looking function because planning is the process of thinking before doing.
> "Planning is deciding in advance what to do, how to do it, when to do it and who is to do it".

13. (a)   Production concept

> **Explanation:** Production concept assumes that availability and affordability of the product are the key to the success of a firm and puts greater emphasis on improving the production and distribution efficiency of the firms.

14. (b)   Divisional organisation

> **Explanation:** Divisional organisation is a type of organisational structure that groups each organisational function into a division. Each division contains all the necessary resources and functions within it to support that product line or geography.

15. (a)   Employees

> **Explanation:** Employees are not the characteristics of business environment because they are the persons who work under the business environment not a feature of that environment.

16. (b)   Harold Koontz

> **Explanation:** In 1910, owing to the Eastern Rate Case, Frederick Winslow Taylor and his Scientific Management methodologies became famous worldwide. In 1911, Taylor introduced his The Principles of Scientific Management paper to the ASME, eight years after his Shop Management paper.

17. (a)   Marketing management

> **Explanation:** Marketing management is a process of controlling the marketing aspects, setting the goals of a company, organising the plans step by step, taking decisions for the firm, and executing them to get the maximum turn over by meeting the consumers' demands.

18. (b)   Divisional structure

> **Explanation:** The divisional organisational structure organises the activities of a business around geographical, market, or product and service groups. Divisional structure also comprise of separate business units or divisions.

19. (a)   Technology

> **Explanation:** Specific forces of the business environment refer to those forces which does not affect every department of the business organisation. It includes investors, customers, competitors and supplier.

20. (c)   Follow-up action

> **Explanation:** Follow-up action to see whether plans are being implemented and activities are performed according to schedule is also part of the planning process. Monitoring the plans is equally important to ensure that objectives are achieved properly.

21. (c) business environment

> **Explanation:** The term business environment the sum total of all individuals, institutions and other forces that are outside the control of a business enterprise but that may affect its performance.

22. (a) dynamic

> **Explanation:** Business environment is dynamic in nature, i.e. nothing is constant. Sometimes planning fails to foresee the changes and there are obstacles in effective planning. Hence, planning can be detrimental.

23. (c) Different piece wage system

> **Explanation:** Under piece system of payment, wages is based on output and not on time. There is no consideration for time taken in completing a task. A fixed rate is paid for each unit produced, job completed or an operation performed. Workers are not guaranteed minimum wages under this system of wage payment.

24. (b) Delegation

> **Explanation:** Elements of delegation are:
>
> (a) Authority: Authority refers to the right of an individual to command his subordinates and to take action within the scope of his position. It flows from top to bottom.
>
> (b) Responsibility: Responsibility refers to the obligation of a subordinate to properly perform the assigned duty. It flows upwards.
>
> (c) Accountability: Accountability refers to answerability to the outcome of the assigned task.

Section - B

25. (c) Organising

> **Explanation:** The function of management highlighted in the above case is "Organising". Organising can be defined as "identifying and grouping different activities in the organisation and bringing together the physical, financial and human resources to establish most productive relations for the achievement of specific goal of organisation".

26. (d) Setting objectives, Developing premises, Identifying alternative course of actions, Evaluating alternative courses.

> **Explanation:** The correct sequence of steps involved in the planning process is:
>
> First step is setting objectives
>
> Second step is developing premises
>
> Third step is identifying alternatives course of actions
>
> Forth step is evaluating alternatives courses

27. (b) Interrelatedness

> **Explanation:** Interrelated different elements of business environment are closely interrelated and interdependent. A change in one element affects the other elements. Economic environment influences the non-economic environment which in turn affects the economic conditions.

28. (b) Branding

> **Explanation:** Branding is the function of marketing that facilitates product differentiation. By giving a unique name, sign or symbol to a product, branding enables a firm to distinguish its product from that of its competitors.

29. (d) Packaging

Explanation: Labelling is a concept of marketing that serves as a communication channel that helps to give proper instruction, information, and knowledge to the customer about the product.

30. (a) effective

Explanation: Effective management refers to the extent to which managers achieve their targets with the assistance of organisational resources.

31. (c) Grading of products

Explanation: The function performed by labelling is to help grading the products into different categories. Sometimes marketer assign different grades to indicate different features or quality of the product.

32. (a) Statement I is correct and II is wrong

Explanation: Statement I is correct and II is wrong because principles of management are in evaluation phase as these principles have evolved over a long period of time with continuous practice and experimentation.
Management Principles are very flexible whereas pure science principles are rigid.

33. (b) Branding

Explanation: Branding is the process of communicating a unique selling proposition, or differential, that set a product or service apart from the competition.

34. (a) (i), (iii), (ii), (iv)

Explanation: Correct sequence of Fayol's Principles of Management is
Division of work, Unity of command, Unity of direction, Stability of personnel

35. (a) Organisational structure

Explanation: The framework created by Amit within which all managerial and operating tasks are to be performed in his organisation is organisational structure.

36. (c) Principles are behaviourial

Explanation: Management Principles are formed to Guide and Influence the behaviour of employees. These Principles insist on improving relationship between Superior, Subordinates and All the Members of the Organization. They also establish relations between Human and Material Resources.

37. (c) Social objective

Explanation: The objective depicted in the given lines is social objectives. It creates the benefit for the society. Business has various social responsibilities towards different interested groups.

38. (a) Production Concept

Explanation: This concept is known as Production Concept. It assumes that availability and affordability of the product are the key to the success of a firm and puts greater emphasis on improving the production and distribution efficiency of the firms.

39. (c) Usable benefit

Explanation: Under this method, coupons are distributed among the consumers on behalf of the producer. Coupon is a kind of certificate telling that the product mentioned there, can be obtained at special discount.

40. (b) Organising

Explanation: The function of management performed by the headmistress by dividing the activities and assigning the duties is organising. She properly segregated all the activities into the tasks groups. Each group was put under the charge of one teacher in order to make the 'Annual Day' of the school a successful event.

All the task is performed by the headmistress and teachers according to the work comes under the organising.

41. (c) technological environment

Explanation: The dimension of business environment is highlighted in the above case is technological environment which includes forces relating to scientific improvements and innovations, which provide new ways of producing goods and services and new methods and techniques of operating business. A businessman must closely monitor the technological changes taking place in the industry as it helps in facing competition and improving quality of the product.

42. (c) Departmentalisation

Explanation: The process is carried out by him is known as Departmentalisation. Departmentalisation refers to the process of grouping activities into departments. Division of labour creates specialists who need coordination. This coordination is facilitated by grouping specialists together in departments.

43. (a) Statement I is correct and II is wrong

Explanation: Statement I is correct and statement II is wrong as the production concept is based on the idea that a company should make low cost products in large quantities rather than products that suit customers' particular needs while the selling concept is based on the concept that customers, be individual or organizations will not buy enough of the organization's products unless they are persuaded to do so through selling effort.

44. (d) Science not rule of thumb

Explanation: The principle of scientific management is being highlighted in the given statement is science not rule of thumb. In order to increase organisational efficiency, the 'Rule of Thumb' method should be substituted by the methods developed through scientific analysis of work. Rule of Thumb means decisions taken by manager as per their personal judgments.

45. (a) identifying alternative course of action

Explanation: The step of planning being described in the given lines is identifying alternatives courses of actions.

Identifying Alternative Courses of Action:

(i)   Once objectives are set, assumptions are made.

(ii)   Then the next step is to act upon them.

(iii) There may be many ways to act and achieve objectives.

(iv) All the alternative courses of action should be identified.

46. (a) efficient, effective

Explanation: Efficiency is doing things the right way, while effectiveness is doing the right things. Something is effective if it produces the intended result, whereas it is efficient if it functions with the least use of resources. It is possible to be effective without being efficient and vice versa.

47. (a) Labelling

Explanation: Labelling is a part of branding and enables product identification. It is printed information that is bonded to the product for recognition and provides detailed information about the product. Customers make the decision easily at the point of purchase seeing the labelling of the product.

48. (a) Both (A) and (R) are correct

> **Explanation:** However, since management deals with human beings and human behaviour, the outcomes of these experiments are not capable of being accurately predicted or replicated. Therefore, management can be called an inexact science. Management as an art and a science are therefore not mutually exclusive but complement each other.

Section – C

49. (b) Planning is a mental exercise

> **Explanation:** The feature of planning is highlighted in the above case study is planning is a mental exercise as it involves thinking and deciding in advance what is to be done, when it is to be done and how it is to be done to accomplish organisational objective.

50. (d) Planning reduces the risks of uncertainty

> **Explanation:** The importance of planning which Neeru hints at while guiding Malini is planning reduce the risk of uncertainty. Planning is always done for future and future is uncertain. Planning helps to anticipate possible changes in future and various activities are planned in the best possible way. In this way, the risk of future uncertainties can be minimised.

51. (b) Developing premises

> **Explanation:** The step of planning process taken by Malini is developing premises as it is necessary to make certain assumptions for the future and such assumptions are necessary to develop proper plan.

52. (a) Planning reduces creativity

> **Explanation:** The limitation of planning highlighted in the above case is planning reduces creativity as subordinates merely follow the plans and are not permitted to act on their own Hence, this reduces the creativity.

53. (c) It reduces the risk of uncertaintly

> **Explanation:** The importance of planning highlighted in the given lines is it reduces the risk of uncertainty.

54. (a) Planning

> **Explanation:** The concept highlighted in the given lines is planning.

55. (c) Product

> **Explanation:** Firms which follow the product concept propose that the way to realise business goal is by making products that are of high quality. These firms manufacture the products of superior quality but they must keep in mind that customers will buy the high quality only when they need or want it, only quality is not enough force.

56. (d) Marketing planning

> **Explanation:** Marketing planning is the process of improvising a marketing plan incorporating overall marketing objectives and goals and designing strategies and programs of actions to achieve those objectives. ... Companies can adopt a marketing plan to suit the situations and their requirements.

57. (b) Social environment

> **Explanation:** The social environment consists of the sum total of a society's beliefs, customs, practices and behaviours. A business also has its own social environment. It can refer to this as its internal social environment, which is simply the customs, beliefs, practices, and behaviours within the confines of the business.

58. (c) Assignment of duties

> **Explanation:** After dividing the organisation into specialised departments each individual working in different departments is assigned a duty matching to his skill and qualifications. The work is assigned according to the ability of individuals.

59. (b) Middle level

> **Explanation:** Middle level managers can include general managers, branch managers and department managers. They are accountable to the top level management for their department's function and they devote more time to organisational and directional functional than the upper management.

60. (b) ₹ 1,965

> **Explanation:** A worker making 60 units earn = 60 × 75 = ₹ 4500
> A worker making 49 units earn = 39 × 65 = ₹ 2535
> Difference between the two = ₹ 1965
> A worker making 60 units earn ₹ 1965 more as compared to a worker making 39 units

Sample Paper 2

Section - A

1. (b) Marketing concept

> **Explanation:** -"They don't sell what they can make, but they make what they can sell" this statement is related to marketing concept. It is a philosophy that encourages firms to analyses the needs of their customers and then develop products to satisfy those needs better than the competitors.

2. (a) Coordination

> **Explanation:** The process by which a manager synchronizes the activities of different departments is known as coordination.

3. (d) All of these

> **Explanation:** Planning function is conducted at all the three levels of management. Strategic planning or long-range planning is related to top management, while intermediate and short-range planning are the concern of middle and operative management respectively.

4. (b) Middle level

> **Explanation:** – Priyansh is working as a middle level manager in cello limited. He is responsible for overall working of his department. He is responsible for ensuring that his department has the necessary personnel.

5. (b) Rebate

> **Explanation:** The method of sales promotion in which Telecall mobile company is offering products at special prices, to clear off excess inventory is known as rebate.

6. (b) Divisional organisation structure

> **Explanation:** Grouping of activities on the basis of product lines is called as Divisional organizational structure. It comprises of separate business units or divisions. Each division is self-contained as it develops expertise in all functions related to a product line. However, functions may vary across divisions in accordance with a particular product line.

7. (a) Planning leads to rigidity

> **Explanation:** The limitation of planning is highlighted in the above statement is a well-defined plan is drawn up with specific goals to be achieved within a specific time frame. These plans then decide the future course of action and managers may not be in a position to change it. This kind of rigidity in plans may create difficulty.

8. (d) values

> **Explanation:** While practicing principles of management values cannot be neglected, as businesses have to fulfill social and ethical responsibilities towards the society.

9. (a) Enchancing customer satisfaction and confidence

> **Explanation:** The features of advertising identifies here is enhancing customer satisfaction and confidence.

10. (a) Selling concept

> **Explanation:** The concept of marketing management referred here is the Selling Concept. It proposes that customers, be individual or organizations will not buy enough of the organization's products unless they are persuaded to do so through selling effort.

11. (c) Social

> **Explanation:** The dimension of business environment identified here is social environment.

12. (d) Risk of uncertainty

> **Explanation:** Planning helps in reducing uncertainties of future as it involves anticipation of future events. Although future cannot be predicted with cent percent accuracy but planning helps management to anticipate future and prepare for risks by necessary provisions to meet unexpected turn of events.

13. (a) Divisional structure

> **Explanation:** The organisational structure here referred to here is divisional structure. It is an organization structure in which various departments are created on the basis of products, territory or region. Each unit has a divisional manager, who is responsible for performance and has authority over their division. Each division is further divided into functional units like production, sales, finance; etc. The divisional head is solely responsible for the profit or loss of their division.

14. (b) Pricing objective

> **Explanation:** Pricing objectives are the goals that guide the business in setting the cost of a product or service to the existing or potential consumers. Some examples of pricing objectives include maximising profits, increasing sales volume, matching competitors' prices, deterring competitors or just pure survival, thus it is not the function of the Packaging.

15. (d) Policy-making

> **Explanation:** Policy making is not an objective of management. It is in fact a process that involves the setting up of goals and objectives for the organization and the determining the ways to achieve the desired goals.

16. (c) Operational management

> **Explanation:** Foremen and supervisors comprise the lower level (operational management) in the hierarchy of the organisation. Supervisors directly oversee the efforts of the workforce. They interact with the actual work force and pass on instructions of the middle management to the workers

17. (a) Place mix

Explanation: The concept referred here is Place mix refers to all the activities required to physically move the goods from manufacturers to customers.

18. (a) Product concept

Explanation: The marketing philosophy being described here is product concept. It implies that the customer is attracted towards the product of good quality. In this case the company has added value to the product in terms of inbuilt air purifier and attractive colours to attract the customers.

19. (a) Grading

Explanation: The process of classification of products into different groups on the basis of their important characteristics refers to grading. It is the process of classification of products into different groups, on the basis of some of its important characteristics such as quality, size, etc. Grading ensures that goods belong to a particular quality and helps in realizing higher prices for high quality output.

20. (c) Delegation

Explanation: Delegation involves giving authority and responsibility to subordinates to operate within the prescribed limits.

21. (b) dynamic

Explanation: Management is a dynamic activity as it changes with the changing environment.

22. (d) All of the above

Explanation: Planning focusses on achieving goals, is pervasive and is a sort of mental exercise where lot of thinking and understanding of the current, future and past situations is needed.

23. (a) Standardisation and simplification

Explanation: The technique of Taylor which is based on his scientific principles of management, 'science not rule of thumb' is standardisation and simplification. 'science not rule of thumb principle says that we should not stuck in the set routine with the old techniques of doing work, rather we should be constantly experimenting to develop new techniques which makes the work more simpler.

24. (d) Gathering and analysing market information

Explanation: The marketing function being used by Atulya Limited is gathering and analysing market information. It is the most the important functions of a marketer to identify the needs and wants of the customers and thus to produce such products which makes the customers satisfied.

Section - B

25. (a) Top Level

Explanation: Sunder is working at the top level management. Functions performed at top level management are:

(i) Responsible for welfare and survival of the organisation.

(ii) Analyse business environment.

(iii) Formulate overall organisational goals and strategies.

(iv) Integrate diverse elements and coordinate the activities of different departments.

26. (d) Follow-up action

> **Explanation:** The concept here referred to is Follow-up action. Follow-up action is to see whether plans are being implemented and activities are being performed according to schedule. The moment there appears to be change in the assumptions on which plan is based there should be corresponding change in the plan also.

27. (b) Social environment

> **Explanation:** The dimension of environment is affected due to such direction is social environment. It includes various social forces such as customs, beliefs, literacy rate, educational levels, lifestyle, values etc. Changes in social environment affect an organization in the long run. Here government has directed all the leading companies to voluntarily participate in the Clean India Mission and asked them to make toilets in cities and villages which is included in Social Environment.

28. (a) Idea

> **Explanation:** Idea is being marketed by the famous actress Vidya Balan with a punchline 'Jaha Soch Waha Shauchalay' to promote cleanliness and hygiene in the country. Every marketer offers some idea. Social marketing comprises of creating awareness on few ideas like family planning, AIDS awareness, discouraging-smoking, child labour, domestic violence, wearing of helmet while driving, blood and eye donation etc.

29. (c) Uncertainty

> **Explanation:** The feature of business environment being described in the given case is uncertainty. The business environment is uncertain in nature so it is very difficult to predict future events.

30. (c) Political environment

> **Explanation:** The dimension of business environment highlighted in the question is political environment. Political factors usually go hand in hand with the legal ones and are generally viewed as the non-market forces. The actions were taken by the government, which potentially affect the routine activities and leads to the creation of the negative impact on business.

31. (b) Stability of personnel

> **Explanation:** Stability of personnel is the concept highlighted in the question. According to the principle of Stability of personnel the tenure of the employee should be stable so that the work continues efficiently.

32. (c) Both the statements are correct

> **Explanation:** The first step in the process of organising involves identifying and dividing the work that has to be done in accordance with previously determined plans. Work is divided into manageable tasks, so that duplication can be avoided and workload can be shared among employees.

33. (d) Societal marketing concept

> **Explanation:** The marketing management philosophy being followed by 'Beauty Product Ltd' is societal marketing concept. Joe Ltd. is a natural and ethical beauty brand famous for offering organic beauty products for men and women to satisfy its customers and also protecting the planet.

34. (b) (ii), (iv), (i),(iii)

> **Explanation:** The correct sequence of the elements of promotion is Advertising, Sales Promotion, public relation and Personal selling.

35. (a) Coordination ensures unity of action

Explanation: The characteristics of coordination that have been highlighted in the above case is coordination ensures unity of action. Coordination is the orderly arrangement of group efforts to provide unity of action in pursuit of common purpose. It involves unifying, integrating and harmonizing the activities of different departments and individuals for the achievement of common goal.

36. (c) Transportation

Explanation: The function of marketing which makes possible the availability of aluminum foil manufactured at Hyderabad but was available for sale in many states across the country is transportation.

37. (d) Gang boss

Explanation: Gang Boss work is described by this sentence under functional foremanship. Gang boss keeps everything and everyone in line. He reads and explains the blueprints, takes care of material delivery on time, and instructs on different techniques to be used for production.

38. (a) Management of work

Explanation: All organizations are set up to perform some task or goal. Management activities aim at achieving goals or tasks to be accomplished. The task or work depends upon the nature of Business for example, work to be accomplished in a school is providing education, in hospital is to treat patient, in industry to manufacture some product. Management makes sure that work is accomplished effectively and efficiently.

39. (a) Public relations

Explanation: The concept of marketing management which will help the manager to get the firm to get out of the crisis is public relations. It includes the various activities that help promote and protect the image of the company and its products and services in the eyes of the public.

40. (d) Order

Explanation: The principle of management violated here is order. According to the principle of order people and material must be in their appropriate place at appropriate time which led to wastage of time and efforts.

41. (c) Product combinations

Explanation: Sales promotion technique used by the company in the given case is Product combination. It is the unique technique of sales promotion in which a product is offered as a gift along with the main product.

42. (a) Discipline

Explanation: According to Fayol, "Discipline means sincerity, obedience, respect of authority and observance of rules and regulations of the enterprise". This principle applies that subordinate should respect their superiors and obey their order. It is an important requisite for smooth running of the enterprise.

43. (a) Statement I is correct and II is wrong

Explanation: Statement I is correct and statement II is wrong because the elements of economic environment consist of economic policies and industrial policies but the economic environment is not the part of micro environment. It is the part of macro environment.

44. (c)   Functional

> **Explanation:** The type of the organizational structure described in the case is functional structure. A functional organizational structure is one wherein the activities of a similar nature are grouped together in departments, and all departments in turn report to head.

45. (c)   Identifying alternative courses of action

> **Explanation:** The step of planning function of management highlighted here is identifying alternative courses of action. Once objectives are set and assumptions are made. Then the next step would be to act upon them. All the alternative courses of action should be identified. An innovative course may be adopted by involving more people and sharing their ideas.

46. (b)   Science, Art

> **Explanation:** Derivation of management principles can be said to be a matter of Science as in science, practical events are observed and analyzed by managerial researchers to derive management principles. The application of the principles of management remains a matter of art. The success of managers depends upon how skillfully they put these principles into practice.

47. (b)   Technological environment

> **Explanation:** The dimension of business environment affecting the local companies' revenue is the technological environment. It is a part of the company's external environment related to developments and changes in technology. In this case market is flooded with better quality toys of foreign origin as a result there is fall in revenue of the indigenous or local companies due to inferior quality products.

48. (b)   (A) is correct (R) is incorrect

> **Explanation:** (A) is correct (R) is incorrect as business environment is a relative concept since it differs from country to country and even region to region. All companies participate in the same general environment, but each company's specific environment is distinct, based on its business and industry.

Section – C

49. (a)   Planning

> **Explanation:** The function of management that has been discussed in the above case is planning Planning is deciding in advance what to do, how to do, when to do and who has to do it. Thus, it involves setting objectives and developing an appropriate course of action to achieve these objectives.

50. (b)   Planning involves huge costs

> **Explanation:** The limitation of planning that has been highlighted in the above case is planning involves huge costs

51. (a)   Planning is a primary function of management

> **Explanation:** The feature of planning is highlighted in the given case is planning is a primary function of management.

52. (c)   Planning provides direction

> **Explanation:** The Importance of planning highlighted in the above case is planning provides direction.

53. (c) Both

> **Explanation:** Planning is closely related with creativity and innovation.

54. (a) Planning focuses on achieving objectives

> **Explanation:** The feature of planning given in the above statement is planning focuses on achieving objectives.

55. (a) It helps in coping with rapid changes

> **Explanation:** The above case highlights one of the points related to the importance of business environment and its understanding by managers as it helps in coping with rapid changes.

56. (a) effective

> **Explanation:** In this case management was effective. Effective management refers to the extent to which managers achieve their targets with the assistance of organizational resources.

57. (b) Planning may not work in a dynamic environment

> **Explanation:** The above situation the limitation of planning which led to decline in it sales, is planning which may not work in a dynamic environment. If the environment is not static and keeps on changing. The organisation has to constantly adapt itself to such changes. It becomes difficult to access future trends in the environment. Hence, planning cannot foresee everything and fail to work in dynamic environment.

58. (c) Planning

> **Explanation:** The function of management involved in the above case is planning. If Rahul has to diversify the business, he needs to make proper plan based on the information he has gathered to accomplish his objectives.

59. (a) Yes because management is being recognised as a profession to a great extent

> **Explanation:** Management is a well-defined body of knowledge. It is considered as a profession, skills, special knowledge, as well as the act of coordination and administration which eventually will help Kapoor son's to be a good businessman.

60. (b) Dynamic nature

> **Explanation:** The feature of business environment which has influenced the business of 'Seven Stars' is business environment is of dynamic nature. Business environment keeps on changing and such changes could be triggered by internal or external factors and it can affect the growth and even the survival of business.

Sample Paper 3

Section - A

1. (b) Initiative

> **Explanation:** 1.The principle of management discussed here is initiative. Initiative means Workers should be encouraged to develop and execute their plan for achieving the organisational objectives.

2. (c) Packaging

> **Explanation:** The process of creating and producing package for a product is known as Packaging. Packing is used to enclose or protect the products from damage and facilitates distribution, storage. It is also used to differentiate the product from other.

3. (b) Efficient

> **Explanation:** Efficiency involves cost-benefit analysis and the relationship between inputs and outputs. It is about making the best possible use of resources. Efficient firms maximise outputs from given inputs, at minimum costs.

4. (b) Age of an organisation

> **Explanation:** Factors is not relevant in price fixation is age of an organisation.

5. (d) Options (b) and (c)

> **Explanation:** The factors that Mary consider to determine the price of his book are demand for the book in the market and price of other competitive books.

6. (c) Decentralisation

> **Explanation:** Decentralisation is not a part of organising process. The process of organizing consists of following steps-Identification and division of work, grouping the jobs and departmentalisation, assignment of duties, establishing reporting relationship.

7. (a) Mental Exercise

> **Explanation:** The feature of planning is highlighted here as planning is a 'mental exercise' because it requires application of the mind involving foresight, intelligent imagination and sound judgement.

8. (b) Disadvantages

> **Explanation:** One of the disadvantages of planning is planning involves lot of cost because it is an intellectual process and companies need to hire the professional experts to carry on this process and Planning is also a time consuming process as lot of time is needed in developing planning premises.

9. (b) Planning is continuous

> **Explanation:** The feature of planning highlighted here is Planning is a never ending or continuous process because even after making plans managers has to be in touch with the changes in dynamic environment and modify the plan accordingly.

10. (a) Price

> **Explanation:** The component of marketing mix used here is price. Price is the monetary value paid in consideration for purchase of a product or service by a buyer.

11. (b) Place

> **Explanation:** The component of marketing mix highlighted here is place or physical distribution. It includes all the activities and decisions related to physical distribution of goods and services so that firms' products are available to the target customers.

12. (b) Responsibility

> **Explanation:** Properly perform the assigned duty, is known as responsibility.

13. (b) Management as an Art

> **Explanation:** The aspect of nature of management highlighted here is management as an art. Like an art, management is a personalised and skilful application of existing knowledge to achieve desired results.

14. (c) Promotion

> **Explanation:** The component of marketing mix highlighted in the above statement is promotion. It is a marketing tool, used as a strategy to communicate between the sellers and buyers. Through this, the seller tries to influence and convince the buyers to buy their products or services.

15. (a) Advertising

> **Explanation:** Advertisement is a tool having mass reach. It is a visual or audio way to communicate with the masses through all forms of media. Advertising is promoting a company, brand, product or a service through social media, television, radio, magazines, or even websites.

16. (c) Operational level of management

> **Explanation:** Foreman and supervisors comprise of Supervisory / Lower / Operational level management. It operates between middle-level management and operative workforce.

17. (b) Organising

> **Explanation:**Organising is process that initiates the implementation of plans by clarifying jobs and working relationships and effectively deploying resources for attainment of identified and desired goals.

18. (b) Providing managers with useful insights into reality

> **Explanation:** The principles of management provide the managers with useful insights into real life situations. The principles add manager's knowledge, ability and understanding of managerial situations and circumstances as he deals with exceptional circumstances by focusing on strategic activities and leaving daily tasks to subordinates which helps them to solve problems quickly and increase managerial efficiency.

19. (d) All of these

> **Explanation:** Business environment consists of both general and specific forces. General forces such as economic, social, political, legal, natural and technological conditions influence all business enterprises. Specific forces such as investors, customers, competitors, suppliers, etc.

20. (a) Functional structure

> **Explanation:** An organisational design that groups similar or related jobs together on the basis of function is known as functional organizational structure. It is a structure used to organize workers. They are grouped based on their specific skills and knowledge.

21. (c) Decentralisation

> **Explanation:** Decentralisation are related to delegation of authority. It is the organizational process of a manager dividing their own work among all their subordinates.

22. (b) Controlling

> **Explanation:** Controlling is concerned with monitoring organisational performance towards the attainment of organisational goals. The controlling function helps in measuring the progress towards the organizational goals to brings any deviations, and ensure corrective action.

23. (b) Organising

> **Explanation:** The function of management which establishes relation between authority and responsibility is organising. It involves assigning duties, setting up authorities and allocating resources to execute a plan. It groups the tasks into manageable work units. Thus, it establishes the authority/responsibility relationship.

24. (b) Science not Rule of Thumb

> **Explanation:** Principle of management emphasize in the given situation is Science not Rule of Thumb. In order to increase organisational efficiency, the 'Rule of Thumb' method should be substituted by the methods developed through scientific analysis of work. Rule of Thumb means decisions taken by manager as per their personal judgments. According to Taylor, even a small production activity like loading iron sheets into box cars can be scientifically planned. This will help in saving time as well as human energy. Decisions should be based on scientific enquiry with cause and effect relationships.

Section – B

25. (c) Societal concept

> **Explanation:** The marketing philosophy highlighted here is societal concept. It is the new concept of marketing which aims at satisfying customer needs with taking proper care of society and environment.

26. (d) Follow-up action

> **Explanation:** Follow-up action is the step in the planning process to see whether plans are being implemented and activities are being performed according to schedule. The managers need to carefully check that the premises are holding true in the existing conditions.

27. (a) Place

> **Explanation:** 'Visit Kerala for Health Tourism is the marketing of place'.

28. (c) Centralisation and Decentralisation

> **Explanation:** The principle of Fayol that has been violated by Ramesh here is 'centralisation and decentralisation'. This principle explains the need of balance between centralisation and decentralisation. He is making all the decisions on his own and he is not giving any decision making authority to his subordinates so he is not following this principle.

29. (c) Place

> **Explanation:** The variable highlighted in the case is place. It refers to the distribution or the methods and location for the products or services to be easily accessible to the target customers.

30. (c) production

> **Explanation:** Large scale production done to reduce the average cost of production is the production concept of marketing management. Large scale production helps to achieve the economies of scale.

31. (b) Product concept

> **Explanation:** Nisha adopted the product concept. With the increase in the supply of goods, customers started looking for products which are of high quality. Thus, the firm in this case emphasises on quality and extra features in the product.

32. (c) Both the statements are correct

> **Explanation:** Both the statements are correct because marketing helps to find the needs and wants of the customers and see how those needs can be fulfilled.
>
> On the other hand marketing is one of the most important activity of the organisation as it helps to generate revenue for the organisation.

33. (a) Organisational structure

> **Explanation:** The framework created by Amit within which all managerial and operating tasks are to be performed in his organisation is organisational structure.

34. (b) (i), (iii), (ii), (iv)

> **Explanation:** The correct sequence of the Henry Fayol's principle of management are Division of work, Unity of command, Unity of direction and Scalar chain.

35. (c) Social and Technological environment

> **Explanation:** The dimensions of the business environment discussed in the above case are social environment and technological environment. The social environment of business includes the social forces like customs, habits and traditions, values, social trends, society's expectations from business, etc. Technological environment includes forces relating to scientific improvements and innovations which provide new ways of producing goods and services and new methods and techniques of operating a business.

36. (d) Pervasive

> **Explanation:** The feature of planning in being referred to in the above statement is planning is pervasive because planning is done by all the managers, working in all departments of an enterprise.

37. (a) Benefits of specialisation

> **Explanation:** The importance of organising is highlighted here is benefits of specialisation It helps in increasing coordination among the various activities of the business as the closely related activities are grouped under the same department. This reduces the work load as well as enhances productivity because of the specific workers performing a specific job on regular basis. By doing a job on regular basis, a worker gets experience in that area and leads to specialisation.

38. (c) Promotion and selling

> **Explanation:** The activities which are undertaken to communicate with the customer and increase the sale is known as promotion and selling.

39. (b) Decision-Making

> **Explanation:** The feature of planning is being highlighted here is decision making It is the process of making choices by identifying a decision, gathering information, and assessing alternative resolutions.

40. (b) Production concept

> **Explanation:** The marketing philosophy being adopted by the company is production concept. It holds that consumers will prefer products that are widely available and inexpensive.

41. (b) an art

> **Explanation:** The given statement indicates that management is an art. A manager applies various theories of management in his unique personalised way by using art of management.

42. (b) Social

> **Explanation:** Dimension of the business environment is discussed here is social environment. The plastic items are creating many environmental problems which affect the lives of people and society in general is more concerned about quality of life.

43. (c) Both the statements are correct

> **Explanation:** Both the statements are correct as the management principles are not exact it can be modifies as per the situation and management principles enhances the understanding of relationship between human and material resource for the achievement of organisational goals.

44. (a) Social

> **Explanation:** The objective depicted in the given lines is social objectives. It creates the benefit for the society. Business has various social responsibilities towards different interested groups.

45. (c) Follow up action

> **Explanation:** The step of planning process highlighted here is follow-up action It refers to the process of monitoring the plans, whether they are implemented properly or not.

46. (a) Authority, Responsibility

> **Explanation:** According to Henri Fayol, "Authority is the right to give orders and the power to exact obedience." Responsibility is the obligation of a subordinate to perform a duty, which has been assigned to him by his superior. Responsibility comes after authority.

47. (d) Help to identify opportunity and getting first mover advantage

> **Explanation:** The importance of business environment is highlighted in the given case is it help to identify opportunity and getting first mover advantage. The ability to identifying the external opportunities early and to make the first move, makes an organisation the market leader.

48. (a) Both (A) and (R) are true and (R) is the correct explanation of (A)

> **Explanation:** Every organisation has a pre-determined goals. Goals need to be explicitly mentioned. By setting clear, realistic goals, organizations have a clearer path to achieve success and realize its vision. Goal setting, and attaining them, can also help an organization achieve increased efficiency, productivity and profitability.

Section – C

49. (c) Organising

> **Explanation:** The function of management performed by Skin Care is organising. It is the process of identifying and grouping the work to be performed, defining and delegating responsibility and authority, and establishing relationships for the purpose of enabling people to work most effectively together in accomplishing objectives.

50. (a) Decenteralisation

> **Explanation:** The concept of management used by Skin Care is decentralisation is referred to as a form of an organisational structure where there is the delegation of authority by the top management to the middle and lower levels of management in an organisation. In this type of organisation structure, the duty of daily operations and minor decision-making capabilities are transferred to the middle and lower levels which allow top-level management to focus more on major decisions like business expansion, diversification etc.

51. (b) Accountability

Explanation: The element of directing is being highlighted here is accountability. It implies 'being answerable for the final outcome of the assigned task'. Accountability flows upwards, *i.e.* a subordinate will be accountable to his superior for satisfactory performance of the assigned work.

52. (c) Planning is primary function of management

Explanation: The feature of planning from above statement is planning is primary function of management. Planning is the basis for all other functions of management.

53. (d) It involves decision making

Explanation: The feature highlighted in the above statement is decision making. The need of planning arises because of the availability of various alternatives to achieve specified objectives. It evaluates the best alternative. Decision-making is an integral part of planning. A manager is surrounded by number of alternatives. He has to pick the best depending upon requirements and resources of the enterprises.

54. (a) Authority

Explanation: The element of directing is being highlighted here is authority. It refers to the right of an individual to command his subordinates and to take action within the scope of his position. It flows from top to bottom of the scalar chain. The superior has authority over the subordinates. It is highest at the top management. However, it reduces as we move downward in the corporate hierarchy.

55. (b) Authority and responsibility

Explanation: The relevant principle associated in the given case is authority and responsibility. According to Henri Fayol, "Authority is the right to give orders." Responsibility is the obligation of a subordinate to perform a duty, which has been assigned to him by his superior. responsibility comes after authority.

56. (d) Unity of command

Explanation: The principle of Unity of Command is violated in this case. The principle states that a worker should take orders from only one manager and should be answerable to him only. In this case the salesman is getting two different orders from two managers which makes him confused and does not allow him to come to a decision.

57. (d) All of these

Explanation: The plan failed and company suffered a huge loss because planning is time consuming and a costly process. It is not suitable for the dynamic business environment.

58. (d) Identifying alternatives

Explanation: The step of the planning process has been performed by Ms. Rajni is identifying the various courses of action. She did a detailed study of the various options and now the company will choose the best alternative which is profitable, feasible and with the least negative consequences.

59. (a) Personal objectives

Explanation: The objective being fulfilled by the GMIR Internationals Ltd are Organisational objectives which strives to achieve multiple organisational objectives, mainly survival, growth and Profit

Personal objectives which are relate to the needs of the employees of the organization which must be given due consideration. In this case

the employees of the company are happy and satisfied with their remuneration, working conditions, promotion policy etc.

Social objectives states that every organization should undertake certain initiatives for the welfare of the society at large. As a part of its moral obligation, the company has taken many initiatives for providing employment to especially abled persons and promoting literacy in the villages adopted by it.

60. (b) Divisional structure

Explanation: The framework which the diversified organisation should adopt to enable it to cope with the emerging complexity is divisional structure. When the organisation is a large organisation and is producing more than one product, then the activities related to one product are grouped together or clubbed under one department.

Sample Paper 4

Section – A

1. (c) Management is all pervasive

Explanation: The activities involved in managing an enterprise are common to all organisations whether economic, social or political.

2. (c) effectiveness

Explanation: Effectiveness refers to complete the task within the time.

3. (a) Standardisation

Explanation: Standardisation ensures that goods or services produced in a specific industry come with consistent quality and a equivalent to other comparable products or services in the same industry.

4. (a) Functional foremanship

Explanation: Taylor advocated separation of planning and execution functions. This concept was extended to the lowest level of the shop floor. It was known as functional foremanship.

5. (c) Functional structure

Explanation: A functional structure leads to occupational specialisation since emphasis is placed on specific functions.

6. (c) Development of personnel

Explanation: Organising enables managers to delegate authority to their subordinates. It develops the ability to deal challenges effectively and help them to realise their full potential.

7. (b) Planning is futuristic

Explanation: Planning essentially involves looking ahead and preparing for the future. The purpose of planning is to meet future events effectively to the best advantage of an organisation.

8. (a) labelling

Explanation: It refers to the process of preparing labels for the product. It describes the product and specifies its content.

9. (b) Equity

   Explanation: Principle of equity states that there should be no discrimination against anyone on account of sex, religion, language, caste, belief or nationality etc.

10. (b) Order

    Explanation: According to Fayol, "People and materials must be in suitable places at appropriate time for maximum efficiency." The principle of order states that 'A right person should be placed at the right job and a right thing should be placed at the right place.

11. (d) Management creates dynamic organisation

    Explanation: The importance of management highlighted in the question is management creates dynamic organisation as it includes goals, objectives and other activities which keeps on changing according to the changes taking place in the business environment.

12. (c) trademark

    Explanation: Trademark provides protection to the product of a particular business firm from other firms against its usage.

13. (d) Usable benefit

    Explanation: When seller gives some usable product along with the main product. It means that if a customer has a coupon of some product he will get the discount mentioned therein whenever he buys it, are known as usable benefit.

14. (a) Equity

    Explanation: Principle of equity states that there should be no discrimination against anyone on account of sex, religion, language, caste, belief or nationality etc.

15. (b) Planning is a mental exercise.

    Explanation: Planning is a mental exercise and is not a benefit of planning. This is because it is a feature of planning.

16. (b) Developing premises

    Explanation: Development of premises is a logical and systematic estimate of the future factors that can affect planning.

17. (b) Organising

    Explanation: Organising is the process of identifying and grouping the work to be performed, defining and delegating responsibility and authority, and establishing relationships for the purpose of enabling people to work most effectively together in accomplishing objectives.

18. (d) Product combination or free products

    Explanation: The technique of sales promotion used by the company in the above case is product combination or free product which means offering another product or gift along with the purchase of a main product.

19. (b) Economic environment

    Explanation: The dimension of business environment, highlighted in the question is economic environment which includes economic forces like economic policies, economic system, economic conditions, economic development, etc.

20. (b) Product Mix

Explanation: Product mix also known as product assortment or product portfolio, refers to the complete set of products or services offered by the firm. A product mix consists of product lines, which are associated items that consumers tend to use together or think of as similar product or services.

21. (c) Supervisory

Explanation: Operational management refers to the bottom level in the management hierarchy of the organization. It consists of Supervisors and Foreman. Supervisory management is the act of over seeing teams of employees and guiding daily operations in a business.

22. (a) Full finance @ 0%

Explanation: Zero percent financing means that a borrower can finance a car without paying any interest charges on the loan.

23. (d) Planning involves decision-making

Explanation: The feature of planning, depicted in the question is planning involves through examination and evaluation of each alternative and choosing the most appropriate one.

24. (c) Inter-relatedness

Explanation: The feature of business environment, highlighted in question is different elements or parts of business environment is closely inter-related.

Section - B

25. (b) Customers and Technological forces

Explanation: Specific forces affect the individual enterprises directly and general forces affect all business of the industry as a whole.

26. (c) Evaluating Alternative Courses

Explanation: The next step or planning is evaluating alternative courses is to weigh the pros and cons of each alternative. Each course will have many variables which have to be weighed against each other. Alternatives are evaluated in the light of their feasibility and consequences.

27. (a) Planning focuses on achieving objectives

Explanation: The features of planning, depicted in the question is planning focuses on achieving objective which include specific goals that are set out in the plans along with the activities to be undertaken to achieve the goals.

28. (a) Production concept

Explanation: Production concept focuses on production at large scale. Profit can be earned maximum by producing mass production as it reduces the cost.

29. (a) Development of each and every person to his or her greatest efficiency and prosperity

> **Explanation:** Taylor's scientific principle of management is followed in the question according to the concept development of each and every person to his or her greatest efficiency and prosperity which assure that the training is given to the right employee, the right steps should be taken at the time of selection and recruiting candidates based on a scientific selection.

30. (a) Economic environment

> **Explanation:** The economic environment comprises of the components such as interest rate, changes in disposable income, economic factors, volume of imports and exports etc.

31. (d) Planning is a mental exercise

> **Explanation:** The feature of planning depicted in the question is planning is a mental exercise. It requires application of the mind involving foresight, intelligent imagination and sound judgement. It is basically an intellectual activity of thinking rather than doing.

32. (b) Statement II is correct and I is wrong

> **Explanation:** Statement I is correct and II is wrong because branding is the process of communicating a unique selling proposition, or differential, that set a product or service apart from the competition. It includes the use of logos, taglines, Jingles or mascots.

33. (a) Top level

> **Explanation:** The level of management at which Ashutosh Goenka was working is top level, because he has responsibility for controlling and overseeing the entire organisation.

34. (a) (ii); (iv); (iii); (i)

> **Explanation:** The correct sequence of elements of marketing mix are: product, price, place and promotion.

35. (d) Product

> **Explanation:** Product is anything that is offered to sale. It includes both goods as well as services.

36. (b) Planning may not work in a dynamic environment.

> **Explanation:** The business environment is dynamic, nothing is constant. Plans are drawn on premises, and these premises may change as per the changes in the environment. Hence, planning may not work in dynamic environment.

37. (a) Relativity

> **Explanation:** The feature of business environment highlighted in the above question is relativity whose impact differs from country to country, region to region and firm to firm. Business environment is dynamic as it keeps changing as shift in consumer preference.

38. (c) penetrating pricing

> **Explanation:** The strategy discussed in the question is known as penetrating pricing when seller charge low prices in the initial stages to capture the market share.

39. (c) Espirit de Corps

> **Explanation:** According to Fayol Management should promote a team spirit of unity and harmony among employees. Management should promote teamwork especially in large organisations.

40. (a) Product designing and development

> **Explanation:** The marketing function being explained in the question is product designing and development which includes the process of imaging, creating and iterating products that solve users problems or address specific needs in a given market. The key to successful product design is understanding the end user customer, the person for whom the product is being created.

41. (a) coordination

> **Explanation:** Coordination is the essence of management. It is the force that binds all other functions of management.

42. (a) Dynamic function

> **Explanation:** The highlighted characteristics in the question is Management is a dynamic function and has to adapt itself to the changing environment.

43. (a) Statement I is correct and II is wrong

> **Explanation:** Statement I is correct and statement II is wrong because there should be complete cooperation between the labour and the management instead of individualism. This principle is an extension of principle of 'Harmony not discord'.

44. (c) It helps in improving performance

> **Explanation:** When Nokia lost its market share, microsoft absorbed it, which helps the organisation in dealing with these changes in an appropriate manner.

45. (a) Authority and Responsibility

> **Explanation:** The step of principle of management is highlighted in the question is authority and responsibility. Authority refers to the right of an individual to command his subordinates and to take action within the scope of his position. Responsibility is the obligation of a subordinate to properly perform the assigned duty.

46. (a) Labelling

> **Explanation:** The concept of marketing discussed in the above question is labelling. Which helps to provide information about a product to the customers and give them knowledge about the product. It is also an effective way of branding the product to the customer. The label design should be such that it gives out the necessary information to the user so that it knows what the supplier has provided and how to handle the item.

47. (d) Personal selling

> **Explanation:** The elements of promotion mix is personal selling which is used by Britanica. It is a personal form of promotion. It involves oral presentation of messages.

48. (a) Both A and R are true and R is the correct explanation of A

> **Explanation:** The activities associated with managing a firm are Familiar to all companies.

Section - C

49. (b) Organising

> **Explanation:** Organising is the process of identifying and grouping the work to be performed, defining and delegating responsibility and authority, and establishing relationships for the purpose of enabling people to work most effectively together in accomplishing objectives.

50. (b) Delegation

> **Explanation:** Delegation of authority merely means the granting of authority to subordinates to operate within prescribed limits.

51. (b) Division of work

> **Explanation:** The concept of principle of management identified in point is division of work. It is the course of task assigned to and completed by, a group of workers in order to increase efficiency.

52. (a) The manager

> **Explanation:** Manager will be accountable because accountability cannot be delegated.

53. (d) All of the above

> **Explanation:** Organising is the process of defining and grouping the activities of the enterprise and establishing authority relationships among them.

54. (b) Organisational structure

> **Explanation:** Organisational structure is the Framework within which managerial and operating tasks are performed.

55. (a) Coordination

> **Explanation:** The concept which was required by the CEO Mr. Raman, to reconcile the differences in approach, interest or opinion in the organisation is coordination. It is the essence of management and the force that binds all other functions of management.

56. (b) Legal environment

> **Explanation:** The dimension of business environment highighted in the above question is legal environment which includes any order or judgement passed by the Court related to the decisions of business environment.

57. (c) Relativity

> **Explanation:** The feature of business environment highlighted in the question is relativity as business environment is a relative concept it differs from country to country and region to region.

58. (b) Developing premises

> **Explanation:** The manager is required to make certain assumptions about the future. Assumptions are the base material upon which plans are to be drawn.

59. (c) Decentralisation

> **Explanation:** The concept which is used by Sumit Rathore is decentralisation. It is the process by which the activities of an organisation, particularly those regarding planning and decision making are distributed or delegated away from a central, authoritative location or group.

60. (a) Yes

> **Explanation:** Yes, because according to the principle of absolute responsibility, authority can be delegated but responsibility and accountability cannot be delegated by a manager. The manager is responsible or accountable to his own superior for both, the tasks that he has assigned to his subordinates and the acts of his subordinates.

Sample Paper 5

Section – A

1. (b) Technological environment

> **Explanation:** Any changes taking place in the method of production, use of new equipment and machineries to improve, the quality of product comes under technological environment.

2. (c) promotion

> **Explanation:** Any activity done with the aim of pursuading buyer to purchase the product is called promotion.

3. (d) management

> **Explanation:** Management is the process of planning, organising, staffing, directing and controlling of the resources with the aim to achieve organisational objectives.

4. (a) Planning reduces creativity

> **Explanation:** Planning is an activity which is done by the top management. Usually the rest of the members just implements these plans.

5. (b) Inter-relatedness

> **Explanation:** Different elements or parts of business environment is closely inter-related.

6. (a) Advertising

> **Explanation:** 6.It is an impersonal form of communication, which is paid for by the marketers (sponsors) to promote some goods or service. The most common modes of advertising are 'newspapers', 'magazines', 'television', and 'radio'.
> The activities involved in managing an enterprise are common to all organisations whether economic, social or political.

7. (a) Planning

> **Explanation:** The function of management highlighted in the given statement is planning. Planning is looking ahead, as it is based on forecasting and is prepared for the future. It is a futuristic process. The purpose of planning is to meet future events effectively to the best advantage of an organisation

8. (b) social

   Explanation: Social environment includes the social forces like, customs and traditions, social trends, Society's expectations from business and Values.

9. (a) Principle of Equity

   Explanation: Principle of equity states that there should be no discrimination against anyone on account of sex, religion, language, caste, belief or nationality etc.

10. (c) Social environment

    Explanation: Social environment includes the social forces like, customs and traditions, social trends, Society's expectations from business and Values.

11. (b) Legal environment

    Explanation: Any order or judgement passed by the Court related to the decisions of business environment comes under Legal environment.

12. (a) essence

    Explanation: Coordination is the essence of management. It is the force that binds all other functions of management.

13. (b) Legal environment

    Explanation: Any order or judgement passed by the Court related to the decisions of business environment comes under Legal environment.

14. (a) Organisational objective

    Explanation: Management is responsible for setting and achieving objectives for the organisation. It has to achieve a variety of objectives in all areas considering the interest of all stakeholders. It includes profit, survival and growth.

15. (b) Functional Foremanship

    Explanation: It is a technique of scientific management.

16. (b) Planning may not work in a dynamic environment.

    Explanation: The business environment is not static, it keeps on changing. The organisation has to constantly adapt itself to such changes. It becomes difficult to access future trends in the environment. Hence, planning cannot foresee everything and fail to work in dynamic environment.

17. (d) marketing

    Explanation: In marketing concept the main focus is on consumer. So, first need is identified and then according to this need product is made.

18. (b) Divisional structure

    Explanation: In a divisional structure, the organisation structure comprises of separate business units or divisions.

19. (c) Implementation of plan

    Explanation: The next step Kapil should follow is Implementation of plan. Implementation is the process that turns strategies and plans into actions in order to accomplish strategic objectives and goals

20. (d) All of the these

> **Explanation:** All of these are the part of micro environment of business. It is a collection of forces or factors that are close to the organization and can influence the performance as well as the day to day activities of the firm.

21. (d) planning

> **Explanation:** It is one of the basic managerial functions. Before doing something, the manager must formulate an idea of how to work on a particular task.

22. (c) Setting objectives, Developing premises, Identifying alternative course of actions, Evaluating alternative courses

> **Explanation:** The steps taken by the business organization in the planning process are setting objectives, Developing premises, Identifying alternative course of actions, Evaluating alternative courses.

23. (a) Standardisation

> **Explanation:** Standardisation refers to the process of setting standards for every business activity.

24. (d) Management is a continuous process

> **Explanation:** The process of management is a series of continuous, composite, but separate functions (planning, organising, directing, staffing and controlling). These functions are simultaneously performed by all managers all the time.

Section - B

25. (b) Uncertainty

> **Explanation:** Business environment is uncertain as it is difficult to predict future events.

26. (b) Identify alternative courses of action

> **Explanation:** Planning involves thorough examination and evaluation of each alternative and choosing the most appropriate one.

27. (b) extends throughout the organisation.

> **Explanation:** Pervasiveness of planning indicates that planning is required at all levels of management as well as in all departments of the organisation.

28. (c) Societal marketing concept

> **Explanation:** The societal marketing concept is the extension of the marketing concept as supplemented by the concern for the long-term welfare of the society. Apart from the customer satisfaction, it pays attention to the social, ethical and ecological aspects of marketing.

29. (b) Dynamic nature

> **Explanation:** Business environment is dynamic as it keeps changing as shift in consumer preference.

30. (b) planning is pervasive

> **Explanation:** Planning is required at all levels of management as well as in all departments of the organisation.

31. (c) Management is all pervasive

> **Explanation:** The activities involved in managing an enterprise are common to all organisations whether economic, social or political.

32. (b) Statement II is correct and I is wrong

> **Explanation:** Appropriate packaging contributes to the convenience in handling the product whereas used and discarded packaging does not contributes to the consumer protection problem.

33. (c) Uncertainty

> **Explanation:** Business environment is uncertain as it is difficult to predict future events.

34. (a) (i), (ii), (iii), (iv)

> **Explanation:** Production concept, Product concept, selling concept and Marketing concept is the correct sequence of the marketing management philosophies.

35. (b) Planning is a mental exercise

> **Explanation:** The feature of planning which is highlighted here is planning is a mental exercise. Planning is called a mental exercise in management because it involves application of high order thinking skills and intellectual faculties, involving vision and foresightedness to decide the things to be done in the future.

36. (a) Product concept

> **Explanation:** The emphasis of the firms shifted from quantity of production to quality of products. The focus of business activity changed to bringing continuous improvement in the quality, incorporating new features etc.

37. (a) Functional structure

> **Explanation:** A functional straucture leads to occupational specialisation since emphasis is placed on specific functions.

38. (b) Restricted entry

> **Explanation:** The entry in a profession is restricted through an examination or through acquiring special knowledge.

39. (a) Planning reduces creativity

> **Explanation:** Planning reduce creativity, as all plans are drawn by the top managers. Subordinates in the organisation is bound to follow these plans made at top level.

40. (a) Functional structure

> **Explanation:** A functional straucture leads to occupational specialisation since emphasis is placed on specific functions viz. production, finance, marketing, etc.

41. (b) Planning may not work in dynamic environment

> **Explanation:** One of the limitation of management highlighted in the above case is planning may not work in dynamic environment. It becomes difficult to access future trends in the environment. Hence, planning cannot foresee everything and fail to work in dynamic environment as a result Bawa Cycle was not able to achieve its target.

42. (b) Production

> **Explanation:** Production concept focuses on production at large scale. Profit can be earned maximum by producing mass production as it reduces the cost.

43. (c) Both the statements are correct

> **Explanation:** Planning reduces overlapping and wasteful activities as it serves as the basis for coordinating the activities and efforts of different divisions and individuals and is pervasive as it is required at all the levels of management but its scope may vary.

44. (a) Functional Structure

> **Explanation:** A functional straucture leads to occupational specialisation since emphasis is placed on specific functions viz. production, finance, marketing, etc.

45. (a) Rebate

> **Explanation:** When seller offers products at special prices, to clear off excess inventory, it is called rebate.

46. (c) organising , decentralised

> **Explanation:** Everything which goes to increase the importance of subordinates, called decentralisation.

47. (c) Principle of contingent

> **Explanation:** A contingency theory is an organizational theory that claims that there is no best way to organize a corporation, to lead a company, or to make decisions. Instead, the optimal course of action is contingent (dependent) upon the internal and external situation.

48. (b) (A) is correct (R) is incorrect

> **Explanation:** Organising is the process of identifying and grouping the work to be performed, defining and delegating responsibility and authority, and establishing relationships for the purpose of enabling people to work most effectively together in accomplishing objectives.

Section - C

49. (b) trademark

> **Explanation:** Trademark provides protection to the product of a particular business firm from other firms against its usage.

50. (a) Marketing methods used

> **Explanation:** Here promotion of product is used by different promotional tools such as providing free home delivery.

51. (b) Regarding the channels or using intermediaties

> **Explanation:** They want that their product must reachable to mass. So they use different distribution techniques.

52. (d) Any of the above

> **Explanation:** The department in the organisation which is generally responsible for performing the important task of managing public opinion are the Marketing department, a separate department created in the firm for the purpose and an outside agency.

53. (a) Societal marketing concept

> **Explanation:** The societal marketing concept is the extension of the marketing concept as supplemented by the concern for the long-term welfare of the society. Apart from the customer satisfaction, it pays attention to the social, ethical and ecological aspects of marketing.

54. (c) Physical distribution

> **Explanation:** Once goods are manufactured, packaged, branded, priced, and promoted, these must be made available to customers at the right place, in right quantity and at the right time.

55. (a) Coordination

> **Explanation:** Coordination is the essence of management. It is the force that binds all other functions of management.

56. (a) Setting objecitves

> **Explanation:** The first and foremost step is setting objectives. Every organisation must have certain objectives. Objectives may be set for the entire organisation and each department or unit within the organisation.

57. (a) Setting objectives

> **Explanation:** The first and foremost step is setting objectives. Every organisation must have certain objectives. Objectives may be set for the entire organisation and each department or unit within the organisation.

58. (d) Identifying alternative courses of action

> **Explanation:** Planning involves thorough examination and evaluation of each alternative and choosing the most appropriate one.

59. (c) Technological dimension

> **Explanation:** The dimension of business environment highlighted in the given case is technological environment. It involves the primary forces that are responsible for the improvement in the scientific field and new innovations being introduced in the market for improving the quality of goods and services and techniques for operating business more efficiently.

60. (c) Subordination of individual interest to general interest

> **Explanation:** The interests of an organisation should take priority over the interests of any one individual employee according to Fayol.

Sample Paper 6

Section - A

1. (a) Planning

> **Explanation:** Growth, Survival and Profit are organisational objectives.

2. (c) human betterment & social justice

> **Explanation:** In planning, the best alternative is chosen among available alternatives.

3. (c) marketing concept

> **Explanation:** Marketing concept focuses on the demands and needs of the customer

4. (b) Effectiveness

> **Explanation:** Effectiveness is concerned with doing the right tasks and achieving goals within the prescribed time.

5. (a) One head one plan

Explanation: According to Principle of Unity of Direction, all the team members should share the same objectives in order to work toward common results, using one plan.

6. (a) Physical distribution

Explanation: Physical distribution is the set of activities concerned with efficient movement of finished goods from the end of the production operation to the consumer.

7. (c) Management is pervasive

Explanation: Management is required in all type of organisations whether it is big or small, public or private.

8. (a) People, work & resources

Explanation: Product promotion, Product identification and Product protection are the essential function of packaging because the fundamentals function of packaging is that it protects the product from damage. With the help of packaging the product can be easily identified. Packaging plays a role of silent salesman because it promotes or enhances the sale of the product.

9. (d) All of the above

Explanation: Organisation is successful when it utilises people, work and resources.

10. (a) Social objective

Explanation: It is trying to fulfill its objectives of social responsibility. Every firm has a social responsibility to work for the welfare of the society along with the objective of profit maximization. By offering job to the physically challenged persons it is helping the society.

11. (a) Functional Structure

Explanation: Functional structure is one of the most common organisational structures. Under this structure, the organisation groups, employees according to a specialised or similar set of roles of tasks.

12. (d) Leads to rigidity

Explanation: Leads to rigidity is not a benefit of planning. It is a limitation of planning.

13. (d) Promotion

Explanation: Discount is being given to promote the sales.

14. (b) Promotion

Explanation: The promotion element of marketing mix is concerned with activities that are undertaken to communicate with customers and distribution channels to enhance the sales of the firm.

15. (d) It includes both tangible and intangible attributes

Explanation: It does not include both tangible and intangible attributes because product is tangible and services are intangible.

16. (b) Planning establishes standards for controlling

Explanation: Planning establishes the standards which the manufacturer or manager tries to maintain with the help of controlling function by comparing actual with planned performance.

17. (c) Packaging

Explanation: Packaging is a set of tasks or activities which are concerned with the designing, production of an appropriate wrapper, container or bag for the product.

18. (c) Both (a) and (b)

Explanation: Prime Minister of India has announced indicate (Political Environment) an economic relief package indicate (Economic Environment)

19. (a) applicable only in large firms

Explanation: Principles of Management can be applied in each and every firm.

20. (c) Increase

Explanation: Span of Management means number of subordinates under one manager. So as there is increase in span of management there will increase in levels

21. (a) Public relation

Explanation: Public Relation is referred to as strategic communication process that helps in building mutually beneficial relationships between organisations and their publics.

22. (a) Divisional structure

Explanation: The divisional structure is a type of organisational structure that groups each organisational function into a division. These divisions can be based on different products or geographies

23. (b) Legal environment

Explanation: Administrative orders and legislations comes under the Legal Environment

24. (d) Equity

Explanation: According to Principle of Equity, while dealing with people there should not be any discrimination on the basis of caste, religion or gender etc.

Section - B

25. (a) Interrelatedness

Explanation: Different elements of business environment are closely interrelated and interdependent. A change in one element affects the other elements

26. (d) Selection of best alternative

Explanation: Selection of best alternative is considered the "real point of decision making" because it is a combination of plans which appears to be most feasible.

27. (a) Brand Name

Explanation: That part of a brand, which can be spoken is called a brand name. In other words, brand name is the verbal component of a brand. For example: Asian Paints, Safola, Maggie, etc.

28. (d) Technological environment

Explanation: Due to new technology, Syska was able to produce an energy efficient light bulb that lasts at least ten times as long as a standard bulb.

29. (c) Planning

> **Explanation:** Planning means looking ahead and chalking out future courses of action to be followed. It is a preparatory step. It is a systematic activity which determines when, how and who is going to perform a specific job. Planning is a detailed programme regarding future courses of action.

30. (a) production

> **Explanation:** Production Philosophy focuses on maximising the profit by producing and distributing at large scale and thereby reducing the average cost of production.

31. (c) Management is a group activity

> **Explanation:** Management is group activity as management includes the managing of business environment and it cannot be done by a single person, as it involves huge and wide variety of process.
>
> In this given case, "This requires team work and integration of efforts of all individuals, departments and specialists. This is because all the individuals and departments depend on each other for information and resources to perform their respective activities."

32. (c) Both the statements are correct

> **Explanation:** As per this principle, authority can be delegated but accountability is absolute and cannot be delegated. The person who delegates authority remains accountable to his own boss for the work performance of his subordinates.

33. (a) Decentralisation

> **Explanation:** "To handle the situation CEO of Digital Ltd. starts delegating some of his authority to the General Manager, who also felt himself overburdened and with the approval of CEO disperses some of his authority to various levels throughout the organisation." These line Indicates that Digital Ltd. Uses concept of decentralization as they delegate it to the immediate junior not to the each and every level systematically.

34. (b) (ii); (iv); (i); (iii)

> **Explanation:** The process of Scientific Techniques in the correct sequence is:
> 1. Functional formanship.
> 2. Standardisation.
> 3. Simplication of work.
> 4. Fatigue study.

35. (d) Both (a) and (b)

> **Explanation:** It has devoted a lot of time and money to this plan. But the competition increases and they were not able to change its plan to beat its competitors because huge amount of money had already been devoted to the pre-decided plan.

36. (b) Middle level

> **Explanation:** Lower Level managers act as a link between workers and middle level managers.

37. (d) Both (a) and (b)

> **Explanation:** Rajiv Bhatt has been appointed as Vice President so he is working at top level manager. To frame policies and plans and to take care of survival and growth of the company are functions of top level manager.

38. (a) Societal marketing concept

> **Explanation:** As company considered environmental friendly techniques to reduce pollution that means company is following Societal Marketing Concept.

39. (a) Cooperation

> **Explanation:** All of them they help each other which leads to a great environment in the company.

40. (a) Management as an art

> **Explanation:** "They tend to deal with a given situation, an issue or a problem through a combination of their own experience, creativity, imagination, initiative and innovation." This line shows Management as an art.

41. (d) reduces creativity

> **Explanation:** As Vishal has an idea regarding assembling of computers which would not only reduce the assembling time of computers but would also reduce the cost of production of the computers. Vishal's supervisor instead of appreciating him, ordered him to complete the work as per the methods and techniques decided earlier as nothing could be changed at that stage. In this case, Vishal was not allowed to use the new method or creativity.

42. (b) stability of personnel

> **Explanation:** According to Principle of Stability of personnel in an organisation personnel must not frequently enter and exit the organisation to run smoothly.

43. (b) Statement II is correct and I is wrong

> **Explanation:** Pricing is a crucial decision regarding product and it can greatly influence the demand of the product.

44. (c) Helps in achieving group goals

> **Explanation:** The importance of management highlithed in the given case is management helps in achieving group goals as it arranges the factors of production, assembles and organizes the resources, integrates the resources in effective manner to achieve goals.

45. (b) implementation

> **Explanation:** In this question, the author is talking about evaluation of alternatives (step of planning process) and after that the selected step is being implemented.

46. (d) Gang boss

> **Explanation:** Gang Boss has to ensure that all the required material to get the things done is available for workers to start the work. He is under the reporting of production as per functional foremanship.

47. (c) Marketing concept

> **Explanation:** Marketing concept the identification of market or customer who are chosen as the target of marketing effort, understanding needs and wants of customers in the target market, development of products or services for satisfying needs of the target market. Satisfying needs of target market better than the competitors & doing all this at a profit.

48. (c) Both (A) and (R) are correct, and (R) is the correct explanation of (A)

> **Explanation:** Planning is the foremost function in sports because it seeks to meet future events effectively to the best advantages in sports. Planning is, therefore, called a forward looking function.

Section – C

49. (b) Organising

> **Explanation:** As Mansi has created fourteen job positions divided into different departments on the basis of functions. It comes under organisation.

50. (a) Functional structure

> **Explanation:** Functional Structure divides the jobs according to their functions.

51. (a) Organisational structure

> **Explanation:** As Mansi has created all the responsibility and authority are to be performed at different levels. It comes under organisation.

52. (b) Delegation

> **Explanation:** Delegation has three elements that are Authority, Responsibility and Accountability.

53. (a) Formal Communication

> **Explanation:** Formal communication takes place between different departments in Travels Organiser.

54. (c) Authority

> **Explanation:** Responsibility is derived from Authority and Accountability is derived from Responsibility. Responsibility arises out of superior subordinate relationship, once a task is assigned to subordinate by his superior it is his duty to perform task perfectly.

55. (c) Relativity

> **Explanation:** Business environment is a relative concept since it differs from country to country and even region to region.

56. (c) Labelling

> **Explanation:** Labeling is the process of attaching a label to the product to aid product recognition and provide necessary information about the product. In this case appropriate safety warning for use were not mentioned on the bottles that it should be used carefully.

57. (a) Product

> **Explanation:** Product mix refers to the complete set of products and/or services offered by a firm.

58. (d) Implementing the plan

> **Explanation:** (a) Setting objectives: increasing profits
> (b) Developing planning premises: making certain assumptions about future.
> (c) Identifying alternative course of action: Purchasing new high speed machines, increasing the sale price, Using waste material in manufacturing stuffed toys
> (d) Evaluating alternatives and selecting an alternative:
>   So the next step will be implementing the action

59. (c) Anish–Saru-Atul-Aman- Lalit-Tanu-Vanshika

> **Explanation:** Anish has to follow the scalar chain to communicate with Vanshika

60. (d) ₹ 995

> **Explanation:** The worker who is making 50 units will earn 55 × 50 = ₹ 2750
> The worker who is making 39 units will earn 39 × 45 = ₹ 1755
> A worker making 50 units will earn ₹ 995 (2750-1755) more as compared to a worker making 39 units.

Sample Paper 7

Section – A

1. (d) Management is intangible

> **Explanation:** Management is an intangible force as it cannot be seen but its presence can be felt when targets are met and there is orderliness and coordination in the work environment.

2. (b) Organising

> **Explanation:** Organising includes structuring, integrating and coordinating task goals and activities to attain objectives.

3. (a) Market

> **Explanation:** A market is a place where buyers and sellers can meet to facilitate the exchange or transaction of goods and services.

4. (c) Lower level management

> **Explanation:** Providing good and healthy working conditions to workers is a function of Lower Level Management.

5. (c) Place mix

> **Explanation:** The place mix handling and movement of goods from place of production to the place of distribution is referred to as physical distribution.

6. (d) Market research

> **Explanation:** Market research is the process of determining the viability of a new service or product through research conducted directly with potential customers. Market research allows a company to discover the target market and get opinions and other feedback from consumers about their interest in the product or service

7. (b) Management of work

> **Explanation:** Management of work is concerned with performance of tasks in an organisation.

8. (c) Advertising

> **Explanation:** Advertising is a marketing communication tool which is used by the manufacturer. It is openly sponsored, non-personal message to promote or sell a product, service or idea.

9. (d) All of the above

Explanation: In Functional Structure, each department has a functional manager responsible for performance and who has authority over the department. All departments are under the charge of a coordinating head. These departments may be further divided into sections.

10. (d) Planning involves decision-making

Explanation: On the basis of advantages and disadvantages of available options, manager chooses the best option to achieve his/her target.

11. (b) Organising

Explanation: As Parul has assigned task to two persons it involves organising function of management.

12. (b) Planning

Explanation: Planning is defined as deciding in advance what to do, when to do and what have to do it.

13. (d) Both (a) and (b)

Explanation: Market includes buyers and geographical locations.

14. (b) Social dimension and economic dimension

Explanation: In the given case the social dimensions and economic dimensions are highlighted.
The social environment of the business consits of forces like traditions, values and social trends etc. which is used to improve the tax compliance. The economic environment consists of factors such as tax rates, environment consists of factors such as tax rates, interest rate, and unemployment rate is used to increase the tax collection by influcencing the people to pay tax on time.

15. (a) Technological conditions

Explanation: Specific forces include investors, customers, competitors, suppliers.

16. (a) purposeful

Explanation: Planning is done with some purpose which helps in achieving goal.

17. (a) Promotion

Explanation: Promotion helps in making people aware about the product and its features.

18. (c) Interrelatedness

Explanation: The concept given in the case is interrelatedness. The different factors of business environment are co-related. In this case the porportion of childrens are decreasing as a result the porportion of old age population becomes more which results in increase in retirement age and shortage of hospital bed.

19. (b) flexible

Explanation: The principle of management is flexible in guidelines providing ample scope for making changes according to the nature of the enterprise, its size, competitive.

20. (c) Span of management

> **Explanation:** Span of Management defines the levels of management and also gives the shape to the organisational structure.

21. (d) Personal selling

> **Explanation:** Personal selling is where organisations use people to sell the product after meeting face-to-face with the customer.

22. (b) Delegation of authority

> **Explanation:** Delegation of authority means division of authority and powers downwards to the subordinate in a systematic way.

23. (b) Social environment

> **Explanation:** The social environment of business encompasses the values, attitudes, beliefs, wants, and desires of the consuming public. The demographics that describe the American population by gender, age, ethnicity, location, occupation, education and income are constantly evolving.

24. (c) Espirit De Corps

> **Explanation:** Esprit de Corps means "Team Spirit". Therefore, the management should create unity, co-operation, and team-spirit among the employees.

Section - B

25. (d) Social environment

> **Explanation:** The social environment of business encompasses the values, attitudes, beliefs, wants, and desires of the consuming public. The demographics that describe the American population by gender, age, ethnicity, location, occupation, education and income are constantly evolving.

26. (a) Setting objectives, Developing Premises, Identifying alternative course of action, Evaluating alternative courses.

> **Explanation:** The correct sequence of steps involved in planning process:
> (i)   The first step is to determine the objectives for the entire organisation and each department or unit within the organisation.
> (ii) The second step is to reflect the assumptions about the future that the manager is required to make since the future is uncertain.
> (iii) The third step dentifying alternatives course of actions through which the desired goals can be achieved.
> (iv) The fourth step evaluating alternatives courses to analyse the relative pes and cons of each alternatives in light of their feasibility and consequences.

27. (c) Societal marketing concept

> **Explanation:** Societal marketing concept is the entension of the marketing concept as supplemented by the concern for the long-term welfare of the society.

28. (d) Social environment

> **Explanation:** The social environment of business encompasses the values, attitudes, beliefs, wants, and desires of the consuming public. The demographics that describe the American population by gender, age, ethnicity, location, occupation, education and income are constantly evolving.

29. (c) Coordination

> **Explanation:** Coordination refers to organising the activities of two or more groups so that they work together efficiently and know what the others are doing.
>
> In the above case Krishna (Manager), ensures that there is adequate workforce and production proceeds according to plans. He also asks the marketing department to prepare their promotional and advertising campaigns also. He coordinated all the activities for winter collection

30. (b) product

> **Explanation:** As Nandini has improved the product by adding water bottle holder.

31. (b) Efficiency

> **Explanation:** As Pankaj provides more discount to complete its targets, he lacks in efficiency.

32. (a) Statement I is correct and II is wrong

> **Explanation:** Accountability flows upwards from a subordinate to the superior.

33. (b) Subordination of individual interest to general interest

> **Explanation:** According to Fayol, where any individual's interest that conflicts with an organizational interest must be subordinated to the interests of the organization. In this case also an employee has the objective of maximizing his salary, whereas the objective of organization is to maximize output at competitive cost. In last the organization's interest was given priority over employees' interest.

34. (a) (ii); (i); (iv); (iii)

> **Explanation:** Top level management includes responsible for determining overall objectives, framing plans and policies, organising activities, assembling all the resources.

35. (c) Coordination

> **Explanation:** Coordination is the process by which a manager synchronises the activities of different departments towards the achievement of a common goal. It is the essence of management as it is needed in all management functions and at all levels of management.

36. (d) May not work in dynamic environment

> **Explanation:** Planning may not work in dynamic environment as Khush Ltd. made all their plans to achieve this target. But due to change in technology adapted by competitors which leads to reduction in their (competitor) cost, the Khush Ltd. could not achieve their target. So, due to change in technology the planning did not work.

37. (b) Link between top and lower level management

> **Explanation:** Radhika is working at middle level management and link between top and lower level management is function of middle level management.

38. (b) Societal marketing concept

> **Explanation:** This team will help the local people in cleaning the polluted river in the country and the cost will be borne by the company. This shows that company is following societal marketing concept.

39. (b) Coordination

> **Explanation:** In the above case "they do not know how to synchronize the work". It is require the proper coordination because coordination is the essence of management as it is needed in all management functions and at all levels of management.

40. (c) Management as profession

> **Explanation:** Management is a discipline, restricted entry are the features of profession which management is being trying to adopt.

41. (d) follow-up action

> **Explanation:** After implementing the plan, Mr. A decides to follow up by seeing in what ways and up to what accuracy has his plan been implemented.

42. (b) cooperation, not individualism

> **Explanation:** There should be complete co-operation between the labour and management instead of individualism; competition should be replaced by co-operation. In decision-making, they should also be involved.

43. (a) Statement I is correct and II is wrong

> **Explanation:** Packaging gives protection to the product and it also helps in promotion of product.

44. (d) Increases efficiency

> **Explanation:** If resources are used optimum then it will lead to efficiency.

45. (b) Developing premises

> **Explanation:** Developing Premises is a second step in planning process which means the certain assumptions are made about futures.

46. (b) Science, not rule of thumb

> **Explanation:** According to the principle Taylor insits that each job performed in the organisation should be based on scientific enquiry and not on intuition, experience and hit and miss methods. He says that there must be thinking before doing which is not in case of rule of thumb. Rule of thumb means dictatorship of manager whereas scientific decisions are based on cause and effect and scientific measurement of methods and ways of production.

Section - C

47. (a) product design and development

> **Explanation:** The process of imagining, creating and iterating products that solve user's problems or address specific needs in a given market.

48. (c) Both (A) and (R) are correct, and (R) is the correct explanation of (A)

> **Explanation:** Planning is time consuming activity as it requires lots of research, study and interpretation on the basis of that managers take the decisions.

49. (b) Organising

> **Explanation:** Naman performed organising function because he identifies the various activities involved and divides the whole work into various task groups like Seating arrangement committee, Security committee and reception committee. In order to facilitate coordination within and among committees, he appoints a supervisor of each group.

50. (a) Division of Work

> **Explanation:** Naman divides the work among the people by identifying the various activities to be performed.

51. (d) Departmentalisation

> **Explanation:** Departmentalisation is the process of grouping activities into departments. Division of labor creates specialists who need coordination.

52. (a) Establishing reporting relationships

> **Explanation:** Establishing Reporting Relationship means to develop the accountability structure within an organisation. It defines to whom each employee reports and is accountable to. This structure was developed by Naman by appointing a supervisor of each group. Each member in the group is asked to report to their respective supervisors and all the supervisors are expected to work as per Naman 's orders.

53. (b) Organisational structure

> **Explanation:** Organisational structure is a system that outlines how certain activities are directed in order to achieve the goals of an organisation.

54. (a) Functional structure

> **Explanation:** A functional organisational structure is an organisational structure that groups employees by specialty, skill or related roles.

55. (d) Political environment

> **Explanation:** The bureaucratic and red tapism in government offices comes under political environment.

56. (a) Branding

> **Explanation:** As products of Yummy Chocolates Ltd became status symbol that is related to branding.

57. (a) Advertising

> **Explanation:** In the above case highlighted that advertising. It is the component of promotion mix. It is an impersonal form to communication, which is paid by the marketers to promote goods and services.

58. (c) Implementation of plan

> **Explanation:** The next step to be followed by Rahim is implementation of plan. Implementation is the process of turning strategies and plans into actions to achieve strategic objective and goals.

59. (b) R-Q-P-A-B-C-D

> **Explanation:** R has to follow Scalar Chain to talk to D who is working in other department at same level.

60. (d) ₹450

> **Explanation:** The worker who is making 45 units will earn 45 × 50 = ₹ 2,250
>
> The worker who is making 35 units will earn 35 × 40 = ₹ 1,800
>
> A worker making 45 units will earn ₹ 450 (2250-1800) more as compared to a worker making 35 units.

❑❑

Economics

Sample Question Paper

Economics

Term – I

Time : 90 Minutes   Max. Marks : 40

General Instructions :

1. There are total 60 questions in this paper out of which 50 questions are to be attempted.
2. This paper is divided into three Sections:
    a. Section A – Contains 24 questions. Attempt any 20 questions.
    b. Section B – Contains 24 questions. Attempt any 20 questions.
    c. Section C – Contains 12 questions. Attempt any 10 questions.
3. All questions carry equal marks.
4. There is no negative marking.

SECTION-A

(20 questions out of 24 questions are to be attempted)

1. The Government can achieve its budget objective of 'Redistribution of Income' by_____________.

(Fill up the blank with correct alternative)

   (a)   managing the General Price Level in the economy to the desired level.

   (b)   increasing the Gross Domestic Products (GDP) of the economy.

   (c)   bringing the production of goods and services under its direct and absolute control.

   (d)   rationalisation of taxes in pro-poor direction.

Ans. (d)   rationalisation of taxes in pro-poor direction.

> **Explanation:** Re-distribution of income and wealth is the transfer of income and wealth from some individual to others through a social mechanism such as taxation, welfare services, etc.

2. Balance of Payments of an economy records_____________ for a fiscal year.

(Fill up the blank with correct alternative)

   (a)   income and expenditure of the government

   (b)   inflow and outflow of funds of the government

   (c)   inflow and outflow of foreign exchange to/from the economy

   (d)   inflow and outflow of loans to/from the rest of the world

Ans. (c)   inflow and outflow of foreign exchange to/from the economy

> **Explanation:** Because the balance of payment of a country is a systematic record of all economic transactions between its residents and residents of foreign countries during a given period of time.

3. Identify which of the following bank does not interact directly with the general public?

(Choose the correct alternative)

   (a) Bank of India   (b) State Bank of India

   (c) Central Bank of India   (d) Reserve Bank of India

Ans. (d) Reserve Bank of India

> **Explanation:** R.B.I. works for the welfare of the country as a whole and without regards to profit as primary consideration. It is an apex institution of a country's monetary system. The design and control of the country's monetary policies is its main responsibility. R.B.I. does not interact directly with the general public, but it manages, supervises and facilitates the other banks of the country.

4. Identify which of the following is not an example of 'invisible item' under Current Account of the Balance of Payments transactions: (Choose the correct alternative)
   (a) Air and sea transport
   (b) Postal and courier services
   (c) Education-related travel
   (d) Merchandise linked transactions

Ans. (d) Merchandise linked transactions

> **Explanation:** Merchandise or good trades are transactions involving the transfer of ownership of a tangible and movable object from a seller to a buyer.

5. Read the following statements carefully and choose the correct alternative from the following:

   Statement 1: Demonetisation was the step taken by the Government of India in order to tackle the problems of corruption, black money, terrorism and circulation of fake currency in the Indian Economy.

   Statement 2: Demonetisation has ensured improved tax compliance in India over the period of time.

   Alternatives:
   (a) Both the statements are true.
   (b) Both the statements are false.
   (c) Statement 1 is true and Statement 2 is false.
   (d) Statement 2 is true and Statement 1 is false.

Ans. (a) Both the statements are true.

> **Explanation:** Demonetisation is advantageous in short, medium and long-term. It is compulsory step to tackle the problem of black money and corruption as it push informal economic activity into more transpareny.

6. Ms. Sakshi, an economics teacher, was explaining the concept of 'minimum percentage of the total deposits to be kept by any Commercial Bank with the Central Bank of the country, as per norms and statute prevailing in the country'.

   From the following, choose the correct alternative which specifies towards the concept explained by her?
   (a) Cash Reserve Ratio
   (b) Repo Rate
   (c) Bank Rate
   (d) Statutory Liquidity Ratio

Ans. (a) Cash Reserve Ratio

> **Explanation:** In simple terms, the cash reserve ratio is a certain percentage of cash that all the banks have to keep with the R.B.I. as a deposit. This percentage is fixed by the R.B.I. and is changed from time to time by the Central Bank.

7. Two friends Mira and Sindhu were discussing the exchange rate systems.

   'Under this system, the exchange rates are determined by the market forces of demand and supply. However, deliberate efforts are made by the competent authority to keep the exchange rates within a specific range'.

   The above-mentioned statement was given by Sindhu, identify the type of exchange rate system was she talking about?
   (a) Fixed Exchange Rate
   (b) Floating Exchange Rate
   (c) Managed Floating Exchange Rate
   (d) Managed Fixed Exchange Rate

Ans. (c) Managed Floating Exchange Rate

> **Explanation:** It is a hybrid of fixed and flexible exchanges rate. It is characterized by some intervention in the exchange rate movements but the intervention is discretionary on the part of monetary authorities.

8. Read the following statements carefully and choose the correct alternative from the following:

    Statement 1: Public goods are those goods and services that are collectively consumed by the public.

    Statement 2: Public goods are excludable and rivalrous in nature.

    Alternatives:

    (a) Both the statements are true.

    (b) Both the statements are false.

    (c) Statement 1 is true and Statement 2 is false.

    (d) Statement 2 is true and Statement 1 is false.

Ans. (c) Statement 1 is true and Statement 2 is false.

> **Explanation:** Public goods are non-excludable and non-rival. Individuals cannot be excluded from using them and use by one individual does not reduce the goods availability to others.

9. Under the Balance of Payments structure of a nation, the two main categories of accounts for the classification of the transactions are________ and ________. (Fill up the blank with correct alternative)

    (i)   current account

    (ii) unilateral transfer account

    (iii) capital account

    (iv) loan account

    (a) (i) and (ii)   (b) (i) and (iii)   (c) (iii) and (iv)   (d) (iv) and (i)

Ans. (b) (i) and (iii)

> **Explanation:** The Balance of payments on current account include items like import and export, expenses on travel, transportation, insurance, investment income etc. On the other hand capital transactions are borrowing and lending of capital, repayment of capital, sale and purchase of securities etc.

10. Identify which of the following is not a function of the Reserve Bank of India?

    (Choose the correct alternative)

    (a) To act as the banker to the Government of India

    (b) To act as the custodian of the gold Reserve of India

    (c) To act as the financial advisor to the Government of India

    (d) To issue coins and one rupee note

Ans. (d) To issue coins and one rupee note

> **Explanation:** Reserve Bank of India has the sole right to issue currency notes of various denominations expect one rupee notes under section 22 of R.B.I. Act. The one rupee note and coins are issued by Ministry and it bears the signature of Finance Secretary.

11. Industrial Policy Resolution (IPR) 1956 formed the basis of the ________ Five Year Plan.

    (Fill up the blank with correct alternative)

    (a) First   (b) Fourth   (c) Second   (d) Third

Ans. (c) Second

> **Explanation:** This resolution formed the basis of the second five year plan, the plan which tried to build the basis for a socialist pattern of the society. This resolution classified industries into three categories, Section A, Section B, Section C.

12. Occupational structure refers to__________.   (Fill in the blank with correct alternative)

    (a) size of labour force in a country

    (b) number of people living in a country

    (c) distribution of workforce among different sectors of an economy

    (d) nature of different occupations

Ans. (c) distribution of workforce among different sectors of an economy

> **Explanation:** It refers to the distribution of its people according to three different occupation. These are primary, secondary and tertiary activities. In India about 64% population engaged only in Agriculture.

13. _____________ is the portion of agricultural produce which is sold in the market by the farmers, after meeting their self-consumption requirements. *(Fill in the blank with correct alternative)*

    (a) Trade Surplus
    (b) Marketable Surplus
    (c) Producer Surplus
    (d) Consumer Surplus

Ans. (b) Marketable Surplus

> **Explanation:** It refers to the difference between the total output produced by a farmer and his on farm consumption.
> Market surplus = Total farm output produced by farmers – Own consumption of farm output.

14. Read the following statements carefully and choose the correct alternatives given below:

    Statement 1: Poverty line in India is defined in terms of monetary value of the minimum nutritional (calorific) requirements of an individual in a day.

    Statement 2: The definition of poverty line in monetary terms has not changed over the years.

    Alternatives:

    (a) Both the statements are true.
    (b) Both the statements are false.
    (c) Statement 1 is true and Statement 2 is false.
    (d) Statement 2 is true and Statement 1 is false.

Ans. (c) Statement 1 is true and Statement 2 is false.

> **Explanation:** A person is considered poor if his or her income or consumption level falls below a given minimum level necessary to fulfill the basic needs. The minimum level is called the poverty line. The Census Bureau determines the poverty line.

15. Read the following statements carefully and choose the correct alternatives given below:

    Statement 1: India is often called as the 'outsourcing hub' of the world.

    Statement 2: Availability of skilled manpower is one of the prime factors responsible for the status gained by India at the international platform.

    Alternatives:

    (a) Both the statements are true.
    (b) Both the statements are false.
    (c) Statement 1 is true and Statement 2 is false.
    (d) Statement 2 is true and Statement 1 is false

Ans. (a) Both the statements are true.

> **Explanation:** India has certain advantages which makes it a favourite outsourcing destination. One of them is the reasonable degree of skills. Indians have fairly reasonable skills and techniques that need low training period and thus, low cost of training.

16. Before the advent of Green Revolution in 1960's, India was primarily dependent on _________ for the supply of foodgrains. *(Fill in the blank with correct alternative)*

    (a) United States of America (USA)
    (b) Britain (United Kingdom)
    (c) Mexico
    (d) Union of Soviet Socialist Republics (USSR)

Ans. (a) United States of America (USA)

> **Explanation:** Before the Green Revolution, approx 75% population depends on Agriculture. The productivity was very low, and Indian farmers basically depend on Monsoon because of lack of irrigation and other infrastructure. That's why, India was dependent on USA for the supply of foodgrains.

17. From the following given sets of statements in column-I and column-II, choose the correct pair of statements.

Column-I	Column-II
(A) Exports of goods and services	(i) Excess of Exports of goods over the Imports of goods
(B) Trade Surplus	(ii) An element of invisible items
(C) Current Transfers to rest of the world	(iii) Recorded as a positive item in the BOP account
(D) Portfolio Investments	(iv) Foreign Institutional Investors

Alternatives:

(a) A-(i)   (b) B-(ii)   (c) C-(iii)   (d) D-(iv)

Ans. (d) D-(iv)

> **Explanation:** Portfolio investment refers to the purchase of securities and other financial assets by investors from another country. There are following types of portfolio investment.
> The Aggressive portfolio, The Defensive Portfolio, Income portfolio, The Hybrid Portfolio.

18. National Bank for Agricultural and Rural Development (NABARD) was set up in 1982 as a/the__________ body to coordinate the activities of all institutions involved in the rural financing system.

    (Fill in the blank with correct alternative)

    (a) cooperative   (b) apex   (c) micro-credit   (d) private-credit

Ans. (b) apex

> **Explanation:** The main objectives of NABARD are Agriculture Development, Rural Development, Credit Planning, Refinance, Regulation of regional Rural Bank.

19. The Government of India has decided to vaccinate the adult population of India (with Covaxin/Covishield), without any charge. This would be categorized as ____________.

    (Fill in the blank with correct alternative)

    (a) revenue nature income   (b) capital nature expenditure

    (c) revenue nature expenditure   (d) capital nature income

Ans. (c) revenue nature expenditure

> **Explanation:** Revenue nature expenditure means that part of Govt. expenditure that does not result in the creation of assets. For example : Expenses of Covaxin, Payment of salaries ,pensions etc.

20. ____________ is not a reason for poverty in India.   *(Fill in the blank with correct alternative)*

    (a) Population explosion   (b) Rise in per capita GDP

    (c) Low capital formation   (d) Socio-economic exclusion

Ans. (b) rise in per capita GDP

> **Explanation:** Main reason for poverty in India:
> Less productivity in Agriculture, Increasing pricing rise, Unemployment, Less utilisation of resources etc. It is widely believed that economic growth measured in terms of GDP growth is related to poverty reduction.

21. In a hypothetical economy, Mr. Neeraj has deposited ₹100 in the bank. If it is assumed that there is no other currency circulation in the economy, then the total money supply in the economy will be _______________.   *(Fill up the blank with correct alternative)*

    (a) zero   (b) ₹100   (c) not defined   (d) ₹120

Ans. (b) ₹100

22. 'Since independence, India has witnessed a considerable fall in the Infant Mortality Rate in India'. Identify which of the following may not be one of the reasons for the fall in the Infant Mortality Rate?

    (Choose the correct alternative)

    (a) Improvement in health facilities over the years

    (b) Improvement in educational standards over the years

    (c)   Fall in standard of living of the population of the nation over the years

    (d)   Technological expansion over the years

Ans. (c)   Fall in standard of living of the population of the nation over the years

23. Read the following statements carefully and choose the correct alternatives given below:

Statement 1: Subsidies do not add any burden on the financial health of a nation.

Statement 2: Complete removal of subsidies may violate the aim of equitable distribution of income.

Alternatives:

    (a)   Both the statements are true.   (b)   Both the statements are false.

    (c)   Statement 1 is true and Statement 2 is false.   (d)   Statement 2 is true and Statement 1 is false.

Ans. (d)   Statement 2 is true and Statement 1 is false.

24. Prior to India's independence, the stagnation in the agricultural sector was mainly caused by ____________.

                        (Fill up the blank with correct alternative)

    (a)   investment in technology   (b)   investment in agriculture facilities

    (c)   advanced infrastructural facilities   (d)   land settlement system

Ans. (d)   land settlement system

SECTION-B

(20 questions out of 24 questions are to be attempted)

25. Read the following statements - Assertion (A) and Reason (R):

Assertion (A): Acquisition of a domestic (Indian) company by a foreign (Australian) company will be recorded on the credit side of Balance of Payment Account.

Reason (R): It leads to outflow of foreign exchange from the domestic economy.

From the given alternatives choose the correct one.

Alternatives:

    (a)   Both Assertion (A) and Reason (R) are true and Reason (R) is the correct explanation of Assertion (A).

    (b)   Both Assertion (A) and Reason (R) are true and Reason (R) is not the correct explanation of Assertion (A).

    (c)   Assertion (A) is true but Reason (R) is false.

    (d)   Assertion (A) is false but Reason (R) is true.

Ans. (c)   Assertion (A) is true but Reason (R) is false.

26. Suppose in an economy, the initial deposits of ₹400 crores lead to the creation of total deposits worth ₹4,000 crores.

Under the given situation the value of reserve requirements would be________.

                        (Fill up the blank with correct alternative)

    (a)   0.01   (b)   1   (c)   0.1   (d)   0.4

Ans. (c)   0.1

Explanation: As we know that,

$$\text{Total money creation} = \frac{\text{Initial deposit}}{\text{Reserve requirement}}$$

$$4{,}000 = \frac{400}{\text{Reserve requirement}}$$

$$\text{Reserve requirement} = \frac{400}{4{,}000} = 0.1$$

- Higher the Reserve requitement, Lower the total money creation.
- Higher the total money creation, Lower the reserve requirement.

27. Read the following statements - Assertion (A) and Reason (R):

Assertion (A): Major policy initiatives (land reforms and Green Revolution) helped India to become self-sufficient in foodgrains production.

Reason (R): The proportion of people depending on agriculture did not decline as expected after the Green Revolution.

From the given alternatives choose the correct one.

Alternatives:

(a) Both Assertion (A) and Reason (R) are true and Reason (R) is the correct explanation of Assertion (A).

(b) Both Assertion (A) and Reason (R) are true and Reason (R) is not the correct explanation of Assertion (A).

(c) Assertion (A) is true but Reason (R) is false.

(d) Assertion (A) is false but Reason (R) is true.

Ans. (b) Both Assertion (A) and Reason (R) are true and Reason (R) is not the correct explanation of Assertion (A).

28. Identify the incorrect statement from the following: (Choose the correct alternative)

(a) Diversification in agriculture sector provides sustainable livelihood rural population.

(b) Diversification includes - change in cropping pattern, shift of workforce from agriculture to other allied activities and non-agriculture sector.

(c) Objective of investment in new agricultural avenues (non-farm activities) increases financial risks for the rural population.

(d) Diversification reduces the proportion of unemployed population in the rural areas to considerable limits.

Ans. (c) Objective of investment in new agricultural avenues (non-farm activities) increases financial risks for the rural population.

29. Read the following statements - Assertion (A) and Reason (R):

Assertion (A): Human Capital Treats human beings as a means to an end (increase in productivity).

Reason (R): Human Capital Formation decreases by way of investments in education and health.

From the given alternatives choose the correct one.

Alternatives:

(a) Both Assertion (A) and Reason (R) are true and Reason (R) is the correct explanation of Assertion (A).

(b) Both Assertion (A) and Reason (R) are true and Reason (R) is not the correct explanation of Assertion (A).

(c) Assertion (A) is true but Reason (R) is false.

(d) Assertion (A) is false but Reason (R) is true.

Ans. (c) Assertion (A) is true but Reason (R) is false.

30. From the set of statements given in Column-I (Name of the Scheme) and Column-II (Objective of Poverty Alleviation Program), choose the correct pair of statements:

Column-I (Name of the Scheme)	Column-II (Objective of Poverty Alleviation Program)
(A) Mahatma Gandhi National Rural Employment Guarantee Act	(i) Developing infrastructure and housing conditions
(B) Poshan Abhiyan (Mid-Day Meal Programme)	(ii) Guaranteed wage employment to rural unskilled worker
(C) National Social Assistance Programme	(iii) Helping specific group–elderly people by giving them pensions
(D) Valmiki Ambedkar Awas Yojana	(iv) Improving food and nutritional status of the poor

Alternatives:

(a) A-(i) (b) B-(ii) (c) C-(iii) (d) D-(iv)

Ans. (c) C-(iii)

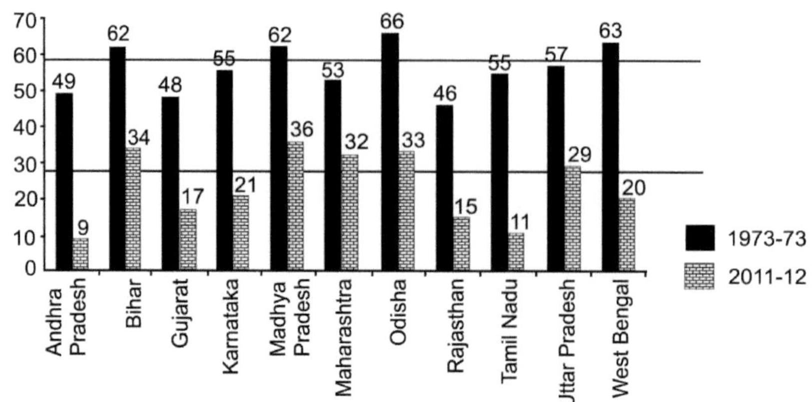

Figure showing Population Below Poverty Line in some Large States, 1973–2012 (%)

Note: For the year 1973, Uttar Pradesh includes the present Uttarakhand, Madhya Pradesh includes Chhattisgarh and Bihar includes Jharkhand.

31. On the basis of the given bar diagram, identify the states which are able to reduce the poverty level as compared to other states between 1973–2012.

(a) Tamil Nadu, Gujarat, Bihar, Andhra Pradesh

(b) Bihar, Madhya Pradesh, West Bengal and Odisha

(c) Rajasthan, Madhya Pradesh, Bihar and Uttar Pradesh

(d) Andhra Pradesh, Rajasthan, West Bengal and Tamil Nadu

Ans. (d) Andhra Pradesh, Rajasthan, West Bengal and Tamil Nadu

32.

Select Indicators of Development in Education and Health Sectors						
Particulars		**1951**	**1981**	**1991**	**2001**	**2016-17**
Real per Capital Income (in ₹)		7,651	12,174	15,748	23,095	77,659
Crude Death Rate (per 1,000 Population)		25.1	12.5	9.8	8.1	6.3
Infant Mortality Rate		146	110	80	63	33
Life Expectancy at	Male	37.2	54.1	59.7	63.9	67
Birth (in years)	Female	36.2	54.7	60.9	66.9	70
Literacy Rate (%)		16.67	43.57	52.21	65.20	76

Source: Economic Survey for various years, Ministry of Finance National Statistical Office & Ministry of Statistics and Programme Implementation: Government of India.

On the basis of the above-mentioned information answer the following question:

The Real per Capital Income of India (as per the given data) has increased by _________ (approximately) between 1951 to 2016-17. (Fill in the blank with correct alternative)

(a) 915% (b) 1015% (c) 815% (d) 715%

Ans. (a) 915%

33. Read the following statements - Assertion (A) and Reason (R):

Assertion (A): The goal of equitable distribution of land was fully served by abolition of intermediaries, in the post-independence India.

Reason (R): Big landlords challenged the land ceiling legislation, delaying the implementation and subsequently escaping from the legislation.

From the given alternatives choose the correct one.

Alternatives:

(a) Both Assertion (A) and Reason (R) are true and Reason (R) is the correct explanation of Assertion (A).

   (b) Both Assertion (A) and Reason (R) are true and Reason (R) is not the correct explanation of Assertion (A).

   (c) Assertion (A) is true but Reason (R) is false.

   (d) Assertion (A) is false but Reason (R) is true.

Ans. (d) Assertion (A) is false but Reason (R) is true.

34. Read the following statements carefully and choose the correct alternatives given below:

Statement 1: The emergence of Self-help Groups (SHG's) ensured the reduction in the fissures of the formal credit system.

Statement 2: The borrowings from SHGs mainly confined to consumption purposes by its members.

Alternatives:

   (a) Both the statements are true.   (b) Both the statements are false.

   (c) Statement 1 is true and Statement 2 is false.   (d) Statement 2 is true and Statement 1 is false.

Ans. (a) Both the statements are true.

35. Read the following statements carefully and choose the correct alternatives given below:

Statement 1: The value of money multiplier is determined by the reserve ratio prevailing in the monetary system.

Statement 2: The process of credit creation directly relates to the value of reserve ratio.

Alternatives:

   (a) Both the statements are true.   (b) Both the statements are false.

   (c) Statement 1 is true and Statement 2 is false.   (d) Statement 2 is true and Statement 1 is false.

Ans. (c) Statement 1 is true and Statement 2 is false.

36. Arrange the following event in the correct chronological order: (Choose the correct arrangements)

   (i) The year of great divide

   (ii) Establishment of Tata Iron and Steel Company (TISCO)

   (iii) Introduction of Railways in India by the British

   (iv) Opening of Suez Canal

Alternatives:

   (a) (iv), (ii), (i), (iii)   (b) (i), (iv), (iii), (ii)

   (c) (ii), (iii), (iv), (i)   (d) (iii), (iv), (ii), (i)

Ans. (d) (iii), (iv), (ii), (i)

> **Explanation:** Correct chronological order:
>
> The years of great divided ------ 1921
>
> Establishment of TISCO ------ 1907
>
> Introduction of Railways in India by the British ----- 1850
>
> Opening of Suez Canal ------ 1869

37. Read the following statements - Assertion (A) and Reason (R). Choose one of the correct alternatives given below.

Assertion (A): Trade of invisible items between two nations is a part of capital account of Balance of Payment.

Reason (R): Transactions that affect the asset-liability status of a country in relation to the rest of the world are known as Capital Account transaction.

Alternatives:

   (a) Both Assertion (A) and Reason (R) are true and Reason (R) is the correct explanation of Assertion (A).

   (b) Both Assertion (A) and Reason (R) are true and Reason (R) is not the correct explanation of Assertion (A).

   (c) Assertion (A) is true but Reason (R) is false.

   (d) Assertion (A) is false but Reason (R) is true.

Ans. (d)   Assertion (A) is false but Reason (R) is true.

38. Demand Deposits include_________ and _________.   (Fill up the blank with correct alternative)
    (i)   Saving account deposits
    (ii) Fixed deposits
    (iii) Current Account Deposits
    (iv) Post Office Savings

    Alternatives:
    (a)   (i) and (ii)   (b)   (ii) and (iii)   (c)   (i) and (iii)   (d)   (i) and (iv)

Ans. (c)   (i) and (iii)

> **Explanation:** Saving account is an interest bearing deposit account held at a bank or other financial institutions.
>
> Current account deposit means amount can be deposited and withdrawn at any time without giving any notice.

39. Read the following statements - Assertion (A) and Reason (R). Choose one of the correct alternatives given below.

    Assertion (A): Since the default rates of farm loans have become chronically high due to multiple reasons, the rural banks are facing a lot of cash crunch.

    Reason (R): Due to lack of proper storage facilities a lot of farm produce is wasted.

    Alternatives:
    (a)   Both Assertion (A) and Reason (R) are true and Reason (R) is the correct explanation of Assertion (A).
    (b)   Both Assertion (A) and Reason (R) are true and Reason (R) is not the correct explanation of Assertion (A).
    (c)   Assertion (A) is true but Reason (R) is false.
    (d)   Assertion (A) is false but Reason (R) is true.

Ans. (b)   Both Assertion (A) and Reason (R) are true and Reason (R) is not the correct explanation of Assertion (A).

40. Read the following statements - Assertion (A) and Reason (R). Choose one of the correct alternatives given below.

    Assertion (A): Since Independence, the economic condition of many farmers across India has improved as they have adopted horticulture as a secondary source of income.

    Reason (R): Varying climatic and soil conditions have given India an added advantage to be the producer of diverse horticultural crops.

    Alternatives:
    (a)   Both Assertion (A) and Reason (R) are true and Reason (R) is the correct explanation of Assertion (A).
    (b)   Both Assertion (A) and Reason (R) are true and Reason (R) is not the correct explanation of Assertion (A).
    (c)   Assertion (A) is true but Reason (R) is false.
    (d)   Assertion (A) is false but Reason (R) is true.

Ans. (a)   Both Assertion (A) and Reason (R) are true and Reason (R) is the correct explanation of Assertion (A).

41. Read the following statements - Assertion (A) and Reason (R). Choose one of the correct alternatives given below.

    Assertion (A): Demand Deposits are considered as a convenient mode of payment for execution of even the high value transactions.

    Reason (R): Demand Deposits are non-withdrawable in nature and cannot be withdrawn against issue of cheques and other similar instruments of payment.

    Alternatives:
    (a)   Both Assertion (A) and Reason (R) are true and Reason (R) is the correct explanation of Assertion (A).

(b) Both Assertion (A) and Reason (R) are true and Reason (R) is not the correct explanation of Assertion (A).

(c) Assertion (A) is true but Reason (R) is false.

(d) Assertion (A) is false but Reason (R) is true.

Ans. (c) Assertion (A) is true but Reason (R) is false.

42. Choose the correct alternatives to be filled in given blanks A and B.

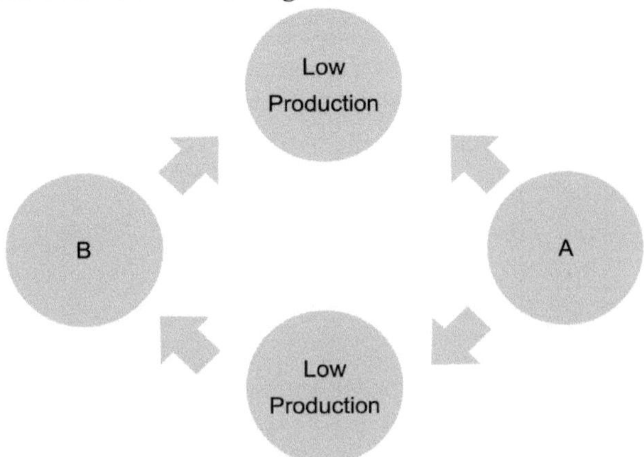

(a) Low level of income and low level of investment

(b) Low level of investment and low level of Income

(c) Low Mobilisation of savings and low level of investment

(d) Low level of Investment and low savings

Ans. (a) Low level of income and low level of investment

43. Ms Ramanpreet has started a new business venture, she intends to spend a huge amount towards 'on-the-job training' of her workers before putting them to work. It exhibits the right step in the direction of Human Capital Formation.

Spot which of the following does not directly contributes to the process of human capital formation by Ms. Ramanpreet:

(a) adds skills and expertise   (b) improves efficiency

(c) ensures gender equity   (d) increases output productivity

Ans. (c) ensures gender equity

44. Suppose that the Balance of Trade (BOT) of a nation, exhibits a surplus of ₹20,000 crores. The import of merchandise of the nation is half of the exports of merchandise to the rest of the world.

The value of exports would be ₹________ crores.   (Fill up the blank with correct alternative)

(a) ₹30,000   (b) ₹40,000   (c) ₹24,000   (d) ₹35,000

Ans. (b) ₹40,000

> **Explanation:** Given,
>
> $$\text{Balance of trade} = ₹20{,}000 \text{ crores}$$
>
> According to the question,
>
> $$\text{Import} = \frac{\text{Export}}{2}$$
>
> $$\text{Balance of trade} = \text{Value of export} - \text{Value of import}$$
>
> $$₹20{,}000 = \text{Value of export} - \frac{\text{Value of export}}{2}$$
>
> $$₹20{,}000 = \frac{\text{Value of export}}{2}$$
>
> $$\text{Value of export} = 20{,}000 \times 2$$
>
> $$\text{Value of export} = ₹40{,}000 \text{ crores}$$

45. Read the following statements carefully and choose the correct alternatives given below:

    Statement 1: Government of India adopted 'Trickle Down Approach' to alleviate poverty to benefit the last man at the bottom of the pyramid.

    Statement 2: Empirical data over the years have shown that trickle-down theory did not yield desired results in India.

    Alternatives:

    (a) Both the statements are true.

    (b) Both the statements are false.

    (c) Statement 1 is true and Statement 2 is false.

    (d) Statement 2 is true and Statement 1 is false.

Ans. (a) Both the statements are true.

46. Read the following statements - Assertion (A) and Reason (R). Choose one of the correct alternatives given below.

    Assertion (A): If the receipts and payments on the current account are equal to each other, it depicts a situation of Current Account Surplus.

    Reason (R): A surplus current account means that the nation is a lender to other countries and a deficit current account means that the nation is a borrower from other countries.

    Alternatives:

    (a) Both Assertion (A) and Reason (R) are true and Reason (R) is the correct explanation of Assertion (A).

    (b) Both Assertion (A) and Reason (R) are true and Reason (R) is not the correct explanation of Assertion (A).

    (c) Assertion (A) is true but Reason (R) is false.

    (d) Assertion (A) is false but Reason (R) is true.

Ans. (d) Assertion (A) is false but Reason (R) is true.

47. Identify the correct statement from the following: (Choose the correct alternative)

    (a) Restrictive policies of commodity production, trade and tariff pursued by the colonial government adversely affected the structure, composition and volume of India's foreign trade.

    (b) Effective trade policies of commodity production, trade and tariff pursued by the colonial government favourably affected the structure, composition and volume of India's foreign trade.

    (c) Liberal policies of commodity production, trade and tariff pursued by the colonial government adversely affected the structure, composition and volume of India's foreign trade.

    (d) Restrictive policies of commodity production, trade and tariff pursued by the colonial government favourably affected the structure, composition and volume of India's foreign trade.

Ans. (a) Restrictive policies of commodity production, trade and tariff pursued by the colonial government adversely affected the structure, composition and volume of India's foreign trade.

48. Match the situations given in Column-I with their respective implications given in Column-II:

    Choose the correct alternative:

Column-I	Column-II
(A) Migration	(i) Reduced in per capita economic growth
(B) Low level of academic standards	(ii) Imbalance between demand and supply of human resource
(C) Population- High Growth rate	(iii) Brain Drain
(D) Lack of proper manpower planning	(iv) Mismatch between required skill and academic standards

    Alternatives:

    (a) A-(ii); B-(iii); C-(iv); D-(i)   (b) A-(iii); B-(iv); C-(i); D-(ii)

    (c) A-(i); B-(ii); C-(iii); D-(iv)   (d) A-(ii); B-(iv), C-(i); D-(iii)

Ans. (b) A-(iii); B-(iv); C-(i); D-(ii)

SECTION-C

(10 questions out of 12 questions are to be attempted)

Q.No. 49 – 54 are to be answered on the basis of the following data: (in ₹ Crores)

		2019-20 Actual
1.	**Revenue Receipts**	**16,84,059**
	2. Tax Revenue (Net to centre)	13,56,902
	3. Non-Tax Revenue	3,27,187
4.	**Capital Receipts**	**10,02,271**
	5. Recovery of Loans	18,316
	6. Other Receipts	50,304
	7. Borrowings and other Liabilities	9,33,651
8.	**Total Receipts (1 + 4)**	**26,86,330**
9.	**Total Expenditure (10 + 13)**	26,86,330
	10. On Revenue Account	23,50,604

Source: indialbudget.gov.in

49. The value of recovery of loans has____________ crores between 2019-20 (Actual) and 2020-21 (Budgeted Estimate). (Fill up the blank with correct alternative)

(a) fallen by ₹3,349 (b) risen by ₹3,349 (c) fallen by ₹3,439 (d) risen by ₹3,439

Ans. (a) fallen by ₹3,349

50. The percentage change in the Non-Tax Revenue, between 2019-20 (Actual) and 2020-21 (Budgeted Estimate), taking the 2019-20 as base, would be __________. (Fill up the blank with correct alternative)

(a) 15.02% (b) 16.20% (c) 17.68% (d) 20.01%

Ans. (c) 17.68%

51. Identify which of the following is not an example of tax revenue for the government:

(Choose the correct alternative)

(a) Wealth Tax (b) Special Assessments
(c) Income Tax (d) Corporate Tax

Ans. (b) Special Assessments

52. Identify the correct formula to calculate Fiscal Deficit

(a) Total Expenditure – Total Receipt (other than borrowings)
(b) Revenue Expenditure – Revenue Receipt
(c) Capital Expenditure – Capital Receipt
(d) Revenue Expenditure + Capital expenditure – Revenue Receipt

Ans. (a) Total Expenditure – Total Receipt (other than borrowings)

53. Read the following statements carefully and choose the correct alternatives given below:

Statement 1: Revenue and Capital receipts are increasing but borrowings and other liabilities are reducing.

Statement 2: Grants and aid for creation of capital assets decreased from 2019 to 2021

Alternatives:
(a) Both the statements are true. (b) Both the statements are false.
(c) Statement 1 is true and Statement 2 is false. (d) Statement 2 is true and Statement 1 is false.

Ans. (c) Statement 1 is true and Statement 2 is false.

54. The value of Primary Deficit for the year 2020-21, would be ₹____________ crores.

(Fill up the blank with correct alternative))

(a) ₹88,134 (b) ₹3,21,581 (c) ₹96,133 (d) ₹6,09,219

Ans. (a) ₹88,134

Directions: Q.No. 55-60 are to be answered on the basis of the following data:

India's post-1990 economic strategy entailed three important breaks with the past:

- To dismantle the vast network of controls and permits that dominated the economic system.
- To redefine the role of the state as a facilitator of economic transactions and as a neutral regulator rather than the primary provider of goods and services.
- To move away from a regime of import substitution and to integrate fully with the global trading system.

The 1991 reforms unleashed the energies of Indian entrepreneurs and gave untold choice to the consumers and changed the face of the Indian economy. The reform agenda constituted a paradigm shift, and has defined the broad contours of economic policy-making for three decades.

Liberalisation was adopted as the guiding principle of governance and all governments since 1991, have broadly stuck to that path.

Today we don't need a paradigm shift. We need to look at individual sectors and see which one of these needs, reforms to create a competitive environment and improve efficiency. The power sector, the financial system, governance structures and even agricultural marketing need reforms.

Today's reforms also require much more discussion and consensus-building. The Central Government needs to work in tandem with state governments and consult different stakeholders impacted by reform decisions. Timing and sequencing are critically important in the new reforms' agenda.

Source: Excerpts from 'Like 1991, the 2021 crisis presents an opportunity, by C.Rangarajan, 22nd January 2021(livemint.com)

55. According to the given text, ________ was adopted as the guiding principle of governance and all governments since 1991.

    (a) modernisation   (b) liberalisation   (c) privatisation   (d) globalisation

Ans. (b) liberalisation

> **Explanation:** Liberalisation refers to a relaxation of government restrictions in the areas of social, political and economic policies. It is a process to removing controls ystems in order to encourage economic development.

56. Read the following statements carefully and choose the correct alternatives given below:

Statement 1: 1991 was a landmark moment in India's post-independence history as that changed the nature of the economy in fundamental ways.

Statement 2: India's economic establishment launched a multipronged reforms agenda to repair India's macroeconomic balance sheet and ignite growth.

Alternatives:

    (a) Both the statements are true.   (b) Both the statements are false.

    (c) Statement 1 is true and Statement 2 is false.   (d) Statement 2 is true and Statement 1 is false.

Ans. (a) Both the statements are true.

57. Read the following statements - Assertion (A) and Reason (R):

Assertion (A): India's pre-1990 economic strategy dismantles the vast network of controls and permits that dominated the economic system.

Reason (R): The 1991 reforms unleashed the energies of Indian entrepreneurs, gave untold choice to consumers and changed the face of the Indian economy.

From the given alternatives choose the correct one:

Alternatives:

    (a) Both Assertion (A) and Reason (R) are true and Reason (R) is the correct explanation of Assertion (A).

    (b) Both Assertion (A) and Reason (R) are true and Reason (R) is not the correct explanation of Assertion (A).

    (c) Assertion (A) is true but Reason (R) is false.

    (d) Assertion (A) is false but Reason (R) is true.

Ans. (d) Assertion (A) is false but Reason (R) is true.

58. In the light of the given text and common knowledge, identify the incorrect statement:
  (a) A severe balance of payments problem triggered an acute economic crisis in 1991.
  (b) In 1991, the economic and political leadership launched a multipronged reforms agenda to repair the macro-economic situation of the nation.
  (c) In post 1991 situation, the state was given the role of primary regulator of the economy.
  (d) Post pandemic, individual sectors should be looked closely. Sectors that need reforms should be identified and corrective action should be taken.

Ans. (c) In post 1991 situation, the state was given the role of primary regulator of the economy.

59. Read the following statements carefully and choose the correct alternatives given below:

Statement 1: Timing and sequencing are critically important in the post-economic reform agenda.

Statement 2: Post pandemic reforms in India require a paradigm shift.

Alternatives:
  (a) Both the statements are true.
  (b) Both the statements are false.
  (c) Statement 1 is true and Statement 2 is false.
  (d) Statement 2 is true and Statement 1 is false.

Ans. (c) Statement 1 is true and Statement 2 is false.

60. Read the following statements - Assertion (A) and Reason (R):

Assertion (A): The 1991 reforms released the vitalities of Indian business persons.

Reason (R): The reform agenda established a paradigm shift and defined the broad outlines of economic policy making for years to come.

From the given alternatives choose the correct one:

Alternatives:
  (a) Both Assertion (A) and Reason (R) are true and Reason (R) is the correct explanation of Assertion (A).
  (b) Both Assertion (A) and Reason (R) are true and Reason (R) is not the correct explanation of Assertion (A).
  (c) Assertion (A) is true but Reason (R) is false.
  (d) Assertion (A) is false but Reason (R) is true.

Ans. (a) Both Assertion (A) and Reason (R) are true and Reason (R) is the correct explanation of Assertion (A).

❏❏

Sample Paper 1

Economics

SECTION-A

(20 questions out of 24 questions are to be attempted)

1. People who are always poor and those who are usually poor but who may sometimes have a little more money (example: casual workers) are grouped together as the______________
   (a) transient poor   (b) occasionally poor   (c) churning poor   (d) chronic poor

2. Institutional sources of agricultural credit are ________________.
   (a) land development banks   (b) NABARD
   (c) self-help group   (d) all of these

3. Identify which of the following items is entered on the credit side of BOP account?
   (a) Repayment of foreign loan   (b) Gifts paid to foreigners
   (c) Investment from abroad   (d) Import of goods

4. Which of the following is not a non-tax source of revenue for the government?
   (a) Interest received   (b) Fees   (c) Fines   (d) GST

5. Read the following statements carefully and choose the correct alternatives given below:

   Statement 1: Central bank controls credit, whereas commercial banks create credit with the currency held by the public.

   Statement 2: Currency notes are backed by a legal promise from the central bank and central government of the country.

   Alternatives:
   (a) Both the statements are true   (b) Both the statements are false
   (c) Statement 1 is true and Statement 2 is false   (d) Statement 2 is true and Statement 1 is false

6. "A lower trade deficit along with strong FDI and portfolio flows in FN 19 January March quarter may help the external sector balance sheet and pop up both current account as well as the overall balance of payments numbers."

   Identify which of the following is not the benefit of a lower trade deficit?
   (a) Help the external sector balance sheet   (b) Prop up the current account.
   (c) Increase the balance of payment numbers   (d) Increase the capital account deficit

7. 'We need good human capital to produce other human capital (say, doctors, engineers etc.). It means that we need investment in human capital to produce more human capital out of human resources' Identify in which of the following sector we need to invest to produce more human capital.?
   (a) Investment in education   (b) Investment in health
   (c) Both (a) and (b)   (d) None of these

8. Read the following statements carefully and choose the correct alternatives given below:

   Statement 1: Balance of payments is the difference between inflow of foreign exchange and outflow of foreign exchange on account of economic transactions.

   Statement 2: Balance of payments always balances.

   Alternatives:
   (a) Both the statements are true   (b) Both the statements are false.
   (c) Statement 1 is true and Statement 2 is false   (d) Statement 2 is true and Statement 1 is false

9. ______________ and ______________ tax rate are not applicable under the GST.
   (i) 25   (ii) 18   (iii) 5   (iv) 8

Identify the correct alternative from the following:

Alternatives:

(a) (i) and (ii) (b) (i) and (iii) (c) (iii) and (iv) (d) (i) and (iv)

10. Identify which of the following is not included in the Money supply measure?

(a) Currency and coins with the public (b) Inter-Bank deposits

(c) Other deposits with RBI (d) Net demand deposits with banks

11. First Industrial Policy was adopted in _______________.

(a) 1949 (b) 1948 (c) 1947 (d) 1950

12. The concept of Five Year Planning is outsourced from _______________.

(a) USA (b) Brazil (c) Mexico (d) Russia

13. _______________ is the originator of Green Revolution in India.

(a) Dr. Manmohan Singh (b) Mr. M.S. Swaminathan

(c) Mr. Jawaharlal Nehru (d) None of these

14. Read the following statements carefully and choose the correct alternatives given below:

Statement 1: Money supply includes the least liquid measure of the money supply.

Statement 2: Money supply includes the currency with public outside banks and demand deposits with banks.

Alternatives:

(a) Both the statements are true (b) Both the statements are false

(c) Statement 1 is true and Statement 2 is false (d) Statement 2 is true and Statement 1 is false

15. Read the following statements carefully and choose the correct alternatives given below:

Statement 1: Government imposes taxes on wealthy section and gives subsidies to the weaker section of the society.

Statement 2: Government imposes heavy taxes on harmful products like tobacco and gives subsidies on LPG.

Alternatives:

(a) Both the statements are true (b) Both the statements are false.

(c) Statement 1 is true and Statement 2 is false (d) Statement 2 is true and Statement 1 is false

16. The stock of skill and expertise of nation at a point of time is called _______________

(a) physical capital (b) human capital formation

(c) human development (d) human capital

17. Match the following:

Column-A	Column-B
(A) People who are always poor	(i) Basic Information
(B) On the job training	(ii) Indicator of educational achievement
(C) Rural Development requires	(iii) Chronic poor
(D) Adult Literacy Rate	(iv) Increase in productivity of labour

(a) A-(ii), B-(iii), C-(i), D-(iv) (b) A-(iii), B-(iv), C-(i), D-(ii)

(c) A-(i), B-(ii), C-(iii), D-(iv) (d) A-(iv), B-(iii), C-(ii), D-(i)

18. A low or zero, _______________ deficit indicates that interest commitments (on earlier loans) have compelled the government to borrow.

(a) revenue (b) budgetary (c) fiscal (d) primary

19. A company located in India receives a loan from a company located abroad. This transaction is recorded in _______________ of India's Balance of payments account.

(a) credit side of current account (b) debit side of current account

(c) credit side of capital account (d) debit side of capital account

20. Revenue deficit is equal to _____________.
    (a) Total expenditure – capital expenditure
    (b) Revenue expenditure – revenue receipts
    (c) Total expenditure – revenue expenditure
    (d) Fiscal deficit – interest payment

21. The GOI has a Revenue expenditure of ₹40,000 crores, revenue receipts are ₹34,000 crores and borrowings are ₹5000 crores; then fiscal deficit will be ₹_______________.
    (a) ₹6000 crores
    (b) ₹40,000 crores
    (c) ₹11,000 crores
    (d) ₹5,000 crores

22. 'India's balance of payments this year is going to be very strong on the back of significant improvement in exports and a fall in imports, as stated by Commerce and Industry Minister Piyush Goyal.' Identify which of the following is the main reason for strong balance of payments?
    (a) Excess of imports
    (b) Excess of exports
    (c) Restrictions on exports
    (d) None of these

23. Read the following statements carefully and choose the correct alternatives given below:
    Statement 1: Commercial banks create credit out of primary deposits.
    Statement 2: Central Bank mints coins in India.
    Alternatives:
    (a) Both the statements are true
    (b) Both the statements are false.
    (c) Statement 1 is true and Statement 2 is false
    (d) Statement 2 is true and Statement 1 is false

24. Full bodied money is that money whose money value and commodity value are:
    (a) Equal in the market
    (b) Declared as equal by the government
    (c) Declared as equal by the RBI
    (d) Different in the market

SECTION-B

(20 questions out of 24 questions are to be attempted)

25. Read the following statements–Assertion (A) and Reason (R), choose one of the correct alternatives given below:

    Assertion (A): Over the years, the government has been following three approaches to reduce poverty in India. Growth oriented development, specific poverty alleviation program and meeting the minimum needs of the poor.

    Reason (R): Poverty can effectively be eradicated only when the poor start contributing to growth by their active involvement in the growth process.
    (a) Both assertion (A) and reason (R) are true and reason (R) is the correct explanation of assertion (A).
    (b) Both assertion (A) and reason (R) are true, but reason (R) is not the correct explanation of assertion (A).
    (c) Assertion (A) is true, but reason (R) is false.
    (d) Assertion (A) is false, but reason (R) is true.

26. In government budget, primary deficit is ₹10,000 crore, interest payment is ₹6,000 crore, then fiscal deficit is ₹_____________ crore.
    (a) ₹16,000
    (b) ₹17,000
    (c) ₹18,000
    (d) ₹5,000

27. Read the following statements–Assertion (A) and Reason (R), choose one of the correct alternatives given below:

    Assertion (A): Double coincidence of wants means that, the two individuals are in possession of such goods which they are willing to exchange for the satisfaction of their wants.

    Reason (R): Double coincidence of wants is an important feature of the barter system of exchange.
    (a) Both assertion (A) and reason (R) are true and reason (R) is the correct explanation of assertion (A).
    (b) Both assertion (A) and reason (R) are true, but reason (R) is not the correct explanation of assertion (A).
    (c) Assertion (A) is true, but reason (R) is false.
    (d) Assertion (A) is false, but reason (R) is true.

28. Identify the incorrect statement about Indian economy.
    (a) Indian agriculture was flourishing before the advent of the British.
    (b) India had a sound industrial base under the British.

    (c) India's foreign trade throughout the colonial period was marked by a large export surplus.

    (d) British developed the Railway system in India for their own benefit.

29. Read the following statements–Assertion (A) and Reason (R), choose one of the correct alternatives given below:

Assertion (A): Capital receipts are those receipts that do not lead to a claim on the government.

Reason (R): All those receipts of the government which create liability or reduce financial assets are termed as capital receipts.

    (a) Both assertion (A) and reason (R) are true and reason (R) is the correct explanation of assertion (A).

    (b) Both assertion (A) and reason (R) are true, but reason (R) is not the correct explanation of assertion (A).

    (c) Assertion (A) is true, but reason (R) is false.

    (d) Assertion (A) is false, but reason (R) is true.

30. Match the following:

Column-A	Column-B
(a) Stock variable	(i) Cheque
(b) Fiduciary money	(ii) Against which cheques are issued
(c) Demand deposits	(iii) Components of money supply
(d) Currency and demand deposits	(iv) Money supply

    (a) A-(i), B-(iii), C-(iv), D-(ii)

    (b) A-(ii), B-(i), C-(iii), D-(iv)

    (c) A-(iv), B-(i), C-(ii), D-(iii)

    (d) A-(iii), B-(ii), C-(i), D-(iv)

31.

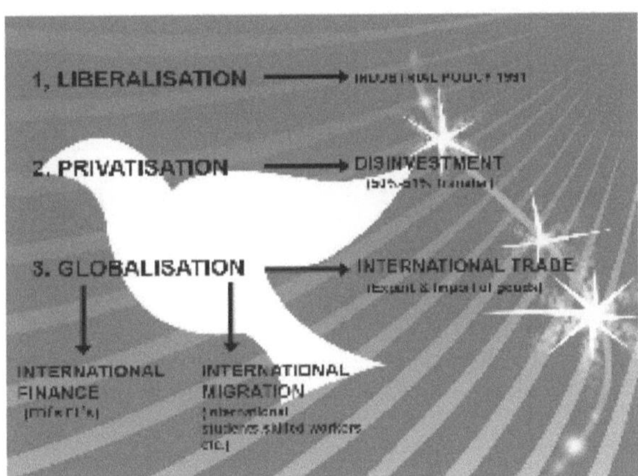

In the above figure, according to privatisation, the rate of disinvestment is:

    (a) 50-51%   (b) 49-51%   (c) 55-69%   (d) None of these

32. The balance of payments on Current Account could be re-written as:

$$(X - M) = (T - G) + (S - I)$$
or
$$(M - X) = (G - T) + (I - S)$$

Trade deficit = Government Balance + Private sector balance

Based on the information mentioned above, answer the following question:

_______________ is the formula of a balance of payment?

    (a) Government balance + Private sector balance

    (b) Government balance + Trade deficit

    (c) Private sector + Trade deficit

    (d) None of these

33. Read the following statements–Assertion (A) and Reason (R), choose one of the correct alternatives given below:

Assertion (A): The Indian economy under the British rule was in a stagnant and backward state.

Reason (R): Land settlement systems were implemented by the colonial government.

    (a) Both assertion (A) and reason (R) are true and reason (R) is the correct explanation of assertion (A).

    (b) Both assertion (A) and reason (R) are true, but reason (R) is not the correct explanation of assertion (A).

    (c) Assertion (A) is true, but reason (R) is false.

    (d) Assertion (A) is false, but reason (R) is true.

34. Read the following statements carefully and choose the correct alternatives given below:
    Statement 1: Recoveries of loans and advances are capital receipts of the government.
    Statement: Capital receipts decrease the assets of the government.
    Alternatives:
    (a) Both the statements are true
    (b) Both the statements are false.
    (c) Statement 1 is true and Statement 2 is false
    (d) Statement 2 is true and Statement 1 is false

35. Read the following statements carefully and choose the correct alternatives given below:
    Statement 1: In the first seven plans after independence, India's trade policies were based on import substitution trade strategy.
    Statement 2: Five year plans gave a big push to the basic and capital goods industries.
    Alternatives:
    (a) Both the statements are true
    (b) Both the statements are false.
    (c) Statement 1 is true and Statement 2 is false
    (d) Statement 2 is true and Statement 1 is false

36. In India, expenditure on education and health is the responsibility of _____________ and ____________.
    (i)   Union Government
    (ii) State Government
    (iii) Regional Rural Banks
    (iv) Cooperative Banks
    Identify the correct alternative from the following:
    Alternatives:
    (a) (i) and (ii)   (b) (i) and (iii)   (c) (iii) and (iv)   (d) (i) and (iv)

37. Read the following statements–Assertion (A) and Reason (R), choose one of the correct alternatives given below:
    Assertion (A): Balance of trade is the difference between the value of exports and value of imports of goods of a country in a given period of time.
    Reason (R): Export of goods is entered as a credit item in BOT.
    (a) Both assertion (A) and reason (R) are true and reason (R) is the correct explanation of assertion (A).
    (b) Both assertion (A) and reason (R) are true, but reason (R) is not the correct explanation of assertion (A).
    (c) Assertion (A) is true, but reason (R) is false.
    (d) Assertion (A) is false, but reason (R) is true.

38. A __________ or __________, primary deficit indicates that interest commitments (on earlier loans) have compelled the government to borrow.
    (i)   Zero   (ii) Low   (iii) High   (iv) Negative
    Identify the correct alternative from the following:
    Alternatives:
    (a) (i) and (ii)   (b) (i) and (iii)   (c) (iii) and (iv)   (d) (iv) and (i)

39. Read the following statements–Assertion (A) and Reason (R), choose one of the correct alternatives given below:
    Assertion (A): On the eve of independence Indian economy was a Stagnant economy.
    Reason (R): Between 1860-1925 it was as low as 0.5% per annum and between 1925-1950 it was 0.1% per annum.
    (a) Both assertion (A) and reason (R) are true and reason (R) is the correct explanation of assertion (A).
    (b) Both assertion (A) and reason (R) are true, but reason (R) is not the correct explanation of assertion (A).
    (c) Assertion (A) is true, but reason (R) is false.
    (d) Assertion (A) is false, but reason (R) is true.

40. Read the following statements–Assertion (A) and Reason (R), choose one of the correct alternatives given below:
    Assertion (A): The Green Revolution resulted in multiple rise in food production. It helped in recovering the country from regular food shortages in the pre-revolution period. Green Revolution resulted in Marketable or Marketed surplus.
    Reason (R): The use of High Yielding Variety (HYV) seeds, fertilizers and pesticides in the correct quantities as well as regular supply of water caused large increase in production and productivity of food grains in India.

(a) Both assertion (A) and reason (R) are true and reason (R) is the correct explanation of assertion (A).
(b) Both assertion (A) and reason (R) are true, but reason (R) is not the correct explanation of assertion (A).
(c) Assertion (A) is true, but reason (R) is false.
(d) Assertion (A) is false, but reason (R) is true.

41. Read the following statements–Assertion (A) and Reason (R), choose one of the correct alternatives given below:

Assertion (A): Income tax is a direct tax.

Reason (R): This is because the impact and incidence lies on the same person.
(a) Both assertion (A) and reason (R) are true and reason (R) is the correct explanation of assertion (A).
(b) Both assertion (A) and reason (R) are true, but reason (R) is not the correct explanation of assertion (A).
(c) Assertion (A) is true, but reason (R) is false.
(d) Assertion (A) is false, but reason (R) is true.

42. Read the following statements carefully and choose the correct alternatives given below based on the information given:

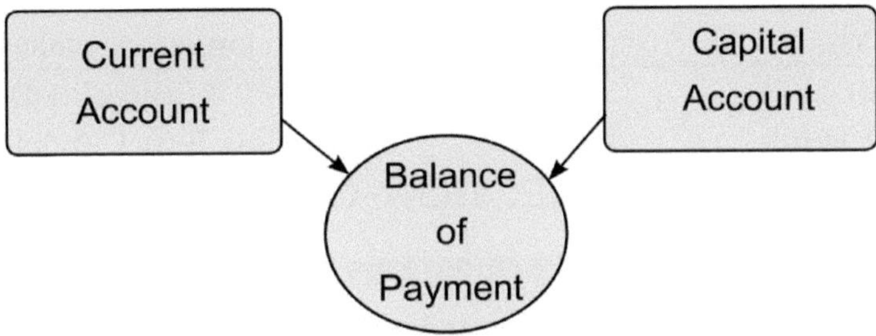

Statement 1: A deficit on the current account means that the value of imports is greater than exports.
Statement 2: A surplus on the current account means that the value of imports is less than the value of exports.
Alternatives:
(a) Both the statements are true
(b) Both the statements are false
(c) Statement 1 is true and Statement 2 is false
(d) Statement 2 is true and Statement 1 is false

43. Seema is an economics teacher, and she explains - A small-scale industry is presently defined as the one whose investment does not exceed ₹5 crores. According to the meaning of SSI, the characteristic of SSI are:
(a) Labour intensive-employment oriented
(b) Self-employment
(c) Less capital is intensive
(d) All the above

44. A government expenditure budget shows primary deficit of ₹4,400 crore. The government expenditure on the interest payment is ₹400 crore. The fiscal deficit will be ₹_______________.
(a) ₹4,800
(b) ₹4,000
(c) ₹4,600
(d) None of these

45. Read the following statements carefully and choose the correct alternatives given below:

Statement 1: Current account of Balance of Payment account records only export and import of goods and services.
Statement 2: Foreign investments are recorded in the capital account of Balance of Payments.
Alternatives:
(a) Both the statements are true
(b) Both the statements are false
(c) Statement 1 is true and Statement 2 is false
(d) Statement 2 is true and Statement 1 is false

46. Read the following statements–Assertion (A) and Reason (R), choose one of the correct alternatives given below:

Assertion (A): Domestic industries were protected from foreign competition through heavy duty on imports to make these costlier in order to discourage imports and fixation of import quotas to specify the quantity of goods which can be imported.

Reason (R): Industries in India were not able to compete worldwide and if these industries were given protection they would be able to face world competition and foreign exchange could also be saved.
(a) Both assertion (A) and reason (R) are true and reason (R) is the correct explanation of assertion (A).

(b) Both assertion (A) and reason (R) are true, but reason (R) is not the correct explanation of assertion (A).

(c) Assertion (A) is true, but reason (R) is false.

(d) Assertion (A) is false, but reason (R) is true.

47. Identify the correct statement from the following:

(a) Supply of money refers to stock of money held by public at a point of time

(b) Supply of money is a flow variable

(c) Supply of money includes cash reserve of banks

(d) Supply of money refers to bank money

48. Match the following:

Column-A	Column-B
(A) Tariff barriers	(i) Imposed on the amounts of imports and exports
(B) Minority sale	(ii) Handicraft industries
(C) Competition from machine	(iii) Equity is offered to investors through domestic public issue
(D) Non-Tariff Barriers	(iv) Imposed on imports to make them costly

(a) A-(iv), B-(iii), C-(ii), D-(i)   (b) A-(i), B-(ii), C-(iii), D-(iv)

(c) A-(iv), B-(i), C-(ii), D-(iii)   (d) A-(iii), B-(i), C-(iv), D-(ii)

SECTION-C

(10 questions out of 12 questions are to be attempted)

Directions: Q. No. 49 – 54 are to be answered based on the following data:

(A) Malnutrition is alarmingly high among the poor. Starvation and hunger are the key features of the poorest households.

(B) The poor people possess few assets. They lack proper housing.

(C) Ill health, disability or severe illness, and poor access to medical facilities make them physically weak.

(D) Their children are less likely to survive or be born healthy.

(E) They have limited economic opportunities as the poor person lacks basic literacy and skills. So, they face unstable unemployment. Moreover, lack of income-yielding assets such as land etc., leads to unemployment.

(F) They borrow from money lenders who charge high rates of interest that lead them into chronic indebtedness.

(G) The poor are highly vulnerable. They are not able to negotiate their legal wages from employers and are exploited.

(H) Most poor households have no access to safe drinking water and electricity. As a result, their primary cooking fuel is firewood and cow dung cakes.

(I) Gender inequality prevails within the family regarding the participation of gainful employment, education, and decision-making.

Attempts made to identify several poor in the country after independence:

(A) In 1962, Planning Commission now called NITI Aayog formed a Study Group. In 1979, another body called the 'Task Force on Projections of Minimum Needs and Effective.

(B) Consumption Demand' was formed.

(C) In 1989 and 2005, 'Expert Groups' were constituted for the same purpose.

Estimation of poverty line:

(a) **Calorie-based estimation:** The Planning Commission has defined the poverty line based on recommended nutritional requirements of 2400 calories per person per day for rural areas and 2100 calories per person per day for urban areas.

(b) **Per capita expenditure-based estimation:** The government of India uses Monthly Per Capita Expenditure (MPCE) as a proxy for the income of households to identify the poor.

Based on 2011-12 prices, the poverty line was defined for rural areas as consumption worth Rs 816 per person a month, and for urban areas, it was Rs 1,000 per person per month.

49. ___________ is alarmingly high among the poor.
    (a) Malnutrition   (b) Hunger   (c) Weakness   (d) All the above
50. The poor people possess few assets. They lack___________.
    (a) high earning   (b) good food   (c) proper housing   (d) None of these
51. In 1962, Planning Commission, now called NITI Aayog, formed which Group.
    (a) Study   (b) Class   (c) Poor   (d) All of these
52. Identify the incorrect statement in the following:
    (a) They borrow from money lenders who charge high rates of interest that lead them into chronic indebtedness.
    (b) The poor are highly vulnerable.
    (c) Most poor households have no access to safe drinking water and electricity.
    (d) The poor are highly rich.
53. Read the following statements carefully and choose the correct alternatives given below:

    Statement 1: The Planning Commission has defined the poverty line based on recommended nutritional requirements of 2400 calories per person per day for rural areas and 2100 calories per person per day for urban areas.

    Statement 2: The government of India uses Monthly Per Capita Expenditure (MPCE) as a proxy for the income of households to identify the poor.

    Alternatives:
    (a) Both the statements are true   (b) Both the statements are false
    (c) Statement 1 is true and Statement 2 is false   (d) Statement 2 is true and Statement 1 is false
54. ___________ is a cut-off point on the line of distribution, which usually divides the country's population as poor and non-poor.
    (a) Security line   (b) Chronic poor   (c) Poverty line   (d) None of these

    Directions: Q. No. 55-60 are to be answered based on the following data:

    Economic reforms in India refer to the neo-liberal policies introduced by the Narsimha-Rao government in 1991 when India faced a severe economic crisis due to external debt. This crisis happened primarily due to inefficiency in economic management in the 1980s. As a result, the revenues that the government was generating were not enough to meet the expenses. Hence, it had to make hefty borrowings from foreign banks to pay the debt. Hence, they were caught up in a debt trap.

    (A) To curb this crisis, India approached the world bank and the international monetary fund (IMF) for the loan and received $7 million to manage their crisis. As a result, these international organisations expected India to open its door to trade with other countries by removing the strict restrictions hitherto present. Hence India adopted the LPG (Liberalisation, Privatisation and Globalisation) reforms under the Economic Reforms. Let us look at each one of them:

    (B) **Liberalisation:** Liberalisation was brought about with the idea that any regulations or restrictions imposed on free trade must loosen up its grip to allow trade. It allowed opening up the economic borders for foreign investments and MNCs. Several economic reforms imposed under Liberalisation include expansion of production capacity, de-servicing producing areas, abolishing industrial licensing by the government, and freedom to import goods.

    (C) **Privatisation:** Privatisation refers to giving more opportunities to the private sector in regulating different services and reducing the role of the public sector(government-owned enterprises) in them. With privatisation, FDI (Foreign Direct Investment) was introduced in India, giving Indian goods and services healthy competition.

    (D) **Globalisation:** In the context of economic reforms, Globalisation means integrating the Indian economy with the world economy. It means that the economy of India will now also depend on the world economy and vice versa. Therefore, it encourages FDI and foreign trade with different countries.

55. In ___________ economic reforms were introduced in India.
    (a) 1991   (b) 1992   (c) 1993   (d) 1989

56. Read the following statements carefully and choose the correct alternatives given below:

    Statement 1: Economic crisis happened mainly due to inefficiency in economic management in the 1980s.

    Statement 2: Economic crisis happened primarily due to inefficiency in economic management in the 1970s.

    Alternatives:

    (a) Both the statements are true
    (b) Both the statements are false
    (c) Statement 1 is true and Statement 2 is false
    (d) Statement 2 is true and Statement 1 is false

57. Read the following statements -Assertion (A) and Reason (R):

    Assertion (A): Per Capita income increased due to an increase in employment.

    Reason (R): Several economic reforms imposed under Liberalisation include expansion of production capacity, de-servicing producing areas, abolishing industrial licensing by the government, and freedom to import goods.

    From the given alternatives, choose the correct one:

    Alternatives:

    (a) Both assertion (A) and reason (R) are true and reason (R) is the correct explanation of assertion (A).
    (b) Both assertion (A) and reason (R) are true, but reason (R) is not the correct explanation of assertion (A).
    (c) Assertion (A) is true, but reason (R) is false.
    (d) Assertion (A) is false, but reason (R) is true.

58. In the light of the given text and shared knowledge, identify the incorrect statement:

    (a) Privatisation aims at providing a solid base for the inflow of FDI.
    (b) With privatisation, FDI (Foreign Direct Investment) was introduced in India, giving healthy competition to Indian goods and services.
    (c) Economic planning is a mechanism for the misallocation of resources.
    (d) Globalisation encourages FDI and foreign trade with different countries.

59. Read the following statements carefully and choose the correct alternatives given below:

    Statement 1: Globalisation means the integration of the Indian economy with the world economy. It means that the economy of India will now also depend on the world economy and vice versa. Therefore, it encourages FDI and foreign trade with different countries.

    Statement 2: Globalisation refers to the expansion of economic activities across the political boundaries of nation-states.

    Alternatives:

    (a) Both the statements are true
    (b) Both the statements are false
    (c) Statement 1 is true and Statement 2 is false
    (d) Statement 2 is true and Statement 1 is false

60. Read the following statements -Assertion (A) and Reason (R):

    Assertion (A): The Narasimha Rao Government, in 1991, started the economic reforms to rebuild internal and external faith in the Indian economy.

    Reason (R): Economic reforms typically indicate deregulation or, at times, a decrease in government size to eliminate deformities caused by the management or the presence of administration, rather than current or raised regulations or government plans to lessen the perversions created by market failure.

    From the given alternatives, choose the correct one:

    Alternatives:

    (a) Both assertion (A) and reason (R) are true and reason (R) is the correct explanation of assertion (A).
    (b) Both assertion (A) and reason (R) are true, but reason (R) is not the correct explanation of assertion (A).
    (c) Assertion (A) is true, but reason (R) is false.
    (d) Assertion (A) is false, but reason (R) is true.

❑❑

Sample Paper 2

Economics

(20 questions out of 24 questions are to be attempted)

1. The effect of a deficit budget on aggregate demand is ______________.
   (a) AD remains constant
   (b) AD increases
   (c) AD decreases
   (d) None of these

2. The impact of British policy on Indian economic structure was ______________.
   (a) India became supplier of finished industrial products and consumer of raw materials from Britain
   (b) India became supplier of finished product to Britain
   (c) India becomes supplier of raw materials and consumer of finished industrial products from Britain
   (d) Both (b) and (c)

3. Identify which one of the following is not a capital expenditure?
   (a) Construction of school building
   (b) Repayment of loans
   (c) Loans advanced by World Bank
   (d) None of these

4. Identify which one of the following is not the objective of government budget?
   (a) Reduction of poverty and unemployment
   (b) Reallocation of resources
   (c) Economic growth
   (d) Maintaining law and order

5. Read the following statements carefully and choose the correct alternative from the following:
   Statement 1: In India, the concept of poverty line is used as a measure of absolute poverty.
   Statement 2: Poverty can be reduced by using labour intensive technique of production.
   Alternatives:
   (a) Both the statements are true
   (b) Both the statements are false.
   (c) Statement 1 is true and Statement 2 is false
   (d) Statement 2 is true and Statement 1 is false

6. "Capital expenditure - the money spent on creating, maintaining, or improving fixed assets like roads and factories - stood at 40% of the budgeted amount in the six months to September, down from 55.5% in the year-ago period, data from the government's Controller General of Accounts show."
   Identify the correct statement regarding capital expenditure.
   (a) It reduces the assets of the government
   (b) It reduces the liabilities of the government
   (c) There is no reduction or increment
   (d) None of these

7. 'Prime Minister Narendra Modi in recent weeks has emphasized on the idea of an 'Atmanirbhar Bharat' or a self-reliant India.' Identify the important objective of Atmanirbhar Bharat from the options below.
   (a) Self-reliance
   (b) Isolationism
   (c) Flexibility
   (d) None of these

8. Read the following statements carefully and choose the correct alternative from the following:
   Statement 1: Interest on loan received from foreign country will be recorded on the debit side of BOP account.
   Statement 2: Borrowing from abroad is treated as credit item in balance of payment account.
   Alternatives:
   (a) Both the statements are true
   (b) Both the statements are false.
   (c) Statement 1 is true and Statement 2 is false
   (d) Statement 2 is true and Statement 1 is false

9. To provide rural credit, the following were established:
   (i)   Land development banks   (ii) Commercial banks
   (iii) NABARD   (iv) SHGs
   Identify the correct alternatives from the following alternatives:
   (a) (i), (ii), (iii)   (b) (ii), (iii), (iv)
   (c) (i), (ii), (iv)   (d) All of these

10. Identify which of the following is not true for fiscal deficit?
    (a) Represent the borrowings of the government
    (b) Is the difference between total expenditure and total receipts of government
    (c) Is the difference between total expenditure and total receipts other than borrowings
    (d) Increases future liability of the government

11. Poverty index developed by Nobel Laureate Amartya Sen was named as ___________.
    (a) Poverty gap index   (b) Sen's index
    (c) Squared poverty gap   (d) None of these

12. ___________ is a primary function of money.
    (a) Medium of exchange   (b) Transfer of value
    (c) Standard of deferred payment   (d) Store of value

13. The institutional source of credit whose area of operation is the one where banking facilities and cooperatives are absent and which operate at the district level is ___________.
    (a) Self-help group   (b) Commercial bank
    (c) Regional rural bank   (d) NABARD

14. Read the following statements carefully and choose the correct alternatives given below:
    Statement 1: Capital receipts are those receipts that do not lead to a claim on the government.
    Statement 2: Escheat is a revenue receipt.
    Alternatives:
    (a) Both the statements are true   (b) Both the statements are false
    (c) Statement 1 is true and Statement 2 is false   (d) Statement 2 is true and Statement 1 is false

15. Read the following statements carefully and choose the correct alternatives given below:
    Statement 1: Difference between value of exports and imports of goods and services is called Balance of Trade.
    Statement 2: External assistance is not recorded in Balance of Payments account.
    Alternatives:
    (a) Both the statements are true   (b) Both the statements are false
    (c) Statement 1 is true and Statement 2 is false   (d) Statement 2 is true and Statement 1 is false

16. The exports surplus during the British rule was used___________.
    (a) to meet expenses on war fought by the British government.
    (b) to make payments for expenses incurred by an office set up by the colonial government in Britain.
    (c) to import invisible items.
    (d) all of these

17. Match the following:

Column-A	Column-B
(A) Depreciation of currency	(i) Positively related to exchange rate
(B) Appreciation of currency	(ii) Inversely related to exchange rate
(C) Demand for foreign currency	(iii) Rise in exports fall in imports
(D) Supply of foreign currency	(iv) Fall in export, rise in imports

   (a) A-(iii), B-(iv), C-(ii), D-(i)   (b) A-(iv), B-(iii), C-(ii), D-(i)
   (c) A-(i), B-(ii), C-(iii), D-(iv)   (d) A-(ii), B-(iv), C-(iii), D-(i)

18. An account indicating a systematic record of all economic transactions between residents of a country and residents of foreign countries during a period of time is called ___________account.
    (a) balance of payment
    (b) balance of Trade
    (c) government budget
    (d) None of these

19. There is___________ relationship between exchange rate and supply of foreign exchange.
    (a) an inverse
    (b) a direct
    (c) both (a) and (b)
    (d) None of these

20. ______________ is called for land reforms in India soon after independence ?
    (a) Equity in agriculture
    (b) Agriculture development
    (c) Growth with equity
    (d) Self-sufficiency in food grains

21. The total indirect tax collected by the government is ₹500 crores while the total subsidy provided by the government on various programs costs ₹300 crores to the government. ______________ is the value of Net Indirect Tax of the economy.
    (a) ₹800 crores
    (b) (–) ₹200 crores
    (c) ₹200 crores
    (d) (–) ₹800 crores

22. "Government decides what goods are to be produced in accordance with the needs of society"
    Identify which of the following type of economic system is described here?
    (a) Capitalist economy
    (b) Socialist economy
    (c) Both (a) and (b)
    (d) None of these

23. Read the following statements carefully and choose the correct alternatives given below:

    Statement 1: Steps can be taken to reduce the current account deficit in India by setting an import quota limit, reducing export duty, and setting a restriction on the repatriation of profit earned on foreign investment.

    Statement 2: Steps that can be taken to reduce the current account deficit in India are setting export quota limits, reducing import duty, and setting a restriction on repatriation of profit earned on foreign investment.

    Alternatives:
    (a) Both the statements are true
    (b) Both the statements are false
    (c) Statement 1 is true and Statement 2 is false
    (d) Statement 2 is true and Statement 1 is false

24. IPR 1956 laid emphasis on the role of ______________.
    (a) Large scale industries
    (b) FDI
    (c) Private sector
    (d) Public sector

SECTION-B

(20 questions out of 24 questions are to be attempted)

25. Read the following statements - Assertion (A) and Reason (R), choose the correct alternative given below:
    Assertion (A): High powered money is money produced by the RBI and the government.
    Reason (R): It consists of two things currency held by public and cash and vault reserve with the banks.
    From the given alternatives choose the correct one.
    Alternatives:
    (a) Both assertion (A) and reason (R) are true and reason (R) is the correct explanation of assertion (A).
    (b) Both assertion (A) and reason (R) are true, but reason (R) is not the correct explanation of assertion (A).
    (c) Assertion (A) is true, but reason (R) is false.
    (d) Assertion (A) is false, but reason (R) is true.

26. Those who regularly move in and out of poverty are called___________.
    (a) Chronically poor
    (b) Churning poor
    (c) Occasionally poor
    (d) Transient poor

27. Read the following statements - Assertion (A) and Reason (R), choose the correct alternative given below:
    Assertion (A): Five year plans gave a big push to the basic and capital goods industries.
    Reason (R): Indian economy is now ranked as the eleventh largest industrial economy in the world.

From the given alternatives choose the correct one.

Alternatives:

(a) Both assertion (A) and reason (R) are true and reason (R) is the correct explanation of assertion (A).

(b) Both assertion (A) and reason (R) are true, but reason (R) is not the correct explanation of assertion (A).

(c) Assertion (A) is true, but reason (R) is false.

(d) Assertion (A) is false, but reason (R) is true.

28. Identify the incorrect statement about the foreign trade in context of Indian Economy during the British rule?

(a) India became exporter of primary products and an importer of finished consumer goods and capital goods from Britain.

(b) India traded with many countries of the world despite discriminatory tariff policy pursued by the British Government.

(c) India generated huge export surplus.

(d) Britain had a monopoly control over India's Foreign Trade.

29. Read the following statements - Assertion (A) and Reason (R):

Assertion (A): Buying foreign goods is expenditure from our country and it becomes the income of that foreign country.

Reason (R): The purchase of foreign goods or imports decreases the domestic demand for goods and services in our country.

From the given alternatives choose the correct one.

Alternatives:

(a) Both assertion (A) and reason (R) are true and reason (R) is the correct explanation of assertion (A).

(b) Both assertion (A) and reason (R) are true, but reason (R) is not the correct explanation of assertion (A).

(c) Assertion (A) is true, but reason (R) is false.

(d) Assertion (A) is false, but reason (R) is true.

30. Match the following:

Column-A	Column-B
(A) Policy of surplus budget	(i) Capital expenditure
(B) Policy of deficit budget	(ii) Capital receipt
(C) Creates liability of the government	(iii) To overcome inflation in the economy
(D) Creates assets of the government	(iv) To overcome deflation in the economy

(a) A-(i), B-(ii), C-(iii), D-(iv)   (b) A-(ii), B-(i), C-(iv), D-(iii)

(c) A-(iv), B-(i), C-(iii), D-(ii)   (d) A-(iii), B-(iv), C-(ii), D-(i)

31. **Funds Allocation for Education and Various Schemes (in ₹crores)**

	Revised Estimate 2020-21	Budget Estimate 2021-22
School Education and Literacy	52,189.07	54,873.66
National Education Mission	28,077.58	31,300.16
Mid-Day Meals in Schools	12,900	11,500
Department of Higher Education	32,900	38,350.65
Digital e-learning	305.38	645.61
Indian Institutes of Technology	6,840.65	7,686.02
Indian Institutes of Management	465.29	476

Based on the given table, the estimated budget for digital e-learning is:

(a) 305.38   (b) 645.61   (c) 465.29   (d) 545.06

32.

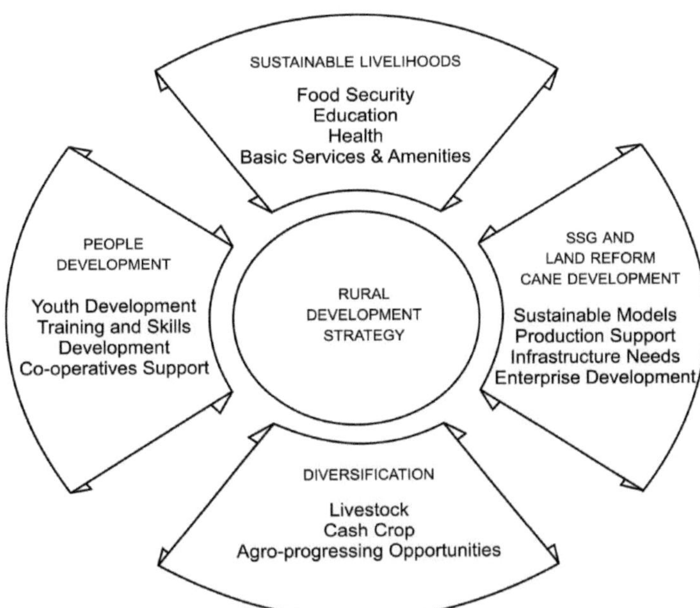

In the above figure, rural development strategies are SSG, Diversification, people development; which is missing?

(a) Sustainable livelihood (b) Diversification

(c) Both (a) and (b) (d) None of these

33. Read the following statements - Assertion (A) and Reason (R):

Assertion (A): According to human capital, humanbeings are ends in themselves.

Reason (R): Human capital considers education and health as means to increase labour productivity.

From the given alternatives choose the correct one.

Alternatives:

(a) Both assertion (A) and reason (R) are true and reason (R) is the correct explanation of assertion (A).

(b) Both assertion (A) and reason (R) are true, but reason (R) is not the correct explanation of assertion (A).

(c) Assertion (A) is true, but reason (R) is false.

(d) Assertion (A) is false, but reason (R) is true.

34. Read the following statements carefully and choose the correct alternatives given below:

Statement 1: The government budget is an annual statement.

Statement 2: The government budget shows the government's actual receipts and expenditure.

Alternatives:

(a) Both the statements are true (b) Both the statements are false.

(c) Statement 1 is true and Statement 2 is false (d) Statement 2 is true and Statement 1 is false

35. Read the following statements carefully and choose the correct alternatives given below:

Statement 1: The current account deficit is because of the net import of services.

Statement 2: The capital account surplus is because of a large amount of external assistance received on a bilateral basis.

Alternatives:

(a) Both the statements are true (b) Both the statements are false.

(c) Statement 1 is true and Statement 2 is false (d) Statement 2 is true and Statement 1 is false

36. Arrange the following in the correct chronological order :

(i) Establishment of TISCO

(ii) British introduced railways in India

(iii) First railway bridge linking Bombay with Theme

(iv) The year of great divide

Alternatives:

(a) (ii), (iv), (iii) and (i)   (b) (i), (iv), (iii) and (ii) (c) (iii), (iv), (i), (ii)   (iv) (ii), (iii), (i), (iv)

37. Read the following statements - Assertion (A) and Reason (R). Choose one of the correct alternatives given below.

    Assertion (A): GST is an indirect tax.

    Reason (R): All indirect taxes are imposed on the production and sale of goods and services.

    Alternatives:

    (a) Both assertion (A) and reason (R) are true and reason (R) is the correct explanation of assertion (A).
    (b) Both assertion (A) and reason (R) are true, but reason (R) is not the correct explanation of assertion (A).
    (c) Assertion (A) is true, but reason (R) is false.
    (d) Assertion (A) is false, but reason (R) is true.

38. Arrange the following government policy in chronological order and choose the correct alternatives:
    I.   Study group formed by planning commission for poverty
    II. Task force on projections of the minimum needs and effective consumption demand
    III. Mahatma Gandhi National Rural Employment Guarantee Act
    IV. Jan Dhan Yoyana

    Choose the correct alternative:

    (a) II, III, IV, I   (b) III, II, I, IV   (c) I, II, III, IV   (d) II, IV, I, III

39. Read the following statements - Assertion (A) and Reason (R). Choose one of the correct alternatives given below.

    Assertion (A): The major policy initiatives *i.e.,* land reforms and green revolution helped India to become self-sufficient in food grains production.

    Reason (R): The proportion of people depending on agriculture did not decline as expected

    Alternatives:

    (a) Both Assertion (A) and Reason (R) are true and Reason (R) is the correct explanation of Assertion (A).
    (b) Both Assertion (A) and Reason (R) are true and Reason (R) is not the correct explanation of Assertion (A).
    (c) Assertion (A) is true but Reason (R) is false.
    (d) Assertion (A) is false but Reason (R) is true.

40. Read the following statements - Assertion (A) and Reason (R). Choose one of the correct alternatives given below.

    Assertion (A): Farmers were forced to shift to commercial crops from the conventional subsistence crops.
    Reason (R): Commercial crops are more profitable.

    Alternatives:

    (a) Both Assertion (A) and Reason (R) are true and Reason (R) is the correct explanation of Assertion (A).
    (b) Both Assertion (A) and Reason (R) are true and Reason (R) is not the correct explanation of Assertion (A).
    (c) Assertion (A) is true but Reason (R) is false.
    (d) Assertion (A) is false but Reason (R) is true.

41. Read the following statements - Assertion (A) and Reason (R). Choose one of the correct alternatives given below.

    Assertion (A): India is a favourite destination for outsourcing.
    Reason (R): India offers an abundant supply of labour at a low wage rate.

    Alternatives:

    (a) Both Assertion (A) and Reason (R) are true and Reason (R) is the correct explanation of Assertion (A).
    (b) Both Assertion (A) and Reason (R) are true and Reason (R) is not the correct explanation of Assertion (A).

(c) Assertion (A) is true but Reason (R) is false.

(d) Assertion (A) is false but Reason (R) is true.

42.

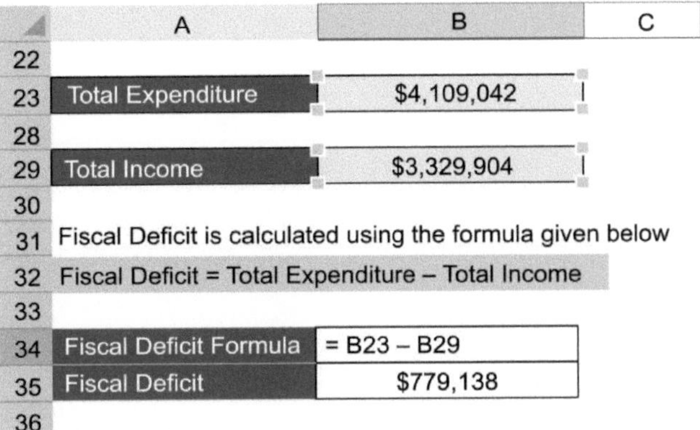

In the above table, fiscal deficit is:

(a) $779,138   (b) $769,138   (c) $679,138   (d) $769,18

43. Suppose if a person does not have access to basic amenities like safe drinking water, electricity, etc., then what do you understand from this situation.

(a) Lack of basic amenities   (b) Starvation and hunger

(c) Malnutrition   (d) None of these

44. Suppose if we want to open economic borders to foreign companies and investments, then which reform are we required to bring so that the government has regulated the private sector organisations to conduct business transactions with fewer restrictions.

(a) Liberalisation   (b) Privatisation

(c) Globalisation   (d) All of these

45. Read the following statements carefully and choose the correct alternatives given below:

Statement 1: In India, the concept of poverty line is used as a measure of absolute poverty.

Statement 2: Poverty alleviation programmes failed to deliver the desired result.

Alternatives:

(a) Both the statements are true.

(b) Both the statements are false.

(c) Statement 1 is true and Statement 2 is false.

(d) Statement 2 is true and Statement 1 is false.

46. Read the following statements - Assertion (A) and Reason (R). Choose one of the correct alternatives given below.

Assertion (A): Wage goods are luxuries of life.

Reason (R): Agriculture provides wage goods to about 121 crore people in India.

Alternatives:

(a) Both Assertion (A) and Reason (R) are true and Reason (R) is the correct explanation of Assertion (A).

(b) Both Assertion (A) and Reason (R) are true and Reason (R) is not the correct explanation of Assertion (A).

(c) Assertion (A) is true but Reason (R) is false.

(d) Assertion (A) is false but Reason (R) is true.

47. Identify the correct statement from the following:

(a) Major share of education expenditure goes to higher education.

(b) No education cess is imposed by the government on all union taxes.

(c) Human development is based on the idea that education and health are integral to human well-being.

(d) Education and literacy can be used as synonyms of each other.

48. Match the following:

Column-A	Column-B
(A) NITI Aayog	(i) 1990-91
(B) Gulf crisis	(ii) World Bank
(C) Policy of liberalisation	(iii) 1929
(D) Great depression	(iv) 2015

   (a) A-(i), B-(iv), C-(ii), D-(iii)
   (b) A-(ii), B-(iii), C-(i), D-(iv)
   (c) A-(iv), B-(i), C-(ii), D-(iii)
   (d) A-(iii), B-(ii), C-(iv), D-(i)

SECTION–C

(10 questions out of 12 questions are to be attempted)

Directions: Q. No. 49 – 54 are to be answered based on the following data:

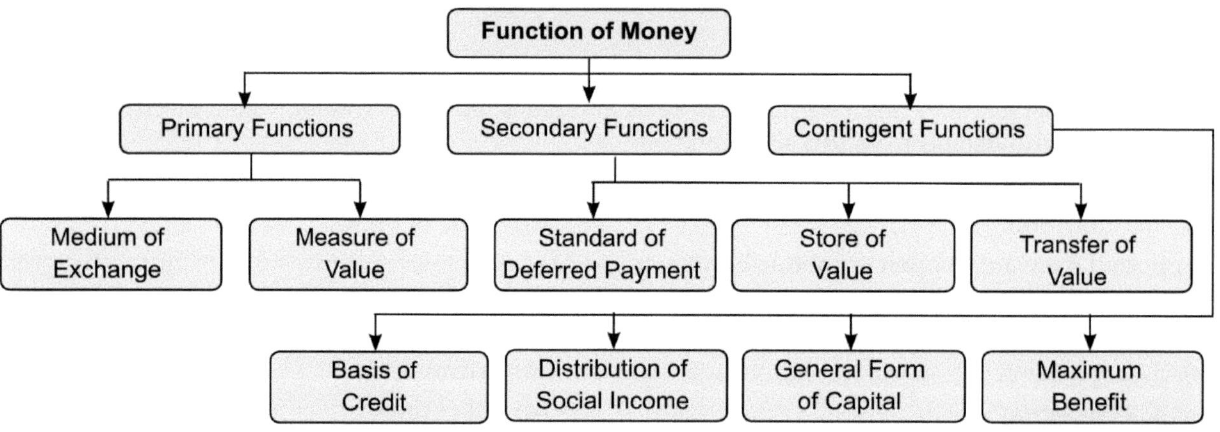

49. Function of money is ______________.

   (a) Primary   (b) Secondary   (c) Contingent   (d) All of these

50. ____________ is the function of being a commonly accepted way to value a debt, thereby allowing goods and services to be acquired now and paid for in the future.

   (a) Standard of deferred payment   (b) Transfer of value

   (c) Basis of credit   (d) All of these

51. Identify the secondary function of money?

   (a) Basis of credit   (b) Transfer of value

   (c) Measure of value   (d) All of these

52. Identity the incorrect contingent functions of money.

   (a) Medium of exchange   (b) Facilitates the distribution of social income

   (c) Maximum benefit   (d) None of these

53. Read the following statements carefully and choose the correct alternatives given below:

Statement 1: The store of value function of money suggests that money can easily store in the method of wealth and can be stored and used as a medium of exchange in the future.

Statement 2: A store of value is an asset that maintains its value rather than depreciating.

Alternatives:

   (a) Both the statements are true

   (b) Both the statements are false.

   (c) Statement 1 is true and Statement 2 is false

   (d) Statement 2 is true and Statement 1 is false

54. The goods could also be exchanged for other cargo or services. For example, Rina is a teacher, so she do some tutoring after school. She has a student that she works with whose mother is a hairstylist. Instead

of getting money from her for the "exchange" of services for her son, she cuts Rina's hair. Identify the function of money given here.

(a) Medium of exchange

(b) Transfer of money

(c) Manage money

(d) None of these

Directions: Q. No. 55-60 are to be answered based on the following data:

Economic reforms in India refer to the neo-liberal policies introduced by the Narsimha-Rao government in 1991 when India faced a severe economic crisis due to external debt. This crisis happened primarily due to inefficiency in economic management in the 1980s. As a result, the revenues that the government was generating were not enough to meet the expenses. Hence, it had to make hefty borrowings from foreign banks to pay the debt. Hence, they were caught up in a debt trap.

(A) To curb this crisis, India approached the world bank and the international monetary fund (IMF) for the loan and received $7 million to manage their crisis. As a result, these international organisations expected India to open its door to trade with other countries by removing the strict restrictions hitherto present. Hence India adopted the LPG (Liberalisation, Privatisation and Globalisation) reforms under the Economic Reforms. Let us look at each one of them:

(B) **Liberalisation:** Liberalisation was brought about with the idea that any regulations or restrictions imposed on free trade must loosen up its grip to allow trade. It allowed opening up the economic borders for foreign investments and MNCs. Several economic reforms imposed under Liberalisation include expansion of production capacity, de-servicing producing areas, abolishing industrial licensing by the government, and freedom to import goods.

(C) **Privatisation:** Privatisation refers to giving more opportunities to the private sector in regulating different services and reducing the role of the public sector(government-owned enterprises) in them. With privatisation, FDI (Foreign Direct Investment) was introduced in India, giving Indian goods and services healthy competition.

(D) **Globalisation:** In the context of economic reforms, Globalisation means integrating the Indian economy with the world economy. It means that the economy of India will now also depend on the world economy and vice versa. Therefore, it encourages FDI and foreign trade with different countries.

55. Economic reforms in India refer to the neo-liberal policies introduced by______________.

(a) Narasimha Rao government

(b) Jawaharlal Nehru

(c) Natwar Singh

(d) Indian National Congress

56. Read the following statements carefully and choose the correct alternatives given below:

Statement 1: To curb this crisis, India approached the world bank and the international monetary fund (IMF) for the loan and received $7 million to manage their crisis.

Statement 2: To curb this crisis, India approached only the world bank for the loan and received $9 million to manage their crisis.

Alternatives:

(a) Both the statements are true

(b) Both the statements are false.

(c) Statement 1 is true and Statement 2 is false

(d) Statement 2 is true and Statement 1 is false

57. Read the following statements -Assertion (A) and Reason (R):

Assertion (A): Abolition of Industrial licensing is Liberalisation.

Reason (R): Liberalisation refers to the process of making policies less constraining of economic activity and also reduction of tariff or removal of non-tariff barriers.

From the given alternatives, choose the correct one:

Alternatives:

(a) Both assertion (A) and reason (R) are true and reason (R) is the correct explanation of assertion (A).

(b) Both assertion (A) and reason (R) are true, but reason (R) is not the correct explanation of assertion (A).

(c) Assertion (A) is true, but reason (R) is false.

(d) Assertion (A) is false, but reason (R) is true.

58. In the light of the given text and shared knowledge, identify the incorrect statement:
    (a) Privatisation refers to giving more opportunities to the private sector in regulating different services
    (b) Expansion of economic activities across political boundaries of nation-states is privatisation.
    (c) Some 65% of the country's population continued to be employed in agriculture even as late as 1990.
    (d) India's New Economic Policy was announced on July 24, 1991.

59. Read the following statements carefully and choose the correct alternatives given below:

    Statement 1: Privatisation can mean different things, including moving something from the public sector into the private sector. It is also sometimes used as a synonym for deregulation when a heavily regulated private company or industry becomes less regulated.

    Statement 2: Privatisation can mean different things, including moving something from the public sector into the private sector. It is also sometimes used as a synonym for regulation when a heavily regulated public company or industry becomes more regulated.

    Alternatives:
    (a) Both the statements are true.   (b) Both the statements are false.
    (c) Statement 1 is true and Statement 2 is false. (d) Statement 2 is true and Statement 1 is false.

60. Read the following statements -Assertion (A) and Reason (R):

    Assertion (A): Every year government fixes a target for disinvestment for public sector enterprises.

    Reason (R): Disinvestment is an excellent tool for discarding the loss incurring public sector enterprises

    From the given alternatives, choose the correct one:

    Alternatives:
    (a) Both assertion (A) and reason (R) are true and reason (R) is the correct explanation of assertion (A).
    (b) Both assertion (A) and reason (R) are true, but reason (R) is not the correct explanation of assertion (A).
    (c) Assertion (A) is true, but reason (R) is false.
    (d) Assertion (A) is false, but reason (R) is true.

❑❑

Sample Paper 3

Economics

SECTION-A

(20 questions out of 24 questions are to be attempted)

1. Traditional sources of rural credit in India are ____________.
   - (a) money lenders
   - (b) traders
   - (c) relatives and friends
   - (d) All of these

2. The Tata Iron and Steel Company (TISCO) was incorporated in ____________
   - (a) 1907
   - (b) 1920
   - (c) 1880
   - (d) 1930

3. Identify which of the following is not concerned with banking organisation?
   - (a) Credit creation
   - (b) Fiscal deficit
   - (c) Cash reserve ratio
   - (d) Bank rate

4. Identify which of the following is a non-farm area of employment?
   - (a) Livestock farming
   - (b) Horticulture
   - (c) Fisheries
   - (d) All of these

5. Read the following statements carefully and choose the correct alternative from the following:

   Statement 1: On the eve of independence Indian agriculture was backward.

   Statement 2: During the British Rule, production of cash crops improved the economic condition of farmers.

   Alternatives:
   - (a) Both the statements are true
   - (b) Both the statements are false
   - (c) Statement 1 is true and Statement 2 is false
   - (d) Statement 2 is true and Statement 1 is false

6. Raju told to Sunil that the Central Bank of India *i.e.,* Reserve Bank of India, is the apex institution that control the entire financial market. It's one of the major functions is to maintain the reserve of foreign exchange. Also, it intervenes in the foreign exchange market to stabilise the excessive fluctuations in the foreign exchange rate.

   From the following discussion between Raju and Sunil, identify who is the Apex institute that controls the entire finance system of financial market?
   - (a) Ministry of Finance
   - (b) Central Government
   - (c) Central Bank of India
   - (d) All of these

7. The teacher asked a student in the class that which government deficit indicates his borrowing requirements. The Student answered "primary deficit".

   Identify from the above statement, the type of deficit indicates the borrowing requirements of the Government.
   - (a) Revenue deficit
   - (b) Fiscal deficit
   - (c) Primary deficit
   - (d) None of these

8. Read the following statements carefully and choose the correct alternative from the following:

   Statement 1: Over the years, the government has been following three approaches to reduce poverty in India. Growth oriented development, specific poverty alleviation program and meeting the minimum needs of the poor.

   Statement 2: Poverty can effectively be eradicated only when the poor start contributing to growth by their active involvement in the growth process.

   Alternatives:
   - (a) Both the statements are true
   - (b) Both the statements are false
   - (c) Statement 1 is true and Statement 2 is false
   - (d) Statement 2 is true and Statement 1 is false

9. Arrange the following government policy in chronological order and choose the correct alternatives.

   I. New economic policy

   II. First official census

   III. Start of first five year plan

   IV. Second stage of demographic transition

   Choose from the given alternatives:

   (a) I, II, III, IV   (b) III, IV, I, II   (c) I, II, IV, III   (d) IV, III, II, I

10. Identify which of the following is not a means of human capital formation?

    (a) Improves technical knowledge   (b) Enlarges the size of business

    (c) Increases cost of production   (d) Changes social outlooks

11. Tools of ___________ policy are government expenditure, taxes, public borrowing and borrowing from Central Bank.

    (a) fiscal   (b) monetary   (c) both (a) and (b)   (d) exim

12. We need good human capital to produce other human capital (say, doctors, engineers etc.). It means that we need investment in human capital to produce more human capital out of human resources.

    For that we need___________.

    (a) investment in education   (b) investment in health

    (c) Both (a) and (b)   (d) None of these

13. The selling of public sector enterprises to the public under privatisation is known as ___________.

    (a) disinvestment   (b) denationalisation

    (c) equity sell-off   (d) joint stock company

14. Read the following statements carefully and choose the correct alternative from the following:

    Statement 1: M_1 = C + OD + Time deposits with the bank.

    Statement 2: M_1 = C + OD + Demand deposits with the bank

    Alternatives:

    (a) Both the statements are true   (b) Both the statements are false.

    (c) Statement 1 is true and Statement 2 is false   (d) Statement 2 is true and Statement 1 is false

15. Read the following statements carefully and choose the correct alternatives given below:

    Statement 1: Poverty can effectively be eradicated only when the poor start contributing to growth by their active involvement in the growth process.

    Statement 2: Human capital formation has nothing to do with the productivity of physical capital.

    Alternatives:

    (a) Both the statements are true   (b) Both the statements are false.

    (c) Statement 1 is true and Statement 2 is false   (d) Statement 2 is true and Statement 1 is false

16. ___________ means the fixing the maximum size of land which could be owned by an individual.

    (a) Land reforms   (b) Land ceiling

    (c) Zamindari   (d) Land holdings

17. Identify the correct sequence of alternatives given in Column-B by matching them with respective terms in Column-A.

Column-A	Column-B
(A) Basis of credit	(i) Contingent function
(B) Exchange of goods for goods	(ii) Secondary function
(C) Accepting deposits	(iii) Barter system
(D) Standard of deferred payment	(iv) Primary function

    (a) A-(ii), B-(iii), C-(iv), D-(i)   (b) A-(iii), B-(ii), C-(i), D-(iv)

    (c) A-(i), B-(ii), C-(iii), D-(iv)   (d) A-(i), B-(iii), C-(iv), D-(ii)

18. ___________ introduced the poverty line, in pre-independent India that proved beneficial for the government to make policies for the weaker section.

    (a) Jawaharlal Nehru   (b) Dadabhai Naoroji

    (c) Mahatma Gandhi   (d) Sardar Vallabhbhai Patel

19. In the present situation of COVID, many banks would have faced financial emergency. If you own a bank and there is financial emergency in your bank, then __________ is the only institution that can come to the rescue of your bank.
    (a) Central Bank
    (b) Commercial bank
    (c) Financial institution
    (d) None of these

20. __________ refers to increase in the country's capacity to produce the output of goods and services within the country.
    (a) Modernisation   (b) Production   (c) Development   (d) Growth

21. Initial deposits made by the people from their resources are called__________.
    (a) Time deposits
    (b) Secondary deposits
    (c) Primary deposits
    (d) Term deposits

22. India's economy under the British colonial rule remained fundamentally agrarian. However despite being the occupation of about 85% of the country's population, the agricultural sector continued to experience stagnation and deterioration.
    Identify which of the following are the reason behind this situation of Indian agriculture under British rule?
    (a) Lack of government initiative to develop means of irrigation
    (b) Production of cash crops
    (c) Exploitation of tillers
    (d) All of these

23. Read the following statements carefully and choose the correct alternatives given below:
    Statement 1: The institution that accepts deposits for lending purposes is known as a commercial bank.
    Statement 2: The institution that accepts deposits for lending purposes is known as the Central Bank.
    Alternatives:
    (a) Both the statements are true
    (b) Both the statements are false.
    (c) Statement 1 is true and Statement 2 is false
    (d) Statement 2 is true and Statement 1 is false

24. Human Development Index (HDI) include __________.
    (a) Quantitative aspect
    (b) Qualitative aspect
    (c) Both (a) and (b)
    (d) None of these

SECTION-B

(20 questions out of 24 questions are to be attempted)

25. Read the following statements - Assertion (A) and Reason (R), choose the correct alternative given below:
    Assertion (A): Double coincidence of wants means that, the two individuals are in possession of such goods which they are willing to exchange for the satisfaction of their wants.
    Reason (R): Double coincidence of wants is an important feature of the barter system of exchange.
    (a) Both assertion (A) and reason (R) are true and reason (R) is the correct explanation of assertion (A).
    (b) Both assertion (A) and reason (R) are true, but reason (R) is not the correct explanation of assertion (A).
    (c) Assertion (A) is true, but reason (R) is false.
    (d) Assertion (A) is false but reason (R) is true.

26. If in an economy the value of Net Indirect Taxes is ₹50 crores and the value of subsidies is ₹40 crores. The value of Net Indirect Tax is __________.
    (a) ₹90 crores   (b) ₹80 crores   (c) ₹10 crores   (d) ₹50 crores

27. Read the following statements - Assertion (A) and Reason (R), choose the correct alternative given below:
    Assertion (A): Capital receipts are those receipts that do not lead to a claim on the government.
    Reason (R): All those receipts of the government which create liability or reduce financial assets are termed as capital receipts.
    (a) Both assertion (A) and reason (R) are true and reason (R) is the correct explanation of assertion (A).
    (b) Both assertion (A) and reason (R) are true, but reason (R) is not the correct explanation of assertion (A).

(c) Assertion (A) is true, but reason (R) is false.

(d) Assertion (A) is false but reason (R) is true.

28. Identify the incorrect statement of industrial sector during British rule?

(a) There was decline in handicraft industries

(b) The British Government promoted capital goods industries

(c) Public sector played a significant role

(d) Both (b) and (c)

29. Read the following statements - Assertion (A) and Reason (R), choose the correct alternative from the following:

Assertion (A): Invisibles include services, transfers and flows of income that take place between different countries.

Reason (R): Services trade includes only non-factor income.

(a) Both assertion (A) and reason (R) are true and reason (R) is the correct explanation of assertion (A).

(b) Both assertion (A) and reason (R) are true, but reason (R) is not the correct explanation of assertion (A).

(c) Assertion (A) is true, but reason (R) is false.

(d) Assertion (A) is false but reason (R) is true.

30. Match the following:

Column-A	Column-B
(A) In a Five Year Plan	(i) Hiring services from external sources
(B) Land reforms	(ii) Composition of trade
(C) Types of goods and services exported and imported	(iii) Institutional changes in ownership
(D) Outsourcing	(iv) Agricultural production

(a) A-(iv), B-(iii), C-(ii), D-(i)

(b) A-(i), b-(ii), C-(iv), D-(iii)

(c) A-(ii), B-(i), C-(iv), D-(iii)

(d) A-(iii), B-(iv), C-(i), D-(ii)

31.

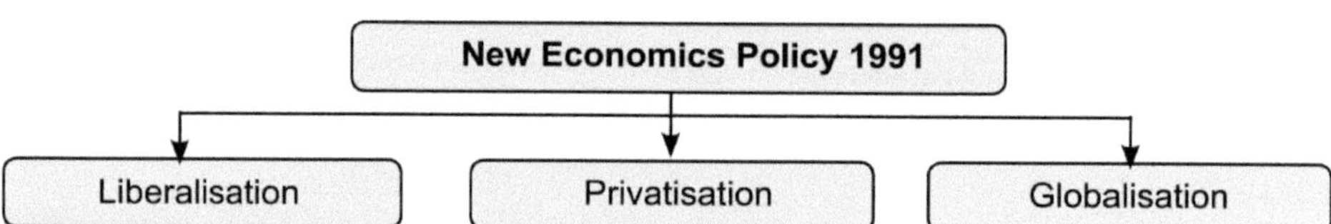

In the above figure, the branches of the new economic policy are:

(a) Liberalisation   (b) Privatisation   (c) Globalisation   (d) All of these

32.

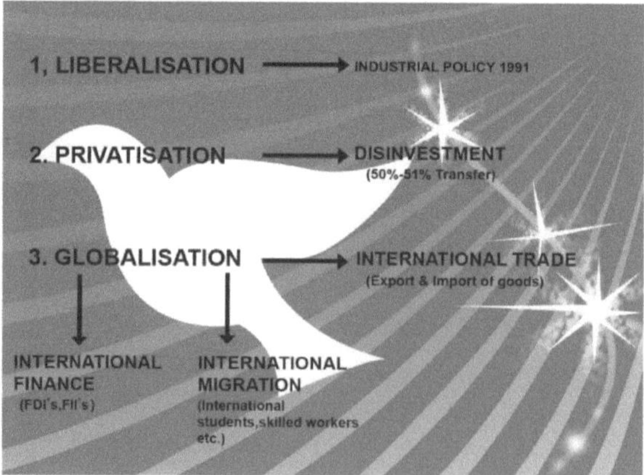

In the above figure, if a person wants to do business at the international level, then in which category he will come:

(a) Liberalisation   (b) Privatisation   (c) Globalisation   (d) None of these

33. Read the following statements - Assertion (A) and Reason (R), choose the correct alternative given below:

Assertion (A): The tax reductions in the reform period, aimed at yielding larger revenue and curb tax evasion, have not resulted in increase in tax revenue for the government.

Reason (R): The reform policies, involving tariff reduction, have curtailed the scope for raising revenue through custom duties.

Alternatives:

(a) Both assertion (A) and reason (R) are true and reason (R) is the correct explanation of assertion (A).

(b) Both assertion (A) and reason (R) are true, but reason (R) is not the correct explanation of assertion (A).

(c) Assertion (A) is true, but reason (R) is false.

(d) Assertion (A) is false but reason (R) is true.

34. Read the following statements carefully and choose the correct alternatives given below:

Statement 1: With the economic reforms, the GDP growth rate of India is increased.

Statement 2: Due to the opening up of the Indian economy to foreign competition, more MNCs are competing with local businesses and companies, facing problems due to financial constraints, lack of advanced technology, and production inefficiencies.

Alternatives:

(a) Both the statements are true.

(b) Both the statements are false.

(c) Statement 1 is true and Statement 2 is false.

(d) Statement 2 is true and Statement 1 is false.

35. Read the following statements carefully and choose the correct alternatives given below:

Statement 1: The amount collected by the government as taxes and duties is known as Tax revenue receipts.

Statement 2: The amount collected by the government as taxes and duties are known as Non-tax revenue receipts.

Alternatives:

(a) Both the statements are true

(b) Both the statements are false.

(c) Statement 1 is true and Statement 2 is false

(d) Statement 2 is true and Statement 1 is false

36. Arrange the following budget in the correct chronological order:

(i) Union budget of independent India

(ii) Interim budget

(b) Union budget for the fiscal period

(d) Union budget of India

Alternatives:

(a) (iv), (ii), (i), (iii)

(c) (ii), (iii), (iv), (i)

(b) (i), (ii), (iii), (iv)

(d) (iii), (iv), (ii), (i)

37. Read the following statements - Assertion (A) and Reason (R). Choose one of the correct alternatives given below.

Assertion (A): Information technology is an important element of knowledge economy.

Reason (R): It highlights the significance of human capital as a tool of growth.

Alternatives:

(a) Both assertion (A) and reason (R) are true and reason (R) is the correct explanation of assertion (A).

(b) Both assertion (A) and reason (R) are true, but reason (R) is not the correct explanation of assertion (A).

(c) Assertion (A) is true, but reason (R) is false.

(d) Assertion (A) is false but reason (R) is true.

38. ______________ and ______________ are primary functions of money.

(i) Medium of exchange

(iii) store of value

(ii) measure of value

(iv) standard for deferred payments

Alternatives:

(a) (i) and (ii)   (b) (ii) and (iii)   (c) (i) and (iii)   (d) (i) and (iv)

39. Read the following statements - Assertion (A) and Reason (R). Choose one of the correct alternatives given below.

Assertion (A): Five year plans gave a big push to the basic and capital goods industries.

Reason (R): Indian economy is now ranked as the eleventh largest industrial economy in the world.

Alternatives:

(a) Both Assertion (A) and Reason (R) are true and Reason (R) is the correct explanation of Assertion (A).

(b) Both Assertion (A) and Reason (R) are true and Reason (R) is not the correct explanation of Assertion (A).

(c) Assertion (A) is true but Reason (R) is false.

(d) Assertion (A) is false but Reason (R) is true.

40. Read the following statements - Assertion (A) and Reason (R). Choose one of the correct alternatives given below.

    Assertion (A): Economic and social equality was considered as the principal goal of planning.

    Reason (R): Real income of the people decreased due to high rate of inflation.

    Alternatives:

    (a) Both Assertion (A) and Reason (R) are true and Reason (R) is the correct explanation of Assertion (A).

    (b) Both Assertion (A) and Reason (R) are true and Reason (R) is not the correct explanation of Assertion (A).

    (c) Assertion (A) is true but Reason (R) is false.

    (d) Assertion (A) is false but Reason (R) is true.

41. Read the following statements - Assertion (A) and Reason (R). Choose one of the correct alternatives given below.

    Assertion (A): The intervention of the government whether to expand demand or reduce it constitutes the stabilisation function.

    Reason (R): The government may need to correct fluctuations in income and employment.

    Alternatives:

    (a) Both Assertion (A) and Reason (R) are true and Reason (R) is the correct explanation of Assertion (A).

    (b) Both Assertion (A) and Reason (R) are true and Reason (R) is not the correct explanation of Assertion (A).

    (c) Assertion (A) is true but Reason (R) is false.

    (d) Assertion (A) is false but Reason (R) is true.

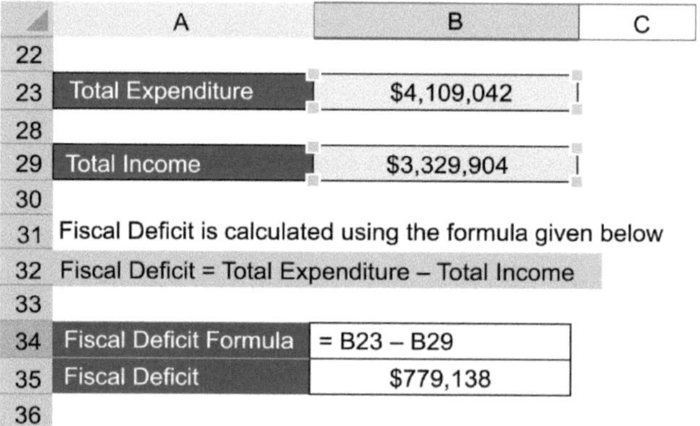

42. Read the following statements carefully and choose the correct alternatives given below based on the information given:

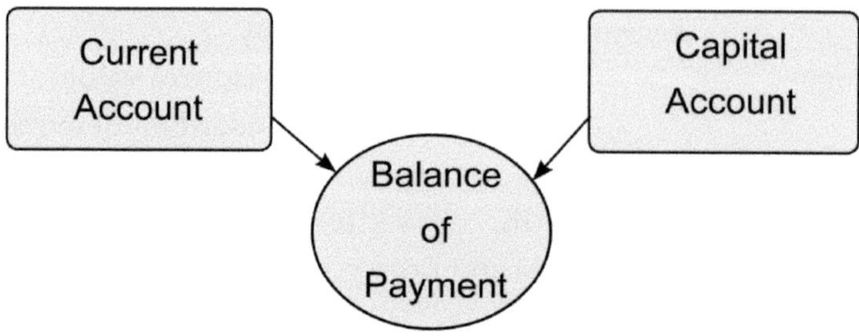

Statement 1: A deficit on the current account means that the value of imports is greater than exports.

Statement 2: A surplus on the current account means that the value of imports is less than the value of exports.

Alternatives:

(a) Both the statements are true

(b) Both the statements are false

(c) Statement 1 is true and Statement 2 is false

(d) Statement 2 is true and Statement 1 is false

43. Seema is an economics teacher, and she explains - A small-scale industry is presently defined as the one whose investment does not exceed ₹5 crores.

According to the meaning of SSI, the characteristic of SSI are:

(a) Labour intensive-employment oriented

(b) Self-employment.

(c) Less capital is intensive.

(d) All of these

44. If the government withdraws from the ownership and management of public sector companies and the outright sale of public sector companies, _____________ will happen?

(a) Transfer of ownership

(b) Disinvestment

(c) Origin of private sector

(d) None of the above

45. Read the following statements carefully and choose the correct alternatives given below:

Assertion (A): Capital receipts are those receipts that do not lead to a claim on the government.

Reason (R): All those receipts of the government which create liability or reduce financial assets are termed as capital receipts.

Alternatives:

(a) Both Assertion (A) and Reason (R) are true and Reason (R) is the correct explanation of Assertion (A).

(b) Both Assertion (A) and Reason (R) are true and Reason (R) is not the correct explanation of Assertion (A).

(c) Assertion (A) is true but Reason (R) is false.

(d) Assertion (A) is false but Reason (R) is true.

46. Read the following statements - Assertion (A) and Reason (R). Choose one of the correct alternatives given below.

Assertion (A): The government may spend an amount equal to the revenue it collects.

Reason (R): When tax collection exceeds the required expenditure, the budget is said to be in surplus.

Alternatives:

(a) Both Assertion (A) and Reason (R) are true and Reason (R) is the correct explanation of Assertion (A).

(b) Both Assertion (A) and Reason (R) are true and Reason (R) is not the correct explanation of Assertion (A).

(c) Assertion (A) is true but Reason (R) is false.

(d) Assertion (A) is false but Reason (R) is true.

47. Identify the correct statement of the following:

(a) Overall balance is positive in case of balanced BOP.

(b) Reserve of foreign exchange could be used to balance any deficit in the balance of payments account.

(c) The market is responsible for exchange rate determination under fixed exchange rate.

(d) Portfolio investment is a type of external assistance

48. Identify the correct pair from column-A and column-B:

Column-A	Column-B
(A) Budget	(i) Parliament
(B) Budget is presented in	(ii) Last day of february
(C) Budget is presented on	(iii) Finance Minister
(D) Budget is presented by	(iv) Annual statement of estimated receipts and estimate expenditure by the government

(a) A-(ii), B-(i), C-(iii), D-(iv)

(b) A-(i), B-(iii), C-(ii), D-(iv)

(c) A-(iv), B-(i), C-(ii), D-(iii)

(d) A-(iii), B-(ii), C-(i), D-(iv)

SECTION-C

(10 questions out of 12 questions are to be attempted)

Directions: Q. No. 49 – 54 are to be answered based on the following data:

India's current account balance posted a marginal surplus of USD 0.6 billion (0.1% of GDP) in the Jan.-Mar. quarter 2020, as against a deficit of USD 4.7 billion in Jan-Mar 2019 and USD 2.6 billion in the previous quarter. It is noteworthy that this is the first quarterly current account surplus since the Jan-Mar quarter of 2007. It is primarily on account of lower trade deficit at USD 35 billion and a rise in net invisible receipts (which includes services, primary and secondary income) at USD 35.6 billion.

The lower trade deficit is a result of the sharp decline in demand at both the national and international levels following the implementation of COVID-19 lockdowns and a fall in global crude oil prices since the beginning of this year.

In the financial account, net foreign direct investment at USD 12 billion was higher than USD 6.4 billion in Jan-March quarter 2019. On the portfolio investment side, there was a net outflow of USD 13.7 billion compared to USD 9.4 billion inflow the same quarter last year on account of money being pulled out from both debt and equity markets. A surplus at both current and capital account has resulted in a forex reserve accretion of USD 18.8 billion in the Jan.-Mar. quarter 2020.

Generally, a current account surplus is a piece of welcome news; however, in the current scenario, it is a major worry for the Indian economy as it reflects a drop in economic activity. Given that the imports collapsed more than the exports and overall trade balance (services + goods) posted a surplus in the month of April and May, the current account will likely remain in surplus in the June quarter.

49. India's current account balance posted a __________ USD 0.6 billion (0.1% of GDP) in the Jan-Mar quarter 2020.

    (a) Marginal deficit   (b) Marginal surplus

    (c) Both (a) and (b)   (d) None of the above

50. __________ is a result of the sharp decline in demand at both the national and international levels?

    (a) Lower trade deficit   (b) Higher trade deficit

    (c) Medium trade deficit   (d) None of the above

51. The Balance of Payments (BOP) records which type of transactions between residents of a country and the rest of the world.

    (a) Monetary   (b) Economic   (c) Physical   (d) None of these

52. A surplus at both current and capital account has resulted in a__________.

    (a) Forex reserve accretion   (b) Resident reserve   (c) Both (a) and (b)   (d) None of these

53. Read the following statements carefully and choose the correct alternatives given below:

    Statement 1: The capital account comprises credit and debit transactions under non-produced non-financial assets and capital transfers between residents and non-residents.

    Statement 2: The current account comprises credit and debit transactions under non-produced non-financial assets and capital transfers between residents only.

    Alternatives:

    (a) Both the statements are true.   (b) Both the statements are false.

    (c) Statement 1 is true and Statement 2 is false.   (d) Statement 2 is true and Statement 1 is false.

54. In the current scenario, it is a major worry for the Indian economy as it reflects a ______ and given that the imports collapsed more than the exports and overall trade balance (services + goods) posted a surplus.

    (a) Rise in economic activity   (b) Stop in economic activity

    (c) Drop in economic activity   (d) None of the above

Directions: Q. No. 55-60 are to be answered based on the following data:

Rural development actions are intended to further the social and economic development of rural communities.

Rural development programs were historically top-down approaches from local or regional authorities, regional development agencies, NGOs, national governments, or international development organizations. However, a critical 'organization gap' identified during the late 1960s, reflecting on the disjunction between national organizations and rural communities, led to a significant focus on community participation in rural development agendas. Frequently this was achieved through political decentralisation policies in developing countries, prevalent among African countries, or policies that shift the power of socio-politico-economic decision-making and the election of representatives and leadership from centralized governments to local governments. As a result, local populations can also bring about endogenous initiatives for development. The term rural development is not limited to issues of developing countries. Many developed countries have very active rural development programs.

Rural development aims at finding ways to improve rural lives with the participation of rural people themselves, to meet the critical needs of rural communities. The outsider may not understand the setting, culture, language, and other things prevalent in the local area. As such, rural people themselves have to participate in their sustainable rural development. In developing countries like Nepal, Pakistan, India, Bangladesh, and China, integrated development approaches are being followed up. In this context, many approaches and ideas have been developed and implemented, for instance, bottom-up approaches, PRA- Participatory Rural Appraisal, RRA- Rapid Rural Appraisal, Working With People (WWP), etc. The New Rural Reconstruction Movement in China has been actively promoting rural development through its ecological farming projects.

55. Rural development actions are intended to____________.
    (a) Economic development
    (b) Social development
    (c) Both (a) and (b)
    (d) None of the above

56. Read the following statements carefully and choose the correct alternatives given below:

    Statement 1: Rural development programs were historically top-down approaches from local or regional authorities, regional development agencies, NGOs, national governments or international development organizations.

    Statement 2: Rural development programs were futuristically bottom approaches from local or regional authorities, regional development agencies, NGOs, national governments, or international development organizations.

    Alternatives:
    (a) Both the statements are true
    (b) Both the statements are false.
    (c) Statement 1 is true and Statement 2 is false
    (d) Statement 2 is true and Statement 1 is false

57. Read the following statements -Assertion (A) and Reason (R):

    Assertion (A): Rural banking has always given lesser attention to the credit requirement of small and marginal farmers.

    Reason (R): Marginal farmers enjoys better creditworthiness.

    From the given alternatives, choose the correct one:

    Alternatives:
    (a) Both assertion (A) and reason (R) are true and reason (R) is the correct explanation of assertion (A).
    (b) Both assertion (A) and reason (R) are true, but reason (R) is not the correct explanation of assertion (A).
    (c) Assertion (A) is true, but reason (R) is false.
    (d) Assertion (A) is false, but reason (R) is true.

58. In the light of the given text and shared knowledge, identify the incorrect statement:
    (a) Local populations can also bring about endogenous initiatives for development.
    (b) The term rural development is not limited to issues of developing countries.
    (c) Rural development aims at finding ways to improve rural lives with the participation of rural people.
    (d) None of the above

59. Read the following statements carefully and choose the correct alternatives given below:

    Statement 1: Rural people themselves have to participate in their sustainable rural development. In developing countries like Nepal, Pakistan, India, Bangladesh and China, integrated development approaches are being followed up.

Statement 2: The New Rural Reconstruction Movement in China has actively promoted rural development through ecological farming projects.

Alternatives:

(a) Both the statements are true

(b) Both the statements are false.

(c) Statement 1 is true and Statement 2 is false

(d) Statement 2 is true and Statement 1 is false

60. Read the following statements -Assertion (A) and Reason (R):

Assertion (A): The problem of rural credit is not primarily one of rural credit; it may be said to be one of rural minded credit.

Reason (R): The Indian economy has yet to come out of rural mentality.

From the given alternatives, choose the correct one:

Alternatives:

(a) Both assertion (A) and reason (R) are true and reason (R) is the correct explanation of assertion (A).

(b) Both assertion (A) and reason (R) are true, but reason (R) is not the correct explanation of assertion (A).

(c) Assertion (A) is true, but reason (R) is false.

(d) Assertion (A) is false, but reason (R) is true.

❑❑

Sample Paper 4

Economics

SECTION-A

(20 questions out of 24 questions are to be attempted)

1. The fiscal deficit is the difference between the government's total expenditure and its total receipts excluding ___________.
   (a) Interest   (b) Taxes   (c) Spending   (d) Borrowings

2. The categories of transactions that are included in the capital account of the balance of payment are________.
   (a) Investment from and to abroad   (b) Borrowing and lending from and abroad
   (c) Changes in foreign exchange reserves   (d) All of these

3. Identify which of the following is known as annual statement of the estimated receipts and expenditure of the government over the fiscal year.
   (a) Budget   (b) Income estimates   (c) Account   (d) Expenditure

4. Identify the given below options; when will the trade deficit situation arise?
   (a) Export of goods more than the import of goods
   (b) Export of goods less than the import of goods
   (c) Export of services more than the import of services
   (d) Export of services less than the import of services

5. Read the following statements carefully and choose the correct alternative from the following:
   Statement 1: Industrial revolution came first in England.
   Statement 2: Industrial revolution came first in Germany.
   Alternatives:
   (a) Both the statements are true.   (b) Both the statements are false.
   (c) Statement 1 is true and Statement 2 is false.   (d) Statement 2 is true and Statement 1 is false.

6. Ms Sakshi, an economics teacher, asked the students about the nationalization of the commercial bank. When has it happened?
   From the following, choose the correct alternative, which specifies the concept explained by her?
   (a) 1966   (b) 1968   (c) 1967   (d) 1969

7. Two friends, Radha and Simran, were discussing the exchange rate systems.
   It allows a nation's central bank to intervene regularly in foreign exchange markets to change the direction of the currency's float and reduce currency volatility.
   Sindhu gave the statement mentioned above, identify the type of exchange rate system was she talking about?
   (a) Fixed Exchange Rate   (b) Floating Exchange Rate
   (c) Managed Floating Exchange Rate   (d) Managed Fixed Exchange Rate

8. Read the following statements carefully and choose the correct alternative from the following:
   Statement 1: Accommodating items are only recorded in the capital account of BOP.
   Statement 2: Import of machinery will be recorded in the capital account of BOP
   Alternatives:
   (a) Both the statements are true.
   (b) Both the statements are false.
   (c) Statement 1 is true and Statement 2 is false.
   (d) Statement 2 is true and Statement 1 is false.

9. Current account record all payment to rest of world as _________ and all receipt from rest of the world as __________.

    (i) Debit   (ii) Credit   (iii) Credit   (iv) Debit

    Identify the correct alternatives from the following:

    Alternatives:

    (a) (i) and (ii)   (b) (i) and (iii)   (c) (iii) and (iv)   (d) (iv) and (i)

10. Identify which of the following is the credit money?

    (a) Cheque and draft   (b) Promissory note

    (c) Exchange note   (d) All of these

11. In India, to date, we have used ___________ five-year plans.

    (a) 10   (b) 12   (c) 13   (d) 14

12. In India , poverty in urban areas is ______________than the poverty in rural areas.

    (a) lesser   (b) more   (c) equal   (d) None of these

13. The poverty line is identical for rural and urban areas ____________.

    (a) false   (b) may be   (c) true   (d) None of these

14. Read the following statements carefully and choose the correct alternative from the following:

    Statement 1: Poverty Alleviation Programmes could succeed because the resources allocated to different programmes were far less than required, considering the magnitude of poverty.

    Statement 2: Poverty Alleviation Programmes could not succeed because resources allocated to different programmes were far less than required, considering the magnitude of poverty.

    Alternatives:

    (a) Both the statements are true.   (b) Both the statements are false.

    (c) Statement 1 is true and statement 2 is false.   (d) Statement 2 is true and statement 1 is false.

15. Read the following statements carefully and choose the correct alternative from the following:

    Statement 1: Human capital formation improves the quality of life as it provides better jobs, high income and improves health.

    Statement 2: Human capital formation degrades the quality of life as it provides no job, less income and improves health.

    Alternatives:

    (a) Both the statements are true.   (b) Both the statements are false.

    (c) Statement 1 is true and statement 2 is false.   (d) Statement 2 is true and statement 1 is false.

16. Green Revolution led to an increase in the production of food __________.

    (a) grain   (b) wheat   (c) fruits   (d) None of these

17. From the following given sets of statements in columns I and II. Choose the correct pair of statements Balance of invisible trade is equal to:

Column-I	Column-II
(A) Export of goods	(i) Import of goods
(B) Export of services	(ii) Import of services
(C) Import of goods	(iii) Export of goods
(D) Import of services	(iv) Export of services

    Alternatives:

    (a) A-(i)   (b) B-(ii)   (c) C-(iii)   (d) D-(iv)

18. ___________ is an apex body that coordinates the functioning of different financial institutions working on expanding rural credit.

    (a) NABARD   (b) Self-Help Group   (c) Both (a) and (b)   (d) None of these

19. One-time large purchases of fixed assets that will be used for revenue generation over a longer period. This would be categorized as ____________.

    (a) Revenue nature income   (b) Capital nature expenditure

    (c) Revenue nature expenditure   (d) Capital nature income

20. ____________ is an indicator of poverty in India.

    (a) Illiteracy level

    (b) Income level

    (c) Employment level

    (d) All of these

21. In the present world, the act of purchase of goods and sale of goods have been separated due to the existence of money. This has been facilitated by the ___________ function of money.

    (a) Measure of money

    (b) Medium of exchange

    (c) Store of value

    (d) None of these

22. Disguised unemployment is unemployment that does not affect aggregate economic output. Identify which of the following one are the type :

    (a) Over employment

    (b) Natural Unemployment

    (c) Underemployment

    (d) None of these

23. Read the following statements carefully and choose the correct alternative from the following:

Statement 1: An annual statement of the estimated receipts and expenditure of the government over the fiscal year is known as a budget.

Statement 2: An annual statement of the estimated receipts and expenditure of the government over the fiscal year is known as expenditure.

Alternatives:

    (a) Both the statements are true.

    (b) Both the statements are false.

    (c) Statement 1 is true and Statement 2 is false.

    (d) Statement 2 is true and Statement 1 is false.

24. Small scale industry is_____________.

    (a) Labour intensive

    (b) Capital intensive

    (c) Complementary to large scale industries

    (d) None of these

SECTION-B

(20 questions out of 24 questions are to be attempted)

25. Read the following statements - Assertion (A) and Reason (R):

Assertion (A): Balance of Payments' represents a better picture of a country's economic transactions with the rest of the world than the 'Balance of Trade'.

Reason (R): Balance of Payments'considers the exchange of both visible and invisible items, whereas 'Balance of Trade' does not.

From the given alternatives, choose the correct one:

Alternatives:

    (a) Both Assertion (A) and Reason (R) are true, and Reason (R) is the correct explanation of Assertion (A).

    (b) Assertion (A) and Reason (R) are true, and Reason (R) is not the correct explanation of Assertion (A).

    (c) Assertion (A) is true, but Reason (R) is false.

    (d) Assertion (A) is false, but Reason (R) is true.

26. The main function of NABARD is to _______________.

    (a) serve as an apex funding agency

    (b) coordinate the rural financing activities

    (c) monitor and evaluate the refunded projects

    (d) All of these

27. Read the following statements - Assertion (A) and Reason (R):

Assertion (A): The Green revolution was comparatively less effective in developing countries, where farmers depended on conventional breeding.

Reason (R): The inability to buy expensive agrochemicals forced farmers to rely on conventional breeding in the developing world.

From the given alternatives, choose the correct one:

Alternatives:

(a) Both Assertion (A) and Reason (R) are true, and Reason (R) is the correct explanation of Assertion (A).

(b) Both Assertion (A) and Reason (R) are true, and Reason (R) is not the correct explanation of Assertion (A).

(c) Assertion (A) is true, but Reason (R) is false.

(d) Assertion (A) is false, but Reason (R) is true.

28. Identify the incorrect statement from the following:

(a) Poverty Reduction and Growth Facility (PRGF) has been established by the International Development Association (IDA) to provide further assistance to low-income countries facing a high level of indebtedness.

(b) Singapore Regional Training Institute (STI) provides training in macro-economic analysis and policy and related subjects as part of the IMF institute programme.

(c) Both (a) and (b)

(d) None of the above

29. Read the following statements - Assertion (A) and Reason (R):

Assertion (A): Human capital treats human beings as a means to an end (increase in productivity).

Reason (R): Human Capital Formation decreases by way of investments in education and health.

From the given alternatives, choose the correct one:

Alternatives:

(a) Both Assertion (A) and Reason (R) are true, and Reason (R) is the correct explanation of Assertion (A).

(b) Both Assertion (A) and Reason (R) are true, and Reason (R) is not the correct explanation of Assertion (A).

(c) Assertion (A) is true, but Reason (R) is false.

(d) Assertion (A) is false, but Reason (R) is true.

30. From the set of statements given in Column I and Column II, choose the correct pair of statements:

Column-I	Column-II
(A) Economic growth	(i) Eradicate poverty
(B) Uttar Pradesh	(ii) Rich people
(C) Increase in the population	(iii) Reduce expenses
(D) Unemployment	(iv) Reduce poverty

Alternatives:

(a) A-(i) (b) B-(ii) (c) C-(iii) (d) D-(iv)

31. Figure showing Population below the poverty line in some large states, 1973-2000.

Population below Poverty Line in Some Large States. 1973-2000 (%)

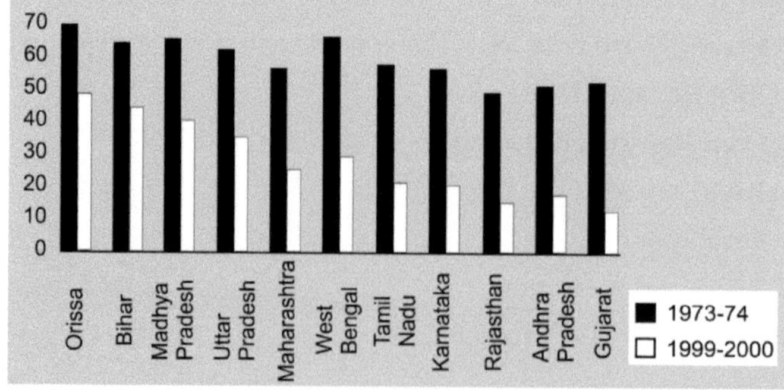

Figure Showing Population below the poverty line in some large states, 1973-2000

Note: Uttar Pradesh includes the present Uttaranchal, Madhya Pradesh includes Chhattisgarh and Bihar includes Jharkhand.

Based on the given bar diagram, identify the states which can reduce the poverty level as compared to other states between 1973-2000.

(a) Gujarat (b) West Bengal (c) Uttar Pradesh (d) None of these

COVID CASTS A LONG SHADOW OVER GROWTH PROSPECTS

GDP Growth Forcast by Various Agencies for India

32.

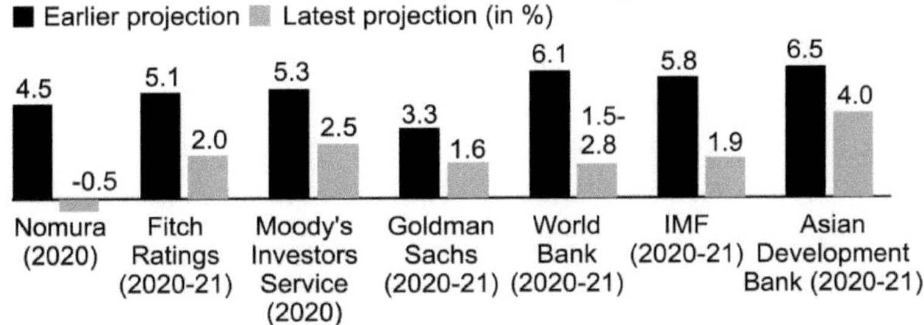

Based on the information mentioned below, answer the following question:

In 2021 earliest projection of Asian development bank is ___________.

(a) 4.0　　　　　　(b) 6.5　　　　　　(c) 5.8　　　　　　(d) 6.1

33. Read the following statements - Assertion (A) and Reason (R):

Assertion (A): Indian economy is predominantly a rural economy.

Reason (R): As per census 2011, the rural country population is almost 83.25 crore.

From the given alternatives, choose the correct one:

Alternatives:

(a) Both Assertion (A) and Reason (R) are true, and Reason (R) is the correct explanation of Assertion (A).

(b) Both Assertion (A) and Reason (R) are true, and Reason (R) is not the correct explanation of Assertion (A).

(c) Assertion (A) is true, but Reason (R) is false.

(d) Assertion (A) is false, but Reason (R) is true.

34. Read the following statements carefully and choose the correct alternative from the following:

Statement 1: In an SHG (Self-Help Group), group members make essential decisions regarding loans and savings.

Statement 2: Self Help Groups issue loans (credit) at a reasonable rate of interest.

Alternatives:

(a) Both the statements are true.　　　　　(b) Both the statements are false.

(c) Statement 1 is true and Statement 2 is false.　　(d) Statement 2 is true and Statement 1 is false.

35. Read the following statements carefully and choose the correct alternative from the following:

Statement 1: Present currency can work as money as it is a legal tender

Statement 2: Central Bank mints coins in India

Alternatives:

(a) Both the statements are true.　　　　　(b) Both the statements are false.

(c) Statement 1 is true and Statement 2 is false　　(d) Statement 2 is true and Statement 1 is false

36. Arrange the following events of China in correct chronological order.

(i)   Great Proletarian Cultural Revolution　　(ii) Great Leap Forward Campaign

(iii) Introduction of Economic Reforms　　　(iv) First Five-Year Plan

Alternatives:

(a) (ii), (iv), (iii), (i)　　　　　　　　(b) (iv), (ii), (i), (iii)

(c) (ii), (iv), (i), (iii)　　　　　　　　(d) (iv), (i), (ii), (iii)

37. Read the following statements - Assertion (A) and Reason (R):

Assertion (A): The 'Balance of Payments' presents a classified record of all receipts on account of goods exported, services rendered and capital received by 'residents' and payments made by them on account of goods imported and services received from capital transferred to 'non-residents' or 'foreigners".

Reason (R): The 'Balance of Payments is a systematic record of all economic transactions between the 'residents' of a country and the rest of the world.

From the given alternatives, choose the correct one:

Alternatives:

(a) Both Assertion (A) and Reason (R) are true, and Reason (R) is the correct explanation of Assertion (A).

(b) Both Assertion (A) and Reason (R) are true, and Reason (R) is not the correct explanation of Assertion (A).

(c) Assertion (A) is true, but Reason (R) is false.

(d) Assertion (A) is false, but Reason (R) is true.

38. ____________ will be the impact on the credit creation ability of commercial banks if the government reduces income tax slabs.

(a) There will be more credit creation in the economy.

(b) There will be less credit creation in the economy.

(c) There will be no impact on credit creation.

(d) It depends upon the behaviour of the targeted population.

39. Read the following statements - Assertion (A) and Reason (R):

Assertion (A): Rural development includes only agricultural development.

Reason (R): Rural development aims at improving the economic and social conditions of people living in villages.

From the given alternatives, choose the correct one:

Alternatives:

(a) Both Assertion (A) and Reason (R) are true, and Reason (R) is the correct explanation of Assertion (A).

(b) Both Assertion (A) and Reason (R) are true, and Reason (R) is not the correct explanation of Assertion (A).

(c) Assertion (A) is true, but Reason (R) is false.

(d) Assertion (A) is false, but Reason (R) is true.

40. Read the following statements - Assertion (A) and Reason (R):

Assertion (A): Economic condition of many farmers.

Reason (R): Two third of its population is engaged in agricultural activity.

From the given alternatives, choose the correct one:

Alternatives:

(a) Both Assertion (A) and Reason (R) are true, and Reason (R) is the correct explanation of Assertion (A).

(b) Both Assertion (A) and Reason (R) are true, and Reason (R) is not the correct explanation of assertion (A).

(c) Assertion (A) is true, but Reason (R) is false.

(d) Assertion (A) is false, but Reason (R) is true.

41. Read the following statements - Assertion (A) and Reason (R):

Assertion (A): Currency held by the public is a monetary liability of the central bank.

Reason (R): Central Bank controls credit, whereas commercial banks create credit with the currency held by the public.

From the given alternatives, choose the correct one:

Alternatives:

(a) Both Assertion (A) and Reason (R) are true, and Reason (R) is the correct explanation of Assertion (A).

(b) Both Assertion (A) and Reason (R) are true, and Reason (R) is not the correct explanation of Assertion (A).

(c) Assertion (A) is true, but Reason (R) is false.

(d) Assertion (A) is false, but Reason (R) is true.

42. Choose the correct alternatives to be filled in the given blank :

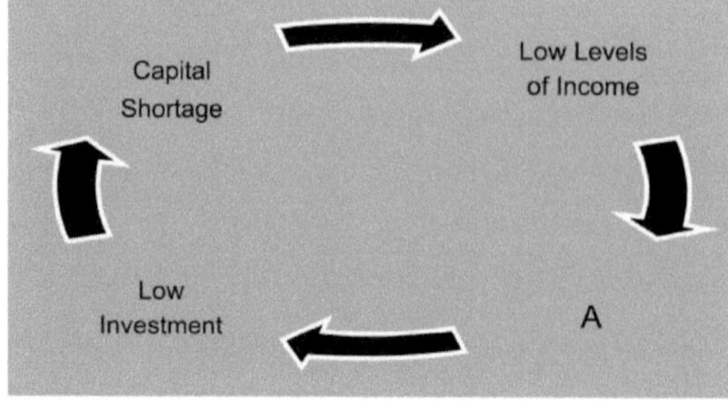

Economic growth and development process are Capital storage, low level of income, _________ and low investment.

(a) Capital storage   (b) low level of income (c) low savings   (d) low investment

43. Seema is discussing a job training role. Which of the following is not the role of on-the-job training?

   (a) Eradicates inequality   (b) Encourages innovation
   (c) Promotes modern methods   (d) Enhances productivity

44. If the country's balance of payment is ₹ (–) 100 crores and the total payments are ₹500 crores. Its total receipts will be ___________.

   (a) ₹100 crore   (b) ₹200 crore   (c) ₹400 crore   (d) None of these

45. Read the following statements carefully and choose the correct alternative from the following:

   Statement 1: Economic growth means the increase in the real national income of a country.
   Statement 2: Economic growth means a decrease in the real national income of a country.
   Alternatives:
   (a) Both statements are true.   (b) Both statements are false.
   (c) Statement 1 is true and Statement 2 is false. (d) Statement 2 is true and Statement 1 is false.

46. Read the following statements - Assertion (A) and Reason (R):

   Assertion (A): A high average income is not indicative of a country's overall well-being or human development.
   Reason (R): Average income does not cover indicators like level of literacy rate, health facilities in a country.
   Alternatives:
   (a) Both Assertion (A) and Reason (R) are true, and Reason (R) is the correct explanation of Assertion (A).
   (b) Both Assertion (A) and Reason (R) are true, and Reason (R) is not the correct explanation of Assertion (A).
   (c) Assertion (A) is true, but Reason (R) is false.
   (d) Assertion (A) is false, but Reason (R) is true.

47. Identify the correct statement from the following :

   (a) Trade policies determine the size of markets for firms' output and strongly influence both foreign and domestic investment.
   (b) Over time, the influence of trade policies on the investment climate is decreasing.
   (c) Over time, the influence of tariff policies on the investment climate is growing.
   (d) Trade policies determine the number of markets for the input of firms.

48. From the set of statements given in Column I and Column II, choose the correct pair of statements:

Column-I	Column-II
(A) Intangible item in the balance of payments statement	(i) Banking services provided in other countries
(B) Debts and claims of a country	(ii) Balance of current account
(C) Current transactions	(iii) Stock
(D) Intangible item	(iv) Food grains

(a) A-(i)   (b) B-(ii)   (c) C-(iii)   (d) D-(iv)

SECTION-C

(10 questions out of 12 questions are to be attempted)

Direction: Q. No. 49 – 54 are to be answered basis of the following data:

From the given information, calculate: (a) Revenue Receipts (b) Fiscal Deficit and (c) Primary Deficit

Particulars	(₹ in crore)
(i) Revenue Deficit	6,000
(ii) Revenue Expenditure	11,000
(iii) Capital Expenditure	14,000
(iv) Non-debt Creating Capital Receipts	8,000
(v) Interest Payments	7,000

49. From the given information, Revenue Receipts would be___________.
    (a) ₹5,000 (b) ₹6,000 (c) ₹4,000 (d) ₹7,000
50. From the given information, Fiscal Deficit would be___________.
    (a) ₹1,200 (b) ₹15,000 (c) ₹10,000 (d) ₹12,000
51. Identify which of the following is not an example of revenue receipt?
    (a) Rent received (b) Borrowings
    (c) Recovery of Loans and (d) Other Capital Receipts
52. Identify the correct formula to calculate the primary deficit.
    (a) Total revenue – Total expenditure excluding interest payments on its debt.
    (b) Revenue Expenditure – Revenue Receipt
    (c) Capital Expenditure – Capital Receipt
    (d) Revenue Expenditure + Capital Expenditure – Revenue Receipt
53. Read the following statements carefully and choose the correct alternatives given below:
    Statement 1: Capital receipts are the income received by the company which is non-recurring.
    Statement 2: Revenue Receipts are the receipts that arise through the core business activities.
    Alternatives:
    (a) Both the statements are true. (b) Both the statements are false.
    (c) Statement 1 is true and Statement 2 is false. (d) Statement 2 is true and Statement 1 is false.
54. From the given information, Primary Deficit would be___________.
    (a) ₹6,000 (b) ₹4,000 (c) ₹5,000 (d) ₹7,000

    Direction: Q. No. 55-60 are to be answered basis of the following data:
    (A) **Industrial Policy Reforms:** To consolidate the gains already achieved during the 1980s and provide more significant competitive stimulus to the domestic industry, a series of reforms were introduced in the Industrial Policy. The government announced a New Industrial Policy on 24 July 1991. The New Industrial Policy established in 1991 sought substantially to deregulate industry to promote a more efficient and competitive industrial economy. The central elements of industrial policy reforms were as follows:
    (B) Industrial licensing was abolished for all projects except in 18 industries. With this, 80 per cent of the industry was taken out of the licensing framework.
    (C) The Monopolies & Restrictive Trade Practices (MRTP) Act was repealed to eliminate large companies' need for prior capacity expansion or diversification approval.
    (D) Areas reserved for the public sector were narrowed down, and private sector participation was permitted in core and primary industries. The new policy reduced the number of areas reserved from 17 to 8. These eight are mainly those involving strategic and security concerns. (Example, railways, atomic energy etc.)
    (E) The policy encouraged disinvestment of government holdings of the equity share capital of public sector enterprises.
    (F) The public sector units were provided greater autonomy and professional management that could help generate reasonable profits through an MOU(Memorandum of Understanding) between the enterprise and the concerned Ministry. The targets that the enterprise had to achieve were set up.
55. The New Industrial Policy established in __________.
    (a) 1991 (b) 1990 (c) 1992 (d) None of these
56. Read the following statements carefully and choose the correct alternatives given below:
    Statement 1: Industrial licensing was abolished for all projects except in 18 industries. With this, 80 per cent of the industry was taken out of the licensing framework.
    Statement 2: Industrial licensing was abolished for all projects except in 18 industries. With this, 60 per cent of the industry was taken out of the licensing framework.
    Alternatives:
    (a) Both the statements are true. (b) Both the statements are false.
    (c) Statement 1 is true and Statement 2 is false. (d) Statement 2 is true and Statement 1 is false.

57. Read the following statements - Assertion (A) and Reason (R):

Assertion (A): Delicensing of industries was an important step taken under liberalisation.

Reason (R): Unwanted control and restrictions led to economic stagnation before 1991.

From the given alternatives, choose the correct one:

Alternatives:

(a) Both Assertion (A) and Reason (R) are true, and Reason (R) is the correct explanation of Assertion (A).

(b) Both Assertion (A) and Reason (R) are true, and Reason (R) is not the correct explanation of Assertion (A).

(c) Assertion (A) is true, but Reason (R) is false.

(d) Assertion (A) is false, but Reason (R) is true.

58. In the light of the given text and shared knowledge, identify the incorrect statement:

(a) Areas reserved for the public sector were narrowed down, and private sector participation was permitted in core and primary industries.

(b) The Monopolies & Restrictive Trade Practices (MRTP) Act was repealed to eliminate large companies' need for prior capacity expansion or diversification approval.

(c) The public sector units were provided greater autonomy.

(d) The limit was raised to 74 per cent and subsequently to 100 per cent for many chemical industries.

59. Read the following statements carefully and choose the correct alternatives given below:

Statement 1: The policy encouraged investment of government holdings of the equity share capital of public sector enterprises.

Statement 2: The policy encouraged disinvestment of government holdings of the equity share capital of public sector enterprises.

Alternatives:

(a) Both the statements are true.

(b) Both the statements are false.

(c) Statement 1 is true and Statement 2 is false.

(d) Statement 2 is true and Statement 1 is false.

60. Read the following statements - Assertion (A) and Reason (R):

Assertion (A): The New Industrial Policy established in 1991 sought substantially to deregulate industry to promote a more efficient and competitive industrial economy.

Reason (R): To consolidate the gains already achieved during the 1980s and provide more significant competitive stimulus to the domestic industry, a series of reforms were introduced in the Industrial Policy to bring out rapid and sustained improvement in the quality of the people of India. From the given alternatives, choose the correct one:

Alternatives:

(a) Both Assertion (A) and Reason (R) are true, and Reason (R) is the correct explanation of Assertion (A).

(b) Both Assertion (A) and Reason (R) are true, and Reason (R) is not the correct explanation of Assertion (A).

(c) Assertion (A) is true, but Reason (R) is false.

(d) Assertion (A) is false, but Reason (R) is true.

❑❑

Sample Paper 5

Economics

SECTION-A

(20 questions out of 24 questions are to be attempted)

1. Institution that accepts deposits for lending purpose is known as ___________.
   - (a) Commercial Bank
   - (b) Central Bank
   - (c) Government
   - (d) Public

2. When Government spends more than it collects by way of revenue, it incurs __________.
   - (a) Budget surplus
   - (b) Budget deficit
   - (c) Capital expenditure
   - (d) Revenue expenditure

3. Identify the year in which the 'Liberalised Industrial Policy' in India was announced for the first time?
   - (a) 1992
   - (b) 1995
   - (c) 1991
   - (d) 1996

4. Identify which of the following is an increase in the aggregate output of goods and services.
   - (a) Economic development
   - (b) Economic planning
   - (c) Economic growth
   - (d) Economy

5. Read the following statements carefully and choose the correct alternative from the following :

   Statement 1 : Although there has been a steady decline in the poverty over last two decades. Still, the total number of poor people has remained constant.

   Statement 2 : There has been a considerable growth in the population.

   Alternatives:
   - (a) Both the statements are true.
   - (b) Both the statements are false.
   - (c) Statement 1 is true and Statement 2 is false.
   - (d) Statement 2 is true and Statement 1 is false.

6. Ms. Srishti, an economics teacher, explained a condition characterised by severe deprivation of basic human needs, including food, safe drinking water, sanitation facilities, health, shelter, education, and information. It depends not only on income but also on access to services.

   From the following, choose the correct alternative which specifies the concept explained by her?
   - (a) Absolute poverty
   - (b) Relative poverty
   - (c) Unemployment
   - (d) None of these

7. Two friends, Lovely and Kanika, were discussing the poverty 'the condition in which people lack the minimum amount of income needed to maintain the average standard of living in the society.'

   Identify the type of measure they were talking about.
   - (a) Absolute poverty
   - (b) Relative poverty
   - (c) Unemployment
   - (d) None of these

8. Read the following statements carefully and choose the correct alternative from the following :

   Statement 1: Money acts as a medium of exchange.

   Statement 2: Law legalizes the use of money as a medium of exchange.

   Alternatives:
   - (a) Both the statements are true
   - (b) Both the statements are false
   - (c) Statement 1 is true and Statement 2 is false
   - (d) Statement 2 is true and Statement 1 is false

9. Difference between the fiscal deficit and interest payment is called __________.
   (a) Primary deficit   (b) Budget deficit   (c) Revenue deficit   (d) Capital deficit

10. Identify the number of industries reserved for the public sector under the industrial policy of 1991.
   (a) 8   (b) 6   (c) 3   (d) 5

11. The economic reforms were intended to take the Indian economy into three specific directions, which are :
   (a) LPG   (b) DPG   (c) LDG   (d) DLP

12. The priority areas of the public sector industries, according to New Industrial Policy, 1997 are__________.
   (a) essential infrastructure goods and services
   (b) exploration and exploitation of oil and mineral resources
   (c) technology development and building up of manufacturing capacities in crucial areas
   (d) All of the above

13. According to the Industrial Policy Resolution of 1956, Schedule B has __________ Industries.
   (a) 12   (b) 15   (c) 16   (d) 17

14. Read the following statements carefully and choose the correct alternatives given below:
   Statement 1: Government budget is an annual estimated statement of revenue and expenditure during the coming fiscal year.
   Statement 2: Through the government budget, it tries to reduce the regional variations.
   Alternatives:
   (a) Both the statements are true   (b) Both the statements are false
   (c) Statement 1 is true and Statement 2 is false   (d) Statement 2 is true and Statement 1 is false

15. Read the following statements carefully and choose the correct alternatives given below:
   Statement 1: India's net export of services have a positive balance.
   Statement 2: India is the largest receiver of remittances around the world.
   Alternatives:
   (a) Both the statements are true   (b) Both the statements are false
   (c) Statement 1 is true and Statement 2 is false   (d) Statement 2 is true and Statement 1 is false

16. Human Development as its main locus in the __________.
   (a) eighth plan   (b) ninth plan   (c) seventh plan   (d) twelfth plan

17. From the following given sets of statements in columns I and II. Choose the correct pair of statements :

Column-I	Column-II
(A) Industrial Development Act	(i) 1944
(B) Employment in agriculture	(ii) 1951
(C) Second industrial policy	(iii) 50%
(D) Privatisation	(iv) Transfer of public ownership to private

   Alternatives:
   (a) A-(i)   (b) B-(ii)
   (c) C-(iii)   (d) D-(iv)

18. LQP raj refers to______________.
   (a) license, quota, privatisation raj   (b) liberalisation, quota, permit raj
   (c) license, quota, permit raj   (d) license, quarter, privatisation raj

19. Those who regularly move in and out of poverty are called ________________.
   (a) Chronically poor   (b) Churning poor
   (c) Occasionally poor   (d) Transient poor

20. The process of removal of import restrictions which began in 1991 completed in a phased manner with the removal of restrictions on__________.
   (a) 515 items   (b) 735 items   (c) 715 items   (d) 550 items

21. In the present scenario, the most precious stock is the stock of skill, ability, expertise, education, and knowledge in a nation. This is known as _______________.
    (a) Human Development   (b) None   (c) Human Resource   (d) Human Capital
22. These reserves are assets denominated in foreign currency held by the Central Bank (RBI) and not by commercial banks. These are known as:
    (a) Foreign Exchange Reserves   (b) Workman Compensation Reserve
    (c) Investment Fluctuation Fund   (d) None of these
23. Read the following statements carefully and choose the correct alternatives given below:
    Statement 1: A current account deficit is financed by attracting capital inflows, *e.g.,* foreigners are buying domestic assets.
    Statement 2: Current account deficit may cause depreciation as there is greater demand for imports and foreign currency.
    Alternatives:
    (a) Both the statements are true   (b) Both the statements are false
    (c) Statement 1 is true and Statement 2 is false (d) Statement 2 is true and Statement 1 is false
24. Balance in capital account refer to the.
    (a) Nation's net exports of goods and services
    (b) Nation's net exports of financial claims
    (c) Nation's net exports of international official reserve assets
    (d) Nation's sum of net exports of goods, services and financial claims

SECTION-B

(20 questions out of 24 questions are to be attempted)

25. Read the following statements - Assertion (A) and Reason (R):
    Assertion (A): A country is in a debt trap if it faces difficulties in repayments.
    Reason (R): It is required to borrow money to make interest payments on outstanding loans .
    From the given alternatives choose the correct one:
    Alternatives:
    (a) Both Assertion (A) and Reason (R) are correct, and Reason is the correct explanation for Assertion (A).
    (b) Both Assertion (A) and Reason (R) are correct, but Reason is not the correct explanation for Assertion (A).
    (c) Assertion (A) is false, but Reason (R) is true.
    (d) Both Assertion and Reason are incorrect.
26. SHGs promoted the habit of savings among ____________ households.
    (a) Rural   (b) Urban   (c) Foreign   (d) None of these
27. Read the following statements - Assertion (A) and Reason (R):
    Assertion (A): Commercial Banks contribute to the quantum of money supply in the economy through credit creation.
    Reason (R): As they do have note-issuing authority.
    From the given alternatives choose the correct one:
    Alternatives:
    (a) Both Assertion (A) and Reason (R) are true, and Reason (R) is the correct explanation of Assertion (A).
    (b) Both Assertion (A) and Reason (R) are true, and Reason (R) is not the correct explanation of Assertion (A).
    (c) Assertion (A) is true but Reason (R) is false.
    (d) Assertion (A) is false but Reason (R) is true.
28. Which is incorrect from the following highlights of the New Small Scale Industrial Policy, 1991?
    (a) Launch of factoring services by SIDBI
    (b) Permission to other units to invest up to 24 per cent in the SSI
    (c) Package for handloom and the aircraft sector
    (d) Tiny sector investment limit raised to ₹7 lakhs

29. Read the following statements - Assertion (A) and Reason (R):

Assertion (A): The monetary policy is a policy formulated by the Central Bank.

Reason (R): The policy involves measures taken to regulate the economy's money supply, availability, and cost of credit.

From the given alternatives choose the correct one:

Alternatives:

(a) Both Assertion (A) and Reason (R) are true, and Reason (R) is the correct explanation of Assertion (A).

(b) Both Assertion (A) and Reason (R) are true, and Reason (R) is not the correct explanation of Assertion (A).

(c) Assertion (A) is true, but Reason (R) is false.

(d) Assertion (A) is false, but Reason (R) is true.

30. From the set of statements given in Column I and Column II, choose the correct pair of statements:

Column-I	Column-II
(A) Economic development programme	(i) Liberalisation, privatisation and globalisation.
(B) Privatisation	(ii) Economic exploitation
(C) Industrial Development Act	(iii) Economic immobility
(D) Employment in agriculture	(iv) 1944

Alternatives:

(a) A-(i)   (b) B-(ii)   (c) C-(iii)   (d) D-(iv)

31. The following figure showing, rates of extreme poverty in different countries.

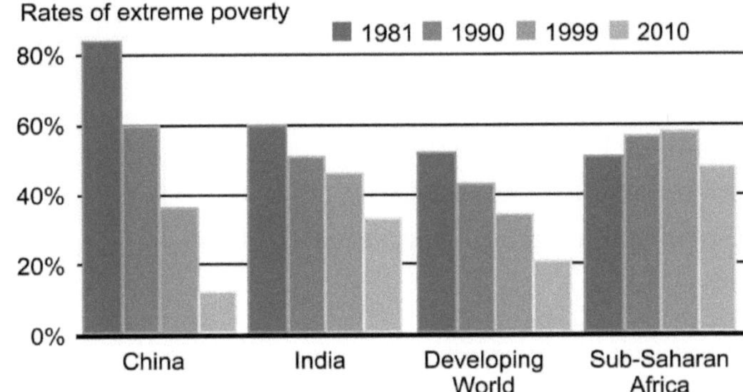

Based on the given bar diagram, identify the country which has been able to achieve the highest reduction in poverty from 1981 to 2010.

(a) India   (b) China

(c) Developing World   (d) Sub-Saharan Africa

32.

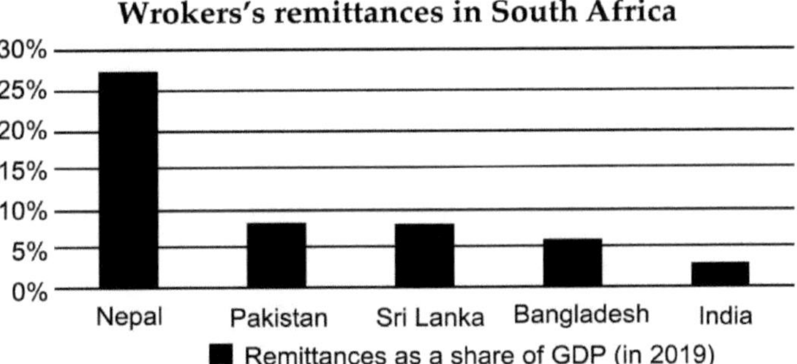

Based on the information mentioned above, answer the following question:

_____________ depicts the least remittances as a share of GDP.

(a) Nepal   (b) Pakistan   (c) India   (d) None of these

33. Read the following statements - Assertion (A) and Reason (R):

    Assertion (A): The modern currency is used as a medium of exchange; however, it does not use its own.

    Reason (R): Modem currency is easy to carry

    From the given alternatives choose the correct one:

    Alternatives:

    (a) Both Assertion (A) and Reason (R) are true, and Reason (R) is the correct explanation of Assertion (A).

    (b) Both Assertion (A) and Reason (R) are true, and Reason (R) is not the correct explanation of Assertion (A).

    (c) Assertion (A) is true, but Reason (R) is false.

    (d) Assertion (A) is false, but Reason (R) is true.

34. Read the following statements carefully and choose the correct alternatives given below:

    Statement 1: Human capital formation in raises production and leads to economic growth.

    Statement 2: Human capital formation possess innovative skills.

    Alternatives:

    (a) Both the statements are true.　　　　(b) Both the statements are false.

    (c) Statement 1 is true and Statement 2 is false.　　　　(d) Statement 2 is true and Statement 1 is false.

35. Read the following statements carefully and choose the correct alternatives given below:

    Statement 1: The capital account only consists of long-term capital transactions.

    Statement 2: The current account includes all transactions which give rise to or use up national income.

    Alternatives:

    (a) Both the statements are true.　　　　(b) Both the statements are false.

    (c) Statement 1 is true, and Statement 2 is false.　　　　(d) Statement 2 is true, and Statement 1 is false.

36. Arrange the following poverty alleviation programmes in India in chronological order and choose the correct alternatives :

    (i) National Rural Employment Programme (NREP).

    (ii) Integrated Rural Development Programme (IRDP).

    (iii) Rural Landless Employment Guarantee Programme (RLEGP).

    (iv) Jawahar Rozgar Yojana (JRY).

    Alternatives:

    (a) (ii), (i), (iv), (iii)　　　　(b) (ii), (iv), (i), (iii)

    (c) (iv), (i), (iii), (ii)　　　　(d) (iii), (iv), (i), (ii)

37. Read the following statements -Assertion (A) and Reason (R), choose one of the correct alternatives given below:

    Assertion (A): Banks charge a higher interest rate on loans than what they offer on deposits.

    Reason (R): The difference between what is charged from borrowers and what is paid to depositors is their primary source of income.

    Alternatives:

    (a) Both Assertion (A) and Reason (R) are true, and Reason (R) is the correct explanation of Assertion (A).

    (b) Both Assertion (A) and Reason (R) are true, and Reason (R) is not the correct explanation of Assertion (A).

    (c) Assertion (A) is true, but Reason (R) is false.

    (d) Assertion (A) is false, but Reason (R) is true.

38. __________ and __________ is an institutional source of rural credit.

    (i) Moneylenders　　　　(ii) Regional Rural Banks

    (iii) Traders　　　　(iv) Commercial Banks

    Alternatives:

    (a) (i) and (ii)　　　　(b) (ii) and (iv)　　　　(c) (i) and (iii)　　　　(d) (i) and (iv)

39. Read the following statements -Assertion (A) and Reason(R); choose one of the correct alternatives given below:

Alternatives:

Assertion (A): Money Multiplier refers to the creation of credit by the Commercial Bank.

Reason (R): Money creation by Commercial Bank raises the National Income

(a) Both Assertion (A) and Reason (R) are true, and Reason (R) is the correct explanation of Assertion (A).

(b) Both Assertion (A) and Reason (R) are true, and Reason (R) is not the correct explanation of Assertion (A).

(c) Assertion (A) is true, but Reason (R) is false.

(d) Assertion (A) is false, but Reason (R) is true.

40. Read the following statements -Assertion (A) and Reason (R); choose one of the correct alternatives given below:

Assertion (A): The Public Distribution System (PDS), which evolved as a management system for food and distribution of foodgrains, plays a significant role in poverty alleviation.

Reason (R): Allocations of commodities such as rice, wheat, kerosene, and sugar to below poverty line families.

Alternatives:

(a) Both Assertion (A) and Reason (R) are true, and Reason (R) is the correct explanation of Assertion (A).

(b) Both Assertion (A) and Reason (R) are true, and Reason (R) is not the correct explanation of Assertion (A).

(c) Assertion (A) is true, but Reason (R) is false.

(d) Assertion (A) is false, but Reason (R) is true.

41. Read the following statements -Assertion (A) and Reason(R); choose one of the correct alternatives given below:

Assertion (A): Schemes like Pradhan Mantri Awas Yojana and Housing for All by 2022 were developed to provide housing to the rural and urban poor.

Reason (R): Poverty Alleviation is the set of steps taken in an economic and humanitarian way for eradicating poverty from a country.

Alternatives:

(a) Both Assertion (A) and Reason (R) are true, and Reason (R) is the correct explanation of Assertion (A).

(b) Both Assertion (A) and Reason (R) are true, and Reason (R) is not the correct explanation of Assertion (A).

(c) Assertion (A) is true, but Reason (R) is false.

(d) Assertion (A) is false, but Reason (R) is true.

42. Choose the correct alternatives which can be included under the current account?

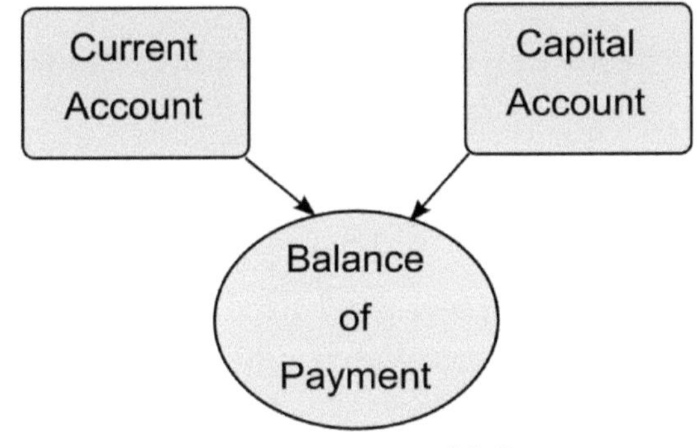

(a) Foreign Investment

(b) Loans

(c) Banking

(d) The nation's earnings and spending abroad

43. ___________means giving loans to individuals for establishing self-employment.

(a) Macro Credit   (b) Micro Credit   (c) Both (a) and (b)   (d) None of these

44. The balance of trade shows a deficit of ₹300 crores. The value of exports is ₹500 crores. The value of imports would be ______________.

(a) ₹200 crores   (b) ₹800 crores   (c) – ₹800 crores   (d) None of these

45. Read the following statements carefully and choose the correct alternatives given below:

Statement 1: The total of the current account must balance with the total of capital and financial accounts in ideal situations.

Statement 2: The current account is used to mark the inflow and outflow of goods and services into a country.

Alternatives:

(a) Both the statements are true.
(b) Both the statements are false.
(c) Statement 1 is true and Statement 2 is false.
(d) Statement 2 is true and Statement 1 is false.

46. Read the following statements -Assertion (A) and Reason (R); choose one of the correct alternatives given below:

Assertion (A): To curb inflation, the RBI should sell the Government securities.

Reason (R): When RBI sells government securities to the people and Commercial Banks, money will flow to RBI, reducing Commercial Banks' lending capacity.

Alternatives:

(a) Both Assertion (A) and Reason (R) are true, and Reason (R) is the correct explanation of Assertion (A).

(b) Both Assertion (A) and Reason (R) are true, and Reason (R) is not the correct explanation of Assertion (A).

(c) Assertion (A) is true, but Reason (R) is false.

(d) Assertion (A) is false, but Reason (R) is true.

47. Identify which of the following is the correct process involving assembling, storing, processing, transportation, packaging, grading, and distributing different agricultural commodities across the country?

(a) Agricultural Management
(b) Agricultural Banking
(c) Agricultural Diversification
(d) Agricultural Marketing

48. From the set of statements given in Column I and Column II, choose the correct pair of statements:

Column-I	Column-II
(A) Machines and buildings are	(i) Natural capital
(B) The stock of skill, ability expertise	(ii) Human capital
(C) HDI index rates	(iii) 0 to 10
(D) Human capital	(iv) Quantitative improvement

(a) A-(i)
(b) B-(ii)
(c) C-(iii)
(d) D-(iv)

SECTION-C

(10 questions out of 12 questions are to be attempted)

Direction: Q. No. 49 – 54 are to be answered on the basis of the following data:

Particulars	(₹ in crore)
(i) Revenue Expenditure	70,000
(ii) Borrowings	15,000
(iii) Revenue Receipt	50,000
(iv) Interest Payment	25% of revenue deficit

49. Interest payment using the above given information would be ____________.

(a) ₹5,000 crores
(b) ₹10,000 crores
(c) ₹15,000 crores
(d) ₹20,000 crores

50. Revenue Deficit using the above given information would be _________.

(a) ₹8,000 crores
(b) ₹10,000 crores
(c) ₹15,000 crores
(d) ₹20,000 crores

51. Identify which of the following is not an example of capital receipt.

(a) Dividend received.

(b) Cash received from the sale of fixed assets.

(c) Amount received from Shareholders and debentureholders.

(d) Borrowings include loans, disinvestment, insurance claims etc.

52. Identify the formula to calculate Revenue Deficit?

(a) Revenue expenditure + Revenue receipt

(b) Revenue expenditure – Revenue receipt

(c) Revenue expenditure ÷ Revenue receipt

(d) Revenue expenditure × Revenue receipt

53. Read the following statements carefully and choose the correct alternatives given below:

Statement 1: Capital receipts are receipts that create liabilities or reduce financial assets.

Statement 2: Revenue receipts can be defined as those receipts which neither create any liability nor cause any reduction in the assets of the Government.

Alternatives:

(a) Both the statements are true.

(b) Both the statements are false.

(c) Statement 1 is true and Statement 2 is false.

(d) Statement 2 is true and Statement 1 is false.

54. Calculate Primary Deficit using the above-given information. It would bne ___________.

(a) ₹5,000 crores

(b) ₹10,000 crores

(c) ₹15,000 crores

(d) ₹20,000 crores

Direction: Q. No. 55-60 are to be answered based on the following data:

Liberalisation, Privatisation and Globalisation.

In the early nineties, India's economy faced a significant crisis, followed by a foreign exchange crunch that pushed the economy down. As a result, the country exhausted its foreign exchange reserves. To face the crisis, the Government came up with new economic adjustments by bringing new reforms.

These reforms were known as 'structural adjustments'. In addition, the Government announced a New Economic Policy on July 24, 1991. This new model of economic reforms is commonly known as the LPG or Liberalisation, Privatisation and Globalisation model.

The main objective was to put the Indian economy into the arena of "Globalisation" and to give it a new thrust on market orientation. The policy was intended to move towards a higher economic growth rate and build sufficient foreign exchange reserves.

Liberalisation:

Liberalisation removes state control over economic activities. It provides better autonomy to the businesses in decision-making without government interference. It was assumed that demand and supply market forces would automatically operate to achieve better efficiency, and economic health would recover. Internally, this was enacted by bringing reforms in the fundamental and financial sectors and externally by releasing foreign exchange and trade from state governments grip.

Privatisation:

It means withdrawing the ownership or management of a government enterprise. Government companies are converted into private companies in two ways.

(i) Government is shredded from the ownership or management of the public-sector companies.

(ii) By the blatant sale of public sector companies.

Privatisation is the transfer of the control and ownership of businesses from the public sector to the private sector. It means a decline in the role of the Government as the property rights shaft from Public to private.

Since planning, the public sector enterprises had been experiencing challenges, such as low efficiency, low profitability, growing losses, political interference, lack of autonomy, labour issues, etc. Therefore, to address this situation, the Government introduced privatisation in the economy.

Conditions to be Met Before Privatisation:

Liberalisation and deregulation of the economy is a significant prerequisite for privatisation to set foot. Capital markets should be developed to bear the brunt of disinvested public sector shares.

Globalisation:

Globalisation can be defined as the integration of the national economy with the world economy. It enables a free flow of information, technology, goods and services, capital investments and even people across different countries. It brings the trade, investments and markets from various countries under one umbrella. Thus, it promotes a more lucid economy. Globalisation is also divided into three types.

The Main Elements of Globalisation are:

(i) To open the domestic markets for the steady flow of foreign manufactured goods, India reduced customs duties on imports.

(ii) The amount of foreign capital in a country is a good indicator of the growth and globalisation of an economy.

(iii) The Foreign Exchange Regulation Act (FERA) was liberalised in 1993, the Foreign Exchange Management Act (FEMA) 1999 was passed to start transactions in foreign currency.

55. Opening up the Indian economy to foreign investors and allowing Indian investors to invest abroad is known as _______________.

   (a) Globalisation   (b) None

   (c) Privatisation   (d) Liberalisation

56. Read the following statements carefully and choose the correct alternatives given below:

   Statement 1: Rapid improvement in technology has been one major factor that has stimulated the globalisation process.

   Statement 2: Developing countries are likely to become at par with developed countries in terms of technological development due to globalisation.

   Alternatives:

   (a) Both the statements are true.   (b) Both the statements are false.

   (c) Statement 1 is true and Statement 2 is false.   (d) Statement 2 is true and Statement 1 is false.

57. Read the following statements - Assertion (A) and Reason (R):

   Assertion (A): Global Production has a complex structure.

   Reason (R): Production of one good may take in different parts of the world. For Instance, equipment may be formed by combining the components produced in different countries.

   From the given alternatives, choose the correct one:

   Alternatives:

   (a) Both Assertion (A) and Reason (R) are true, and Reason (R) is the correct explanation of Assertion (A).

   (b) Both Assertion (A) and Reason (R) are true, and Reason (R) is not the correct explanation of Assertion (A).

   (c) Assertion (A) is true, but Reason (R) is false.

   (d) Assertion (A) is false, but Reason (R) is true.

58. In the light of the given text and common knowledge, identify the incorrect statement, regarding the steps that are taken towards liberalisation.

   (a) Delicensing of industries   (b) Dereservation of industries

   (c) Conflict of values   (d) Delicensing of imports

59. Read the following statements - Assertion (A) and Reason (R):

   Statement 1: The removal of trade barriers is known as liberalisation.

   Statement 2: Federalisation of trade allows businesses to decide which goods to import and which to export freely is the outcome of liberalisation.

Alternatives:

(a) Both the statements are true.

(b) Both the statements are false.

(c) Statement 1 is true and Statement 2 is false.

(d) Statement 2 is true and Statement 1 is false.

60. Read the following statements - Assertion (A) and Reason (R):

Assertion (A): Globalisation leads to increased competition in international trade and domestic markets.

Reason (R): Globalisation also makes consumers better off as they have a wider variety of goods to choose from at lower prices.

From the given alternatives, choose the correct one:

Alternatives:

(a) Both Assertion (A) and Reason (R) are true, and Reason (R) is the correct explanation of Assertion (A).

(b) Both Assertion (A) and Reason (R) are true, and Reason (R) is not the correct explanation of Assertion (A).

(c) Assertion (A) is true, but Reason (R) is false.

(d) Assertion (A) is false, but Reason (R) is true.

❑❑

Sample Paper 6

Economics

SECTION-A

(20 questions out of 24 questions are to be attempted)

1. Spot the capital receipt__________.
   - (a) Tax received
   - (b) External grants received
   - (c) Dividend received
   - (d) Disinvestment

2. __________ is not formed part of current account under the balance of payments.
   - (a) Export and import of goods
   - (b) Export and import of services
   - (c) Income receipts and payments
   - (d) Capital receipts and payments

3. Identify which of the following is the impact of the government budget on the economy, excluding.
   - (a) Bring better allocation of resources
   - (b) Implement government welfare programs
   - (c) Bring aggregate fiscal indiscipline level
   - (d) Better access to public goods

4. Identify the term whose definition is given below?

   Those items, whose transactions are done by consideration of profit (economic motive).
   - (a) Autonomous items
   - (b) Accommodating items
   - (c) Both (a) and (b)
   - (d) None of these

5. Read the following statements carefully and choose the correct alternative from the following:

   Statement 1: Primary Deficit is the difference between Fiscal Deficit and interest payment.

   Statement 2: Primary Deficit is the difference between imports and exports.

   Alternatives:
   - (a) Both the statements are true.
   - (b) Both the statements are false.
   - (c) Statement 1 is true and Statement 2 is false.
   - (d) Statement 2 is true and Statement 1 is false.

6. Ms. Sakshi, an economics teacher, explained the concept that it is required to borrow money to make interest payments on outstanding loans by country then the country is said to be in:

   From the following, choose the correct alternative, which specifies the concept explained by her.
   - (a) Debt trap
   - (b) Good Cash Flow
   - (c) Insolvent
   - (d) None of these

7. Two friends, Radha and Simran, discussed the Declaration of National Policy Farmers had provided a holistic approach to the development of the farm sector. The broad areas of its coverage includes: Focus will be on the economic well-being of the farmers in addition to production and productivity.

   Simran gave the statement mentioned above; identify the year of the declaration of national policy.
   - (a) 2006
   - (b) 2008
   - (c) 2007
   - (d) 2009

8. Read the following statements carefully and choose the correct alternative from the following:

   Statement 1: India's net export of services have a positive balance.

   Statement 2: India is the largest receiver of remittances around the world.

   Alternatives:
   - (a) Both the statements are true.
   - (b) Both the statements are false.
   - (c) Statement 1 is true and Statement 2 is false.
   - (d) Statement 2 is true and Statement 1 is false.

9. __________and __________on health makes human more efficient and productive.
   - (i) Expenditure
   - (ii) Investment
   - (iii) Income
   - (iv) None of these

Identify the correct alternatives from the following :

Alternatives :

(a) (i) and (ii)   (b) (i) and (iii)   (c) (iii) and (iv)   (d) (iv) and (i)

10. Poverty is a state in which a person is?

(a) poor   (b) does not have the proper home

(c) inability to fulfil basic requirements   (d) None of these

11. __________ refers to the ability of humans to contribute to the process of value addition in the economy.

(a) Human capital   (b) Human resource

(c) Human development   (d) Human being

12. India adopted __________ approach in 1969 to meet the need for Rural Credit.

(a) social banking   (b) multi-agency

(c) both (a) and (b)   (d) none of these

13. The person who made the most notable attempt to calculate India's national income during the British rule in India, on the eve of independence was __________.

(a) O. Hume   (b) Dadabhai Naoroji

(c) Surendra Nath Bonnerji   (d) Mahatma Gandhi

14. Read the following statements carefully and choose the correct alternative from the following:

Statement 1: In absolute poverty, a person fails to reach the standard minimum level of consumption.

Statement 2: In absolute poverty, a person fails to reach the standard maximum level of consumption.

Alternatives:

(a) Both the statements are true.   (b) Both the statements are false.

(c) Statement 1 is true and Statement 2 is false.   (d) Statement 2 is true and Statement 1 is false.

15. Read the following statements carefully and choose the correct alternative from the following:

Statement 1: Physical capital is tangibly sold in the market.

Statement 2: Sources of human capital refer to adding to the stock of capital.

Alternatives:

(a) Both the statements are true.   (b) Both the statements are false.

(c) Statement 1 is true and Statement 2 is false.   (d) Statement 2 is true and Statement 1 is false.

16. __________ means giving small loans to an individual for establishing self-employment.

(a) Macro-credit   (b) Micro-credit

(c) Both (a) and (b)   (d) None of these

17. From the following given sets of statements in columns I and II. Choose the correct pair of statements :

Balance of invisible trade is equal to :

Column-I	Column-II
(A) Import of goods and services	(i) Credit in the current account
(B) Credit in the current account	(ii) Debit in the current account
(C) Direct investment receipt	(iii) Credit in the capital account
(D) Portfolio investment payments	(iv) Debit in the current account

Alternatives:

(a) A-(i)   (b) B-(ii)   (c) C-(iii)   (d) D-(iv)

18. Giving permission to withdraw money by an amount more than deposited to is known as __________.

(a) advance   (b) overdraft   (c) loan   (d) None of these

19. __________ is a non tax receipt.

(a) Sale tax   (b) Gift and Grants   (c) Gift tax   (d) Excise duty

20. __________ is a minimum calories intake for people in the urban area.

(a) 2400   (b) 2000   (c) 2200   (d) 2100

21. Anything which is generally acceptable by the people as medium of exchange, measure of value, standard of deferred payment and performs the function of store of value. It is known as__________.
    (a) Measure of Money
    (b) Medium of Exchange
    (c) Money
    (d) None of these

22. Balance in capital account refer to the:
    (a) Nation's net exports of goods and services
    (b) Nation's net exports of financial claims
    (c) Nation's net exports of international official reserve assets
    (d) Nation's sum of net exports of goods, services and financial claims

23. Read the following statements carefully and choose the correct alternative from the following:
    Statement 1: Budget is a statement of expected annual receipt and expenditure.
    Statement 2: Government budget indicates the BOP status of the economy.
    Alternatives:
    (a) Both the statements are true.
    (b) Both the statements are false.
    (c) Statement 1 is true and Statement 2 is false.
    (d) Statement 2 is true and Statement 1 is false.

24. The enrolment ratio of female students in school is__________ and their drop out ratio is __________.
    (a) high, less
    (b) less, high
    (c) less, less
    (d) None of these

SECTION-B

(20 questions out of 24 questions are to be attempted)

25. Read the following statements - Assertion (A) and Reason (R):
    Assertion (A): Increased lending abroad is recorded on the debit side of the capital account.
    Reason (R): Lending affects the asset and liabilities of the economy and involves the outflow of income.
    From the given alternatives, choose the correct one:
    Alternatives:
    (a) Both Assertion (A) and Reason (R) are true, and Reason (R) is the correct explanation of Assertion (A).
    (b) Both Assertion (A) and Reason (R) are true, and Reason (R) is not the correct explanation of Assertion (A).
    (c) Assertion (A) is true, but Reason (R) is false.
    (d) Assertion (A) is false, but Reason (R) is true.

26. _________ are the alternative measures of money supply in India?
    (a) M_1
    (b) M_2
    (c) M_3 and M_4
    (d) All of these

27. Read the following statements - Assertion (A) and Reason (R):
    Assertion (A): Britishers destroyed indigenous handicraft market in India.
    Reason (R): India was made markets for British manufactured products.
    From the given alternatives, choose the correct one:
    Alternatives:
    (a) Both Assertion (A) and Reason (R) are true, and Reason (R) is the correct explanation of Assertion (A).
    (b) Both Assertion (A) and Reason (R) are true, and Reason (R) is not the correct explanation of Assertion (A).
    (c) Assertion (A) is true, but Reason (R) is false.
    (d) Assertion (A) is false, but Reason (R) is true.

28. Identify the correct statements regarding post-liberalisation India's balance of payments position.
    (i) The current account deficit is on account of the net import of services.
    (ii) The capital account surplus accounts for a large amount of external assistance received on a bilateral basis.
    (iii) The balance of payments situation has improved post-liberalisation.

Alternatives:

(a) Only (iii)   (b) (ii) and (iii)   (c) (i) and (ii)   (d) (i) and (iii)

29. Read the following statements - Assertion (A) and Reason (R):

Assertion (A): There was a significant need to introduce a policy measure which could improve the efficiency and productivity in an economy.

Reason (R): As a result, LPG model of growth was introduced in 1991 which provided a structural shift in the policy perspective of Indian economy.

From the given alternatives, choose the correct one:

Alternatives:

(a) Both Assertion (A) and Reason (R) are true, and Reason (R) is the correct explanation of Assertion (A).

(b) Both Assertion (A) and Reason (R) are true, and Reason (R) is not the correct explanation of Assertion (A).

(c) Assertion (A) is true, but Reason (R) is false.

(d) Assertion (A) is false, but Reason (R) is true.

30. From the set of statements given in Column-I and Column-II, choose the correct pair of statements:

Column-I	Column-II
(A) Integrated Rural Development Programme (IRDP)	(i) 1978
(B) Mid-Day Meal Scheme (MDMS)	(ii) 1998
(C) Pradhan Mantri Jan DhanYojana (PMJDY)	(iii) 2014
(D) Pradhan Mantri Gramin Awaas Yojana (PMGAY)	(iv) 2018

Alternatives:

(a) A-(i)   (b) B-(ii)   (c) C-(iii)   (d) D-(iv)

31.

Poverty Rate

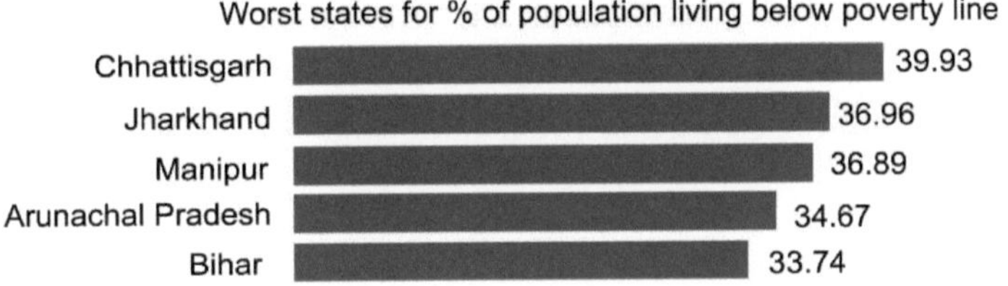

Figure showing Poverty Rate

Based on the given bar diagram, identify the state which is more population of poverty.

(a) Chhattisgarh   (b) Jharkhand   (c) Manipur   (d) None of these

32.

Rate of growth of GDP by Industrial Origin at Factor Cost

(Compound Annual Growth Rate at 1980-81 Prices)

Sectors	1950-51 to 1960-61	1960-61 to 1970-71	1970-71 to 1980-81	1980-81 to 1990-91	1950-51 to 1990-91	1990-91 to 1996-97
(1)	(2)	(3)	(4)	(5)	(6)	(7)
I. Agriculture and allied activities	3.0	2.3	1.5	3.6	2.6	2.8
II. Mining and manufacturing etc.	6.2	5.4	4.0	6.7	5.6	6.6
III. Service sector	4.1	4.6	4.3	6.6	4.9	7.4
GDP at Factor cost	3.9	3.7	3.1	5.6	4.1	5.8

Based on the information mentioned above, answer the following question:

In the 1980s, GDP at factor cost is _____________ (Indian Economic Development)

(a) 4.0   (b) 5.6   (c) 3.1   (d) 6.1

33. Read the following statements - Assertion (A) and Reason (R):

Assertion (A): Non-institutional finance forms an integral part of rural Credit.

Reason (R): Small farmers cannot access bank credit because of borrowers' unfriendly products.

From the given alternatives, choose the correct one:

Alternatives:

(a) Both Assertion (A) and Reason (R) are true, and Reason (R) is the correct explanation of Assertion (A).

(b) Both Assertion (A) and Reason (R) are true, and Reason (R) is not the correct explanation of Assertion (A).

(c) Assertion (A) is true, but Reason (R) is false.

(d) Assertion (A) is false, but Reason (R) is true.

34. Read the following statements carefully and choose the correct alternative from the following:

Statement 1: Total stock of money held by the public at a particular time in an Economy is known as a credit multiplier.

Statement 2: Total stock of money held by the public at a particular time in an Economy is known as money supply.

Alternatives:

(a) Both the statements are true.
(b) Both the statements are false.

(c) Statement 1 is true and Statement 2 is false.
(d) Statement 2 is true and Statement 1 is false.

35. Read the following statements carefully and choose the correct alternative from the following:

Statement 1: RBI is the sole authority to issue and manage currency in India.

Statement 2: A nationalized bank is the sole authority to issue and managed currency in India.

Alternatives:

(a) Both the statements are true.
(b) Both the statements are false.

(c) Statement 1 is true and Statement 2 is false
(d) Statement 2 is true and Statement 1 is false

36. Arrange the following events in chronological order and choose the correct

(i) Cheap imports of British manufactured goods increase in the country.

(ii) The growth rate of the industrial sector was minimal.

(iii) India was reduced to be a mere exporter of raw material.

(iv) India faced a shortage of locally made goods.

Alternatives:

(a) (iii), (iv), (i), (ii)　　　(b) (iv), (ii), (i), (iii)　　(c) (ii), (iv), (i), (iii)　　(d) (iv), (i), (ii), (iii)

37. Read the following statements - Assertion (A) and Reason (R):

Assertion (A): Balance of trade is also referred to as the balance of payments.

Reason (R): Balance of trade includes the value of imports and exports of visible goods and invisible goods.

From the given alternatives, choose the correct one:

Alternatives:

(a) Both Assertion (A) and Reason (R) are true, and Reason (R) is the correct explanation of Assertion (A).

(b) Both Assertion (A) and Reason (R) are true, and Reason (R) is not the correct explanation of Assertion (A).

(c) Assertion (A) is true, but Reason (R) is false.

(d) Assertion (A) is false, but Reason (R) is true.

38. _______________ of the following makes a financial institution a bank.

(a) accepting borrowing
(b) lending

(c) accepting demand deposits
(d) accepting time deposits

39. Read the following statements - Assertion (A) and Reason (R):

Assertion (A): India became an exporter of primary products and an importer of finished consumer and capital goods produced in Britain.

Reason (R): A restrictive policy of commodity production, trade, and tariff pursued by the colonial Government adversely affected India's foreign trade structure, composition, and volume.

From the given alternatives, choose the correct one:

Alternatives:
(a) Both Assertion (A) and Reason (R) are true, and Reason (R) is the correct explanation of Assertion (A).
(b) Both Assertion (A) and Reason (R) are true, and Reason (R) is not the correct explanation of Assertion (A).
(c) Assertion (A) is true, but Reason (R) is false.
(d) Assertion (A) is false, but Reason (R) is true.

40. Read the following statements - Assertion (A) and Reason (R):

Assertion (A): The major policy initiatives, *i.e.,* land reforms and the green revolution, helped India become self-sufficient in foodgrain production.

Reason (R): The proportion of people depending on agriculture did not decline as expected.

From the given alternatives, choose the correct one:

Alternatives:
(a) Both Assertion (A) and Reason (R) are true, and Reason (R) is the correct explanation of Assertion (A).
(b) Both Assertion (A) and Reason (R) are true, and Reason (R) is not the correct explanation of Assertion (A).
(c) Assertion (A) is true, but Reason (R) is false.
(d) Assertion (A) is false, but Reason (R) is true.

41. Read the following statements - Assertion (A) and Reason (R):

Assertion (A): Reserve Bank of India constantly regulates the supply of money.

Reason (R): A Central Bank can undertake actions that follow an expansionary or contractionary policy through monetary policy.

From the given alternatives, choose the correct one:

Alternatives:
(a) Both Assertion (A) and Reason (R) are true, and Reason (R) is the correct explanation of Assertion (A).
(b) Both Assertion (A) and Reason (R) are true, and Reason (R) is not the correct explanation of Assertion (A).
(c) Assertion (A) is true, but Reason (R) is false.
(d) Assertion (A) is false, but Reason (R) is true.

42. Choose the correct alternatives to be filled in given blank:

Rise in Human Capital	Rise Economic Growth
↓	↓
⇒ Modern attitude and outlook better quality of life, higher life expectancy.	⇒ Rise in per capital income
↓	↓
⇒ More efficiency	⇒ More investment in education and health
↓	↓
⇒ More production	⇒ Rise in human capital
↓	
⇒ More economic growth	

If rise in human capital, then ultimate it rises___________.
(a) economic growth   (b) capital growth   (c) quality growth   (d) None of these

43. Seema is discussing if Individuals become landless. Which of the following example is landless labourer?
(a) Urban poor   (b) Rural poor   (c) Both (a) and (b)   (d) None of these

44. If the country's balance of payment is ₹ (–) 200 crores and the total payments are ₹1,000 crores. Its total receipts would be ___________.
(a) ₹100 crore   (b) ₹200 crore   (c) ₹800 crore   (d) None of these

45. Read the following statements carefully and choose the correct alternative from the following:
    Statement 1: During British rule, India saw a massive drain of wealth.
    Statement 2: India generated a large export surplus during the period.
    Alternatives:
    (a) Both the statements are true.
    (b) Both the statements are false.
    (c) Statement 1 is true and Statement 2 is false.
    (d) Statement 2 is true and Statement 1 is false.
46. Read the following statements - Assertion (A) and Reason (R):
    Assertion (A): Rapid improvement in technology has been one of the major factor that has stimulated the globalisation process.
    Reason (R): Developing countries are likely to become at par with developed countries in terms of technological development due to globalisation.
    Alternatives:
    (a) Both Assertion (A) and Reason (R) are true, and Reason (R) is the correct explanation of Assertion (A).
    (b) Both Assertion (A) and Reason (R) are true, and Reason (R) is not the correct explanation of Assertion (A).
    (c) Assertion (A) is true, but Reason (R) is false.
    (d) Assertion (A) is false, but Reason (R) is true.
47. Identify the correct statement from the following.
    (a) Development plans started in India on which year 1st April 1951.
    (b) In the year 1951, what % of contribution was from agriculture towards national income 72%
    (c) Trade policies determine the number of markets for the input of firms.
    (d) In India green revolution was successful for; Wheat and Potato.
48. From the set of statements given in Column-I and Column-II, choose the correct pair of statements:

Column-I	Column-II
(A) Long-term credit	(i) For purchasing land or tractor
(B) Duration of the long term credit	(ii) 1 year
(C) Duration of the short term credit	(iii) 10 year
(D) Co-operative credit	(iv) NABARD

Alternatives:
    (a) A-(i)
    (b) B-(ii)
    (c) C-(iii)
    (d) D-(iv)

SECTION-C

(10 questions out of 12 questions are to be attempted)

Q. No. 49 – 54 are to be answered based on the following data:

Particulars	(₹ in crore)
(i) Revenue Deficit	8,000
(ii) Revenue Expenditure	14,000
(iii) Capital Expenditure	16,000
(iv) Non-debt Creating Capital Receipts	10,000
(v) Interest Payments	7,000

49. As per the given information, Revenue Receipts would be__________.
    (a) ₹5,000
    (b) ₹6,000
    (c) ₹4,000
    (d) ₹7,000
50. As per the given information, Fiscal Deficit would be__________.
    (a) ₹1,200
    (b) ₹15,000
    (c) ₹10,000
    (d) ₹14,000
51. Identify which of the following is an example of revenue receipt.
    (a) Money received for services provided to customers
    (b) Rent received
    (c) Discount received from suppliers, vendors, or creditors
    (d) All of the above

52. Identify the correct formula to calculate the Total Revenue.

    (a) Total expenditure excluding interest payments on its debt – Primary Deficit

    (b) Revenue Expenditure – Revenue Receipt

    (c) Capital Expenditure – Capital Receipt

    (d) Revenue Expenditure + Capital Expenditure – Revenue Receipt

53. Read the following statements carefully and choose the correct alternative from the following:

Statement 1: Primary Deficit is the difference between the current year's fiscal Deficit and the interest paid on the borrowings of the previous year.

Statement 2: Revenue deficit occurs when realized net income is less than the projected net income.

Alternatives:

    (a) Both the statements are true.   (b) Both the statements are false.

    (c) Statement 1 is true and Statement 2 is false.   (d) Statement 2 is true and Statement 1 is false.

54. From the given information, Primary Deficit would be__________.

    (a) ₹6,000   (b) ₹4,000   (c) ₹5,000   (d) ₹7,000

Q. No. 55-60 are to be answered based on the following data:

    (A) The 'Land Reform' measures and 'Green Revolution' were the most outstanding achievements of the Indian Government in increasing agricultural production and productivity. As a result, by the late 1960s, Indian agricultural productivity had increased sufficiently to enable the country to be self-sufficient in foodgrains.

    (B) On the negative side, some 65% of the country's population continued to be employed in agriculture even as late as 1990.

    (C) Economists have found that as a nation becomes more prosperous, the proportion of GDP contributed by agriculture and the proportion of the population working in this sector declined considerably. But in India, between 1950 and 1990, the proportion of GDP contributed by agriculture declined significantly but not the population depending on it (67.5% in 1950 to 64.9% in 1990).

    (D) Agricultural output could have been grown with much fewer people working in the sector. However, the engagement of such a large proportion of the population in agriculture shows that industrial and service sectors did not absorb the people working in the agricultural sector. This is regarded as an essential failure of our policies followed during 1950-1990.

55. __________ were the most significant achievements of the Indian Government.

    (a) Land Reform   (b) Green Revolution

    (c) Both (a) and (b)   (d) None of these

56. Read the following statements carefully and choose the correct alternative from the following:

Statement 1: By the late 1960s, Indian agricultural productivity had increased sufficiently to enable the country to be self-sufficient in foodgrains.

Statement 2: By the late 1960s, Indian agricultural productivity had increased sufficiently to enable the country to be self-sufficient in wheat and oil.

Alternatives:

    (a) Both the statements are true.   (b) Both the statements are false.

    (c) Statement 1 is true and Statement 2 is false.   (d) Statement 2 is true and Statement 1 is false.

57. Read the following statements - Assertion (A) and Reason (R):

Assertion (A): Land Reforms refers to change in the ownership of land Holdings.

Reason (R): At the time of independence, the land tenure system was characterized by intermediaries such as zamindars, who merely collected rent from the actual tillers without contributing towards improvements on the farm.

Alternatives:

    (a) Both Assertion (A) and Reason (R) are true and Reason (R) is the correct explanation of Assertion (A).

    (b) Both Assertion (A) and Reason (R) are true and Reason (R) is not the correct explanation of Assertion (A).

    (c) Assertion (A) is true but Reason (R) is false.

    (d) Assertion (A) is false but Reason (R) is true.

58. In the light of the given text and shared knowledge, identify the incorrect statement:
    (a) Economists have found that as a nation becomes more prosperous, the proportion of GDP contributed by agriculture and the proportion of the population working in this sector declined considerably.
    (b) Agricultural output could have been grown with much fewer people working in the sector.
    (c) Some 65% of the country's population continued to be employed in agriculture even as late as 1990.
    (d) Land reforms (Institutional reforms) – for increasing productivity.

59. Read the following statements carefully and choose the correct alternative from the following:

    Statement 1: – In India, between 1950 and 1990, the proportion of GDP contributed by agriculture declined significantly but not the population depending on it.

    Statement 2: – In India, between 1990 and 2005, the proportion of GDP contributed by agriculture declined significantly but not the population depending on it.

    Alternatives:
    (a) Both the statements are true.
    (b) Both the statements are false.
    (c) Statement 1 is true and Statement 2 is false.
    (d) Statement 2 is true and Statement 1 is false.

60. Read the following statements - Assertion (A) and Reason (R):

    Assertion (A): This refers to the significant increase in the production of foodgrains result from the use of high yielding variety (HYV) seeds, especially for wheat and rice, and the use of fertilizer and pesticide in the correct quantities and a regular supply of water.

    Reason (R): At the time of independence, about 75% of the country's population was dependent on agriculture, and productivity in the agricultural sector was very low because of the use of old technology and the absence of required infrastructure for the vast majority of farmers.

    Alternatives:
    (a) Both Assertion (A) and Reason (R) are true and Reason (R) is the correct explanation of Assertion (A).
    (b) Both Assertion (A) and Reason (R) are true and Reason (R) is not the correct explanation of Assertion (A).
    (c) Assertion (A) is true but Reason (R) is false.
    (d) Assertion (A) is false but Reason (R) is true.

❑❑

Sample Paper 7

Economics

SECTION-A

(20 questions out of 24 questions are to be attempted)

1. Initial deposits made by the people from their resources are called___________.
   (a) time deposits
   (b) secondary deposits
   (c) primary deposits
   (d) term deposits

2. Balance of Payment (BOP) of a country can be defined as_____________.
   (a) a systematic statement of all economic transactions between different states to estimate the GST generated from each state.
   (b) it is the balance of loans to be paid to other countries and organizations like the IMF only.
   (c) balance of Payment (BOP) of a country can be defined as a systematic statement of a country's economic transactions with the rest of the world during a specific period.
   (d) all of the above

3. Identify which objectives the Government attempts to obtain through Budget.
   (a) To Promote Economic Development
   (b) Balanced Regional Development
   (c) Redistribution of Income and Wealth
   (d) All of these

4. Identify which of the following does not form a part of the current account under the balance of payments?
   (a) Export and import of goods
   (b) Export and import of services
   (c) Income receipts and payments
   (d) Capital receipts and payments

5. Read the following statements carefully and choose the correct alternatives from the following:

   Statement 1: Demonetisation is the act of stripping a currency unit of its status as legal tender.

   Statement 2: It occurs whenever there is a change of national currency.

   Alternatives:
   (a) Both the statements are true.
   (b) Both the statements are false.
   (c) Statement 1 is true, and Statement 2 is false.
   (d) Statement 2 is true, and Statement 1 is false.

6. Ms. Srishti, an economics teacher, explained an account that represents a country's imports and exports of goods and services, payments made to foreign investors, and transfers such as Foreign Aid.

   From the following, choose the correct alternative which specifies the concept explained by her?
   (a) Current Account
   (b) Capital Account
   (c) Foreign exchange rate
   (d) None of these

7. Two friends, Lovely and Kanika, were discussing the budget 'Government estimated receipts are less than government estimated expenditure in the budget.

   Identify the type of measure which were they talking about?
   (a) Budget Deficit
   (b) Budget Surplus
   (c) Government Expenditure
   (d) None of these

8. Read the following statements carefully and choose the correct alternatives from the following:

   Statement 1: Money supply does not include money held by Government and Commercial Banks.

   Statement 2: Government and Commercial Banks are themselves the supplier of money.

   Alternatives:
   (a) Both the statements are true.
   (b) Both the statements are false.
   (c) Statement 1 is true, and Statement 2 is false.
   (d) Statement 2 is true, and Statement 1 is false.

9. Which of the following features pertains to the economy of India?
   (i) Mixed economy   (ii) High density of population
   (iii) Less fertility rate   (iv) One-child norm
   Alternatives:
   (a) (i) and (ii)   (b) (i) and (iii)   (c) (i) and (iv)   (d) (ii) and (iv)

10. __________ is the narrow measure of the money supply?
    (a) M_2 (b) M_3 (c) M_1 (d) M_4

11. The main objective of the first five-year plan of India was__________.
    (a) development of infrastructure
    (b) development of ports
    (c) development of the industries
    (d) correct the damage done to the economy by partition

12. MSP is determined with the recommendation of the commission for__________.
    (a) Agricultural Cost and Prices   (b) Aggregated Cost and Prices
    (c) Agricultural Cost and Production   (d) Agricultural Consumption and Prices

13. The development of rural marketing relates to__________.
    (a) transportation   (b) storage   (c) regulated market   (d) all of these

14. Read the following statements carefully and choose the correct alternatives given below:
    Statement 1: Eradication of poverty leads to economic development.
    Statement 2: When the economy grows, employment opportunities are generated for the people below the poverty line, leading to poverty eradication.
    Alternatives:
    (a) Both the statements are true.   (b) Both the statements are false.
    (c) Statement 1 is true, and Statement 2 is false.   (d) Statement 2 is true, and Statement 1 is false.

15. Read the following statements carefully and choose the correct alternatives given below:
    Statement 1: Human Capital formation is required for the effective use of physical capital.
    Statement 2: The formation of human capital raises the life expectancy of people.
    Alternatives:
    (a) Both the statements are true.   (b) Both the statements are false.
    (c) Statement 1 is true, and Statement 2 is false.   (d) Statement 2 is true, and Statement 1 is false.

16. The main aim of the Eleventh Five Year Plan was__________.
    (a) Eradication of regional imbalances   (b) Food, Work and Productivity
    (c) Inclusive Growth in all sectors   (d) Eradication of Poverty

17. Choose the correct pair of statements from the following given sets of statements in columns I and II.

Column-I	Column-II
(A) Regional Rural Banks	(i) Adequate credit for agriculture
(B) Kisan Credit Card	(ii) Certain portion to agriculture and MSMEs
(C) Micro Finance Institutions (MFI)	(iii) Timely credit support from the banking system
(D) Priority Sector Lending (PSL)	(iv) Give loans (usually up to ₹50000) to the poor Farmers

   (a) A-(i)   (b) B-(ii)   (c) C-(iii)   (d) D-(iv)

18. In India green revolution was successful for__________.
    (a) wheat and potato   (b) wheat and rice   (c) cereals and rice   (d) pulses and com

19. The expenditures which do not create assets for the Government is called__________.
    (a) Revenue Expenditure   (b) Capital Expenditure
    (c) Both (a) and (b)   (d) None of these

20. The most urgent problem which prompted the introduction of New Economic Policy in 1991 was__________.
    (a) Poor performance of public sector   (b) High tax rate leading to tax evasion
    (c) Foreign exchange crisis   (d) All of these

21. In a hypothetical situation, if 60 people are poor in a survey that samples 300 people, calculate the proportion of population that is counted as poor?
     (a) 20%   (b) 28.88%   (c) 25%   (d) 23.8%
22. Financial institutions provide financial services to the unserved and unbanked region of the country. These are___________.
     (a) Small Finance Banks (SFBs)
     (b) National Bank for Agriculture and Rural Development (NABARD)
     (c) Kisan Credit Card (1998)
     (d) None of the above
23. Read the following statements carefully and choose the correct alternatives given below:
     Statement 1: This new Green Revolution is leading to foreign ownership over most of India's farmland, undermining farmers' interests.
     Statement 2: New Green Revolution is driven by private (and foreign) interest—notably MNCs.
     Alternatives:
     (a) Both the statements are true.   (b) Both the statements are false.
     (c) Statement 1 is true, and Statement 2 is false.   (d) Statement 2 is true, and Statement 1 is false.
24. The rural population needs a long-term loan________________.
     (a) for making minor improvements on land   (b) to buy seeds
     (c) for buying fertilizers   (d) for buying agricultural machinery

SECTION-B

(20 questions out of 24 questions are to be attempted)

25. Read the following statements - Assertion (A) and Reason (R):
     Assertion (A): Most of the economies these days follow managed exchange rate system.
     Reason (R): The only way government tries to manipulate the exchange rate in a 'managed exchange rate' is by buying and selling foreign currency or indirectly by monetary policy.
     From the given alternatives choose the correct one:
     Alternatives:
     (a) Both Assertion (A) and Reason (R) are true, and Reason (R) is the correct explanation of Assertion (A).
     (b) Both Assertion (A) and Reason (R) are true, and Reason (R) is not the correct explanation of Assertion (A).
     (c) Assertion (A) is true, but Reason (R) is false.
     (d) Assertion (A) is false, but Reason (R) is true.
26. ___________ is the component of M_1 measure of money supply?
     (a) Time deposit   (b) Bill of exchange   (c) Treasury bill   (d) None of these
27. Read the following statements - Assertion (A) and Reason (R):
     Assertion (A): Rural Banking has always given less attention to the credit requirements of small and marginal farmers.
     Reason (R): Marginal farmers enjoy better worthiness.
     From the given alternatives choose the correct one:
     Alternatives:
     (a) Both Assertion (A) and Reason (R) are true, and Reason (R) is the correct explanation of Assertion (A).
     (b) Both Assertion (A) and Reason (R) are true, and Reason (R) is not the correct explanation of Assertion (A).
     (c) Assertion (A) is true, but Reason (R) is false.
     (d) Assertion (A) is false, but Reason (R) is true.
28. Identify the incorrect statement from the following highlights of the Capital Account convertibility.
     (a) Freedom to invest in financial assets of other countries.
     (b) It does not allow foreign investors to purchase Indian financial assets.
     (c) Capital account convertibility is a feature of a nation's financial regime that centres on the ability to conduct transactions of local financial assets into foreign financial assets freely
     (d) It is sometimes referred to as capital asset liberation or CAC.

29. Read the following statements - Assertion (A) and Reason (R):

    Assertion (A): Expenditure on migration is a source of Human Capital Formation.

    Reason (R): Migration to other countries involves the cost of production from one place to another and the higher cost of living to migrated places.

    From the given alternatives choose the correct one:

    Alternatives:

    (a) Both Assertion (A) and Reason (R) are true, and Reason (R) is the correct explanation of Assertion (A).

    (b) Both Assertion (A) and Reason (R) are true, and Reason (R) is not the correct explanation of Assertion (A).

    (c) Assertion (A) is true, but Reason (R) is false.

    (d) Assertion (A) is false, but Reason (R) is true.

30. From the set of statements given in Column-I and Column-II, choose the correct pair of statements:

Column-I	Column-II
(A) Rural development	(i) Additional tools and implements
(B) Human resources	(ii) Improvement in the living conditions of the weaker sections of the population
(C) Infrastructure development	(iii) Electricity, irrigation, transport facilities
(D) Alleviation of poverty	(iv) Literacy

    Alternatives:

    (a) A-(i) (b) B-(ii) (c) C-(iii) (d) D-(iv)

31.

Evolution of Poverty

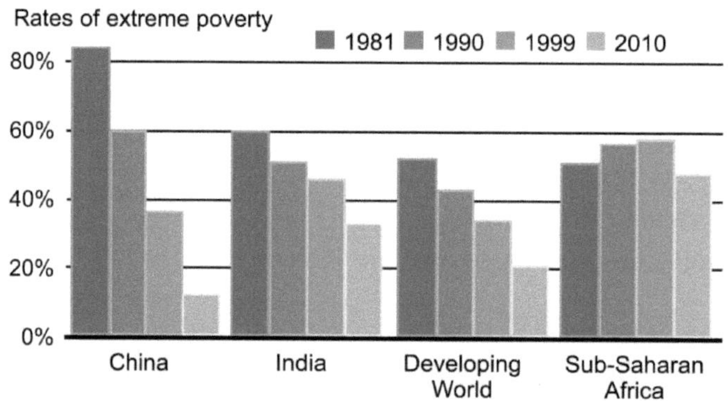

Figure Showing, rates of extreme poverty in different countries

    Based on the given bar diagram, identify the country which has achieved significantly less decline in poverty from the year 1981 to 2010.

    (a) India (b) China (c) Developing World (d) Sub-Saharan Africa

32.

Workers' remittances in South Africa

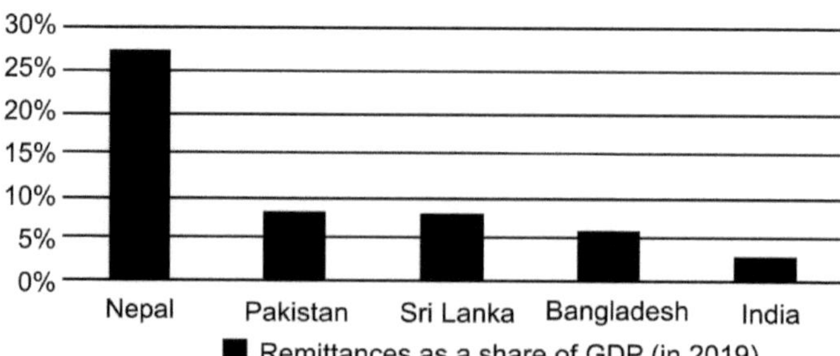

Source : West Bank April 2020

    Based on the information mentioned above, identify,

    which country depicts the highest remittances as a share of GDP?

    (a) Nepal (b) Pakistan (c) India (d) None of these

33. Read the following statements - Assertion (A) and Reason (R):
    Assertion (A): The facilities of human capital have remained adequate.
    Reason (R): The resources allocated to human capital formation have been much less than required.
    From the given alternatives choose the correct one:
    Alternatives:
    (a) Both Assertion (A) and Reason (R) are true, and Reason (R) is the correct explanation of Assertion (A).
    (b) Both Assertion (A) and Reason (R) are true, and Reason (R) is not the correct explanation of Assertion (A).
    (c) Assertion (A) is true, but Reason (R) is false.
    (d) Assertion (A) is false, but Reason (R) is true.

34. Read the following statements carefully and choose the correct alternative:
    Statement 1: On-the-job training is the source of human capital formation.
    Statement 2: After on-the-job training of employees, firm insists that the workers should work for a specific period of time.
    Alternatives:
    (a) Both the statements are true.　　　　　(b) Both the statements are false.
    (c) Statement 1 is true, and Statement 2 is false.　　(d) Statement 2 is true, and Statement 1 is false.

35. Read the following statements carefully and choose the correct alternative:
    Statement 1: Currency held by the public is a monetary liability of the Central Bank.
    Statement 2: Central bank controls credit, whereas Commercial Banks create credit with the currency held by the public.
    Alternatives:
    (a) Both the statements are true.　　　　　(b) Both the statements are false.
    (c) Statement 1 is true, and Statement 2 is false.　　(d) Statement 2 is true, and Statement 1 is false.

36. Arrange the following poverty alleviation programmes in India in chronological order and choose the correct alternatives :
    (i) Growth with Stability.　　　　　(ii) Self-sufficiency in food .
    (iii) A self-generating economy.　　　(iv) Rapid industrialisation.
    (a) (ii), (i), (iv), (iii)　　　　(b) (ii), (iv), (i), (iii)　　　(c) (iv), (i), (iii), (ii)　　　(d) (ii), (iv), (iii), (i)

37. Read the following statements -Assertion (A) and Reason (R), choose one of the correct alternatives given below:
    Assertion (A): The BOP statement helps the Government decide on fiscal and trade policies.
    Reason (R): Depending upon the status of BOP, the country formulates the fiscal (tax-related) and trade policies, as it acts as a report card and exposes the areas which need attention.
    Alternatives:
    (a) Both Assertion (A) and Reason (R) are true, and Reason (R) is the correct explanation of Assertion (A).
    (b) Both Assertion (A) and Reason (R) are true, and Reason (R) is not the correct explanation of Assertion (A).
    (c) Assertion (A) is true, but Reason (R) is false.
    (d) Assertion (A) is false, but Reason (R) is true.

38. _______________and____________ are the functions of a Central Bank.
    (i) Issue of notes
    (ii) Banker to the Government and Banks
    (iii) Money serves as a standard for deferred payments
    (iv) Money serves as a store of value
    (a) (i) and (ii)　　　　(b) (ii) and (iii)　　　(c) (i) and (iii)　　　(d) (i) and (iv)

39. Read the following statements -Assertion (A) and Reason (R), choose one of the correct alternatives given below:
    Assertion (A): One of the pillars of IPR 1956 was to check concentration of economic power in few individuals, groups or business houses.
    Reason (R): It established the public sector as epicentre of industrialisation.

Alternatives:
(a) Both Assertion (A) and Reason (R) are true, and Reason (R) is the correct explanation of Assertion (A).
(b) Both Assertion (A) and Reason (R) are true, and Reason (R) is not the correct explanation of Assertion (A).
(c) Assertion (A) is true, but Reason (R) is false.
(d) Assertion (A) is false, but Reason (R) is true.

40. Read the following statements -Assertion (A) and Reason (R), choose one of the correct alternatives given below:

Assertion (A): The Public Distribution System (PDS), which evolved as a management system for food and distribution of food grains, plays a significant role in poverty alleviation.

Reason (R): Allocations of commodities such as rice, wheat, kerosene, and sugar to below poverty line families.

Alternatives:
(a) Both Assertion (A) and Reason (R) are true, and Reason (R) is the correct explanation of Assertion (A).
(b) Both Assertion (A) and Reason (R) are true, and Reason (R) is not the correct explanation of Assertion (A).
(c) Assertion (A) is true, but Reason (R) is false.
(d) Assertion (A) is false, but Reason (R) is true.

41. Read the following statements -Assertion (A) and Reason (R), choose one of the correct alternatives given below:

Assertion (A): Diversification into non-farm activities is essential because it will reduce the risk from the agriculture sector.

Reason (R): Diversification into non-farm activities is essential because it will provide ecological balance.

Alternatives:
(a) Both Assertion (A) and Reason (R) are true, and Reason (R) is the correct explanation of Assertion (A).
(b) Both Assertion (A) and Reason (R) are true, and Reason (R) is not the correct explanation of Assertion (A).
(c) Assertion (A) is true, but Reason (R) is false.
(d) Assertion (A) is false, but Reason (R) is true.

42. Choose the correct alternatives which can also be included under functions of money?

Roles of Money

(a) Accepting deposits
(b) Standard of deferred payments
(c) Issuing loans
(d) None of these

43. Ms. Tanvi has started a new business venture, she intends to spend a huge amount on education of labourers before putting them to work which enables her to generate more income than an uneducated person. It exhibits the right step towards human capital formation.
Spot which of the following does not directly contributes to the process of human capital formation by Ms. Tanvi.
(a) Better productivity
(b) Adaptation of new technologies
(c) Stimulates Innovation
(d) Good sanitation facilities

44. What will be the value of fiscal deficit if primary deficit is 53000 crores and interest on borrowing is ₹5,000 crore?
(a) ₹55,000
(b) ₹57,000
(c) ₹58,000
(d) ₹60,000

45. Read the following statements carefully and choose the correct alternatives given below:

    Statement 1: The urban poor include people from the rural areas who migrate to cities in search of employment.

    Statement 2: The poverty line expresses the per capita average monthly expenditure by which people can satisfy their minimum needs.

    Alternatives:

    (a) Both the statements are true.
    (b) Both the statements are false.
    (c) Statement 1 is true, and Statement 2 is false.
    (d) Statement 2 is true, and Statement 1 is false.

46. Read the following statements -Assertion (A) and Reason (R), choose one of the correct alternatives given below:

    Assertion (A): Balance of trade is the difference between the value of a country's export and the value of the country's import.

    Reason (R): Economists use the Balance of Trade to measure the relative strength of a country's economy.

    Alternatives:

    (a) Both Assertion (A) and Reason (R) are true, and Reason (R) is the correct explanation of Assertion (A).
    (b) Both Assertion (A) and Reason (R) are true, and Reason (R) is not the correct explanation of Assertion (A).
    (c) Assertion (A) is true, but Reason (R) is false.
    (d) Assertion (A) is false, but Reason (R) is true.

47. Identify the correct one who has the right of note issue?

    (a) Central Bank
    (b) Commercial Bank
    (c) Government
    (d) Co-operative Bank

48. From the set of statements given in Column-I and Column-II, choose the correct pair of statements:

Column-I	Column-II
(A) Balance of trade	(i) Value of import and export of the country.
(B) Current account	(ii) Transactions leading to changes in financial assets and liabilities of a country.
(C) Balance of payments	(iii) Unilateral transfer of goods and services.
(D) Capital account	(iv) All economic transactions between a country's residence and residents of other countries.

    Alternatives:

    (a) A-(i)
    (b) B-(ii)
    (c) C-(iii)
    (d) D-(iv)

SECTION-C

(10 questions out of 12 questions are to be attempted)

Direction: Q. No. 49 – 54 are to be answered based on the following data:

Particulars	(₹ in crore)
(i) Revenue Expenditure	1,00,000
(ii) Borrowings	25,000
(iii) Revenue Receipt	60,000
(iv) Interest Payment	25% of Revenue Deficit

49. __________ is the formula for calculating Primary Deficit?

    (a) Primary deficit = Fiscal deficit – Interest payment
    (b) Primary deficit = Fiscal deficit + Interest payment
    (c) Primary deficit = Fiscal deficit / Interest payment
    (d) Primary deficit = Fiscal deficit × Interest payment

50. Calculate Revenue Deficit using the above given information.

    (a) ₹40,000 crores
    (b) ₹10,000 crores
    (c) ₹15,000 crores
    (d) ₹20,000 crores

51. ___________ is the source of Non-Tax Revenue of State Government.

   (a) Police services   (b) Income Tax   (c) Wealth Tax   (d) Corporation Tax

52. Calculate Interest payment using the above given information.

   (a) ₹5,000 crores   (b) ₹10,000 crores   (c) ₹15,000 crores   (d) ₹20,000 crores

53. Read the following statements carefully and choose the correct alternatives given below:

Statement 1: A capital expenditure budget is a formal plan that states an organization's amounts and timing of fixed asset purchases.

Statement 2: Revenue expenditure is expenditure for the regular running of government departments and various services.

Alternatives:

   (a) Both the statements are true.   (b) Both the statements are false.

   (c) Statement 1 is true and Statement 2 is false.   (d) Statement 2 is true and Statement 1 is false.

54. From the above given information the value primary deficit will be ___________.

   (a) ₹5,000 crores   (b) ₹10,000 crores   (c) ₹15,000 crores   (d) ₹20,000 crores

Direction: Q. No. 55-60 are to be answered based on the following data:

Liberalisation, Privatisation and Globalisation.

Economic reforms refer to the fundamental changes launched in 1991 to liberalise the economy and quicken its economic growth rate. The Narasimha Rao Government, in 1991, started the economic reforms to re-build internal and external faith in the Indian economy.

The reforms intended at bringing in more considerable cooperation of the private sector in the growth method of the Indian economy. Policy changes were proposed about technology upgradation, industrial licensing, restrictions on the private sector, foreign investments, and foreign trade. The essential features of the economic reforms are – Liberalisation, Privatisation, and Globalisation, commonly known as LPG.

Economic reforms were introduced in India because of the following reasons:

Poor performance of the public sector:

(A) The public sector was given an essential role in development policies during 1951–1990.

(B) However, the performance of the majority of public enterprises was disappointing.

(C) They were incurring huge losses because of inefficient management.

Adverse BOP or imports exceed exports:

(A) Imports grew at a very high rate without matching the growth of exports.

(B) The Government could not restrict imports even after imposing heavy tariffs and fixing quotas.

(C) On the other hand, exports were significantly less due to the low quality and high prices of our goods than foreign goods.

Fall in foreign exchange reserves:

(A) Foreign exchange (foreign currencies) reserves, which the Government generally maintains to import petrol and other essential items, dropped to levels that were insufficient for even a fortnight.

(B) The Government was not able to repay its borrowings from abroad.

Huge debts on Government:

(A) Government expenditure on various developmental works was more than its revenue from taxation.

(B) As a result, the Government borrowed money from banks, public and international financial institutions like the IMF, etc.

Inflationary pressure:

(A) There was a consistent rise in the general price level of essential goods in the economy.

(B) To control inflation, a new set of policies were required.

55. ___________means change in a set of policies and rules and regulations from one period of time to another to achieve economic growth.

   (a) Tax reforms   (b) Economic reforms   (c) Land reforms   (d) None of these

56. Read the following statements carefully and choose the correct alternatives given below:

    Statement 1: Privatisation will shift the position of the RBI from a regulator to a facilitator of the financial sector.

    Statement 2: The government abolished the licensing requirement of all industries, except for the five, under the economic reforms.

    Alternatives:
    (a) Both the statements are true.
    (b) Both the statements are false.
    (c) Statement 1 is true, and Statement 2 is false.
    (d) Statement 2 is true, and Statement 1 is false.

57. Read the following statements -Assertion (A) and Reason(R):

    Assertion (A): The professionals in India are the best at what they do.

    Reason (R): India's skillset and the availability of human resource capital are the most dynamic and effective throughout the world.

    From the given alternatives choose the correct one:

    Alternatives:
    (a) Both Assertion (A) and Reason (R) are true, and Reason (R) is the correct explanation of Assertion (A).
    (b) Both Assertion (A) and Reason (R) are true, and Reason (R) is not the correct explanation of Assertion (A).
    (c) Assertion (A) is true, but Reason (R) is false.
    (d) Assertion (A) is false, but Reason (R) is true.

58. In the light of the given text and common knowledge, identify the correct statement:

    Prior to India's independence, the stagnation in the agricultural sector was mainly caused by
    (a) investment in technology
    (b) investment in agriculture facilities
    (c) advanced infrastructural facilities
    (d) land settlement system

59. Read the following statements carefully and choose the correct alternatives given below:

    Statement 1: The Indian economy under the British rule was in a stagnant and backward state.

    Statement 2: The demand for British goods increased in India.

    Alternatives:
    (a) Both the statements are true.
    (b) Both the statements are false.
    (c) Statement 1 is true, and Statement 2 is false.
    (d) Statement 2 is true, and Statement 1 is false.

60. Read the following statements -Assertion (A) and Reason (R):

    Assertion (A): Globalisation leads to an increase in foreign exchange reserves.

    Reason (R): Increase in foreign investment and foreign direct investments in the Indian economy.

    From the given alternatives choose the correct one:

    Alternatives:
    (a) Both Assertion (A) and Reason (R) are true, and Reason (R) is the correct explanation of Assertion (A).
    (b) Both Assertion (A) and Reason (R) are true, and Reason (R) is not the correct explanation of Assertion (A).
    (c) Assertion (A) is true, but Reason (R) is false.
    (d) Assertion (A) is false, but Reason (R) is true.

□□

Answers

Sample Paper 1

SECTION–A

1. **(d)** chronic poor

   Explanation: These are those poors who are always poor and those who are usually poor but they sometimes may have a little more money.

2. **(d)** all of these

   Explanation: Institutional sources include co-operatives, commercial banks including the SBI Group, RBI and NABARD whereas Non-Institutional sources include moneylenders, traders and commission agents, relatives and landlords.

3. **(c)** Investment from abroad

   Explanation: Investment from abroad is entered in credit side of BOP account as they bring in foreign exchange and add to the capital stock of the country.

4. **(d)** GST

   Explanation: Interest received, fees and fines is a source of non-tax source of revenue because it is revenue received by the government administration, public enterprises, gifts and grants etc.

5. **(a)** Both the statements are true

   Explanation: Central Bank is the sole agency of note issuing and controls the supply of money in the economy. It serves as the banker of the government and manages foreign exchange of the government. Therefore, the main function of the Central Bank is to control of credit in the economy and not create it. It is the commercial bank that deals in the creation of credit in the economy.

6. **(d)** Increase the capital account deficit

   Explanation: A trade deficit occurs when the value of a country's imports exceeds the value of its exports with imports and exports referring both to goods, or physical products, and services. Thus the lower trade deficit will not help to increase the capital account deficit.

7. **(c)** Both (a) and (b)

   Explanation: Investment in Educational Sector and Investment in Health Sector will produce more human capital because education not only raises the standard and quality of living but also encourages modern attitude of the people whereas investment in health sector increases efficiency, efficacy and productivity of a nation's workforce.

8. **(a)** Both the statements are true.

   Explanation: BOP is a systematic record of all economic transactions between its residents and residents of the foreign countries during a given period of time whereas BOP is always in equilibrium because if current account is in deficit, the same is restored (compensated) with capital account. Hence overall balance of payment is always balanced.

9. **(d)** (i) and (iv)

   Explanation: Tax rates under GST are 5%, 12%, 18% and 28%.

10. (b)   Inter-Bank deposits

> **Explanation:** The stock of money held by government and the banking system are not included in the money supply.

11. (b)   1948

> **Explanation:** The Industrial Policy Resolution of 1948 was adopted by the Parliament on April 6, 1948. It was the first official resolution on industrial policy after independence.

12. (d)   Russia

> **Explanation:** The Five year plan was obtained from the USSR (The Union of Soviet Socialist Republics). It is called as the Soviet Union and is composed of Russia and its surrounding countries.

13. (b)   Mr. M.S. Swaminathan

> **Explanation:** Green Revolution in India was founded by M.S. Swaminathan.

14. (d)   Statement 2 is true and Statement 1 is false

> **Explanation:** Money supply includes total stock of money held by the public of an economy at a particular point of time and includes currency components as well as demand deposits of the public with the banks.

15. (a)   Both the statements are true

> **Explanation:** Both statements are the objectives of government budget. In statement 1 the Government tries to bring economic equality of society whereas in statement 2 the government endeavours to equally allocate resources and wealth.

16. (d)   Human capital

> **Explanation:** It refers to the stock of skill, ability, expertise, education and knowledge in a nation at a point of time.

17. (b)   A-(iii), B-(iv), C-(i), D-(ii)

> **Explanation:** (i) People who are always poor are termed as chronic poor.
> (ii) On the job training increases the productivity of labour.
> (iii) Rural development requires all the basic information.
> (iv) Adult literacy rate is the indicator of educational achievement.

18. (d)   primary

> **Explanation:** Primary deficit indicates how much of the government borrowings are going to meet expenses other than the interest payments. The difference between fiscal deficit and primary deficit shows the amount of interest payments on the borrowings made in past.

19. (c)   credit side of capital account

> **Explanation:** This transaction indicates that it is a borrowing from abroad and it will increase the international liability of country.

20. (b)   Revenue expenditure-revenue receipts

> **Explanation:** Revenue deficit can be calculated by subtracting total revenue expenditure from total revenue receipts.

21. (d)   ₹5,000 crore

> **Explanation:** Fiscal Deficit is the excess of total expenditure over total receipts of the country, which often means that fiscal deficit is equal to borrowings of the state. In this case borrowings = ₹5,000, hence fiscal deficit will be ₹5,000.

22. (b) Excess of exports

> **Explanation:** Excess of exports is the main reason for strong balance of payments.

23. (c) Statement 1 is true and Statement 2 is false

> **Explanation:** All commercial banks create credit by advancing loans and purchasing securities whereas all the minting of coins is done by the Finance Ministry not by RBI.

24. (a) Equal in the market

> **Explanation:** Any unit of money, whose face value and intrinsic value are equal, is known as full bodied money *i.e.,* Money value = Commodity value.

SECTION-B

25. (b) Both assertion (A) and reason (R) are true but reason (R) is not the correct explanation of assertion (A).

> **Explanation:** Three dimensions of government approach to reduce poverty are growth oriented approach, Food for work and provide minimum basic amenities to the people.

26. (a) ₹16,000

> **Explanation:**
>
> $$\text{Fiscal Deficit} = \text{Primary Deficit} + \text{Interest Payments}$$
> $$\text{Primary Deficit} = 10,000$$
> $$\text{Interest Payment} = 6,000$$
> $$\text{Fiscal Deficit} = 10,000 + 6,000$$
> $$= ₹16,000 \text{ crores}$$

27. (b) Both assertion (A) and reason (R) are true and reason (R) is not the correct explanation of assertion (A).

> **Explanation:** Double coincidence of wants means that one trader wants what another trade is offering in the market and vice versa and it is an essential feature of a barter system.

28. (b) India had a sound industrial base under the British

> **Explanation:** India failed to develop a sound and strong industrial base during the colonial rule. The status of industrial sector during the British rule can be well defined by the term 'systematic deindustrialisation.'

29. (d) Assertion (A) is false but reason (R) is true.

> **Explanation:** All Government receipts which either create liability or reduce assets are treated as capital receipts.

30. (c) A-(iv), B-(i), C-(ii), D-(iii)

> **Explanation:** (i) Money supply is the stock variable.
> (ii) Cheque is an example of fiduciary money.
> (iii) Demand deposits issues the cheque.
> (iv) Currency and demand deposits are the components of money supply.

31. (a) 50-51%

> **Explanation:** The figure in the question clearly shows that the rate of disinvestment in privatisation is 50-51%

32. (a) Government balance + Private sector balance

> **Explanation:** The formula of the balance of payment is:
>
> Trade deficit = Government balance + Private sector balance

33. (a) Both assertion (A) and reason (R) are true and reason (R) is the correct explanation of assertion (A).

> **Explanation:** India's per-capita income remained mostly stagnant during the Raj, with most of its GDP growth coming from an expanding population and the Zamindari System was introduced by Cornwallis in 1793 through the Permanent Settlement Act.

34. (a) Both the statements are true

> **Explanation:** Recovery of loans is a capital receipt as it reduces government assets. Capital receipts are receipts that create liabilities or reduce financial assets.

35. (a) Both the statements are true

> **Explanation:** During the first seven Five-Year plans, the trade policy was characterised by the inward-looking trade strategy. This strategy is known as import substitution. Five year plans gave push especially to the development of heavy industries and capital goods, like iron, steel, chemicals, etc. and the machine building industries.

36. (a) (i) and (ii)

> **Explanation:** In India, expenditure on education and health is the responsibility of Union and State governments.

37. (b) Both assertion (A) and reason (R) are true but reason (R) is not the correct explanation of assertion (A).

> **Explanation:** BOT refers to the difference between the monetary value of a country's imports and exports over a given time period whereas any time an item (good, service, or asset) is exported from a country, the value of that item is recorded as a credit entry on the balance of payments hence export of goods is entered as a credit item in BOT.

38. (a) (i) and (ii)

> **Explanation:** A zero or low primary deficit indicates government borrowings.

39. (a) Both Assertion (A) and Reason (R) are true and Reason (R) is the correct explanation of Assertion (A).

> **Explanation:** The Indian economy on the eve of independence suffered and continues to suffer the effects of zamindari system.

40. (a) Both Assertion (A) and Reason (R) are true and Reason (R) is the correct explanation of Assertion (A).

> **Explanation:** Green revolution benefitted farmers in various ways. It helped in raising the income of the formers and hence their living standard because now the produce was more and the farmers had marketable surplus to sell in the market. HYV seeds had more success with the wheat crop and were highly effective in regions that had proper irrigation.

41. (a) Both Assertion (A) and Reason (R) are true and Reason (R) is the correct explanation of Assertion (A).

> **Explanation:** A direct tax can be defined as a tax that is paid directly by an individual or organization to the imposing entity. Income tax is an example of direct tax.

42. (a) Both the statements are true.

> **Explanation:** In financial terms, a deficit occurs when expenses exceed revenues, imports exceed exports, or liabilities exceed assets. Thus, a deficit is synonymous with a shortfall or loss and is the opposite of a surplus.

43. (d) All of the above

> **Explanation: SMALL SCALE INDUSTRY (SSI) :** A small-scale industry is presently defined as one whose investment does not exceed ₹5 crores.
>
> **CHARACTERISTICS OF SSI OR ROLE OF SMALL SCALE INDUSTRIES:**
>
> 1. Labour intensive-employment oriented
>
> 2. Self-employment.
>
> 3. Less capital intensive.
>
> 4. Export promotion.
>
> 5. Seedbeds for large-scale industries.
>
> 6. Shows locational flexibility.

44. (a) ₹4,800

> **Explanation:**
>
> $$\text{Fiscal Deficit} = \text{Primary Deficit} + \text{Interest Payments}$$
> $$\text{Primary Defict} = ₹4,400$$
> $$\text{Interest Payments} = ₹400 \text{ crore}$$
> $$\text{Fiscal Deficit} = 4,400 + 400$$
> $$= ₹4,800 \text{ crores}$$

45. (d) Statement 2 is true and Statement 1 is false

> **Explanation:** In addition to exports and imports of goods and services, current account also records unilateral receipts and payments and Foreign investments are recorded in the capital account of balance of payments as such investments cause a change in the assets of the country.

46. (a) Both Assertion (A) and Reason (R) are true and Reason (R) is the correct explanation of Assertion (A).

> **Explanation:** The government protected the domestic industries from foreign competition through this policy. Protection from imports took two forms (i) Tariffs and Quotas specify the quantity of goods which can be imported.

47. (a) Supply of money refers to stock of money held by public at a point of time

> **Explanation:** In macroeconomics, the money supply (or money stock) refers to the total volume of money held by the public at a particular point in time in an economy.

48. (a) A-(iv), B-(iii), C-(ii), D-(i)

> **Explanation:** (i) Tariff barriers are imposed on imports.
> (ii) When equity is offered to investors through domestic public issue is called Minority Sale.
> (iii) Handicraft industries failed miserably as it was competing with the machine made goods.
> (iv) Non-tariff Barriers are imposed on trade.

SECTION-C

49. (a) Malnutrition

> **Explanation:** Malnutrition is alarmingly high among the poor. Starvation and hunger are the key features of the poorest households.

50. (c) proper housing

> **Explanation:** The poor people possess few assets. They lack proper housing.

51. (a) Study

> **Explanation:** In 1962, Planning Commission, now called NITI Aayog, formed a Study Group.

52. (d) The poor are highly rich

> **Explanation:** Poverty refers to a situation where people cannot meet their basic minimum life needs, such as food, clothing, and shelter.

53. (a) Both the statements are true.

> **Explanation: Calorie based estimation:** The Planning Commission has defined a poverty line based on recommended nutritional requirements of 2400 calories per person per day for rural areas and 2100 calories per person per day for urban areas.
>
> **Per capita expenditure-based estimation:** The government of India uses Monthly Per Capita Expenditure (MPCE) as a proxy for the income of households to identify the poor.
>
> Based on 2011-12 prices, the poverty line was defined for rural areas as consumption worth ₹816 per person a month, and it was ₹1,000 per person per month for urban areas.

54. (c) Poverty line

> **Explanation:** The poverty Line is a cut-off point on the line of distribution, which usually divides the country's population as poor and non-poor. It is the minimum amount of money (usually in terms of monthly per capita expenditure) needed to meet his basic needs. Thus, the concept of the poverty line is used to measure the extent of poverty in a country.

55. (a) 1991

> **Explanation:** India's New Economic Policy was announced on July 24, 1991, known as the LPG or Liberalisation, Privatisation, and Globalisation model.

56. (c) Statement 1 is true and Statement 2 is false

> **Explanation:** Economic crisis happened primarily due to inefficiency in economic management in the 1980s of liberalisation. This clearly shows that the reason is the correct explanation of the assertion.

57. (b) Both assertion (A) and reason (R) are true, and reason (R) is not the correct explanation of assertion (A).

> **Explanation:** : Assertion is the positive outcome of LPG Policy, and the reason shows the meaning of liberalisation. This clearly shows that the reason is the incorrect explanation of the assertion.

58. (c) Economic planning is a mechanism for the misallocation of resources.

> **Explanation:** Economic planning is a mechanism for the allocation of resources.

59. (a) Both the statements are true.

> **Explanation:** Globalisation refers to the expansion of economic activities across the political boundaries of nation-states. Globalisation means the integration of the Indian economy with the world economy. It means that the economy of India will now also depend on the world economy and vice versa. Therefore, it encourages FDI and foreign trade with different countries.

60. (a) Both assertion (A) and reason (R) are true, and reason (R) is the correct explanation of assertion (A).

> **Explanation:** The fundamental changes that were launched by the Narashima Rao Government with the plan of liberalising the economy and quickening its rate of economic growth, started the economic reforms to rebuild internal and external faith in the Indian economy. Thus reason is the correct explanation of the assertion.

Sample Paper 2

SECTION-A

1. (b) AD increases

   Explanation: When the government expenditure increases and tax reduces, there is a government deficit and there will be a corresponding increase in the aggregate demand.

2. (c) India becomes supplier of raw materials and consumer of finished industrial products from Britain.

   Explanation: The main focus of the economic policies pursued by the colonial government was to make India a mere supplier of raw materials for Britain's own industrial base. Such exploitative policies created a lopsided structure in the Indian Economy by reducing it to a supplier of raw materials and consumer of finished industrial products Imported from Britain.

3. (c) Loans advanced by World Bank

   Explanation: Loans advanced by World Bank creates liability or reduce assets and thus treated as capital receipt and not a capital expenditure.

4. (d) Maintaining law and order

   Explanation: Objectives of a Government Budget includes Economic growth, Reduction of poverty and unemployment, Reduction of inequalities or the Redistribution of income and Reallocation of resources etc.

5. (a) Both the statements are true

   Explanation: The HCPR is the percentage of the population under the poverty line. This means that it is the absolute poverty that is estimated in India. Therefore Poverty can be reduced by using labour intensive technique of production instead of Capital-intensive technique.

6. (d) None of these

   Explanation: Capital Expenditure increases the value of assets of the government.

7. (a) Self-reliance

   Explanation: The primary aim of this Atmanirbhar Bharat package is to make the country independent and combating the competition in the global market.

8. (d) Statement 2 is true and Statement 1 is false

   Explanation: Interest on loan received will be recorded on the credit side of BOP account because it results in an inflow of foreign currency. Borrowing from abroad is treated as credit item in balance of payment account because it also results in an inflow of foreign currency.

9. (d) All of these

   Explanation: Sources of Rural Credit includes Land Development Banks, Co-operative Credit Societies, Regional Rural Banks, and Commercial Banks.

10. (c) Is the difference between total expenditure and total receipts other than borrowings.

    Explanation: A fiscal deficit refers to a situation when total expenditure exceeds the total receipts. Thus, fiscal deficit is estimated as the difference between total expenditure and total receipts of the government.

11. (b) Sen's index

> **Explanation:** Poverty index developed by Nobel Laureate Amartya Sen was named as Sen's index.

12. (a) Medium of exchange

> **Explanation:** Money has three primary functions. It is a medium of exchange, a unit of account, and a store of value.

13. (c) Regional Rural Bank

> **Explanation:** The institutional source of credit whose area of operation is the one where banking facilities and cooperative are absent and which operate at district level is Regional Rural Bank.

14. (b) Both the statements are false

> **Explanation:** Government receipts which either create liabilities or reduce assets are capital receipts. Escheats is a revenue receipts because it increases the assets of the government.

15. (b) Both the statements are false

> **Explanation:** BOT is the difference between the value of merchandise (goods) exports and imports. External assistance is a part of Balance of payments or external assistance is recorded in Balance of Payments Account.

16. (d) All of these.

> **Explanation:** The export surplus was used for:
> (i) To make payments for administrative expenses incurred by the British government in Britain.
> (ii) To meet expenses on the war fought by the British Government.
> (iii) To import invisible items, etc.

17. (a) A-(iii), B-(iv), C-(ii), D-(i)

> **Explanation:**
> (i)   Depreciation of currency rises the exports and decreases the imports.
> (ii) Appreciation of currency decreases the exports and increases the imports.
> (iii) Demand for foreign currency is inversely proportional to the exchange rate.
> (iv) Supply of foreign currency is directly proportional to the exchange rate.

18. (a) balance of payment

> **Explanation:** Balance Of Payment (BOP) refers to the systematic records of all economic transactions taking place between the residents of one country and resident of foreign countries during a given period of time.

19. (b) a direct

> **Explanation:** Supply curve of foreign exchange slopes upwards due to positive or direct relationship between supply for foreign exchange and foreign exchange rate, which means that supply of foreign exchange increases as the exchange rate increases.

20. (a) Equity in agriculture

> **Explanation:** Equity in agriculture is called for land reforms in India which primarily refer to change in the ownership of landholdings.

21. (c) ₹200 crores

> **Explanation:**
>
> $$\text{Net indirect taxes} = \text{Total indirect tax} - \text{Subsidy}$$
> $$= 500 - 300$$
> $$= ₹200 \text{ crores}$$

22. (b) Socialist economy

> **Explanation:** In Socialist Economy, the government decides what goods are to be produced in accordance with the needs of society. In a socialist economy, the entire foundation is based on socio-economic objectives.

23. (c) Statement 1 is true and Statement 2 is false.

> **Explanation:** These are the steps that can be taken to reduce India's current account deficit: setting an import quota limit, reducing export duty, and setting a restriction on repatriation of profit earned on foreign investment

24. (d) Public sector

> **Explanation:** The Industrial Policy of 1956 laid stress on the role of cottage and small scale industries, *i.e.*, basically on the public sector for generating larger employment opportunities.

SECTION-B

25. (a) Both assertion (A) and reason (R) are true and reason (R) is the correct explanation of assertion (A).

> **Explanation:** High powered money can also be defined as the total liability of monetary authority of the country and RBI. High powered money consists of currency and coins held by the public and deposits held by government and commercial banks.

26. (b) Churning poor

> **Explanation:** The churning poor are the people who go in and out of poverty (for example, small farmers and seasonal workers)

27. (c) Assertion (A) is true, but reason (R) is false.

> **Explanation:** The capital goods sector I that is so indispensable to self-reliant industrialisation got its first big push in India in the Second Five-Year Plan whereas Indian economy is now ranked as the fifth largest industrial economy in the world and not eleventh.

28. (b) India traded with many countries of the world despite discriminatory tariff policy pursued by the British Government

> **Explanation:** The British followed a discriminatory tariff policy under which they imposed heavy tariffs (export duties) on India's export of handicraft products while allowing free export of India's raw material to only Britain and free import of British products to India.

29. (a) Both assertion (A) and reason (R) are true and reason (R) is the correct explanation of assertion (A).

> **Explanation:** The purchase of foreign goods or imports decreases the domestic demand for goods and services in our country.

30. (d) A-(iii), B-(iv), C-(ii), D-(i)

Explanation:
(i)   Surplus budget is related to the inflation of the economy.
(ii) Deficit budget is related to the deflation in the economy.
(iii) Capital receipt creates the liability of the economy.
(iv) Capital expenditure creates the assets of the economy.

31. (b) 645.61

Explanation: The table given in the Question shows that the estimated budget for digital e-learning is 645.61 crore.

32. (a) Sustainable livelihood

Explanation: In the given figure, it is clearly shown that the strategy of rural development are rural development strategy are SSG, Diversification, people development, Sustainable livelihood.

33. (d) Assertion (A) is false but reason (R) is true.

Explanation: Education and health are considered an important input for the development of a nation as much as they are important for the development of an individual.

34. (c) Statement 1 is true and statement 2 is false

Explanation: A government budget is an annual statement of estimated receipts and expenditure during a fiscal year.

35. (b) Both the statements are false.

Explanation:
(i)   A current account deficit occurs when the total value of goods and services a country imports exceeds the total value of goods and services it exports.
(ii) Changes in the rate of domestic saving or domestic investment will cause changes in a country's capital and current account balances. For example, a rise in domestic investment relative to saving will, all else equal, cause the capital account surplus to rise and the current account balance to fall.

36. (d) (ii), (iv), (i) and (iii)

Explanation:
(i)   British introduced railway in India - 1850.
(ii) The year of great divide - 1921.
(iii) Establishment of TISCO - 1907.
(iv) First railway bridge linking Bombay with Thane - 1854.

37. (b) Both assertion (A) and reason (R) are true but reason (R) is not the correct explanation of assertion (A).

Explanation: Goods and Services Tax (GST) is an indirect tax (or consumption tax) used in India on the supply of goods and services. Indirect taxes are imposed on goods and services on the basis of production, supply, sale or purchase of products or provision of services, in the form of goods and services tax.

38. (d) II, IV, I, III

Explanation: Study Group formed by Planning Commission for Poverty came in 1962. 'Task Force on Projections of the Minimum Needs and Effective Consumption Demand' came in 1979. Mahatma Gandhi National Rural Employment Guarantee Act came in 2005. Jan Dhan Yojana came in 2014.

39. (b)   Both assertion (A) and reason (R) are true but reason (R) is not the correct explanation of assertion (A).

> **Explanation:** The green revolution has made India self-sufficient in food grains. India has adopted a new strategy in the field of agriculture.

40. (a)   Both assertion (A) and reason (R) are true and reason (R) is the correct explanation of assertion (A).

> **Explanation:** Farmers were forced to shift because indigo was required by the textile industry in Britain for dyeing or bleaching of the textile. Whereas as commercial crops costs more amount than the seasonal crops so this can bring more profit to the farmer.

41. (a)   Both assertion (A) and reason (R) are true and reason (R) is the correct explanation of assertion (A).

> **Explanation:** The most important point that makes India as the most favourite spot for outsourcing is the favourable government and tax policies.

42. (a) $ 779,138

> **Explanation:** In the given figure, the fiscal deficit is calculated, and we get $ 779,138.

43. (a)   Lack of basic amenities

> **Explanation:** Most poor households do not have access to basic amenities like safe drinking water, electricity, etc. Their primary cooking fuel is firewood and cow dung cake. Thus lack of basic aminities is there.

44. (a)   Liberalisation

> **Explanation:** Liberalisation is the process or means of eliminating control of the state over economic activities. It provides greater autonomy to the business enterprises in decision-making and eliminates government interference.

45. (a)   Both the statements are true

> **Explanation:** In India, Persons having income or consumption expenditure less than the minimum consumption expenditure defined as poverty line are called poor in absolute sense. Whereas the unequal distribution of land and other assets, the benefits from direct poverty alleviation programs have been appropriated by the non-poor.

46. (d)   Assertion (A) is false but Reason (R) is true.

> **Explanation:** Wage goods such as wheat, rice, maize, pulses, oil, sugarcane, etc are necessary goods and not luxuries of life. Whereas agricultural sector in India provides wage goods to 121 crore people and 38 crore animals.

47. (c)   Human development is bases on the idea that education and health are integral to human well-being

> **Explanation:** Human development is based on the idea that education and health are integral to human well-being because only when people have the ability to read and write and the ability to lead a long and healthy life, they will be able to make other choices which they value.

48. (c)   A-(iv), B-(i), C-(ii), D-(iii)

> **Explanation:**
> (i)   NITI Aayog was introduced in 2015.
> (ii)   Gulf Crisis : 1990-91.
> (iii)   Policy of liberalisation was introduced by world Bank.
> (iv)   The year of great depression was 1929.

SECTION-C

49. (d) All of these

> **Explanation:** Three functions of money are primary function, secondary function, and contingent.

50. (a) Standard of deferred payment

> **Explanation:**
> (i)   The standard of deferred payment can be distinguished from the medium of exchange function since its value might change over time. If payment is to be deferred, it should be denominated in a unit expected to maintain its value. Deferred payments need durability when used in trade and a minimum opportunity to cheat others as the diamond or gold examples illustrate.
> (ii) The store of the value function, which relates to the saving, storing, and retrieval of value.
> (iii) The unit of account function requires fund ability so accounts in any amount can be readily settled.

51. (b) Transfer of value

> **Explanation:** Money can be transferred easily from one place to another and from one person to another. Therefore, with the help of money, purchasing power can be transferred.

52. (a) Medium of exchange

> **Explanation:** The following are the various contingent functions that money performs:
> (i)   **Facilitates credit:** Money facilitates credit instruments such as cheques, promissory notes, bills of exchange, etc. Such credit instruments facilitate the transfer of value from one person to another.
> (ii) **Facilitates distribution of income:** Factor payments can be made easily in monetary remunerations such as wages, rent, interest, and profit.
> (iii) **Maximizes consumers' and producers' satisfaction:** Since all goods and services are valued in terms of money, consumers can maximize their satisfaction by equalizing marginal utilities of various goods consumed. Similarly, all the factors of production are valued in monetary terms. Therefore, it becomes possible for a producer to maximize production by equalizing marginal productivity of the different factors of production.
> (iv) **Liquidity:** Money is the most liquid of all assets and wealth. Gold, silver, land, cheques, etc., are not as liquid as money. If the need arises, these assets have to be converted into money. Still, on the other hand, money need not be converted into any other form as it is readily acceptable.

53. (a) Both the statements are true.

> **Explanation:** Money is an asset in an economy that you can use to buy goods and services from other people or businesses. One of the functions of money in an economy is that it serves as a store of value. A store of value is something that people use to transfer purchasing power from the present to the future. While money is an asset that can store value, it is not the only type. Gold and silver, for example, act as stores of value.

54. (a) Medium of exchange

> **Explanation:** The "American Heritage College Dictionary" defines an exchange economy as "an economy in which goods are traded using money or exchanged for other goods." In the "exchange economy," goods and services are produced here and there and elsewhere. Then, the goods arrive in the general market and get traded for others.

55. (a) Narasimha Rao government

> **Explanation:** India's economic reforms refer to the neo-liberal policies introduced by the Narsimha Rao government when India faced a severe economic crisis due to external debt.

56. (c) Statement 1 is true and Statement 2 is false

> **Explanation:** The revenues that the government was generating were not enough to meet the expenses. To curb this crisis, India approached the world bank and the international monetary fund (IMF) for the loan and received $7 million to manage their crisis.

57. (b) Both assertion (A) and reason (R) are true, but reason (R) is not the correct explanation of assertion (A).

> **Explanation:** Both Assertion (A) and Reason (R) explains that Liberalisation led to freedom of trading. However, Reason (R) is not the correct reason for the Assertion (A).

58. (a) Both assertion (A) and reason (R) are true, and reason (R) is the correct explanation of assertion (A).

> **Explanation:** Assertion is the Salient feature of LPG Policy, and the reason shows the meaning of Liberalisation. This clearly shows that the reason is the correct explanation of the assertion.

59. (c) Statement 1 is true and Statement 2 is false

> **Explanation:** Privatisation can mean different things, including moving something from the public sector into the private sector. It is also sometimes used as a synonym for deregulation when a heavily regulated private company or industry becomes less regulated.

60. (a) Both assertion (A) and reason (R) are true, and reason (R) is the correct explanation of assertion (A).

> **Explanation:** Assertion is showing that government fixes a target for disinvestment, and the reason is showing the disinvestment is an excellent tool for discarding the loss incurring public sector enterprises. This clearly shows that the reason is the correct explanation of the assertion.

Sample Paper 3

SECTION-A

1. (d) All of these

> **Explanation:** Traditional sources of rural credit in India include moneylenders, friends and relatives, traders etc. These sources provided the credit at a cheap rate to the people of rural areas for these people do not have access to banks and other financial institutions.

2. (b) 1907

> **Explanation:** Tata Steel Ltd was incorporated in the year 1907 with the name Tata Iron and Steel Company Ltd.

3. (b) Fiscal deficit

> **Explanation:** Fiscal deficit, the condition when the expenditure of the government exceeds its revenue in a year hence it is a part of government budget and not banking organization.

4. (d) All of these

> **Explanation:** Non-farming activities can include various ventures like handicrafts, household as well as non-household small-scale manufacturing, construction etc. But it does not include livestock farming, horticulture, fisheries and animal husbandry.

5. (c) Statement 1 is true and Statement 2 is false

Explanation: Before independence, the economy was 95% dependent on agriculture and the revenues earned from agriculture. Concerning agriculture, the situation of the Indian economy on the eve of independence was disheartening.

There was an increase in the yield of cash crops, but it helped the farmers in no way. Farmers were now mass producing cash crops instead of food crops, which were ultimately used for the benefit of British industries.

6. (c) Central Bank of India

Explanation: From the discussion between Raju and Sunil, Central Bank of India is the right answer. The RBI or Central bank of India is the apex institution organises, runs, supervises, regulates and develops the monetary system and the financial system of the country.

7. (b) Fiscal deficit

Explanation: From the given statement, Fiscal deficit gives an indication to the government about the total borrowing requirements from all sources.

8. (a) Both the statements are true

Explanation: The government's approach to poverty reduction was of three dimensions:

The first one is growth oriented approach. It is based on the expectation that the effects of economic growth, rapid increase in gross domestic product and per capita income would spread to all sections of society and will trickle down to the poor sections also.

The second approach aimed at creation of incremental assets and by means of work generation. This could be achieved through specific poverty alleviation programmes.

The third approach to addressing poverty is to provide minimum basic amenities to the people. Programmes under this approach are expected to supplement the consumption of the poor, create employment opportunities and bring about improvements in health and education.

And poverty can only be eradicated when poor start contributing to growth by their active involvement hence option 1 and 2 both are correct.

9. (d) IV, III, II, I

Explanation: First official census – 1881

Second stage of demographic transition – 1921

Start of first five year plan – 1951

New economic policy – 1991

10. (c) Increases cost of production

Explanation: Improves technical knowledge, Enlarges the size of business and Changes social outlooks contributes to the formation of human capital.

11. (a) fiscal

Explanation: Fiscal policy refers to the use of government spending and tax policies to influence economic conditions. There are three tools inside the fiscal policy toolkit. The tools are the same - government spending, taxes and transfer payments.

12. (c) Both (a) and (b)

Explanation: Investment in Educational Sector and Investment in Health Sector will produce more human capital because education not only raises the standard and quality of living but also encourages modern attitude of the people whereas investment in health sector increases efficiency and productivity of a nation's workforce.

13. (a) disinvestment

> **Explanation:** Privatisation of the public sector undertakings by selling off parts of the equity of PSUs to the private sector is known as disinvestment. The purpose of the sale is mainly to improve financial discipline and facilitate modernisation.

14. (d) Statement 2 is true and Statement 1 is false

> **Explanation:** Money supply refers to the total stock of money of all types (currency as well as demand deposits). M_1 is a type of measurement that measures the money as a medium of exchange function.
> $$M_1 = C + DD + OD$$

15. (c) Statement 1 is true and Statement 2 is false

> **Explanation:** Poverty can only be eradicated when poor start contributing to growth by their active involvement hence option 1 is correct.
>
> Human Capital refers to the stock of skill, ability, expertise, education and knowledge in a nation at a point of time whereas physical capital means all inputs which are required for further production such as machine, tools and implements, factory buildings, etc. So both concepts are totally different which means human capital formation has nothing to do with physical capital.

16. (b) Land ceiling

> **Explanation:** Land Ceiling means fixing the maximum size of landholding that an individual or family can own. Land over and above the ceiling limit is called surplus land.

17. (d) A-(i), B-(iii), C-(iv), D-(ii)

> **Explanation:**
> (i) Basis of credit creation is the contingent function of money.
> (ii) Exchange of goods for goods is called Barter System.
> (iii) Accepting deposits is the primary function of money.
> (iv) Standard of deferred payment is the secondary function of money.

18. (b) Dadabhai Naoroji

> **Explanation:** In pre-independence India, Dadabhai Naoroji was the first to discuss the concept of poverty. The three dimensional attack on poverty adopted by the government has not succeeded in poverty alleviation in India.

19. (a) Central Bank

> **Explanation:** Central Bank is the only institution that can come to the rescue for any bank in case of any emergency or financial crisis. This function of Reserve bank is known as Lender of Last Resort.

20. (d) Growth

> **Explanation:** Economic growth is an increase in the production of goods and services in an economy. Increases in capital goods, labour force, technology, and human capital can all contribute to economic growth.

21. (c) Primary deposits

> **Explanation:** Primary deposits are those deposits that the bank collects from different surplus stakeholders in the economy by different accounts. These consist of cash deposited by the people with the banks in different deposit account such as savings deposits, time or fixed deposits, current or demand deposits and other deposits.

22. (d) All of these

Explanation: The zamindars (owners of land) were required to pay very high revenue (lagaan) to the British government, which they used to collect from the peasants (landless labourers, who were actually cultivating). Moreover, in order to feed British industries with cheap raw materials, the Indian peasants were forced to grow cash crops (such as, indigo, cotton, etc.) instead of food crops.

23. (c) Statement 1 is true, and Statement 2 is false.

Explanation: The term commercial bank refers to a financial institution that accepts deposits, offers checking account services, makes various loans, and offers essential financial products like certificates of deposit (CDs) and savings accounts to individuals and small businesses. A commercial bank is where most people do their banking.

24. (c) Both (a) and (b)

Explanation: Both quantitative aspect and qualitative aspect comprises of Human development Index (HDI). This includes the per capita income as well as the health and sanitation, literary rate, etc.

SECTION-B

25. (b) Both assertion (A) and reason (R) are true, but reason (R) is not the correct explanation of assertion (A).

Explanation: Double coincidence of wants occurs when two individuals swap their goods, in exchange for one another. This is also referred to as the 'perfect barter exchange'. In such cases, both the individuals are happy to exchange their good or commodities. Hence, statement 1 is correct.

Double coincidence of wants is essential because it facilitates the exchange of goods and thus the exchange of goods will occur. Hence it is an important feature of double coincidence of wants.

26. (c) ₹10 crores

Explanation:

$$\text{Net indirect taxes} = \text{Total indirect tax} - \text{Subsidy}$$
$$= 50 - 40$$
$$= ₹10 \text{ crores}$$

27. (d) Assertion (A) is false but reason (R) is true.

Explanation: All Government receipts which either create liability or reduce assets are treated as capital receipts.

28. (d) Both (b) and (c)

Explanation: There were no capital goods industries to promote industrialization in India. As a result, the growth of domestic industries and their contribution to the economic output remained low. When India gained independence in 1947, the economic condition of the country was very poor. There were hardly any public sector enterprises other than the Railways and the Postal Services. Hence both b and c statements are incorrect.

29. (a) Both assertion (A) and reason (R) are true and reason (R) is the correct explanation of assertion (A).

Explanation: Invisible trade refers to an international transaction which does not involve tangible goods, but services, such as consultancy services, insurance, banking, intellectual property, international tourism, etc. In other words, it is the import and export of services between countries.

30. (a) A-(iv), B-(iii), C-(ii), D-(i)

Explanation:
(i) The foremost objective of five year plan was to increase the agricultural production.

    (ii) Land reforms were the changes in ownership.

    (iii) Composition of trade refers to the types of goods and services exported and imported or traded.

    (iv) Outsourcing is hiring services from external sources.

31. (d) All the above

Explanation: Liberalisation: It refers to the process of making policies less constraining of economic activity and also reduction of tariff or removal of non-tariff barriers.

Privatisation: It refers to the transfer of ownership of property or business from a government to a privately owned entity.

Globalisation: It refers to the expansion of economic activities across the political boundaries of nation-states.

32. (c) Globalisation

Explanation: Globalisation is the word used to describe the growing interdependence of the world's economies, cultures, and populations, brought about by cross-border trade in goods and services, technology, and flows of investment, people, and information.

33. (b) Both assertion (A) and reason (R) are true, but reason (R) is not the correct explanation of assertion (A).

Explanation: In order to attract foreign investment, tax incentives were provided to foreign investors which further reduced the scope for raising tax revenues.

34. (a) Both the statements are true.

Explanation: India's GDP growth rate increased. For example, during 1990-91, India's GDP growth rate was only 1.1%, but after 1991 reforms GDP growth rate increased year by year and in 2015-16, it was estimated to be 7.5% by IMF.

Adverse outcomes are due to the opening up of the Indian economy to foreign competition, and more MNCs are competing with local businesses and companies, which are facing problems due to financial constraints, lack of advanced technology, and production inefficiencies.

35. (c) Statement 1 is true and Statement 2 is false

Explanation: The sum of all receipts from the taxes and all other duties under the government are referred to as tax revenue. They are either from direct taxes or indirect taxes. It is the primary source of regular receipts of the government and is categorized into Direct Taxes and Indirect Taxes.

36. (b) (i), (ii), (iii), (iv)

Explanation:

    (i) The first union budget of independent India was presented by R.K. Shanmukham Chetty on 26th November, 1947.

    (ii) The union budgets for the fiscal year 1959-61 to 1963-64, was presented by Morarji Desai.

    (iii) The interim budget for 1962-63, was presented by Mororji Desai.

    (iv) The Union Budget of India for 2012-13 was presented by Pranab Mukherjee.

37. (a) Both assertion (A) and reason (R) are true and reason (R) is the correct explanation of assertion (A).

Explanation: The proposed framework articulates that six elements are essential to generate knowledge outputs: Innovation Capability, Leadership, Human Capital, Information Technology Resources, Financial Resources, and Innovation Climate. Hence both the statements are correct.

38. (a) (i) and (iii)

Explanation: Money has three primary functions. It is a medium of exchange, a unit of account, and a store of value.

39. (c) Assertion (A) is true but Reason (R) is false.

> **Explanation:** The capital goods sector I that is so indispensable to self-reliant industrialisation got its first big push in India in the Second Five-Year Plan whereas Indian economy is now ranked as the fifth largest industrial economy in the world and not eleventh.

40. (b) Both Assertion (A) and Reason (R) are true and Reason (R) is not the correct explanation of Assertion (A).

> **Explanation:** Reduction of economic inequalities and eradication of poverty are the second group of objective of almost all the Five Year Plans of our country particularly since the Fourth Plan. Due to the faulty approach followed in the initial part of our planning, economic inequality widened and poverty became acute. Inflation reduces real wages through (1) a decline of the capital stock, and (2) a shift in relative prices. Hence both of the statements are correct.

41. (b) Both Assertion (A) and Reason (R) are true and Reason (R) is not the correct explanation of Assertion (A).

> **Explanation:** There may be times when demand exceeds available output under conditions of high employment and thus may give rise to inflation. In such situations, restrictive conditions may be needed to reduce demand. The intervention of the government whether to expand demand or reduce it constitutes the stabilisation function. Whereas the overall level of employment and prices in the economy depends upon the level of aggregate demand which depends on the spending decisions of millions of private economic agents apart from the government.

42. (a) Both the statements are true.

> **Explanation:** In financial terms, a deficit occurs when expenses exceed revenues, imports exceed exports, or liabilities exceed assets. Thus, a deficit is synonymous with a shortfall or loss and is the opposite of a surplus.

43. (d) All of these

> **Explanation: SMALL SCALE INDUSTRY (SSI)**
> A small-scale industry is presently defined as one whose investment does not exceed ₹ 5 crores.
> **CHARACTERISTICS OF SSI OR ROLE OF SMALL SCALE INDUSTRIES**
> 1. Labour intensive-employment oriented
> 2. Self-employment.
> 3. Less capital intensive.
> 4. Export promotion.
> 5. Seedbeds for large-scale industries.
> 6. Shows locational flexibility.

44. (a) Transfer of ownership

> **Explanation: Transfer of ownership:** Government companies can be converted into private companies in the following two ways:
> (i) By the withdrawal of the government from the ownership and management of public sector companies
> (ii) By the outright sale of public sector companies.

45. (d) Assertion (A) is false but Reason (R) is true.

> **Explanation:** Capital receipts are receipts that create liabilities or reduces financial assets. They can be both non-debt and debt receipts.

46. (b) Both Assertion (A) and Reason (R) are true and Reason (R) is not the correct explanation of Assertion (A).

> **Explanation:** A budget surplus occurs when income exceeds expenditures. The term often refers to a government's financial state, as individuals have "savings" rather than a "budget surplus." A surplus is an indication that a government's finances are being effectively managed.

47. (b) Reserve of foreign exchange could be used to balance any deficit in the balance of payments account.

> **Explanation:** The country could use its reserves of foreign exchange in order to balance any deficit in its balance of payments. The reserve bank sells foreign exchange when there is a deficit. This is called official reserve sale.

48. (c) A-(iv), B-(i), C-(ii), D-(iii)

> **Explanation:**
> (i) Budget is the annual statement of estimated receipts and estimate expenditure by the Government.
> (ii) Budget is presented in the Parliament.
> (iii) Budget is presented on the last day of february.
> (iv) Budget is presented by the finance Minister.

SECTION-C

49. (b) Marginal surplus

> **Explanation:** India's current account balance posted a marginal surplus of USD 0.6 billion (0.1% of GDP) in the Jan-Mar quarter 2020, as against a deficit of USD 4.7 billion in Jan-Mar 2019 and USD 2.6 billion in the previous quarter.

50. (a) Lower trade deficit

> **Explanation:** The lower trade deficit is a result of the sharp decline in demand at both the national and international levels following the implementation of COVID-19 lockdowns and a fall in global crude oil prices since the beginning of this year.

51. (b) Economic

> **Explanation:** The Balance of Payments (BOP) records all economic transactions between residents of a country and the rest of the world. The BOP account mainly consists of the current account and the capital account.

52. (a) Forex reserve accretion

> **Explanation:** A surplus at both current and capital account has resulted in a For *e.g.,* reserve accretion of USD 18.8 billion in the Jan-Mar quarter 2020.

53. (c) Statement 1 is true and Statement 2 is false

> **Explanation:** : The capital account comprises credit and debit transactions under non-produced non-financial assets and capital transfers between residents and non-residents. Thus, acquisitions and disposals of non-produced non-financial assets, such as land sold to embassies and sales of leases and licenses, as well as transfers which are capital in nature, are recorded under this account.

54. (c) Drop in economic activity

Explanation: A current account surplus is a piece of welcome news; however, in the current scenario, it is a major worry for the Indian economy as it reflects a drop in economic activity. Given that the imports collapsed more than the exports and overall trade balance (services + goods) posted a surplus in the month of April and May, the current account will likely remain in surplus in the June quarter.

55. (c) Both (a) and (b)

Explanation: Rural development actions are intended to further the social and economic development of rural communities.

56. (c) Statement 1 is true and Statement 2 is false

Explanation: Rural development programs were historically top-down approaches from local or regional authorities, regional development agencies, NGOs, national governments or international development organizations.

57. (c) Assertion (A) is true, but Reason (R) is false.

Explanation: : Assertion is about rural banking, and the reason shows the marginal farmers enjoys better creditworthiness. This clearly shows that the reason is the incorrect explanation of the assertion.

58. (d) None of the above

Explanation: All the statement is correct, no one is incorrect

59. (a) Both the statements are true

Explanation: The outsider may not understand the setting, culture, language and other things prevalent in the local area. As such, rural people themselves have to participate in their sustainable rural development. In developing countries like Nepal, Pakistan, India, Bangladesh and China, integrated development approaches are being followed up. In this context, many approaches and ideas have been developed and implemented, for instance, bottom-up approaches, PRA- Participatory Rural Appraisal, RRA- Rapid Rural Appraisal, Working With People (WWP) etc. In addition, the New Rural Reconstruction Movement in China has been actively promoting rural development through its ecological farming projects.

60. (b) Both Assertion (A) and Reason (R) are true, and Reason (R) is not the correct explanation of Assertion (A).

Explanation: Assertion shows the problem of rural credit, and the reason is showing the rural mentality. This clearly shows that the reason is the incorrect explanation of the assertion.

Sample Paper 4

SECTION-A

1. (d) Borrowings

Explanation: Borrowing is a loan taken by the government and falls under capital receipts in the Budget document. It is essentially the total amount of money that the central government borrows to fund its public services and benefits.

2. (d) All of these

Explanation: The capital account of BOP records the financial transaction of a country in foreign exchange with the rest of the world that changes the assets and liabilities status of a country. It includes three transactions Investment from and to abroad, Borrowing and lending from and to abroad and Changes in foreign exchange reserves.

3. (a) Budget

Explanation: A budget estimates revenue and expenses over a specified future time and is usually compiled and re-evaluated periodically. Budgets can be made for a person, a group of people, a business, a government, or just about anything else that makes and spends money.

4. (b) Export of goods less than the import of goods

Explanation: When the export of goods is less than the import of goods, it is the situation of a trade deficit.

5. (c) Statement 1 is true and Statement 2 is false

Explanation: Industrial revolution came first in England.

6. (d) 1969

Explanation: The Government of India issued the Banking Companies (Acquisition and Transfer of Undertakings) Ordinance, 1969 and nationalized the 14 largest Commercial Banks with effect from the midnight of 19 July, 1969. These banks contained 85 per cent of bank deposits in the country. Within two weeks of the ordinance issue, the Parliament passed the Banking Companies (Acquisition and Transfer of Undertaking) Bill, and it received presidential approval on 9 August, 1969.

7. (c) Managed Floating Exchange Rate

Explanation: A managed floating exchange rate is an exchange rate system that allows a nation's Central Bank to intervene regularly in foreign exchange markets to change the direction of the currency's float and reduce the amount of currency volatility. This exchange rate system is also known as a "dirty float".

8. (c) Statement 1 is true, and Statement 2 is false.

Explanation: Accommodating items are only recorded in the capital account of BOP. The main motive of such a transaction is to settle the surplus and deficit of BOP due to autonomous transactions.

9. (a) (i) and (ii)

Explanation: Foreign exchange inflow is recorded on the credit side. And the outflow of foreign exchange is recorded on the debit side of BOP.

10. (d) All of these

Explanation: Credit money is monetary value created as the result of some future obligation or claim. As such, credit money emerges from the extension of credit or issuance of debt.

11. (b) 12

Explanation: The first five-year plan in India was launched in 1951, and since then, India has witnessed twelve Five Year Plans. However, the present government had discontinued the Five-year plan system, and a new mechanism was put into place.

12. (a) Lesser

Explanation: Poverty is urban areas is lesser than poverty in rural areas because Rural poverty is often a product of poor infrastructure that hinders development and mobility. Rural areas tend to lack sufficient roads that would increase access to agricultural inputs and markets. Without roads, the rural poor are cut off from technological development and emerging markets in more urban areas.

13. (a) false

Explanation: The urban poverty line is set higher than the rural poverty line, reflecting the relatively higher living costs in urban areas. For example, the cost of living is typically higher in urban than in rural areas. One reason is that food staples tend to be more expensive in urban areas.

14. (d) Statement 2 is true and Statement 1 is false.

Explanation: Poverty Alleviation Programmes could not succeed because resources allocated to different programmes were far less than required, considering the magnitude of poverty.

15. (c) Statement 1 is true and Statement 2 is false.

Explanation: Human capital formation improves the quality of life as it provides better jobs, high income and improves health. It results in a better standard of living.

16. (a) grain

Explanation: Green Revolution led to an increase in the production of food grains. With the use of modern technology, extensive use of fertilizers, pesticides and HYV seeds, there was a significant increase in the agricultural productivity and product per farmland. In addition, the spread of the marketing system, abolition of intermediaries and easy availability of credit has enabled farmers with a more significant portion of the marketable surplus. All these factors enabled the government to procure sufficient food grains to build the buffer stock and provide a cushion against famines' shocks and shortages.

17. (b) B-(ii)

Explanation: Invisible trade means the trade of intangible goods like services.

18. (a) NABARD

Explanation: NABARD stands for National Bank for Agriculture and Rural Development and is an apex regulatory body in the Indian rural banking system. It is a development bank that aims to provide and regulate credit in rural areas.

19. (b) Capital nature expenditure

Explanation: Capital expenditures (CAPEX) are funds used by a company to acquire, upgrade, and maintain physical assets such as property, buildings, or equipment. Capital expenditures are typically one-time large purchases of fixed assets used for revenue generation over a more extended period.

20. (d) All of these

Explanation: In the past two decades, research in development and poverty has firmly established that poverty is a multi-dimensional phenomenon that can't be adequately described or measured in monetary terms. So the boundary is widening from the economic perspective alone to include social, political and cultural dimensions.

21. (b) Medium of exchange

Explanation: A medium of exchange is an intermediary instrument or system used to facilitate the sale, purchase, or trade of goods between parties. In modern economies, the medium of exchange is currency.

22. (c) Underemployment

    Explanation: Disguised unemployment exists when part of the labour force is either left without work or is working in a redundant manner such that worker productivity is essentially zero.

23. (c) Statement 1 is true and Statement 2 is false.

    Explanation: A budget estimates revenue and expenses over a specified future period and is usually compiled and re-evaluated periodically. Budgets can be made for a person, a group of people, a business, a government, or just about anything else that makes and spends money.

24. (a) Labour intensive

    Explanation: In developing countries like India, these small scale industries are the lifeline of the economy. These are generally labour-intensive industries, so they create much employment. They also help with per capita income and resource utilisation in the economy.

SECTION-B

25. (a) Both Assertion (A) and Reason (R) are true, and Reason (R) is the correct explanation of Assertion (A).

    Explanation: Both Assertion ad Reason are true because Assertion is BOP and reason is the definition of BOP. BOP presents more clear picture of a country's economic transactions with rest of the world and it considers exchange of both visible and invisible items. This clearly shows that the reason is the correct explanation of the assertion.

26. (d) All of these

    Explanation: The primary function of NABARD is to serve as an apex funding agency, coordinate the rural financing activities, monitor and evaluate the refunded projects, etc.

27. (d) Assertion (A) is false, but Reason (R) is true.

    Explanation: Green revolution was the phase of the enormous increase in agricultural production when wide yielding improved varieties of crop plants were used. But the increased yield was partly due to improved crop varieties but mainly due to the use of better management practices and agrochemicals (chemicals and fertilizers). However, these practices and agrochemicals were generally costly in the developing world, which the farmers could not afford. Hence, the developing world's farmers relied mainly on cheaper conventional breeding methods; thus, the green revolution could not become as productive or effective as it was in the developed world.

28. (a) Poverty Reduction and Growth Facility (PRGF) has been established by the International Development Association (IDA) to provide further assistance to low-income countries facing a high level of indebtedness.

    Explanation: In 1999, the IMF established the Poverty Reduction and Growth Facility (PRGF) to make the objectives of poverty reduction and growth more central to lending operations in its poorest member countries.

29. (c) Assertion (A) is true, but Reason (R) is false.

    Explanation: Human capital treats human beings as a means to an end, the end being the increase in productivity, whereas, in the Human development perspective, human beings end in themselves. Human capital includes the skills, abilities, talent, habits etc. and human development is concerned with the development of the same.

30. (a) A-(i)

Explanation: Economic growth leads to economic development only when it helps to eradicate poverty. When the economy grows, employment opportunities get generated for the people below the poverty line, leading to poverty eradication. Therefore, eradication of poverty leads to economic development.

31. (a) Gujarat

Explanation: In this above figure, Gujarat is the state which reduces its poverty line tremendously, and after that, Rajasthan, Andhra Pradesh, Karnataka, etc.

32. (b) 6.5

Explanation: In the given figure, it is clearly shown.

33. (a) Both Assertion (A) and Reason (R) are true, and Reason (R) is the correct explanation of Assertion (A).

Explanation: Assertion is a rural economy, and the reason is the population of the rural economy. This clearly shows that the reason is the correct explanation of the assertion.

34. (a) Both the statements are true

Explanation: SHG is a mutual-help group of people who provide support among themselves.
(i) In an SHG (Self Help Group), group members make essential decisions regarding loans and savings.
(ii) Self Help Groups issue loans (credit) at a reasonable rate of interest.
(iii) They come together to solve their economic issues, earn income and become self-reliant.
(iv) Helped women to discuss relevant issues like health.

35. (a) Both the statements are true.

Explanation: The coins issued by the Government of India under Section 6 of The Coinage Act, 2011, shall be legal tender in payment or on the account provided that a coin has not been defaced and has not lost weight to be less than such weight as may be prescribed in its case.

36. (b) (iv), (ii), (i), (iii)

Explanation: Following is the arrangement of the various events in China in chronological order.
(i) 1953: Five-year plan. This was introduced during the regime of Chairman Mao Zedong.
(ii) 1958 to 1963: Great Leap Forward campaign. It began during the 2nd five-year plan.
(iii) 1966-1976: The Great Proletarian Cultural Revolution was a sociopolitical movement.
(iv) December 1978: Economic reforms came about in China.

37. (a) Both Assertion (A) and Reason (R) are true, and Reason (R) is the correct explanation of Assertion (A).

Explanation: Assertion is showing the BOP receipts, and the reason is the economic transaction of BOP. This clearly shows that the reason is the correct explanation of the assertion.

38. (a) There will be more credit creation in the economy

Explanation: The impact on the credit creation ability of Commercial Banks if the government reduces income tax slabs, then there will be more credit creation in the economy.

39. (d) Assertion (A) is false, but Reason (R) is true.

Explanation: Rural Development is the process of improving the quality of life and economic well-being of people living in rural areas, often relatively isolated and sparsely populated areas like education, entrepreneurship, physical infrastructure, and social infrastructure all play an essential role in developing rural regions

40. (a) Both Assertion (A) and Reason (R) are true, and Reason (R) is the correct explanation of Assertion (A).

> **Explanation:** Assertion shows the economic condition of many farmers, and reason shows the population of agricultural. This shows that the reason is the correct explanation of the assertion.

41. (b) Both Assertion (A) and Reason (R) are true, and Reason (R) is not the correct explanation of assertion (A).

> **Explanation:** A Central Bank is an apex bank that controls the entire banking system of a country. It is the sole agency of note-issuing and controls the supply of money in the economy. It serves as the banker of the government and manages the foreign exchange of the government. Therefore, the Central Bank's primary function is to control credit in the economy and not create it. It is the Commercial Bank that deals in the creation of credit in the economy.

42. (c) low savings

> **Explanation:** In the given figure, it can be seen that capital storage, low level of income, low saving and low investment is the complete process of Economic growth and development.

43. (d) Enhances productivity

> **Explanation:** In this case, the role of on the job training is to Eradicates inequality, Encourages innovation, Promotes modern methods.

44. (c) ₹400 crores

> **Explanation:**
> $$\text{Balance of Payment} = \text{Total receipts} - \text{Total payments}$$
> $$\text{Total receipts} = \text{Total Payment} + \text{BOP}$$
> $$= 500 + (-100) = 500 - 100 = 400 = ₹400 \text{ crores}$$

45. (c) Statement 1 is true and Statement 2 is false.

> **Explanation:** Economic growth refers to an increase in the country's real output of goods and services. Growth relates to a gradual increase in one of the components of Gross Domestic Product: consumption, government spending, investment, net exports. Thus, economic growth reflects the growth of national or per capita income.

46. (a) Both Assertion (A) and Reason (R) are true, and Reason (R) is the correct explanation of Assertion (A).

> **Explanation:** Both assertion and reason are true, and the reason is the correct explanation of assertion. Higher average income is not the only indicator of human development in a country. Factors like the level of literacy rate, health facilities and public facilities are also important.

47. (a) Trade policies determine the size of markets for firms' output and strongly influence both foreign and domestic investment.

> **Explanation:** Trade policies determine the size of markets for firms' output and, hence, strongly influence foreign and domestic investment. Over time, the influence of trade policies on the investment climate is growing. Changes in technology, liberalisation of host country policies towards trade and investment and the growing organization of global production chains within multinational enterprises (MNEs) have all served to make trade policies in home and host countries alike a crucial ingredient in encouraging both foreign and domestic investment and in maximizing the contribution of that investment to development.

48. (a) A-(i)

> **Explanation:** Banking services provided in other countries is an intangible item in the balance of payments statement.

SECTION-C

49. (a) ₹5,000

Explanation:

$$\text{Revenue receipts} = \text{Revenue expenditure} - \text{Revenue deficit}$$
$$= 11,000 - 6,000 = ₹5,000$$

50. (d) ₹12,000

Explanation:

$$\text{Fiscal deficit} = \text{Revenue deficit} + (\text{Capital expenditure} - \text{Non-debt creating capital receipts})$$
$$= 6,000 + (14,000 - 8,000)$$
$$= 6,000 + 6,000 = ₹12,000$$

51. (a) Rent received

Explanation: Some examples of receipts that are routine, *i.e.,* revenue receipts in an organization, are:

(i)   Money received for services provided to customers

(ii) Rent received

(iii) Discount received from suppliers, vendors or creditors

(iv) Dividend received

(v)   Interest earned

(vi) Commission received

52. (a) Total revenue – Total expenditure excluding interest payments on its debt.

Explanation: Primary deficit = Total revenue – Total expenditure excluding interest payments on its debt. Primary deficit = Fiscal deficit – Interest payment. The interest payment will be the payment that a government makes on borrowings to the creditors.

53. (a) Both the statements are true.

Explanation:

(i) Capital receipts are the income received by the company which is non-recurring. They are part of the financing and investing activities rather than operating activities.

(ii) Revenue Receipts are the receipts that arise through the core business activities. These receipts are a part of everyday business operations; they occur repeatedly; however, their benefit can be enjoyed only in the current accounting year as its effect is short-term.

54. (c) ₹5,000

Explanation: Primary deficit = Fiscal deficit – Interest payments = 12,000 – 7,000 = ₹5000

55. (a) 1991

Explanation: The government announced a New Industrial Policy on 24 July, 1991. The New Industrial Policy established in 1991 sought substantially to deregulate industry to promote a more efficient and competitive industrial economy.

56. (c) Statement 1 is true and Statement 2 is false.

Explanation: Industrial licensing was abolished for all projects except in 18 industries. With this, 80 per cent of the industry was taken out of the licensing framework.

57. (b) Both Assertion (A) and Reason (R) are true, and Reason (R) is not the correct explanation of Assertion (A).

> **Explanation:** Assertion shows the delicensing of industries and reason is not correct. This clearly shows that the reason is the incorrect explanation of the assertion.

58. (d) The limit was raised to 74 per cent and subsequently to 100 per cent for many chemical industries.

> **Explanation:** In 1991, the government announced a specified list of high technology and high-investment priority industries wherein automatic permission was granted for foreign direct investment (FDI) up to 51 per cent foreign equity. The limit was raised to 74 per cent and subsequently to 100 per cent for many of these industries. Moreover, many new industries have been added to the list over the years.

59. (d) Statement 2 is true and Statement 1 is false

> **Explanation:** The policy encouraged disinvestment of government holdings of the equity share capital of public sector enterprises.

60. (a) Both Assertion (A) and Reason (R) are true, and Reason (R) is the correct explanation of Assertion (A).

> **Explanation:** Assertion shows the new industrial policy and reason is showing to bring out rapid and sustained improvement in the quality of the people. This clearly shows that the reason is the correct explanation of the assertion.

Sample Paper 5

SECTION-A

1. (a) Commercial Bank

> **Explanation:** The term Commercial Bank refers to a financial institution that accepts deposits, offers checking account services, makes various loans, and offers essential financial products like certificates of deposit (CDs) and savings accounts to individuals and small businesses. Thus, a Commercial Bank is where most people do their banking.
>
> Commercial Banks make money by providing and earning interest from mortgages, auto loans, business loans, and personal loans. Customer deposits provide banks with the capital to make these loans.

2. (b) Budget deficit

> **Explanation:** A budget deficit occurs when expenses exceed revenue and indicate the financial health of a country. The Government generally uses the term budget deficit when referring to spending rather than businesses or individuals.

3. (c) 1991

> **Explanation:** Liberalised Industrial Policy was introduced in 1991 in India. However, before that, all the industries needed licensing and permission from the Government to commence their business, resulting in the depletion of the Entrepreneurial spirit. Hence, resulted in the Backwardness of Indian Industry.

4. (c) Economic growth

> **Explanation:** Economic growth is the increase in the value of the goods and services produced by an economy over time. It is conventionally measured as the percentage rate of real Gross Domestic Product increase or real GDP (GDP adjusted for inflation).

5. (a) Both the statements are true.

   Explanation: Although there has been a steady decline in poverty over the last two decades, the total number of poor people has remained constant because of following reasons:
   (i) Inequality and marginalisation.
   (ii) Conflict.
   (iii) Hunger, malnutrition, and stunting.
   (iv) Poor healthcare systems — especially for mothers and children.
   (v) Little or no access to clean water, sanitation, and hygiene.
   (vi) Climate change.
   (vii) Lack of education.
   (viii) Poor public works and infrastructure.

6. (a) Absolute poverty

   Explanation: Absolute poverty is the state by which an individual is unable to meet their immediate needs. In other words, they cannot obtain basic needs such as shelter, water, food and warmth.

7. (b) Relative poverty

   Explanation: Relative poverty describes circumstances in which people cannot afford actively to participate in society and benefit from the activities and experiences that most people take for granted.

8. (a) Both the statements are true.

   Explanation: Money acts as a medium of exchange in the following ways : (i) Overcomes the double coincidence of wants. For example, if a person needs wheat in exchange for tea, they must search for a person ready to trade wheat for tea. Money made the need for such searches redundant. (ii) Acts as a medium of deferred payment. (iii) Has a store value.

9. (a) Primary deficit

   Explanation: Primary deficit indicates the extent to which the government needs to borrow to implement its budgetary programmes and policies for the upcoming years.

10. (a) 8

   Explanation: Under the industrial policy of 1991, the number of industries reserved for the public sector was reduced from 17 to only 8, which were considered strategic importance. Therefore, a new Industrial Policy was adopted by the Government of India in the year of 1991. It was adopted to create a more accessible and competitive economy. The main objective of any industrial policy is to augment industrial production and thereby enhance industrial growth.

11. (a) LPG

   Explanation: The economic reforms, popularly known as the NEP (New Economic Policy) of 1991, were intended to take the Indian economy in the direction of Liberalisation, Privatisation and Globalisation (LPG) by removing the restrictions on trade, private sector reduced the role of the Government in many areas.

12. (d) All of the above

   Explanation: The Priority areas of the Public Sector Industries, according to the New Industrial Policy, 1991 are:
   1. essential infrastructural goods and services.
   2. exploration and exploitation of oil and mineral resources.

3. technology development and building up of manufacturing capacities in crucial areas.

The Government of India adopted a new Industrial Policy in the year of 1991. It was adopted to create a more accessible and competitive economy. The main objective of any industrial policy is to augment industrial production and thereby enhance industrial growth.

13. (a)   12

Explanation: According to the Industrial Policy Resolution of 1956, Schedule B contains 12 industries. Industrial Policy Resolution of 1956 is a resolution adopted by the Indian Parliament in April 1956. The 1956 policy continued to constitute the primary economic policy for a long-time.

14. (a)   Both the statements are true.

Explanation: The budget is also referred to as the Annual Financial Statement in Article 112 of the Constitution of India. Thus, the Union Budget is the annual financial statement that contains the Government's revenue and expenditure for a fiscal year.

The government budget aims to reduce regional disparities through its taxation and expenditure policy to encourage setting up production units in economically backward regions.

15. (a)   Both the statements are true.

Explanation: The net exports of services enjoy a positive figure of USD 60.44 billion.

India has been the largest recipient of remittances since 2008. However, the remittance received by India in 2020 was over USD 83 billion, which is a drop of 0.2 per cent from 2019 (USD 83.3 billion).

16. (a)   eighth plan

Explanation: Human Development is its primary locus in the eighth plan. The eighth plan focuses on overall human development. Human development can be defined as the process of advancing human well being.

17. (d)   D-(iv)

Explanation: Privatisation is the transfer of publicly owned or publicly operated means of production to private ownership or operation. The argument for this transfer is usually that privately run enterprises are subject to the discipline of the market, and therefore they will be more efficient.

18. (c)   license, quota, permit raj

Explanation: The license, quota, permit raj was the elaborate system of licences, regulations and accompanying red tape required to set up and run businesses in India between 1947 and 1990. The New Economic Policy (NEP) aimed at replacing LQP raj with liberalisation, privatisation and globalisation (LPG) policies.

19. (b)   Churning poor

Explanation: Churning poor are people who keep moving in and out of the poverty line. It is a form of classifying and sub-classifying the poor in different categories. Explanation: The people who keep moving out of the poverty lines are classified as churning poor.

20. (c)   715 items

Explanation: After 1991, India's trade policy was to encourage exports and remove government control on imports. An essential element of India's trade policy changes was removing quantitative restrictions on imports, under which 715 items were freed of quantitative restrictions.

21. (d)   Human Capital

Explanation: This definition states what human capital means. Human capital refers to the skills, knowledge and experience of an individual or a population at large.

22. (a) Foreign Exchange Reserves

Explanation: Foreign exchange reserves are related to India's foreign exchange reserves comprises of FCA (foreign currency assets), gold, SDR with IMF and reserve tranche position in the IMF. It is kept as a cushion against any potential balance of payment-related crisis.

23. (a) Both the statements are true.

Explanation: A deficit-financed by long-term capital investment is more sustainable than a deficit financed by borrowing.
A deficit may occur due to high growth and strong consumer spending – rather than uncompetitiveness.

24. (b) Nation's net exports of financial claims

Explanation: The capital account, on a national level, represents the balance of payments for a country. The capital account keeps track of the net change in a nation's assets and liabilities during a year. The capital account's balance will inform economists whether the country is a net importer or net exporter of capital.

SECTION-B

25. (a) Both Assertion (A) and Reason (R) are correct, and Reason (R) is the correct explanation for Assertion (A).

Explanation: A debt trap is a situation in which a debt is difficult or impossible to repay, typically because high-interest payments prevent repayment of the principal. For example, a country is in a debt trap if it has to borrow to make interest payments on outstanding loans.

26. (a) Rural

Explanation: SHG is a holistic programme of micro-enterprises covering all aspects of self-employment, organization of the rural poor into self-help groups and their capacity building, planning of activity clusters, infrastructure build-up, technology, credit and marketing.
It emphasizes activity clusters based on the resources and the occupational skills of the people and the availability of markets.

27. (c) Assertion (A) is true, but Reason (R) is false.

Explanation: The most crucial purpose of a Commercial Bank is the creation of credit. This is the Reason why the money supplied by Commercial Banks is called credit money. All Commercial Banks create credit by advancing loans and purchasing securities. Thus, they lend money to the individuals and the businesses out of deposits accepted from the Public.
Commercial Banks are not allowed to use the entire amount of public deposits for lending purposes. Instead, they are accepted to keep a certain amount as a reserve with the Central Bank. This is for serving the cash needs of the depositors.
The Commercial Banks can lend the remaining portion of the public deposits after keeping the expected reserves.

28. (d) Tiny sector investment limit raised to ₹7 lakhs

Explanation: Tiny sector investment limit raised to ₹7 lakhs is incorrect from the New Small Scale Industrial Policy highlights, 1991. New Small Scale Industrial Policy, 1991 can be referred to as a reform in the Indian economy. It caused several changes in the small scale industrial sector. First, it helped to create a more free economy.

29. (a)   Both Assertion (A) and Reason (R) are true, and Reason (R) is the correct explanation of Assertion (A).

> **Explanation:** Monetary policy refers to the Central Bank's policy concerning using monetary instruments under its control to achieve the goals specified in the Act. The Reserve Bank of India (RBI) is vested with the responsibility of conducting monetary policy.

30. (a)   A-(i)

> **Explanation:** LPG stands for Liberalisation, Privatisation, and Globalisation. India, under its New Economic Policy, approached International Banks for the development of the country. These agencies asked the Indian Government to open its restrictions on trade done by the private sector and between India and other countries.

31. (b)   China

> **Explanation:** In 1981, the Poverty rate in China was more than 80%, which has been declined to less than 20% in 2010.

32. (c)   India

> **Explanation:** India's remittances as a share of GDP is least of all, that is < 5%

33. (b)   Both Assertion (A) and Reason (R) are true, and Reason (R) is not the correct explanation of Assertion (A).

> **Explanation:** Modern currency is accepted as a medium of exchange without any use of its own because:
> (i)   Modern currency is authorized by the Government of a country.
> (ii)   In India, the Reserve Bank of India issues all currency notes on behalf of the Central Government.
> (iii) No other individual or organization is allowed to issue currency.
> (iv) The law legalizes using a rupee as a medium of payment that cannot be refused in settling transactions in India.
> (v)   No individual in India can legally refuse a payment made in rupees.

34. (a)   Both the statements are true.

> **Explanation:**
> (i)   Inventions, innovations, and technological improvement
>   Human capital leads to more innovations in the areas of production and other related activities.
>   Innovation leads to more growth.
>   Human capital also creates the ability to absorb new technologies.
> (ii) Higher productivity of physical capital
>   Human capital increases labour productivity.
>   Trained workers will use the physical capital (like machines) more efficiently.

35. (d)   Statement 2 is true and Statement 1 is false

> **Explanation:** The capital account records all those transactions between the residents of a country and the rest of the world, which causes a change in assets and liabilities.
> The current account measures only net income.

36. (a)   (ii), (i), (iv), (iii)

Explanation: Following is the arrangement of poverty alleviation programmes in India in chronological order.

(a) Integrated Rural Development Programme (IRDP)

(b) National Rural Development Programme (NREP)

(c) Jawahar Rozgar Yojna (JRY)

(d) Rural Landless Employment Guarantee Programme (RLEGP)

37. (a) Both Assertion (A) and Reason (R) are true, and Reason (R) is the correct explanation of Assertion (A).

Explanation: Banks charge a higher interest rate on loans than what they offer on deposits. They do so to make a profit.

The term interest rate refers to a percentage charged on the principal amount lent by the lenders. The word principal refers to the amount of money lent.

This is how a bank works by providing attractive interest rates to the depositors on their deposits for using their funds.

Banks use the funds lying in the accounts of the individuals by providing funds to the loan seeker. First, the Bank provides attractive interest rates to the depositors, higher than the savings account interest, to garner funds for the loan. Second, once the depositors provide the fund, the Bank then provides funds to the loan seeker at higher rates and profits from the differential interest rates.

38. (b) (ii) and (iv)

Explanation: Regional Rural Banks (RRBs) are Government-owned scheduled Commercial Banks of India that operate at the regional level in different states of India. These banks are under the ownership of the Ministry of Finance, Government of India. They were created to serve rural areas with basic banking and financial services.

This prompted the nationalization of certain banks in 1969. The nationalised Commercial Banks (through their branch expansion programmes) were directed to offer credit directly to the farmers and indirectly through cooperatives societies.

39. (a) Both Assertion (A) and Reason (R) are true, and Reason (R) is the correct explanation of Assertion (A).

Explanation: The money multiplier is a phenomenon of creating money in the economy in the form of credit creation. The money is created in the market based on the fractional reserve banking system. Therefore, it is also sometimes called monetary Multiplier or credit multiplier.

It is the maximum limit to which money supply can be affected by changing the amount of money deposits deposited by the people in the market. The effect of the money multiplier can be seen in commercial banks of the economy. Commercial banks accept money or deposits. They keep some amount as a reserve with them and lend other shares as loans to the people.

The amount of money that is kept as reserves by these commercial banks for the withdrawal purposes of the depositors at any time is known as the reserve ratio or the required reserve ratio or cash reserve ratio.

The lending process of the commercial banks increases the rate of investment and production in the economy, which in turn helps in improving the national income in the economy.

40. (a) Both Assertion (A) and Reason (R) are true, and Reason (R) is the correct explanation of Assertion (A).

Explanation: Issue of Ration Cards for the people below the poverty line.

Identification of families living below the poverty line.

Management of food scarcity and distribution of food-grain.

41. (a) Both Assertion (A) and Reason (R) are true, and Reason (R) is the correct explanation of Assertion (A).

Explanation: Poverty Alleviation Programmes aims to reduce the country's poverty rate by providing proper access to food, monetary help, and essentials to the households and families below the poverty line.

42. (d) The nation's earnings and spending abroad

Explanation: The current account measures the nation's earnings and spending abroad. It consists of the balance of trade, net primary income or factor income (earnings on foreign investments minus payments made to foreign investors) and net unilateral transfers that have taken place over a given time.

43. (a) Macro Credit

Explanation: Micro-finance is an individual based concept to furnish financial services to low-income individuals who have no access to finance conventionally. Macro finance is a whole economy-based concept that is not framed for any particular group to grow the economy at a national level.

44. (b) ₹800 crores

Explanation:

$$\text{Balance of trade} = \text{Exports} - \text{Imports}$$

So,

$$\text{Imports} = \text{Exports} - \text{Balance of trade}$$
$$= 500 - (-)\,300 = ₹800 \text{ crores}$$

45. (a) Both the statements are true.

Explanation: The current account on the balance of payments measures the inflow and outflow of goods, services, investment incomes and transfer payments.

The main components of the current account are:

Trade-in goods (visible balance)

Trade-in services (invisible balance), *e.g.,* insurance and services

Investment incomes, *e.g.,* dividends, interest and migrants remittances from abroad

Net transfers – *e.g.,* International aid.

46. (a) Both Assertion (A) and Reason (R) are true, and Reason (R) is the correct explanation of Assertion (A).

Explanation: The RBI can purchase or sell Government securities from or to the Public. The RBI sells the securities in the money market to control inflation, which sucks out excess liquidity from the market. As the amount of liquid cash decreases, demand goes down. This part of monetary policy is called the open market operation.

47. (d) Agricultural Marketing

Explanation: Agricultural marketing is a process that starts with a decision to produce a saleable farm commodity involves all the aspects of market structure or system, both financial and institutional, based on technical and economic considerations and includes pre-and post-harvest operations, assembling, grading, storage, transportation and distribution.

48. (b) B-(ii)

Explanation: This definition states what human capital means. Human capital refers to the skills, knowledge and experience of an individual or a population at large.

SECTION-C

49. (a) ₹5,000 crores

> **Explanation:** Interest payment = 25% of Revenue deficit = ₹20,000 crores × 25/100[1] = ₹5,000 crores

50. (d) ₹20,000 crores

> **Explanation:**
>
> $$\text{Revenue deficit} = ₹70,000 \text{ crores} - ₹50,000 \text{ crores}$$
> $$= ₹20,000 \text{ crores}$$

51. (a) Dividend received

> **Explanation:** Capital receipts are receipts that create liabilities or reduce financial assets. They also refer to incoming cash flows. Capital receipts can be both non-debt and debt receipts. Loans from the general Public, foreign governments, and the Reserve Bank of India (RBI) form crucial capital receipts.

52. (b) Revenue expenditure – Revenue receipt

> **Explanation:** Revenue deficit is that which occurs when the Government's total revenue expenditure exceeds its total revenue receipts. This includes those transactions that directly impact the Government's current income and expenditure and happen when the actual revenue and spending do not correspond with the budgeted revenue and expenditure.

53. (b) Both the statements are true.

> **Explanation:** Capital receipts are the income received by the company which is non-recurring. They are part of the financing and investing activities rather than operating activities.
>
> Revenue Receipts are the receipts that arise through the core business activities. These receipts are a part of everyday business operations; that is why they occur repeatedly; however its benefit can be enjoyed only in the current accounting year as its effect is short-term.

54. (b) ₹10,000 crores

> **Explanation:**
>
> $$\text{Fiscal deficit} = \text{Borrowings} = ₹15,000 \text{ crores}$$
> $$\text{Primary deficit} = \text{Fiscal deficit} - \text{Interest payment}$$
> $$\text{Primary deficit} = ₹15,000 \text{ crores} - ₹5,000 \text{ crores}$$
> $$= ₹10,000 \text{ crores}$$

55. (a) Globalisation

> **Explanation:** Globalisation is the integration of the domestic economy with the rest of the world through trade and capital (investment) flows.

56. (a) Both the statements are true.

> **Explanation:** Since globalisation leads to the movement of goods, services, people and technology across nations, Developing countries are likely to become at par with developed countries in terms of technological development due to globalisation.

57. (a) Both Assertion (A) and Reason (R) are true and Reason (R) is the correct explanation of Assertion (A).

> **Explanation:** Globalisation leads to the connectivity of different countries, and goods and services can be transported across the world. Goods, Components produced in different parts of the world can be used for production in any country.

58. (c)   Conflict of values

> **Explanation:** To liberalise the Indian economy, industrial licensing was abolished, many industries reserved for the public sector were deserved, and import licensing was also abolished in most industries.

59. (a)   Both the statements are true.

> **Explanation:** The removal of trade barriers is known as liberalisation, and the businesses freely deciding which goods to import and export is an outcome of liberalisation, not a reason for liberalisation.

60. (b)   Both Assertion (A) and Reason (R) are true, and Reason (R) is not the correct explanation of Assertion (A).

> **Explanation:** Globalisation leads to increased competition in international trade and domestic markets as there is free movement of goods and services, labour and funds across countries. Also, consumers are better off as they get better quality and increased variety of goods at lower prices.

Sample Paper 6

SECTION-A

1. (d)   Disinvestment

> **Explanation:** Capital receipts are those receipts that either reduce assets or increase liabilities. Disinvestment reduces assets.

2. (d)   Capital receipts and payments

> **Explanation:** The current account is an essential pointer of an economy's health. It is defined as the sum of the balance of trade (goods and services exports minus imports), net income from abroad, and net current transfers.

3. (c)   Bring aggregate fiscal indiscipline level

> **Explanation:** The impacts of the government budget on the economy are Bring better allocation of resources, Implement government welfare programs, Better access to public goods, etc.
>
> The fiscal measures are undertaken by the Government affect public expenditure. For example, a rise in direct taxes would decrease personal disposable income, consequently reducing demand for goods. This decrease in demand will translate into a decrease in production, therefore affecting the growth of the economy.

4. (a)   Autonomous items

> **Explanation:** Autonomous items, also termed as 'above the line items', are those items, these transactions are done by consideration of profit (economic motive). Hence, these transactions have nothing to do with the state of BOP.

5. (c)   Statement 1 is true and Statement 2 is false.

> **Explanation:** Primary deficit is the difference between fiscal deficit and interest payment on accumulated profits.

6. (a)   Debt trap

> **Explanation:** A debt trap means that one owes a considerable amount of money to various institutions or people, which feels never-ending. Sometimes loans are taken to gain financial advantage, which is a wise decision. But, on the other hand, a debt trap is a situation we never want to be in.

7. (c) 2007

Explanation: The National Policy for Farmers, 2007, on recommendations of the National Commission on Farmers, has provided a holistic approach to the development of the farm sector. The comprehensive areas of its coverage include: (i) Focus will be on the economic well-being of the farmers in addition to production and productivity.

8. (a) Both the statements are true.

Explanation: A positive net export number indicates a trade surplus, while a negative number means a trade deficit. A weak currency exchange rate makes a nation's exports more competitive in price. Countries with comparative advantages and access to natural resources tend to be net exporters. India has been the largest recipient of remittances since 2008.

9. (a) (i) and (ii)

Explanation: : Investment leads to productivity improvements, which in turn lead to increased growth. This then leads to improved profits and additional investment, and in an ideal economy, the cycle continues.

Health expenditure is an important determinant of the health status and economic development of a nation. Experience has revealed that countries which assign due recognition to this aspect have healthier and more productive human capital.

10. (c) inability to fulfil basic requirements

Explanation: Poverty is a state or condition in which a person or community lacks the financial resources and essentials for a minimum standard of living. Poverty means that the income level from employment is so low that basic human needs can't be met.

11. (b) Human resource

Explanation: Human resources is the set of people who make up the workforce of an organisation, business sector, industry, or economy. A narrower concept is human capital, the knowledge and skills which the individuals command. Similar terms include workforce, labour, personnel, associates, or simply: people.

12. (c) Both (a) and (b)

Explanation: In case of monsoon failure, crop yield is low, and farmers need to be shielded against this loss by providing credit and insurance. Keeping the above points in view, major nationalisation of banks was done in 1969, as India adopted social banking and multi-agency approach to meet the needs of rural credit adequately.

13. (b) Dadabhai Naoroji

Explanation: Dadabhai Naoroji made the first attempt to calculate national income.

14. (c) Statement 1 is true, and Statement 2 is false.

Explanation: Absolute poverty is when household income is below a certain level, making it impossible for the person or family to meet the basic needs of life, including food, shelter, safe drinking water, education, healthcare, etc.

In this state of poverty, even if the country is growing economically, it does not affect people living below the poverty line. Absolute poverty compares households based on a set income level, and this level varies from country to country depending on its overall economic conditions.

15. (a) Both the statements are true.

Explanation: Physical capital is tangible, *i.e.*, it can be seen and touched. Unlike human capital is intangible, which can only be experienced. The creation of physical capital is an economic and technical process.

Human capital formation is the process of adding to the stock of human capital over some time. It refers to the development of abilities, skills, education, and experience among the county population.

16. (b) Micro-credit

Explanation: Micro-credit is a method of lending tiny sums to individuals to start or expand a small business. Micro-credit borrowers tend to be low-income individuals living in parts of the developing world; the practice originated in its modern form in Bangladesh.

17. (c) C-(iii)

Explanation: Direct investment receipt is credit in the capital account.

18. (b) Overdraft

Explanation: The overdraft allows the accountholder to continue withdrawing money even when the account has no funds in it or has insufficient funds to cover the amount of the withdrawal.

Basically, an overdraft means that the bank allows customers to borrow a set amount of money.

19. (b) Gift and Grants

Explanation: Public income received through the administration, commercial enterprises, gifts, and grants are the source of non-tax revenues of the Government.

20. (d) 2,100

Explanation: The nutritional requirement recommends a national norm of 2,400 kilo calories a day for rural areas and 2,100 calories a day for urban areas. The difference is attributed to the lower rate of physical activity in urban areas.

21. (c) Money

Explanation: Anything, which is generally accepted by the people as a medium of exchange, measure of value, standard of deferred payment, and performs the function of store of value is known as money.

22. (b) Nation's net exports of financial claims

Explanation: Balance in capital account refer to the Nation's net exports of financial claims.

23. (c) Statement 1 is true, and Statement 2 is false.

Explanation: (a) A budget estimates revenue and expenses over a specified future period and is usually compiled and re-evaluated periodically. Budgets can be made for a person, a group of people, a business, a government, or just about anything else that makes and spends money.

24. (b) less, high

Explanation: The enrolment ratio of girl children has gone up, so has the drop-out ratio. Dealing with puberty is among the significant reasons. According to the latest Child Rights and You (CRY) report, only one in every three school-going children in the country finish class 12 at an appropriate age.

SECTION-B

25. (a) Both Assertion (A) and Reason (R) are true, and Reason (R) is the correct explanation of Assertion (A).

Explanation: Assertion that lending abroad is recorded on the debit side, and the lending affects the asset and liabilities of the economy. This clearly shows that the reason is the correct explanation of the assertion.

26. (d) All of these

Explanation: Following four measures of money stock are used.

$$M_1 = C + DD + OD$$
$$M_2 = M_1 + \text{Saving deposit in Post Office Saving banks.}$$
$$M_3 = M_1 + \text{Net time deposit of banks}$$
$$M_4 = M_3 + \text{Total deposit with post office saving organisation}$$

27. (a) Both Assertion (A) and Reason (R) are true, and Reason (R) is the correct explanation of Assertion (A).

Explanation: Indian handicrafts gained reputation the international markets. But during the British rule, these princely stales were ruined thereby ruining the protection of those handicrafts industries. Thus, Indian handicrafts industries could not survive.

28. (a) Only (iii)

Explanation: The balance of payments situation has improved post-liberalisation because it increases exports, etc.

29. (a) Both Assertion (A) and Reason (R) are true, and Reason (R) is the correct explanation of Assertion (A).

Explanation: Assertion is about direct tax, reason is the meaning of tax, and tax is classified into two parts. Reason is the correct explanation of assertion.

30. (c) C-(iii)

Explanation: To ensure financial inclusion by affordably ensuring access to financial services.

31. (a) Chhattisgarh

Explanation: In this above figure shows, clearly that Chhattisgarh is the state where more population percentage is facing poverty.

32. (b) 5.6

Explanation: In the above figure, it is clearly shown.

33. (b) Both Assertion (A) and Reason (R) are true, and Reason (R) is not the correct explanation of assertion (A).

Explanation: Assertion is non-institutional finance, and the reason is about the small farmers accessing credit. This not shows the correct explanation of the assertion.

34. (d) Statement 2 is true, and Statement 1 is false.

Explanation: Total stock of money held by the public at a particular point of time in an Economy is known as money supply.

35. (c) Statement 1 is true and Statement 2 is False.

Explanation: RBI stands for Reserve Bank of India. It is the Central Bank of India. It is the apex bank and has the sole authority to issue and manage currency in India. Only RBI can issue currency on behalf of the Indian Government. It also manages the money supply in the economy by exercising monetary and fiscal policy.

36. (a)   (iii), (iv), (i), (ii)

> **Explanation:** Following is the arrangement of the various events in chronological order.
> (i)   India was reduced to be a mere exporter of raw material.
> (ii)   India faced a shortage of locally made goods.
> (iii)   Cheap imports of British manufactured goods increase in the country.
> (iv)   The growth rate of the industrial sector was minimal.

37. (d)   Assertion (A) is false, but Reason (R) is true.

> **Explanation:** Assertion is balance of trade is also referred to as the balance of payments, and the reason is a balance of trade includes the value of imports and exports of visible goods and invisible goods. This shows that the assertion is the incorrect and reason is correct.

38. (c)   accepting demand deposits

> **Explanation:** It is only the bank that accepts the demand deposits. The depositor is free to withdraw money out of it on demand through cheque, ATM, and online banking. The saving and current accounts are examples of demand deposits.

39. (a)   Both Assertion (A) and Reason (R) are true, and Reason (R) is the correct explanation of Assertion (A).

> **Explanation:** Assertion shows India became an exporter of primary products and reason shows the restrictive policy of commodity production, trade, and tariff pursued by the colonial Government. This shows that the reason is the correct explanation of the assertion.

40. (a)   Both Assertion (A) and Reason (R) are true, and Reason (R) is the correct explanation of Assertion (A).

> **Explanation:** Assertion shows the policy initiatives and reason the proportion of people depending on agriculture. This shows that the reason is the correct explanation of the assertion.

41. (b)   Both Assertion (A) and Reason (R) are true, and Reason (R) is the correct explanation of Assertion (A).

> **Explanation:** A Central Bank regulates the level of money supply within a country. Through monetary policy, a Central Bank can undertake actions that follow an expansionary or contractionary policy.

42. (a)   economic growth

> **Explanation:** In the above figure, it is mentioned that if human capital will rise then it leads to economic growth.

43. (b)   Rural poor

> **Explanation:** It refers to people who do not have any land for farming or who are prevented from owning the land that they farm by the economic system or by rich people who own a lot of land.

44. (c)   ₹800 crore

> **Explanation:**
> $$\text{Balance of Payment} = \text{Total Receipts} - \text{Total Payments}$$
> $$\text{Total Receipts} = \text{Total Payment} + \text{BOP}$$
> $$= 1,000 + (-)\ 200$$
> $$= 1,000 - 200 = ₹800 \text{ crores}$$

45. (c)   Statement 1 is true and Statement 2 is False.

> **Explanation:** India saw a huge drain because of the British rule due to their policies.

46. (b)   Both Assertion (A) and Reason (R) are true, and Reason (R) is not the correct explanation of assertion (A).

Explanation: Since globalisation leads to movement of goods, services and people and technology across nations, developing countries are likely to become at par with developed countries in terms of technological development due to globalisation.

47. (a) Development plans started in India on which year 1st April, 1951.

Explanation: The planning process was initiated in April 1951 when the First Five Year Plan was launched. Since then, ten five-year plans have been completed, and the Eleventh Plan is in progress.

48. (a) A-(i)

Explanation: Tractor loans are loans provided to farmers or business people to buy new or pre-owned tractors. Such tractors can be used for agricultural or commercial purposes. A farmer has to own a minimum of three acres of agricultural land to qualify for a tractor loan, though this could vary from lender to lender. These are generally for 15-20 years.

SECTION–C

49. (b) ₹6,000

Explanation:
$$\text{Revenue receipts} = \text{Revenue expenditure} - \text{Revenue deficit}$$
$$= 14,000 - 8,000 = ₹6,000$$

50. (d) ₹14,000

Explanation:
$$\text{Fiscal deficit} = \text{Revenue deficit} + (\text{Capital expenditure} - \text{Non-debt creating capital receipts})$$
$$= 8,000 + (16,000 - 10,000)$$
$$= 8,000 + 6,000 = ₹14,000$$

51. (d) All of the above

Explanation: Some examples of receipts that are routine, *i.e.,* revenue receipts in an organisation, are,
(i) Money received for services provided to customers
(ii) Rent received
(iii) Discount received from suppliers, vendors, or creditors
(iv) Dividend received
(v) Interest earned
(vi) Commission received

52. (a) Total expenditure excluding interest payments on its debt- Primary Deficit

Explanation:
Total revenue = Total expenditure excluding interest payments on its debt – Primary Deficit.
Primary deficit = Fiscal deficit – Interest payment. The interest payment will be the payment that a government makes on borrowings to the creditors.

53. (a) Both the statements are true.

Explanation:
(i) Primary Deficit is the difference between the current year's Fiscal Deficit and the interest paid on the borrowings of the previous year.
(ii) Revenue deficit occurs when realized net income is less than the projected net income. This happens when the actual amount of revenue and the actual amount of expenditures do not correspond with budgeted revenue and expenditures

54. (d) 7,000

> **Explanation:**
> $$\text{Primary deficit} = \text{Fiscal deficit} - \text{Interest payments}$$
> $$= 14{,}000 - 7{,}000 = ₹7{,}000$$

55. (c) Both (a) and (b)

> **Explanation:** The 'Land Reform' measures and 'Green Revolution' were the most outstanding achievements of the Indian Government in increasing agricultural production and productivity.

56. (c) Statement 1 is true and Statement 2 is false.

> **Explanation:** By the late 1960s, Indian agricultural productivity had increased sufficiently to enable the country to be self-sufficient in food grains.

57. (a) Both Assertion (A) and Reason (R) are true, and Reason (R) is the correct explanation of Assertion (A).

> **Explanation:** Assertion is the meaning of land reform,and the reason shows the need for reforms. This clearly shows that the reason is the correct explanation of the assertion.

58. (d) Land reforms (Institutional reforms) – for increasing productivity.

> **Explanation:** Land reforms (Institutional reforms) – for promoting equity in agriculture. Land reform means equity in agriculture that also means the shift in the ownership of landholdings. Land reform relates typically to the redistribution of land from the rich to the poor. It involves control of operation, ownership, sales, leasing, and inheritance of land.

59. (c) Statement 1 is true and Statement 2 is false.

> **Explanation:** : In India, between 1950 and 1990, the proportion of GDP contributed by agriculture declined significantly but not the population depending on it (67.5% in 1950 to 64.9% in 1990).

60. (a) Both Assertion (A) and Reason (R) are true, and Reason (R) is the correct explanation of Assertion (A).

> **Explanation:** : Assertion is the showing meaning of green revolution, and the reason is showing the reasons of the green revolution. This clearly shows that the reason is the correct explanation of the assertion.

Sample Paper 7

SECTION-A

1. (c) primary deposits

> **Explanation:** Primary deposits are those deposits that the bank collects from different surplus stakeholders by different accounts. These consist of cash deposited by the people with the banks in different deposit account such as savings deposits, time or fixed deposits, current or demand deposits and other deposits.

2. (c) Balance of Payment (BOP) of a country can be defined as a systematic statement of a country's economic transactions with the rest of the world during a specific period.

> **Explanation:** Balance of payment may sound like a country's debt, but it is not the case.
> (i) The systematic accounting is done based on double-entry bookkeeping (both sides of transactions credit and debit are included).

(ii) Economic transaction includes all such transactions that involve the transfer of title or ownership of goods and services, money, and assets.

(iii) All trades conducted by the private and public sectors are accounted for in the BOP to determine how much money is going in and out of a country.

3. (d) All of these

Explanation: The various objectives of the government budget are:

(i) Reallocation of Resources.

(ii) Reducing inequalities in income and wealth.

(iii) Economic Stability.

(iv) Management of Public Enterprises.

(v) Economic Growth.

(vi) Reducing regional disparities.

4. (d) Capital receipts and payments

Explanation:

(i) The current account represents a country's imports and exports of goods and services, payments made to foreign investors, and transfers such as foreign Aid.

(ii) The current account may be positive (a surplus) or negative (a deficit); positive means the country is a net exporter, and negative means it is a net importer of goods and services.

(iii) A country's current account balance, whether positive or negative, will be equal but opposite to its capital account balance.

5. (a) Both the statements are true, and the reason is not the correct explanation of the Assertion.

Explanation: The main benefit of demonetisation is to curtail criminal activity as their supply of money is no longer legal tender. This affects counterfeiters as well as they cannot exchange their "merchandise" for fear of discovery. Furthermore, it can prevent tax evasion as those who were evading taxes must come forward to exchange their existing currency, at which time the authorities can retroactively tax them. Finally, it can usher in the digital currency age by slowing down the circulation of physical currency.

6. (a) Current account

Explanation:

(i) The current account of the balance of payments includes a country's essential activity, such as capital markets and services.

(ii) The current account balance should theoretically be zero, which is impossible, so in reality, it will tell whether a country is in a surplus or deficit.

(iii) A surplus is indicative of an economy that is a net creditor to the rest of the world. Conversely, a deficit reflects a government and an economy that is a net debtor to the rest of the world.

7. (a) Budget Deficit

Explanation: A budgetary deficit is referred to as the situation in which the spending is more than the income. In other words, a budgetary deficit is said to have taken place when the individual, government, or business budgets have more spending than the income that they can generate as revenue.

8. (a) Both the statements are true.

Explanation: Money supply includes the currency in circulation with the public at a particular point in time; hence it does not include the money held by the Government or commercial banks. Consequently, it is not in circulation with the public at a given point in time.

9. (a) (i) and (ii)

> **Explanation:** India, as a developing country, features a mixed economy in the world. The major characteristics of developing economy are low per capita income, overpopulation, maximum population below the poverty line, poor infrastructure, agro-based economy and a lower rate of capital formation.

10. (c) M_1

> **Explanation:** The term 'Narrow Money' is derived from the fact that M_1/M_0 are the narrowest or most restrictive types of money that form the basis for an economy's medium of exchange. The narrow supply of money includes only the most liquid financial assets. These funds must be available on-demand.

11. (d) Correct the damage done to the economy by partition

> **Explanation:** The first-year plan (1951–56) was essentially a 'repair plan', made to take care of the severe damage to the country's economy caused by war, famine (1943), and the sub-continent's partition in 1947. The first-year plan was the Harrod – Domar model of development economics. FYP had a target of 2.1% PA growth in national income. Top priority was given to the development of the agricultural sector. The idea was agricultural development would lead to a higher rate of economic growth. The plan's performance was good due to a good harvest and the National income increased at the rate of 3.6% PA.

12. (a) Agricultural Cost and Prices

> **Explanation:** The Government decided the support prices for various agricultural commodities after taking recommendations of the Commission for Agricultural Costs and Prices.

13. (d) All of these

> **Explanation:** Agricultural marketing includes all these processes between harvesting and final sale of the product by the farmers.

14. (a) Both the statements are true.

> **Explanation:** Poverty reduction occurs mainly due to overall economic growth. Aid and government support in health, education, and infrastructure help growth by increasing human and physical capital. Poverty alleviation also involves improving the living conditions of people who are already poor.

15. (a) Both the statements are factual.

> **Explanation:** Human capital formation increases the efficiency of physical capital. Skilled human resources handle the physical capital so that it enhances productivity, which helps in the growth of an economy. Human capital help in the efficient and effective utilisation of physical capital.

16. (c) Inclusive Growth in all sectors

> **Explanation:** The Eleventh Five Year Plan aims to achieve an improved quality of life for the state's citizens and contribute to the larger national goals of socio-economic development. This will require faster and more equitable social and economic development of the state.

17. (a) A-(i)

> **Explanation:**
> (i) RRBs are financial institutions that ensure adequate credit for agriculture and other rural sectors.
> (ii) Regional Rural Banks were set up based on the recommendations of the Narasimham Working Group (1975) and after the legislation of the Regional Rural Banks Act, 1976.

    (iii) **Stakeholders:** The equity of a regional rural bank is held by the Central Government, concerned State Government, and the Sponsor Bank in the proportion of 50:15:35.

    (iv) The main objectives of RRBs are:

        (A) To provide credit and other facilities to the small and marginal farmers, agricultural labourers, artisans, and small entrepreneurs in rural areas.

        (B) To check the outflow of rural deposits to urban areas and reduce regional imbalances and increase rural employment generation.

    (v) The RRBs are required to provide 75% of their total credit as priority sector lending.

18. (b) Wheat and Rice

Explanation: The Green Revolution was a period when agriculture in India was converted into an industrial system due to the adoption of modern methods and technology, such as the use of high yielding variety (HYV) seeds, tractors, irrigation facilities, pesticides, and fertilizers.

19. (a) Revenue Expenditure

Explanation: Revenue expenditures are short-term expenses used in the current period or typically within one year. Revenue expenditures include the expenses required to meet the on going operational costs of running a business and thus are essentially the same as operating expenses (OPEX).

20. (c) Foreign exchange crisis

Explanation: High tax rates leading to tax evasion.

21. (a) 20%

Explanation: By far the most widely-used measure is the headcount index, which simply measures the proportion of the population that is counted as poor, often denoted by P_0. Formally,

$$P_0 = \frac{N_p}{N}$$

Where N_p is the number of poor and N is the total population (or sample). If 60 people are poor in a survey that samples 300 people, then

$$P_0 = \frac{60}{300} = 0.2 = 20\%$$

22. (a) Small Finance Banks (SFBs)

Explanation:

(i) Small Finance Banks are the financial institutions that provide financial services to the unserved and unbanked region of the country.

(ii) They are registered as a public limited company under the Companies Act, 2013.

(iii) They are required to extend 75% of its Adjusted Net Bank Credit (ANBC) to the sectors eligible for classification as priority sector lending by the Reserve Bank of India.

(iv) At least 50% of its loan portfolio should constitute loans and advances of up to ₹25 lakh.

23. (a) Both the statements are true.

Explanation: Under premiership of Congress leader Lal Bahadur Shastri, the Green Revolution within India commenced in 1965, leading to an increase in foodgrain production, especially in Punjab, Haryana, and Uttar Pradesh. Major milestones in this undertaking were the development of high-yielding varieties of wheat, and rust resistant strains of wheat. However, certain social activists like Vandana Shiva are of the opinion that it caused greater long term sociological and financial problems for the people of Punjab and Haryana.

24. (d) For buying agricultural machinery

     Explanation: Longer-term agricultural financing is needed for longer-term investments such as better storage facilities, food/commodity processing facilities and equipment and mechanisation.

SECTION-B

25. (a) Both Assertion and Reason are correct, and the reason is the correct explanation for Assertion.

     Explanation: A country follows a mix of fixed and flexible exchange rate systems wherein the Government attempts to manipulate the exchange rate directly by buying/selling foreign currency or indirectly by monetary policy.

26. (d) None of these

     Explanation: The M_1 measure of money supply includes the following components:
     (i) Currency held by the public in the form of notes and coins.
     (ii) Net Demand Deposits held by the commercial banks.
     (iii) Other deposits held by the RBI.

27. (c) Assertion (A) is true, but Reason (R) is false.

     Explanation: Rural credit agencies and their schemes have ignored the needs of small and marginal farmers. As a result, credit agencies are paying less attention to the credit needs of poor farmers, while credit agencies are paying more attention to the creditworthiness of relatively well-off farmers.

28. (b) It does not allow foreign investors to purchase Indian financial assets.

     Explanation: Similarly, capital account convertibility means the freedom to conduct investment transactions without any constraints. Typically, it would mean no restrictions on the amount of rupees you can convert into foreign currency to enable an Indian resident to acquire any foreign asset.

29. (b) Both Assertion (A) and Reason (R) are true, and Reason (R) is not the correct explanation of Assertion (A).

     Explanation: Expenditure on migration is a source of human capital formation as enhanced earnings in the migrated place is more than the increase in costs due to migration. This also leads to the capital formation through fuller utilisation of skills.

30. (c) C-(iii)

     Explanation: Infrastructure development includes electricity, irrigation, credit, marketing, transport facilities, including building village roads and feeder roads to nearby highways, agriculture research and extension facilities, and information dissemination.

31. (a) India

     Explanation: In 1981and 2010 both the Poverty rate in India was more than 40%. However, it showed a slight decline in 1981 as compared to 2010.

32. (a) Nepal

     Explanation: India's remittances as a share of GDP is the highest of all, that is >25%

33. (d) Assertion (A) is false, but Reason (R) is true.

     Explanation: The resources allocated to the formation of human capital have been much less than the resources required. Due to this reason, the facilities for the formation of human capital have remained grossly inadequate. The cost of such loss of quality human capital is very high.

34. (a) Both the statements are true.

> **Explanation:** Expenditure regarding on-the-job training is a source of human capital formation as the return of such expenditure in the form of enhanced labour productivity is more than the cost of it. People migrate in search of jobs that fetch them higher salaries than what they may get in their native places. Firms will, thus, insist that the workers should work for a specific period of time, after their on-the-job training, during which it can recover the benefits of the enhanced productivity owing to the training.

35. (a) Both the statements are true.

> **Explanation:** The Central Bank controls credit by making variations in the bank rate.
>
> The Central Bank now has the loans (or government bonds) as assets and the cash as liabilities. The cash is a liability because if the commercial bank goes back to the Central Bank and gives back the cash, the Central Bank will have to give back the loans (or government bonds).

36. (a) (ii), (i), (iv), (iii)

> **Explanation:** Therefore, the First Plan had the objectives of rehabilitating refugees, agricultural development, self-sufficiency in food, and controlling inflation.
>
> The focus of the Second Plan was rapid industrialisation, especially the development of heavy industries and capital goods, like iron, steel, chemicals, etc., and the machine-building industries.
>
> The primary goal of the Third Plan was to establish India as a self-reliant and self-generating economy.
>
> This plan's two principal objectives – 'Growth with Stability and 'Progressive Achievement of Self-Reliance'.

37. (a) Both Assertion (A) and Reason (R) are true, and Reason (R) is the correct explanation of Assertion (A).

> **Explanation:** The BOP does not just mean the repayment of loans; it is the transaction statement and includes both credit and debit. If a country has surplus BOP (credit more than debit), which increases the value of that country's currency. So, BOP indicates both the appreciation and depreciation of a country's currency.

38. (a) (i) and (ii)

> **Explanation:** The functions of a central bank can be discussed as follows:
> (i)   Currency regulator or bank of issue.
> (ii)   Bank to the Government.
> (iii) Custodian of Cash reserves.
> (iv)   Custodian of International currency.
> (v)   Lender of last resort.
> (vi)   Clearing house for transfer and settlement.
> (vii) Controller of credit.
> (viii) Protecting depositors interests.

39. (b) Both Assertion (A) and Reason (R) are true, and Reason (R) is not the correct explanation of Assertion (A).

> **Explanation:** The 1956 policy in injunction with the IDA act did just reverse of what it was supposed to do. The licensing policy of the government favoured big business houses who were in better position to raise huge amount of capital and had the better management skills to run the industry. They were also able to secure financial assistance from development and finance institutions. Further, since there was no proper system of allocation of licenses in place; pre-empting of licensing by authorities to select people or groups happened due to an array of reasons. Overall, the freedom of entry into industry was restricted due to licensing and this resulted in the concentration of economic power in few individuals.

40. (a) Both Assertion (A) and Reason (R) are true, and Reason (R) is the correct explanation of Assertion (A).

   Explanation: Issue of Ration Cards for the people below the poverty line.
   Identification of families living below the poverty line.
   Management of food scarcity and distribution of foodgrain.

41. (a) Both Assertion (A) and Reason (R) are true, and Reason (R) is the correct explanation of Assertion (A).

   Explanation: Diversification into non-farm activities is essential because it will:
   1. Reduce the risk from the agriculture sector.
   2. Provide sustainable livelihood options to people living in villages.
   3. Provide ecological balance.

42. (b) Standard of deferred payments

   Explanation: In economics, standard of deferred payment is a function of money. It is the function of being a widely accepted way to value a debt, thereby allowing goods and services to be acquired now and paid for in the future.

43. (d) Good sanitation facilities

   Explanation: Labour skill of an educated person is more than that of an uneducated person, which enables him to generate more income than the uneducated person and hence contributes more to the economic growth.

   Spending on education by individuals is similar to spending on capital goods by companies with the objective of increasing future profits over a period of time. It increases productivity and efficiency of labour. Thus, individuals invest in education with the objective of increasing their future income.

   Education is sought not only as it confers higher earning capacity on people but also for its other highly valued benefits:

   (i) It gives one a better social standing and pride.

   (ii) It enables one to make better choices in life.

   (iii) It provides knowledge to understand the changes taking place in society.

   (iv) It also stimulates innovations.

   (v) It facilitates adaptation of new technologies.

   Thus, expanding educational opportunities in a nation accelerates the development process.

44. (c) ₹58,000

   Explanation:

   $$\text{Fiscal deficit} = \text{Primary deficit} + \text{Interest payment}$$
   $$= 53{,}000 + 5{,}000 = ₹58{,}000$$

45. (a) Both the statements are true.

   Explanation: The urban poor include people from the rural areas who migrate to cities in search of employment. Urban poor include migrants from the rural areas who is in search of employment, casual factory workers and street vendors and other such low-earning self-employed people. The poverty line expresses the per capita average monthly expenditure by which people can satisfy their minimum needs.

46. (a) Both Assertion (A) and Reason (R) are true, and Reason (R) is the correct explanation of Assertion (A).

   Explanation: Economists use the BOT to measure the relative strength of a country's economy. A country that imports more goods and services than exports in terms of value has a trade deficit or a negative trade balance.

Balance of trade, is the difference in value over sometime between a country's imports and exports of goods and services, usually expressed in the unit of currency of a particular country or economic union.

47. (a) Central Bank

Explanation: Central Banks carry out a nation's monetary policy and control its money supply, often mandated with maintaining low inflation and steady GDP growth. On a macro basis, Central Banks influence interest rates and participate in open market operations to control the cost of borrowing and lending throughout an economy.

48. (a) A-(i)

Explanation: Balance of trade is the difference in value over sometime between a country's imports and exports of goods and services, usually expressed in the unit of currency of a particular country or economic union.

SECTION-C

49. (a) Primary deficit = Fiscal deficit – Interest payment

Explanation: Primary deficit is the difference between the fiscal deficit of the current year and the interest paid by the Government on loans obtained in the past. It indicates that the Government's borrowings are utilised to pay the interest on loans rather than capital expenditure.

50. (a) ₹40,000 crores

Explanation:

$$\text{Revenue deficit} = ₹1,00,000 - ₹60,000 = ₹40,000 \text{ crores}$$

51. (a) Police services.

Explanation: Non-Tax Revenue is the recurring income earned by the Government from sources other than taxes. The most important receipts under this head are interest receipts (received on loans given by the Government to states, railways and others) and dividends and profits from public sector companies.

52. (b) ₹10,000 crores

Explanation:

$$\text{Interest payment} = 25\% \text{ of Revenue deficit}$$
$$= 40,000 \times \frac{25}{100} = ₹10,000 \text{ crores}$$

53. (a) Both the statements are true.

Explanation: Revenue expenditure is expenditure for the regular running of government departments and various services, interest charges on debt incurred by the Government, subsidies, etc. But expenditure that does not create assets is treated as revenue expenditure.

54. (c) ₹15,000 crores

Explanation:

$$\text{Fiscal deficit} = \text{Borrowings} = ₹15,000 \text{ crores}$$
$$\text{Primary deficit} = \text{Fiscal deficit} - \text{Interest payment}$$
$$\text{Primary deficit} = ₹25,000 - ₹10,000 = ₹15,000 \text{ crores}$$

55. (b) Economic reforms

   Explanation: The reforms intended at bringing in more considerable cooperation of the private sector in the growth method of the Indian economy. Policy changes were proposed about technology up-gradation, industrial licensing, restrictions on the private sector, foreign investments, and foreign trade.

56. (d) Statement 2 is true and Statement 1 is false.

   Explanation: Liberalisation caused a substantial shift in the role of the RBI from a regulator of the financial sector. Under liberalisation, reforms were introduced in many areas. For example: the government abolished the licensing requirement of all industries except for five *i.e.,* liquor, cigarette, defence equipment, industrial explosives and dangerous chemicals, and drugs and pharmaceuticals industries.

57. (a) Both Assertion (A) and Reason (R) are true, and Reason (R) is the correct explanation of Assertion (A).

   Explanation: The most significant advantage of globalisation and its outcome outsourcing is that large multinational corporations or even small businesses can benefit from good services at a lower rate than their country's standards.

   The low wage rate and highly skilled personnel have made India the most favourable global outsourcing destination in the subsequent phase of the reform.

   It has helped in the growth and development of the tertiary sector of the economy and the creation of more jobs and employment for the people.

58. (d) land settlement system

   Explanation: The stagnation of pre independence India was caused mainly because of various land settlement systems imposed by the colonial government, among the most prominent being the Zamindari system.

59. (a) Both the statements are true.

   Explanation: Under the colonial rule, India was basically an agrarian economy, employing nearly 85% of its population. Nevertheless, the growth of the agriculture sector was meagre. The reasons for stagnancy includes introduction of the land revenue system, forceful commercialisation, and lack of irrigation facilities and resources. Whereas the demand for British goods was increased in India due to deindustrialisation of Indian industries.

60. (a) Both Assertion (A) and Reason (R) are true, and Reason (R) is the correct explanation of Assertion (A).

   Explanation: An increase in foreign exchange reserves raises both liquid and total debt while shortening debt maturity. To the extent that foreign exchange reserve interest rates are low, increased foreign reserves will cause a permanent decline in consumption and move labour from the non-tradable to the tradable sector.

☐☐

Name of Exam : _______________________________

2021-22

OMR Response Sheet

Roll No.

1 ○ ○ ○ ○ ○ ○ ○
2 ○ ○ ○ ○ ○ ○ ○
3 ○ ○ ○ ○ ○ ○ ○
4 ○ ○ ○ ○ ○ ○ ○
5 ○ ○ ○ ○ ○ ○ ○
6 ○ ○ ○ ○ ○ ○ ○
7 ○ ○ ○ ○ ○ ○ ○
8 ○ ○ ○ ○ ○ ○ ○
9 ○ ○ ○ ○ ○ ○ ○
0 ○ ○ ○ ○ ○ ○ ○

Name ____

Class & Section _______________________________________

Subject ____

Subject Code : ☐ ☐ ☐

Date of Exam : D D   M M   YYYY
☐☐/☐☐/☐☐ ☐☐

Candidate's Sign.

Invigilator's Sign.

Instructions for filling the OMR sheet :

1. Use only black blue ballpoint pen to fill the circle
2. Use of pencil is strictly prohibited
3. Circle should be designed completely and properly
4. Cutting and erasing on this sheet is not allowed

Q. No.	A	B	C	D
1.	○	○	○	○
2.	○	○	○	○
3.	○	○	○	○
4.	○	○	○	○
5.	○	○	○	○
6.	○	○	○	○
7.	○	○	○	○
8.	○	○	○	○
9.	○	○	○	○
10.	○	○	○	○
11.	○	○	○	○
12.	○	○	○	○
13.	○	○	○	○
14.	○	○	○	○
15.	○	○	○	○
16.	○	○	○	○
17.	○	○	○	○
18.	○	○	○	○
19.	○	○	○	○
20.	○	○	○	○

Q. No.	A	B	C	D
21.	○	○	○	○
22.	○	○	○	○
23.	○	○	○	○
24.	○	○	○	○
25.	○	○	○	○
26.	○	○	○	○
27.	○	○	○	○
28.	○	○	○	○
29.	○	○	○	○
30.	○	○	○	○
31.	○	○	○	○
32.	○	○	○	○
33.	○	○	○	○
34.	○	○	○	○
35.	○	○	○	○
36.	○	○	○	○
37.	○	○	○	○
38.	○	○	○	○
39.	○	○	○	○
40.	○	○	○	○

Q. No.	A	B	C	D
41.	○	○	○	○
42.	○	○	○	○
43.	○	○	○	○
44.	○	○	○	○
45.	○	○	○	○
46.	○	○	○	○
47.	○	○	○	○
48.	○	○	○	○
49.	○	○	○	○
50.	○	○	○	○
51.	○	○	○	○
52.	○	○	○	○
53.	○	○	○	○
54.	○	○	○	○
55.	○	○	○	○
56.	○	○	○	○
57.	○	○	○	○
58.	○	○	○	○
59.	○	○	○	○
60.	○	○	○	○

Name of Exam : _________________________

2021-22

OMR Response Sheet

Roll No.						

Name _________________________

Class & Section _________________________

Subject _________________________

Subject Code :

Date of Exam : D D   M M   YYYY

☐☐/☐☐/☐☐☐☐

Candidate's Sign.

Invigilator's Sign.

Instructions for filling the OMR sheet :

1. Use only black blue ballpoint pen to fill the circle
2. Use of pencil is strictly prohibited
3. Circle should be designed completely and properly
4. Cutting and erasing on this sheet is not allowed

Q. No.	A	B	C	D	Q. No.	A	B	C	D	Q. No.	A	B	C	D
1.	○	○	○	○	21.	○	○	○	○	41.	○	○	○	○
2.	○	○	○	○	22.	○	○	○	○	42.	○	○	○	○
3.	○	○	○	○	23.	○	○	○	○	43.	○	○	○	○
4.	○	○	○	○	24.	○	○	○	○	44.	○	○	○	○
5.	○	○	○	○	25.	○	○	○	○	45.	○	○	○	○
6.	○	○	○	○	26.	○	○	○	○	46.	○	○	○	○
7.	○	○	○	○	27.	○	○	○	○	47.	○	○	○	○
8.	○	○	○	○	28.	○	○	○	○	48.	○	○	○	○
9.	○	○	○	○	29.	○	○	○	○	49.	○	○	○	○
10.	○	○	○	○	30.	○	○	○	○	50.	○	○	○	○
11.	○	○	○	○	31.	○	○	○	○	51.	○	○	○	○
12.	○	○	○	○	32.	○	○	○	○	52.	○	○	○	○
13.	○	○	○	○	33.	○	○	○	○	53.	○	○	○	○
14.	○	○	○	○	34.	○	○	○	○	54.	○	○	○	○
15.	○	○	○	○	35.	○	○	○	○	55.	○	○	○	○
16.	○	○	○	○	36.	○	○	○	○	56.	○	○	○	○
17.	○	○	○	○	37.	○	○	○	○	57.	○	○	○	○
18.	○	○	○	○	38.	○	○	○	○	58.	○	○	○	○
19.	○	○	○	○	39.	○	○	○	○	59.	○	○	○	○
20.	○	○	○	○	40.	○	○	○	○	60.	○	○	○	○

Roll No. digit rows: 1 2 3 4 5 6 7 8 9 0 (each with seven option circles)

Name of Exam : _______________________________

2021-22

OMR Response Sheet

Roll No.

1	○ ○ ○ ○ ○ ○ ○
2	○ ○ ○ ○ ○ ○ ○
3	○ ○ ○ ○ ○ ○ ○
4	○ ○ ○ ○ ○ ○ ○
5	○ ○ ○ ○ ○ ○ ○
6	○ ○ ○ ○ ○ ○ ○
7	○ ○ ○ ○ ○ ○ ○
8	○ ○ ○ ○ ○ ○ ○
9	○ ○ ○ ○ ○ ○ ○
0	○ ○ ○ ○ ○ ○ ○

Name _____________________________________

Class & Section ___________________________

Subject __________________________________

Subject Code : ☐ ☐ ☐

Date of Exam :   D D   M M   YYYY
☐☐ / ☐☐ / ☐☐ ☐☐

Candidate's Sign.

Invigilator's Sign.

Instructions for filling the OMR sheet :

1. Use only black blue ballpoint pen to fill the circle
2. Use of pencil is strictly prohibited
3. Circle should be designed completely and properly
4. Cutting and erasing on this sheet is not allowed

Q. No.	A	B	C	D
1.	○	○	○	○
2.	○	○	○	○
3.	○	○	○	○
4.	○	○	○	○
5.	○	○	○	○
6.	○	○	○	○
7.	○	○	○	○
8.	○	○	○	○
9.	○	○	○	○
10.	○	○	○	○
11.	○	○	○	○
12.	○	○	○	○
13.	○	○	○	○
14.	○	○	○	○
15.	○	○	○	○
16.	○	○	○	○
17.	○	○	○	○
18.	○	○	○	○
19.	○	○	○	○
20.	○	○	○	○

Q. No.	A	B	C	D
21.	○	○	○	○
22.	○	○	○	○
23.	○	○	○	○
24.	○	○	○	○
25.	○	○	○	○
26.	○	○	○	○
27.	○	○	○	○
28.	○	○	○	○
29.	○	○	○	○
30.	○	○	○	○
31.	○	○	○	○
32.	○	○	○	○
33.	○	○	○	○
34.	○	○	○	○
35.	○	○	○	○
36.	○	○	○	○
37.	○	○	○	○
38.	○	○	○	○
39.	○	○	○	○
40.	○	○	○	○

Q. No.	A	B	C	D
41.	○	○	○	○
42.	○	○	○	○
43.	○	○	○	○
44.	○	○	○	○
45.	○	○	○	○
46.	○	○	○	○
47.	○	○	○	○
48.	○	○	○	○
49.	○	○	○	○
50.	○	○	○	○
51.	○	○	○	○
52.	○	○	○	○
53.	○	○	○	○
54.	○	○	○	○
55.	○	○	○	○
56.	○	○	○	○
57.	○	○	○	○
58.	○	○	○	○
59.	○	○	○	○
60.	○	○	○	○

Name of Exam : ___________________________

2021-22

OMR Response Sheet

Roll No.

1	○ ○ ○ ○ ○ ○ ○
2	○ ○ ○ ○ ○ ○ ○
3	○ ○ ○ ○ ○ ○ ○
4	○ ○ ○ ○ ○ ○ ○
5	○ ○ ○ ○ ○ ○ ○
6	○ ○ ○ ○ ○ ○ ○
7	○ ○ ○ ○ ○ ○ ○
8	○ ○ ○ ○ ○ ○ ○
9	○ ○ ○ ○ ○ ○ ○
0	○ ○ ○ ○ ○ ○ ○

Name ____

Class & Section ___________________________________

Subject ____

Subject Code : ☐ ☐ ☐

Date of Exam :   D D   M M   YYYY
☐☐ / ☐☐ / ☐☐ ☐☐

Candidate's Sign.

Invigilator's Sign.

Instructions for filling the OMR sheet :

1. Use only black blue ballpoint pen to fill the circle
2. Use of pencil is strictly prohibited
3. Circle should be designed completely and properly
4. Cutting and erasing on this sheet is not allowed

Q. No.	A	B	C	D
1.	○	○	○	○
2.	○	○	○	○
3.	○	○	○	○
4.	○	○	○	○
5.	○	○	○	○
6.	○	○	○	○
7.	○	○	○	○
8.	○	○	○	○
9.	○	○	○	○
10.	○	○	○	○
11.	○	○	○	○
12.	○	○	○	○
13.	○	○	○	○
14.	○	○	○	○
15.	○	○	○	○
16.	○	○	○	○
17.	○	○	○	○
18.	○	○	○	○
19.	○	○	○	○
20.	○	○	○	○

Q. No.	A	B	C	D
21.	○	○	○	○
22.	○	○	○	○
23.	○	○	○	○
24.	○	○	○	○
25.	○	○	○	○
26.	○	○	○	○
27.	○	○	○	○
28.	○	○	○	○
29.	○	○	○	○
30.	○	○	○	○
31.	○	○	○	○
32.	○	○	○	○
33.	○	○	○	○
34.	○	○	○	○
35.	○	○	○	○
36.	○	○	○	○
37.	○	○	○	○
38.	○	○	○	○
39.	○	○	○	○
40.	○	○	○	○

Q. No.	A	B	C	D
41.	○	○	○	○
42.	○	○	○	○
43.	○	○	○	○
44.	○	○	○	○
45.	○	○	○	○
46.	○	○	○	○
47.	○	○	○	○
48.	○	○	○	○
49.	○	○	○	○
50.	○	○	○	○
51.	○	○	○	○
52.	○	○	○	○
53.	○	○	○	○
54.	○	○	○	○
55.	○	○	○	○
56.	○	○	○	○
57.	○	○	○	○
58.	○	○	○	○
59.	○	○	○	○
60.	○	○	○	○

Name of Exam : _______________________________

2021-22

OMR Response Sheet

| Roll No. | Name ____ |

1 ○ ○ ○ ○ ○ ○ ○
2 ○ ○ ○ ○ ○ ○ ○
3 ○ ○ ○ ○ ○ ○ ○
4 ○ ○ ○ ○ ○ ○ ○
5 ○ ○ ○ ○ ○ ○ ○
6 ○ ○ ○ ○ ○ ○ ○
7 ○ ○ ○ ○ ○ ○ ○
8 ○ ○ ○ ○ ○ ○ ○
9 ○ ○ ○ ○ ○ ○ ○
0 ○ ○ ○ ○ ○ ○ ○

Name ____

Class & Section _______________________________________

Subject ____

Subject Code : ☐ ☐ ☐

Date of Exam : D D M M YYYY
☐ ☐ / ☐ ☐ / ☐ ☐ ☐ ☐

Candidate's Sign.

Invigilator's Sign.

Instructions for filling the OMR sheet :

1. Use only black blue ballpoint pen to fill the circle
2. Use of pencil is strictly prohibited
3. Circle should be designed completely and properly
4. Cutting and erasing on this sheet is not allowed

Q. No.	A	B	C	D
1.	○	○	○	○
2.	○	○	○	○
3.	○	○	○	○
4.	○	○	○	○
5.	○	○	○	○
6.	○	○	○	○
7.	○	○	○	○
8.	○	○	○	○
9.	○	○	○	○
10.	○	○	○	○
11.	○	○	○	○
12.	○	○	○	○
13.	○	○	○	○
14.	○	○	○	○
15.	○	○	○	○
16.	○	○	○	○
17.	○	○	○	○
18.	○	○	○	○
19.	○	○	○	○
20.	○	○	○	○

Q. No.	A	B	C	D
21.	○	○	○	○
22.	○	○	○	○
23.	○	○	○	○
24.	○	○	○	○
25.	○	○	○	○
26.	○	○	○	○
27.	○	○	○	○
28.	○	○	○	○
29.	○	○	○	○
30.	○	○	○	○
31.	○	○	○	○
32.	○	○	○	○
33.	○	○	○	○
34.	○	○	○	○
35.	○	○	○	○
36.	○	○	○	○
37.	○	○	○	○
38.	○	○	○	○
39.	○	○	○	○
40.	○	○	○	○

Q. No.	A	B	C	D
41.	○	○	○	○
42.	○	○	○	○
43.	○	○	○	○
44.	○	○	○	○
45.	○	○	○	○
46.	○	○	○	○
47.	○	○	○	○
48.	○	○	○	○
49.	○	○	○	○
50.	○	○	○	○
51.	○	○	○	○
52.	○	○	○	○
53.	○	○	○	○
54.	○	○	○	○
55.	○	○	○	○
56.	○	○	○	○
57.	○	○	○	○
58.	○	○	○	○
59.	○	○	○	○
60.	○	○	○	○

Name of Exam : _______________________________

2021-22
OMR Response Sheet

Roll No.						

Name ____

Class & Section __________________________________

Subject ____

Subject Code : ☐ ☐ ☐

Date of Exam :   D D   M M   YYYY
☐☐ / ☐☐ / ☐☐ ☐☐

Roll No. digits:
1 ○ ○ ○ ○ ○ ○ ○
2 ○ ○ ○ ○ ○ ○ ○
3 ○ ○ ○ ○ ○ ○ ○
4 ○ ○ ○ ○ ○ ○ ○
5 ○ ○ ○ ○ ○ ○ ○
6 ○ ○ ○ ○ ○ ○ ○
7 ○ ○ ○ ○ ○ ○ ○
8 ○ ○ ○ ○ ○ ○ ○
9 ○ ○ ○ ○ ○ ○ ○
0 ○ ○ ○ ○ ○ ○ ○

Candidate's Sign.

Invigilator's Sign.

Instructions for filling the OMR sheet :

1. Use only black blue ballpoint pen to fill the circle
2. Use of pencil is strictly prohibited
3. Circle should be designed completely and properly
4. Cutting and erasing on this sheet is not allowed

Q. No.	A	B	C	D	Q. No.	A	B	C	D	Q. No.	A	B	C	D
1.	○	○	○	○	21.	○	○	○	○	41.	○	○	○	○
2.	○	○	○	○	22.	○	○	○	○	42.	○	○	○	○
3.	○	○	○	○	23.	○	○	○	○	43.	○	○	○	○
4.	○	○	○	○	24.	○	○	○	○	44.	○	○	○	○
5.	○	○	○	○	25.	○	○	○	○	45.	○	○	○	○
6.	○	○	○	○	26.	○	○	○	○	46.	○	○	○	○
7.	○	○	○	○	27.	○	○	○	○	47.	○	○	○	○
8.	○	○	○	○	28.	○	○	○	○	48.	○	○	○	○
9.	○	○	○	○	29.	○	○	○	○	49.	○	○	○	○
10.	○	○	○	○	30.	○	○	○	○	50.	○	○	○	○
11.	○	○	○	○	31.	○	○	○	○	51.	○	○	○	○
12.	○	○	○	○	32.	○	○	○	○	52.	○	○	○	○
13.	○	○	○	○	33.	○	○	○	○	53.	○	○	○	○
14.	○	○	○	○	34.	○	○	○	○	54.	○	○	○	○
15.	○	○	○	○	35.	○	○	○	○	55.	○	○	○	○
16.	○	○	○	○	36.	○	○	○	○	56.	○	○	○	○
17.	○	○	○	○	37.	○	○	○	○	57.	○	○	○	○
18.	○	○	○	○	38.	○	○	○	○	58.	○	○	○	○
19.	○	○	○	○	39.	○	○	○	○	59.	○	○	○	○
20.	○	○	○	○	40.	○	○	○	○	60.	○	○	○	○

Printed by Libri Plureos GmbH in Hamburg,
Germany